D1615697

STANFORD'S ORGANIZATION THEORY RENAISSANCE, 1970–2000

RESEARCH IN THE SOCIOLOGY OF ORGANIZATIONS

Series Editor: Michael Lounsbury

Recent Volumes

RESEARCH IN THE SOCIOLOGY OF ORGANIZATIONS
VOLUME 28

STANFORD'S ORGANIZATION THEORY RENAISSANCE, 1970–2000

EDITED BY

CLAUDIA BIRD SCHOONHOVEN
University of California, Irvine, CA, USA

FRANK DOBBIN
Harvard University, Cambridge, MA, USA

United Kingdom – North America – Japan
India – Malaysia – China

Emerald Group Publishing Limited
Howard House, Wagon Lane, Bingley BD16 1WA, UK

First edition 2010

Copyright © 2010 Emerald Group Publishing Limited

Reprints and permission service
Contact: booksandseries@emeraldinsight.com

British Library Cataloguing in Publication Data
A catalogue record for this book is available from the British Library

ISBN: 978-1-84950-930-5
ISSN: 0733-558X

Awarded in recognition of
Emerald's production
department's adherence to
quality systems and processes
when preparing scholarly
journals for print

INVESTOR IN PEOPLE

CONTENTS

PART I: THEORIES

LIST OF CONTRIBUTORS

Howard E. Aldrich	Department of Sociology, University of North Carolina at Chapel Hill, Chapel Hill, NC, USA
Terry L. Amburgey	Joseph L. Rotman School of Management, University of Toronto, Toronto, Ontario, Canada
Christine M. Beckman	The Paul Merage School of Business, University of California, Irvine, CA, USA
Joan R. Bloom	School of Public Health, University of California, Berkeley, CA, USA
J. Adam Cobb	Ross School of Business, University of Michigan, Ann Arbor, MI, USA
Gerald F. Davis	Ross School of Business, University of Michigan, Ann Arbor, MI, USA
Alison Davis-Blake	Carlson School of Management, University of Minnesota, Minneapolis, MN, USA
Jacques Delacroix	Santa Cruz, CA, USA
Kathleen M. Eisenhardt	Department of Management and Science Engineering, Stanford University, Stanford, CA, USA
Martha S. Feldman	School of Social Ecology, University of California, Irvine, CA, USA
Mary L. Fennell	Sociology Department, Brown University, Providence, Rhode Island, USA
Ann Barry Flood	Community and Family Medicine, Dartmouth Medical School, Hanover, New Hampshire, USA

Mary Jo Hatch	University of Virginia, Charlottesville, VA, USA; Copenhagen Business School, Frederiksberg, Denmark; and School of Business, Economics and Law (Business and Design Lab), University of Gothenburg, Gothenburg, Sweden
P. Devereaux Jennings	Alberta School of Business, University of Alberta, Edmonton, Alberta, Canada
Roderick M. Kramer	Graduate School of Business, Stanford University, Stanford, CA, USA
Theresa Lant	Lubin School of Business, Pace University, Pleasantville, NY, USA
Raymond E. Levitt	Civil and Environmental Engineering, Stanford University, Stanford, CA, USA
James G. March	Stanford University, Stanford, CA, USA
Joanne Martin	Graduate School of Business, Stanford University, Stanford, CA, USA
Debra E. Meyerson	School of Education, Stanford University, Stanford, CA, USA
Stephen Mezias	Entrepreneurship and Family Enterprise, INSEAD Abu Dhabi Centre, Abu Dhabi, UAE
Donald Palmer	Graduate School of Management, University of California, Davis, CA, USA
Brian Rowan	School of Education, University of Michigan, Ann Arbor, MI, USA
Martin Ruef	Department of Sociology, Princeton University, Princeton, NJ, USA
W. Richard Scott	Department of Sociology, Stanford University, Stanford, CA, USA
Jitendra V. Singh	The Wharton School, University of Pennsylvania, Philadelphia, PA, USA

Sim B. Sitkin	Fuqua School of Business, Duke University, Durham, NC, USA
Lee Sproull	Stern School of Business, New York University, New York, NY, USA
David Strang	Department of Sociology, Cornell University, Ithaca, NY, USA
Mark C. Suchman	Department of Sociology, Brown University, Providence, Rhode Island, USA
Patricia H. Thornton	Fuqua School of Business, Duke University, Durham, NC, USA
Amy S. Wharton	Department of Sociology, Washington State University, Vancouver, WA, USA
Ezra W. Zuckerman	Sloan School of Management, Massachusetts Institute of Technology (MIT), Cambridge, MA, USA

ADVISORY BOARD

SERIES EDITOR

Michael Lounsbury
Alex Hamilton Professor of Business,
University of Alberta School of Business, and
National Institute for Nanotechnology, Edmonton, Alberta, Canada

ADVISORY BOARD

AN ORGANIZATIONAL SOCIOLOGY OF STANFORD'S ORGANIZATION THEORY RENAISSANCE

If you peruse the table of contents of a textbook on organizational theory or search the web for courses in organizational sociology, you cannot help but notice how many of the key contributors to the field spent time at Stanford between 1970 and 2000, as faculty members, post-docs, or graduate students. Skim a few syllabi, and you will find that many of the seminal articles and books were written at Stanford in those years. Many of the most productive and innovative scholars in the field taught at Stanford or studied there.

Of the five most influential macro-organizational paradigms in play today – institutional theory, network theory, organizational culture, population ecology, and resource dependence theory (in alphabetical order) – Stanford served as an important pillar, if not the entire foundation, for all but network theory. By the 1990s, it became an important site for network theory as well. Today Stanford immigrants, and second-generation offspring of immigrants, hold faculty positions across the country. Visit the web sites of leading sociology departments and business schools and you will find them in profusion.

To date there has been no sustained effort to understand Stanford's influence on organizational research. How did Stanford become so prominent in this field? How has it had such a lasting influence on intellectual develop-ments in organization theory? Armchair theorizing abounds, and pet theories range from Machiavellian meditations on a subterranean "West Coast Mafia," to Malthusian meanderings about the effects of the San Francisco Peninsula's climate, to Saxenian speculation about the proximity of so many open-architecture start-up paradigms in a single zip code.

This volume is an effort to fill that void. Thirty essays from Stanford faculty, Ph.D. students, and post-doctoral fellows from the period of 1970 to 2000 discuss the theoretical and empirical contributions that emerged in those years and turn the sociological lens back on the phenomenon, seeking to explain why Stanford generated so many good ideas and pathbreaking studies. The list of contributors breaks sociology's first methodological dictum: study anything but yourself. While that makes the contributors less than fully objective, it does ensure that they know something about that of which they speak.

ORGANIZATIONAL SOCIOLOGY'S PARADIGMATIC REVOLUTIONS

In 1981, W. Richard (Dick) Scott of Stanford's sociology department described a paradigmatic revolution in organizational sociology that had occurred in the preceding decade. In *Organizations: Rational, Natural, and Open Systems* (Scott, 1981), he depicted the first wave of organizational theory as based in rational models of human action that focused on the internal dynamics of the organization. He described the second wave, found in human relations theory and early institutional theory, as based in natural social system models of human action but still focused on the internal "closed system." A sea change occurred in organizational theory in the 1970s as several camps began to explore environmental causes of organizational behavior. The open-systems approaches that Scott sketched in 1981 were still seedlings, but all would mature. What they shared was an emphasis on relations between the organization and the world outside of it. The roots of these new paradigms can be traced to innovations of the 1960s. Contingency theorists Paul Lawrence and Jay Lorsch (1967) had argued that firms add new practices and programs largely in response to external social demands and not simply to internal functional needs. James Thompson (1967) argued that organizations come to reflect the wider environment and particularly the regulatory environment.

From the late 1970s, resource dependency and institutional theorists expanded on these insights. Both found organizations adopting structures in response to environmental pressures, but the two schools envisioned the environment differently (Oliver, 1991). In *The External Control of Organizations*, resource dependency pioneers Jeffrey Pfeffer and Gerald Salancik (1978) argued that as organizational dependence on suppliers, customers, or regulators increases, so will organizational attention to the expectations and demands of these groups. Strategic response to environmental demands is the key. In "Institutionalized Organizations: Formal Structure as Myth and Ceremony", John Meyer and Brian Rowan (1977) argued that firms choose structures and strategies to symbolize their commitment to norms of efficiency and fairness. Then in "The Population

Ecology of Organizations", population ecologists Michael Hannan and John Freeman (1977) described organizational characteristics as arising from environmental selection. Organizations within a population are founded with an array of different structures and strategies (variation), they compete for environmental resources, and the environment selects for retention those best adapted to survive.

Resource dependency theorists developed a power theory of the organization from an open-systems perspective. Institutionalists developed a social constructionist theory from an open-systems perspective. Ecologists developed a theory of competition from an open-systems perspective.

If three vibrant paradigms at Stanford were contributing to an open-systems revolution, two were contributing to a social constructionist revolution, institutional theory and organizational culture theory. The prevailing theories of the 1960s were broadly functionalist or materialist. Institutionalists now focused on the social construction of common organizational practices across the field of organizations. Organizational culture theorists emphasized the construction of idiosyncratic folkways among the members and sub-groups in an individual firm. Organizational institutionalists were concerned with why organizations portrayed themselves as so much alike. Culture theorists were concerned with why they portrayed themselves as so distinct.

The four paradigms that prevailed at Stanford during this time thus varied on two dimensions. Three were open-systems perspectives, emphasizing power, competition, and social construction, respectively. Two were social constructivist theories, emphasizing the external and internal field, respectively. The ideas spawned by these four paradigms ran the gamut of what was being done in sociology more broadly, from the micro interactionism of organizational culture theory to the macro rationalism of population ecology theory. This much was clear: Stanford's organizational community did not arrive at such prominence on the national and international scene because of groupthink. Despite a couple of common themes across these paradigms, the organizational culture in Stanford's organizational community was characterized by sharply divided subcultures.

In the core of this essay, we take the perspectives of each of these four theories in turn to try to understand the Stanford organizational phenomenon. We find useful insights from each of the theories. But we begin with two important caveats. One caveat is that Stanford was not necessarily the progenitor of these theories. Indeed, all four can be traced to other institutions, as we will see in the chapters that discuss them. Population ecology can be traced to the time that Hannan (Stanford) and Freeman (Berkeley) spent in graduate school at the University of North Carolina, and the influence of the ecologist Amos Hawley. Resource dependence germinated at the University of Illinois where Jeffrey Pfeffer collaborated with Gerald Salancik, although many of the ideas can be traced back to Pfeffer's earlier doctoral dissertation at Stanford. Organizational culture can be traced to Edgar Schein and John Van Maanen at MIT and to the spontaneous generation of similar ideas in a number of European and American universities, as Mary Jo Hatch argues in her essay. Organizational institutionalism can be traced to Peter Berger (Boston University) and Thomas Luckmann's (University of Constance) *The Social Construction of Reality* (1966), as well as to Philip Selznick (Berkeley) and his early work on institutions within organizations.

The other caveat is that there were organizational scholars from a number of other paradigms making important contributions at Stanford in this period as well, including the organizational psychologist Robert Sutton from the School of Engineering, Roderick Kramer the psychologist of trust at the graduate school of business (GSB), the national culture theorist William Ouchi at the GSB, and the network theorist Don Palmer at the GSB. Some of the leading scholars contributed to multiple paradigms – James (Jim) March is an institutionalist in some writings, a learning theorist in others, and the co-founder of Garbage Can theory in still others. The first section of the book covers eight broad theoretical approaches that were represented – resource dependency, institutional theory, ecology, learning theory, organizational culture, labor market theory, network theory, and health care research. We might have included others. In this essay we discuss four of the most influential paradigms to illuminate the organizational phenomenon that was the Stanford organizational community.

FOUR ORGANIZATIONAL THEORIES
APPLIED TO THE CASE

While the origins of the paradigms that are the source of Stanford's prominence in organizational theory can be traced to other institutions, there is little doubt that Stanford became a fount of ideas for a number of different paradigms. Important contributions were published by scholars at Stanford, and in population ecology, institutionalism, resource dependence, and organizational culture, many of the leading second-generation scholars were trained at Stanford. Why did these paradigms flourish as they did at Stanford?

Sociologists of knowledge talk about an array of factors that contribute to paradigmatic vitality. Thomas Kuhn (1970) points out that in science, one paradigm must begin to falter before it can be replaced. Perhaps the impetus for the blossoming of organizational paradigms in the late 1970s was the widespread rejection of functionalism across sociology's subfields. But why did so much paradigmatic innovation occur at Stanford? Harriet Zuckerman and Robert Merton (1972) talk about the accumulation of advantage in science, as centrally located actors in an intellectual field win greater resources than those on the periphery, which in turn helps them to win further resources. Perhaps the accumulation of advantage redounded to the institution itself at a certain point, but the Stanford organizational community moved from being a relatively obscure outpost to being a central player in fairly short order. If the accumulation of advantage was at work, one would have expected Harvard, where Paul Lawrence and Jay Lorsch and Talcott Parsons sat in the 1970s, or Columbia, where Peter Blau and Robert Merton and C. Wright Mills had held court, to have prevailed in the 1980s and beyond. Stanford University itself was just rising to national prominence in the 1970s, as Dick Scott discusses in the concluding chapter.

Diana Crane (1972) argues that invisible colleges, comprising national networks of distributed scholars working together on intellectual projects, generate excitement and innovation and dynamism. Stanford was more of a visible college, with a significant concentration of organizational scholars on one campus, and the paradigmatic differences across the different subgroups might have been expected to divide that college. On other campuses, competing paradigms have played out the roles of the Hatfields and the McCoys. Stanford saw some healthy sibling rivalry between paradigms, but the groups never came to blows. Perhaps Stanford achieved some of the benefits of invisible colleges and some of the benefits of visible ones.

Actor network theorists trace the use of particular scientific devices that help paradigmatic groups to cohere and to spread their techniques and ideas (Callon, 1998). We can identify some cross-usage of methodological tools and even theoretical components. For instance, both institutional theorists and population ecologists made use of new event history techniques (Tuma & Hannan, 1984) to demonstrate their claims and establish beachheads in the leading quantitatively oriented journals (*American Sociological Review*, *American Journal of Sociology*, and *Administrative Science Quarterly*). The same two camps borrowed ideas, as when ecologists embraced the idea of legitimacy, or institutionalists began to use the idea of density. But beyond that, the spread of methods and theoretical concepts was haphazard. Generally, methodological conventions divided rather than united the paradigms. Organizational culture theorists used ethnography

(Martin, 1992), garbage can theorists relied on mathematical models (Cohen, March, & Olsen, 1972), and resource dependence theorists employed cross sectional statistical models (e.g. Pfeffer & Cohen, 1984). The semiconductor certainly explained the rise of early entrepreneurial groups in Silicon Valley, but there was no analogous technology to explain the rise of Stanford's entrepreneurial paradigmatic groups in organization theory.

The approach we take is not to build on insights from the sociology of science, but to apply some of the organizational theories that were being developed at Stanford to the case of Stanford's success in organizational theory. We ask: Can Stanford's theories help explain the proliferation of theories that emerged at Stanford between 1970 and 2000? We follow this path for two reasons. First, in applying four organizational theories to the case of the rise of one particular organization (Stanford University) in one particular domain (organizational analysis), we set the scene without simply previewing the chapters and potentially stealing the authors' best lines. More formal reviews of these four paradigms, and four other approaches and substantive areas that were developed at Stanford, appear in the eight chapters that make up the first section of this volume.

The second reason we apply organizational paradigms to the question of Stanford's peculiar success is that, by contrast to most scientific phenomena, the case of Stanford's preeminence as a place for organizational analysis seems to us to be a specifically organizational phenomenon. Most works in the sociology of science trace the rise of a paradigm, scientist, or type of scientist. The paradigm or the scientist is the unit of analysis. In this case, the phenomenon occurred at the level of an organization, Stanford University, and so the organization seems to us to be the appropriate focus. The typical caveats about drawing conclusions from a case study apply. But we view the chapter, and the book more generally, as an exercise in grounded theory. What lessons do a bunch of certified social scientists take from an exceptional case, and one they know well? Following the chapters that sketch the remarkable contributions of Stanford's organizational paradigms, most of the essays from former faculty and students take up the question of what made Stanford "work." One can read them as 22 efforts at grounded theory, or as 22 different Rashomon-like angles on the same event, Stanford's rise in organizational theory.

The chapters in the Theories section of this volume chronicle the evolution of each of eight theoretical and substantive approaches. Here, we sketch one or two ideas from each of four theories that might help to explain Stanford's phenomenal intellectual dynamism in the field of organizational sociology between 1970 and 2000.

Resource Dependence

Resource dependence theory suggests that organizational structure and strategy are influenced importantly by the resource flows available from the environment. Organizations succeed by adapting to their environments. Where resource streams are available, organizations that decode the best means for drawing those resources are most likely to prosper. In the case of academic research, dimensions of the resource environment are multiple. Each university must draw talented students to its degree programs, grants from federal agencies and private foundations, gifted faculty to staff teaching and research positions, and substantial donations to build its endowment.

From the perspective of resource dependence, Stanford's organizational community of the 1970s and 1980s succeeded by adapting to two sorts of financial resource flows with particular agility. First, in the sociology department Dick Scott spearheaded efforts to attract federal dollars that would provide support for graduate students and post-docs, who are the lifeblood of university-based research. Beginning in 1972, Scott spearheaded efforts to win a series of training grants first from the National Institute of Mental Health (NIMH) and later from the National Institute of Aging (NIA) that would support successive cohorts of graduate and post-doctoral students. That Scott's grant proposals would be successful was far from a foregone conclusion. Neither Scott nor his primary collaborators were experts in mental health or in aging when they began their quests for funding. Their claim was that they could strengthen organizational scholarship in ways that would improve our understanding of all organizations, including mental health systems and organizations serving the elderly, and could examine the ways in which all organizations affected the mental health of their participants. The federal model of supporting basic research and research training through grants for institutional development was the root of Stanford's success, and so was the entrepreneurship of one particular sociology faculty member.

Scott's success in attracting NIMH and NIA funding provided a research foundation for attracting another important resource: graduate students and post-docs. Many graduate students (including the authors of this chapter) benefitted from pre-doctoral training grants that allowed them to pursue the research interests that inspired them and to collaborate on research projects with their choice of faculty. The grants allowed sociology and the business school, in particular, to expand their doctoral programs by providing funding to scores of advanced students. At the same time, generation upon generation of post-doctoral students came to Stanford and developed collaborative projects with graduate students and faculty members. The appendices list the dozens of graduate students and post-docs who benefitted from these grants.

The training grants also stipulated that pre-doctoral trainees would participate in a regular seminar. From its inception in 1972, the weekly organizations research training program (ORTP) seminars were led by successive faculty members, first by Jim March, then Gene Webb, next by Bill Ouchi, and then others in subsequent years as faculty rotated through the responsibility. In addition to the incredible faculty students were able to work with and learn from, the students themselves contributed substantially to the quality of these weekly seminars. Many early dissertation ideas were vetted and nourished as seminar papers in this context. In addition to the pre-doctoral seminars, lively colloquia were organized each quarter. These featured a series of visiting and local scholars who helped infuse additional perspectives into the emerging interdisciplinary community. With students and faculty drawn from sociology, the business school, industrial engineering, education, psychology, and other units meeting weekly to hear presentations by students, faculty, and visitors, a strong interdisciplinary community began to flourish. Subsequently faculty were able to leverage additional funds, principally from the Graduate School of Business, to support a monthly colloquium series to host leading organizational scholars from outside the University. The seminars and colloquia proved key to creating an ongoing interdisciplinary community.

The NIMH funding also helped to finance an annual conference for the Stanford organizational community, held most years between the mid-1970s and the early 1990s. While the first conference was a commuter event held at the local Atherton House and featured James Coleman, the organizers soon took advantage of Stanford's proximity to the Pacific Ocean. As the organization community grew, the event graduated to a cluster of private homes at Pajaro Dunes and finally moved further south along the coast to the Asilomar conference grounds in Monterey. Each year 100 or more Stanfordites got together for several days to listen to plenary speakers from outside, to discuss their own work, and to build community by walking along the beach and partying through the night.

Stanford's organizational community emerged from a combination of Dick Scott's institution-building efforts, which were informed by the grant requirements of the National Institute of Mental Health, and later the National Institute of Aging. With a strong history of collaboration, with Peter Blau, Sanford Dornbusch, and John Meyer to name just a few, Scott was able to entice others to join him. The collective organization theory resources helped to draw faculty to Stanford, and keep many there, for faculty benefitted from subsidized graduate student research assistants and post-docs as well as the research seminars, colloquia, and annual conferences that helped to build national as well as local network ties. Faculty also benefitted from strong theory and methods courses in the business school, the sociology department, and beyond that created a flow of sophisticated research assistants/collaborators. The educational resources benefitted both sides, for faculty could rely on the statistical skills and theoretical knowledge of students, and well-trained students hired to code data or conduct interviews often found themselves as full collaborators on research articles.

Pfeffer and Salancik's resource dependence theory suggests that organizations that are able to take advantage of environmental resource pools will prosper, and that is certainly what happened when Stanford was able to support organizational scholars at the pre- and post-doc levels. The program drew unlikely candidates into a field of sociology, organization theory, that had recently been dominated by functionalist thinking. The institution was built out to meet resource flows, such that people who had not worked on health systems or aging previously moved in that direction. Amy Wharton's essay tells of how the grants influenced her research and Mary Fennell and Anne Flood's essay describes the multiple studies in health systems and the accompanying theoretical development.

As federal agencies began to decommission the programs that had funded the Stanford community through the late 1980s, Dick Scott and Jim March scanned the resource environment for alternative venture capitalists and came up with an inside and an outside source of capital. Scott drew on the emergent university model of inter-disciplinary centers to found the Stanford Center for Organizational Research (SCOR), drawing on short-term university funding to continue the tradition of interdisciplinary colloquia, workshops, and the post-doc program from 1988 to 1995. Thus as the resource environment changed, the implicit CEO of Stanford's organizational community pursued a new institutional funding model, in which Stanford (like its peers) provided venture capital to a start-up center in the hope that the center would attract new investors for the second round of funding.

In the spring of 1989, Jim March negotiated for a Scandinavian organizational research center at Stanford, under the auspices of the Scandinavian Consortium for Organizational Research. SCANCOR created a U.S. outpost for Scandinavian organizational researchers for pre-doctoral, post-doctoral, and sabbatical visits. Its festive opening celebration was attended by Denmark's Crown Prince Frederik, and SCANCOR continues to this day, with support from Finland, Denmark, Iceland, Norway, and Sweden, under the leadership of institutionalist and network theorist Walter (Woody) Powell.

From a resource dependence perspective, then, Stanford's success in organizational sociology was a consequence of a federal funding model for supporting basic science and research training that provided funds not only for specific research projects but also for institutional development and staffing. A core set of entrepreneurs at Stanford brought the community together to apply for several rounds of funding. The university's capacity to adapt to the resource environment made it a success in this domain.

Population Ecology

Ecologists began with the insights that organizations compete with others in their populations, and that those best adapted to their environments are most likely to survive. The characteristics of any particular population of organizations are driven by conditions at the time of founding (birth) and then by natural selection. Theirs is not simply a theory of competition and selective survival, but of the creation of new industries through processes such as legitimacy. Hannan and Freeman (1989) argued that when a new industry is emerging, the establishment of each new enterprise contributes to the legitimacy of the industry in the eyes of investors and clients. With each new Argentine newspaper, American labor union, Irish micro-brewery, or California vintner, investors and consumers gain confidence that the industry as a whole will survive and prosper, and thus the survival chances of individual firms increase. Until, that is, the market approaches saturation, at which point, each additional founding will increase competition and the survival chances of incumbents will decline. This approach is very much at the heart of the work of current Stanford Graduate School of Business faculty Michael Hannan, Glenn Carroll, and William Barnett.

If academic paradigms are like enterprises and if intellectuals are like entrepreneurs, the "density dependence" thesis of organizational ecologists may offer insight into why so many different intellectual groups flourished at Stanford at the same time. Intellectual entrepreneurs established a number of different academic enterprises side-by-side in the 1970s. There was Jim March, housed in the Hoover Institution but with joint appointments in sociology, education, political science, and the business school. His enterprise contributed generations of graduate students and post-docs working on learning theory, garbage can theory, and decision-making. There was Mike

Hannan in sociology, whose closest early collaborator was John Freeman at Berkeley, but who soon had a lab employing a host of graduate students on population ecology projects. There was Dick Scott, the original organizational sociologist in sociology proper, who collaborated with Sandy Dornbusch on studies of authority systems in organizations and later with John Meyer on institutional studies. Together they trained generations of graduate students working on education, health systems, and institutional theory. There was John Meyer, who worked with Hannan and students on studies of the diffusion of public policies and with Scott and students on the diffusion of organizational policies. There was Jeffrey Pfeffer in the Graduate School of Business, who collaborated with graduate students and post-docs on resource dependence studies. There was Joanne Martin in the Graduate School of Business who developed her own organizational culture lab that trained cohorts of graduate students.

These labs were in full swing by 1980, and rather than competing for scarce resources, they seemed to build upon one another. The importance of organizational analysis in the sociology department was bolstered by its role in the graduate school of business and, later, in the school of engineering's management program. The presence of organizational theorists in education, health systems, and engineering confirmed the salience of the research in other domains. Most importantly, as each paradigm began to win legitimacy in the publishing world, by taking up pages in the *Administrative Science Quarterly* (ASQ), the *American Sociological Review* (ASR), and the *American Journal of Sociology* (AJS), the others seemed to gain legitimacy. If each paradigm was an enterprise, the vitality of one paradigm in the population fueled the success of paradigms that economists might have seen as competitors.

This environment might have proven toxic to start-up paradigms competing in the resource space. As enterprises grow in size, conventional industrial organization theorists suggest (Tirole, 1988), they achieve economies of scale and scope that make it difficult for small upstarts to survive. Population ecologists recognize another dynamic at work with the growth of dominant firms in an industry, which they term resource partitioning (Carroll & Swaminathan, 2000). Dominant firms in the core of an industry (think of Honda) may come to produce for the average consumer, leaving space for specialty producers in niche markets (think of Maserati or the Mini Cooper). Honda may provide little competition to those brands. The same process may operate in academic markets. Where a dominant theory exists, attracting the bulk of graduate students and research resources, that theory may leave unexplored intellectual terrain for other theories. Other theories may prosper in niche markets.

One might describe the initial rise of organizational culture theory in these terms. Where the population ecologists, resource dependence theorists, and institutionalists had engaged the interest of the quantitative, macro, graduate students and post-docs, Joanne Martin was able to attract a sizeable group of students with qualitative and micro orientations. They came to Stanford to work with her, in one of the liveliest organizational communities around. Or they came with uncertain interests and were drawn to her more micro and qualitative approach. Others as well prospered in this environment, such as the trust theorist Rod Kramer, Steve Barley, who brought his own brand of organizational culture theory to Stanford, and Don Palmer, who was developing an open-systems network approach inspired by power theory.

To move up a level, from treating the university as a field to treating the system of universities as a field, one can see evidence that the Stanford model of fostering an organizations community spread to other universities. Beginning first in the San Francisco Bay Area, faculty and students at nearby universities began to organize themselves to send delegations of students and faculty to the Asilomar conference. Soon, UC Berkeley, UC San Francisco, UC Davis, UCLA, and USC were regular participants, some helping to co-fund the annual conference. Soon doctoral students and post-docs moved on to assume faculty positions at other universities, and as they did replications of Stanford's organizations model began to appear. First at the University of Texas and then at Illinois, Michigan, Northwestern, Pennsylvania, and Minnesota centers or networks of organizations scholars were created (see Scott's concluding chapter). Each program gathered ideas, support, and legitimacy from the existence of the others. The idea of bringing organizational sociologists in sociology departments, business schools, engineering schools, medical schools, law schools, together in a university-wide interdisciplinary program became institutionalized. Appendix D lists the domestic and international university-based organizations centers in operation circa 1995.

Neo-Institutionalism

The classical organizational institutionalism of Selznick (1949, 1957), Zald and Denton (1963), and Clark (1960) focused on the natural history of an organization, charting how practices and programs became taken for granted and developed a life of their own as institutions. The new institutionalism that was introduced by faculty member John Meyer and graduate student Brian Rowan (1977) in "Institutionalized Organizations: Formal Structure as Myth and Ceremony" focused on the rise and spread of new practices and programs in the organizational field, emphasizing not the inner workings of the organization, but the external sources of organizational ideas and programs. Both approaches emphasized the social construction of particular organizational regimes as fair, efficient, appropriate, and even optimal – the best possible way to proceed.

The organizational institutionalists working at Stanford, led by sociology faculty members John Meyer and Dick Scott, and later Walter (Woody) Powell, and encompassing several generations of graduate students and post-docs as well as other faculty members, took a new approach to understanding organizations. They paid little attention to an organization's internal dynamics or functional needs, and instead traced the spread of innovations across the population of organizations. How did school reforms, corporate due process mechanisms, total quality management, or the poison pill spread from one firm to another?

As students in Dick Scott's famous graduate/undergraduate class on organizational sociology, we all learned about organizational boundary spanning. We also learned about the multiplicity of particular organizations. The federal government could be treated as a single organization, or as hundreds of distinct organizations with different missions and purposes under a broad umbrella. Likewise, the university could be viewed as a singular entity, or as dozens of organizations with distinct structures and missions.

New organizational institutionalism, like population ecology, can be applied to the case of Stanford University if we treat the different theoretical camps, or research labs, as distinct organizations with their own personnel and missions, albeit with personnel and missions that sometimes overlapped and that existed under the same umbrella. Perhaps the research university is best viewed as a network organization, with hundreds of entrepreneurial faculty building their own project-based teams to conduct research, and then disassembling and reassembling teams as they initiate new projects (Powell, 1990).

A key insight from the new institutionalism is that innovations gain legitimacy as they spread through the population, of firms or government agencies or schools or (in this case) research labs. As they diffuse, they confer legitimacy on adopters. To be modern is to be on alert for the latest innovation that will make your firm, agency, school, or lab more efficient, adaptable, rational, equitable, etc. Four new organization-theory institutions spread among the Stanford paradigms we are focusing on in this chapter. Each innovation gained legitimacy in the local community and soon influenced the field of organizational sociology more generally. As these approaches gained in popularity at Stanford, they also gained in popularity in the journals. In institutional terms, each innovation helped to legitimate the research labs that adopted it, and each adoption by a lab helped to legitimate the innovation.

The first innovation was a focus on the effects of the organizational population, field, or network. Contingency theorists like Lawrence and Lorsch (1967) had already turned their attention to the environment, but they focused on the relations between an individual firm and specific organizational partners in the environment; partners that influenced the firm's life chances. For contingency theory, it was the relations between a firm and its buyers, or a firm and its regulators – its "organization set" – that mattered. The firm was still the focus, and the environment was viewed as comprising several dyadic relationships with outsiders.

Ecologists, institutionalists, resource dependence theorists, and network theorists moved toward making the constellation of organizations in the environment the focus. They turned their attention from ego, to all of the others in the environment and the overall structure of their relations. These theories were based on relational approaches found in the human ecology of Amos Hawley, the social constructionism of Peter Berger and Thomas Luckmann (1966), the power theory of Mills (1956), and the network approach of Georg Simmel (1964), respectively. Those theorists had explored the wider social arena as the main object of study, and the new paradigms found at Stanford brought a relational approach to the study of the organization. Functionalist and neo-Marxist theorists of the firm had long operated with a wider view of the role of the firm in society, but organizational studies had come to focus on the internal mechanisms determining organizational structure and strategy.

Ecologists took the most revolutionary position, focusing on the formal characteristics of the population rather than on those of the firm itself, and nearly denying the capacity of the individual organization to act on its environment and affect its life chances. Network theorists likewise focused on the formal characteristics of the other organizations in the environment. Institutionalists took an intermediate position, describing in statistical studies the behavior of the individual firm as a result both of internal characteristics and external trends in the field. New models of organizational behavior were devised and legitimated in the organizational field. For resource dependence theorists, the entire constellation of suppliers, customers, competitors, and regulators shaped the firm's strategy. The empirical focus was on ego's network rather than on the population. Because each organizational theory imported a conception of the relational environment from the meta-theory it drew inspiration from, it is not quite accurate to say that the population approach spread from one paradigm to the next. Instead, the use of a population or field approach in one domain of organizational research helped to legitimate it in other domains. As these paradigms gained ground they reinforced – and in important ways, reinvented – the "open-systems" approach.

The second innovation to gain legitimacy from common use was event history analysis. In the 1970s, the gold standard in quantitative organizational study was the large N cross-sectional study. Everything we knew about organizations based on quantitative analysis came from such research. In Stanford's sociology department, Nancy Tuma and Michael Hannan built on survival techniques in demography to develop event history techniques to analyze divorce rates – a dichotomous dependent variable – in the Seattle-Denver Income Maintenance research program. Tuma pioneered the RATE statistical program to run event history analyses at a time when the prevailing statistical software packages, SPSS and SAS, had nothing of the kind in their toolkits. Tuma and Hannan published their opus on time series modeling, *Social Dynamics: Models and Methods* in 1984, but by the late 1970s they and their students were using event history modeling and the RATE program widely.

In 1979, Meyer and Hannan published an edited volume, *National Development and the World System*, in which they used longitudinal data and dynamic techniques to analyze the diffusion of policies across countries and the effects of those policies. Meanwhile, both population ecologists and institutionalists began to use the modeling techniques to study organizational change, though in different ways. For the ecologists, the events were vital rates of organizational births and failures. For the institutionalists, the events were organizational program adoptions. By the late 1970s, an event history course was required as part of the sociology doctoral course sequence, and in short order, students working in both research labs had lost interest in cross sectional data and were collecting longitudinal data. Moreover, students of organizations from across the University flocked to these courses. The ecologists collected data on foundings and failures in a wide range of organizational populations. The institutionalists first collected longitudinal data for the world polity studies, focusing on policy diffusion across countries, and then began to work at the organizational level, focusing on the spread of policies across schools and firms. Others outside of the population ecology and institutional labs, including GSB faculty member Don Palmer and doctoral student Jerry Davis, were soon using dynamic modeling techniques as well.

Scholars from other organizational paradigms began to use longitudinal modeling techniques and by the end of the 1980s, a strong preference for dynamic modeling could be found in the leading outlets for organizational sociology, particularly the *Administrative Science Quarterly, American Sociological Review*, and *American Journal of Sociology*. The approach had gained wide legitimacy for its capacity to better specify causality by identifying the organizational and environmental shifts that immediately precede events of interest, which ranged from organizational failure to adoption of safety departments.

The third factor to spread across labs was the theoretical concept of legitimacy. The institutionalists infected the ecologists with their theory of legitimacy, or perhaps both were infected by the work of Stanford sociologist Morris (Buzz) Zelditch Jr., a social psychologist who had long worked on legitimacy (Evan & Zelditch, Jr., 1961), and whose interest was stimulated in part by Dornbusch and Scott's (1975) examination of the role of legitimacy in authority processes. Influenced by Buzz Zelditch's social psychology and John Meyer's developing institutional ideas, Lynne Zucker's (1977) dissertation focused on the role of institutionalization in cultural persistence. For ecologists, the concept of legitimacy provided a solution to an empirical quandary. Resource competition is a key mechanism for human as well as biological ecologists. The ecologists noticed that in organizational populations, an increase in competition for resources threatened the survival of incumbent firms, but only after population density reached a certain level. In the early years of an organizational population, or industry, each new birth improved the life chances of incumbents. Ecologists borrowed the idea of legitimacy to explain their particular version of the ecological concept of population density dependence (Hannan & Freeman, 1989, p. 131). They argued that as organizational populations increase in size from zero, density has a positive effect on the life chances of organizations because each new organization increases the legitimacy of the form. Greater theoretical precision and some rapprochement between the two theories was facilitated by a spirited exchange in the ASR between Lynne Zucker (1989, p. 542) and Carroll and Hannan (1989), in which Zucker argued that both historical context and legitimacy should be measured directly to adequately account for increasing rates of organizational foundings. Nonetheless, diffusion of the idea of legitimacy from institutional theory to ecology helped to legitimate the legitimacy concept, and in so doing helped to legitimate both theories. Institutional theory added a cultural mechanism to the much more rationalist population ecology theory, and ecology broadened its theoretical base by borrowing from a constructionist paradigm.

The fourth innovation that gained legitimacy by being employed across paradigms was the metatheoretical approach of social constructionism, shared by the new institutionalists and organizational culture theory. Here again, it was not so much that a concept spread from one research lab/paradigm to another, as that mutual adoption of a concept bolstered the paradigms and the concept. Organizational culture theory, as we see below in the essays by Mary Jo Hatch and Joanne Martin, emerged out of the work of people such as Edgar Schein and John Van Maanen at MIT and Linda Smircich at the University of Massachusetts at Amherst. The approach was based in social psychology and anthropology and it was, in the instantiation that Joanne Martin and others developed at Stanford, social constructionist. The local culture and its meanings were developed through social networks. Cultural practices gained meaning through interaction, ritual, repetition, and myth. The social constructionism found in the new institutionalism was based to a greater extent in the phenomenology of Peter Berger and Thomas Luckmann (1966) who were strongly influenced by Alfred Schutz (1970). While the two paradigms can be traced to different sources, the core ideas about the role of social construction in meaning-making and in the persistence of organizational practices were strikingly similar. The two theories lent credence to one another by making parallel arguments about how the social construction of reality contributed to the persistence of cultural forms and practices. The intersubjective objectivation of organizational customs became a focus of both approaches.

If we look across these four paradigms, there were some instances of diffusion, as when event history methods were taken up by the institutionalists or when the concept of legitimation was taken up by ecologists. But the focus on the field or population, and the concept of social construction, were out there in the ether somewhere, and they were taken up at about the same time by different paradigms that had strongholds at Stanford. It was their simultaneous adoption and use that helped to legitimate them. Perhaps they were adopted at about the same time because paradigmatic entrepreneurs recognized the same weaknesses in the prevailing functionalist, egocentric, approach to organizations. That is our guess. In Kuhn's (1970) terms, then, a multi-faceted paradigmatic revolution occurred, as the weaknesses of functionalism and a closed-system approach to the organization began to become increasingly apparent. Different innovators recognized the fissures, and sought to repair functionalism with an interactionist and constructionist approach, and to repair the egocentric approach with a field orientation. These were not cases of the rise and spread of entirely new institutions. Rather, they were cases of the contemporaneous embrace of existing theoretical approaches by multiple nascent paradigms. Perhaps reinforcement and learning are better terms for describing this process than diffusion or institutionalization.

Similar weaknesses in the functionalism and behaviorism of the 1950s and 1960s were being addressed by institutional revolutions in other disciplines, and those revolutions surely reinforced these innovations in organizational sociology. Closest at hand was the world polity approach, a macro-institutional theory that John Meyer and his graduate student colleagues developed in response not only to behaviorism, but to the materialist version of world systems theory that was then in vogue. Meyer in collaboration with Hannan (1979), and with several generations of graduate students, explored the global diffusion of new policy regimes, beginning with education and extending to a wide range of issues. In sociology, then, there was a macro institutionalism and an organizational institutionalism.

Meanwhile in political science, the historical institutionalism of Theda Skocpol (1979) and others began to take hold. In their studies, the focus was on how political institutions shaped future possibilities by imposing constraints on policy alternatives, or by opening up policy possibilities (Thelen, 1999; Thelen & Steinmo, 1992). Historical happenstance was the source of the institutional arrangements that affected policy choices. Rational choice institutionalists in American politics challenged behaviorism but not functionalism, by exploring how state institutions influenced congressional voting patterns even among fully rational political actors (see Campbell, 1998; Hall & Taylor, 1996). Stephen Krasner, Terry Moe, and Barry Weingast, in political science at Stanford, were important contributors to this work. In economics, institutionalists built rational theories of behavior generally, and in the case of Oliver Williamson's (1975) *Markets and Hierarchies*, argued that markets and hierarchical organizations like firms are alternative governance structures which differ in their approaches to resolving conflicts of interest. A key prediction, supported empirically, is that the likelihood of economic agents to conduct transactions within firm boundaries increases with the relationship specificity of their assets. A more historical group in economics took the longue durée as the point of departure, seeking to understand how economic institutions evolved (North, 1981, 1990). Avner Greif (2006) in economics at Stanford has emerged as a champion of this approach. These various institutionalisms reinforced one another, despite the fact that their shared antipathy toward behaviorism covered disparate metatheoretical orientations, ranging from hyper-rationalist, in the case of rational choice institutionalism in political science, to radically social constructionist, in the case of world polity and organizational instituitionalisms. Here as in organizational theory, it is not fair to say that ideas spread from one camp to another; rather, several approaches appeared at about the same time with certain common critiques of behaviorism, and these approaches helped to reinforce one another.

Organizational Culture

The organizational culture paradigm flourished at Stanford, but as Mary Jo Hatch and Joanne Martin observe in their essays in this volume, the earliest pioneers were to be found at MIT and at the University of Massachusetts and in Europe. Culture theorists took very different approaches from one another in the 1980s and 1990s, as Joanne Martin pointed out in 1992. Some focused on the informal and interactional characteristics of organizations. Peters and Waterman's (1982) best selling *In Search of Excellence* suggested that successful companies share a set of common cultural elements that makes them innovative, closer to their customers, and profitable. Others emphasized broad differences across national cultures, as in the case of Graduate School of Business faculty member William Ouchi (1981), whose *Theory Z* described distinctive corporate cultures in the United States and Japan. At the other extreme were ethnographies of individual firms that championed the distinctiveness of their own cultures (Kunda, 1992).

Joanne Martin (1992) charts the variety of approaches taken by culture theorists, and our first thought for the culture section of this chapter was to apply her distinctive organizational culture perspective to the Stanford organizational community. Martin sketches three approaches to culture research, based on existing culture studies. She points out that most researchers look for integration, differentiation, or fragmentation, and that culture can be best understood in terms of all three at once. We thought to apply that model to the Stanford organizational community, but Martin scooped us by using that approach in her chapter in this volume.

We will elaborate, however, on one of her themes: the tension between mainstream cultures and subcultures. In academia, cultures and subcultures exist in universities and colleges, but also in the "invisible colleges" found in disciplines. In the invisible, national (and at times international) college of organizational scholarship circa 1970, there was one mainstream culture, with its stories, routines, practices, and jargon. The dominant culture was functionalist first and foremost and quantitative for the most part. It was connected to the prevailing sociological paradigm, Talcott Parsons' structural functionalism, which dominated the field in the 1950s and 1960s.

The quantitative studies of Peter Blau and colleagues were emblematic. Functionalist assumptions were adapted to fit an open-systems perspective by researchers such as Lawrence and Lorsch (1967) and Thompson (1967).

If there was a subculture in organizational sociology in those days, it was to be found among neo-Marxists. Mills' (1956) *The Power Elite* challenged the managerial view of the firm, suggesting that power not ability was the basis for managerial control of the firm. Harry Braverman's (1974) *Labor and Monopoly Capital: The Degradation of Work in the Twentieth Century* challenged mainstream organizational theory to be sure, but from outside of the fold. He was a socialist, not a sociologist. Michael Burawoy was a sociologist, but his *Manufacturing Consent* (1979) challenged the functionalist view of the firm by treating labor power as inevitably coerced rather than exchanged. But it was not this neo-Marxist counterculture that came to displace the dominant functionalist paradigm.

The dominant culture of the invisible college of organizational theory in the 1950s and 1960s mirrored the culture of Parsonian structural functionalism in sociology more broadly. The key idea behind structural functionalism was that social structures evolved to serve functional needs. Social systems in every society had to serve a set of different functions, of adaptation to the environment, goal attainment, social integration, and latency or the capacity to reproduce themselves. If societies had common features, such as religion, it was because those features were needed to fulfill vital social functions. This dominant paradigm had its methodological rituals. There were case studies, but the ritual that was on the rise was the organizational survey with regression analysis relating certain internal characteristics to other internal characteristics.

In organizational sociology, as in business history, the practices of the firm were viewed as fulfilling functional needs. If two firms had similar hierarchical structures, or finance departments, it was because both had functional needs for command and control, or for the means to finance ongoing activities and future growth. Any practice that was widespread must exist because of an internal functional need of the firm. Joan Woodward (1958), for instance, tried to understand the span of managerial control, the number of levels of hierarchy, and the codification of rules as a function of the organization's production technology rather than as a function of the product. Thus in small batch production, a narrow span of supervisory control is needed because production is not routine. In mass production, firms can get away with a bigger ratio of workers to supervisors, and so on.

The four paradigms that flourished at Stanford at first constituted alternative subcultures to this prevailing paradigmatic culture. Over time they created a new, multiparadigmatic, organizational culture, arguably with its own subcultures.

The four subcultures had their charismatic leaders, as organizational culture theorists predicted they would. Ecology had Mike Hannan at Stanford and John Freeman at Berkeley. Institutional theory had John Meyer and Dick Scott in Stanford sociology, James March with his more political version, and later Paul DiMaggio and Woody Powell, who were together at Yale and who ended up at Princeton and Stanford, respectively. Resource dependence had Jeff Pfeffer at Stanford and Gerald Salancik at the University of Illinois. Organizational culture (as distinct from corporate culture) had John Van Maanen and Edgar Schein at MIT and Joanne Martin and Terrence Deal at Stanford.

They had their origin myths (which we will see in the following chapters) as culture theorists predicted they would. Ecology emerged out of an innovation of two North Carolina doctoral students influenced by Amos Hawley's approach to human ecology. Institutional theory emerged out of the alchemy of Meyer's world polity constructionism and Scott's organizational sociology. Resource dependence theory blossomed when Stanford graduate student Jeff Pfeffer encountered Gerry Salancik when he took his first job at Illinois. Organizational culture theory had roots in social psychology and anthropology, in North America and Europe, and emerged through parallel intellectual processing in that invisible college.

The new countercultural paradigms had their own methodological rituals as well. The ecologists, institutionalists, and resource dependence theorists all challenged the ritual of explaining one internal organizational characteristic in terms of another internal characteristic. In their models, something about the environment explained internal program and structural choices. The organizational culture paradigm challenged the ritual of cross-sectional statistical correlation from the other end of the spectrum, suggesting that organizations have cultures that cannot be discovered through an inventory of practices and structural features. Organizations with identical structures may have very different cultures. As of 1980, these paradigms offered clear countercultures to the dominant culture in the invisible college of organizational sociology. But those countercultures had enough in common, and had a sufficiently coherent critique of the dominant culture, that they came to replace the dominant culture.

Perhaps transforming these theoretically disparate subcultures into a new dominant culture in organizational sociology was easier because the subcultures formed a single culture at Stanford, particularly among graduate students. The NIMH pre-doctoral and post-doctoral fellows created an esprit de corps among the ranks, and brought people from different groups together for regular discussion. The annual conferences at the Asilomar facility in Monterey, California, created a chance for bonding and intellectual cross-fertilization. A community of 100 strong met together in scholarship and fellowship, for days of debate and nights of bonding. There and in the seminars we developed an organizational culture, described fully in the chapters that follow. If Stanford's organizations community created an organizational culture of its own, Peters and Waterman's title, "In Search of Excellence" aptly describes what that culture was about. We felt we were part of a renaissance in organizational theory that challenged the status quo with a range of rich new theories.

CONCLUSION

Learning theory, garbage can theory, cooperation theory, network theory, organizational stratification – beyond the four theories we have focused on here, there was a cornucopia of organizational theories represented at Stanford in the years between 1970 and 2000. To this day there is an active, dynamic, group of organizational scholars working there. Stanford probably continues to have the greatest density of organizational scholars in the world, though it has competition from some of the other organizational centers that Dick Scott assembled into a national cabal, including the Universities of Michigan, Minnesota, Pennsylvania, and Texas.

The essays that follow are grouped into four sections. First is the section on "Theories" which describes the primary paradigms that emerged at Stanford. The essays in this section are authored by the former Stanford Ph.D. students who worked directly on the development of the paradigms they discuss. Some essays focus on specific theoretical paradigms, whereas others describe approaches applied to specific research areas, such as labor markets and health care. Next are observations by Stanford faculty who participated during the prime years of the Organizations Research Training Program and who contributed substantively to the theoretical ideas that developed between 1970 and 2000. This section would be even more representative had it included the considerable wit of the late Gene Webb and the genial thoughtfulness of the late Hal Leavitt. Both were pillars during the early period of the community's development. Then we have a robust section of observations by many of the pre-doctoral and post-doctoral students resident during the program, augmented by remarks by Howard Aldrich, a visiting professor during the very first 12 months of the program who taught many of us. In issuing invitations to former students and post-docs, we did our best to put together a representative sample of theories, departments, and eras. Limitations of space prevented us from inviting everyone who spent time at Stanford as a student or post-doc. The volume concludes with the chapter, "Collegial Capital: the Organizations Research Community at Stanford, 1970–2000," by W. Richard Scott. Dick's energy and intelligence enabled the development of Stanford's organizational community and his wisdom (yes, with much assistance he will remind us all) helped guide its evolution over the 30-year period.

The chapters to come display a fascinating array of insights about the dynamics underlying Stanford's organizational community. We have resisted the temptation to preview them, in part because the sheer number of contributions would make for a dizzying preview, but also because we believe each is best read fresh out of the box. That leaves us only the task of thanking the contributors and facilitators. Many thanks to the more than two dozen contributors for keeping (more or less) to a production schedule and for writing thoughtful, provocative, interesting, and often witty contributions. It was our hope to produce a volume that would be of interest well beyond the Stanford community, and contributors have worked hard to achieve that goal. We are particularly grateful that contributors responded quickly and thoughtfully to our suggestions for revision. Thanks to Michael Lounsbury who, despite not being a Stanford alum himself, as series editor endorsed the project and shepherded it through with enthusiasm and grace. Thanks to Marc Ventresca for being an early and vocal champion of the project. Thanks to Laura Thomas for cheerfully dunning authors and putting the manuscript together. Thanks especially to Dick Scott for providing historical detail and documents key to the project and for doing double duty by writing a reflection on his experience and a wonderful concluding chapter.

REFERENCES

Berger, P. L., & Luckmann, T. (1966). *The social construction of reality: A treatise on the sociology of knowledge.* Garden City, NJ: Doubleday.

Braverman, H. (1974). *Labor and monopoly capital.* New York: Monthly Review.

Burawoy, M. (1979). *Manufacturing consent: Changes in the labor process under monopoly capitalism.* Chicago: University of Chicago Press.

Callon, M. (1998). Introduction: The embeddedness of economic markets in economics. In: M. Callon (Ed.), *The laws of the markets.* Oxford: Blackwell.

Campbell, J. L. (1998). Institutional analysis and the role of ideas in political economy. *Theory and Society, 27*, 377–409.

Carroll, G. R., & Hannan, M. T. (1989). Density dependence and the evolution of populations of organizations. *American Sociological Review, 54*, 524–541.

Carroll, G. R., & Swaminathan, A. (2000). Why the microbrewery movement? Organizational dynamics of resource partitioning in the US brewing industry. *American Journal of Sociology, 106*, 715–762.

Clark, B. R. (1960). *The open-door colleges: A case study.* New York: McGraw Hill.

Cohen, M. D., March, J. G., & Olsen, J. P. (1972). A garbage can model of organizational choice. *Administrative Science Quarterly, 17*, 1–25.

Crane, D. (1972). *Invisible colleges. Diffusion of knowledge in scientific communities.* Chicago: University of Chicago Press.

Dornbusch, S. M., & Scott, W. R. (1975). *Evaluation and the exercise of authority.* San Francisco: Jossey-Bass.

Evan, W. M., & Zelditch, M., Jr. (1961). A laboratory experiment on bureaucratic authority. *American Sociological Review, 26*, 883–893.

Greif, A. (2006). *Institutions and the path to the modern economy: Lessons from medieval trade.* Cambridge: Cambridge University Press.

Hall, P. A., & Taylor, R. C. R. (1996). Political science and the three new institutionalisms. *Political Studies, 44*, 936–958.

Hannan, M. T., & Freeman, J. H. (1977). The population ecology of organizations. *American Journal of Sociology, 72*, 267–272.

Hannan, M. T., & Freeman, J. H. (1989). *Organizational ecology.* Cambridge, MA: Harvard University Press.

Kuhn, T. (1970). *The structure of scientific revolutions.* Chicago: University of Chicago Press.

Kunda, G. (1992). *Engineering culture: Control and commitment in a high-tech corporation.* Philadelphia: Temple University Press.

Lawrence, P., & Lorsch, J. W. (1967). *Organization and environment: Managing differentiation and integration.* Boston: Harvard Graduate School of Business Administration.

Martin, J. (1992). *Cultures in organizations: Three perspectives.* New York: Oxford University Press.

Meyer, J. W., & Hannan, M. T. (Eds). (1979). *National development and the world-system: Educational, economic and political change, 1950–1970.* Chicago, IL: University of Chicago Press.

Meyer, J. W., & Rowan, B. (1977). Institutionalized organizations: Formal structure as myth and ceremony. *American Journal of Sociology, 83*, 340–363.

Mills, C. W. (1956). *The power elite.* New York: Oxford University Press.

North, D. (1981). *Structure and change in economic history.* New York: Norton.

North, D. (1990). *Institutions, institutional change and economic performance.* New York: Cambridge University Press.

Oliver, C. (1991). Strategic responses to institutional processes. *Academy of Management Review, 16*, 145–179.

Ouchi, W. G. (1981). *Theory Z: How American business can meet the Japanese challenge.* Reading, MA: Addison-Wesley.

Peters, T. J., & Waterman, R. H. (1982). *In search of excellence.* New York: Harper & Row.

Pfeffer, J., & Cohen, Y. (1984). Determinants of internal labor markets in organizations. *Administrative Science Quarterly, 29*, 550–572.

Pfeffer, J., & Salancik, G. R. (1978). *The external control of organizations: A resource dependence perspective.* New York: Harper and Row.

Powell, W. W. (1990). Neither market nor hierarchy: Newtork forms of organization. In: L. L. Cummings & B. Shaw (Eds), *Research in organizational behavior* (pp. 295–336). Greenwich, CT: JAI.

Schutz, A. (1970). *On phenemonology and social relations.* Chicago: University of Chicago Press.

Scott, W. R. (1981). *Organizations: Rational natural and open systems.* Englewood Cliffs, NJ: Prentice Hall.

Selznick, P. (1949). *Tva and the grass roots.* Berkeley, CA: University of California Press.

Selznick, P. (1957). *Leadership in administration: A sociological interpretation.* New York: Harper and Row.

Simmel, G. (1964). *The sociology of Georg Simmel.* New York: Free Press.

Skocpol, T. (1979). *States and social revolutions: A comparative analysis of France, Russia, and China.* New York: Cambridge University Press.

Thelen, K. (1999). Historical institutionalism in comparative politics. *Annual Review of Political Science, 2,* 369–404.

Thelen, K., & Steinmo, S. (1992). Historical institutionalism in comparative politics. In: S. Steinmo, K. A. Thelen & F. Longstreth (Eds), *Structuring politics: Historical institutionalism in comparative politics* (pp. 1–32). New York: Cambridge University Press.

Thompson, J. D. (1967). *Organizations in action.* New York: McGraw-Hill.

Tirole, J. (1988). *The theory of industrial organization.* Cambridge, MA: MIT Press.

Tuma, N. B., & Hannan, M. T. (1984). *Social dynamics: Models and methods.* New York: Academic.

Williamson, O. E. (1975). *Markets and hierarchies: Analysis and antitrust implications.* New York: Free Press.

Woodward, J. (1958). *Management and technology.* London: Her Majesty's Stationery Office.

Zald, M. N., & Denton, P. (1963). From evangelism to general service: The transformation of the YMCA. *Administrative Science Quarterly, 8,* 214–234.

Zucker, L. G. (1977). The role of institutionalization in cultural persistence. *American Sociological Review, 42,* 726–743.

Zucker, L. G. (1989). Combining institutional theory and population ecology: No legitimacy, no history. *American Sociological Review, 54,* 542–545.

Zuckerman, H., & Merton, R. K. (1972). Patterns of evaluation in science-institutionalisation, structure, and functions of referee system. *Sociological Review, 20,* 258–260.

Frank Dobbin
Claudia Bird Schoonhoven
Editors

PART I
THEORIES

CHAPTER 1

ORGANIZATIONAL INSTITUTIONALISM AT STANFORD: REFLECTIONS ON THE FOUNDING OF A 30-YEAR THEORETICAL RESEARCH PROGRAM

Brian Rowan

This chapter will *not* be another scholarly review of the "Stanford school" of organizational institutionalism. That is hardly needed given the sustained attention this branch of organization theory has received over the past 30 years. In fact, since John Meyer and I published our widely cited paper on institutionalized organizations in the *American Journal of Sociology* in 1977 (Meyer & Rowan, 1977), Meyer, Scott, and their students have done much more than I can do here to define and polish the brand. In the 1980s and 1990s, Meyer and Scott developed, revised, and applied institutional theory to the study of organizations through publication of several edited volumes of theory and research (Meyer & Scott, 1983; Scott, Meyer, & Associates, 1994; Scott & Christensen, 1995). In addition, over 30 years of work, Scott, Meyer, and their students have published several reviews of institutional theory applied to the study of organizations (Zucker, 1987; Scott, 1987,

Stanford's Organization Theory Renaissance, 1970–2000
Research in the Sociology of Organizations, Volume 28, 3–19
Copyright © 2010 by Emerald Group Publishing Limited
All rights of reproduction in any form reserved
ISSN: 0733-558X/doi:10.1108/S0733-558X(2010)0000028005

2008; Meyer, 2008). More significantly, Scott published a seminal book on institutions and organizations, now in its third edition (Scott, 1995/2000/ 2008). Taken alone, this body of work has been so widely heralded, and so deeply analyzed, that there is little original or profound that I can add to the discussion.[1]

The development of institutional theory at Stanford involved more than just work in the field of organizational studies, however. Meyer, Scott, their students and colleagues also produced a large number of reviews, edited volumes, and monographs contributing to research in a variety of fields, including, a multifaceted body of work on the world polity (Thomas & Meyer, 1984; Meyer, Boli, Thomas, & Ramirez, 1997; Boli & Thomas, 1999; Drori, Meyer, & Hwang, 2006; Kruken & Drori, 2009), major contributions to economic sociology (Dobbin, 1994, 2004), important research on post-secondary and K-12 education (Meyer, Kamens, & Benavot, 1992; Meyer, Ramirez, Frank, & Shofer, 2007; Ramirez & Meyer, 1980; Rowan & Miskel, 1999; Meyer & Rowan, 2006), fundamental studies of health care organization and policy (Fennell & Alexander, 1993; Scott, Ruef, Mendel, & Caronna, 2000), research on law in society (Edelman & Suchman, 1997), and recent work on social movement organization (Davis, McAdam, Scott, & Zald, 2005).

Beyond these efforts, the Stanford group also published literally hundreds of theoretical and empirical papers applying institutional theory to issues ranging from accounting practices in organizations to the world system of societies. As this work gained attention, the group of scholars contributing to institutional theory expanded, as sociologists from other universities, and scholars from disciplines beyond sociology, discovered the power of institutional thinking and built "institutional theory" into what it is today – a sprawling, interdisciplinary, and contested theoretical perspective used not just in the fields of organizational studies and sociology, but also in diverse fields such as business, communications, criminology, economics, education, engineering, health policy research, information science, industrial and labor relations, law, political science and public administration, psychology, and social work.

THE PROBLEM

My intent in this chapter is not to review this ever-expanding body of work, which now encompasses all sorts of "new" institutionalisms applied to micro-, meso-, and macro-levels of social analysis in a wide variety of fields.

Rather, I propose to stay a narrower course, focusing on the "new" organizational institutionalism that emerged at Stanford in the 1970s. To a considerable extent, this focus excludes from sustained attention the growth of world polity theory, a body of work that is closely aligned to organizational institutionalism, but that was developed somewhat independently of Scott by Meyer and his associates (for an excellent, short overview of this line of work, see Jepperson, 2002; otherwise, see Meyer et al., 1997 or Meyer, 2000). In focusing on *organizational* institutionalism, I will add only marginally to what has already been written. My first task will be to describe the earliest developments of this form of analysis in the 1970s and early 1980s at Stanford, since describing how research programs in organizational studies got founded at Stanford is a major theme of the present volume. After that, I will advance some ideas about how and why this research program became so influential, in so many fields of study.

My story begins with Meyer and Scott, acting on their epistemic interests in the immediate context of the Stanford Sociology Department. This immediate context, I will argue, shaped how Meyer and Scott conceived of their epistemic project and brought the two scholars into contact with a continuous pool of talented graduate students and local colleagues, all of whom published widely and well, spreading organizational institutionalism to a broader audience. Beyond this local context, however, I will discuss the larger social networks in which Meyer and Scott were embedded, and beyond that, the larger field(s) in which these social networks were located. Using these ideas, I plan to explain the rise of organizational institutionalism in terms of a primitive sociology of knowledge – a story about Stanford's brand of organizational institutionalism as a theoretical "logic," about the penetration of this logic into the larger field of organizational studies and its progressive linkages to (and disputes with) other theoretical "logics," and finally about the diffuse governance of academic work, which allowed (and continues to allow) multiple "neo-institutionalisms" to flourish, leading to the transfiguration of the Stanford school of institutional theory from an isolated perspective on organizations to a major brand of organization theory.

BEGINNINGS (1975–1977)

An interesting question is what motivated Meyer and Scott to invent a new "school" of organization theory in the first place. One "institutionalist" explanation that comes to mind is the notion of Meyer and Scott as deliberately cognizing actors playing out their *epistemic* interests according to a script that was institutionalized in both their local context and in the larger field of sociology. The script I am referring to is what their colleagues at the Stanford Sociology Department called "a theoretical research program" (Berger, Zelditch, & Anderson, 1966; Berger & Zelditch, 2002). The idea of a script guiding the birth of institutional theory is not as far-fetched as it might seem, for it not only fits with Scott's own accounts of his work (Scott, 2005, 2006) but also with Jepperson's (2002) account of Meyer's work. It also accords well with what was happening in both sociology and organization theory at the time. In the 1970s, sociology was just emerging from the era of grand theory and placing a great deal of emphasis on developing so-called "theories of the middle range" (Merton, 1968). It also was a time of propositional (even hypethetico-deductive) reasoning, especially in organization theory, where, for example, Blau (1970) had developed an elegant and highly regarded formal theory of differentiation in organizations, where Hage and Aiken (1967) had developed an "axiomatic" theory of organization structure, and where Perrow (1972) had distilled a number of "schools" of theorizing about complex organizations.[2]

If the archetypical "script" was available, it took a while to fill in the particulars. The first step toward creation of a Stanford school of organizational institutionalism emerged when Meyer and Scott threw in together, a matter that from Scott's (2006) telling occurred because he and Meyer felt somewhat isolated from their departmental colleagues (who were mostly social psychologists). As far as I can tell, the formal occasion for this coming together was a series of research projects at what was then known as the Stanford Center for Research and Development on Teaching (SCRDT), where Meyer and Scott joined Elizabeth G. Cohen to study the organizational context for classroom teaching. This is also where I enter the story, for after my second year as a sociology graduate student, having written a comprehensive examination on comparative institutions that was evaluated by Meyer, I was taken by Meyer to Scott's office one afternoon to discuss my examination. That long-forgotten exam, it can be noted selfishly, was built around Berger and Luckmann's (1966) work and presaged some of what showed up in Meyer and Rowan (1977) by emphasizing the way "carrier groups" institutionalized ideas and helped spread them through society. It also reflected the strong interest of several graduate students in sociology at Stanford who, at the time, were actively exploring the relevance to sociological theory of the works of Schutz, Garfinkel, Berger and Luckmann, and others. Some time after this meeting, Scott, who was then department chair, called me into his office for what turned out to be the pivotal moment of my career. The conversation at that meeting was brief. Scott said the department was thinking about where to assign me for my research assistantship, and he gave me two choices: schools or hospitals (both areas in which he had active research projects). In that brief moment, I found myself saying "schools" and the rest (as they say) was history.

The SCRDT project where I was assigned was the "birthplace" of the Stanford school of *organizational* institutionalism.[3] Historically, the SCRDT project nicely mirrors developments in organization theory at the time, especially the importance of contingency theory. A core idea guiding the SCRDT work, for example, was that "differentiated teaching" was making the task of teaching more complex, and as this occurred, school organization would need to respond (perhaps by implementing "team teaching" as a coordinative response to complexity, or perhaps by increasing the numbers of administrative and support staff to manage the increased technical demands). Interestingly, while these basic hypotheses from contingency theory received some empirical support (see, Cohen, Deal, Meyer, & Scott, 1979), neither Meyer, nor Scott, nor I were much interested, for two reasons. First, there were far more puzzling results emerging from the work. One was the finding (reported in Meyer & Rowan, 1978; Meyer, Scott, & Deal, 1983) that nobody in schools seemed to be tightly controlling the "core technology" of teaching, whereas on issues other than instruction, a great deal of administrative oversight was being exercised. This corresponded quite well with more conventional thinking on schools as organizations, such as Bidwell's (1965) classic essay on school as a formal organization, published in the first *Handbook of Organizations* (March, 1965), and Lortie's (1975) then new study of teaching as an occupation. Equally important, the National Institute of Education (NIE), which funded the SCRDT work, had convened a meeting (which Meyer attended) to plan out an agenda for educational research, and one of the papers prepared for that meeting was Weick's (1976) now famous paper on educational organizations as loosely coupled systems. So there was already a buzz about loose coupling in the air. Beyond that, however, I was also beginning to see the importance of what later would be called "institutional effects," especially in the finding that levels of state and federal funding in the schools and school districts in the SCRDT study seemed to exercise more influence over both the size and scope of what organization theorists then called the "administrative component" than did variations in the complexity of the teaching task.

In early 1975, Meyer invited me to work with him on a paper to develop these ideas. The basic problem, as we formulated it, was how to explain the rise of a large and highly complex bureaucratic form that (contrary to all reasoning in organization theories of the time) ended up not exercising much coordination or control over its core technology – classroom teaching. And therein was born the Stanford school of organizational institutionalism, not so much as a fully formed theory of organization but rather as a bricolage assembled from many different ideas. The basic idea was true to Meyer's work on education as an institution (Meyer, 1970, 1977), which viewed schooling, not so much as an enterprise exercising strong socializing effects on students, but rather as an institution that functioned in society to bestow statuses and rights on graduates. The key idea in the paper we ended up writing in 1975, and that was published three years later (Meyer & Rowan, 1978), was that the *structure* of educational organizations largely reflected this institutional logic. That is, schools were organized around – and tightly managed – a set of highly institutionalized categories that were central to the school's role as society's "personnel agency." To describe these categories, we invented the idea of a schooling rule – where education is defined as "a certified teacher teaching a standardized curricular topic to a registered student in an accredited school." This was the first statement of the principal of institutional isomorphism, where a set of external agencies (legislatures, accrediting agencies, disciplinary associations, and so on) are seen as institutionalizing a set of deeply taken-for-granted rules about how a particular class of organizations are to be structured, and the target organizations are seen as incorporating these elements into their formal structures to gain support and legitimacy. To be sure, the idea of isomorphism as we developed it contained elements of what later would be called cognitive, regulatory, and even normative elements of institutions. The paper also talked about the benefits of isomorphism not only in terms of legitimacy, but also in terms of resource acquisition. It was only much later that institutionalists (and others) began parsing these various ideas analytically, often without much success.

But identifying the processes that structured schools as organizations was only half the problem Meyer and I wanted to solve, for another problem was to explain why institutional isomorphism would lead to the loose coupling we were observing in schools. A close reading of the 1978 paper shows that we developed a variety of arguments that presage subsequent developments in institutional theory. For one, we contextualized the argument to a particular institutional environment, American education, which was seen as governed in a highly pluralistic and decentralized way (in contrast to educational governance in many other nation states). This was a primitive theory of organizational fields. Second, we noted that institutionalized rules in American education were vague – not at all prescriptive – so that schools in the United States, at least, were not governed by a strong "technical" logic. All of this, we argued, produced a great deal of variation in practice, great potential for conflict among externally constructed organizational routines, and much resulting uncertainty, which if surfaced for inspection would only serve to undermine the institutionalized myth of the schooling rule and associated ritualized categories, like "graduate."

An important question for us, however, was how a bureaucrat could function in good faith to "absorb" these technical uncertainties (rather than act on them), and here we developed two additional lines of thought. One was the idea that schools would segment (or decouple) organizational units from each other so that they did not come into contact, a process that not only required organizational slack, but also prevented technical uncertainties from spilling across units, contaminating technical interdependencies, and revealing "problems" that had to be acted upon. Another line of attack was to invoke the micro-sociology of Erving Goffman, with its emphasis on the naturalness of such interaction rituals as overlooking, maintaining face, and so on, which we called "the logic of confidence" that decouples structure from activity. Our insight was that this process extended beyond face-to-face interactions and was present also in larger, sector-wide processes of control, to wit the use of professional controls like teacher certification and school accreditation, which rely only on the most minimal inspection of the inner workings of schools and school systems and assume good faith action by agents. This, the reader will note, presages the emphasis on "ceremonial" conformity to institutional logics that has been a controversial element of the Stanford school of organizational institutionalism. Also, it positions this brand of institutional theory in a very different space from economistic views of organizations, which tend to analyze the processes I just described at the organizational level and see them as non-rational forms of shirking or as other forms of bureaucratic misfeasance.

EARLY WORK (1977–1991)

The next phase of theoretical development might be called the "childhood" of organizational institutionalism – a period lasting from the publication of Meyer and Rowan (1977) to the publication of Powell and DiMaggio's (1991) edited volume on the "new institutionalism" in organizational studies. This period begins in 1976, when Meyer approached me to write a paper for the *American Journal of Sociology*, which at the time had issued a special call aimed at securing more theory-oriented papers for publication. Meyer took this opening to "generalize" our 1975 work, which I see as the first step in trying to formalize organizational institutionalism into a research program, an action that was perhaps also spurred by a rump group (sometimes called the "West Coast mafia") that received funding from the American Sociological Association to develop organization theory in sociology and that included John Freeman, Mike Hannan, John Meyer, Marshall Meyer, Jeff Pfeffer, and Dick Scott. This group, incidentally, published *Environments and Organizations* (Meyer & Associates, 1978), which included a number of theoretical statements by group members. It also spawned a number of interesting contributions to organization theory.

Since most people see the Meyer and Rowan (1977) paper on institutionalized organizations as a founding document in organizational institutionalism, the paper has been discussed extensively many, many times. For this reason, I will not attempt my own exegesis here, except to note that many of the ideas currently at the center of institutional theorizing in both organizational studies and sociology are present in that work, including primitive ideas about the cognitive, regulatory, and normative bases of institutionalization; the importance of relational networks to institution building; the importance of organizational fields to institutional theory; the role of institutional entrepreneurship; and the global scope of rationalized myths. A more interesting point, however, is that this paper – now viewed as one of the foundational pieces in the whole line of institutional theory – almost did not make it to publication, having been sent originally to two reviewers, who were of split mind, and then sent to a third reviewer, who responded favorably.[4] At issue in the critical review were two ideas that have plagued the Stanford school of organizational institutionalism since its founding. The main problem the critic had with the paper was the idea that organizations could survive without being efficient – something that the reviewer saw as unequivocal grounds for rejection and that many institutionalists also have trouble with (Scott, 2008, pp. 423–424). A related problem is the "fix-up" the editor recommended, which asked us to draw a distinction between technical and institutional environments, a distinction that has drawn criticism from many observers and that has become essentially moot as institutional theorists have come to understand that the very "logics" of rationality, markets, and forms of technology are socially constructed in organizational fields – something the original paper hinted at, but had to mute.

I am not sure how much attention the 1977 paper would have gotten had it not been for two additional events. The first was the publication of Meyer and Scott's (1983) volume, *Organizational Environments: Ritual and Rationality*, which not only reprinted work originating at SCRDT, but also included additional work funded by the NIE under the umbrella of Stanford's Institute for Research on Educational Finance and Governance, as well as work by Scott produced in his role as a health care researcher. To say that this volume represented an important step forward in the formalization of institutional theory would be an understatement, for here was where the Stanford school first began to grapple with, and solidify its understanding of, organizational fields. Two chapters from this volume particularly stand out in my mind, the chapter by Scott and Meyer (1983) on the organization of societal sectors – the first place I encountered sophisticated thinking about organizational fields – and the paper by Meyer (1983) on the centralization of funding and control in educational governance – which remains, in my view, the most sophisticated analysis of American-style governance and its effects on educational organization that I have seen. The other critical event, in my view, was publication of DiMaggio and Powell's (1983) *Iron Cage Revisited*, which is more widely cited than Meyer and Rowan (1977) and stands with it as a foundational contribution to organizational institutionalism. Both works (Meyer & Scott, 1983; DiMaggio & Powell 1983) shifted the focus of organizational institutionalism away from a primary concern with organizations per se (or even the dyadic relationships between organizations and their environments) and toward a focus on institutional fields. As a result, both works positioned institutional theory as a truly sociological (as opposed to strictly organizational) enterprise.

However, even in 1983, the Stanford brand was not all that influential. For example, Meyer and Rowan (1977) was being cited at a growing rate (about 25 times per year in 1983) according to the ISI citation database, a rate that exceeds most papers, but nowhere near the over 100 times per year the paper is now cited. Interestingly enough, even in these early days, the plurality of citations (46%) were coming from business and management journals, with only about 18% coming from sociology journals, and another 17% from education journals. At the same time, from publication to 1990, Meyer and Scott's (1983) edited volume was not yet highly cited, Scott's (1987) review paper on the "adolescence" of institutional theory was too recently published to have gained momentum, and even Zucker's (1977) now well-cited and influential paper on the micro-foundations of institutional theory was far from being highly cited at the time (with just 36 citations from date of publication to 1990).

Importantly, during this early time period, many (but hardly all) of the authors citing works in institutional theory were close colleagues or students at Stanford, including among others, Jim Barron, Glenn Caroll, Mike Hannan, Jim March, Bill Ouchi, and Jeff Pfeffer. Pfeffer and Barron (1988), for example, cited institutional theory in their work on personnel systems; Hannan and Freeman (1984) began citing institutional theory as they formalized their thinking on inertial forces in organizational life and as they incorporated aspects of political and institutional environments into their models; March and Olsen (1984) cited the Stanford brand of institutional theory in their seminal statement on the new institutionalism in political science; and Ouchi (1980) cited the work in his well-known statement on markets, bureaucracies, and clans as organizational forms. A close look at the citations also shows institutional theory being discussed in management research, in particular management research grounded in agency theory, cognitive theories of organizing, and strategic choice; it also was being cited in research on management practices in Japan and other Asian nations, research on organizational innovation and change, and early studies of organizational culture.

CONSOLIDATION, TAKEOFF, AND
TRANSFIGURATION (1991–2008)

Consolidation and Takeoff

It was not until the 1990s that the Stanford brand of organizational institutionalism took off (as confirmed by a sharp rise in citation rates for papers I discussed in first paragraph of this chapter). In my view, two events triggered this takeoff. The first was the publication of Powell and DiMaggio's (1991) edited volume, *The New Institutionalism in Organizational Analysis*; the second was publication of the first edition of Scott's (1995) *Institutions and Organizations*. These efforts were important in several respects. First, they were the first (and highly successful) efforts to consolidate institutional theory as it applied to the study of organizations. Together, the volumes invented an intellectual history for the movement, generated a set of major propositions, and posed some epistemic priorities for future research. In these volumes, for example, we begin to see the contrast between "old" and "new" institutionalisms, learn that institutional theory has been around and is being developed in economics and political science as well as sociology and organization theory, get exposed to some easy-to-understand frameworks describing the bases of institutions and the processes leading to institutional isomorphism. Here, too, we learn about key concepts such as organizational fields and institutional logics, and about some epistemic priorities that need to be addressed in institutional theory – for example, the role of agency in institution building and maintenance, or how the process of institutional change unfolds. We also see in these volumes the beginnings of a self-conscious discourse about the kinds of research designs needed to "test" institutional theories. All of these are crucial advances, opening up the field to a broader audience by inviting linkages to other theoretical logics, formulating the overarching framework in more digestible fashion, pointing out some epistemic priorities to encourage researchers to engage with the perspective, and signaling how research in the field can proceed.

Interestingly, the uptake for this now identified "new" organizational institutionalism was largely centered in North American business schools, not sociology departments, reflecting not only the spectacular growth of business school enrollments from the 1970s onward (Doti & Tuggle, 2005), but also the subsequent location of "organizational studies" as a quasi-disciplinary field of research in these professional schools, and the concurrent development of professional societies and journal outlets closely associated with these business schools (Augier, March, & Sullivan, 2005).[5] This uptake by business school faculty brought what had been heretofore been a theoretical perspective on organizations largely centered around the study of professionalized and public sector domains of organization into confrontation with theoretical perspectives centered around what Augier and colleagues called the "strategic management" of private sector organizations, with its focus on economic thinking and the management of performance. In the organizational field constructed by the rise of business schools, this led to a healthy interchange between the Stanford school of organizational institutionalism and other theoretical "logics," a process well-reflected in Scott's (2008) recounting of changes to organizational institutionalism as it moved into what he called "adulthood." It is to that confrontation that I now turn.

Transfiguration

As organizational institutionalism moved to the business school setting, several processes of transfiguration occurred. One has been noted by

Mizruchi and Fein (1999) in reference to DiMaggio and Powell's (1983) paper, but that also can be applied to the Stanford approach. The key idea here is that the theoretical logic of the Stanford school becomes "selectively appropriated [to] accord with prevalent discourse in the field, and ... centrally located researchers ... [become] more likely than other scholars to invoke this dominant interpretation" (Mizruchi & Fein, 1999, p. 653). A quick look at the ISI citation database reveals some of the centrally located theorists who fit this bill. Of course, the founders and their students remain central to this process, but other scholars also become engaged (e.g., Royston Greenwood, Paul Hirsch, Michael Lounsbury, Christine Oliver, Hayagreeva Rao, Roy Sudaby, and Edward Zajac, to name a few). As this occurs, much more than the selective formulation of a stylized canon results. One process involves the substantial editing of the foundational perspective, as researchers who support the research program work on epistemic priorities identified during the consolidation process and raise new issues. So, the Stanford school of organizational institutionalism confronts structuration theory, revisits the problem of developing a micro-foundational theory of action, elaborates on the concept of legitimacy, and more, as discussed in several papers published in the newly released *Handbook of Organizational Institutionalism* (Greenwood, Oliver, Suddaby, & Sahlin-Andersson, 2008). In addition, scholars working from inside and outside the research program begin to engage in boundary maintenance and border crossings (again as seen in Greenwood et al., 2008). Part of this process involves a confrontation among the logics of "new" and "old" organizational institutionalisms (e.g., Hirsch, 1997; Hirsch & Lounsbury, 1997) or alternative sociological approaches to the study of institutions (e.g., Brinton & Nee, 1998). But theorists also begin to assess the boundaries between organizational institutionalism and other theoretical perspectives in the field, like network theory, organizational economics, organizational ecology, organizational learning theories, globalization theories, and more (again, see various papers in Greenwood et al., 2008). From this lively discourse arises the well-known editing and expansion of organizational institutionalism to include new forms of analyses, as well as a fairly uniform assessment of the epistemic priorities facing the perspective, including the often-noted calls by scholars of different stripes to include in organizational institutionalism a greater attention to the roles of interest, agency and entrepreneurship in the creation of institutions, more attention to the strategic responses of organizational actors to institutional pressures, a greater recognition that institutions often call for consequential rather than superficial responses, a recognition of a need for more attention to the roles of social networks and organizational fields as units of analysis in organization theory and to the role of contestation and conflict within these fields, as well as related concerns calling for institutionalists to attend not only to crescive stages of institutionalization, but also to the processes of de-institutionalization and creative destruction (for review of these themes, see Scott, 2008).[6]

CONCLUSION

Where does all this leave the Stanford approach to organizational institutionalism? It is certainly in a far different place than it was 30 years ago, when a few individuals were working at the edges of organization theory to construct a new theoretical logic that stood in sharp contrast to the reigning theoretical discourse of the day. Now, 30 years later, organizational institutionalism as developed at Stanford has become a part of the standard discourse in the field of organizational studies, and although it might have lost a bit of its original distinctiveness along the way, it has not lost its initial vibrancy, and – judging from citation patterns – still stands on the shoulders of its founders.

NOTES

1. In preparing this chapter, I looked at the ISI Web of Science citation database to get a sense of the impact of the works on organizational institutionalism just cited. Meyer and Rowan (1977) has been cited about 2,300 times since publication, Scott (1995/2000/2008) over 1,000 times, Scott (1987) over 400 times, Zucker (1987) more than 300 times, and Meyer and Scott (1983) nearly 200 times.

2. Meyer and Scott were not the only ones following this script. Hannan and the organizational ecologists also appear to have been operating in this way, as would be true of Pfeffer in the building of resource dependence theory. As an historical footnote, for example, note the tendency in most of the 1970s Stanford sociology work to formulate formal propositions – even in a work as dense as Meyer and Rowan (1977).

3. World polity theory – a related form of institutional theory – grew out of a different work group that was operating at the same time and included Mike Hannan, John Meyer, and a large group of graduate students, including Albert Bergeson, John Boli, Chris Chase-Dunn, Jacques Delacroix, Ylmaz Esmer, Francois Nielsen, Francisco Ramirez, Richard Rubinson, and George Thomas. Even as Meyer, Scott, and I were developing organizational institutionalism at SCRDT, this group, housed in the sociology department, was actively thinking about what was then called "world systems theory" and developing the kinds of archival and quantitative research methods that were later discussed as hallmarks of quantitative research on institutional

theory by Jepperson (2002), Ventresca and Mohr (2002), and Schneiberg and Clemens (2006). This work group spanned multiple perspectives on cross-national research in sociology, published various empirical papers in first-rate journals, and produced an edited volume (Meyer & Hannan, 1979). It was also the spawning ground for the more macro-level brand of Stanford institutionalism – world polity theory.

4. It is interesting to observe that another "founding" paper in institutional theory – DiMaggio and Powell (1983) experienced exactly the same divided response from reviewers (Greenwood & Meyer, 2008).

5. As an example of this uptake process consider that by 2009, about 68% of citations to Meyer and Rowan (1977) listed in the ISI social science citation database were from the fields of management and business, whereas only about 19% were from sociology. Moreover, 75% of all citations came from journals published in North America. Also, about 77% of citations to Scott (1995/2000/2008) in that same database were from the fields of management and business, and only 9% from sociology, with 65% coming from North American journals.

6. It is interesting to note that world polity theory has taken a course of development that differs from organizational institutionalism. In developing this perspective, Meyer and colleagues seem to have stayed more within the field of sociology, as evidenced not only by where the world polity group publishes, but also by the sources of citations to the work. As an example, I looked at the sources of citations to the group's most highly cited work (Meyer et al., 1997). Here, 48% of 364 citations come from journals in sociology, 23% from political science/ international relations, and just 6% from business and management. In my view, location in this field is what has allowed world polity theory to maintain more of an emphasis on the early themes of the Stanford brand of institutional theory, including core commitments to studying crescive institution building, central source diffusion, loose coupling of institutions and activities, and a view of individuals as constituted by (and then enacting) heavily institutionalized scripts, rather than operating as self-interested actors. Still, critiques like those made of organizational institutionalism in the business school field are emerging with respect to world polity theory (see, e.g., Beckfield, 2008), although consistent with the arguments of Augier et al., 2005), the fields of sociology and political science seem more tolerant of the original idealism of the Stanford approach than does scholarship in the business school field.

REFERENCES

Augier, M., March, J. G., & Sullivan, B. N. (2005). Notes on the evolution of a research community: Organization studies in Anglophone North America, 1945–2000. *Organization Science, 16*(1), 85–95.

Beckfield, J. (2008). The dual world polity: Fragmentation and integration in the network of intergovernmental organizations. *Social Problems, 55*(3), 419–442.

Berger, J., & Zelditch, M., Jr. (Eds). (2002). *New directions in contemporary sociological theory.* Lanham, MD: Rowman and Littlefield.

Berger, J., Zelditch, M., Jr., & Anderson, B. (1966). *Sociological theories in progress.* Boston: Houghton Mifflin.

Berger, P. L., & Luckmann, T. (1966). *The social construction of reality: A treatise in the sociology of knowledge*. New York: Irvington Publishers.
Bidwell, C. (1965). The school as formal organization. In: J. G. March (Ed.), *Handbook of organizations* (pp. 972–1019). New York: Rand McNally.
Blau, P. M. (1970). Formal theory of differentiation in organizations. *American Sociological Review, 35*(2), 201–218.
Boli, J., & Thomas, G. M. (Eds). (1999). *Constructing world culture: International nngovernmental oganizations since 1875*. Stanford, CA: Stanford University Press.
Brinton, M. C., & Nee, V. (1998). *The new institutionalism in sociology*. Stanford, CA: Stanford University Press.
Cohen, E. G., Deal, T. E., Meyer, J. W., & Scott, W. R. (1979). Technology and teaming in the elementary school. *Sociology of Education, 52*(1), 20–33.
Davis, G. F., McAdam, D., Scott, W. R., & Zald, M. (Eds). (2005). *Social movements and organization theory*. New York: Cambridge University Press.
DiMaggio, P. J., & Powell, W. W. (1983). The iron cage revisited: Institutional isomorphism and collective rationality in organizational fields. *American Sociological Review, 48*(2), 147–160.
Dobbin, F. (1994). *Forging industrial policy: The United States, Britain, and France in the railway age*. New York: Cambridge University Press.
Dobbin, F. (Ed.) (2004). *The new economic sociology: A reader*. Princeton, NJ: Princeton University Press.
Doti, J. L., & Tuggle, F. D. (2005). Doing the math on B-school enrollments. *BizEd*, (July/August), 46–50.
Drori, G., Meyer, J. W., & Hwang, H. (Eds). (2006). *Globalization and organization: World society and organizational change*. New York: Oxford University Press.
Edelman, L. B., & Suchman, M. C. (1997). The legal environments of organizations. *Annual Review of Sociology, 23*, 479–515.
Fennell, M. L., & Alexander, J. A. (1993). Perspective on organization change in the United States medical sector. *Annual Review of Sociology, 19*, 89–112.
Greenwood, R., & Meyer, R. E. (2008). Influencing ideas: A celebration of DiMaggio and Powell (1983). *Journal of Management Inquiry, 17*(4), 258–264.
Greenwood, R., Oliver, C., Suddaby, R., & Sahlin-Andersson, K. (2008). *The SAGE handbook of organizational institutionalism*. Thousand Oaks, CA: Sage.
Hage, J., & Aiken, M. (1967). Relationship of centralization to other structural properties. *Administrative Science Quarterly, 12*(1), 72–92.
Hannan, M. T., & Freeman, J. (1984). Structural inertia and organizational change. *American Journal of Sociology, 92*, 910–943.
Hirsch, P. M. (1997). Institutions and organizations: Theory and research (book review). *American Journal of Sociology, 102*(6), 1702–1723.
Hirsch, P. M., & Lounsbury, M. (1997). Putting the organization back into organization theory – Action, change, and the "new" institutionalism. *Journal of Management Inquiry, 6*(1), 79–88.
Jepperson, R. (2002). The development and application of sociological neo-institutionalism. In: J. Berger & M. Zelditch, Jr. (Eds), *New directions in contemporary sociological theory* (pp. 229–266). Lanham, MD: Rowman and Littlefield.
Kruken, G., & Drori, G. S. (Eds). (2009). *World society: The writings of John W. Meyer*. New York: Oxford University Press.
Lortie, D. C. (1975). *Schoolteacher: A sociological study*. Chicago: University of Chicago Press.

March, J. G., & Olsen, J. P. (1984). The new institutionalism: Organizational factors in political life. *American Political Science Review, 78*, 734–749.

Merton, R. K. (1968). *Social theory and social structure.* New York: Free Press.

Meyer, H. D., & Rowan, B. (Eds). (2006). *The new institutionalism in education: Advancing research and policy.* Albany, NY: State University of New York Press.

Meyer, J. W. (1970). The charter: Conditions of diffuse socialization in schools. In: W. R. Scott (Ed.), *Social processes and social structures* (pp. 564–578). New York: Holt, Rinehart, and Winston.

Meyer, J. W. (1977). The effects of education as an institution. *American Journal of Sociology, 83*(1), 55–77.

Meyer, J. W. (1983). Centralization and funding and control in educational governance. In: J. W. Meyer & W. R. Scott (Eds), *Organizational environments: Ritual and rationality* (pp. 179–198). Beverly Hills, CA: Sage.

Meyer, J. W. (2000). Globalization: Sources, and effects on national states and societies. *International Sociology, 15*(2), 235–250.

Meyer, J. W. (2008). Reflections on institutional theories of organizations. In: R. Greenwood, C. Oliver, R. Suddaby & K. Sahlin-Andersson (Eds), *The SAGE handbook of organizational institutionalism* (pp. 788–809). Thousand Oaks, CA: Sage.

Meyer, J. W., & Hannan, M. (Eds). (1979). *National development and the world system.* Chicago: University of Chicago Press.

Meyer, J. W., & Rowan, B. (1977). Institutionalized organizations: Formal structure as myth and ceremony. *American Journal of Sociology, 83*(2), 340–363.

Meyer, J. W., & Rowan, B. (1978). The structure of educational organizations. In: M. W. Meyer and Associates (Ed.), *Environments and organizations* (pp. 78–109). San Francisco: Jossey-Bass.

Meyer, J. W., & Scott, W. R. (1983). *Organizational environments: Ritual and rationality.* Beverly Hills, CA: Sage.

Meyer, J. W., Boli, J., Thomas, G. M., & Ramirez, F. (1997). World society and the nation-state. *American Journal of Sociology, 103*(1), 144–181.

Meyer, J. W., Kamens, D., & Benavot, A. (1992). *School knowledge for the masses: World models and national primary curricular categories in the twentieth century.* Philadelphia: Falmer Press.

Meyer, J. W., Ramirez, F. O., Frank, D. J., & Shofer, E. (2007). Higher education as an institution. In: P. Gumport (Ed.), *The sociology of higher education* (pp. 187–221). Baltimore, MD: The Johns Hopkins University Press.

Meyer, J. W., Scott, W. R., & Deal, T. E. (1983). Institutional and technical sources of organizational structure: Explaining the structure of educational organizations. In: J. W. Meyer & W. R. Scott (Eds), *Organizational environments: Ritual and rationality* (pp. 45–70). Beverly Hills, CA: Sage.

Meyer and Associates, M. W. (1978). *Organizations and environments.* San Francisco: Jossey Bass.

Mizruchi, M. S., & Fein, L. C. (1999). The social construction of organizational knowledge: A study of the uses of coercive, mimetic, and normative isomorphism. *Administrative Science Quarterly, 44*(4), 653–683.

Ouchi, W. G. (1980). Markets, bureaucracies, and clans. *Administrative Science Quarterly, 25*, 129–141.

Perrow, C. (1972). *Complex organizations: A critical essay.* Glenview, IL: Scott Foresman.

Pfeffer, J., & Barron, J. N. (1988). Taking the workers back out: Recent trends in the structuring of employment. *Research in Organizational Behavior, 10*, 257–303.

Powell, W. W., & DiMaggio, P. J. (Eds). (1991). *The new institutionalism in organizational analysis.* Chicago: University of Chicago Press.

Ramirez, F. O., & Meyer, J. W. (1980). Comparative education: The social construction of the modern world system. *Annual Review of Sociology, 6*, 369–399.

Rowan, B., & Miskel, C. G. (1999). Institutional theory and the study of educational organizations. In: J. Murphy & K. S. Lewis (Eds), *Handbook of research on educational administration* (pp. 359–383). San Francisco: Jossey Bass.

Schneiberg, M., & Clemens, E. S. (2006). The typical tools for the job: Research strategies in institutional analysis. *Sociological Theory, 24*(3), 195–226.

Scott, W. R. (1987). The adolescence of institutional theory. *Administrative Science Quarterly, 32*, 493–511.

Scott, W. R. (1995/2000/2008). *Institutions and organizations.* Thousand Oaks: Sage.

Scott, W. R. (2005). Institutional theory: Contributing to a theoretical research program. In: K. G. Smith & M. A. Hitt (Eds), *Great minds in management: The process of theory development* (pp. 465–480). New York: Oxford University Press.

Scott, W. R. (2006). Ad Astra per Aspera: A journey from the periphery. *Organization Studies, 27*, 877–897.

Scott, W. R. (2008). Approaching adulthood: The maturing of institutional theory. *Theory and Society, 37*, 427–442.

Scott, W. R., & Christensen, S. (Eds). (1995). *The institutional construction of organizations: International and longitudinal studies.* Thousand Oaks: Sage.

Scott, W. R., & Meyer, J. W. (1983). The organization of societal sectors. In: J. W. Meyer & W. R. Scott (Eds), *Organizational environments: Ritual and rationality* (pp. 129–154). Beverly Hills, CA: Sage.

Scott, W. R., & Meyer and Associates, J. W. (1994). *Institutional environments and organizations: Structural complexity and individualism.* Thousand Oaks: Sage.

Scott, W. R., Ruef, M., Mendel, P., & Caronna, C. (2000). *Institutional change and healthcare organizations: From professional dominance to managed care.* Chicago: University of Chicago Press.

Thomas, G. M., & Meyer, J. W. (1984). The expansion of the state. *Annual Review of Sociology, 10*, 461–482.

Ventresca, M. J., & Mohr, J. (2002). Archival methods in organization studies. In: J. A. Baum (Ed.), *Companion to organizations* (pp. 805–828). Malden, MA: Blackwell.

Weick, K. E. (1976). Educational organizations as loosely coupled systems. *Administrative Science Quarterly, 21*(1), 1–19.

Zucker, L. G. (1977). The role of institutionalization in cultural persistence. *American Sociological Review, 42*(5), 726–743.

Zucker, L. G. (1987). Institutional theories of organization. *Annual Review of Sociology, 13*, 443–461.

CHAPTER 2

RESOURCE DEPENDENCE THEORY: PAST AND FUTURE

Gerald F. Davis and J. Adam Cobb

ABSTRACT

This chapter reviews the origins and primary arguments of resource dependence theory and traces its influence on the subsequent literatures in multiple social science and professional disciplines, contrasting it with Emerson's power-dependence theory. Recent years have seen an upsurge in the theory's citations in the literature, which we attribute in part to Stanford's position of power in the network of academic exchange. We conclude with a review of some promising lines of recent research that extend and qualify resource dependence theory's insights, and outline potentially fruitful areas of future research.

There must have been something in the air during the time of the Ford Administration, as a half-dozen of the enduring paradigms for the study of organizations emerged at roughly the same time – many of them at Stanford. A theoretical Cambrian explosion saw the major statements of transaction cost economics (Williamson, 1975), agency theory (Jensen & Meckling, 1976), new institutional theory (Meyer & Rowan, 1977), population ecology (Hannan & Freeman, 1977), and resource dependence

Stanford's Organization Theory Renaissance, 1970–2000
Research in the Sociology of Organizations, Volume 28, 21–42
ISSN: 0733-558X/doi:10.1108/S0733-558X(2010)0000028006

theory (RDT) (Aldrich & Pfeffer, 1976; Pfeffer & Salancik, 1978). Like other products of the mid-1970s, such as disco and polyester clothing, each of these approaches continues to exercise influence today, even as some of the core questions asked by organization theorists have changed (Davis, 2005). And the Cambrian analogy is appropriate, as all of these approaches except agency theory evolved in part from a common ancestor, Thompson's (1967) masterful synthesis *Organizations in Action*, and spread out in different directions to become (friendly) competitors. Of all these paradigms, RDT is perhaps the most comprehensive in the scope of its approach to organizations, combining an account of power within organizations with a theory of how organizations seek to manage their environments.

This chapter describes the basic elements of RDT and the empirical support for its account of organization-environment relations. We then provide evidence of the theory's ongoing influence across a number of social science fields, drawing on comprehensive data from the Social Science Citation Index (SSCI), and contrast the citation career of *The External Control of Organizations* (Pfeffer & Salancik, 1978) with that of "Power-dependence relations," Emerson's (1962) classic statement of power and exchange. Our analysis shows that RDT has had an expansive influence that spread from management and sociology to education, health care, public policy, and other cognate disciplines. When scholars study power in and around organizations, they are highly likely to draw on RDT. We next propose three alternative hypotheses for RDT's ongoing influence: it is empirically accurate; its imagery of power and conflict fit with the tenor of the times; and it benefited from Stanford's hegemony over doctoral education in organization studies. We close with some thoughts on exemplary recent work and suggestions on future directions.

WHAT DOES RDT SAY?

Although the focus of this volume is on Stanford's contribution to organization studies, resource dependence owes as much to the University of Illinois as it does to Stanford, according to Pfeffer (2003). After receiving his BS and MS degrees from Carnegie-Mellon University, Jeff Pfeffer entered the doctoral program in organizational behavior at the Stanford Graduate School of Business and completed his PhD in under three years (a record subsequently bested only by William Ocasio, now at Northwestern). He went on to faculty positions first at the University of Illinois at Urbana-Champaign and then the University of California at Berkeley, returning to

Stanford as a faculty member in 1979. Pfeffer's dissertation was a remarkable set of demonstrations of the importance of exchange and power relations in and around organizations, and his time at Illinois resulted in a flood of early publications arising from his dissertation (e.g., Pfeffer, 1972a, 1972b, 1972c). The fertile intellectual soil of Urbana-Champaign, coupled with Gerry Salancik's complementary micro-orientation, allowed RDT to grow like a mighty stalk of corn. But to strain the simile to the breaking point, it is fair to say that the seeds for the theory were carried from Stanford and germinated by Jeff Pfeffer's dissertation committee, which included James Miller, Mike Hannan, Dick Scott, and Eugene Webb. Pfeffer credited Gene Webb in particular as an important and under-appreciated influence at Stanford, as Gene had a talent for finding unobtrusive methods of studying organizational phenomena, which contrasted with the dominant survey-based approach of the time.

The External Control of Organizations, the 1978 book that consolidated the work between Jeff's initial time at Stanford and his subsequent move from Illinois to Berkeley, covered a lot of territory, from the internal power struggles among individuals and departments to industry-level dynamics. But the most widely used aspects of the theory outlined in *External Control* analyze the sources and consequences of power in interorganizational relations: where power and dependence come from, and how those that run organizations use their power and manage their dependence. As Jeff Pfeffer put it in the revised edition of the book, "Resource dependence was originally developed to provide an alternative perspective to economic theories of mergers and board interlocks, and to understand precisely the type of interorganizational relations that have played such a large role in recent 'market failures'" (Pfeffer, 2003, p. 25). The motivation of those running the organization was to ensure the organization's survival and to enhance their own autonomy, while also maintaining stability in the organization's exchange relations. These were the drivers behind many of the organization's observed actions. Moreover, when it came to explaining strategy, power often trumped profits, an insight distinctly at odds with the dominant economic approaches of the time.

There are three core ideas of the theory: (1) social context matters; (2) organizations have strategies to enhance their autonomy and pursue interests; and (3) power (not just rationality or efficiency) is important for understanding internal and external actions of organizations. The emphasis on power, and a careful articulation of the explicit repertoires of tactics available to organizations, is a hallmark of RDT that distinguishes it from other approaches, such as transaction cost economics. The basic story of exchange-based power in the theory was derived from Emerson's (1962) parsimonious account: the power of A over B comes from control of resources that B values and that are not available elsewhere. In this account, power and dependence are simply the obverse of each other: B is dependent on A to the degree that A has power over B. Further, power is not zero-sum, as A and B can each have power over each other, making them *interdependent*. Concretely, to use a favorite example of transaction cost theorists, General Motors (GM) was dependent on Fisher Body for auto bodies because these were not readily available in volume elsewhere. At the same time, Fisher was dependent on GM because it was the predominant buyer of Fisher's products. Emerson's account of exchange-based power also found ready operationalization via the industry concentration data published by the Census Bureau and the industry input–output matrices published by Bureau of Economic Analysis, an approach artfully developed by Ron Burt in subsequent work (e.g., Burt, 1983, 1988).

Prior theorists had argued for the relevance of interorganizational power to strategy and structure (e.g., Thompson, 1967), but RDT added an elaborate catalog of organizational responses to interdependence that could inform empirical work. The basic theory might be summarized by a piece of advice to top managers: "Choose the least-constraining device to govern relations with your exchange partners that will allow you to minimize uncertainty and dependence and maximize your autonomy." The array of tactics described by the theory forms a continuum from least- to most-constraining. If dependence comes from relying on a sole-source supplier, then an obvious solution is to find and maintain alternatives. (This is, of course, standard practice in manufacturing.) Growing large in and of itself is also a potential source of advantage – particularly if one grows too big to fail, a tactic that has served several giant American financial institutions well recently. Large size might also allow an organization to call on the government for reinforcement. For instance, when a large national real estate firm headquartered in Michigan faced an unwanted takeover bid from an out-of-state rival a few years ago, it was able to successfully call on the state legislature to pass legislation to prevent the takeover and thus (allegedly) save local jobs – including, of course, those of the company's own managers.

Other tactics require more-or-less coordinated efforts with other organizations, thereby entailing somewhat more constraint. The least entangling of these is to join associations or business groups. A somewhat more constraining choice is to form an alliance or joint venture with the source of one's constraint. Alliances "involve agreements between two or more organizations to pursue joint objectives through a coordination of activities or sharing of knowledge or resources" (Scott & Davis, 2007, pp. 206–207) and can include joint research and development contracts, licensing and franchising agreements, shared manufacturing and marketing arrangements, minority investments, and equity swaps, among other possibilities. The prevalence of alliances has skyrocketed since the publication of *External Control*, as a range of formal and informal alternatives to vertical integration (i.e., solutions that are neither market nor hierarchy, in transaction cost terms) have developed (Gulati, 2007). Early evidence suggested that joint ventures were most common in industries at intermediate levels of concentration (Pfeffer & Salancik, 1978, pp. 152–161), which is where one would expect to see the greatest degree of "manageable interdependence."

A riskier strategy for managing dependence is to co-opt it. Drawing on Selznick's (1949) account of the Tennessee Valley Authority, the theory suggests that an organization can manage uncertainty by inviting a representative of the source of constraint onto its governing board, thus trading sovereignty for support. Firms might invite executives of constraining suppliers or major customers onto their board to gain their support, or startups might add a venture capitalist to the board to maintain sources of funding, or corporations reliant on government contracts might invite former senators and cabinet members to join the board to gain contacts and signal legitimacy. The expectation is that having a representative serving on the board provides the source of constraint with a vested interest in the dependent organization's survival. For the first several years, board ties were probably "the most empirically examined form of intercorporate relation" from a resource dependence perspective (Pfeffer, 1987, p. 42), although the literature on alliances undoubtedly dwarfs all other domains at this point. The evidence on board ties, like that on joint ventures, primarily came from industry-level correlations showing that the prevalence of ties to competitors was related to the level of industry concentration (Pfeffer & Salancik, 1978), while interindustry ties mapped onto the level of exchange-based constraint between the industries (Burt, 1983).

The most constraining method of managing dependence is to incorporate it within the organization's boundary through mergers and acquisitions. The prescription to absorb uncertainty that cannot otherwise be managed dates back to Thompson (1967), but Pfeffer was undoubtedly the person that pursued this idea most vigorously with empirical data. Mergers take three general forms: vertical (buying suppliers or buyers), horizontal (buying competitors), and diversifying or conglomerate mergers (buying organizations in a different domain). *External Control* argued that mergers – seen by those with an efficiency orientation as a means of reducing transaction costs, to the ultimate benefit of consumers – were actually a means of managing interdependence, and may provide little benefit to either consumers or shareholders. "We argue that vertical integration represents a method of extending organizational control over exchanges vital to its operation; that horizontal expansion represents a method for attaining dominance to increase the organization's power in exchange relationships and to reduce uncertainty generated from competition; and that diversification represents a method for decreasing the organization's dependence on other, dominant organizations" (Pfeffer & Salancik, 1978, p. 114).

A distinctive feature of merger as a strategy of managing dependence is that the legality and prevalence of different kinds of mergers varied substantially over the course of the 20th century. Buying competitors was limited by the Sherman Act of 1890 and its subsequent interpretations, and other acquisition strategies were increasingly constrained during the decades prior to the Reagan Administration. Thus, by the 1960s and 1970s, the time period that RDT was developed, American firms were largely limited to diversification as a means of expansion (see Fligstein, 1990 for a brief history of antitrust and its effects on organizational strategies). During the 1980s, on the other hand, antitrust enforcement became substantially more relaxed, and industry deregulation in the 1990s led to waves of horizontal mergers in pharmaceuticals, defense, banking, and other industries.

Early studies at the industry level supported the basic predictions of RDT. Interindustry mergers were more common among transaction partners, consistent with the idea that firm growth was oriented toward sources of constraint. Further, intraindustry mergers were most common at medium levels of concentration – the rationale being that highly concentrated industries were constrained from further consolidation by antitrust concerns (and firms in them could coordinate their actions implicitly), while firms in highly competitive industries would gain little leverage through integration (Pfeffer & Salancik, 1978). For constrained firms without access to horizontal or vertical integration, diversification was a plausible tactic.

The sheer volume and diversity of empirical analyses summarized in *External Control* is surely an important reason for RDT's continuing influence. Also it is hard to disagree with the basic notion that organizational strategies are often driven as much by power dynamics and managerial aggrandizement as by profit (or "shareholder value"), in light of the various financial scandals of the past decade. On the other hand, the evidence behind some of the specific claims of RDT is not always perfect. In particular, as "an alternative perspective to economic theories of mergers and board interlocks," RDT faces two limitations.

First, the analyses of mergers and interlocks were done at the industry level rather than the organizational level, which leaves their results susceptible to claims of an ecological fallacy. Robinson (1950) demonstrated that correlations at the group level need not apply at the individual level. His example compared levels of literacy and immigration: at the state level, having a higher proportion of immigrants was strongly positively related to the rate of literacy, while at the individual level the opposite was true (i.e., immigrants had lower levels of literacy on average than native citizens). A more recent example might be the 2008 presidential election: well over 90% of African-American voters supported Barack Obama, yet the correlation between the percentage of a state that is black and the percentage of the state that voted for Obama was negative (–0.09), and five of the six states with the highest proportion of African-American residents (Mississippi, Louisiana, South Carolina, Georgia, and Alabama) voted heavily in favor of McCain. In other words, a relationship that holds in the aggregate (a state) need not be true for its constituents (individual voters), and vice versa.

Similarly, findings at the highly aggregated industry level may say little about firm-level dynamics. A simple example suffices: Pfeffer and Salancik (1978, p. 166) report that "The amount of competitor interlocking is positively related to the level of [industry] concentration and negatively related to the difference in concentration from an intermediate level," yet at the firm level there are zero true "competitor interlocks." Sharing directors among firms in the same industry has been illegal since the Clayton Act of 1914, and it is one of the easiest provisions to police, given that board memberships are public information. The apparent prevalence of "intraindustry" interlocking most likely reflects the highly aggregated nature of industry boundaries in the data: Zajac (1988) notes that SIC code 28 (Chemicals) included firms in such disparate industries as "Chemicals and Allied Products" (DuPont, Dow, Monsanto), "Drugs" (Merck, Lilly, Pfizer), "Soaps and Detergents" (Procter & Gamble, Colgate-Palmolive), "Perfumes and Cosmetics" (Avon, Revlon), and "Paint, Varnish, and Lacquers" (Sherwin-Williams, Insilco).

A second limitation to the empirical findings in *External Control* is the obverse of one of the theory's strengths. The reported empirical results documented that a parsimonious theory of power predicted a wide range of specific organizational actions, from who was put on the board to what kinds of acquisitions an organization engaged in. But organizational repertoires have evolved enormously, along with their environments.

Organizations that diversified in the 1960s and 1970s were highly likely to be taken over and perhaps split up during the 1980s, as happened to nearly one-third of the 1980 Fortune 500. Relatively few firms diversified outside of a small set of industries (notably finance and media), and by the 1990s layoffs, spinoffs, and outsourcing had replaced growth and diversification as dominant organizational strategies (Davis, Diekmann, & Tinsley, 1994). By the 1990s, evidence suggested that board interlocks never occurred within an industry, and were quite rare among major buyers and suppliers, or between corporations and their bankers – executives tended to find the notion of co-opting a supplier through a board seat to be a bad idea, given the board's legal duty of loyalty (Davis, 1996).

In spite of the changing prevalence of the types of mergers and interlocks described in RDT, it is clear that power and dependence relations among organizations, and the managerial lust for self-aggrandizement, had not gone away due to the advent of "shareholder value" (Pfeffer, 2003) – they had simply found new modes of expression, as shareholders in Enron, WorldCom, AIG, and Citigroup were to discover.

TRACING THE INFLUENCE OF *THE EXTERNAL CONTROL OF ORGANIZATIONS*

The usefulness of a given work is determined in part by the extent to which the ideas contained within it are subsequently utilized by others (Small, 1978). Citations, in particular, play an important role in the development of scholarly work and serve as a form of certification, ascribing merit to the claims made in a given publication. Though an admittedly imperfect means by which to assess the impact and importance of scholarly work, examining citation patterns provides one window through which we can quantify the importance that *External Control of Organizations* has had across academic disciplines. We collected annual citation counts of *External Control of Organizations* from the SSCI database. Although SSCI has its own system of categorizing citations, this system does not, unfortunately, differentiate between sub-disciplines of business (e.g., there is no separate category for "Strategy"). In an effort to capture the influence of *External Control* more granularly, we created our own classification scheme, basing categories on the journal in which the article was published. Our classification scheme allowed us to examine in detail the influence that *External Control* has had across a variety of academic disciplines.

One of the major contributions of RDT was to bring issues of power to the forefront of organizational studies (Pfeffer, 2003); as such, we also analyzed the citation counts of Emerson's (1962) classic article, "Power-dependence relations," which took a more abstract approach to power among "actors" (broadly construed). As of July 2008, *External Control* had been cited 3,334 times over the 30 years since its publication, making it one of the most highly cited works ever in the study of organizations. "Power-dependence relations" was cited roughly 1,000 times over 46 years, 145 of which occurred prior to the publication of *External Control* in 1978. A total of 236 publications cite both works.

Fig. 1 makes clear that *External Control*'s impact is derived not only from its influence in Management and other business fields, such as Marketing,

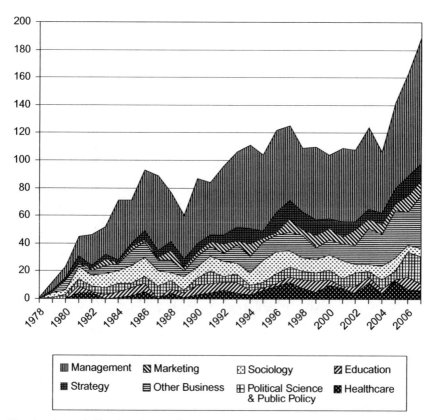

Fig. 1. Annual Citation Counts for *External Control of Organizations*, 1978–2007.

but also in how its arguments and concepts have spread to other disciplines beyond management and sociology. Education and Healthcare, for instance, accounted for 116 and 154 of the total citations, respectively. Interestingly, over the past decade *External Control* has been cited as often in Healthcare journals as in Sociology journals. Additionally, there have been 191 total citations in Political Science and Public Policy journals, 40% of which are from this decade. This pattern of citations indicates a significant scholarly breadth in the impact of *External Control*. In comparison, the trend line in Fig. 2 indicates there was a steady increase in citations to "Power-dependence relations" until around 1984, and since that time there have been a relatively constant number of total annual citations. Whereas *External Control* is most heavily cited in business disciplines,

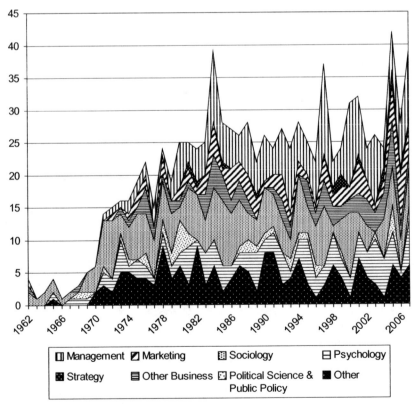

Fig. 2. Annual Citation Counts for *Power-Dependence Relations*, 1962–2007.

particularly in Management and Strategy, "Power-dependence relations" has received more of its attention in the core social science disciplines, particularly in journals of Sociology and Psychology, which account for 23% and 13% of its total citations, respectively.

One explanation for this pattern is the relevant units of analysis in these different domains. RDT works best for describing organizations, whereas Emerson's approach is more descriptive of individuals. Thus, if one needs to cite an authority for the claim that power matters (Stinchcombe's, 1982 "small change" function), then those that focus on individuals (e.g., Psychology, Marketing) will cite Emerson and those that focus on firms (e.g., Management, Strategy, Education, Healthcare) cite Pfeffer and Salancik.

On the other hand, there are 236 articles that cite both *External Control* and "Power-dependence relations." But there were only 14 citations of Emerson (1962) in Management journals between 1962 and 1978, and 102 citations after the publication of *External Control*. This suggests that *External Control* served to draw attention among management scholars to power-dependence relations both within and among organizations. And of the 222 citations of "Power-dependence relations" in management journals, nearly half also cite *External Control*. In other words, the two works are perhaps best thought of as complements rather than competitors. There is much less overlap in citations in Sociology and Psychology, however. This may be because management studies are more likely to cross levels of analysis, making interpersonal and firm dynamics relevant in the same study.

Trends in citations over time indicate two broad conclusions. First, *External Control* continues to influence organizational scholars in a range of diverse domains, from Management and Strategy to Healthcare and Education, indicating that its approach is broadly applicable across a range of organizational types. Second, within Sociology, *External Control's* influence has begun to taper over the past few years. This may be attributable to the rise of economic sociology as a friendly competitor to organization theory. With its focus on markets, networks, institutions, and identity, rather than on organizations as actors, economic sociology provides perhaps a less hospitable home for actor-oriented accounts of power and exchange, such as RDT.

WHAT ACCOUNTS FOR THIS PATTERN?

We propose three distinct hypotheses for the pattern of influence of RDT: (1) it was empirically accurate; (2) it fit with the social environment that researchers operated in; and (3) it reflected a kind of Stanford hegemony in which one university managed to foist its particular worldview off on the field, privileging its local products. We consider each of these hypotheses in turn.

Hypothesis 1. *RDT was successful because it fit with the empirical world of its time.* In the mid-1970s, big corporations seemed to control the world, fulfilling the prophecy set out by Berle and Means (1932): "The rise of the modern corporation has brought a concentration of economic power which can compete on equal terms with the modern state…. The future may see the economic organism, now typified by the corporation, not only on an equal plane with the state, but possibly even superseding it as the dominant form of social organization." Conglomerates, in particular, seemed destined to engulf and devour everything in their path. ("Engulf and Devour" was, of course, a snide sobriquet for Gulf & Western, one of the large conglomerates of the 1970s.) Their growth paths seemed to follow no clear logic other than empire-building for its own sake; certainly, the stock market provided a harsh judgment of their tactics, and their efficiency rationale was singularly unconvincing (Davis et al., 1994).

RDT offered a parsimonious account for perplexing growth machines such as the modern conglomerate. Ultimately it was all about power. Take ITT, which had grown from an obscure Caribbean phone company to America's 10th-largest corporation in 1970 through a string of hundreds of acquisitions during the 1960s that included Sheraton hotels, the producer of Wonder Bread and Twinkies, Avis Rent-A-Car, various auto parts manufacturers, insurance companies, and a chain of vocational schools. What rational model of organizations could account for this crazy industrial archipelago? Certainly, Thompson's dictum to buffer the technical core would never predict using Wonder Bread as the proper material. And what theory of organizational boundaries would lump together the producer of Belgian phone directories with schools for auto mechanics? From the perspective of rationality and efficiency, ITT and its ilk (GE, Gulf & Western, Textron, LTV, Westinghouse, and many of the other largest corporations of the 1970s) were an aberration, whose size and diversity served no economic purpose. But power explained this and more – for instance, ITT's alleged role in the coup against the democratically elected government of Salvador Allende in Chile in September 1973.

By this hypothesis, the popularity of RDT should wax and wane according to the prevalence of the tactics it described. As we noted in the previous section, thanks to the rise of so-called "shareholder capitalism," vertical integration has been largely replaced by alliances and out-sourcing; competitive or co-opting interlocks are nearly non-existent in the United States these days; and diversification is rare outside a handful of industries, and never approaches the brash approach of ITT. (ITT itself endured multiple rounds of restructurings and spinoffs in the 1980s and 1990s, and the remaining stub was acquired by Starwood Hotels in 1997.) Moreover, "size" as traditionally measured is no longer a source of power. Consider that in 2005, GM had 335,000 employees and revenues of over $190 billion, whereas Google had $6 billion in revenues and fewer than 6,000 employees. Which is more powerful? Which is more likely to have influence in Washington? (For comparison purposes, in early 2009 Google's market capitalization was over $100 billion, compared to GM's $2.25 billion.)

We, therefore, would expect to see the popularity of RDT wane with the rise of shareholder capitalism and the associated decline in the prevalence of the tactics favored by RDT: vertical integration, diversifica-tion, and board interlocks with constraining suppliers. Shareholder capitalism has its own repertoire of corporate tactics and privileges market-based measures over traditional indicators of size and power such as sales and employment. One might imagine that RDT would appear outmoded if the outcomes on which it focused became rare, yet this has not happened: the theory continues to have a broad influence among students of organizations across a variety of domains, and even shows signs of a revival. We must, then, look elsewhere for an explanation.

Hypothesis 2. *RDT was successful because it fit with the social and scholarly environment of its time.* It is perhaps not a coincidence that power-based accounts grew in dominance during the time of disillusion that followed the 1960s, just as functionalism was being mothballed in sociology. Who could take Parsons seriously with Nixon in the White House? Jeff Pfeffer attributes some of his thinking to the social environment at the time, with the advent of the civil rights, feminist, and antiwar movements providing daily evidence of power in action, and the illusion of benign governance shattered by the deceptions of Vietnam and Watergate. As Jane Wagner put it, "No matter how cynical you get, it's never enough to keep up."

The empirical implication would seem to be that the popularity of RDT should reflect the ambient cynicism in the world, perhaps with more functionalist approaches such as transaction cost economics or agency theory predominating when cynicism is low. As with the previous hypothesis, however, the prevalence of different theories seems hard to square with our predictions (although it is possible that the Bush Administration is responsible for the recent upsurge of work in RDT, as we describe below). Academic interest in power does not appear to track the salience of power relations in the real world, although a firm conclusion on this would need a more systematic test.

Hypothesis 3. *RDT's popularity reflects Stanford hegemony.* A third possibility is that the popularity of RDT reflects the dominance of Stanford University in controlling scarce resources in organization theory, and thus in compelling its dependents to adopt its worldview. That is, to the extent that Stanford affiliates control the supply of elite journal editors and reviewers, new faculty, and textbooks and other materials used in doctoral training, a Stanford view of which theories are worth studying and testing – and which can be ignored – will come to pervade the academic study of organizations. This Gramscian/Pfefferian hypothesis is an appealing one because it has excess empirical implications, applying not simply to RDT but to the other subjects of this volume. And, of course, it is a direct implication of RDT.

Stanford was a distinctive place during the 1960s and 1970s. The business school, in particular, seemed to take seriously the Ford Foundation and Carnegie Corporation reports of 1959 that chastised business schools in general for their low-caliber students, poorly trained faculty, and weak research. The Carnegie report stated that "Much of the research at these institutions is heavily weighted on the side of description; much of it centers on particular companies or local trade groups; much of it is undertaken because of its practical usefulness; very rarely is emphasis placed on developing analytical findings which can be fitted into a general system of principles and tested in a scientific manner." The Ford report further noted that "more significant research of ultimate value to business has come out of nonbusiness departments of the university" [e.g., psychology, mathematics, statistics, economics, and sociology] "than out of the business schools" (quoted in Daniel, 1998, p. 160). But Stanford's business school came to be singularly devoted to research firmly rooted in the social science disciplines, and embraced an interdisciplinary model of organization studies. Indeed, by the 1980s nearly all the faculty in Organizational Behavior were trained in psychology, sociology, or political science – except, of course, for Jeff Pfeffer. As other business schools adopted the approach to research characteristic of Stanford's business school, perhaps the folkways and values of that institution spread as well.

There are many signs of Stanford hegemony. Scanning the editorial boards of elite journals, for instance, reveals a disproportionate number of current Stanford faculty and graduates (e.g., the editor and three associate editors of one administrative journal we are familiar with are all Stanford fellow travelers). The past four chairs of the Organization and Management Theory division of the Academy of Management (Jerry Davis, Kim Elsbach, Willie Ocasio, and Henrich Greve) were all Stanford graduates. Coincidentally, recent winners of the OMT Distinguished Scholar Award include Woody Powell (2008), Steve Barley (2006), Joanne Martin (2005), and Kathy Eisenhardt (2002) – all Stanford faculty members, joining past winners Jim March, Dick Scott, Mike Hannan, and Jeff Pfeffer for a 29% Stanford market share of the award since its inception. In the Organizations, Occupations & Work section of the American Sociological Association, the best article award itself is titled the "W. Richard Scott Award for Distinguished Scholarship," in honor the man who had seemingly trained half the organizations faculty in America via Sociology 260.

It is a cliché that history is written by the victors. In this case, one of the most potent methods of maintaining Stanford's hegemony is the two books that collectively account for approximately every doctoral course in organization theory and are on every prelim study list in the country for organization studies: Pfeffer's (1982) *Organizations and Organization Theory* and Scott's (1981) *Organizations: Rational, Natural, and Open Systems*. Since their publication in the early 1980s, these two books have crystallized a particular view of organization theory and helped reproduce a canon in which, unsurprisingly, Stanford figures centrally. (Of course, this volume further reproduces this canon.) Independent of empirical validity or social context, Stanford-based theories of the mid-1970s benefited from being canonized within the sandstone walls of the institution that Berkeley-based scholars call "the world's largest Taco Bell."

If this hypothesis is accurate, we should expect the influence of RDT to wax and wane with the market share of Stanford-associated textbooks, faculty, and journal control. But while a sudden drop in sales of the latest incarnation of Dick Scott's book (Scott & Davis, 2007) might be an interesting natural experiment, we cannot advocate it due to humanitarian objections (also known as "kid's tuition bills").

THE REVIVAL OF RDT

Jeff Pfeffer lamented the fact that RDT has been reduced to a "metaphorical statement about organizations" (Pfeffer, 2003, p. 16). One explanation for this is the absence of empirical examination and clarification of the theory's basic premises. In the section that follows, we highlight some of the efforts taken to address this issue, which have led to a "recent renaissance of resource dependence theory" (Katila, Rosenberger, & Eisenhardt, 2008, p. 321).

Pfeffer and Salancik (1978) suggest that certain benefits accrue to firms through their board members: advice and expertise, access to resources, and legitimacy. Given the importance of corporate boards in obtaining these critical benefits, Pfeffer has called for additional work to test the predictions put forth by resource dependence and other theories concerning the determinants of the size and composition of boards (Pfeffer, 2003, p. 18). In answering that call, Amy Hillman (2005) found that firms in heavily regulated industries have more former politicians on their boards than firms in less-regulated industries, and further found some evidence that this is associated with higher levels of financial performance. She inferred that ex-politicians serve as conduits of information and offer access to important political resources that are extremely beneficial to firms operating in highly regulated environments, an interpretation highly consistent with RDT.

Additionally, Hillman, Shropshire, and Cannella (2007) found that the presence of women on corporate boards is consistent with the predictions put forth by RDT. Specifically, large firms that face legitimacy pressures, companies operating in industries that are heavily dependent on female employees, and firms with ties to companies with female board members are likely to have women directors on their board. Thus, the composition of boards seemingly mirrors the environmental constraints faced by firms, giving some credence to the proposition that firms strategically select board members as a means to reduce uncertainty.

RDT also argues that in situations of uncertainty, one strategy is to put representatives of competitors, key suppliers, or customers on the board as a means of co-optation. As we argued earlier, and Jeff Pfeffer (2005, p. 450) himself has admitted, the theory has not had much success in explaining patterns of corporate interlock behavior. The reconstitution of broken ties, for instance, shows at best limited support for resource dependence predictions (e.g., Palmer, 1983). But the insight behind the co-optation hypothesis is still valid. Thus, Westphal, Boivie, and Chng (2006) studied the reconstitution of friendship ties among board members to determine whether these individuals use informal links in lieu of formal board appointments. While companies may not place key suppliers, buyers or competitors on their board, the study shows that individual board members seek to reconstitute broken friendship ties with members of these firms for instrumental reasons. This study extends RDT by showing that the proposed mechanisms motivating the hypotheses related to co-optation through board appointments are captured through less obtrusive means (i.e., friendship ties). In short, the diagnosis of the motivation was apt, but the outlet required modest tweaking of the theory.

External Control of Organizations focuses considerable attention on the ways in which firms become constrained by their environment and the strategies they can employ to manage these dependencies. Because the theory focuses upon the dependent firm, a natural question which arises is, "How do powerful firms exercise their influence and what tactics do they employ to avoid being co-opted by their dependents?" From this starting point, Casciaro and Piskorski (2005) reanalyze Pfeffer and Salancik's concept of interdependence. Pfeffer and Salancik argue that mutual dependence and power imbalance combine to create interdependence – a notion challenged by Casciaro and Piskorski. In a study on merger and acquisition (M&A) activity, these authors argue that power imbalance and mutual dependence have *opposing* effects on the propensity for firms to engage in mergers and acquisitions. By separating and measuring power imbalance and mutual dependence independently, the authors find that power imbalance is an obstacle in M&A activity while mutual dependence drives M&A activity. Their argument is that more powerful firms are less willing to enter into a merger with their dependents, lest they lose the advantages of being the power-holder in the relationship.

In a study of entrepreneurial ventures in U.S. technology-based industries, Katila and colleagues (2008) examine the conditions under which entrepreneurial ventures are likely to be part of a corporate investment relationship. The fundamental tension for the entrepreneur underlying this decision is the tradeoff between access to resources and the potential of being taken advantage of in the relationship. Resource dependence research has focused primarily on the cooperative side of relationship formation while ignoring the potential that one party can be manipulated. Moreover, research has not investigated whether the propensity of being exploited influences the decision to enter into a relationship with another party. As such, Katila and colleagues (2008) find that new firms enter corporate investment relationships when (1) financial resource needs are high, (2) managerial resource needs are great, and

(3) firms can defend themselves against resource misappropriation through defense mechanisms. The authors argue that RDT overlooks the competitive side of tie formation. But these findings show entrepreneurs consider resource needs and defense mechanisms simultaneously when considering relationship formation.

These and other recent contributions to RDT (e.g., Gulati & Sytch, 2007; Ozcan & Eisenhardt, 2009) suggest that there is currently a revival of interest in the theory and offer some clues on where the theory may be heading. One commonality among many of these studies is that they offer some challenge to the basic tenets put forth in *External Control*. Assumptions are being tested (Casciaro & Piskorski, 2005), alternative strategies are being offered (Westphal et al., 2006), and gaps in the theory are being filled (Katila et al., 2008). While these works offer an excellent starting point, it seems there are numerous opportunities for scholarly contribution to RDT.

CONCLUSION

After an unfortunate period of dormancy, there is evidence that interest in RDT is on the rise. In some respects this is not surprising. The status of global affairs is markedly similar to the period in which Jeff Pfeffer conceptualized the theory – economic crisis, dissatisfaction with political leadership, increased social activism – all of which make issues of power and dependency more salient. It is an opportune time for revitalizing RDT for a different economy.

One of the challenges for RDT is that its prescriptions are intertwined with its theoretical predictions (Casciaro & Piskorski, 2005). The prescriptions that arise from *External Control* undoubtedly require modification today – tactics like co-opting suppliers by putting them on the board, or diversifying, probably would do most firms more harm than good. But the underlying theoretical approach of diagnosing the sources of power and dependence and predicting when and in what direction organizations are likely to respond still yields great insight into organizational behavior. Thus, the most useful future work will address one or both of these issues: updating the sources of power and dependence, and cataloging the new set of available tactics for managing dependence. We conclude with some suggestions regarding where to look.

Three master trends that have altered the profiles of power and dependence, and the methods of managing the organization's environment, are the ubiquity of information and communication technologies (ICTs), the rise of finance, and globalization in trade. ICTs (computers, the Internet, mobile telephony) can lower transaction costs by making information about prices and alternatives more readily available, generically lowering dependence among buyers and suppliers able to develop alternatives more readily. It has also altered power relations within firms, as "internal suppliers" (e.g., human resource or IT departments) find that they face potential outside competitors. Fidelity can do payroll and benefits management; united parcel service (UPS) can do assembly and logistics; IDEO can do design. As a result, there has been an explosion of outsourcing, which is not limited to business: families with a fast internet connection and Skype find that they can use offshore vendors to file their taxes, edit their wedding videos, plan their family reunions, and tutor their children (Davis, 2009). Maintaining alternatives has perhaps never been easier; on the other hand, establishing a long-lasting monopoly is increasingly difficult (cf. Alta Vista, AT&T).

Finance has altered power relations within firms by privileging one particular constituency (shareholders), changing metrics of performance (shareholder value), and re-orienting pay and human resource practices (to promote increases in share price). It has also ushered in a stunning array of new tactics for managing dependence, from the creation of investor relations offices (to deal with equity analysts and institutional investors) to the expansive use of exotic off-balance-sheet entities to disguise the financial shape of the organization. As the example of Google suggested, the size that gets a firm power today is market capitalization, not sales or employees, which creates rather different power dynamics.

Finally, globalization has changed the range of potential competitors and the possible outlets for expansion, as well as the typical forms of organization. Adam Smith's pin factory today would undoubtedly be organized as a global supply chain spanning three continents and a half-dozen vendors, with the "original equipment manufacturer" responsible primarily for brand management and licensing its intellectual property from a subsidiary based in Bermuda. Globalization has also put multinational corporations (which includes nearly every U.S. firm outside the retail, banking, and utility industries) into the international relations business, as they now face European administrators that want to regulate them, sovereign wealth funds that want to invest in them, foreign suppliers that want to compete with them, and social movements that want to hold them responsible for the labor practices of their suppliers and the human rights abuses of the governments running the countries where they operate. Firms can now manage legal uncertainty by choosing their preferred "legal vendor" (e.g., Miami-based Royal Caribbean Cruises is incorporated in Liberia for tax purposes), but new forms of uncertainty have a way of finding firms (e.g., the revival of the Alien Tort Claims Act, created in the late 18th century to prosecute pirates but now used by foreign nationals to sue multinationals in U.S. courts).

RDT is rightly regarded as a seminal contribution to organization theory and a proud Stanford product. Events in the 30 years since *External Control* was first published have altered both the sources of organizational power and dependence and the means of their management. But as long as power plays a part in the conduct of organizational life, RDT will continue to provide insight.

ACKNOWLEDGMENTS

We appreciate the helpful comments of Frank Dobbin, Amy Hillman, Jeff Pfeffer, and Flannery Stevens.

REFERENCES

Aldrich, H. E., & Pfeffer, J. (1976). Environments of organizations. *Annual Review of Sociology*, 2, 79–105.

Berle, A. A., & Means, G. C. (1932). *The modern corporation and private property*. New York: MacMillan.

Burt, R. S. (1983). *Corporate profits and cooptation: Networks of market constraints and directorate ties in the American economy*. New York: Academic Press.

Burt, R. S. (1988). The stability of American markets. *American Journal of Sociology*, 94, 356–395.

Casciaro, T., & Piskorski, M. J. (2005). Power imbalance, mutual dependence, and constraint, absorption: A close look at resource dependence theory. *Administrative Science Quarterly*, 50, 167–199.

Daniel, C. A. (1998). *MBA: The first century*. Lewisburg, PA: Bucknell University Press.

Davis, G. F. (1996). The significance of board interlocks for corporate governance. *Corporate Governance*, 4, 154–159.

Davis, G. F. (2005). Firms and environments. In: N. J. Smelser & R. Swedberg (Eds), *Handbook of economic sociology*. (2nd ed., pp. 478–502). Princeton, NJ: Princeton University Press.

Davis, G. F. (2009). *Managed by the markets: How finance reshaped America*. Oxford, UK: Oxford University Press.

Davis, G. F., Diekmann, K. A., & Tinsley, C. H. (1994). The decline and fall of the conglomerate firm in the 1980s: The de-institutionalization of an organizational form. *American Sociological Review*, 59, 547–570.

Emerson, R. M. (1962). Power-dependence relations. *American Sociological Review, 27*, 31–40.

Fligstein, N. (1990). *The transformation of corporate control.* Cambridge, MA: Harvard University Press.

Gulati, R. (2007). *Managing network resources: Alliances, affiliations, and other relational assets.* Oxford, UK: Oxford University Press.

Gulati, R., & Sytch, M. (2007). Dependence asymmetry and joint dependence in interorganizational relationships: effects of embeddedness on manufacturers' performance in procurement relationships. *Administrative Science Quarterly, 52*, 32–69.

Hannan, M. T., & Freeman, J. (1977). The population ecology of organizations. *American Journal of Sociology, 82*, 929–964.

Hillman, A., Shropshire, C., & Cannella, A. (2007). Organizational predictors of women on corporate boards. *Academy of Management Journal, 50*, 941–952.

Hillman, A. C. (2005). Politicians on the board: do connections affect the bottom line? *Journal of Management, 31*, 464–481.

Jensen, M. C., & Meckling, W. H. (1976). Theory of the firm: managerial behavior, agency cost, and ownership structure. *Journal of Financial Economics, 3*, 305–360.

Katila, R., Rosenberger, J., & Eisenhardt, K. (2008). Swimming with sharks: Technology ventures, defense mechanisms and corporate relationships. *Administrative Science Quarterly, 53*, 295–332.

Meyer, J. W., & Rowan, B. (1977). Institutionalized organizations: Formal structure as myth and ceremony. *American Journal of Sociology, 83*, 41–62.

Ozcan, P., & Eisenhardt, K. (2009). Origin of portfolios: Entrepreneurial firms and strategic action. *Academy of Management Journal, 52*, 246–279.

Palmer, D. A. (1983). Broken ties: Interlocking directorates and intercorporate coordination. *Administrative Science Quarterly, 28*, 40–55.

Pfeffer, J. (1972a). Interorganizational influence and managerial attitudes. *Academy of Management Journal, 15*, 317–330.

Pfeffer, J. (1972b). Merger as a response to organizational interdependence. *Administrative Science Quarterly, 17*, 382–394.

Pfeffer, J. (1972c). Size and composition of corporate boards of directors: The organization and its environment. *Administrative Science Quarterly, 17*, 218–228.

Pfeffer, J. (1982). *Organizations and organization theory.* Marshfield, MA: Pitman.

Pfeffer, J. (1987). A resource dependence perspective on interorganizational relations. In: M. S. Mizruchi & M. Schwartz (Eds), *Intercorporate relations: The structural analysis of business* (pp. 25–55). Cambridge, UK: Cambridge University Press.

Pfeffer, J. (2003). Introduction to the classic edition. In: J. Pfeffer & G. R. Salancik (Eds), *The external control of organizations: A resource dependence perspective (classic edition).* Stanford, CA: Stanford University Press.

Pfeffer, J. (2005). Developing resource dependence theory: How theory is affected by its environment. In: K. G. Smith & M. A Hitt (Eds), *Great minds in management: The process of theory development.* New York: Oxford University Press.

Pfeffer, J., & Salancik, G. R. (1978). *The external control of organizations: A resource dependence perspective.* New York: Harper & Row.

Robinson, W. S. (1950). Ecological correlations and the behavior of individuals. *American Sociological Review, 15*, 351–357.

Scott, W. R. (1981). *Organizations: Rational, natural, and open systems.* Englewood Cliffs, NJ: Prentice-Hall.

Scott, W. R., & Davis, G. F. (2007). *Organizations and organizing: Rational, natural, and open system perspectives.* Upper Saddle River, NJ: Pearson Prentice Hall.

Selznick, P. (1949). *TVA and the grass roots.* Berkeley, CA: University of California Press.

Small, H. (1978). Cited documents as concept symbols. *Social Studies of Science, 8,* 327–340.

Stinchcombe, A. L. (1982). Should sociologists forget their mothers and fathers? *The American Sociologist, 17,* 2–11.

Thompson, J. D. (1967). *Organizations in action.* New York: McGraw Hill.

Westphal, J. D., Boivie, S., & Chng, D. H. M. (2006). The strategic impetus for social network ties: Reconstituting broken CEO friendship ties. *Strategic Management Journal, 27,* 425–445.

Williamson, O. E. (1975). *Markets and hierarchies: Analysis and antitrust implications.* New York: Free Press.

Zajac, E. J. (1988). Interlocking directorates as an interorganizational strategy: A test of critical assumptions. *Academy of Management Journal, 31,* 428–438.

CHAPTER 3

POPULATION ECOLOGY

Terry L. Amburgey

INTRODUCTION

Every paper needs a theme. Luckily, the venue defines the theme for me: how did the initial conditions at Stanford affect the development and diffusion of population ecology as a theoretical research program. I use the term theoretical research program reluctantly, especially considering the context of the department of sociology at Stanford University during the 1970s and 1980s (Lakatos & Musgrave, 1970). Nonetheless, I believe that population ecology can be usefully described as such. It is not a theory but rather a collection of theories developing over time with progressive problem shifts. There are methodological rules that define what paths of research to pursue and to avoid (Pfeffer, 1993, p. 613).

In the first section of the paper, I want to briefly describe the setting. Others undoubtedly will do the same and in greater detail. I want to focus on aspects of the setting that, to my mind, had an important impact on population ecology. To that end, I will discuss the department of sociology, The Organizational Research Training Program (ORTP), and inter-campus ties with the University of California at Berkeley. In the second section, I will briefly discuss two aspects of early theoretical integration in population ecology, institutional theory and organizational learning and change. In the third section I will discuss the diffusion of population ecology as a result of migration as well as a broadcast process and a contagion process. I will finish the chapter with a discussion of a potential new

Stanford's Organization Theory Renaissance, 1970–2000
Research in the Sociology of Organizations, Volume 28, 43–57
Copyright © 2010 by Emerald Group Publishing Limited
ISSN: 0733-558X/doi:10.1108/S0733-558X(2010)0000028007

direction for population ecology (the evolution of inter-organizational networks) and a summary and conclusion.

THE DEPARTMENTAL SETTING

I will argue two factors within the department of sociology that had an important impact on the early development of population ecology: the development of neo-institutional theory and the development of hazard rate methodology. I have argued elsewhere that the late 1970's were unusual in the near simultaneous emergence of four major theoretical perspectives: population ecology, institutional theory, resource dependence theory, and transactions cost economics (Amburgey & Rao, 1996). The department of sociology at that time contained Michael Hannan, one of the originators of population ecology as well as John W. Meyer and W. Richard Scott, two originators (listed alphabetically) of Institutional Theory. As I will discuss shortly, I believe that the co-development of these two research programs in the same department had a profound impact on population ecology.

The second factor is the development of hazard rate software by Nancy Tuma, who was also resident in the department of sociology at that time. Jeffrey Pfeffer (1993, p. 613) has noted the universal usage of Professor Tuma's RATE program by early researchers in population ecology and it is difficult to overstate its importance to the research program. Although there are now choices for software to use in modeling hazard rates when population ecology was initially developing, there was not. Without the RATE program as an enabling technology, empirical research on (for example) the factors influencing the exit rates of organizations would not have been able to proceed. The utilization of hazard rate analysis and of the RATE program was greatly facilitated by the publication of the book *Social Dynamics: Models and Methods* (Tuma & Hannan, 1984).

THE ORTP

A second important factor in the setting is the ORTP initiated and managed by W. Richard Scott. The salient feature of the ORTP for me is the extent to which it brought students of organizations from a wide variety of locations across the Stanford campus together. I want to discuss three features of the program in particular: the School of Business, the conference series at Asilomar, and post-doctoral fellows.

The exposure of PhD students to the Graduate School of Business was consequential in several ways. First, sociology students were in contact with faculty that we would normally not meet. Jeffrey Pfeffer moved to the school of business during this time frame. Since Professor Pfeffer is one of the originators of Resource Dependence Theory, the local environment now housed three of the four major theoretical frameworks that developed in the late 1970s. Along the same lines, it brought sociology students into contact with James G. March. Although Professor March is a polymath with academic appointments seemingly everywhere, ecologists were somewhat more likely to meet him in the context of the School of Business than in Education or Sociology. As a consequence, Sociology students were put in contact with the Behavioral Theory of the Firm and the literature on organizational learning.

Second, PhD students in the School of Business were exposed to faculty and theories in Sociology since PhD students from Sociology and the School of Business intermingled in courses. This provided the foundation for a social network that would elaborate over time. It also seeded the world of management education with faculty that were appreciative of organizational sociology in general and population ecology in particular.

As Dick Scott (2006, p. 891) has pointed out "A conference, held at the Asilomar Center, near Monterey, California, provided an annual focal event around which an even larger community routinely gathered, as we were joined by faculty and students from neighboring universities, including UC Berkeley, UCLA, and USC, for three days of intensive talk about organizations." Needless to say, much of the intensive talk involved population ecology and it brought people from the sociology department into contact with others that became involved in ecological analyses such as Meyer and Zucker (1989) and Bill McKelvey and Aldrich (1983).

The last aspect of the ORTP that I want to mention is the post-doctoral fellowships. The ORTP "…supported an average of 10 trainees, 6 pre-doctoral and 4 post-doctoral students, who annually formed the inner core of a much larger community of graduate students and faculty." (Scott, 2006, p. 891). One of those post-doctoral fellows was Jacques Delacroix who had graduated from the sociology department earlier. Jacques was acquainted with Glenn Carroll from his time at Indiana University but it was not until his return as an ORTP post-doctoral fellow that he became involved in research in population ecology and became one of its most prolific early contributors (Delacroix & Carroll, 1983; Carroll & Delacroix, 1982; Delacroix & Swaminathan, 1991; Swaminathan & Delacroix, 1991; Delacroix & Rao, 1994).

THE BERKELEY CONNECTION

One aspect of the setting that I think may be unique to population ecology
is the connection to UC Berkeley. The tie between Michael Hannan and
John Freeman was long and strong. When Mike came to the sociology
department at Stanford, John went to the Haas School at Berkeley. As Mike
began training students in organization theory at Stanford, John was doing
the same at Berkeley. There was a great deal of interaction between the
PhD students at the two campuses, not just at the Asilomar conferences
mentioned above but in seminars and ad hoc meetings. Jack Brittain and
Douglas Wholey, in particular, were Berkeley students at that time who
spent a great deal of time on the Stanford campus and who also hosted
Stanford students at Berkeley. Jack and Doug were also early and prolific
researchers in population ecology (Freeman & Brittain, 1977; Brittain &
Freeman, 1980; Wholey & Brittain, 1986; Brittain & Wholey, 1988;
Wholey & Brittain, 1989).

THEORETICAL REFINEMENT

One way in which the setting at Stanford influenced the development of
population ecology is the incorporation of neo-institutional theory into the
theoretical research program. I have argued elsewhere (Amburgey & Rao,
1996, p. 1267) that by 1988 "The demarcation between ecological theory
and institutional theory had, at least from the ecological perspective, largely
disappeared." I would argue that the integration of institutional theorizing
into ecological theorizing occurred very early. For reasons of simplicity,
I will restrict the discussion to one central feature of population ecology,
structural inertia.

In the article generally taken as the starting point, Hannan and Freeman
(1977) delineate a number of processes that restrict the ability of organizations to systematically respond to environmental contingencies through
adaptation. They briefly describe four factors internal to organizations
that constrain adaptation and four factors external to organizations that
constrain adaptation (1977, pp. 931–932). Both lists contain arguments that
are *institutional* in nature. The fourth internal factor involves normative
agreements: "Once standards of procedure and the allocation of tasks and
authority have become the subject of normative agreement, the costs of
change are greatly increased. Normative agreements constrain adaptation
in at least two ways. First, they provide a justification and an organizing

principle for those elements that wish to resist reorganization (i.e., they can resist in terms of a shared principle). Second, normative agreements preclude the serious consideration of many alternative responses" (Hannan & Freeman, 1977, p. 931). Similarly, the third external factor involves legitimation: "Legitimacy constraints also emanate from the environment. Any legitimacy an organization has been able to generate constitutes an asset in manipulating the environment. To the extent that adaptation (e.g., eliminating undergraduate instruction in public universities) violates the legitimacy claims, it incurs considerable costs. So external legitimacy considerations also tend to limit adaptation" (Hannan & Freeman, 1977, p. 932).

In their initial paper, Hannan and Freeman provide an argument describing selection processes as a necessary counterpoint to adaptation because of the existence of inertial processes "We argue that in order to deal with the various inertial pressures the adaptation perspective must be supplemented with a selection orientation" (Hannan & Freeman, 1977, p. 933). I think it is important to note that in this initial formulation structural inertia and its causes are exogenous to the theorizing and the theory.

In 1984, Hannan and Freeman wrote a paper devoted specifically to the topic of structural inertia. This paper is important here for two reasons, but for now I want to focus on the continuing integration with neo-institutional theorizing. In short, structural inertia is developed as a consequence of selection processes rather than an exogenous precursor to selection processes and the argumentation draws upon institutional thinking. The two organizational characteristics at the core of their thinking are reliability and accountability (Hannan & Freeman, 1984, p. 154). The argumentation about accountability is where neo-institutional thinking is involved in the theoretical reorientation of structural inertia.

In one sense the role of institutional thinking, in the 1984 article, is a continuation of the role in the 1977 article.

> In general, organizations attain reproducibility of structure through processes of institutionalization ... institutionalization, is a two-edged sword. It greatly lowers the cost of collective action by giving an organization a taken-for-granted character such that members do not continually question organizational purposes, authority relations, etc. Reproduction of structure occurs without apparent effort in highly institutionalized structures. The other edge of the sword is inertia. The very factors that make a system reproducible make it resistant to change. (Hannan & Freeman, 1984, p. 154)

However, the work of Meyer and Rowan (1977) shows its influence in Hannan and Freeman's repeated use of the phrases "the modern world" and "modern societies." Meyer and Rowan (1977, pp. 343–344) point out that "In modern societies, the myths generating formal organizational structure have two key properties. First they are rationalized and impersonal prescriptions that identify various social purposes as technical ones and specify in a rulelike way the appropriate means to pursue these technical purposes rationally... Second, they are highly institutionalized and thus in some measure beyond the discretion of any individual participant or organization."

The impact of neo-institutional theorizing has continued to this day. An excellent example is the recent work of Michael Hannan, Pólos, and Carroll (2007) on organizations and audiences. Although the central purpose of this work is a fundamental reformulation and formalization of population ecology, Part 1 of the book is avowedly institutional in nature: "In this chapter and the next three (Chapters 3–5) we attempt to develop a fresh perspective on forms and populations. This approach retains a focus on forms and features (defined broadly to include relations, as noted above). However, it also emphasizes the social construction of categories, forms, and populations" (Hannan et al., 2007, p. 31).

It is possible that the early development of population ecology would have included neo-institutional thinking even if Mike Hannan, John Meyer, and Dick Scott had not been resident in the department of sociology at the same time. It is hard to evaluate counterfactuals. On the other hand, the sociological literature has abundant theorizing and empirical evidence on the importance of propinquity.

Transformation and Learning

The refinements to structural inertia in the 1984 article are due, at least in part, to the ongoing tension between population ecology and the adaptation oriented theories that it was intended to complement. In an understated way, Hannan and Freeman (1984, p. 150) acknowledge that "... the claim that organizational structures rarely change is the subject of dispute." This acknowledgement appears to be due (at least in part) to a review of the literature on organizational change by James G. March which is quoted in the paper. In the quote Hannan and Freeman (1984, p. 150) have a review which argues that organizations are not rigid and inflexible but rather that they are continually changing; changing routinely, easily, and responsively. The quote by March is followed quickly, by a quote from W. Richard Scott arguing that some features are more fundamental or *core* with changes occurring over long periods of time while other features are more peripheral with change occurring more rapidly.

In this refinement of structural inertia, Hannan and Freeman (1984, p. 149) go on to develop a framework that "... goes beyond our earlier theory in acknowledging that organizational changes of some kinds occur frequently and that organizations sometimes even manage to make radical changes in strategies and structures." The two key features of this refinement (other than making structural inertia an endogenous outcome of selection) are recognition of the role of relative timing and a hierarchical differentiation of organizational features.

The first feature concerns the correspondence between the time required by an organization to learn and change and the rate of change in relevant environments. Thus "Learning and adjusting structure enhances the chance of survival only if the speed of response is commensurate with the temporal patterns of relevant environments" (Hannan & Freeman, 1984, p. 151). Structural inertia is no longer defined in an absolute way but in a relative way, "... structural inertia must be defined in relative and dynamic terms" (Hannan & Freeman, 1984, p. 151). The second feature is presaged by the quote from Scott and also goes back as far as Talcott Parsons: organizations are not unitary but can be viewed as consisting of layers with different properties. Thus Hannan and Freeman (1984, p. 156) "... conceptualize organizational structure as composed of hierarchical layers of structural and strategic features that vary systematically in flexibility and responsiveness." Structural inertia not only is defined on the basis of the correspondence between an organization's speed of response and an environment's speed of change but also on different layers of an organization. *Core* features such as goals and forms of authority are relatively inflexible and change both rarely and slowly. *Peripheral* features such as numbers and sizes of subunits or inter-organizational linkages are flexible and change frequently and quickly.

As with the integration with neo-institutional theory, it is impossible to say that the substantial reworking of structural inertia is due to the setting in which it occurred. I will just point out the quotes from both W. Richard Scott and James G. March as well as cite to Jeffrey Pfeffer and let readers draw their own conclusions. Whether or not the refinement of structural inertia was due to the setting, it had important consequences for the later development of population ecology.

SOCIOLOGY MEETS MAMMON

Although population ecology was developed in part within sociology, it did not remain there. A substantial portion of subsequent developments occurred within schools of business or management. This is partly due to the attractiveness of some of population ecology's theoretical content. The core of the theoretical research program is differential entry and exit of organizations. The entry component is of interest to management scholars involved in the study of entrepreneurship. The exit component (both exit through failure and exit through acquisition) is of interest to scholars involved in the study of organizational strategy. Similarly, a consistent focus on *competition* made much of ecological theorizing of interest to strategic management. The largest impediment to the diffusion of population ecology into schools of business or management was the (whether actual or perceived) denial of managerial efficacy contained in the concept of structural inertia. The re-conceptualization of structural inertia by Hannan and Freeman (1984) removed that impediment. In a general way, the relationship between selection and transformation becomes an empirical question and an interesting one at that. In a more specific way, the peripheral features of an organization such as the lines-and-boxes of structure or specific inter-organizational linkages can be incorporated into the framework. Although these aspects may be less interesting to some sociologists, they were and remain interesting to scholars of management.

How did the initial setting influence the diffusion of population ecology into schools of business and management? Using the terms very broadly, there was migration, broadcast, and contagion. At this point I want to make two apologies. First, I am not attempting a complete sociometry or enumeration of important scholars. What I write is idiosyncratic and personal; I apologize for any missing names. Second, I apologize for any inappropriate familiarity; I am going to use the casual names of people that I know.

Migration

When Glenn Carroll graduated, he took a job in the department of sociology at Brown University. The following year he moved to the business school at Berkeley. That same year, I graduated and took a job at the school of management at Northwestern University. At roughly the same time, PhD students in business at Stanford and Berkeley graduated and (naturally enough) took jobs in schools of business. Jack Brittain and Doug Wholey left Berkeley for the University of Texas and Arizona University, respectively. Similarly, Jitendra Singh, Anne Miner, and Richard Harrison graduated from Stanford and took business school jobs at the University of Toronto, the University of Wisconsin, and the University of Arizona, respectively.

The initial setting had a strong impact on both the migration of sociology students into schools of business and the subsequent work of business students. Glenn and I were familiarized with business schools through close contact with both professors and students at Stanford as well as the strong ties to Berkeley through John Freeman and his students. The annual get-togethers at Asilomar served to acquaint us with organizational scholars elsewhere, some of whom were resident in schools of business or management. Similarly, the broad *tent* of organizational scholars created by the ORTP and Stanford Center for Organizational Research (SCOR) programs brought a deep awareness of population ecology to PhD students in business and management (Scott, 2006, pp. 890–891).

Broadcast

The diffusion of population ecology into schools of business and management also occurred through a broadcast process; not everyone involved in ecological theorizing and research has a direct tie to Mike Hannan, John Freeman, or their students. As ecological work was published in various outlets, it became accessible to students of organizations everywhere. This is how much of academia is intended to operate of course. Just two examples help illustrate the broadcast process. Elaine Romanelli (1989a, 1989b, 1991) was a PhD student in the School of Business at Colombia working with Michael Tushman. Similarly, Rao and Neilsen (1992) and Rao (1994) was a PhD student at Case Western Reserve University. To my knowledge neither Elaine nor Hayagreeva developed their interest in ecological processes as a consequence of a direct tie.

Contagion

The final aspect of the diffusion of population ecology into schools of business and management is what I will call contagion, direct contact with someone involved with the research program. I will focus on another common activity within academia, the education and training of students. One good example of this is Jitendra Singh's move to the University of Toronto. After moving to Toronto, Jitendra became deeply involved in ecological research (e.g., Singh, Tucker, & House, 1986a; Singh, House, & Tucker, 1986b). Two of the PhD students in the faculty of management subsequently became involved in ecological work, Joel Baum and Tina Dacin. An MBA student, Heather Haveman, subsequently entered the PhD program at Berkeley and became involved in ecological research.

Glenn Carroll and John Freeman at Berkeley also produced several students who went on to work in organizational ecology. In addition to Heather Haveman, William Barnett and Anand Swaminathan are Berkeley graduates. When I took the job at Northwestern University, I met a PhD Student, Kelly and Amburgey (1991) and Amburgey, Kelly, and Barnett (1993), that I collaborated with on a several studies. When I moved to the University of Wisconsin I began working with Miner, Amburgey, and Stearns (1990), Barnett and Amburgey (1990), Amburgey, et al. (1993), and Barnett (1997). Amburgey and Dacin (1994) had moved from Toronto with her husband and I was on Tina's dissertation committee and also worked with her on subsequent research.

The wide diffusion of population ecology into schools of business through migration, broadcast, and contagion has had, in my opinion, a substantial effect on both the type of research carried out and on its sheer volume. The refinement of structural inertia made the *peripheral* elements of organizational structure and activities suitable areas of research within the program. At the same time, the orientations of schools of business and management make such topics desirable. The growing popularity of the MBA and other practitioner programs provided positions well beyond what was (and still is) available in departments of sociology.

RECENT CONTENT

Future Development

More than a decade ago Hayagreeva Rao and I (1996, p. 1281) edited a special issue on organizational ecology that discussed past, present, and future directions. One of the future directions was "... organizational networks created through strategic alliances, joint ventures, and other forms of relational linkages (the blending of competition and cooperation into 'coopetition')." Such research was already underway; the next month saw the publication of ecological research on technological networks among semiconductor firms (Podolny, Stuart, & Hannan, 1996). Since that time a substantial amount of research has been conducted on inter-organizational ties and the networks that result from such ties. This work adds considerably to the literature on the evolution of organizational populations within organizational fields. Perhaps the best example is the research on the shifting network typology and logics of attachment over time in biotechnology by Walter Powell and colleagues (Powell, White, Koput, & Owen-Smith, 2005). The work of Freeman and Audia (2006) is another example. They analyze the interplay of different types of organizational *location*, including inter-organizational relations within organizational communities.

Following both Podolny (Podolny et al., 1996) and Powell (Powell et al., 2005), I want to briefly describe a potentially useful integration of population ecology and network analysis. It is widely recognized that biotechnology is an area where technological innovation is important. Podolny and his colleagues focus upon patent citations for their analysis. Powell and colleagues (2005) take a broader view; they recognize that organizational networks are multiplex and consider a number of different types of ties such as R&D agreements, licensing agreements, etc. In both cases the important point is that they are instances of endogenous population structuring (Podolny et al., 1996, p. 662). The networks produced by inter-organizational ties define both internal structure of the population at an aggregate level and also aspects of an organization's realized niche at the level of individual organizations.

One aspect of the structure of a network concerns variations in the cohesiveness of different regions. A k-core decomposition is one way of determining strata in networks. The *k-core* measure indicates the cohesivenenss of subsets in the network, based upon the degree centrality of the nodes in the subset. A *k-core* is a subset in which each node is adjacent to at least a minimum number k of the other nodes in the subset (Wasserman & Faust, 1994, p. 266). The larger the value of k, the higher the degree of connectedness of the node under observation, and the larger the cohesiveness of its region of the network. See Fig. 1 (Batagelj & Zaversnik, 2002, p. 2) for a graphical representation of a *k-core* decomposition.

In Fig. 2 we provide the *k-core* values of the quarterly R&D network of U.S. biotechnology firms from 1983 to 1999 (Amburgey, Al-Laham, Tzabbar, & Aharonson, 2008). We have summed the number of nodes in the respective *k-core strata* over the time periods under observation (quarters). There are several aspects of interest. First, the number of layers increases over time, indicating an increasing structural differentiation of the network. At the end of the period there are six layers in the R&D network from the sparse outermost periphery to the more densely connected core. Second, the number of organizational nodes is unequally distributed across the layers. The largest absolute number of nodes as well as the steepest increase over time takes place in the 1-*core* layer. This layer represents the

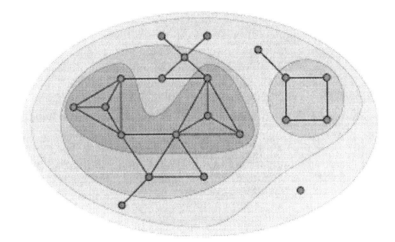

Fig. 1. 0, 1, 2, and 3 Cores.

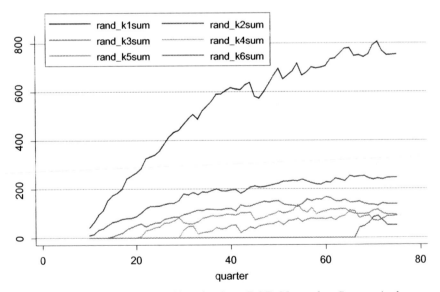

Fig. 2. Coreness Strata. U.S. Biotechnology R&D Networks. *Source:* Amburgey et al. (2008).

periphery of the network, where organizations are only sparsely connected to each other. The lowest number of nodes is located in the 6-*core* area of the network, which represents the innermost core. This is the layer with the highest connectivity and robustness due to multiple linkages between nodes.

The endogenous generation of population structure and creation of differentiated organizational niches are topics well within the domain of population ecology. The rise of inter-organizational ties among firms and other organization since the mid-1980s offers a new venue for ecological analysis in two related venues. The first is an examination of network structure and its effects on vital rates. The second is the obverse, the effect of vital rates on the evolution of network structure. This sort of research matches James G. March's call for work with "...the emphasis on endogenous environments, on the ways in which the convergence between an evolving unit and its environment is complicated by the fact that the environment is not only changing, but changing partly as part of a process of coevolution" (1994, p. 43).

CONCLUSION

The context in which population ecology developed had a profound impact on its initial form and its subsequent developments. Although my tastes run more to the nomothetic than the idiographic, the specifics of time and place were immensely consequential. I have attempted to describe some of the ways in which Stanford has had and will continue to have a legacy within the theoretical research program of population ecology. Some of these (e.g., the ORTP) were widely shared across different people and activities. The close ties to Berkeley were, I believe, unique to population ecology and ecologists. I have long been interested in evolutionary processes and phenomena such as initial condition imprinting and path dependence. Population ecology's initial creation and later development are good examples of both.

REFERENCES

Amburgey, T. L., Al-Laham, A., Tzabbar, D., & Aharonson, B. (2008). The structural evolution of multiplex organizational networks: Research and commerce in biotechnology. In: J. A. C. Baum & T. J. Rowley (Eds), *Advances in strategic management: Network strategy*. Bingley: JAI Press.

Amburgey, T. L., & Dacin, T. (1994). As the left foot follows the right? The dynamics of strategic and structural change. *Academy of Management Journal, 37,* 1427–1452.
Amburgey, T. L., & Rao, H. (1996). Organizational ecology: Past, present, and future directions. *Academy of Management Journal, 39,* 1265–1286.
Amburgey, T. L., Kelly, D., & Barnett, W. P. (1993). Resetting the clock: The dynamics of organizational change and failure. *Administrative Science Quarterly, 38,* 51–73.
Barnett, W. P. (1997). The dynamics of competitive intensity. *Administrative Science Quarterly, 42,* 128–160.
Barnett, W. P., & Amburgey, T. L. (1990). Do larger organizations generate stronger competition? In: J. V. Singh (Ed.), *Organizational evolution: New directions* (pp. 78–102). Newbury Park, CA: Sage Publications.
Batagelj, V., & Zaversnik, M. (2002). Generalized cores. *Journal of the ACM, 5,* 1–8.
Brittain, J., & Freeman, J. (1980). Organizational proliferation and density-dependent selection. In: J. Kimberly & R. Miles (Eds), *Organizational life cycles* (pp. 291–338). San Francisco: Jossey-Bass.
Brittain, J. W., & Wholey, D. R. (1988). Competition and coexistence in organizational communities: Population dynamics in electronic components manufacturing. In: G. R. Carroll (Ed.), *Ecological models of organizations.* Cambridge: Ballinger Publishing Company.
Carroll, G. R., & Delacroix, J. (1982). Organizational mortality in the newspaper industries of Argentina and Ireland: An ecological approach. *Administrative Science Quarterly, 27*(2), 169–198.
Delacroix, J., & Carroll, G. R. (1983). Organizational foundings: An ecological study of the newspaper industries of Argentina and Ireland. *Administrative Science Quarterly, 28*(2), 274–291.
Delacroix, J., & Rao, H. (1994). Externalities and ecological theory: Unbundling density dependence. In: J. Singh & J. Baum (Eds), *Evolutionary dynamics of organizations.* Oxford University Press.
Delacroix, J., & Swaminathan, A. (1991). Cosmetic, speculative, and adaptive organizational change in the wine industry: A longitudinal study. *Administrative Science Quarterly, 36*(4), 631–661.
Freeman, J. H., & Audia, P. G. (2006). Community ecology and the sociology of organizations. *Annual Review of Sociology, 32,* 145–169.
Freeman, J. H., & Brittain, J. (1977). Union merger process and industrial environment. *Industrial Relations, 16,* 173–185.
Hannan, M. T., & Freeman, J. (1977). The population ecology of organizations. *American Journal of Sociology, 82*(5), 929–964.
Hannan, M. T., & Freeman, J. (1984). Structural inertia and organizational change. *American Sociological Review, 49*(2), 149–164.
Hannan, M. T., Pólos, L., & Carroll, G. G. (2007). *Logics of organization theory: Audiences, codes and ecologies.* Princeton, NJ: Princeton University Press.
Kelly, D., & Amburgey, T. L. (1991). Organizational inertia and momentum: A dynamic model of strategic change. *Academy of Management Journal, 34,* 591–612.
Lakatos, I., & Musgrave, A. (Eds). (1970). *Criticism and the growth of knowledge.* Cambridge: Cambridge University Press.
March, J. G. (1994). The evolution of evolution. In: J. A. C. Baum & J. V. Singh (Eds), *Evolutionary dynamics of organizations* (pp. 39–49). New York: Oxford University Press.

McKelvey, B., & Aldrich, H. (1983). Populations, natural selection, and applied organizational science. *Administrative Science Quarterly, 28*, 101–128.

Meyer, J. W., & Rowan, B. (1977). Institutionalized organizations: Formal structure as myth and ceremony. *The American Journal of Sociology, 83*(2), 340–363.

Meyer, M. W., & Zucker, L. (1989). *Permanently failing organizations.* Newbury Park, CA: Sage Publications.

Miner, A. S., Amburgey, T. L., & Stearns, T. (1990). Interorganizational linkages and population dynamics: Buffering and transformational shields. *Administrative Science Quarterly, 35*, 689–713.

Pfeffer, J. (1993). Barriers to the advance of organizational science: Paradigm development as a dependent variable. *The Academy of Management Review, 18*(4), 599–620.

Podolny, J. M., Stuart, T. E., & Hannan, M. T. (1996). Networks, knowledge, and niches: Competition in the worldwide semiconductor industry, 1984–1991. *The American Journal of Sociology, 102*, 659–689.

Powell, W. W., White, D. R., Koput, K., & Owen-Smith, J. (2005). Network dynamics and field evolution: The growth of interorganizational collaboration in the life sciences. *American Journal of Sociology, 111*, 1463–1568.

Rao, H. (1994). The social construction of reputation: Certification contests, legitimation, and the survival of organizations in the American automobile industry: 1895–1912. *Strategic Management Journal, 15*(Winter, Special Issue: Competitive Organizational Behavior), 29–44.

Rao, H., & Neilsen, E. H. (1992). An ecology of agency arrangements: Mortality of savings and loan associations, 1960–1987. *Administrative Science Quarterly, 37*(3), 448–470.

Romanelli, E. (1991). The evolution of new organizational forms. *Annual Review of Sociology, 17*, 79–103.

Romanelli, E. (1989a). Environments and strategies of organizational start-up: Effects on early survival. *Administrative Science Quarterly, 34*, 369–387.

Romanelli, E. (1989b). Organization birth and population variety: A community perspective on origins. In: L. L. Cummings & B. Staw (Eds), *Research in organizational behavior* (Vol. 11, pp. 211–246). Greenwich, CT: JAI Press.

Scott, W. R. (2006). Ad Astra per aspera: A journey from the periphery. *Organization Studies, 27*, 877–897.

Singh, J. V., House, R. J., & Tucker, D. J. (1986b). Organizational change and organizational mortality. *Administrative Science Quarterly, 31*, 587–611.

Singh, J. V., Tucker, D. J., & House, R. J. (1986a). Organizational legitimacy and the liability of newness. *Administrative Science Quarterly, 31*, 171–193.

Swaminathan, A., & Delacroix, J. (1991). Differentiation within an organizational population: Additional evidence from the wine industry. *The Academy of Management Journal, 34*(3), 679–692.

Tuma, N. B., & Hannan, M. T. (1984). *Social dynamics: Models and methods.* Orlando, FL: Academic Press.

Wasserman, S., & Faust, K. (1994). *Social network analysis: Methods and applications.* Cambridge: Cambridge University Press.

Wholey, D. R., & Brittain, J. W. (1986). Organizational ecology: Findings and implications. *The Academy of Management Review, 11*(3), 513–533.

Wholey, D. R., & Brittain, J. W. (1989). Characterizing environmental variation. *The Academy of Management Journal, 32*(4), 867–882.

CHAPTER 4

ORGANIZATIONAL LEARNING

Lee Sproull

ABSTRACT

This chapter comments on organizational learning research produced by scholars who studied or taught at Stanford University during the last third of the 20th century. Challenging classical learning models, Stanford scholars have demonstrated how cognitive and social processes attenuate connections between environmental action and the lessons learned from it. They have demonstrated how goals change over time as a partial function of prior performance and the importance of temporal processes in learning rates. They have shown how rules and routines encode only imperfectly lessons learned from organizational action. Their research has deepened and enriched our understanding of organizational learning.

INTRODUCTION

Organizational learning scholars who studied or taught at Stanford are members of a broad scholarly community that collectively has published scores of books and articles on the topic of organizational learning. This chapter traces some of the Stanford-school contributions to this broad community. In so doing, it constructs a truly peculiar history of the development of a few ideas about organizational learning. In fact, this chapter, itself, serves as an object lesson in the perils of learning from

Stanford's Organization Theory Renaissance, 1970–2000
Research in the Sociology of Organizations, Volume 28, 59–69
ISSN: 0733-558X/doi:10.1108/S0733-558X(2010)0000028008

small-sample history. It ignores many of the most important scholars of organizational learning – including those such as Karl Weick and Sidney Winter – simply because they did not study or teach at Stanford, even though they significantly influenced Stanford scholars. It ignores the influence of universities other than Stanford where Stanford graduates continued their research on organizational learning, found new colleagues, and built their own scholarly careers. Two simple categorization rules simplify and distort the history that follows (Stanford: yes/no; work related to organizational learning: yes/no). Fortunately, Stanford-school scholars have produced more beautiful and comprehensive commentaries on organizational learning on other occasions. These scholars and commentaries include: Michael Cohen, Stanford post-doc, 1972–1973 (Cohen & Sproull, 1996); Theresa Lant, Stanford PhD, 1987 (Lant & Shapira, 2000); Barbara Levitt, Stanford PhD, 1988 (Levitt & March, 1988); Steve Mezias, Stanford PhD, 1987 (Miner & Mezias, 1996); Anne Miner, Stanford PhD, 1985 (Miner & Haunschld, 1995); Lee Sproull, Stanford PhD, 1978 (Sproull, 1981); and Jim March, Stanford faculty member from 1970 to 1995 and emeritus from 1995 to the present (March, 1988, 1999, 2008).

Classical models of learning, including organizational learning, rest on conceptions of behavior that is goal-oriented and feedback-driven. In these models, people and organizations know their goals and "learn" how to achieve them by taking action and adjusting subsequent action based on environmental feedback to it. Feedback is causally related to actions taken. Actions producing positive feedback are repeated or intensified; actions producing negative feedback are modified or eliminated. Learning efficiency is improved by embodying actions that produce positive feedback or reduce negative feedback in organizational routines. Over time, routine-driven behavior will lead people and organizations closer and closer to their goals. One pragmatic application of these models can be found in "learning curve" research that demonstrates, for example, how industrial plants improve the speed and quality of their output by fine-tuning their performance over time. See Argote (1999) for an extensive treatment of this research.

Fig. 1 displays the components in a conventional model of organizational learning. People take actions based on their beliefs and aspirations or goals. For example, a manager may recommend hiring a particular job candidate, renewing a contract with a supplier, launching a new product. Individual actions are translated into organizational actions via organizational processes: for example, the hiring process, the contracting process, the

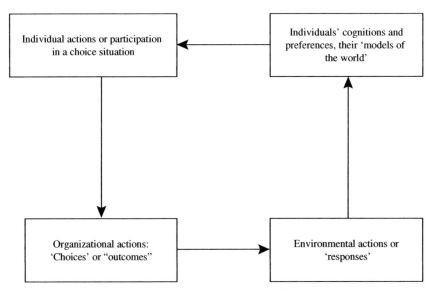

Fig. 1. Conventional Model of Organizational Learning.

product-launch process. The environment responds to these organizational actions with, for example, positive or negative business press stories about the new appointment, positive or negative contractor performance, higher or lower new product sales. People and organizations record those responses, learn from them, and modify their subsequent behavior accordingly.

For more than 30 years as a Stanford faculty member, Jim March has fixed his congenial, Midwestern skeptical squint on standard models of learning, observing that they rest on assumptions of logic and rationality and tight coupling between action and lessons learned from it (e.g., March & Olsen, 1975). Under conditions of ambiguity and rapid change, which are hallmarks of life in modern organizations, these assumptions become problematic and the models become more complicated. Stanford students and colleagues have heard (and helped develop) Jim March's ideas about organizational learning through courses, seminars, and Friday afternoon wine. Some of them have even developed a bit of a skeptical squint of their own. This paper describes how some of Jim's Stanford colleagues have amplified some themes in Jim's work on organizational learning in their own scholarly careers.[1]

BELIEFS: COGNITIVE AND SOCIAL PROCESSES

Classical learning models assume that beliefs and cognitions – that is, the "lessons" people learn from environmental response to their actions – result causally from the objective environment and accurately reflect its signals. Stanford-school scholars have made substantial contributions to our understanding of how and why "lessons" can be incomplete, inaccurate, and only loosely connected to environmental action.

Cognitive Processes

By the early 1980s basic research in cognitive and social psychology had begun to focus on how memory structures and category schemes affect people's ability to encode, store and retrieve information from memory. Concurrent work demonstrated how peoples' use of information processing heuristics results in predictably biased inference. This basic science demonstrated how peoples' cognitive and inferential processes loosened the connections between environmental action and the lessons learned from that action. Sproull and her colleagues, including Stephen Weiner, an Organizational Research Training Program (ORTP) faculty member, and David Wolf, Stanford PhD, 1984 (Sproull, Weiner, & Wolf, 1978; Sproull, 1981; Kiesler & Sproull, 1982) were among those who offered organizational scholars an early introduction to some of the then-new ideas about cognitive structures and heuristic processing and how they influence the development of beliefs. Research on managerial cognition, based on advances in cognitive psychology, burgeoned in the 1980s and 1990s with more than 350 articles and books on cognitive processes in organizational learning published between 1980 and 2005. (See Walsh, 1995; Hodgkinson & Healey, 2008 for papers surveying research over this period.)

Most learning is incremental, takes place over repeated learning cycles, and exhibits a positivity bias. Sim Sitkin, Stanford PhD, 1986, emphasized the importance of learning from "small failures" in building organizational resilience and long-term performance (Sitkin, 1992). Dramatic events – often crises or "large failures" – may engender one-trial learning. Michal Tamuz, Stanford PhD, 1988, demonstrated how the cognitive process of categorizing rare events acts as a toggle switch triggering different information processing routines depending upon how an event is categorized (e.g., Tamuz, 1987, 2001). Building on Tamuz' field work and other studies of rare and catastrophic events, March, Sproull, and Tamuz (1991) described how organizations can learn, not only from rare events but also from events that never occurred, through creating and interpreting hypothetical histories. This work remains influential among scholars interested in vicarious learning, rare events, and near failures (e.g., Carroll, Rudolph, & Hatakenaka, 2002; Kim & Miner, 2007).

Narrative Knowing

Concurrent with and complementary to research on managerial cognition is research on "narrative knowing" (Czarniawska-Joerges, 1998; Polkinghorne, 1988). This work, in the sense-making tradition of Weick (1995), emphasizes that people do not simply process information inside their heads; they socially construct interpretations of environmental action by creating and sharing stories and other cultural artifacts. Joanne Martin, who was an ORTP faculty member, and her students contributed early work to this theme (Martin, 1982; Martin, Feldman, Hatch, & Sitkin, 1983; Martin, Sitkin, & Boehm, 1985; Siehl & Martin, 1984; Feldman, 1991). Constructing and sharing stories, myths, rites, and ceremonies transform individual learning into organizational learning. These cultural artifacts can take on a life of their own, thereby supporting vicarious learning and socialization across the organization.

GOALS AND ASPIRATIONS

Classical learning models assume that goals are exogenous and fixed. Stanford-school scholars have produced a body of work demonstrating how goals, instead of being fixed, adjust over time. In early simulation models Daniel Levinthal, Stanford PhD, 1984, and Jim March demonstrated that goals are modified as a weighted function of prior goals and prior performance (Levinthal & March, 1981). Theresa Lant (1992) extended these ideas empirically and demonstrated not only that aspirations adjust to feedback over time but also that aspirations can sometimes adjust more rapidly than performance. In the context of a marketing strategy game, she also demonstrated that managers consistently set aspirations higher than actual performance.

With Scott Herriott, Stanford PhD, 1984, Levinthal and March extended their earlier simulation work to consider the effect of learning rates on performance (Herriott, Levinthal, & March, 1985). Simple learning over repeated trials will lead people and organizations to repeat <extinguish>

what they are rewarded <punished> for doing and to become better
<worse> at it. Fast learning about rewarded behavior can lead to
competence traps, which is repetition of positive, but sub-optimal, behavior.
The same reinforcement dynamics can lead to failure traps in which people
and organizations rapidly abandon behavior that is not rapidly rewarded.
In each case, rapid learning in the short-run is likely to prevent the discovery
of superior alternatives in the long-run.

Fast learning, whether driven by success or failure, leads organizations to
ignore distant times – both the long-run historical past and the long-run
future. It leads them to ignore distant places – that is, ones outside their near
neighborhood. Success-driven fast learning, resulting in self-assurance and
over-confidence, leads them to ignore failures. Levinthal and March (1993)
describe all of these behaviors as facets of the myopia of learning, pointing
out that they make it difficult to maintain a balance between exploitation
and exploration (March, 1991). Slow learning – skepticism in the face
of success and persistence in the face of failure – runs against the apparatus
of classical learning theory and the advice of management consultants.
But under conditions of complexity and rapidly changing environments,
it may produce superior outcomes.

ROUTINES

Organizational action associated with positive outcomes becomes embodied
over time in organizational routines; action associated with negative
outcomes leads to revising or extinguishing routines. (See, for example,
Lant, Milliken, & Batra, 1992, for a study of deliberate replacement of
routines at the firm level after poor past performance.) Whatever the level
of analysis – individual, group, or organization – routines are guides to
behavior or programs for behavior that are often tacit rather than explicit.
They are stimulus-driven and can run without people's explicit awareness or
articulation of them. They are conventionally thought of as mechanisms for
stability, supporting the efficient operation of repeated action and the
exploitation of previously learned lessons. They are also conventionally
thought of as impeding improvisation and innovation through limiting or
foreclosing the exploration of new ideas. Michael Cohen, with Paul
Bacdayan, produced a particularly elegant experimental demonstration
of the development of outcomes-based routines that are characterized by
reliability, efficiency, and sub-optimal performance when confronted with
novelty (Cohen & Bacdayan, 1994).

Rules – a written codification of organizational routines – are visible evidence of history-based organizational learning and are usually considered to be particularly strong impediments to improvisation and innovation. Xueguang Zhou, Stanford PhD, 1991 and now a faculty member in the Stanford sociology department, demonstrated how rules are institutionalized over time. Martin Schulz, Stanford PhD, 1993, who demonstrated that the birth rate of new rules declines with the number of rules in a rule population over time, concluded that "[existing] rules reduce the likelihood that new problems will be seen as opportunities to draw new lessons" (Schultz, 1998, p. 872). Schulz, Zhou, and March (March, Schulz, & Zhou, 2000) produced a more comprehensive analysis of the dynamics of rules: they documented that rule creation and rule revision follow different dynamics, with rule creation responsive to exogenous shocks, but imprecisely so, and rule revision responsive to rule histories.

Despite a general emphasis on the history-preserving nature of routines, several Stanford-school scholars have analyzed how routines change and support change. Miner, Bassoff, and Moorman (2001) demonstrated that routines can be both cause and consequence of improvisation, which they define as real-time, short-term situational learning. In an investigation of improvisation in new product development, they discovered that routines can serve as referents for improvisation. They also documented how improvisations can be retained over time in the form of new or revised routines, some of which are codified in new organizational rules. Dan Levinthal, with Wes Cohen, argued that routines may contribute to an organization's capacity to benefit from R&D (Cohen & Levinthal, 1990). In contrast with models assuming that the most efficient way for a firm to learn from R&D is to appropriate results from other firms, Cohen and Levinthal argue that internal R&D enhances a firm's ability to learn both from its own behavior and from the work of other firms. Internal R&D builds organizational scaffolding, which includes new and revised routines, to play a role similar to cognitive scaffolding in individual learning processes.

Martha Feldman, Stanford PhD, 1983, introduces agency into theorizing about routines, thereby producing a richer conceptualization of routines as a source of flexibility and continuous change (Feldman, 2000; Feldman & Pentland, 2003). Following Latour (1986) she theorizes that routines have both an ostensive component (the idea and ideal) and performative component (the action/enactment). People who carry out routines reflect on, react to, and modify previous iterations of them. The two components together constitute opportunities for learning and change via routine-based everyday work.

LOOKING BACKWARD, LOOKING FORWARD

Stanford-school organizational scholars have made substantial contributions to our understanding of organizational learning. Their work, collectively, is both broad and deep. Their PhD home departments include economics, political science, sociology, business, and education. They have studied learning in government agencies, schools and universities, business organizations, and industries. They have collected data using computer simulations, laboratory experiments, archival studies, and multi-year multi-method field studies. No one scholar (except for Jim March himself!) has worked within all of these disciplines and methods. Yet the work of each has enriched and been enriched by membership in the broader Stanford organizational learning community.

Looking forward, changes in the global political economy will afford opportunities for research on more non-US-owned organizations. Indeed these words are being written as the US automobile industry – the canonical subject of organizational learning curve research – is being deconstructed and reconstituted with Asian and European owners. Additionally, new measurement tools and analytic techniques will broaden the range of phenomena and deepen the level of understanding available to organizational learning scholars. Brain imaging and hormonal assay are increasingly used in studies of individual and small group choice and learning (e.g., Glimscher, Camerer, Fehr, & Poldrack, 2008). Results from these studies will find their way to new models of organizational learning. Extremely large social networks, with nodes numbering in the millions, are now supported by and visible on the Internet, giving scholars the opportunity to investigate models of learning by diffusion and imitation at a new scale (Kleinberg, 2008). Developments such as these may result in an increasing balkanization of organization scholarship in which brain imagers do not talk to data miners and political scientists do not talk to business school faculty. One can only hope for the emergence of a 21st-century version of the Stanford ORTP to support the broadest possible conception of organizational learning.

NOTE

1. Because this volume focuses on the Stanford-school community, it omits reference to many of Jim's colleagues and collaborators on organizational learning from other institutions.

REFERENCES

Argote, L. (1999). *Organizational learning: Creating, retaining and transferring knowledge.* Norwell, MA: Kluwer Academic Publishers.

Carroll, J. S., Rudolph, J. W., & Hatakenaka, S. (2002). Learning from experience in high-hazard organizations. *Research in Organizational Behavior, 24*, 87–137.

Cohen, M. D., & Bacdayan, P. (1994). Organizational routines are stored as procedural memory: Evidence from a laboratory study. *Organization Science, 5*, 554–568.

Cohen, M. D., & Sproull, L. S. (Eds). (1996). *Organizational learning.* Thousand Oaks, CA: Sage.

Cohen, W. M., & Levinthal, D. A. (1990). Absorptive capacity: A new perspective on learning and innovation. *Administrative Science Quarterly, 35*, 128–152.

Czarniawska-Joerges, B. (1998). *A narrative approach to organization studies.* Thousand Oaks, CA: Sage.

Feldman, M. S. (1991). The meanings of ambiguity: Learning from stories and metaphors. In: P. J. Frost, L. Moore, M. Louis, C. Lundberg & J. Martin (Eds), *Reframing organizational culture* (pp. 145–156). Thousand Oaks, CA: Sage.

Feldman, M. S. (2000). Organizational routines as a source of continuous change. *Organization Science, 11*, 611–629.

Feldman, M. S., & Pentland, B. T. (2003). Reconceptualizing organizational routines as a source of flexibility and change. *Administrative Science Quarterly, 48*, 94–118.

Glimscher, P. W., Camerer, C. F., Fehr, E., & Poldrack, R. A. (2008). *Neuroeconomics: Decision making and the brain.* New York: Academic Press.

Herriott, S. R., Levinthal, D., & March, J. G. (1985). Learning from experience in organizations. *American Economic Review, 75*, 298–302.

Hodgkinson, G. P., & Healey, M. P. (2008). Cognition in organizations. *Annual Review of Psychology, 59*, 387–417.

Kiesler, S., & Sproull, L. (1982). Managerial response to changing environments: Perspectives on problem sensing from social cognition. *Administrative Science Quarterly, 27*, 548–570.

Kim, J., & Miner, A. S. (2007). Vicarious learning from the failures and near-failures of others: Evidence from the U.S. commercial banking industry. *Academy of Management Journal, 50*, 687–714.

Kleinberg, J. (2008). The convergence of social and technological networks. *Communications of the ACM, 51*(11), 66–72.

Lant, T. K. (1992). Aspiration level updating: An empirical exploration. *Management Science, 38*, 623–644.

Lant, T. K., Milliken, F. J., & Batra, B. (1992). The role of managerial learning and interpretation in strategic persistence and reorientation: An empirical exploration. *Strategic Management Journal, 13*, 585–608.

Lant, T. K., & Shapira, Z. (Eds). (2000). *Organizational cognition: Computation and interpretation.* Mahwah, NJ: Lawrence Erlbaum.

Latour, B. (1986). The powers of association. In: J. Law (Ed.), *Power, action and belief* (pp. 264–280). London: Routledge and Kegan Paul.

Levinthal, D., & March, J. G. (1981). A model of adaptive organizational search. *Journal of Economic Behavior and Organization, 2*, 307–333.

Levinthal, D., & March, J. G. (1993). The myopia of learning. *Strategic Management Journal,* *14*, 95–112.
Levitt, B., & March, J. G. (1988). Organizational learning. *Annual Review of Sociology, 14,* 319–340.
March, J. G. (1988). *Decisions and organizations.* Cambridge, MA: Blackwell.
March, J. G. (1991). Exploration and exploitation in organizational learning. *Organization Science, 2,* 71–87.
March, J. G. (1999). *The pursuit of organizational intelligence.* Cambridge, MA: Blackwell.
March, J. G. (2008). *Explorations in organizations.* Stanford, CA: Stanford University Press.
March, J. G., & Olsen, J. P. (1975). The uncertainty of the past: Organizational learning under ambiguity. *European Journal of Political Research, 3,* 147–171.
March, J. G., Schulz, M., & Zhou, X. (2000). *The dynamics of rules: Change in written organizational codes.* Stanford, CA: Stanford University Press.
March, J. G., Sproull, L., & Tamuz, M. (1991). Learning from samples of one or fewer. *Organization Science, 2,* 1–13.
Martin, J. (1982). Stories and scripts in organizational settings. In: A. Hastorf & A. Isen (Eds), *Cognitive social psychology.* New York: Elsevier-North Holland.
Martin, J., Feldman, M., Hatch, M. J., & Sitkin, S. (1983). The uniqueness paradox in organizational stories. *Administrative Science Quarterly, 28,* 438–453.
Martin, J., Sitkin, S., & Boehm, M. (1985). Founders and the elusiveness of a cultural legacy. In: P. Frost, L. Moore, M. Louis, C. Lundberg & J. Martin (Eds), *Organizational culture* (pp. 99–124). New York: Sage Publications.
Miner, A. S., Bassoff, P., & Moorman, C. (2001). Organizational improvisation and learning: A field study. *Administrative Science Quarterly, 46,* 304–337.
Miner, A. S., & Haunschld, P. R. (1995). Population level learning. *Research in Organizational Behavior, 17,* 115–166.
Miner, A. S., & Mezias, S. J. (1996). Ugly duckling no more: Pasts and futures of organizational learning research. *Organization Science, 7,* 88–99.
Polkinghorne, D. (1988). *Narrative knowing and the human sciences.* Albany, NY: State University of New York Press.
Schultz, M. (1998). Limits to bureaucratic growth: The density dependence of organizational rule births. *Administrative Science Quarterly, 43,* 845–876.
Siehl, C., & Martin, J. (1984). The role of symbolic management: How can managers effectively transmit organizational culture? In: J. G. Hunt, D. Hosking, C. Schriesheim & R. Stewart (Eds), *Leaders and managers: International perspectives on managerial behavior and leadership* (Vol. 7, pp. 227–239). Elmsford, NY: Pergamon Press.
Sitkin, S. (1992). Learning through failure: The strategy of small losses. *Research in Organizational Behavior, 14,* 231–266.
Sproull, L. (1981). Beliefs in organizations. In: P. Nystrom & W. Starbuck (Eds), *Handbook of organization design* (Vol. 2, pp. 203–224). London: Oxford University Press.
Sproull, L. S., Weiner, S. W., & Wolf, D. (1978). *Organizing an anarchy: Beliefs, bureaucracy, and politics in the national institute of education.* Chicago: University of Chicago Press.

Tamuz, M. (1987). The impact of computer surveillance on air safety reporting. *Columbia Journal of World Business, 22*(1), 69–77.

Tamuz, M. (2001). Learning disabilities for regulators: The perils of organizational learning in the air. *Administration & Society, 33*, 276–302.

Walsh, J. P. (1995). Managerial and organizational cognition: Notes from a trip down memory lane. *Organization Science, 6*(3), 280–321.

Weick, K. (1995). *Sense making in organizations.* Thousand Oaks, CA: Sage.

CHAPTER 5

CULTURE STANFORD'S WAY

Mary Jo Hatch

ABSTRACT

Stanford contributed significantly to the organizational culture movement that occurred in organization studies from 1970–2000. This chapter traces developments at Stanford and puts the contributions of its researchers and scholars in the context of the many influences that shaped the study of organizational culture during this period. In addition to the historical account, there is speculation about why the culture movement at Stanford more or less ended but might yet be revived, either by those studying institutionalization processes or by those who resist them.

There is no denying that Stanford positions itself on the frontier of research into most new ideas. Organizational culture was no exception and, in the early 1980s, three books extolling the importance of corporate culture were written or co-authored by individuals associated with the Stanford Graduate School of Business (GSB): William Ouchi, one time faculty member; Richard Pascale, adjunct lecturer; and Tom Peters who earned his MBA (1972) and PhD (1977) at the GSB and also worked for a period as an adjunct lecturer there. Both Ouchi's *Theory Z* and Pascale's (and Anthony Athos's) *The Art of Japanese Management* appeared in 1981 (Pascale & Athos, 1981) amid national concern over the economic challenge posed by Japanese manufacturing (particularly in the automotive industry).

Stanford's Organization Theory Renaissance, 1970–2000
Research in the Sociology of Organizations, Volume 28, 71–95
Copyright © 2010 by Emerald Group Publishing Limited
ISSN: 0733-558X/doi:10.1108/S0733-558X(2010)0000028009

Both books brought corporate culture to the attention of managers by addressing the burning question of the day: Can successful Japanese management practices be transferred to other cultures?

As high profile as the two Japanese management books were, Peters and Bob Waterman's (1982) *In Search of Excellence* soon overshadowed them, this one focusing not just on what makes companies excellent, but the role organizational culture plays in their success. This book was so popular – topping the New York Times bestseller list for over 60 weeks and staying on the list for more than three years – that some say it spawned the lucrative market segment of guru management books (Collins, 2007, p. 12).

Of course, Stanford cannot lay claim to the popularity Peters and Waterman's book enjoyed. Consulting house McKinsey, in which Peters was then a partner, suggested the project and funded data collection, as well as supported the two researchers while they wrote the book. And of course there is much to be said for good timing. But Peters' ties to Stanford not only provided him a seedbed to nurture the ideas behind *In Search of Excellence*, they enabled students to read an early draft. I read the manuscript in 1981 as part of a PhD seminar on culture offered by Joanne Martin, who was at that time an untenured assistant professor at the GSB. It was typical of Stanford to introduce its students to what would become influential new works before most others knew about them.

Neither can Stanford lay claim to creating the academic field of organizational culture studies, though it was an early player. Other academics started looking into organizational culture around the time the books by Ouchi, Pascale, and Peters were being written. In my memory the most notable outside influences on Stanford's organizational culture researchers were Edgar Schein and John Van Maanen at MIT; Linda Smircich at UMASS Amherst; Lou Pondy and Meryl Louis at the University of Illinois; and folklorist Michael Owen Jones at UCLA. Soon to be influential researchers from outside the United States, with interests primarily in symbolic approaches to organizations, were Barry Turner in the United Kingdom, Pasquale Gagliardi in Italy, P. O. Berg in Sweden, Peter Frost in Canada, and Kristian Kreiner in Denmark. In 1981, this group would found the Standing Conference on Organizational Symbolism (SCOS, a subgroup of EGOS, the European Group for Organization Studies), whose conferences provided sites for some of the most productive meetings between culture researchers from North America and Europe, beginning with the Milan conference held in 1987.

But considerably before the 1987 "invasion" of SCOS by US culture researchers, a number of important small conferences had taken place around the United States. The first of these, billed as "Organizational Symbolism," was held in 1979 at the home of Louis Pondy and resulted in a book by the same title edited by Pondy, Frost, Morgan, and Dandridge (1983) – notably, Frost and Morgan came from Canada. Two more small conferences took place in 1983, one organized at UCLA and hosted by Jones called "Myth, Symbols & Folklore: Expanding the Analysis of Organizations"; the other entitled "Organizational Culture and the Meaning of Life in the Workplace," held at the University of British Columbia in Vancouver hosted by the Research Group for the Study of Organizational Life at UBC, of which Frost was a member (P. O. Berg from Sweden attended this meeting as well). Conferees at these latter meetings jointly produced three books: *Inside Organizations* (Jones, Moore, & Snyder, 1988), *Organizational Culture* (Frost, Moore, Lundberg, Louis, & Martin, 1985), and *Reframing Organizational Culture* (Frost, Moore, Lundberg, Louis, & Martin, 1991). Martin, along with various of her PhD students, presented Stanford's organizational culture research at these meetings, and Martin herself co-edited and/or wrote chapters for all the books (Martin & Powers, 1983b; Martin, Sitkin, & Boehm, 1985; Siehl & Martin, 1988; Martin, 1991). Martin's student, Deb Meyerson, wrote two chapters for the second Frost et al. book based on her culturally rich qualitative study of the effects of ambiguity on social work and social workers in a hospital (Meyerson, 1991a; Meyerson, 1991b).

The books these small conferences produced were, for a time, nearly the only place to find the controversial studies on organizational culture then on offer, though, significantly, *Administrative Science Quarterly* (*ASQ*) published a special issue on the topic in 1983 (edited by Jelenik, Smircich, & Hirsch, 1983). Until the mid-1990s, on the other side of the Atlantic, one place to find SCOS member's organizational culture research was in the pages of their obscure newsletter *Dragon*. Access to European work on organizational culture became easier in 1995 when SCOS founded its own journal under the title *Studies in Cultures, Organizations and Societies* (recently renamed *Culture and Organization*). Prior to the founding of the journal, two edited books comprising articles based on papers presented at SCOS conferences had significant influence on the by-then fairly established field (Turner, 1990; Gagliardi, 1990), as did the few studies by European culture researchers reported in the EGOS journal *Organization Studies* (e.g., Gagliardi, 1986; Linstead & Grafton-Small, 1992; Young, 1989).

As Smircich recalled the 1970s and 1980s, organizational researchers interested in culture, who were often marginalized at their own institutions, were likely to be found at relatively marginal business schools, so organizational culture studies, in the United States at least, was doubly marginalized. This context made the research done at Stanford and MIT extremely important; these institutions bestowed much sought after legitimacy to the entire field. But even though Stanford and MIT quickly became US hubs for organizational culture research, the importance of the conferences held on both sides of the Atlantic should not be underestimated. It was in these venues that organizational culture's contours were defined and the politics of doing culture research were analyzed and engaged.

As compared to the development of other schools in organizational studies that trace their roots to Stanford (e.g., institutional theory, population ecology, resource dependence theory), the genesis of organizational culture studies was much more widely distributed. As a result, organizational culture studies was intellectually diverse from its beginnings, which may account for the lack of a dominant paradigm in this field of study. On the other hand, if cultural researchers are to explore the many informal and symbolic ways that humans meaningfully organize themselves, particularly in the lower regions of organizational hierarchies, such diversity is extremely useful.

At this point I hope you can see the complications I face in telling the story of culture research at Stanford. The context of a rapidly growing and geographically distributed set of research activities with their attendant politics is but one of them. Additional complications arise from the tension most business schools maintain between the worlds of practice and academic research. For example, at least from 1981 to 1985 while I was a student there, the Stanford GSB maintained two mainframe computers, one for the use of MBA students and administrators called "How," and the other for researchers and PhD students named "Why." This tension is important in understanding the role Stanford played in the organizational culture field because it was books written for managers by Ouchi, Pascale, and Peters that first aligned Stanford's name with the topic of culture in organizations.

There are many "hardcore" researchers (quite a few prominent ones are at Stanford) that to this day believe culture is unworthy of scientific study, mainly because they cannot relax their assumption that all research needs to be designed around testable hypotheses that can be disproved and evaluated using criteria of reliability and validity. Thus, a subplot of the practice–theory complication is the long fought philosophical war that, at the time organizational culture was emerging as a research topic, took shape as a battle between qualitative and quantitative research methods (see Martin & Frost, 1996). John Van Maanen, who edited a (Van Maanen, 1979) special issue of *Administrative Science Quarterly* focused on qualitative methods, became an important influence on the developing culture scene at Stanford because he argued loudly, persuasively, and with considerable panache for the relevance of ethnographic and other qualitative approaches to the study of organizations.

A last complication I have confronted in telling my story of Stanford's contribution to culture research arose from the close relationship between Stanford's GSB and its Sociology faculty (many organization studies faculty at the GSB at the time held courtesy appointments in Sociology). Institutional theory was just coming to prominence in sociology as organizational culture appeared on the horizon. Inspired by Philip Selznick's early work on institutional theory, W. Richard Scott, John Meyer, and Meyer's student Brian Rowan developed one important strand of new institutionalism at Stanford (see Scott, 2008; Rowan, this volume).

I do not remember anyone at the time making much of the overlap between the concepts of institutionalization and culture (see Dobbin, 1994; Pedersen & Dobbin, 2006, for latter expressions of this concern), or the important distinctions eventually drawn between ethnomethodology and ethnography. But to understand how organizational culture research at Stanford's GSB developed beginning in the 1970s, and perhaps why it had all but disappeared by 2000, it is necessary to consider the relationship of the GSB culture researchers to the Sociology Department's new institutionalists, which I will do at the end of the chapter.

It was into this complex world I stumbled in 1981 when I arrived in Palo Alto to start my PhD. To the best of my limited memory, complemented by the reminiscences of key culture researchers I spoke with while writing this chapter, I will reconstruct the story of Stanford's role in relation to the tensions between theory and practice, and between qualitative and quantitative research methods; the often tentative but always productive dialog between US and non-US culture researchers; and the influence of new institutionalism as it was being developed in Stanford's Sociology Department while over at the GSB organizational culture became a fulcrum of debate.

ORGANIZATIONAL CULTURE AT STANFORD: THE 1970s

The GSB's two most recognizable claims to fame around the world are its record of outstanding academic achievement and its renowned MBA program. Prior to the 1970s, the push to do internationally recognized scholarly work alongside teaching practically minded future managers did not produce much strain for organizational researchers. Hal Leavitt, David Bradford, Richard Pascale, and Jerry Porras, all representatives of the Human Relations tradition, published works that were respected by academics *and* built on their interests in the practical concerns of managers and the practices of management. But academia was changing the way business schools defined themselves and writing for managers was no longer as appreciated as it once had been by those who decide who gets tenure and who does not.

Ever since joining their universities, business faculties have been accused or suspected of using inferior methods by colleagues in other parts of the academy. The great rigor vs. relevance conundrum is one expression of the tension that business schools have provoked in the larger academic community. In the 1980s, Stanford was a world leader in forming a business faculty that could compete with other university departments for academic respectability. This it achieved in part by promoting only those with the strongest records of publication in top academic journals. But this change to a publish-or-perish mentality never reduced the importance of management practice to the GSB and its students. As is the case at other business schools, academic researchers at Stanford continued to teach MBA classes, and PhD students maintained strong applied interests.

Ouchi's two most enduring contributions to organizational culture studies appear to me to pivot around the growing tension between theory (or, perhaps more accurately, scholarly publication) and practice at Stanford in the 1970s. Ouchi (1980) made the case that organizational culture marked the latest institutional development in the evolutionary path leading from markets to bureaucracies, and now, according to Ouchi, clans (his term for organizational cultures). While this article, published in a top journal (*ASQ*), claimed space for organizational culture within the discourses of institutional economics and sociology fomenting at Stanford during this period, Ouchi's other major contribution forged a continuation of the interests of Leavitt, Bradford, and Porras in promoting the value of humanistic management practices. *Theory Z* (Ouchi, 1981) presented organizational culture as an important context for assessing alternatives to both the command and control model of management that Douglas McGregor (1960) called Theory X, and McGregor's own Theory Y, the definitive statement of the Human Relations approach. By simultaneously writing works positioning culture in relation to institutional economics and human relations, as well as prescribing tenets of Japanese management practice, Ouchi had stretched himself between the poles of theory and practice and made a connection between organizational culture and the new institutionalism then under development in Stanford's Sociology Department.

In writing their respective books for managerial audiences, Ouchi, Pascale, and Peters had employed case-based argumentation, which was not necessarily problematic; there is a long tradition in sociology supporting the use of case studies. But the issue of not including any controls caused the works of these authors to be regarded with suspicion if not condescension. Academic critics accused the authors of relying on anecdote instead of evidence and described their efforts as journalistic. Anecdotal and journalistic were terms of opprobrium within Stanford's research community, a culture shaped, at least for its organizational culture researchers, by strong association with Stanford's Sociology Department. Thus, the books written by Ouchi, Pascale, and Peters supplied hardcore researchers with ammunition to strike at all organizational culture research.

To be fair, Ouchi used comparisons between more and less Japanese-like organizations in the United States for his evidence, which at least implied the use of controls. Peters and Waterman, however, relied purely on success stories to argue their case and their massive success along with later exposure of the weaknesses in their method (*Business Week* ran a cover story decrying the later failures of some of the "excellent" companies Peters and Waterman identified), tainted all the corporate culture books of the era. The criticism of these popular books haunted the organizational culture researchers who came to Stanford after Peters and Ouchi had left, and who operated under the watchful gaze of the Stanford Sociology Department.

The uphill battle with the then dominant positivist methodology preferred by Stanford sociologists would continue to be fought in large part by Joanne Martin (see Martin, 1990a, for an early account of this battle), at the time a new and untenured member of the GSB faculty with courtesy appointments in Psychology and Sociology. According to Martin (2003), whose PhD training at Harvard had been in experimental social psychology, her interest in culture traces to Alan Wilkins. Wilkins asked Martin to take over as his PhD thesis advisor after Ouchi left for UCLA. At that time Martin was deeply involved in social injustice research, so she was surprised by Wilkins's request. She knew almost nothing about organizational culture, how could she help?

To address her concerns Wilkins started leaving copies of his favorite culture papers on her desk, most of which came from anthropology. As Martin recalls, she found herself turning to these papers whenever she had time to read, instead of to the justice literature that she then regarded as her specialty. She soon recognized that she was developing interest in culture and began formulating research plans. Not long after, Wilkins graduated and Martin began working with two new PhD students, Caren Siehl and Melanie Powers. Wilkins (1989) would eventually write his own popular management book, *Developing Corporate Character*, in the Stanford tradition of providing theoretically grounded practical advice, much as Ouchi, Pascale, and Peters had done before him, and as Jeffrey Pfeffer (1994, 1998, 2007) and others, including Deb Meyerson and myself (Meyerson, 2003; Hatch & Schultz, 2008), would do much later.

Caren Siehl entered the GSB's PhD program after a career as a practicing manager and consultant. Her practical orientation can be seen in the work she and Martin published, consisting of articles based on case studies built from secondary sources and on field studies involving innovative measures of the extent to which cultures are shared (Martin & Siehl, 1983; Siehl & Martin, 1984, 1988). The most influential of these was a study of John DeLorean's division at General Motors that observed and described subcultures in this large business organization. In their article, Martin and Siehl (1983) described subcultures in terms of their relationship with the dominant corporate (sub)culture represented by the values and beliefs of top executives. In their framework, subcultures were typecast as either enhancing (supportive), orthogonal (neutral), or countercultural (subversive).

In another paper, Siehl and Martin (1984) linked culture to learning, using both qualitative and quantitative methods to explore the ways managers used distinctive jargon, stories, rituals, and dress norms to transmit cultural knowledge to newcomers. They showed that new employees first learned technical jargon followed by socio-emotional jargon that was unique to their culture. It was only over time that they became familiar with commonly told organizational stories and learned to interpret them the way old-guard employees did. At the conclusion of their socialization, most newcomers could fill in random blanks their researchers left in copies of their boss' memos, a development they identified as tacit cultural knowledge. This building-block model of cultural learning showed each new type of cultural knowledge enabling the next.

Along with PhD student Melanie Powers, Martin conducted a series of laboratory studies showing that information presented as a story is significantly more memorable than information presented in non-narrative ways (Martin, 1982; Martin & Powers, 1983a, 1983b). Just as she was wrapping up her studies of subcultures and cultural transmission, a new crop of PhD students arrived for whom Martin designed a PhD seminar focused on organizational culture.

ORGANIZATIONAL CULTURE
AT STANFORD: THE 1980s

Sim Sitkin, Tom Kosnik, and I were among the group that signed up for Martin's culture seminar in 1982. The comradeship we developed in the classroom spilled over into a research group Martin created to keep us together. Along with Michael Boehm, a new PhD student with an undergraduate degree in anthropology, and Martha Feldman, a doctoral student in political science, both of whom joined a little later, the group produced several academic articles. One particularly influential one, entitled "The Uniqueness Paradox in Organizational Stories," landed on the pages of the special issue of *Administrative Science Quarterly* on organizational culture mentioned earlier. Karl Weick, then *ASQ*'s editor-in-chief, who had attended one or two of the small culture conferences in the United States, proposed the idea for the special issue to Jelinek, Smircich, and Hirsch who became its guest co-editors. Among the influential articles published there, Martin, Feldman, Hatch, and Sitkin's (1983) "The Uniqueness Paradox" remains one of the most frequently cited papers on organizational culture.

"The Uniqueness Paradox" reported the results of a theme-based content analysis of the stories told in corporate biographies. This study showed that organizational claims to uniqueness were based on stories that were themselves not unique because they always fell into one of seven basic thematic categories (e.g., Is the big boss human? How will mistakes be handled?). The paradox is still important today, not only because it shows that cultural manifestations are not unique, as often claimed, but also because it suggests that perceptions of uniqueness, formed within the cultural context of the organization, contribute to the construction of organizational identity (e.g., Hatch & Schultz, 1997, 2000, 2002).

Appearing in the same *ASQ* special issue was Stephen Barley's (1983) "The Semiotics of Funeral Work." Barley, who would later join Stanford's School of Engineering, was then a PhD student at MIT's Sloan School of Management where he studied with Edgar Schein and John Van Maanen. The appearance in the special issue of representatives of both Stanford and MIT was itself symbolic. There was a friendly rivalry between the two business schools that took shape in an often intense debate between Martin and Schein over how best to define and study culture.

About the same time that Ouchi, Pascale, and Peters were writing their books on corporate culture for managers, MIT's Schein developed his theory of culture as the shared assumptions and values underpinning cultural artifacts (1981, 1984, 1985). Schein's work was partly the product of his early Human Relations training, and so his contributions to culture are not surprisingly directed to managers as well as to academic researchers. In the early 1980s, Martin began taking issue with Schein's views mainly because she felt he denied the importance of subcultures. According to Schein, at the time anyway, if it is not shared universally throughout the organization, then it is not culture. Martin saw subcultures as rife with meanings not shared throughout the organization and felt that these meanings must be acknowledged and studied if culture in organizations is to be fully addressed (later she would conclude that even subcultural differentation was insufficient to account for the myriad meanings that articulate a culture).

Meanwhile, Van Maanen, also at MIT and a close colleague of Schein's, was much more sanguine about subcultures, having staked his claim in the territory of developing ethnographic methods for organizational culture research. His *Tales of the Field* (Van Maanen, 1988) would become a classic among culture researchers, and his example as an organizational ethnographer inspired many a Stanford culture researcher (e.g., Van Maanen, 1973, 1975, 1976, 1991). Schein's culture theory was likewise a staple in the diet of organizational researchers including those at Stanford, albeit often read in the context of Martin's criticisms of his "integrationist" (read "managerialist") view.

Schein's model was particularly attractive to me because it offered the only theoretical foundation available and I began to develop my own theory of the dynamics of organizational culture by articulating the relationships between the concepts of assumption, value, and artifact. In my first year at Stanford, I wrote a paper for James March's PhD seminar with my initial thoughts on extending Schein's model to symbols and making it more dynamic. Jim wrote but one dismal comment next to my concluding statement: "This is not yet an interesting idea." Concentrating on "yet," I remained undeterred, only later realizing, after many longer conversations with Jim, that he was one of culture's constant critics, often asking: "When are you people ever going to get around to some reliability and validity?"

In this spirit, and contrary to our hopes and expectations of acceptance if not celebration upon publication of the *ASQ* special issue, all hell broke loose. While we had been alerted to the virulent objections raised by our quantitatively inclined colleagues to the prescriptive work of Ouchi, Pascale, and Peters, the extension of this argument to what we regarded as our much more "scientific" approach caught us by surprise. Martin and other culture researchers had by now organized symposium after symposium at the Academy of Management annual conferences to provide a venue for debate and to garner attention and gain legitimacy (Martin 1980, 1981, 1982; Martin, Hatch, Kosnik, & Sitkin, 1983; Martin, Sitkin, Kosnik, & Boehm, 1983) and Martin participated in the many smaller conferences around the United States. That the marginalization of culture research and researchers continued was almost too much to bear. But the final straw was the persistence of the assumption that culture could be managed, a view promoted in the early prescriptive books by Stanford's own faculty and students. Martin went on the warpath.

In the early 1980s, most cultural researchers in the United States were arguing that cultural change was a form of "value engineering," whereby top managers could articulate values that would, if reinforced consistently, come to be shared by employees throughout an organization. Martin, Sitkin, and Boehm's (1985) research in Silicon Valley produced a study showing that, even an extremely charismatic leader of a very small firm, found it hard to create a culture reflecting his (the leaders studied were all men) own values. This study reported that, within months of the company's founding, employees began forming subcultures that embraced different patterns of values than those of their leader. Based on analysis of key event histories told to them by employees, Martin, Sitkin, and Boehm found that, while the leader saw himself as critical to each of the key events, employees often saw his role as less central and many made members of their own subculture the heroes who "saved the day" in their stories.

By the mid-1980s a new set of doctoral students had become ensconced at Stanford, including Deb Meyerson who soon became Martin's student and co-author (after some years on the faculty at the University of Michigan, she would rejoin Stanford first as a visiting professor at the GSB and later as a faculty member at the School of Education, where she sits today). Together Meyerson and Martin created a framework that Martin would later use to categorize the different ways organizational researchers study culture (Meyerson & Martin, 1987; Martin & Meyerson, 1988). Their thesis was that organizational cultures can be viewed as integrated wholes (the view promoted by Schein's model); as sets of differentiated subcultures; or as fragmented pieces that do not in any way support the assertions of uniformity made by (some of) their members, a view suggested by postmodernism. In their study of the Peace Corps in Africa, Meyerson and Martin (1987) showed that a variety of change processes altered organizational culture, for example by creating subcultural differences that exacerbated conflicts between the leadership and rank and file employees, and fostered ambiguity rather than clarity. This longitudinal study showed that there was more to culture than the integration perspective reveals.

In the mid-1980s, Martin and her students began to travel outside the United States, particularly to Europe to attend SCOS meetings. Organizational scholars from Europe have always been a bit put off by what they may have good reason to describe as the hegemony of American research. At least in the 1980s they were only infrequently published in high profile US management and organization journals. SCOS became a place where organizational culture scholars from the European tradition of doing research could exercise their mutual frustration about not getting appropriately recognized. Not only was it nearly impossible to get your work published in US journals if you were non-US based, but for the time being the authors who did publish in these journals almost never cited work done outside the US. So when Martin and Smircich accompanied by an entourage of US students began attending SCOS conferences, they were often given a somewhat hostile welcome (it was nice to be recognized by American scholars, but the suspicion of hegemony put them on guard). Nonetheless, as the decade wore on, SCOS increasingly, if begrudgingly, accepted at least some Americans, and one graduate of the Stanford PhD program, yours truly, even migrated to Europe.

I had naïvely presented a quantitative study based on my dissertation at the watershed 1987 SCOS conference in Milan. The presentation was given considerable attention, first of all because it was part of the opening session of the conference, and also because my quantitative methods (ANOVA) violated the norm for doing qualitative research embedded deeply in SCOS culture. Nonetheless, my methods produced the finding that symbolism explained the perceived effects of physical structure (how subjects thought their space affected them) that endured in spite of demonstrated behavioral effects that were contrary to these expectations (Hatch, 1990). That is to say, open space office environments were interpreted as supporting open communication when in behavioral fact they resulted in their inhabitants spending less time working together than did occupants of private offices (the control group).

After being confronted, singly or in small groups, by the love–hate of what felt like every last SCOS conferee (they loved that I found empirical evidence of an effect for symbolism, they hated that I did it using quantitative methods), Martin and Smircich dragged me off to the farewell lunch and advised me not to reject my experience at SCOS, but rather to savor it. I wanted desperately to tell all these critical people that they were plain wrong to reject my methods, when it occurred to me that this was the flip side of the treatment from which I had been suffering in the United States where the only conversation I seemed able to have started and ended with "Why are you still doing those ♯(*$&@* qualitative studies?"'. What is more, SCOS provided the antidote. Jesper Strandgaard Pedersen, of the Copenhagen Business School (CBS), would soon take a study tour of the United States visiting Van Maanen and Schein at MIT, and Martin at Stanford followed by a three-week stay with me in San Diego during which we endlessly discussed the ideas provoked by his visits to Martin and Schein. Pedersen would soon thereafter contact me about becoming a visiting professor at CBS.

ORGANIZATIONAL CULTURE AT STANFORD: THE 1990s

The beginning of the 1990s found Martin busy reworking the framework she had developed with Meyerson for her 1992 book *Cultures in Organizations*. There she would apply the integration, differentiation, and fragmentation perspectives to data collected in a Silicon Valley high tech company, presenting the three perspectives as complementary rather than competing alternatives. This book had enormous impact on both sides of the Atlantic. In the United States it became *the* framework with which to organize the by-now almost overwhelmingly complex literature on organizational culture, while in Europe it was more likely to be reviled because it did not make room for the nuances of interpretation Europeans felt was needed to prevent their research being inappropriately pigeonholed, or worse ignored because it did not fit any category (a version of the complaint that US researchers do not give European scholarship its due).

By this time Martin's PhD students, Meyerson and Maureen Scully, had developed the concept of tempered radicalism (Meyerson & Scully, 1995; Meyerson, 2003; Meyerson & Tomkins, 2007). Their work, informed by feminism, was inspired in part by how Martin managed to do highly risky culture research and still earn tenure. Meyerson and Scully's interests in feminism in turn sparked a kindred spirit in Martin that can be found represented in the integration, differentiation, and fragmentation perspectives on organizational cultures (Martin, 1992). There one can discern a clear path from the theme of alterity in feminist studies to the themes of differentiation and fragmentation that Martin argues lead to different ways of understanding culture in organizations. That is to say, while Martin equated the integration perspective with a hegemonic (white male) order, the differentiation perspective argues that subcultures may harbor harmony within their borders, but that cross border relations with other subcultures often involve conflict and, in the case of relationships with the dominant subculture of top management, invoke significant power differentials as well. Fragmentation took the logic of internal conflict and divisiveness further by acknowledging that, no matter how hard a group of individuals tries to share values, purpose, beliefs, and ideals, there are simply too many dimensions along which individuals can vary to find harmony with other cultural members for long.

Throughout the 1990s, Martin's interests in postmodernism and feminism began to work their way into her research agenda (Martin, 1990a, 1990b, 2000; Martin & Meyerson, 1998). Although Martin would continue to contribute to the field of organizational culture studies through her review of the field with Peter Frost (Martin & Frost, 1996) and her *Organizational Culture: Mapping the Terrain* (Martin, 2002), no new PhD students interested in pursuing culture as their primary dissertation topic appeared on the horizon and Martin turned her attention back to injustice. Nonetheless, for Martin it is the same as for her students who have moved beyond culture to do research in other areas – such as Feldman on stories and narratives (Feldman, 1991, 1995; Feldman & Sköldberg, 2002; Feldman, Sköldberg, Brown, & Horner, 2004), Sitkin on sense-making (see his contribution to this volume), Meyerson on ambiguity (1991a, 1991b), Meyerson and Maureen Scully on tempered radicalism (Meyerson & Scully, 1995; Meyerson, 2003; Meyerson & Tomkins, 2007), and Kathy Knopoff on emotional labor (Martin, Knopoff, & Beckman, 1998) – all they have done since the culture years at Stanford is colored by the sensitivities developed as they pursued the qualitative study of organizational culture.

As for myself, in the 1990s I began to expand on that not-yet-interesting dynamic theory of organizational culture begun in March's seminar, first publishing the theory of cultural dynamics (Hatch, 1993) and later writing handbook chapters to relate cultural dynamics to Weber's theory of the routinization of charisma and the problem of leadership within organizational cultures (Hatch, 2000), and to acknowledge the extensive work done on cultural dynamics by cultural anthropologists during the first half of the 20th century, exploring how their ideas inform research on organizational culture (Hatch, 2004).

Had it not been for Joanne Martin, and Bill Ouchi and Tom Peters before her, I do not believe that any of the PhD students who worked at Stanford from 1970 to 2000 would have pursued organizational culture as a research topic or become a proponent of the ethnographic methods that have contributed to the remarkable development of organization studies during this period at Stanford and beyond. My culture student cohort at Stanford – Siehl, Sitkin, Feldman, Meyerson, and Boehm – appear to feel much the same way, as collectively they have contributed a wealth of culturally informed, ethnographically rich studies in and of organizations.

Martin herself has not given up on culture; she has recently begun a revision of *Cultures in Organizations* (Martin, 1992). But, since her retirement from Stanford in 2007, organizational culture seems to exist as a topic only for select researchers in the Schools of Engineering and Education (where, respectively, Barley and Meyerson sit) and among the new institutionalists in sociology who are theorizing culture in organizations without making reference to the concept, being inclined to attribute everything once called organizational culture to processes of institutionalization.

CULTURE BEYOND STANFORD 1970–2000

It is likely that my impressions of organizational culture research at Stanford are heavily colored by my living and working in Denmark and the United Kingdom throughout nearly the whole of the 1990s, so I think it is important to return to the matter of culture research that was taking place outside Stanford during the period covered by this chapter. So I will now return to the beginning of my saga and to the context within which Stanford's research on organizational culture developed, for though there were perhaps too few references to European researchers in the papers produced at Stanford during most of the culture years, views framed outside of the United States were part of the development of the culture perspective at Stanford. Of particular note was the considerable influence on Martin and her students of those European scholars who were steeped in the philosophical traditions of symbolism.

By the early 1980s, when organizational culture research really got going in the United States, a tradition of studying symbolism in organizations using qualitative methods had already produced a significant body of research in more critically oriented European management studies programs. For example, nearly three decades before the culture concept made its presence felt in the United States, Elliott Jaques (1951) published the influential Tavistock study of Glacier Metal Company under the title *The Changing Culture of a Factory*. And in 1971, a decade before Ouchi, Pascale, and Peters published their books, Barry Turner wrote *Exploring the Industrial Subculture*, in which he treated industry as an alien subculture, examining its beliefs and patterns of meaning as communicated through ritual and language.

It would be misleading to suggest that symbolism was only of concern in the European context. It was rife in non-business school approaches to the topic of culture such as in sociology programs throughout the world (particularly those engaged in the new institutionalism about which I will say more momentarily), and within organization studies it was apparent, for example, in the ethnographic studies of the police written by Van Maanen (1973, 1975, 1976, 1978) and in organizational folklore promoted by Jones (1988, 1991, 1994, 1996). The loudest proponent of symbolism in a US business school was probably Lou Pondy, whose untimely death ended his program of studying organizations symbolically, a program that would surely have made a significant contribution. Canadians Frost (originally South African) and Morgan, who had ties to both European as well as US researchers, were the main connections between European and US culture scholars during the 1970s.

The 1970s and 1980s brought many PhD students to Stanford to study at SCANCOR, a program founded by Jim March to bring Scandinavian scholars to Stanford. March always sent visiting scholars interested in culture to meet Martin over at the GSB. For example, Majken Schultz and Jesper Strandgaard Pedersen of CBS had both visited MIT on their study tours on their way to Stanford. Each of them produced dissertations on organizational culture and wrote articles that were influenced by culture research produced at both institutions. Schultz, for example, built a major piece of her dissertation published as *Diagnosing Organizational Cultures* (Schultz, 1995) directly on Schein's model and the book reflected many ideas she developed in her conversations with Martin. Schultz and my joint work reflects much of the influence Martin and Schein had on us both (Hatch & Schultz, 1997, 2000, 2002; Schultz & Hatch, 1996; Schultz, Hatch, & Larsen, 2000).

I have already said enough about the tensions between theory and practice at Stanford and their complicating effects on telling the story of culture research at Stanford. And much of the groundwork for what I wanted to say about the gap between European and US approaches to culture research has been laid. It remains for me to explain why I think this difference is so important to telling the Stanford story, which I will now attempt to do, concluding with a few comments about the new institutionalism at the Stanford Sociology Department and why I feel it contributed to the tailing off of culture research in the GSB at the end of the 20th century. Please forgive me for personalizing the story at this point.

My experiences living and working in Denmark from 1990 to 1995 when I moved to the United Kingdom are worth reporting, as I believe they reveal, in microcosm, the difficulties and opportunities that appeared in the gap between European and US approaches to the study of organizational culture at the time, and the relationship between this gap and the one I misread at first as a distinction between qualitative and quantitative methods.

My reasons for moving to Denmark were many, but chief among them was the post-Stanford frustration I experienced when I found myself repeatedly defending my position as a qualitative culture researcher. I had earned an MBA in finance, written a dissertation based on a quantitative study, and soon after my 1985 graduation published my second *Administrative Science Quarterly* article, a quantitative investigation into how physical settings in organizations correspond to the way people spend their time at work (Hatch, 1987).

In spite of what I felt was paying my dues in the currency of quantitative research, I found I could not engage anyone outside my old circle of Stanford cronies on issues of substance concerning qualitative culture research. All anyone wanted to talk about, it seemed to me, was why I was not doing more quantitative studies. Why on Earth would I persist in researching culture? No matter how many times or in how many ways I answered this question, I could not escape the fact that I was not getting the support I needed to further my ability to do what I found myself constantly defending.

Times were changing and my dean at San Diego State University was president of the AACSB the year CBS invited me for a visit. The AACSB was on its initial kick to internationalize US business schools and my proposal to live abroad for a year met with his hearty support, as did my request to extend the stay to a second year when I found I had not yet absorbed the lessons of culture to be learned from my Danish hosts. But a better reason to request an extension had emerged during my stay. I found in Denmark a faculty department (IOA, Institute for the Study of Organization and Work) composed entirely of social constructionists. I had landed right in the heart of a group that was remarkably suited to expanding my limited understanding of the philosophical differences between European and US-based research, and it was clear my education was going to take a little longer.

While in Denmark, via my colleagues at IOA and CBS's support of my involvement in many European conferences, larger perspectives on doing organization theory would be revealed and work their way into a textbook I was writing at the time: *Organization Theory: Modern, Symbolic and Postmodern Perspectives* (Hatch, 1997). It was in developing the framework for this book that I first recognized a profound methodological difference between my European colleagues and the training I had received at Stanford. Whereas my research training in the United States emphasized the need to match theory and method, the emphasis in Europe involved taking a position on ontology and epistemology. While at first I glossed over this distinction, equating theory with ontology and method with epistemology, later I came to understand the need for thinking in terms of all four concerns, which is why I now believe that researchers who cross the Atlantic are such a different breed to those who stay on one side or the other. Put it down to American pragmatism, but in relation to organizational culture studies, my new appreciation made the study of culture much more relevant to me and to my work. At last I was able to embrace fully what subjectivist ontology and interpretive epistemology meant for culture studies and to explain to others what I had learned by studying culture and organizations on both sides of the Atlantic (see Hatch & Yanow, 2003, 2008 for more on these differences and their implications for methodology).

It was this tension, in my view, that explains why Martin's work (e.g., Martin, 1992, 2002), which never fully accounted for the ontological and epistemological differences behind her integration, differentiation, and fragmentation perspectives, led to continued friction between researchers trained in the United States and those who trained in Europe. This impasse, I believe, ultimately contributed to limiting the future of organizational culture studies at Stanford by cutting many US researchers off from the interpretive paradigm shift that more fully took hold of European trained researchers. One final tension that in my opinion marginalized organizational culture studies at Stanford remains to be examined is the one between the institutionalists in sociology and organizational culture researchers at the GSB.

ORGANIZATIONAL CULTURE AND THE NEW INSTITUTIONALISM AT STANFORD

The trajectory of organizational culture studies at Stanford, it seems to me, can be described by the pattern Kroeber (1944, p. 774) referred to as the florescence and decline of cultural forms, about which he remarked tellingly:

> Soon after culmination, ... [the cultural form, such as drama, or in this case organizational culture studies] usually becomes fairly repetitive at a constant low level of quality; but it continues on this level. It has become a fairly fixed or institutionalized activity, well rooted in its culture and affording unquestionable satisfactions; an activity

which does not aim at, nor can any longer achieve, high values, though it may be practiced with genuine competence.

Organizational culture theory at Stanford may well be a case of cultural florescence and decline. Having enjoyed a useful and creative florescence, culture was no longer on the cutting edge of organizational research and so lost support. Though it might have continued to be done competently, it had lost the power to endow researchers with tenure and slipped into decline.

But the story of organizational culture at Stanford may not yet be over. The institutional theorists in the Department of Sociology, who were always a bit suspicious of the methodology employed by the GSB's organizational culture researchers, must find it difficult to confront demands to explain how institutions change when the role of organizational culture is removed from view. Realizing that organizational culture provides a good explanation for what is currently referred to as institutionalization processes, yet wanting to avoid the term organizational culture, keeps the old tensions alive but does little to advance knowledge. The double irony here is that institutional theory provides a framework for understanding what happened to organizational culture research at Stanford (its institutionalization within the larger Academy marked its decline at Stanford), while organizational culture theory may yet solve the current dilemma confronting institutional theorists – how to explain institutional change when the theory itself purports to explain why and how institutionalized order stays the same.

To suggest one possible way forward, I quote myself in a passage that builds on Kroeber's (1944) ideas as quoted above (Hatch, 2004, p. 198):

> Whereas institutional theory presents institutions as explanations of cultural conservatism, Kroeber maintained that they are merely artifacts. Moreover, most institutionalists argue that institutions maintain and transfer knowledge and meaning from one generation to the next... whereas Kroeber's views suggest that institutionalization is a process by which knowledge and meaning are lost. Kroeber's theory makes institutions complicit in the decline of particular cultural patterns. When you look at institutions you look into the past without much hope of recovering the meanings that once made these fossilized cultural patterns flourish.

If, as Kroeber insisted, institutions are rote repetitions of the past, whereas culture is the site of dynamism and change in human affairs, then perhaps change in institutions must occur through the mechanisms and dynamics of culture. What is more, the dynamics of culture can breath new life into institutionalized behavior by revivifying its origins.

Looking backward we have the chance to correct missteps that led to the divide between institutional and cultural theorists at Stanford in the first place and move in a new direction. Zucker's (1977) paper on the

micro-foundations of institutions was perhaps the point of greatest
historical overlap with organizational culture theory at Stanford, but this
was never adequately explored on either side of this interdisciplinary fence,
possible because, though influence always flows from sociology to
organization studies, there is precious little going in the opposite direction.
Had it done so, Ouchi's work on clans as alternative economic forces to
markets and bureaucracies might have provided fruitful ground for working
out how institutions like those of Western management practice change
through contact with other cultures. This could lead, for example, to our
learning from communities in Africa who use a clan-type of organizing as
they develop economies on the back of micro-lending practices. Or perhaps,
we might derive fresh insights into institutional change by investigating how
ongoing cultural change (organizational and/or societal) offers a platform
for building corporate strategy that better serves the organization's
stakeholders than do current practices of driving the strategy formulated
by executives (presumably on the basis of institutionalized expectations of
what their strategy should be) "down" (into employees) and "outward"
(to stakeholders). Seeing change in this way could lead researchers to see
how culture and institution cannot be fully separated.

In my view, there remains important work to be done exploring the
similarities and differences between institutional and organizational culture
theory, work I am happy to report was started by Stanford Sociology
graduate Frank Dobbin (PhD 1987) who is also co-editor of this volume.
Dobbin, joined by CBS and former SCANCOR visiting student Jesper
Strandgaard Pedersen, are among the few to have tackled this complex topic
to date (Dobbin, 1994; Pedersen & Dobbin, 2006). In my view this matter
deserves much more attention than it has been given thus far and it is my
hope that more debate will soon occur, whether it takes place at Stanford or
beyond. By the way, there is going to be a symposium on the topic at the
next Academy of Management meeting (Aten & Howard-Grenville, 2009)
that will include Stanford PhD in Sociology Marc Ventresca, former
Stanford SCANCOR visiting PhD student Majken Schultz, and myself, so
please stay tuned for further developments from the Stanford crowd.

ACKNOWLEDGMENTS

Thanks go to Martha Feldman, Kristian Kreiner, Joanne Martin, Jesper
Strandgaard Pedersen, Majken Schultz, Sim Sitkin, Linda Smircich, and
John Van Maanen for the many memories and important insights they

shared with me as I constructed this story. Frank Dobbin was a good collaborator as well, offering astute comments and suggestions, and much encouragement along the way. I also want to thank Frank, Kaye Schoonhoven, and Joanne Martin for talking me into taking this instructive journey into our collective past.

REFERENCES

Aten, K., & Howard-Grenville, J. (2009). Culture and institutions: Initiating a conversation between scholars, Symposium, Academy of Management Annual Meeting.

Barley, S. (1983). Semiotics and the study of occupational and organizational culture. *Administrative Science Quarterly, 28*, 393–413.

Collins, D. (2007). *Narrating the management guru: In search of Tom Peters*. Oxford, UK: Routledge.

Dobbin, F. (1994). Culture models of organization: The social construction of rational organizing principles. In: D. Crane (Ed.), *The sociology of culture* (pp. 117–141). Oxford, UK: Blackwell.

Feldman, M. S. (1991). The meaning of ambiguity: Learning from stories and metaphors. In: P. Frost, L. Moore, C. Lundberg, M. Louis & J. Martin (Eds), *Reframing organizational culture*. Newbury Park, CA: Sage.

Feldman, M. S. (1995). *Strategies for interpreting qualitative data*. Newbury Park, CA: Sage.

Feldman, M. S., & Sköldberg, K. (2002). Stories and the rhetoric of contrariety: Subtexts of organizing (change). *Culture and Organization, 8*(4), 275–292.

Feldman, M. S., Sköldberg, K., Brown, R. N., & Horner, D. (2004). Making sense of stories: A rhetorical approach to narrative analysis. *Journal of Public Administration Research and Theory, 14*(2), 147–170.

Frost, P., Moore, L., Lundberg, C., Louis, M., & Martin, J. (Eds). (1985). *Organizational culture*. Newbury Park, CA: Sage.

Frost, P., Moore, L., Lundberg, C., Louis, M., & Martin, J. (Eds). (1991). *Reframing organizational culture*. Newbury Park, CA: Sage.

Gagliardi, P. (1986). The creation and change of organizational cultures: A conceptual framework. *Organization Studies, 7*, 117–134.

Gagliardi, P. (Ed.) (1990). *Symbols and artifacts: Views of the corporate landscape*. Berlin, Germany: Walter de Gruyter.

Hatch, M. J. (1987). Physical barriers, task characteristics, and interaction activity in research and development firms. *Administrative Science Quarterly, 32*, 387–399.

Hatch, M. J. (1990). The symbolics of office design: An empirical exploration. In: P. Gagliardi (Ed.), *The symbolics of corporate artifacts* (pp. 129–146). Berlin, Germany: de Gruyter.

Hatch, M. J. (1993). The dynamics of organizational culture. *Academy of Management Review, 18*(4), 657–693.

Hatch, M. J. (1997). *Organization theory: Modern, symbolic-interpretive and postmodern perspectives*. Oxford, UK: Oxford University Press.

Hatch, M. J. (2000). The cultural dynamics of organizing and change. In: N. Ashkanasy, C. Wilderom & M. Peterson (Eds), *Handbook of organizational culture and climate* (pp. 245–260). Newbury Park, CA: Sage.

Hatch, M. J. (2004). Dynamics in organizational culture. In: M. S. Poole & A. Van de Ven (Eds), *Handbook of organizational change and innovation* (pp. 190–211). Oxford, UK: Oxford University Press.

Hatch, M. J., & Schultz, M. (1997). Relations between organizational culture, identity and image. *European Journal of Marketing, 31*(5), 356–365.

Hatch, M. J., & Schultz, M. S. (2000). Scaling the Tower of Babel: Relational differences between identity, image and culture in organizations. In: M. Schultz, M. J. Hatch & M. H. Larsen (Eds), *The expressive organization: Linking identity, reputation, and the corporate brand* (pp. 13–35). Oxford, UK: Oxford University Press.

Hatch, M. J., & Schultz, M. S. (2002). The dynamics of organizational identity. *Human Relations, 55,* 989–1018.

Hatch, M. J., & Schultz, M. (2008). *Taking brand initiative: How corporations can align strategy, culture and identity through corporate branding.* San Francisco, CA: Wiley/Jossey-Bass.

Hatch, M. J., & Yanow, D. (2003). Organization theory as an interpretive science. In: C. Knudsen & H. Tsoukas (Eds), *The Oxford handbook of organization theory: Meta-theoretical perspectives* (pp. 61–87). Oxford, UK: Oxford University Press.

Hatch, M. J., & Yanow, D. (2008). Methodology by metaphor: Ways of seeing in painting and research. *Organization Studies, 29,* 23–44.

Jaques, E. (1951). *The changing culture of a factory.* London, UK: Tavistock Publications.

Jelenik, M., Smircich, L., & Hirsch, P. (1983). Special issue: Organizational culture. *Administrative Science Quarterly, 28*(3).

Jones, M. O. (1988). *How does folklore fit in?* Paper given at the Academy of Management Meeting, Anaheim, CA.

Jones, M. O. (1991). Why folklore and organizations? *Western Folklore, 50,* 29–41.

Jones, M. O. (Ed.) (1994). *Putting folklore to use.* University Press of Kentucky.

Jones, M. O. (Ed.) (1996). *Studying organizational symbolism.* Thousand Oaks, CA: Sage.

Jones, M. O., Moore, M. D., & Snyder, R. C. (Eds). (1988). *Inside organizations: Understanding the human dimension.* New York, NY: Sage.

Kroeber, A. L. (1944). *Configurations of culture growth.* Berkeley, CA: University of California Press.

Linstead, S., & Grafton-Small, R. (1992). On reading organizational culture. *Organization Studies, 13,* 331–356.

Martin, J. (1980). Truth and corporate propaganda: The value of a good war story. In J. Martin (chair), *Stories and symbolism in organizations.* Symposium presented at the annual meeting of the Academy of Management, Detroit, MI.

Martin, J. (1981). Better ways of making judgment calls in methodological decision making. In: R. Daft (chair), *Methodological innovations for studying organizations.* Symposium, Academy of Management, San Diego, CA.

Martin, J. (1982). Stories and scripts in organizational settings. In: A. H. Hastorf & A. M. Isen (Eds), *Cognitive social psychology* (pp. 255–305). New York, NY: Elsevier-North Holland.

Martin, J. (1990a). Breaking up the mono-method monopolies in organizational research. In: J. Hassard & D. Pym (Eds), *Theory and philosophy of organizations* (pp. 30–43). London, UK: Routledge.

Martin, J. (1990b). Deconstructing organizational taboos: The suppression of gender conflict in organizations. *Organizational Science, 1*(4), 339–359.

Martin, J. (1991). From integration to differentiation to fragmentation to feminism. In: P. Frost, P. L. Moore, C. Lundberg, M. Louis & J. Martin (Eds), *Reframing organizational culture* (pp. 352–355). Newbury Park, CA: Sage.

Martin, J. (1992). *Cultures in organizations: Three perspectives.* New York, NY: Oxford University Press.

Martin, J. (2000). Hidden gendered assumptions in mainstream organizational theory and research. *Journal of Management Inquiry, 9*, 207–216.

Martin, J. (2002). *Organizational culture: Mapping the terrain.* Newbury Park, CA: Sage.

Martin, J. (2003). Swimming against the tide: Aligning values and work. In: R. Stablein & P. Frost (Eds), *Renewing research practice* (pp. 29–53). Stanford, CA: Stanford University Press.

Martin, J., Feldman, M., Hatch, M. J., & Sitkin, S. (1983). The uniqueness paradox in organizational stories. *Administrative Science Quarterly, 28*, 438–453.

Martin, J., & Frost, P. (1996). The organizational culture war games: A struggle for intellectual dominance. In: S. Clegg, C. Hardy & W. Nord (Eds), *Handbook of organizational studies* (pp. 598–621). Newbury Park, CA: Sage.

Martin, J., Hatch, M. J., Kosnik, T., & Sitkin, S. (1983). Entrepreneurial control of the culture creation process. In: Martin, J. (chair), *Organizational culture and the institutionalization of charisma.* Symposium presented at the annual meeting of the Academy of Management, Dallas, TX.

Martin, J., Knopoff, K., & Beckman, C. (1998). An alternative to bureaucratic impersonality and emotional labor: Bounded emotionality at the Body Shop. *Administrative Science Quarterly, 43*, 429–469.

Martin, J., & Meyerson, D. (1988). Organizational cultures and the denial, channeling, and acknowledgment of ambiguity. In: L. R. Pondy, R. J. Boland & H. Thomas (Eds), *Managing ambiguity and change* (pp. 93–125). New York, NY: Wiley.

Martin, J., & Meyerson, D. (1998). Women and power: Conformity, resistance, and disorganized co-action. In: R. Kramer & M. Neale (Eds), *Power and influence in organizations* (pp. 311–348). Thousand Oaks, CA: Sage.

Martin, J., & Powers, M. (1983a). Organizational stories: More vivid and persuasive than quantitative data. In: B. Staw (Ed.), *Psychological foundations of organizational behavior* (2nd ed., pp. 162–168). Glenview, IL: Scott, Foresman.

Martin, J., & Powers, M. (1983b). Truth or corporate propaganda: The value of a good war story. In: L. Pondy, P. Frost, G. Morgan & T. Dandridge (Eds), *Organizational symbolism* (pp. 93–107). Greenwich, CT: JAI Press.

Martin, J., & Siehl, C. (1983). Organizational culture and counter culture: An uneasy symbiosis. *Organizational Dynamics, Fall*, 52–64.

Martin, J., Sitkin, S., & Boehm, M. (1985). Founders and the elusiveness of a cultural legacy. In: P. Frost, L. Moore, M. Louis, C. Lundberg & J. Martin (Eds), *Organizational culture* (pp. 99–124). New York, NY: Sage.

Martin, J., Sitkin, S., Kosnik, T., & Boehm, M. (1983). Wild-eyed guys and old salts: The birth of organizational sub-cultures. In: S. Barley and M. R. Louis (chairs), *Many in one: Organizations as multi-cultural entities.* Symposium presented at the meeting of the Academy of Management, Dallas, TX.

McGregor, D. (1960). *The human side of enterprise.* McGraw-Hill.

Meyerson, D., & Tomkins, M. (2007). Tempered radicals as institutional change agents: The case of advancing gender equity at the University of Michigan, *Harvard Journal of Law and Gender, 30*, 303–322.

Meyerson, D. E. (1991a). 'Normal' ambiguity? In: P. Frost, P. L. Moore, C. Lundberg, M. Louis & J. Martin (Eds), *Reframing organizational culture* (pp. 131–144). Newbury Park, CA: Sage.

Meyerson, D. E. (1991b). Acknowledging and uncovering ambiguities in cultures. In: P. Frost, P. L. Moore, C. Lundberg, M. Louis & J. Martin (Eds), *Reframing organizational culture* (pp. 254–270). Newbury Park, CA: Sage.

Meyerson, D. E. (2003). *Tempered radicals: How people use difference to inspire change at work.* Cambridge, MA: Harvard Business School Press.

Meyerson, D. E., & Martin, J. (1987). Culture change: An integration of three different views. *Journal of Management Studies, 24*, 623–648.

Meyerson, D. E., & Scully, M. A. (1995). Tempered radicalism and the politics of ambivalence and change. *Organization Science, 6*, 585.

Ouchi, W. G. (1980). Markets, bureaucracies, and clans. *Administrative Science Quarterly, 25*, 129–141.

Ouchi, W. G. (1981). *Theory Z: How American business can meet the Japanese challenge.* Reading, MA: Addison-Wesley.

Pascale, R. T., & Athos, A. G. (1981). *The art of Japanese management.* New York, NY: Simon & Schuster.

Pedersen, J. S., & Dobbin, F. (2006). In search of identity and legitimation: Bridging organizational culture and neoinstitutionalism. *American Behavioral Scientist, 49*, 897–907.

Peters, T. J., & Waterman, R. H. (1982). *In search of excellence: Lessons from America's best run companies.* New York, NY: Harper & Row.

Pfeffer, J. (1994). *Managing with power: Politics and influence in organizations.* Cambridge, MA: Harvard Business School Press.

Pfeffer, J. (1998). *The human equation: Building profits by putting people first.* Cambridge, MA: Harvard Business School Press.

Pfeffer, J. (2007). *What were they thinking?: Unconventional wisdom about management.* Cambridge, MA: Harvard Business School Press.

Pondy, L., Frost, P., Morgan, G., & Dandridge, T. (Eds). (1983). *Organizational symbolism.* Greenwich, CT: JAI Press.

Schein, E. H. (1981). Does Japanese management style have a message for American managers? *Sloan Management Review, 23*, 55–68.

Schein, E. H. (1984). Coming to a new awareness of organizational culture. *Sloan Management Review, 25*, 3–16.

Schein, E. H. (1985). *Organizational culture and leadership.* San Francisco, CA: Jossey-Bass. (Second edition 1992).

Schultz, M. (1995). *On studying organizational cultures: Diagnosis and understanding.* Berlin, Germany: Walter de Gruyter.

Schultz, M., & Hatch, M. J. (1996). Living with multiple paradigms: The case of paradigm interplay in organizational culture studies. *Academy of Management Review, 21*, 529–557.

Schultz, M., Hatch, M. J., & Larsen, M. H. (Eds). (2000). *The expressive organization: Identity, reputation and corporate branding.* Oxford, UK: Oxford University Press.

Scott, W. R. (2008). Approaching adulthood: The maturing of institutional theory. *Theory and Society, 37*, 427–442.

Siehl, C., & Martin, J. (1984). The role of symbolic management: How can managers effectively transmit organizational culture? In: J. G. Hunt, D. Hosking, C. Schriesheim & R. Stewart (Eds), *Leaders and managers: International perspectives on managerial behavior and leadership* (Vol. 7, pp. 227–239). Elmsford, NY: Pergamon Press.

Siehl, C., & Martin, J. (1988). Measuring organizational culture: Mixing qualitative and quantitative methods. In: M. O. Jones, M. D. Moore & R. C. Snyder (Eds), *Inside organizations: Understanding the human dimension* (pp. 79–104). New York, NY: Sage.

Turner, B. (1971). *Exploring the industrial subculture*. New York, NY: Seabury Press.

Turner, B. A. (Ed.) (1990). *Organizational symbolism*. Berlin, Germany: Walter de Gruyter.

Van Maanen, J. (1973). Observations on the making of policemen. *Human Organization, 32*(4), 407–418.

Van Maanen, J. (1975). Police socialization. *Administrative Science Quarterly, 20*(3), 207–228.

Van Maanen, J. (1976). Breaking in: Socialization to work. In: R. Dubin (Ed.), *Handbook of work, organization, and society* (pp. 67–130). Chicago: Rand McNally.

Van Maanen, J. (1978). The asshole. In: P. K. Manning & J. Van Maanen (Eds), *Policing: A view from the streets* (pp. 221–238). New York, NY: Random House

Van Maanen, J. (1979). Special issue: Qualitative methods. *Administrative Science Quarterly, 24*(4).

Van Maanen, J. (1988). *Tales of the field: On writing ethnography*. Chicago, IL: University of Chicago Press.

Van Maanen, J. (1991). The smile factory. In: P. Frost, P. L. Moore, C. Lundberg, M. Louis & J. Martin (Eds), *Reframing organizational culture*. London: Sage.

Wilkins, A. (1989). *Developing corporate character*. San Francisco: Jossey-Bass.

Young, E. (1989). On naming the rose: Interests and multiple meanings as elements of organizational change. *Organization Studies, 10*, 187–206.

Zucker, L. G. (1977). The role of institutionalization in cultural persistence. *American Sociological Review, 42*(5), 726–743.

CHAPTER 6

ORGANIZATIONS AND LABOR MARKETS

Alison Davis-Blake

ABSTRACT

The 1980s and 1990s at Stanford University were a uniquely productive era for research on organizations and labor markets. I describe three important, interconnected themes that characterize the research on organizations and labor markets that emerged from Stanford during this era: the central role of the firm in a multi-level system that determines labor market outcomes, the role of institutions in both creating and constraining labor market outcomes, and the dynamic, often unexpected, consequences of labor market outcomes. I describe the genesis and development of each theme and conclude by discussing what lessons can be learned from this era about creating an innovative and productive research culture.

One of my most vivid memories from my first year in the doctoral program at Stanford's Graduate School of Business is taking Jim March's seminar on organizations. The seminar was required of all first-year students in the business school, regardless of discipline, and was a forum for the kind of sharp, engaging, multi-disciplinary dialog which only Jim March was capable of hosting. About half way through the semester, we

Stanford's Organization Theory Renaissance, 1970–2000
Research in the Sociology of Organizations, Volume 28, 97–117
Copyright © 2010 by Emerald Group Publishing Limited
ISSN: 0733-558X/doi:10.1108/S0733-558X(2010)0000028010

read Baron & Bielby's (1980) classic *American Sociological Review* article "Bringing the Firms Back In: Stratification, Segmentation, and the Organization of Work." Because I was not familiar with much of the existing research on social stratification, I found the article quite difficult to follow. As I was reading it for perhaps the third time, I received a frantic telephone call from a fellow student in a discipline other than organizations telling me that he simply could not understand the article at all and asking if I could explain it, which I could not do with much clarity. Late into the evening, the essential message of the article finally started to become clear: if one wishes to understand the highly heterogeneous outcomes individuals experience in the labor market, one cannot simply examine the causes and consequences of individual ascription or achievement, neither can one rely on gross differences between industries or labor market sectors. Rather, one must get inside the firm where decisions about allocating money, opportunity, status, and a variety of other intangible rewards are actually made. Only by understanding how allocation decisions are made within firms and the individual, group, firm, and industrial factors that shape those decisions can one truly understand both the genesis and consequences of individual labor market outcomes.

This insight about the role of the firm and about the multi-level, interconnected individual, organizational, and institutional landscape that creates labor market outcomes is at the heart of a particularly vibrant period in the study of organizations and labor markets. The space available in this chapter is not sufficient to do justice to the many contributions that emerged from Stanford faculty and the post-doctoral and doctoral students who trained at Stanford during this period. However, I believe that three important and interconnected themes characterize the research about organizations and labor markets that emerged from Stanford during the 1980s and 1990s: the central role of the firm in a multi-level system that determines labor market outcomes, the role of institutions in both creating and constraining labor market outcomes, and the dynamic, often unexpected, consequences of labor market outcomes, particularly for firms. Each of these themes had its genesis in the unique environment that existed at Stanford at that time, and each of these themes continues to be important in contemporary research on organizations and labor markets. Below, I describe each theme and explain the role that the environment at Stanford played in its emergence. I then briefly explore some of the ways in which each theme developed and continues to influence the literature on organizations and labor markets today. I conclude by exploring what can be learned from this era about creating a vibrant and productive research culture and discuss what causal factors behind this uniquely productive period might be replicated elsewhere.

In this chapter, my primary focus is on the critical intellectual contributions by Stanford faculty and students through which each of these themes was developed during the 1980s and 1990s. As each of these themes has spawned a rich and varied literature, my treatment of the many ways in which each of these themes is currently manifest in the literature is illustrative rather than exhaustive.

THE CENTRAL ROLE OF THE FIRM

A key theme that emerged from research on organizations and labor markets at Stanford during the 1980s and 1990s was the recognition of the central role of the firm in both shaping labor markets and in creating outcomes previously attributed to worker decisions or to sectoral or industrial forces. Stanford researchers not only "brought the firms back in" to research on labor market outcomes but also explored in detail the implications of the firm as a primary driver of these outcomes. Early empirical work in this tradition focused on challenging the dual economy and dual labor markets explanations for labor market outcomes. Post-doctoral student Yinon Cohen (now a sociology faculty member at Columbia) and Stanford GSB (Graduate School of Business) faculty member Jeff Pfeffer (Cohen & Pfeffer, 1984) found little evidence of the existence of primary and secondary labor market sectors which had previously been used to explain individual differences in wages, opportunities, and related outcomes. Further, Jim Baron (a GSB faculty member now on the business school faculty at Yale) and Bill Bielby (1984, p. 454) assessed sectors organizationally rather than using industry boundaries and reported that "while coarse taxonomies of economic segmentation may accurately represent the economic extremes, however, they obscure the diversity of enterprises between those extremes. Stratification and work arrangements can be better understood by analyzing their specific organizational and environmental determinants." However, the true power of the Stanford perspective on labor markets was that it did not merely replace sectoral or industrial forces with firm forces as the key explanatory variable in labor market outcomes. Rather, it highlighted the central role of the firm in a multi-level system where each component had important effects.

One of the hallmarks of Stanford during the 1980s and 1990s was interdisciplinary training and collaboration. Doctoral students in the business school regularly took courses with faculty such as Amos Tversky and Lee Ross in psychology and Dick Scott and Mike Hannan in sociology, with leading economists in the business school, as well as with a variety of business school faculty who had different disciplinary orientations and worked at a variety of levels of analysis (such as Jim Baron, Jim March, Joanne Martin, Don Palmer, and Jeff Pfeffer). There was a strong tradition, exemplified by Dick Scott, of individuals attending research seminars across campus and of faculty serving on doctoral committees of students in a variety of departments. The annual conference on organizations at Asilomar was a substantive and symbolic lynchpin of this multi-disciplinary approach (this annual conference for the entire Stanford organizations community, regardless of discipline, was held each year at Asilomar, California on the Pacific Ocean. Faculty, post-doctoral students, and doctoral students all participated). One of the consequences of this extensive contact across disciplines was a high level of sensitivity to the idea that forces at multiple levels of analysis typically shape important outcomes in organizations and an awareness of the need to clearly understand and unpack the effects of forces at different levels of analysis. During her dissertation defense, I recall my contemporary in the GSB doctoral program, Mary Jo Hatch (most recently on the faculty at the University of Virginia), stating that one of the most critical things she had learned while at Stanford was to attend to and differentiate effects on organizational phenomenon that derived from processes operating at multiple levels of analysis.

At times, key collaborations between specific people shape the direction of research in a multi-disciplinary environment. The collaboration between Bill Bielby and Jim Baron was a collaboration that had a significant impact on the direction of research on organizations and labor markets at Stanford. Bill Bielby was on the sociology faculty at the University of California, Santa Barbara where Jim Baron was his doctoral student. Jim received his Ph.D. in 1982, and his dissertation, "Economic Segmentation and the Organization of Work," was, in part, a call for more focused, disciplined examination of the role of firms in creating labor market outcomes. When Jim arrived at the GSB as a faculty member in 1982, his seminal conceptual work with Bill Bielby on the role of the firm in creating labor market outcomes had already been published. Further, he and Bill had already started a line of research demonstrating the critical roles of firm structures and processes in creating and maintaining gender segregated work (see, e.g., Bielby & Baron, 1986). Shortly after Jim came to Stanford, Bill spent a year as a fellow at Stanford's Center for Advanced Study in the Behavioral Sciences. Having Jim and Bill together at Stanford caused many members of the Stanford community from different disciplinary traditions to focus their attention on how firms, the forces that shape firms' structures and processes, and decision makers inside firms all affect labor market outcomes.

This idea of attending to effects at multiple levels of analysis is very evident in meticulous empirical research on determinants of internal labor market formation and operation, much of which was pioneered at Stanford. Research on internal labor markets addressed critical problems in the two extant traditions that explained differences in individual labor market outcomes: the status attainment tradition and the dual economy tradition. The status attainment tradition argued that differences in individual labor market outcomes derived largely from differences in individual human capital (whether ascribed such as race, gender, or class or achieved such as education, total labor market experience, or job tenure). The status attainment tradition had documented in great detail the returns to various types of human capital (Featherman & Hauser, 1978; Hauser & Featherman, 1974; Mincer, 1974; Sewell & Shah, 1968). However, the status attainment tradition left unanswered the fundamental question of *how* differences in human capital were translated into differences in labor market outcomes. In labor markets where the buyers of labor were largely firms rather than individuals or small groups, an examination of the specific ways in which firms valued (or did not value) various types of human capital was necessary in order to understand the processes through which differences in human capital led to differences in labor market outcomes.

While the status attainment tradition focused on individual human capital as the key causal factor in labor market outcomes, the dual economy tradition highlighted economic sector as the key determinant of individual labor market outcomes. The dual economy tradition argued that the economy could be divided into two basic sectors (typically operationalized along industrial lines although sometimes operationalized along occupational lines): a primary sector and a secondary sector. Individuals employed in the primary sector enjoyed good labor market outcomes (high wages, job security, access to training, and promotional opportunities) while individuals employed in the secondary sector received poor labor market outcomes (Averitt, 1968; Beck, Horan, & Tolbert, 1978; Tolbert, Horan, & Beck, 1980). While the dual economy was perhaps a necessary corrective to the status attainment tradition's focus on the characteristics of individual sellers of labor as key determinants of labor market outcomes, the dual economy tradition painted the characteristics of buyers of labor in broad, overly monolithic strokes suggesting that, within a sector, all jobs were either good or bad. However, the dual economy tradition could not explain how and

why individuals who occupied different kinds of jobs within the same sector
or worked for different kinds of firms within the same sector experienced
radically different labor market outcomes. For example, although the health
care sector is the kind of industry typically classified in the dual labor
markets tradition as part of the primary sector, the career trajectories and
labor market outcomes of nurses are quite different from those of laboratory
assistants. Similarly, even controlling for human capital, the labor market
outcomes of nurses in large multi-hospital systems are typically different
than those of a nurses working for physicians in a small group practice.

The study of internal labor markets solved the problems inherent in both
the status attainment and dual economy traditions. Research on internal
labor markets emphasized that individual, occupational, firm, and institutional forces caused firms to develop internal opportunity systems which
then created differential outcomes for individuals depending on the type of
firm in which they were employed and where they were located inside the
firm. The focus on a detailed understanding of the operation of opportunity
systems inside firms answered the question from the status attainment
tradition of *how* buyers of labor assigned returns to human capital. The
focus on understanding specific opportunity systems inside of firms and how
those systems might vary for different types of jobs and workers addressed
the issue of intrasectoral heterogeneity in labor market outcomes that had
plagued the dual economy tradition.

While the idea that firms have internal labor markets was not new
(Doeringer & Piore, 1971), the notion of studying in detail the specific
attributes of internal labor markets and the multi-level forces that created
those attributes was something that gained traction at Stanford during the
1980s. For example, Pfeffer and Cohen (1984) documented that both
institutional and industry level forces (unions, the professions as represented
by personnel departments, and being in the industrial core) as well as firm
level factors (being a branch unit of a firm and a firm's commitment to
training) were important determinants of the extent to which internal labor
markets were present in firms. Baron, Davis-Blake, and Bielby (1986, p. 248)
used a more fine-grained analysis to examine the characteristics of job
ladders and found that the existence and characteristics of job ladders were
linked to "firm-specific skills, organizational structure, gender distinctions,
technology, occupational differentiation, the institutional environment, and
the interests of unions." The unpacking within a single study of the effects
on internal labor markets of features of jobs, occupations, organizations,
and institutions was a novel approach and characterized research on labor
markets in the Stanford tradition.

This early attention to effects on internal labor markets from factors at multiple levels of analysis has spawned three important traditions that continue in the literature today. First, as internal labor markets have decreased in importance and new forms of work organization have emerged, students trained in the Stanford tradition and those they have influenced have continued to examine these new forms using a multi-level lens. For example, as employment has been increasingly externalized and as various forms of nonstandard work have proliferated, individuals touched by the Stanford tradition have continued to examine how factors at multiple levels of analysis shape these new forms of employment. For example, Davis-Blake and Uzzi (1993) (a doctoral student, now faculty member at Northwestern's business school, with whom I worked after leaving Stanford), in one of the earliest comprehensive empirical examinations of determinants of firms' use of nonstandard workers, found that skills required in specific jobs, organizational size and bureaucratization, and government oversight of employment all affected firms' utilization of temporary workers and independent contractors. Similarly, Uzzi and Barsness (1998) reported that organizational age and size, the involvement of unions, the detailed organization of jobs, and job technologies all affected firms' use of contractors and part-time employees.

Second, as the multi-level determinants of employment systems have become clear, there has been increased interest in understanding how factors at different levels of analysis can interact, often in unexpected ways, to affect both individuals and firms. For example, in a series of papers, Bielby and Baron (1986, p. 759) documented the pervasiveness and causes of gender segregation at work, noting that there is little evidence that "employers' practices reflect efficient and rational responses to sex differences in skills and turnover costs"; instead they argued that gender segregation is due to a pattern of statistical discrimination where employers reserve some jobs for men and others for women. Later, Amy Wharton (a post-doctoral student in sociology and now on the sociology faculty at Washington State University) and Jim Baron (1987) reported that gender segregation, which typically has deleterious effects on the career prospects of women, can actually be psychologically beneficial for men. They found that men in work groups where the gender composition was balanced had lower levels of job satisfaction and self-esteem and higher levels of job-related depression than men in gender segregated work groups. This is an excellent example of how decisions and actions at the firm level of analysis can interact with the dynamics of work groups to create quite unexpected consequences for individuals.

Similarly, a very interesting and initially Stanford-centric line of work examined some of the unexpected consequences of wage dispersion in organizations for individuals and work groups. This work demonstrated that wage dispersion, which can result from a variety of factors, including strong links between pay and performance, can have unexpected and potentially undesirable consequences for work groups and their members. Pfeffer and Davis-Blake (1990) documented the variety of factors at multiple levels of analysis that drive salary dispersion in organizations including public control, specialization and proliferation of jobs, and gender composition. Later research documented that, like gender segregation, wage dispersion had some unexpected and perhaps unintended consequences within organizations. Pfeffer and Langton (a doctoral student in sociology, now a business school faculty member at the University of British Columbia) (Pfeffer & Langton, 1993) reported that in colleges and universities with high levels of wage dispersion, faculty members were less satisfied with their work, less research productive, and less likely to collaborate with others. Wage dispersion may be potentially beneficial for firms if it results from a strong linkage between pay and performance. For example, Pfeffer and Davis-Blake (1992) found that wage dispersion interacted with individual salary level and had a negative effect on turnover of those with high salaries and a positive effect on turnover of those with low salaries, an outcome that may be desirable from an organizational perspective if salary and performance are highly correlated. However, Pfeffer and Langton's research documented how the organizational and institutional forces that create wage dispersion can interact with work group dynamics to create negative effects on individuals and work groups.

Finally, and perhaps most recently, there has been increased attention to the idea that some of these interactions across factors at different levels of analysis can be quite positive and that firms can intentionally design employment systems that intentionally combine features at different levels of analysis to create highly synergistic and effective employment systems. During the 1990s, Jeff Pfeffer (1998) documented a number of case studies of firms who had intentionally used levers at multiple levels of analysis to create work arrangements that yielded exceptional individual and firm performance. These firms typically selected individuals with attitudes highly consonant with the firm culture, embedded these individuals in very intensive socialization and training programs designed to reinforce and refine the values individuals already possessed, and designed jobs and reward systems that would encourage individuals to act in a manner consistent with these values. This layering of individual, job, and organizational features toward a common end is a key attribute of high performance work systems, which continues to be a robust area of research on labor markets (see, e.g., Applebaum, Bailey, Berg, & Kalleberg, 2000).

INSTITUTIONAL CONDUITS
AND CONSTRAINTS

Although the Stanford approach to determinants and consequences of labor markets was multi-level and explored everything from the psychology of the individual to the role of the nation-state in employment practices, a distinguishing theme of the Stanford approach to organizations and labor markets was a broad and deep exploration of institutional effects on labor markets. As the birthplace of neoinstitutional theory (Meyer & Rowan, 1977; see Scott, 2008 for a summary), Stanford was home to a special emphasis on understanding institutions as both conduits for the emergence of new labor market phenomenon and constraints that shaped how labor markets emerged and evolved.

Clearly, one reason for the prominence of institutional thinking at Stanford was the presence of key thinkers in the area such as sociology faculty John Meyer and Dick Scott. However, as with most things at Stanford during that time period, the intellectual vitality of the place was generated not just by the presence of a few key people but rather by formal and informal systems and structures that directed attention and effort to specific problems and ideas. During the 1980s, Dick Scott headed an National Institute of Health (NIH) training program designed to prepare social scientists to do research on health care organizations and health care systems (see Scott, Ruef, Mendel, & Caronna, 2000 for an example of the kinds of thinking that emerged from this program). Many Stanford graduate students and post-doctoral students were touched by that training program, either as formal trainees or as participants in classes and seminars connected to the program. Thus, there was a very broad awareness of the health care industry and health care issues among the intellectual community at Stanford. Given the highly institutionalized nature of the American health care system with its dynamic interplay of federal, state, and local governments, the professions, and a myriad of interest groups, advocacy groups, and professional organizations, anyone who was touched by the NIH training program was highly sensitized to institutional effects on organizations. Just as it was impossible to be around Stanford during that time period without thinking about levels of analysis, it was impossible to participate in the Stanford intellectual community without thinking about institutions and institutional effects on just about every conceivable organizational phenomenon.

The area of organizations and labor markets was particularly fertile territory for budding institutional theorists for two reasons. First, institutional effects on labor market phenomenon are both numerous and strong. Second, extant explanations of labor market phenomenon during that era tended to be economic or technical. Thus, any enterprising student or faculty member with an interest in examining labor market issues through an institutional theory lens had a myriad of potentially good topics to choose from.

Early efforts from an institutional perspective focused on documenting the significant role of two key institutional forces, the state and the professions, on the emergence of bureaucratic control of the employment relationship and bureaucratic features of internal labor markets, often as described by Weber (1946, trans). For example, Jim Baron, Frank Dobbin (a doctoral student in sociology now on the sociology faculty at Harvard), and Dev Jennings (a doctoral student in sociology now on the faculty of the business school at the University of Alberta) (Baron, Dobbin, & Jennings, 1986) documented the critical role played by labor unions, personnel professionals, and the state in the movement away from personal control of work by the supervisor and the emergence and widespread implementation of bureaucratic and technical control of work within firms (see also Baron, Jennings, & Dobbin, 1988 for a discussion of factors that led to the emergence of bureaucratic control). Cohen and Pfeffer (1986) provided evidence that personnel departments were a significant force in the adoption of formalized hiring standards that moved firms away from particularistic hiring criteria and toward standardized, universalistic hiring criteria. Similarly, Baron and Bielby (1986) documented that proximity to the state was associated with the proliferation of specific job titles associated with specialized roles and responsibilities, another feature of classical Weberian bureaucracy.

These early efforts were quite successful in demonstrating that key institutional forces had specific effects on the organization of work. However, this emphasis on the isolated effects of specific institutional forces on broad features of work soon became more sophisticated in three important ways, each of which continues to influence the literature on organizations and labor markets: (1) scholars from the Stanford tradition began examining the interplay between institutional forces, particularly the interplay between the state and the professions, (2) many of these same scholars began examining specific employment practices in much more detail rather than relying on broad constructs such as the presence of bureaucratic control, and (3) following a broader trend in research on institutions, scholars interested in employment practices began examining how the interplay between institutions and interests affected the organization of work. Below, I describe each of these lines of thinking in more detail.

One of the critical contributions of scholars from the Stanford tradition was to recognize and document the many ways that institutional forces previously treated as independent had interdependent and even interactive effects on employment practices. The interplay between the state and the professions, particularly the human resource management profession, was a topic that received particular attention. A number of pieces of research documented how legal mandates which at first glance might appear to have unambiguous effects on personnel practices caused human resource managers to devise systems that went well beyond the original legislative intent. For example, Dobbin, Sutton, Meyer, and Scott (1993, p. 396) reported that, in response to the emergence of federal Equal Employment Opportunity (EEO) legislation and case law (which were intended to prevent employment discrimination based on race, gender, ethnicity, and similar individual attributes), "personnel managers devised and diffused employment practices that treat all classes of workers as ambitious and achievement oriented."

While the latitude of human resource managers to interpret and respond to the law sometimes caused the emergence of systems that expanded the law's intended benefits, human resource managers could also use that latitude to create the appearance of legal compliance while changing little about the internal operations of their firms. For example, sociology doctoral student Lauren Edelman (now on the law faculty at Berkeley) (Edelman, 1992) documented how firms responded to the passage of the 1964 Civil Rights Act by creating organizational structures (such as affirmative action offices) that generated the appearance of legal compliance but which actually generated little change in employment practices. In a study of EEO grievance procedures, Edelman (1999) argued that as human resource professionals constructed rational responses to particular pieces of legislation, courts begin to recognize as legitimate and appropriate certain organizational responses that began merely as "gestures of compliance." Over time, courts further legitimated these organizational responses, even if there was little or no evidence that they achieve the intended purposes of the legislation that prompted their creation. In an examination of the implementation of comparable worth, Steven Mezias (a doctoral graduate in business now on the faculty at NYU's business school) and his NYU doctoral student Rikki

Abzug (Abzug & Mezias, 1993) argued that the fragmentation of the state due to the separation of powers and the divisions between federal, state, and local authorities further empowered human resource managers to interpret and create what would become generally accepted specific solutions to sweeping legal mandates.

Just as scholars from the Stanford tradition moved away from an overly simplified model of institutional forces acting in isolation to a more complex and sophisticated model of interacting institutional forces, many of these same scholars also moved away from thinking about the organization of work and employment in very broad terms (e.g., whether control in the workplace was particularistic or bureaucratic) to examining specific structures, processes, and protections that could be present in the workplace. This movement toward examining specific employment structures often required the collection of detailed, often longitudinal, data about employment practices and institutional forces, permitting much more fine-grained conclusions than could be achieved with earlier approaches. For example, Edelman (1990) documented in detail how degree of proximity to the public sphere and the level of differentiation of the personnel function affected not only the diffusion of grievance procedures across firms but the rate of diffusion such that firms further from the public sphere and with less differentiated personnel functions were much slower to adopt grievance procedures than firms with the opposite characteristics. Edelman's work on the diffusion of grievance procedures is an excellent example of how focusing on one specific employment practices allows more nuanced conclusions. Rather than reaching a conclusion such as the presence of a personnel function is associated with the adoption of grievance procedures (which would have characterized earlier work on this topic), Edelman was able to go beyond this simple conclusion to show how attributes of the personnel function affected the speed of adoption of grievance procedures. The practice of fine-grained examination of causes and consequences of specific employment practices continues in current research on the employment relationship. For example, Frank Dobbin and Erin Kelly (a doctoral student of Dobbin at Princeton) (Dobbin & Kelly, 2007) examined the adoption of sexual harassment grievance procedures and sensitivity training. By focusing on these specific employment practices, they were able to document in a detailed way how specific landmark judicial decisions about sexual harassment provided human resource professionals with the ability to argue that grievance procedures and training would minimize legal risk, despite widespread opinions from lawyers to the contrary. This is a good example of how focusing on a specific employment practice allows a much deeper longitudinal examination of how the interplay over time between legislation, judicial interpretations, and the actions and advocacy of human resources professionals shapes employment practices.

Several robust streams of research on the interplay between institutional forces (typically the state and the human resources profession) in shaping the employment relationship developed over time. However, as the role of interests in shaping institutions became more predominant in the thinking of neoinstitutional theorists (Scott, 2008), the interplay between interests and institutions also emerged in the work of Stanford trained scholars interested in the organization of work. For example, David Strang (a doctoral student in sociology now a faculty member in sociology at Cornell) and Jim Baron (Strang & Baron, 1990) described how specific occupational groups advocated for the emergence and proliferation of certain job titles and job ladders (and associated rewards), often using the human resource profession as their ally in the process. Similarly, Dobbin (1992) documented how the passage of the Wagner Act and Social Security energized union and business support for the private insurance and how this interaction between a change in the legal landscape and union and business interests led to the emergence of the types of fringe benefits that are common in today's workplace.

DYNAMIC CONSEQUENCES OF LABOR MARKET OUTCOMES

Interest among Stanford scholars trained in neoinstitutional theory in the dynamic evolution of personnel practices was just one manifestation of the third important theme that characterized research on organizations and labor markets at Stanford during the 1980s and 1990s: an interest in the dynamic, often unintended or unexpected, consequences of the labor market outcomes generated by organizational employment systems. This interest in dynamic analysis was not necessarily driven by scholars interested in labor markets; rather, it was initially driven by another emerging area of interest at Stanford: organizational ecology. During the 1980s and 1990s, many graduate and post-doctoral students training at Stanford were exposed to a growing number of scholars interested in organizational ecology and trained in the longitudinal methods necessary to study ecological phenomenon. With the presence of Mike Hannan at Stanford and John Freeman at Berkeley, there was a strong core of faculty and students throughout the Bay Area interested in organizational ecology. Soon, everyone found themselves learning not only ecological theory but the associated methods as well. During my time at Stanford, it seemed that everyone learned RATE (one of the few available statistical tools for event history analysis, see Tuma, 1979; Tuma & Hannan, 1984) whether one had a clear purpose for doing so or not. This rapid diffusion of longitudinal thinking and expertise in longitudinal analysis influenced many students and faculty to consider how they might apply longitudinal thinking and analysis to problems in their own areas of expertise beyond organizational ecology.

At the same time that facility with longitudinal methods was increasing, many Stanford students were also becoming exposed to ideas about organizational demography, a process where the essential and critical effects were longitudinal (Pfeffer, 1983). The core notion behind organizational demography was quite straightforward: the employment practices that a firm put in place generated a distribution of employees along a particular demographic dimension of interest (initially organizational tenure received much of the research attention). That demographic distribution, which was typically an unintended consequence of an organization's employment practices, could then exert significant effects on the organization (early research focused on effects in the form of increased turnover as the consequences of demographic dissimilarity exerted themselves over time). A number of empirical studies documented that demographic diversity in tenure or age led to increased turnover rates among faculty (McCain, O'Reilly, & Pfeffer, 1983), members of top management teams (Wagner, Pfeffer, & O'Reilly, 1984), and nurses (Pfeffer & O'Reilly, 1987). This early research on organizational demography has spawned a vast amount of research on the consequences of demographic differences in firms that continue as a robust area of research today (Tsui & Ellis, 2005).

This interest in the longitudinal effects of organizational employment practices led to several lines of research that documented how the conditions created by an organization's employment practices could have unexpected consequences over time. For example, several institutional and economic forces were causing more women to enter the workforce and were causing organizations to adopt practices that facilitated the employment of women and nonwhites. However, research initiated at Stanford indicated that the entry of women into the work groups and jobs occupied by men could have negative consequences, over time, for men and women. Pfeffer and Davis-Blake (1987) reported that, as the proportion of women employed in the central administration of a university increased, salaries of both men and women declined. Similarly, Jim Baron, Brian Mittman (a doctoral student in business now Director of the VA Center for Implementation Practice and

Research Support), and Andy Newman (a doctoral student in sociology) (Baron, Mittman, & Newman, 1991) found that the number of women and nonwhites already in an organization hastened the rate of gender integration, and thus the onset of the economic dynamics described by Pfeffer and Davis-Blake (1987).

While some employment practices, such as a reduction in barriers to the employment of women and nonwhites in a variety of jobs, could have unanticipated negative consequences for an organization or its members, other employment practices could create unexpected positive changes over time. For example, Roberto Fernandez (a faculty member at the business school during the 1990s), Emilio Castilla (a sociology doctoral student now on the faculty at MIT's business school), and Paul Moore (a doctoral student in business) (Fernandez, Castilla, & Moore, 2000) demonstrated how the use of employee referrals in hiring led, as employers hoped and expected, to better hiring outcomes such as greater longevity of new employees. However, Castilla (2005) further reported that the use of referral networks in hiring led to stronger performance among employees hired through referral networks (compared to employees hired through other means).

As described earlier, research from Stanford scholars in the neoinstitutional tradition also became more focused on the interplay over time of specific institutional forces as well as the interplay between institutions and interests. Dobbin and Sutton (1998, p. 441) documented how, over time, the dynamic interactions between these forces could even change the nature of the forces themselves. They studied how human resource professionals' interpretations of the law spurred the adoption of a number of new offices such as benefits and antidiscrimination departments. They further reported that "as institutionalization proceeded, middle managers came to disassociate these new offices from policy and to justify them in purely economic terms, as part of the new human resource management paradigm."

During the 1990s, the strong ecological and labor market traditions at Stanford merged with the creation of the Stanford Project on Emerging Companies (SPEC) under the leadership of Jim Baron and Mike Hannan. This ambitious data collection and analysis effort followed a large sample of high-technology Silicon Valley startups from birth forward for several years. The project examined how firms addressed the major organizational and human resource challenges they encountered during their early years and the consequences of firms' early decisions for the subsequent evolution and performance of firms (Baron & Hannan, 2002). The research that has been emerging from the SPEC studies has been influenced by ecologists' interest in founding conditions and thus has paid particular attention to the longitudinal consequences of early decisions about human resource management practices. For example, Baron, Hannan, and Diane Burton (a sociology doctoral student now on the industrial and labor relations faculty at Cornell) (Baron, Hannan, & Burton, 1999) examined how a firm's initial gender mix and the employment model of its founder influenced subsequent managerial intensity. They reported that firms where the founder held a bureaucratic model of organization became more administratively intense while firms that initially employed more women were less administratively intense in subsequent years. Subsequently, Baron, Hannan, and Burton (2001) reported that changes in the initial employment model adopted by the founder were, as ecologists would predict, quite disruptive to firms, leading to increased turnover of individuals (particularly individuals with longer tenure) and decreased organizational performance.

WHAT CAN BE LEARNED FROM THE STANFORD EXPERIENCE?

As I reflect on this enormously productive era at Stanford, an obvious question is whether such an environment can be replicated. While any uniquely productive environment is probably the result of some highly specific, nonreplicable factors, I believe that productivity of this era at Stanford was the product of three important tensions that could be introduced and managed into other academic settings: tensions between independence and integration, between serendipity and planning, and between single-discipline and multi-discipline training. First, Stanford obviously had outstanding scholars and scholars in training who were, according to the traditions of the academy, free to choose their own intellectual pursuits and to act independently in matters of research. However, those scholars did not exist in isolation but rather were embedded in a set of formal and informal structures that brought them together in ways that generated fruitful collaboration. Some of these structures were probably unintentional, such as the tradition of doctoral students taking courses in a wide variety of disciplines across the campus. But, some of these traditions, such as the annual Asilomar Conference and Dick's Scott's multi-disciplinary NIH training program, were intentional and planned in order to achieve cross-fertilization of ideas. The business school's doctoral curriculum required that all students, regardless of discipline, take three courses together during their first year as doctoral students. Since one of those courses was a course on organizations, GSB students with organizational interests were exposed to a wider than normal variety of paradigms and approaches for thinking about organizations. Similarly, the presence of the Center for Advance Study in the Behavioral Sciences on the Stanford campus was an important vehicle for bringing a variety of scholars interested in organizations to Stanford. Bill Bielby's presence at the Center was particularly important in shaping research at Stanford on organizations and labor markets. As in any academic setting, participation in these traditions was voluntary and thus subject to degradation over time. However, the notion of introducing structures for cross-disciplinary interaction that capture the imagination (and thus the voluntary participation) of students and faculty is one that seems possible to introduce in other settings.

Second, many of the ideas and collaborations at Stanford came about through serendipitous and unplanned encounters between people. Such chance encounters are a necessary engine of creativity in a setting where the next important idea cannot be known in advance. However, part of the essence of the Stanford experience was that innovation and creativity were not left solely to chance but rather were facilitated by planned encounters designed specifically to get people with different areas of interest and expertise together to focus on a particular topic. Dick Scott's NIH training program was one such longstanding, planned mechanism to generate encounters between people with different skills, interests, and stage of intellectual development. An interesting observation about the NIH training program is that, I believe, many of the participants did not make health care a primary focus of their research. However, as a result of those planned encounters around health care topics, many of the participants did become deeply steeped in the workings of critical institutions such as the state and the professions and brought that expertise to other areas of interest, such as organizations and labor markets.

Another forum for convergence of people with a variety of interests and backgrounds was the School of Education at Stanford where several faculty and doctoral students had organizational interests and were regular participants in doctoral seminars, research colloquiua, and the Asilomar Conference. Like the health care sector, the education sector is one where the state and the professions play an important role in shaping work and employment (although the effects sometimes look quite different than those observed in the health care sector). Frequent interaction with colleagues from the School of Education not only highlighted the importance of these types of institutional forces in organizations but also emphasized the viability of educational institutions as research sites to study organizations and labor markets. For example, the work that both Nancy Langton and

I did with Jeff Pfeffer on determinants and consequences of wage dispersion was conducted using data from higher education settings. Unlike the NIH training program, the presence of the School of Education on campus was not explicitly intended to promote multi-disciplinary collaboration. Nevertheless, because it was a permanent fixture of the campus and continually attracted people with an interest in educational institutions who then participated in the broader community interested in organizations, it shaped the dialog about organizations at Stanford. Again, the notion of systematic, planned encounters that create a shared language, expertise, and set of interests also seems transportable to another setting.

Finally, deep, discipline-based training was a hallmark of the Stanford experience. Graduate and post-doctoral students were expected, as in most places, to become thoroughly steeped in the knowledge and traditions of a particular discipline. However, at Stanford, unlike some other places with which I am familiar, the expectation of deep disciplinary training existed alongside an equally strong, although at times unspoken, expectation that individuals being trained at Stanford would learn from a broad range of intellectual traditions and would not be afraid to participate in settings where they had less expertise than others in the room. In my experience, this expectation was not transmitted formally but rather was simply part of the essence of being at Stanford. Whether I was in Dick Scott's doctoral student discussion group for those enrolled in his seminar on organizations or in Lee Ross' course on social psychology, I knew that I was expected not simply to understand how those with more formal training than I in sociology or psychology thought but to critique, challenge, and, ultimately, extend their thinking. No one ever told me that this was the expectation; however, like most deeply embedded cultural norms, the expectation was clear and powerful. And that, perhaps, is what may make the Stanford experience difficult to replicate. While some of the traditions and practices of that time were formal, visible, and relatively easy to embed elsewhere, some remained unspoken and eluded codification. Thus, while critical aspects of the Stanford experience can be transported to other settings, the absence of those more elusive elements may make the replication imperfect.

REFERENCES

Abzug, R., & Mezias, S. J. (1993). The fragmented state and due-process protections in organizations: The case of comparable worth. *Organization Science, 4*(3), 433–453.

Applebaum, E., Bailey, T., Berg, P., & Kalleberg, A. L. (2000). *Why high-performance work systems pay off*. Ithaca, NY: Cornell University Press.

Averitt, R. T. (1968). *The dual economy: The dynamics of American industry structure*. New York: Norton.

Baron, J. N., & Bielby, W. T. (1980). Bringing the firms back in: Stratification, segmentation, and the organization of work. *American Journal of Sociology, 45*(5), 737–765.

Baron, J. N., & Bielby, W. T. (1984). The organization of work in a segmented economy. *American Sociological Review, 49*(4), 454–473.

Baron, J. N., & Bielby, W. T. (1986). The proliferation of job titles in organizations. *Administrative Science Quarterly, 41*(4), 561–586.

Baron, J. N., Davis-Blake, A., & Bielby, W. T. (1986). The structure of opportunity: How promotion ladders vary within and among organizations. *Administrative Science Quarterly, 31*(2), 248–273.

Baron, J. N., Dobbin, F. R., & Jennings, P. D. (1986). War and peace: The evolution of modern personnel administration in U.S. industry. *American Journal of Sociology, 92*(2), 350–383.

Baron, J. N., & Hannan, M. T. (2002). Organizational blueprints for success in high-tech start-ups: Lessons from the Stanford Project on emerging companies. *California Management Review, 44*(3), 8–36.

Baron, J. N., Hannan, M. T., & Burton, M. D. (1999). Building the iron cage: Determinants of managerial intensity in the early years of organizations. *American Sociological Review, 64*(4), 527–547.

Baron, J. N., Hannan, M. T., & Burton, M. D. (2001). Change in organizational models and employee turnover in young, high-tech firms. *American Journal of Sociology, 106*(4), 960–1012.

Baron, J. N., Jennings, P. D., & Dobbin, F. R. (1988). Mission control? The development of personnel systems in U.S. industry. *American Sociological Review, 53*(4), 497–514.

Baron, J. N., Mittman, B. S., & Newman, A. E. (1991). Targets of opportunity: Organizational and environmental determinants of gender integration within the California civil service, 1979–1985. *American Journal of Sociology, 96*(6), 1362–1401.

Beck, E. M., Horan, P. M., & Tolbert, C. M., III. (1978). Stratification in a dual economy: A sectoral model of earnings determination. *American Sociological Review, 43*(5), 704–720.

Bielby, W. T., & Baron, J. N. (1986). Men and women at work: Sex segregation and statistical discrimination. *American Journal of Sociology, 91*(4), 759–799.

Castilla, E. J. (2005). Social networks and employee performance in a call center. *American Journal of Sociology, 110*(5), 1243–1283.

Cohen, Y., & Pfeffer, J. (1984). Employment practices in the dual economy. *Industrial Relations, 23*(1), 58–72.

Cohen, Y., & Pfeffer, J. (1986). Organizational hiring standards. *Administrative Science Quarterly, 31*(1), 1–24.

Davis-Blake, A., & Uzzi, B. (1993). Determinants of employment externalization: A study of temporary workers and independent contractors. *Administrative Science Quarterly, 38*(2), 195–223.

Dobbin, F., & Kelly, E. L. (2007). How to stop harassment: Professional construction of legal compliance in organizations. *American Journal of Sociology, 112*(4), 1203–1243.

Dobbin, F., & Sutton, J. R. (1998). The strength of a weak state: The rights revolution and the rise of human resources management divisions. *American Journal of Sociology, 104*(2), 441–476.

Dobbin, F., Sutton, J. R., Meyer, J. W., & Scott, W. R. (1993). Equal opportunity law and the construction of internal labor markets. *American Journal of Sociology, 99*(2), 396–427.

Dobbin, F. R. (1992). The origins of private social insurance: Public policy and fringe benefits in American, 1920-1950. *American Journal of Sociology, 97*(5), 1416–1450.

Doeringer, M. J., & Piore, P. B. (1971). *Internal labor markets and manpower analysis.* Heath Lexington Books.

Edelman, L. B. (1990). Legal environments and organizational governance: The expansion of due process in the American workplace. *American Journal of Sociology, 95*(6), 1401–1440.

Edelman, L. B. (1992). Legal ambiguity and symbolic structures: Organizational mediation of civil rights law. *American Journal of Sociology, 97*(6), 1531–1576.

Edelman, L. B. (1999). The endogeneity of legal regulation: Grievance procedures as rational myth. *American Journal of Sociology, 105*(2), 406–454.

Featherman, D. L., & Hauser, R. M. (1978). *Opportunity and change.* New York: Academic.

Fernandez, R. M., Castilla, E. J., & Moore, P. (2000). Social capital at work: Networks and employment at a phone center. *American Journal of Sociology, 105*(5), 1288–1356.

Hauser, R. M., & Featherman, D. L. (1974). Socioeconomic achievements of U.S. men, 1962 to 1972. *Science, 185*, 325–331.

McCain, B. E., O'Reilly, C. A., & Pfeffer, J. (1983). The effects of departmental demography on turnover: The case of a university. *Academy of Management Journal, 26*(4), 626–641.

Meyer, J. W., & Rowan, B. (1977). Institutionalized organizations: Formal structure as myth and ceremony. *American Journal of Sociology, 83*(2), 340–363.

Mincer, J. (1974). *Schooling, experience, and earnings.* New York: National Bureau of Economic Research.

Pfeffer, J. (1983). Organizational demography. In: L. L. Cummings & B. M. Staw (Eds), *Research in Organizational Behavior* (Vol. 5, pp. 299–357). Greenwich, CT: JAI Press.

Pfeffer, J. (1998). *The human equation: Building profits by putting people first.* Cambridge, MA: Harvard Business School Press.

Pfeffer, J., & Cohen, Y. (1984). Determinants of internal labor markets in organizations. *Administrative Science Quarterly, 29*(4), 550–572.

Pfeffer, J., & Davis-Blake, A. (1987). The effect of the proportion of women on salaries: The case of college administrators. *Administrative Science Quarterly, 32*(1), 1–24.

Pfeffer, J., & Davis-Blake, A. (1990). Determinants of salary dispersion in organizations. *Industrial Relations, 29*(1), 38–57.

Pfeffer, J., & Davis-Blake, A. (1992). Salary dispersion, location in the salary distribution, and turnover among college administrators. *Industrial and Labor Relations Review, 45*(4), 753–763.

Pfeffer, J., & Langton, N. (1993). The effects of wage dispersion on satisfaction, productivity, and working collaboratively: Evidence from college and university faculty. *Administrative Science Quarterly, 38*(3), 382–407.

Pfeffer, J., & O'Reilly, C. A. (1987). Hospital demography and turnover among nurses. *Industrial Relations, 26*(2), 158–173.

Scott, W. R. (2008). *Institutions and organizations: Ideas and interests* (3rd ed.). Thousand Oaks, CA: Sage Publications.

Scott, W. R., Ruef, M., Mendel, P. J., & Caronna, C. (2000). *Institutional change and health care organizations: From professional dominance to managed care.* Chicago, IL: University of Chicago Press.

Sewell, W. H., & Shah, V. P. (1968). Parents' education and children's educational aspirations and achievements. *American Sociological Review, 33*(1), 191–209.

Strang, D., & Baron, J. N. (1990). Categorical imperatives: The structure of job titles in California state agencies. *American Sociological Review, 55*(4), 475–495.

Tolbert, C. M., III., Horan, P. M., & Beck, E. M. (1980). The structure of economic segmentation: A dual economy approach. *American Journal of Sociology, 85*(6), 1095–1116.

Tsui, A. S., & Ellis, A. (2005). Organizational demography. *Blackwell encyclopedic dictionary of organizational behavior.* Oxford, UK: Blackwell Publishing.

Tuma, N. B. (1979). *Invoking RATE.* Palo Alto, CA: DMA Press.

Tuma, N. B., & Hannan, M. T. (1984). *Social dynamics: Models and methods.* New York: Academic.

Uzzi, B., & Barsness, Z. I. (1998). Contingent employment in British establishments: Organizational determinants of the use of fixed-term hire and part-time workers. *Social Forces, 76*(3), 967–1005.

Wharton, A. S., & Baron, J. N. (1987). So happy together? The impact of gender segregation on men at work. *American Sociological Review, 52*(5), 574–587.

Wagner, W. G., Pfeffer, J., & O'Reilly, C. A. (1984). Organizational demography and turnover in top-management groups. *Administrative Science Quarterly, 29*(1), 74–92.

Weber, M. (1946). In: H. H. Gerth & C. W. Mills (Eds, Tans.) [*From Max Weber: Essays in sociology*]. New York: Oxford University Press.

CHAPTER 7

THE HISTORY OF CORPORATE NETWORKS: EXPANDING INTELLECTUAL DIVERSITY AND THE ROLE OF STANFORD AFFILIATIONS

Christine M. Beckman

INTRODUCTION

When first asked to write a chapter on "Corporate Networks," I was flummoxed by the Stanford focus. Unlike many of the other theories in this volume, where a game of word association by theory results in a roster of current or emeritus Stanford faculty members, corporate network has roots in many institutions. Indeed, institutions such as University of Chicago or Stonybrook may make a claim for being at the forefront of research on corporate networks, and University of Michigan is the current home to three of the top researchers in the area. Yet, among the core network researchers, a good number of them either spent their early faculty years at Stanford (e.g., Pam Haunschild, Don Palmer, Joel Podolny) or completed doctoral training at Stanford (e.g., Jerry Davis, Henrich Greve, Toby Stuart, Christine Beckman). And this list does not include those that came to Stanford later in their careers (e.g., Mark Granovetter and Woody

Stanford's Organization Theory Renaissance, 1970–2000
Research in the Sociology of Organizations, Volume 28, 119–143
Copyright © 2010 by Emerald Group Publishing Limited
ISSN: 0733-558X/doi:10.1108/S0733-558X(2010)0000028011

Powell). Furthermore, the history of corporate network research is intertwined with many of the theories developed at Stanford during the late 1970s. To understand this influence, I begin with a brief but broad history of research on corporate networks, a history that begins somewhat earlier than 1970 and continues to the present. Then I turn to the question of Stanford's role in supporting this research stream and intellectual life more broadly.

First, the boundary question: what are corporate networks? I use the term synonymously with interorganizational or interfirm relationships and focus primarily (although not exclusively) on horizontal linkages between firms. The first corporate network to receive empirical attention was interlocking directorates or boards of directors (Dooley, 1969; Levine, 1972). I consider research that focuses on interpersonal in addition to that which examines interorganizational factors driving boards, such as the influence of personal ties in obtaining board appointments (Westphal & Stern, 2006). As other sources of data became available, alliances, market exchanges, collaboration and innovation networks, and more recently investment ties have been regularly examined. I consider corporate networks, then, more narrowly than some views of interorganizational networks (Baker & Faulkner, 2002) but more widely than interlocks alone (Mizruchi, 1996).

Excellent reviews of interorganizational networks have appeared with regularity (Galaskiewicz, 1985; Oliver, 1990; Mizruchi & Galaskiewicz, 1993; Podolny & Page, 1998; Baker & Faulkner, 2002; Gulati, Dialdin, & Wang, 2002; Provan, Fish, & Sydow, 2007; Stuart, 2007). Many of these reviews catalog the antecedents and consequences of corporate networks, and I generally concur with these views. For example, Stuart (2007) suggests that corporate networks serve several key functions: information diffusion, attributions of competence, brokerage, embeddedness that ensures trust and generates obligation, and sanctions. My addition to the conversation is not a hitherto antecedent or consequence that has been excluded but, in the spirit of this volume, an exploration of the origin and evolution of corporate network research and how it has altered its theoretical and empirical focus over the past four decades. In order to create this history, I collected roughly 250 articles on corporate networks. With the help of a doctoral student, I searched the titles and abstracts of 13 major journals for relevant articles in management and sociology. Because there is not a common language to capture research on corporate networks (e.g., an article on corporate networks may refer to interlocks, alliances, interorganizational, interfirm, partner, or embedded ties), there was some imprecision in our collection of articles and we undoubtedly missed some relevant articles. Thus, we undersampled rather than oversampled our area of interest. I supplemented this list with articles from the above-mentioned reviews of interorganizational networks and my own knowledge of the literature. To understand how research on corporate networks has evolved, I ran some descriptive statistics on these articles (as well as a few regressions). In the tables presented, I focused on those 212 articles in the eight journals where more than 10 articles on corporate networks have been published since 1970 (*Administrative Science Quarterly, American Journal of Sociology, American Sociological Review, Organization Science, Academy of Management Journal, Academy of Management Review,* and *Strategic Management Journal, Research Policy*). I coded these articles by theory, method, and empirical context. I coded by theory (e.g., institutional theory, diffusion, embeddedness) in order to demonstrate how research on corporate networks fits within the larger organizational context and to see changes over time. Thus, this overview is based on an empirical analysis of trends in corporate networks.

To preview, although research on corporate networks began with a tight focus on interlocking directorates as a tool of organizational and class interests, research in the 1990s rapidly expanded to new areas, spurred in large part by new theoretical developments in embeddedness, diffusion, and institutional theory. Subsequent work in large part focused on population ecology, positional power (here I include work on brokerage as well as work on status), and economic theories in the context of corporate networks. In the 21st century, embeddedness has emerged as the dominant theory for research on corporate networks, and research has moved from a stable home in the sociology and organization theory journals to a wider audience in strategy and general management journals. Today, corporate network scholars study alliances, exchange relationships and collaborative ties both within and outside the United States.

Stanford scholars have played an important part in this research trajectory, particularly from the 1990s; however, with the arrival of Jeff Pfeffer and Don Palmer, in 1979 and 1980, respectively, Stanford has always had a scholar of corporate networks on the faculty or among the doctoral students. Corporate networks, as an area of study, is not dominated by a single Stanford-affiliated faculty member, but the field is not dominated by any one person or perspective. Because corporate networks are a phenomenon rather than a theory, many scholars use corporate networks as a key construct across a range of theoretical perspectives and empirical settings (e.g., Dyer, Gulati, Mizruchi, Stearns, Uzzi, and Westphal). I argue that this breadth of use is exactly why Stanford affiliated scholars have a continued interest in and influence on corporate networks. Many theories developed at Stanford are able to draw on corporate networks as a key conduit of information, social standing, and organizational legitimacy as well as a means of managing dependency and economic relations. Like Stanford, corporate networks are a "place" where researchers develop ideas across a wide intellectual landscape. In other words, there is not a dense collection of scholars in corporate networks but rather a number of loosely connected scholarly groups that each focus on a different aspect of what, together, I call corporate networks. The depth of Stanford's influence on corporate networks is obscured by this breadth, and my goal is to illuminate both this intellectual diversity and the underlying Stanford connections.

THE EARLY YEARS: 1970–1989

The earliest management research on corporate networks emerged from a focus on how the social relations across corporations support class interests. The availability of interlock data, because federal filing regulations require firms to disclose their directors and their director's affiliations, spurred early interest and empirical work along these lines. Indeed, the vast majority of the research in the 1970s and 1980s focused on interlocking directorates (72%). It accounts for 28% of the research on corporate networks over the past four decades, making it still the most prevalent data source for research on corporate networks (see Table 1). Inspired in large part by Mills (1956), early scholars viewed interlocking directorates as a mechanism of capitalist

Table 1.   Type of Corporate Network by Decade.

	Interlocks	Alliances	Market	Collaboration	Other	Total Articles
1970s	4	1	1	1	1	8
	50%	13%	13%	13%		
1980s	19	0	1	1	3	24
	79%	0	4%	4%		
1990s	24	22	26	17	2	91
	27%	24%	29%	19%		
2000s	12	25	28	19	5	89
	13%	28%	31%	21%		
Total	59	48	56	38	11	212
	28%	23%	26%	18%		

class cohesion. Bunting (1983) found banks and insurance companies in New York to be a cohesive corporate network by 1816, and the interlock network continued to be cohesive as we moved into the 20th century (Mizruchi, 1982; Roy, 1983). With the passage of the Clayton Act of 1914, prohibiting competitors from sitting on each other's boards, board composition and the resulting interlocking network of corporations changed. Yet Dooley (1969), in a comparison of interlocks in 1935 and 1965, found that interlocks reflected local interests and the dominance of financial institutions well into the 20th century. Although the centrality of financial institutions faded in the latter portion of the 20th century, as financial firms no longer serve as the primary intermediary between firms (Davis & Mizruchi, 1999), the overall stability of the corporate interlock network remains strong into the 21st century (Davis, Yoo, & Baker, 2003). These early studies examined the structure of corporate interlocks to make arguments about the integration of the elite class (Levine, 1972; Zeitlin, 1974; Useem, 1979; Mintz & Schwartz, 1981). For example, the similarity of political views among interlocked firms can be seen as a signal of class cohesion (Clawson & Neustadtl, 1989; Mizruchi, 1989).

Although the very earliest work viewed corporate networks as a source of class power, a perspective that has been called power-structure theory, a parallel track of thinking quickly emerged arguing that corporate networks are a means of managing resource dependence (Pfeffer, 1972; Pfeffer & Nowak, 1976). Interlocks, as well as joint ventures, allow firms to co-opt firms across sectors in the face of market constraints (Burt, Christman, & Kilburn, 1980; Burt, 1980a, 1983). Although some of this research examines constraints across industries rather than firms (Burt, 1980b), the logic is that relationships are used to reduce a firm's dependence on other organizations and leverage a firm's own interests. Thus, rather than serve class interests, corporate networks serve organizational interests. Early work contrasted these perspectives. For example, Palmer (1983) examined whether, when an interlock between two companies is inadvertently broken, the interlock is reconstituted between the same two firms. Ties that are not replaced with another tie from the same firm are seen as evidence of intraclass ties rather than interfirm ties (see Stearns & Mizruchi, 1986, for a discussion of functional reconstitution). Although scholars have found that roughly 50% of interlock ties are not reconstituted at all, research using these and other empirical techniques generally concludes that interlocks serve to support both class and organizational interests (e.g., Palmer, Singh, & Friedland, 1986).

Clearly, the dominant perspectives in this time period were class and resource dependence theories (see Table 2). Yet, near the end of the 1980s,

Table 2. Theoretical Perspective by Decade.

	Class Theory	Resource Dependence Theory	Positional Power Theories	Institutional Theory	Embeddedness Theory	Evolution Emergence Theories	Diffusion Learning Theories	Ecology Theories	Economic Theories	Strategy Theories	Perform. DV	Total Articles
1970s	3 37%	4 50%	0 0%	0 0%	0 0%	0 0%	0 0%	0 0%	1 14%	0 0%	0 0%	8
1980s	11 46%	9 38%	0 0%	1 4%	1 4%	1 4%	0 0%	0 0%	0 0%	2 8%	0 0%	24
1990s	9 10%	19 21%	12 13%	20 22%	20 22%	10 11%	20 22%	11 12%	18 20%	10 11%	6 7%	91
2000s	4 5%	9 10%	18 21%	7 8%	27 30%	18 20%	12 14%	9 10%	8 9%	14 16%	24 28%	89
Total	27 13%	41 20%	30 14%	28 13%	48 23%	29 14%	32 15%	20 9%	27 13%	26 12%	30 14%	212

scholars began to consider the relevance of corporate networks for understanding institutional theory (Galaskiewicz & Wasserman, 1989), population ecology (Miner, Amburgey, & Stearns, 1990), and the field of strategy (Jarillo, 1988; Zajac, 1988). The other shift that occurred was from an early focus on the antecedents of corporate networks (i.e., are interlocks formed to serve organizational or class interests?) to a focus on the consequences of these networks. In the 1970s, the majority of articles published looked at the precursors to corporate networks. During the 1980s, this focus shifted and research primarily highlighted the consequences of corporate networks. This trend toward consequences continued into the 1990s (54% in the 1980s then 73% of the articles in the 1990s).

EXPLODING INTEREST IN CORPORATE NETWORKS: THE 1990s

Several important developments marked research in the 1990s. First, there was an enormous leap in the number of articles published on corporate networks: the sheer number almost quadrupled from 24 articles in the 1980s, to 91 articles in the 1990s. The 1990s were the decade when research on corporate networks broadened its appeal. In looking at where these articles were published, we saw a dramatic increase in the proportion of corporate networks articles in all of the journals; with the exceptions of *Academy of Management Review*, which does not peak until this decade, and *American Sociological Review*, which was an early leader in corporate networks and published at nearly the same rate in the 1980s and 1990s (7 and 10 articles, respectively).

Along with this growth in the number of articles, we also saw a greatly expanded theoretical breadth of research on corporate networks in the 1990s. Studies focused on the relevance of corporate networks for economic theories, such as agency theory and transaction cost economics, made a dramatic surge, as did studies of diffusion and learning, embeddedness, and institutional theory (see Table 2). Furthermore, a healthy minority of articles explored corporate networks and population ecology (e.g., Podolny et al, 1996; Ingram & Baum, 1997), network position or status (e.g., Podolny, 1994; Stuart, 1998), and network evolution (e.g., Hagedoorn, 1995; Koza & Lewin, 1998).

Despite these important new arenas for corporate networks, over a quarter of the articles published in the 1990s examined corporate networks in relation to social class or resource dependence (e.g., Baker, 1990;

D'Aveni & Kesner, 1993). Many articles compared resource dependence and economic predictions for firm action (e.g., Galaskiewicz, 1997; Mizruchi & Stearns, 1994). In addition, Palmer and colleagues continued to demonstrate the importance of both class cohesion and organizational dependence (e.g., Palmer, Jennings, & Zhou, 1993; Palmer, Barber, Zhou, & Soysal, 1995). However, the multiple predictors demonstrated by these results suggest a complex set of forces shaping firm action and signaled the move toward a broader array of explanatory factors. Furthermore, Davis (1996) has argued that interlocks were no longer a source of co-optation by 1994, and this may account for some of the shift in interlock research. Thus, even within resource dependence and class theories, research moved into new directions.

Although early considerations of resource dependence measured constraint using industry-level data (e.g., industry-level input–output tables; Burt, 1980a, 1980b; Burt et al., 1980; Pfeffer & Salancik, 1978), firm-level measures of dependence emerged in the early 1990s (e.g., Baker, 1990; Palmer et al., 1995). In this time period, there were two different conceptualizations of resource dependence. In the tradition of Pfeffer and Salancik (1978), there were those that measured dependence according to asymmetry between two organizational actors (such as the ownership of outside investors or the proportion of business received from another firm). In the later tradition of Burt (1992), others measured power accrued by structural position in the network (such as structural holes in Walker, Kogut, & Shan, 1997). It is this latter focus that began to attract more attention in the 1990s, although the former perspective continued to develop as well (e.g., Galaskiewicz, 1997). In this latter stream, we see an interest in how status within a market shapes economic activities (Podolny, 1993). Toby Stuart and colleagues used these ideas of position and status in the context of corporate networks to demonstrate how the prominence of network partners provided organizational advantage (Stuart, 1998; Stuart, Hoang, & Hybels, 1999). This important area of research on positional advantage continues to attract attention in the most recent decade (growing from 13% to 21% of the articles).

In the 1990s, two important shifts also occurred within those studies coded as class and focused primarily on managerial interests and corporate cohesion. In the first twist on traditional class research, Zajac and Westphal (1996) examined how individual interests of CEOs and board members, and the intraorganizational contests for power, play a role in shaping the overall corporate network (see also Westphal & Zajac, 1997). It is the group interaction and exchange between CEOs and the board that was their focal point, not the overall corporate network. The second twist was to focus on the mechanism (often interlocks) by which ideas and practices supporting managerial control diffuse. For example, Davis (1991) found interlocks acted as a means of maintaining managerial control despite agency theory predictions about the role of the corporate board. The anti-takeover defense of poison pills diffused through the corporate network, protecting managerial interests, and it is both the service of managerial interests and the diffusion process itself that are of note. Thus, diffusion processes and individual interests have implications for corporate control, but it is the process of diffusion or group interaction and contestation that was the focus of these studies.

Emerging from the earlier interlock research, like Davis (1991), studies of diffusion through corporate interlocks developed into a major area of research in the 1990s. Rather than considering interlocks purely as an indicator of corporate control, networks were seen as a means of communicating and diffusing new ideas (often, although not exclusively, through interlocks). For example, Haunschild (1993) found that firms imitate their interlock partners by making similar types of acquisitions (e.g., vertical, horizontal, conglomerate); furthermore, firms imitated those partners even when they were engaging in dissimilar actions. Diffusion and learning through corporate networks accounted for a full 22% of studies during the 1990s (see Strang & Soule, 1998, for a review). Of particular note are studies that began to examine the contingencies of corporate networks. For example, Davis and Greve (1997) examined the different diffusion patterns of two corporate governance practices, poison pills and golden parachutes, and found that diffusion could be explained by interlock and geographic proximity, respectively. The cultural meanings of the practices themselves shaped the particular pattern and source of diffusion. As another example, Haunschild and Beckman (1998) explored how the combination of information sources shaped acquisition decisions. They found that interlocks were more influential when complementary sources of information, such as the mass media, focused attention on acquisitions. Rather than focus on how practices diffuse through corporate networks, these studies explored what accounts for differences in diffusion patterns.

Related to these studies, and included with the studies coded as diffusion in Table 2, are those studies focused on learning through corporate networks. Some of these studies resemble those above in that they examined differences in who adopts particular practices. For example, Kraatz (1998) found that similarity between the focal organization and adopters in the organization's network accounted for the adoption of major curriculum changes in liberal arts colleges. Haunschild and Miner (1997) found that firms imitated the frequent practices of other firms and those practices with salient outcomes (importantly, both positive and negative outcomes). An important subset of these articles focused not on dyads but on the network itself (Podolny & Page, 1998). For example, Powell, Koput, and SmithDoerr (1996) found that firms embedded in a network of R&D alliances, with experience in interorganizational relationships, grew more quickly and developed richer networks than other firms. They argued for networks of learning where innovation is found through interorganizational collaborations rather than individual firms. This focus on the network level of analysis remains understudied but began to gather attention in the 1990s (Provan et al., 2007).

A closely related theoretical perspective that garnered significant attention during the 1990s is institutional theory. A few articles focused exclusively on institutional theory; for example, Burns and Wholey (1993) found institutional pressures predicted the adoption but not the abandonment of matrix management programs. However, most articles in the 1990s drew on multiple theoretical perspectives. For example, some of the articles linked diffusion with institutional processes, such as Westphal and Zajac's (1997) discussion of how the practice of total quality management (TQM) looked different depending on when firms' adopted (early or late in the diffusion process) and how the role of networks changed over time. Other articles explored the role of power and institutional processes in the adoption of particular practices or the continuity and dissolution of corporate networks (e.g. Palmer et al., 1993; Baker, Faulkner, & Fisher, 1998).

Research on embeddedness emerged as a leading area of interest in the 1990s. Following the logic of Granovetter (1985), these articles focused on how social relations constrain organizational economic actions. This work builds from theories of class and power-structure, at least implicitly, because to argue that corporate networks serve class interests acknowledges that embeddedness exists. The difference between these views is the focus on networks as a source of elite cohesion or as an enabler of economic action. This shift in attention has changed the tone of the discussion from somewhat critical or suspicious of managerial motivations to a generally positive discussion of how embedded relationships can benefit firms (Uzzi 1996, 1997, 1999). For example, Uzzi (1996) found that a mix of embedded and arm's length ties improved the survival chances of firms (completely embedded ties were detrimental). In a similar vein, Gulati and Gargiulo (1999) argued prior alliances and common ties facilitated the development of new alliances (see also Gulati, 1995a, 1995b, 1998, 1999).

Relationships are embedded in an existing social structure which shapes future ties as well as firm performance.

A final series of articles in the 1990s examined economic theories within the context of corporate networks. The vast majority of these articles discussed transaction cost economics (e.g., Parkhe, 1993; Dyer, 1996, 1997), although a significant number addressed agency theory. Some of these articles compared organizational and economic views; for example, Galaskiewicz (1997) compared agency, resource dependence, and institutional explanations to predict corporate charitable giving. Scholars also used corporate networks to discuss strategy theories such as the resource-based view (Eisenhardt & Schoonhoven, 1996; Dyer & Singh, 1998; Gulati, 1999). Some of the articles suggested that corporate networks add a social or symbolic component to economic or rational processes in the firm (Wade, O'Reilly, & Chandrahat, 1990; Zajac & Westphal, 1995).

In addition to this vast theoretical breath (seen in Table 2), research on corporate networks expanded beyond the study of interlocks during the 1990s (see Table 1). However, board interlocks continued to be a focus of study, accounting for 27% of the total articles. Of these interlock studies, half focused on class or resource dependence theories (e.g., Palmer et al., 1995; Kono, Friedland, & Palmer, 1998; Gulati & Westphal, 1999), with a good number considering diffusion or institutional processes (Davis, 1991; Haunschild, 1993; Davis & Greve, 1997). In the 1990s, however, alliance networks, market relationships, and collaboration ties all became important corporate networks of study – emerging virtually from nowhere. Studies of alliance networks and embeddedness were clearly linked: 50% of all embeddedness articles in the 1990s examined alliance networks (e.g., Gulati, 1995a, 1995b, 1998, 1999). That said, articles examining alliances drew on a range of theories (e.g., resource dependence, institutional theory, embeddedness, evolutionary theory, diffusion) because these networks offered a new empirical context to study a number of important ideas. The focus on alliances has increased our understanding of both the emergence and evolution of corporate networks (Hagedoorn, 1995; Koza & Lewin, 1998; Gulati & Gargiulo, 1999) and the role of corporate networks outside the United States (e.g., Dyer, 1996; Lincoln, Gerlach, & Ahmadjian, 1996). The research on market relationships, in contrast, focused primarily within the United States. Those studying market relationships have informed our understanding of theories such as embeddedness (Uzzi, 1996), resource dependence (Baker, 1990), and institutional theory (Haunschild & Miner, 1997). Finally, research that explored collaborative networks found that institutional linkages reduced organizational mortality (Baum & Oliver, 1991) as well as increased innovation and change (Smith, Dickson, & Smith, 1991; Powell et al., 1996; Kraatz, 1998). Despite this theoretical and empirical breadth, however, the vast majority of research considered the consequences rather than the antecedents of corporate networks during this time period (73%).

RESEARCH IN THE 21ST CENTURY: 2000 TO THE PRESENT

Although this volume highlights research between 1970 and 2000, it is worth noting the directions that corporate network research has moved in this decade. Corporate networks remain a vibrant area of research, and more articles will be published on the topic in this decade than the last. However the favored empirical context has continued to shift. In the current decade, interlock research accounts for only 13% of articles, with other corporate networks becoming more prevalent (again see Table 1). This change in empirical context coincides with a shift in theoretical focus as well.

In this decade we see a clear focus on the performance consequences of corporate networks. For example, Shipilov and Li (2008) demonstrated that an open network, or one with structural holes, had both positive and negative effects on market performance and aided firms in status accumulation. Furthermore, more articles draw on strategy theories (e.g., Gimeno, 2004; Zaheer & Bell, 2005). This shift to performance and strategic consequences can also be seen in the changing publication outlets for corporate network research. Over the past four decades, *Administrative Science Quarterly* (ASQ) has been the key outlet for corporate network research (32% of all articles) but in this decade *Strategic Management Journal* (SMJ) has matched ASQ for articles published on corporate networks (both publishing roughly 20 articles between 2000 and 2008). This is notable as much for the drop in articles published in ASQ from the prior decade (from 32 to 22) as for the growth in SMJ (from 11 to 20).

Another key development is the dominance of the embeddedness perspective through empirical examinations of market relationships (e.g., Davis, Rao, & Ward, 2000; Gulati & Sytch, 2007; Uzzi & Lancaster, 2004) and collaborative relationships (e.g., Ahuja, 2000; Galaskiewicz, Bielefeld, & Dowell, 2006; Owen-Smith & Powell, 2003). Of particular importance has been understanding the importance of geography in creating embedded corporate networks. Kono et al. (1998) spurred this resurgence of interest in space (the importance of propinquity is an old concept: Festinger, Schachter, & Back, 1950) by demonstrating how the formation of interlocks are predicted by the other companies and elite clubs in a city. They suggest that local and nonlocal interlocks have different determinants. Sorenson and Stuart (2001) focused on the consequences of geographic proximity and demonstrate that geographic distance predicts venture capital investments (see also Marquis, 2003, for a discussion of geographically focused imprinting).

A final growing theoretical focus considers the emergence and evolution of corporate networks (e.g., Human & Provan, 2000; Neuman, Davis, & Mizruchi, 2008; Stuart, Ozdemir, & Ding, 2007). The growth has refocused research on the antecedents of networks (although consequences continue to be the dominant focus and more research on antecedents is needed, see Stuart, 2007). This growth has also fueled longitudinal research (28% of the research on corporate networks in this decade examine networks over time). For example, at the field level, Powell, White, Koput, and Owen-Smith (2005) explored how networks within the biotechnology industry changed over time according to different logics of attachment. Focusing instead on dyadic networks, Beckman, Haunschild, and Phillips (2004) suggested levels of uncertainty lead firms to broaden or reinforce their alliance and interlock networks. Building from this, recent work has examined the role of uncertainty, contextual factors, and shortcuts in establishing new market or alliance relationships (Rosenkopf & Padula, 2008; Sorenson & Stuart, 2008). Also at the dyadic level, Hallen (2009) examined the role of founder human capital in explaining the origin of corporate networks (see also Schoonhoven, Beckman, & Rottner, 2010).

In addition to the above-mentioned areas, new theoretical developments have occurred within the foundational perspectives of corporate networks. In the area of diffusion of learning, for example, work in this decade has moved beyond the diffusion of a particular practice through the intercorporate network. For example, Beckman and Haunschild (2002) explored how the diversity of network experiences, rather than particular dyadic ties, resulted in learning about acquisition premiums. Further, Westphal, Seidel, and Stewart (2001) demonstrated second-order imitation effects through interlocks rather than the diffusion of specific policies. Others have explored global diffusion patterns (e.g., Guler, Guillen, & MacPherson, 2002) or the impact of illegitimate practices on the overall network structure (Sullivan, Haunschild, & Page, 2007).

In the area of resource dependence, scholars have deepened our understanding of the role of power asymmetry and interdependence in interfirm relations (Casciaro & Piskorski, 2005; Gulati & Sytch, 2007) as well as demonstrated the penetration of interfirm dependence to influence on internal promotion decisions (Beckman & Phillips, 2005).

However, rather than focusing on the traditional resource dependence view, more attention has turned to consideration of brokerage, structural holes, and measures of network position. This focus on position and status has been taken up by a wide number of scholars (e.g., Galaskiewicz et al., 2006; Soda, Usai, & Zaheer, 2004).

This decade has also brought increasing methodological sophistication. We see the incorporation of sophisticated network methods and graphics to examine existing theories (e.g., Powell et al., 2005). For example, Cattani, Ferriani, Negro, and Perretti (2008) used network methods and graphics to demonstrate that interorganizational relations are key to the legitimation processes and reduced organizational mortality rates (reminiscent of Miner et al., 1990). Other recent work has drawn on small-world network techniques to better understand embeddedness, innovation, and the emergence and evolution of networks (e.g., Fleming, King, & Juda, 2007; Rosenkopf & Padula, 2008; Schilling & Phelps, 2007). These studies have investigated the effects of cohesion and reachability at the network level and linked it to firm- and network-level outcomes. This latter work, in particular, offers great promise to developing our understanding of corporate networks. In addition, researchers are using new empirical techniques to deal with problems of endogeneity (Lomi & Pattison, 2006; Stuart & Yim, 2008). For example, Stuart & Yim (2008) reported extensive additional analyses to demonstrate that the influence of interlocks on the likelihood of receiving a private-equity offer has a causal relationship. Finally, we have also seen a few studies examining different types of networks simultaneously (e.g., Beckman et al., 2004; Lee, Lee, & Pennings, 2001) and the study of multiplex as well as cross-sector networks should prove to be a fruitful area for additional research and may shed new light on the development of communities (e.g., Marquis, 2003).

Finally, beginning in the 1990s and continuing to this decade we finally see growth in comparative studies or studies looking outside of the United States (39% of the research in this decade consider non-U.S. contexts). Recent research on corporate networks has not only included those focused on Japan (Ahmadjian & Lincoln, 2001) but also considers networks in South Korea (Siegel, 2007), Europe (Starkey, Barnatt, & Tempest, 2000; Windolf, 2002), China (Keister, 2001), and Australia (Ingram & Roberts, 2000).

THE STANFORD CONNECTION

In this final section, I link Stanford to this broad array of research on corporate networks. Given my lack of objectivity, I looked to my empirical analysis to answer the question of how much Stanford contributed to the development of corporate networks. First, I tried to answer the question: was Stanford a leading contributor to research on corporate networks? The empirical answer is clearly a resounding "yes." Overall, 23% of the research on corporate networks has been done by Stanford-affiliated scholars. Is this a large percentage? When I tallied the other institutions that can claim influence through the publishing of affiliated scholars, Stanford takes the lead. This accounts for the multiple institutions that can claim a scholar. For instance, Stanford, Michigan, Columbia, and Northwestern can all claim Jerry Davis; Northwestern, Michigan, and Texas can claim Jim Westphal. Despite this, Stanford-affiliated scholars fare well, publishing the largest number of articles (with 48, followed by Kellogg and Michigan with 31 and 30, respectively). Admittedly, my tallies likely undercounted for some institutions as I relied on my own knowledge of people's career trajectories and doctoral training and only limited archival research. As another check, I created a table of the 19 most prolific scholars of corporate networks (those publishing four or more articles in the selected journals). Eight on the list have Stanford affiliations (Kellogg claims five; Michigan and Harvard, each three; see Table 3). Although these are measures of quantity and not necessarily of overall influence, they are indicative that Stanford had a role in the development of this research stream. I find this reassuring, as it validates having a chapter on corporate networks in this volume. However, the qualitative story is perhaps more interesting and more revealing than the quantitative story.

The story was quite simple in the beginning. The two early Stanford faculty members to play a role in corporate networks were Jeff Pfeffer and Don Palmer. Initially, each represented a key early view: either interlocks as representing organizational dependence (Pfeffer) or as representing class cohesion (Palmer). Pfeffer returned to Stanford in 1979 (where he had received his PhD in 1972), and, although his primary focus was the development of resource dependence theory (see Davis, this volume), his influence on early corporate network research is clear. Pfeffer wrote two corporate network papers, one on interlocks and the other on joint ventures (Pfeffer, 1972; Pfeffer & Nowak, 1976). These papers, along with Pfeffer and Salancik (1978) and other writings, set the stage for what has accounted for 20% of all corporate network research to date. The other key scholar, Palmer, arrived at Stanford in 1980 as a freshly minted PhD from Stonybrook. Palmer focused his early research on corporate networks and became one of the leading scholars to integrate and test class theory and resource dependence both during and after he left Stanford (Palmer et al.,

Table 3. Authors Publishing on Corporate Networks (in Journals Publishing 10 or More Network Articles since 1970).

Author	Number of Articles in Eight Select Journals[a]
Gulati, R.	12
Stuart, T.[b]	9
Westphal, J.	9
Mizruchi, M.	8
Dyer, J.	7
Galaskiewicz, J.	7
Haunschild, P.[b]	7
Davis, G.[b]	6
Palmer, D.[b]	6
Baum, J.	5
Brewster Stearns, L.	5
Hagedoorn, J.	5
Podolny, J.[b]	5
Singh, H.	5
Uzzi, B.	5
Beckman, C.[b]	4
Greve, H.[b]	4
Powell, W.[b]	4
Zajac, E.	4

[a]Administrative Science Quarterly, American Journal of Sociology, American Sociological Review, Organization Science, Academy of Management Journal, Academy of Management Review, and Strategic Management Journal, Research Policy.
[b]Denotes Stanford affiliated scholars (8 total).

1986, 1995; Barber & Palmer, 2001). As discussed earlier, the theories these two faculty members studied were at the heart of early research on corporate networks. And without corporate networks, these important theories would have lacked the inspiration and empirical context in which to develop.

The next wave of corporate network research at Stanford occurred in the shadow of great new theoretical developments (such as learning, institutional theory, and population ecology). The shift of focus from corporate networks as a means of corporate control to a mechanism of communication and legitimacy occurred as these new theoretical developments took hold. During this time where Stanford flourished (Scott, this volume), so too did research on corporate networks. Joel Podolny joined the faculty in 1991, followed by Pam Haunschild in 1994. Podolny (followed by his student, Stuart) conducted important work on status and position in corporate networks in the context of investment banking and alliances. This work has been at the forefront of emerging research on positional power (along, of course, with Ron Burt; see Table 2). Haunschild (followed by her student, Beckman) conducted early work on the diffusion and learning that occurs through corporate interlocks. Greve, a student of Jim March, conducted his own research on diffusion patterns. These and other Stanford scholars published eight articles drawing on institutional theory; nine on diffusion and learning. In terms of empirical contexts, the majority of the Stanford-affiliated scholars studied interlocks during the 1990s (e.g., Beckman, Davis, Haunschild, Palmer; indeed, almost half of all interlock research in the 1990s has a Stanford-affiliation). Scholars central to corporate network research continued to be drawn to Stanford: Granovetter joined the faculty in 1995 and Powell in 1999.

Perhaps because corporate networks offered a tool for testing core ideas within theories such as institutional theory, resource dependence and diffusion, and learning, a number of Stanford doctoral students of the late 1980s and early 1990s (e.g., Davis, Greve, Stuart) emerged as key players in research on corporate networks. The diversity of thought around corporate networks (rather than a single dominant personality) provided students with an array of possibilities, and networks were very much a part of what students attended to during their studies. It is important to point out that two of the most prolific scholars of corporate networks in Table 3 were on the faculty (Haunschild and Palmer) and two were Stanford doctoral students (Davis and Stuart); and these people did not work together. They all made independent contributions to the field of corporate networks, which speaks to the rich diversity of thought at Stanford. Palmer and Davis, for example, both continue to be leading voices in our understanding of class but have clearly distinct voices (Barber & Palmer, 2001; Davis et al., 2003).

I will say only a word or two about where Stanford scholars have been less visible. The recent move to predicting firm performance from corporate networks and to focus on traditional strategy theories has not been led by Stanford scholars. Stanford-affiliated corporate network scholars, consistent with the hallmarks of the "Stanford School," have tended to focus on the "non-rational" or social components of corporate networks (Scott, this volume). As might be expected then, the more sociologically oriented Stanford-scholars have been over-represented in studying the antecedents rather than the consequences of corporate networks (accounting for 39% of the research on antecedents). Stanford-scholars have also been U.S. focused, perhaps as a result of interlock research.

Although I have talked about specific Stanford-affiliated scholars of corporate networks, I have neglected thus far to talk about the role of

Stanford as a place. As many of the scholars in this volume note, Stanford as a place was important to the development of many ideas, including corporate networks. As Scott rightfully points out (this volume), it is not just the aggregation of smart individuals that explains Stanford's preeminence. Indeed, network research suggests that relationships among faculty members are an important source of diffusion for new ideas. The constellation of people at Stanford during the 1980s and 1990s certainly facilitated this diffusion. The close proximity of these departments in space (the sociology department and the education, business, and engineering schools are not more than a half a mile away from each other) also clearly plays a role in understanding the innovations that occurred (Sorenson & Stuart, 2001). The abundant, co-located, and diverse intellectual resources resulted in high rates of learning and creative outcomes (Beckman & Haunschild, 2002; Singh & Fleming, 2010).

As Scott details, however, it was not just the mutual stimulation of people at Stanford day-to-day that was important; it was the infrastructure put in place to support the development of new ideas. In the case of corporate networks, early leaders in corporate networks visited Stanford. For example, Ed Laumann (Laumann, Marsden, & Galaskewicz, 1977) was an Asilomar presenter. Mark Granovetter spent the year on a faculty fellowship in 1986–1987 (and then joined the Stanford faculty in 1995). Having Granovetter as part of the fabric of Stanford for that year, given that Granovetter (1985) has probably inspired more research on corporate network research than any single article (25% of all research since it was published), is another example of how Stanford managed to be at the center of new ideas.

Although not all roads lead to or from Stanford in this case, it is also true that many of the leading scholars in my review have been connected to Stanford at one time or another. This mixture of scholars is responsible not for a single perspective or viewpoint, but rather for a diversity of influential ideas that continue to lead the field. That this diversity of views and scholars flourished at Stanford serves as a perfect example of the unique collegial capital described by Dick Scott. Stanford was a remarkable place to be during the latter part of the 20th century, and I am indebted to the institution, as well as to the faculty, for the experience.

ACKNOWLEDGMENTS

Thanks to the editors and Pam Haunschild for helpful comments and to Sung Namkung for his research assistance.

REFERENCES

Ahmadjian, C. L., & Lincoln, J. R. (2001). Keiretsu, governance, and learning: Case studies in change from the Japanese automotive industry. *Organization Science, 12*(6), 683–701.

Ahuja, G. (2000). Collaboration networks, structural holes and innovation: A longitudinal study. *Administrative Science Quarterly, 45*(3), 425–455.

Baker, W. E. (1990). Market networks and corporate behavior. *American Journal of Sociology, 96*(2), 589–625.

Baker, W. E., & Faulkner, R. R. (2002). Interorganizational networks. In: J. A. C. Baum (Ed.), *The Blackwell companion to organizational studies* (pp. 520–540). Malden, MA: Basil Blackwell.

Baker, W. E., Faulkner, R. R., & Fisher, G. A. (1998). Hazards of the market: The continuity and dissolution of interorganizational market relationships. *American Sociological Review, 63*(2), 147–177.

Barber, B. M., & Palmer, D. (2001). Challengers, elites, and owning families: A social class theory of corporate acquisitions in the 1960s. *Administrative Science Quarterly, 46*(1), 87–120.

Baum, J. A. C., & Oliver, C. (1991). Institutional linkages and organizational mortality. *Administrative Science Quarterly, 36*(2), 187–218.

Beckman, C. M., & Haunschild, P. R. (2002). Network learning: The effects of partners' heterogeneity of experience on corporate acquisitions. *Administrative Science Quarterly, 47*(1), 92–124.

Beckman, C. M., Haunschild, P. R., & Phillips, D. J. (2004). Friends or strangers? Firm-specific uncertainty, market uncertainty, and network partner selection. *Organization Science, 15*(3), 259–275.

Beckman, C. M., & Phillips, D. J. (2005). Interorganizational determinants of promotion: Client leadership and the attainment of women attorneys. *American Sociological Review, 70*(4), 678–701.

Bunting, D. (1983). Origins of the American corporate network. *Social Science History, 7*(2), 129–142.

Burns, L. R., & Wholey, D. R. (1993). Adoption and abandonment of matrix management programs – Effects of organizational characteristics and interorganizational networks. *Academy of Management Journal, 36*(1), 106–138.

Burt, R. S. (1980a). Cooptive corporate actor networks – A reconsideration of interlocking directorates involving American manufacturing. *Administrative Science Quarterly, 25*(4), 557–582.

Burt, R. S. (1980b). Autonomy in a social topology. *American Journal of Sociology, 85*, 892–925.

Burt, R. S. (1983). *Corporate profits and cooptation: Networks of market constraints and directorate ties in the American economy.* New York: Academic Press.

Burt, R. S. (1992). *Structural holes: The social structure of competition.* Cambridge: Harvard University Press.

Burt, R. S., Christman, K. P., & Kilburn, H. C. (1980). Testing a structural theory of corporate cooptation – Interorganizational directorate ties as a strategy for avoiding market constraints on profits. *American Sociological Review, 45*(5), 821–841.

Casciaro, T., & Piskorski, M. J. (2005). Power imbalance, mutual dependence, and constraint absorption: A closer look at resource dependency theory. *Administrative Science Quarterly, 50*, 167–199.

Cattani, G., Ferriani, S., Negro, G., & Perretti, F. (2008). The structure of consensus: Network ties, legitimation, and exit rates of U.S. feature film producer organizations. *Administrative Science Quarterly, 53*(1), 145–182.

Clawson, D., & Neustadtl, A. (1989). Interlocks, PACs, and corporate conservatism. *American Journal of Sociology, 94*(4), 749–773.

D'Aveni, R. A., & Kesner, I. F. (1993). Top managerial prestige, power and tender offer response – A study of elite social networks and target firm cooperation during takeovers. *Organization Science, 4*(2), 123–151.

Davis, G. (1996). The significance of board interlocks for corporate governance. *Corporate Governance, 4*, 154–159.

Davis, G. F. (1991). Agents without principles – The spread of the poison pill through the intercorporate network. *Administrative Science Quarterly, 36*(4), 583–613.

Davis, G. F., & Greve, H. R. (1997). Corporate elite networks and governance changes in the 1980s. *American Journal of Sociology, 103*(1), 1–37.

Davis, G. F., & Mizruchi, M. S. (1999). The money center cannot hold: Commercial banks in the U.S. system of corporate governance. *Administrative Science Quarterly, 44*(2), 215–239.

Davis, G. F., Rao, H., & Ward, A. (2000). Embeddedness, social identity and mobility: Why firms leave the NASDAQ and join the New York Stock Exchange. *Administrative Science Quarterly, 45*(2), 268–292.

Davis, G. F., Yoo, M., & Baker, W. E. (2003). The small world of the American Corporate elite, 1982–2001. *Strategic Organization, 1*(3), 301–326.

Dooley, P. C. (1969). The interlocking directorate. *American Economic Review, 59*(3), 314–323.

Dyer, J. H. (1996). Does governance matter? Keiretsu alliances and asset specificity as sources of Japanese competitive advantage. *Organization Science, 7*(6), 649–666.

Dyer, J. H. (1997). Effective interfirm collaboration: How firms minimize transaction costs and maximize transaction value. *Strategic Management Journal, 18*(7), 535–556.

Dyer, J. H., & Singh, H. (1998). The relational view: Cooperative strategy and sources of interorganizational competitive advantage. *Academy of Management Review, 23*(4), 660–679.

Eisenhardt, K. M., & Schoonhoven, C. B. (1996). Resource-based view of strategic alliance formation: Strategic and social effects in entrepreneurial firms. *Organization Science, 7*(2), 136–150.

Festinger, L., Schachter, S., & Back, K. W. (1950). *Social pressure in informal groups.* New York: Harper.

Fleming, L., King, C., & Juda, A. I. (2007). Small worlds and regional innovation. *Organization Science, 18*(6), 938–954.

Galaskiewicz, J. (1985). Interorganizational relations. *Annual Review of Sociology, 11*, 281–304.

Galaskiewicz, J. (1997). An urban grants economy revisited: Corporate charitable contributions in the Twin Cities, 1979–81, 1987–89. *Administrative Science Quarterly, 42*, 445–471.

Galaskiewicz, J., Bielefeld, W., & Dowell, M. (2006). Networks and organizational growth: A study of community based nonprofits. *Administrative Science Quarterly, 51*, 337–380.

Galaskiewicz, J., & Wasserman, S. (1989). Mimetic processes within an interorganizational field – An empirical-test. *Administrative Science Quarterly, 34*(3), 454–479.

Gimeno, J. (2004). Competition within and between networks: The contingent effect of competitive embeddedness on alliance formation. *Academy of Management Journal, 47*(6), 820–842.

Granovetter, M. (1985). Economic-action and social-structure – The problem of embeddedness. *American Journal of Sociology, 91*(3), 481–510.

Gulati, R. (1995a). Does familiarity breed trust – The implications of repeated ties for contractual choice in alliances. *Academy of Management Journal, 38*(1), 85–112.

Gulati, R. (1995b). Social structure and alliance formation patterns: A longitudinal analysis. *Administrative Science Quarterly, 40*(4), 619–652.

Gulati, R. (1998). Alliances and networks. *Strategic Management Journal, 19*(4), 293–317.

Gulati, R. (1999). Network location and learning: The influence of network resources and firm capabilities on alliance formation. *Strategic Management Journal, 20*(5), 397–420.

Gulati, R., Dialdin, D., & Wang, L. (2002) Organizational Networks. In: J. A. C. Baum (Ed.), *The Blackwell Companion to Organizational Studies* (pp. 281–303). Malden, MA: Basil Blackwell.

Gulati, R., & Gargiulo, M. (1999). Where do interorganizational networks come from? *American Journal of Sociology, 104*(5), 1439–1493.

Gulati, R., & Sytch, M. (2007). Dependence asymmetry and joint dependence in interorganizational relationships: Effects of embeddedness on a manufacturer's performance in procurement relationships. *Administrative Science Quarterly, 52*(1), 32–69.

Gulati, R., & Westphal, J. D. (1999). Cooperative or controlling? The effects of CEO-board relations and the content of interlocks on the formation of joint ventures. *Administrative Science Quarterly, 44*(3), 473–506.

Guler, I., Guillen, M. F., & MacPherson, J. M. (2002). Global competition, institutions, and the diffusion of organizational practices: The international spread of ISO 9000 quality certificates. *Administrative Science Quarterly, 47*(2), 207–232.

Hagedoorn, J. (1995). A note on international market leaders and networks of strategic technology partnering. *Strategic Management Journal, 16*(3), 241–250.

Hallen, B. L. (2009). The causes and consequences of the initial network positions of new organizations: From whom do entrepreneurs receive investments? *Administrative Science Quarterly, 53*(4), 685–718.

Haunschild, P. R. (1993). Interorganizational imitation – The impact of interlocks on corporate acquisition activity. *Administrative Science Quarterly, 38*(4), 564–592.

Haunschild, P. R., & Beckman, C. M. (1998). When do interlocks matter?: Alternate sources of information and interlock influence. *Administrative Science Quarterly, 43*(4), 815–844.

Haunschild, P. R., & Miner, A. S. (1997). Modes of interorganizational imitation: The effects of outcome salience and uncertainty. *Administrative Science Quarterly, 42*(3), 472–500.

Human, S. E., & Provan, K. G. (2000). Legitimacy building in the evolution of small-firm multilateral networks: A comparative study of success and demise. *Administrative Science Quarterly, 45*(2), 327–365.

Ingram, P., & Baum, J. A. C. (1997). Chain affiliation and the failure of Manhattan hotels, 1898–1980. *Administrative Science Quarterly, 41*(4), 629–658.

Ingram, P., & Roberts, P. W. (2000). Friendships among competitors in the Sydney hotel industry. *American Journal of Sociology, 106*(2), 387–423.

Jarillo, J. C. (1988). On strategic networks. *Strategic Management Journal, 9*(1), 31–41.

Keister, L. A. (2001). Exchange structures in transition: Lending and trade relations in Chinese business groups. *American Sociological Review, 66*(3), 336–360.

Kono, C., Friedland, R., & Palmer, D. (1998). Lost in space: The geography of corporate interlocking directorates. *American Journal of Sociology, 103*(4), 863–911.

Koza, M. P., & Lewin, A. Y. (1998). The co-evolution of strategic alliances. *Organization Science, 9*(3), 255–264.

Kraatz, M. S. (1998). Learning by association? Interorganizational networks and adaptation to environmental change. *Academy of Management Journal, 41*(6), 621–643.

Laumann, E. O., Marsden, P. V., & Galaskewicz, J. (1977). Community influence structures: A replication and extension of a network approach. *American Journal of Sociology, 83*(3), 594–631.

Lee, C., Lee, K., & Pennings, J. M. (2001). Internal capabilities, external networks, and performance: A study on technology-based ventures. *Strategic Management Journal, 22*(6-7), 615–640.

Levine, J. H. (1972). The Sphere of Influence. *American Sociological Review, 37*(1), 14–27.

Lincoln, J. R., Gerlach, M. L., & Ahmadjian, C. L. (1996). Keiretsu networks and corporate performance in Japan. *American Sociological Review, 61*(1), 67–88.

Lomi, A., & Pattison, P. (2006). Manufacturing relations: An empirical study of the organization of production across multiple networks. *Organization Science, 17*(3), 313–332.

Marquis, C. (2003). The pressure of the past: Network imprinting in intercorporate communities. *Administrative Science Quarterly, 48*(4), 655–689.

Mills, C. W. (1956). *Power elite*. Ann Arbor, MI: Oxford Press.

Miner, A. S., Amburgey, T. L., & Stearns, T. M. (1990). Interorganizational linkages and population-dynamics – Buffering and transformational shields. *Administrative Science Quarterly, 35*(4), 689–713.

Mintz, B., & Schwartz, M. (1981). Interlocking directorates and interest group formation. *American Sociological Review, 46*(6), 851–869.

Mizruchi, M. S. (1982). *The American corporate network: 1904–1974*. Beverly Hills, CA: Sage.

Mizruchi, M. S. (1989). Similarity of political-behavior among large American corporations. *American Journal of Sociology, 95*(2), 401–424.

Mizruchi, M. S. (1996). What do interlocks do? An analysis, critique, and assessment of research on interlocking directorates. *Annual Review of Sociology, 22*, 271–298.

Mizruchi, M. S., & Galaskiewicz, J. (1993). Networks of interorganizational relations. *Sociological Methods and Research, 22*, 46–70.

Mizruchi, M. S., & Stearns, L. B. (1994). A longitudinal-study of borrowing by large American corporations. *Administrative Science Quarterly, 39*(1), 118–140.

Neuman, E. J., Davis, G. F., & Mizruchi, M. S. (2008). Industry consolidation and network evolution in U.S. global banking, 1986–2004. *Advances in Strategic Management, 25*, 211–245.

Oliver, C. (1990). Determinants of interorganizational relationships – Integration and future-directions. *Academy of Management Review, 15*(2), 241–265.

Owen-Smith, J., & Powell, W. W. (2003). The expanding role of university patenting in the life sciences: assessing the importance of experience and connectivity. *Research Policy, 32*(9), 1695–1711.

Palmer, D. (1983). Broken ties – Interlocking directorates and intercorporate coordination. *Administrative Science Quarterly, 28*(1), 40–55.

Palmer, D., Barber, B. M., Zhou, X. G., & Soysal, Y. (1995). The friendly and predatory acquisition of large U.S corporations in the 1960s – The other contested terrain. *American Sociological Review, 60*(4), 469–499.

Palmer, D., Jennings, P. D., & Zhou, X. (1993). Late adoption of the multidivisional form by large U.S. corporations: A further exploration of the institutional, political, and economic accounts. *Administrative Science Quarterly, 38*(1), 100–131.

Palmer, D., Singh, J. V., & Friedland, R. (1986). The ties that bind – Organizational and class bases of stability in a corporate interlock network. *American Sociological Review, 51*(6), 781–796.

Parkhe, A. (1993). Strategic alliance structuring – A game-theoretic and transaction cost examination of interfirm cooperation. *Academy of Management Journal, 36*(4), 794–829.

Pfeffer, J. (1972). Size and composition of corporate boards. *Administrative Science Quarterly, 17*(2), 218–228.

Pfeffer, J., & Nowak, P. (1976). Joint ventures and interorganizational interdependence. *Administrative Science Quarterly, 21*(3), 398–418.

Pfeffer, J., & Salancik, G. R. (1978). *The external control of organizations: A resource dependence perspective.* New York: Harper and Row.

Podolny, J. M. (1993). A status-based model of market competition. *American Journal of Sociology, 98,* 829–872.

Podolny, J. M. (1994). Market uncertainty and the social character of economic exchange. *Administrative Science Quarterly, 39*(3), 458–483.

Podolny, J. M., & Page, K. L. (1998). Network forms of organization. *Annual Review of Sociology, 24,* 57–76.

Podolny, J. M., Stuart, T. E., & Hannan, M. T. (1996). Networks, knowledge, and niches: Competition in the worldwide semiconductor industry, 1984–1991. *American Journal of Sociology, 102*(3), 659–689.

Powell, W. W., Koput, K. W., & SmithDoerr, L. (1996). Interorganizational collaboration and the locus of innovation: Networks of learning in biotechnology. *Administrative Science Quarterly, 41*(1), 116–145.

Powell, W. W., White, D. R., Koput, W., & Owen-Smith, J. (2005). Network dynamics and field evolution: The growth of interorganizational collaboration in the life sciences. *American Journal of Sociology, 110*(4), 1132–1205.

Provan, K. G., Fish, A., & Sydow, J. (2007). Interorganizational networks at the network level: A review of the empirical literature on whole networks. *Journal of Management, 33,* 479–516.

Rosenkopf, L., & Padula, G. (2008). Investigating the microstructure of network evolution: Alliance formation in the mobile communications industry. *Organization Science, 19*(5), 669–687.

Roy, W. G. (1983). Interlocking directorates and the corporate revolution. *Social Science History, 7*(2), 143–164.

Schilling, M. A., & Phelps, C. C. (2007). Interfirm collaboration networks: The impact of large-scale network structure on firm innovation. *Management Science, 53*(7), 1113–1126.

Schoonhoven, C. B., Beckman, C. M., & Rottner, R. (2010). *Alliance portfolio emergence and its consequences in new organizations.* Working Paper. The Paul Merage School of Business, Irvine, CA.

Shipilov, A. V., & Li, S. X. (2008). Can you have your cake and eat it too? Structural holes' Influence on status accumulation and market performance in collaborative networks. *Administrative Science Quarterly, 53,* 73–108.

Siegel, J. (2007). Contingent political capital and international alliances: Evidence from South Korea. *Administrative Science Quarterly, 52*(4), 621–666.

Singh, J., & Fleming, L. (2010). *Lone inventors as sources of breakthroughs: Myth or reality?* *Management Science, 56*(1), 41–56.

Smith, H. L., Dickson, K., & Smith, S. L. (1991). There are 2 sides to every story – Innovation and collaboration within networks of large and small firms. *Research Policy, 20*(5), 457–468.

Soda, G., Usai, A., & Zaheer, A. (2004). Network memory: The influence of past and current networks on performance. *Academy of Management Journal, 47*(6), 893–906.

Sorenson, O., & Stuart, T. E. (2001). Syndication networks and the spatial distribution of venture capital investments. *American Journal of Sociology, 106*(6), 1546–1588.

Sorenson, O., & Stuart, T. E. (2008). Bringing the context back in: Settings and the search for syndicate partners in venture capital investment networks. *Administrative Science Quarterly, 53*(2), 266–294.

Starkey, K., Barnatt, C., & Tempest, S. (2000). Beyond networks and hierarchies: Latent organizations in the U.K. television industry. *Organization Science, 11*(3), 299–305.

Stearns, L. B., & Mizruchi, M. S. (1986). Broken-ties reconstitution and the functions of interorganizational interlocks – A reexamination. *Administrative Science Quarterly, 31*(4), 522–538.

Strang, D., & Soule, S. A. (1998). Diffusion in organizations and social movements: From hybrid corn to poison pills. *Annual Review of Sociology, 24*(4), 265–290.

Stuart, T. E. (1998). Network positions and propensities to collaborate: An investigation of strategic alliance formation in a high-technology industry. *Administrative Science Quarterly, 43*(3), 668–698.

Stuart, T. E. (2007). The formation of inter-organizational networks. In: J. Rauch (Ed.), *The missing links: Formation and decay of economic networks.* Russell Sage Foundation.

Stuart, T. E., & Yim, S. (2008). *Board interlocks and the propensity to be targeted in private equity transactions.* Working Paper. Series, No. 14189, NBER.

Stuart, T. E., Hoang, H., & Hybels, R. C. (1999). Interorganizational endorsements and the performance of entrepreneurial ventures. *Administrative Science Quarterly, 44*(2), 315–349.

Stuart, T. E., Ozdemir, S. Z., & Ding, W. W. (2007). Vertical alliance networks: The case of university-biotechnology-pharmaceutical alliance chains. *Research Policy, 36*(4), 477–498.

Sullivan, B. N., Haunschild, P. R., & Page, K. (2007). Organizations non gratae? The impact of unethical corporate acts on interorganizational networks. *Organization Science, 18*(1), 55–70.

Useem, M. (1979). Social-organization of the American-business elite and participation of corporation directors in the governance of American institutions. *American Sociological Review, 44*(4), 553–572.

Uzzi, B. (1996). The sources and consequences of embeddedness for the economic performance of organizations: The network effect. *American Sociological Review, 61*(4), 674–698.

Uzzi, B. (1997). Social structure and competition in interfirm networks: The paradox of embeddedness. *Administrative Science Quarterly, 42*(1), 35–67.

Uzzi, B. (1999). Embeddedness in the making of financial capital: How social relations and networks benefit firms seeking financing. *American Sociological Review, 64*(4), 481–505.

Uzzi, B., & Lancaster, R. (2004). Embeddedness and price formation in the corporate law market. *American Sociological Review, 69*(3), 319–344.

Wade, J., O'Reilly, C. A., & Chandratat, I. (1990). Golden parachutes – CEOs and the exercise of social-influence. *Administrative Science Quarterly, 35*(4), 587–603.

Walker, G., Kogut, B., & Shan, W. J. (1997). Social capital, structural holes and the formation of an industry network. *Organization Science, 8*(2), 109–125.

Westphal, J. D., Seidel, M. D. L., & Stewart, K. J. (2001). Second-order imitation: Uncovering latent effects of board network ties. *Administrative Science Quarterly, 46*(4), 717–747.

Westphal, J. D., & Stern, I. (2006). The other pathway to the boardroom: Interpersonal influence behavior as a substitute for elite credentials and majority status in obtaining board appointments. *Administrative Science Quarterly, 51*(2), 169–204.

Westphal, J. D., & Zajac, E. J. (1997). *Defections from the inner circle: Social exchange, reciprocity, and the diffusion of board independence in U.S. corporations.* Administrative.

Windolf, P. (2002). *Corporate networks in Europe and the United States.* Oxford: Oxford University Press.

Zaheer, A., & Bell, G. G. (2005). Benefiting from network position: Firm capabilities, structural holes, and performance. *Strategic Management Journal, 26*(9), 809–825.

Zajac, E. J. (1988). Interlocking directorates as an interorganizational strategy – A test of critical assumptions. *Academy of Management Journal, 31*(2), 428–438.

Zajac, E. J., & Westphal, J. D. (1995). Accounting for the explanations of CEO compensation – Substance and symbolism. *Administrative Science Quarterly, 40*(2), 283–308.

Zajac, E. J., & Westphal, J. D. (1996). Director reputation, CEO-board power, and the dynamics of board interlocks. *Administrative Science Quarterly, 41*(3), 507–529.

Zeitlin, M. (1974). Corporate ownership and control: The large corporation and the capitalist class. *American Journal of Sociology, 79*(5), 1073–1119.

CHAPTER 8

HEALTHCARE ORGANIZATIONS AND THE STANFORD SCHOOL OF ORGANIZATIONAL SOCIOLOGY

Mary L. Fennell and Ann Barry Flood

ABSTRACT

The Stanford School of Organizational Sociology has influenced the development and direction of healthcare organizations as a field of research in several very significant ways. This chapter will provide a focused review of the major paradigms to develop from work at Stanford from 1970 to 2000, much of which involved the study of processes and structures within and surrounding healthcare organizations during this period. As a subarea of organizational theory and health services research, healthcare organizations embrace both theory-based research and applied research, and they borrow concepts, theories, and methods from medical sociology, organizational theory, healthcare administration and management, and (to a more limited extent) health economics and decision theory. The bulk of this chapter will focus on four major themes or paradigms from research on healthcare organizations that grew from work by faculty and students within the Stanford School of Organizational Sociology: Health Care Outcomes, Internal Organizational Dynamics, Organizations and Their Environments, and Organizational Systems of Care and Populations of Care Providers.

Stanford's Organization Theory Renaissance, 1970–2000
Research in the Sociology of Organizations, Volume 28, 145–169
Copyright © 2010 by Emerald Group Publishing Limited
All rights of reproduction in any form reserved
ISSN: 0733-558X/doi:10.1108/S0733-558X(2010)0000028012

Following our examination of these four paradigms, we will consider their
implications for current and future debates in health services research and
healthcare policy.

INTRODUCTION

The field of research known as "healthcare organization theory" developed
fairly recently, even given the context of its being embedded in the young
discipline of health services research. For example, although early attempts
to evaluate performance of hospitals (cf. Georgopoulos & Mann, 1962;
Roemer & Friedman, 1971) and healthcare clinics (cf. Freidson, 1975) began
in the 1960s and 1970s, they were usually case studies using qualitative
approaches and surveys. Computerized records helped revolutionize the field,
permitting both the development of detailed and sophisticated measures of
patient care and comparisons across healthcare organizations (HCOs). These
developments have helped propel this field into a recognized area for study
with important policy implications (cf. the Robert Wood Johnson Foundation's Health Care Financing and Organization program, and the Agency for
Healthcare Research and Quality's outcomes research efforts).

Those who do research on HCOs typically describe this area as the study
of the organizations involved in healthcare delivery from the perspective
of organizational theory. Beyond this rather simplistic insider definition,
however, many health policy analysts and others in related areas of public
health or health services research – and even most informed consumers – do
not recognize HCOs as a field of inquiry. These unresolved definitional
challenges make it difficult to offer a clear statement of what is inside the
gates of this field and what stands outside.

Most would agree with our claim that the study of HCOs sits within the
larger field of *health services research*, given the central importance of HCOs
in delivering care at all levels of the healthcare system and across stages of
the care continuum. Health services research is itself a specialized area built
from borrowed research traditions in health economics, medical sociology,
epidemiology, health policy, and public health disciplines.

As a subarea of organizational theory *and* health services research,
HCO constitutes something of a "hybrid cross-over" (borrowing terminology from the US auto industry). It embraces both theory-based research and
applied research, and it borrows concepts, theories and methods from
medical sociology, organizational theory, healthcare administration and

management, and (to a more limited extent) health economics and decision theory.

The interdisciplinarity of those who study HCOs is both a boon (i.e., it enhances its impact and deepens the interest in studying organizational influences across the various disciplines) and a barrier to its being recognized as a defined subarea. For example, while professional associations from several disciplines address organizational issues in healthcare to various extents (see American Sociological Association, Academy of Management, and AcademyHealth), the Healthcare Organization Research Association (HORA) – an organization founded in 1999 – is the most directly focused on the subarea itself.

Perhaps the two most influential volumes to foster recognition of the field of HCOs and further its development are the edited collections led by Stephen Mick: *Innovations in Health Care Delivery* (Mick & Associates, 1990) and *Advances in Health Care Organization Theory* (Mick & Wyttenbach, 2003a, 2003b). The subtitle of the first Mick volume, "Insights *for* Organization Theory" (emphasis added), illustrates the growing recognition that the study of HCOs offers theoretical and methodological advances in its own right that should inform the larger field.

The authors' intent in the first volume was not to *define* the field of research on HCOs but rather to trace how studies of HCOs can change our more general theoretical notions of organizational change and environmental influence "... to advance the field of organizational theory" (Mick, 1990, p. 1). More specifically, the overall aim of this volume was "... to present diverse views on what the turmoil in the healthcare environment of the 1980s implied for organizational theory" (Mick, 1990, p. xi). Thus, the study of the unusual environmental changes occurring in healthcare in the 1980s and their impact on HCOs provided a very special category of exemplar cases that led to more general changes and developments in the way we think about organizations and organizational change – most notably in the development and refinement of institutional theory.

Mick and Wyttenbach's (2003a) later book, "Advances in Health Care Organization Theory" promulgated a wider view and greater legitimacy of *healthcare organization theory* as a field. The book enumerates large-scale environmental shifts in the healthcare field during the 1990s such as increased market and political uncertainty, a greater cost consciousness in delivering care, continuing technological innovation, rapid organizational adaptation and change to political and market-based influences, and workforce turbulence.

The enormity of those changes touched every sector linked to healthcare as well as HCOs per se and swept away all previous "normative" assumptions about how the US healthcare system does or should operate. As the editors noted: "The convergence of thinking in a field of inquiry, of which the study of HCOs is but one example, is influenced by the problems and issues in a historically grounded period of time" (Mick & Wyttenbach, 2003b, p. 13). Hence this second volume distinctly implies that a field of inquiry can become legitimated (and more prominently recognized) due to unique historical events or trends of unprecedented importance.

These two Mick volumes include chapters written by Stanford organizational sociologists and Stanford-trained organizational sociologists. For example, see chapters by Scott and Backman (1990), Alexander and D'Aunno (1990), and Hurley and Fennell (1990) in the first volume and Scott (2003), Alexander and D'Aunno (2003), and Shortell and Rundall (2003) in the second volume. Although significant chapters in their own right, the overarching contribution of the Mick volumes has been to focus attention on HCOs and to gradually define the nature of this field. Specifically, Mick and colleagues provided overviews of the dominant themes within the study of HCOs at two points in time, and it is within many of those dominant themes that Stanford scholars have made important contributions.

More generally, the Stanford School of Organizational Sociology has significantly influenced the development and direction of HCOs as a field of research in several ways. This chapter provides a focused review of the major paradigms that developed from work at Stanford from 1970 to 2000, much of which involved the study of processes and structures within and surrounding HCOs during this period. Much of that early work was an attempt to apply organizational theory to interesting problems and issues that were of distinct importance within care delivery organizations.

As argued by Mick and others, attempts to apply current theory to practical problems in healthcare threw into the spotlight the ways in which those theories were limited in their application to service organizations, especially in healthcare. As a consequence, major organizational theories were enhanced during the 1970s and 1980s by studying HCOs. This redirection was followed in the late 1990s and early 2000s by increasing interest in the major changes taking place in the environments of HCOs, as chronicled by Mick and Wyttenbach and others, and in a shift in focus from intra- to interorganizational dynamics, to more meso and macro levels of analysis and to systems of care with multiple levels of governance, structures, and markets.

The bulk of this chapter will focus on four major themes or paradigms from research on HCOs that grew from work by faculty and students within the Stanford School of Organizational Sociology. We will explore these themes as they developed in a somewhat sequenced fashion through the 1970–2000 period. Our review will be selective, rather than comprehensive and will connect work at Stanford to the work of other influential scholars in the study of HCOs. Please note: although this review emphasizes the impact of work by Stanford scholars, we do not intend to argue that the field of HCO research was solely the result of work by the Stanford group. Far from it! In fact, part of what has distinguished this school of thought has been its emphasis on collaboration across disciplines, and with various scholars worldwide, rather than its mainstream perspectives.

In the following sections, we discuss four broad-based paradigms relevant to HCO theory, to which the Stanford School of Organizational Sociology contributed heavily: (1) Early work: internal dynamics and organizational performance; (2) Internal organizational dynamics: modeling work and performance; (3) organizations and their environments; and (4) breaking down old boundaries: organizational systems of care and multiple levels of influence. Following our examination of these four paradigms, we consider their implications for current and future debates in health services research and healthcare policy.

EARLY WORK: INTERNAL DYNAMICS AND ORGANIZATIONAL PERFORMANCE

Using an organization level of analysis, the Stanford group's early work attempted to examine and explain variation in HCO performance based on care outcomes. This work focused on identifying the within-organization structures and care delivery processes that might influence the likelihood of good outcomes.

Work at Stanford was linked to two nation-wide studies of care outcomes. The first was the National Halothane Study, funded by the National Academy of Sciences (NAS), to investigate suspicions that the anesthetic halothane caused incidental liver damage resulting in serious morbidity and death. This study pioneered using electronic records of surgical outcomes to investigate quality of care in hospitals and its results had two important implications for health services research: (1) it basically cleared halothane of the suspicion and (2) it found evidence (based on adjusted death rates) of major variation in the quality of surgical care at US hospitals (Moses & Mosteller, 1968).

Following the publication of these results, the NAS decided it was more prudent to use the remaining money from the Halothane Study to fund the "Institutional Differences Study" to follow-up on the second implication: whether quality of care truly varied across hospitals. The alternative explanation most providers offered was that some hospitals only appeared to have higher death rates than expected because the Halothane Study inadequately accounted for differences in the types of patients being treated at each hospital or the difficulty of the work (e.g., type of surgery).

In 1971, the NAS selected Stanford's Center for Health Care Research to spearhead the Institutional Differences Study (IDS), and its principal investigators were W. Richard Scott (organizational sociology), William Forrest, Jr. (anesthesiology), and Byron W. Brown, Jr. (biostatistics) along with principal research scientists: Ann Barry Flood (organizational sociology) and Wayne Ewy (biostatistics). Subsequent related work to examine HCO structure and performance was funded by the National Center for Health Services Research and Technology Assessment (the federal precursor to the current Agency for Healthcare Research and Quality, Department of Health and Human Services (DHHS)).

The IDS produced historic data about the impact of hospital characteristics on surgical outcomes and hospital length of stay and was the first to examine quality of care in a large number of hospitals based on risk-adjusted outcome measures. [This work is summarized in Flood & Scott (1987).] This study drew upon models developed by the structural comparative school within organizational theory, professional models of work, and models to assess quality of care in HCOs. The latter were heavily influenced by theoretical models being developed by Avis Donabedian (1980) to help understand the relationships between healthcare structure, processes carried out in the performance of work, and the outcomes of patients. Work at RAND led by Robert Brook (Brook, 1973; Brook et al., 1977; Brook & Lohr, 1985) was also instrumental in helping the Stanford group tease out how to use outcomes following surgery to measure *quality* of care, when outcomes were also influenced by patient health prior to surgery as well as the type and difficulty of the surgery being performed. Statisticians were called upon to develop new models of risk adjustment, based on the emerging computer technology with the capacity to process large databases and the nascent electronic medical record summaries being promoted by the Commission of Professional and Hospital Activities of Ann Arbor.

The models that evolved to link HCO structures, work, and performance led the Stanford group to focus on both the major professional groups involved in surgical care (nurses, surgeons, and anesthesiologists) and the settings and organizational contexts for their work and workflow. The latter included a focus on key subunits where the technical work was performed such as the various postsurgical wards where surgical patients were typically grouped for care, the Operating Room (OR) suite, the recovery room, and intensive care units. The larger organizational context included factors such as teaching; size and complexity of the hospital; how the medical staff were organized to conduct peer review, recruit, and oversee credentials; how the hospital and nursing administration created policies about transfer of responsibility across shifts and in emergencies; and how and when surgeons could make demands on hospital resource use.

There were several important findings from this work: Hospitals did appear to vary significantly on the *quality* of care their patients received – which did not "disappear" when even the most stringent measures and details about difficulty of the surgery and patient factors were taken into account. Medical staff organization – including how stringently and systematically senior physicians evaluated new members and reviewed their quality systematically – was strongly associated with better care. Hospital context and major organizational features also mattered. This evidence largely supported organizational theories about work in complex organizations with embedded professional groups.

The models tested also led to some surprising results that influenced how organizational theorists conceptualized HCOs. For example, Schoonhoven, Scott, Flood, and Forrest (1980) work to develop and characterize the difficulty of the surgical mix in a unit (by assessing the relative complexity and uncertainty of individual surgical procedures) helped uncover several important facts. Nurses (rating postsurgical care) and surgeons (rating the procedure itself) agreed remarkably closely about which procedures were more difficult to care for. The ranking of difficulty of a given procedure mattered little whether raters were asked about the complexity of the steps or the uncertainty of what would happen – that is, difficult work is "difficult" irrespective of why. And, when the ratings were applied to the mix of procedures in a given hospital to rank the overall difficulty of surgeries, we noted that hospitals – regardless of whether they were large academic centers or small community hospitals – mostly treated rather routine cases. And even more interestingly, when nurses were asked to rate what made their work difficult, they did not talk about the patients or the type of surgery, rather they named the complexity of the numbers and types of surgeons they had to deal with and their unique requests for "the proper way" to care for their patients (Comstock & Scott, 1977).

Another surprise was the unwillingness of nurses or surgeons to describe power and influence over hospital policies as potentially shared by different groups, all of whom were influential (or none were). Instead, they used zero-sum terms to describe power, for example if doctors were very powerful then nurses could not be. Professional power was also different than expected in two ways: Counter to our hypothesis that hospitals that had very explicit, definite policies governing nurses' work would have poorer care, we found that they were the highest quality hospitals. Investigating this finding post hoc, we found that nurses did not find that explicit policies "threatened" their professionalism; instead, they helped people to know what their responsibilities were and how to manage work better especially in emergencies. The other "surprise" (well, a surprise to the physicians on the team) was that hospital-related factors were more influential in explaining variations in quality than were surgeon characteristics, such as their experience and training.

Another finding that evolved from IDS was in follow-up to work by Luft, Bunker, and Enthoven (1979). Working with another large database of surgical patients, Luft and colleagues found evidence that the volume of cases of a particular type treated at the hospital predicted better-than-expected outcomes. They argued that their findings suggest that hospital care would be improved by concentrating patients into a given regional hospital, based on treatments needed.

Using the rich database on patient health and surgery and outcomes available from the IDS studies, the Stanford group examined whether volume of patients was associated with better care and, if so, whether the volume was really associated with the surgical team or with the hospital irrespective of surgeon volume (Flood, Scott, & Ewy, 1984a, 1984b). They found evidence that the volume that was most predictive of better outcomes than expected was associated with the hospital, not with individual surgeons within the hospital. The Stanford group also examined whether *overall* volume of surgical cases (i.e., not specific to the type of surgery) or other associated factors such as overall size of hospital and teaching status would make the finding disappear – but they did not. They argued that the evidence was that "practice makes perfect" and a whole series of factors associated with hospital volume – from more experience in postsurgical and intensive care as well as more opportunities to build effective work processes – were operating. Luft then countered with a study that asserted we had it backwards – it was just that patients went to better hospitals and so the volume increased as a result, but found evidence to suggest that both factors existed. This debate has continued throughout the subsequent decades, with numerous studies finding the same basic relationship but the explanation is still elusive. (See Luft, Garnick, Mark, & McPhee, 1990 for a review of all the initial work in this area.)

In summary, the IDS studies made significant advances in performance measures and added to the understanding of how well these organizational models served to explain and elucidate HCOs. However, these designs were built on the organizational theories and specifically the worldviews of HCOs of the 1960s and 1970s – which were decidedly internally focused. (See Scott, 2004 for a review.) With hindsight, they curiously omitted noticing the complex interorganizational networks and the organizational environments that constrained and motivated how HCOs evolved and how well they performed. We turn next to the Stanford School's evolving contributions in these areas.

INTERNAL ORGANIZATIONAL DYNAMICS: MODELING WORK AND PERFORMANCE

First, we briefly outline the work expanding theories about work and dynamics within the HCO. The Stanford IDS project, with its focus on hospitals and hospital performance, provided a basis for expanding theories about internal organizational dynamics. By exploring their ability (and inability) to explain healthcare organizational performance, theoretical refinements could be identified and explored. Hospitals offered a rich testing ground by being complex, very hierarchical organizations with multiple goals; by having a multitude of ownership types and connections to teaching and research centers; and by needing to integrate work across multiple professional groups in which the most powerful group (physicians) were seldom on-site, were not employees, and indeed usually had competing loyalties at other hospitals and HCOs.

Of particular importance was further refinement of the professional model of work based on Freidson's (1970a, 1970b, 1975) work on professional control and Scott's (1982) three tiers of hierarchical control: autonomous, heteronomous, and conjoint. IDS's work to characterize the "difficulty" of tasks helped spawn some refinements of the assumptions behind contingency theory (Schoonhoven, 1981). Another key area of early work influenced by the IDS project studied the influence of internal HCO structure and processes on professional work, organizational culture, and organizational performance. Finally, a general model of performance evaluation within organizations developed at Stanford in the early 1970s (Dornbusch & Scott, 1975) examined the importance of evaluation processes in the work setting on job satisfaction and performance, particularly when there was a mismatch between employee expectations about fair dimensions of task performance to be evaluated and their perceptions about how they were actually evaluated. This model is relevant to performance evaluation methods within organizations where professionals work both as autonomous individuals, in collaborative teams, and in cross-cutting matrices of work teams, oftentimes with continually changing membership.

Professional Model Refinements

Scott (1982) expanded on the notion of hospitals as "dual hierarchies" in which medical staff were organized into a relatively flat hierarchy of departments and members where physician-leaders had a very constrained ability to control and evaluate professional work. This half of the dual hierarchy was based on professional models of control, mostly acting through committees to offer peer review of problem cases and credential review of new members. The second hierarchy consisted of all the other workers and departments at the hospital; it was much more differentiated and based on bureaucratic forms of control over work, that is, assignment of tasks and evaluation of work with strong ability to sanction infractions or poor performance, using differentiation and specialization to match workers to tasks, etc.

Scott's insight was to note that nurses had a separate hierarchy which was a hybrid between one that was based on professional norms and control and one that used bureaucratic controls and was a richly layered hierarchy based on units of care and shifts. This led the way toward examining the nuances of how professionals worked together as teams in the various units and on committees with oversight over clinical policies (such as control hospital-acquired infectious disease).

Fennell and Leicht (Fennell & Leicht, 1997; Leicht & Fennell, 2001), expounding on how professional work is organized, noted how technology and evolving arrangements have further transformed the settings for professionals. They argue that hierarchies in which professionals work are more likely to be flat (as technology eliminates the need for some middle layers) and employ temporary or subcontracted workers (which decreases the need for long-term commitments and benefits for employees and increases organizational flexibility to handle work fluctuations). Some changes are harder for HCOs to use (such as allowing workers to work offsite through virtual interactions). Others are more complex (such as attracting a stable workforce while facing a nursing shortage and reduced unionization and bargaining power for employees). Normative pressures to have a more diverse workforce have also influenced hiring and promotions in subtle ways, impacting HCOs in general and their professional workforce in particular. Of overriding importance, however, is the encroachment of professional managers/administrators over physician autonomy in the practice of medicine within HCOs, an example of the ascendance of the "managerial project" (Leicht & Fennell, 2001) within HCOs, and the decline of the medical half of the "dual hierarchy."

Technological Contingency Theory

Schoonhoven (1981) used the IDS study to examine the usefulness of contingency theory to examine organizational effectiveness in Operating Rooms. When the more traditional contingency hypotheses did not fit well, Schoonhoven reexamined them for the healthcare context and identified several problems, which she then addressed by formulating more precise contingency hypotheses. Tests of these revised hypotheses resulted in much stronger empirical support, suggesting that relationships between technology, structure, and organizational effectiveness are more complicated than Galbraith's (1973) original formulations assumed. Contingency theory needs to be revised, at least to capture its relationship to organizational effectiveness in HCOs, to take into account subtleties such as the interactive, nonmonotonic, and symmetrical interrelationships between structure and technology.

Internal Dynamics, Incentives, and Organizational Performance

Flood and colleagues (Flood, Bott, & Goodrick, 2000; Flood et al., 1998; Goodrick, Flood, & Fremont, 1998) examined how a large clinic with managed care and fee-for-service patients tried to change its incentives, evaluations, and structure to influence the overall cost of providing care to its patients. It was a detailed study of how changing professional control and norms can backfire in its impact on performance if not done well. It also builds on the Dornbusch and Scott (1975) general model of performance evaluation and the institutional theory concept of mimetic isomorphism

(DiMaggio & Powell, 1983) concerning why organizations imitate successful models.

Here is the tale of caution in brief: The clinic administration was worried about cost increases in their own managed care insurance, with pressures from local employers to keep premiums from escalating. To address this problem, they used a benchmarking procedure to identify a "well run" managed care clinic with lower costs and then succeeded in making a series of changes to bring their clinic in line with the benchmark and set standards to match their care.

Unfortunately, they made a series of errors, starting with the choice of benchmark. They assumed that their clinic (where doctors treated both fee-for-service and managed care patients) should be organized the same way and could use the same incentives as a clinic that had only managed care patients (the benchmark). They also failed to note that they were already treating their managed care patients with lower services than fee-for-service (they never compared their own populations to each other). If they had, they might have noticed that their strategy to encourage managed care patients to use branch clinics and family practice doctors explained most of their lower resource use.

Instead, the clinic administration decided that all doctors must "mend their ways" and learn to treat managed care patients at the benchmark level. To accomplish this change, the clinic introduced a dual financial structure, rewarding a doctor for treating fee-for-service patients with billable services but putting the same doctor on a "diet," that is, requiring a strict budget of acceptable average expenses for services provided to their managed care patients, beyond which the doctor would be financially penalized.

The clinic failed to appreciate how much chaos their financial incentive plan would cause. The doctors were upset, not only because it was a change per se with uncertain financial implications, but it meant a practically difficult and professionally untenable clinic-wide strategy to provide lower resources based on insurance (performing a "wallet biopsy" first). Heretofore, they had been proud of their clinic's "culture," that is, their doctors provided the "best care" while also practicing appropriate cost efficiencies regardless of insurance.

Meanwhile, the role of department leaders changed from policy-making and problem-solvers to doling out financial warnings and penalties. This power shift caused its own problems since the leaders had not been selected for their skills in dealing with such "problems"; some actually refused to carry out their responsibilities to "punish" some members for providing too many services to managed care patients.

ORGANIZATIONS AND THEIR
ENVIRONMENTS

The former world of the independent physician ministering to the medical needs of his patients under simple fee-for-service arrangements ... seems a distant dream. These arrangements, so stable for so long – (from the 1920s into the 1960s) – appeared largely impervious to change. One would be hard-pressed to find a comparably stable instance among other arenas of social activity during the first half of the twentieth century. It would be equally difficult to identify a large system that has changed so quickly. ... Highly institutionalized sectors, by definition, resist change, but when change occurs, they can become transformed rapidly.

– Scott (2003, pp. 23–24)

Indeed, Scott's description of the rapidity of change in the healthcare system from 1960 through the late 1990s could end with an exhortation to "Stand Back! Watch out for the flying debris from disintegrating ideologies and organizational arrangements!" The catalysts behind those enormous changes were often found within the resource and institutional environments facing HCOs during the latter part of that period.

In a somewhat parallel fashion, the 1980s and 1990s were an explosive period of growth in the development of theory and research about the environments of organizations. Incredible pressures to curtail growth of spending while increasing production and quality were building during these two decades within the US healthcare system. Critics frequently made comparisons to better controls and better access and less administrative waste in national healthcare systems in Europe. At the same time, the US system was pressured to lead in developing medical technology breakthroughs while being criticized for its spiraling healthcare costs and flat-of-the-curve care (i.e., care that offered no benefit for its increased costs). These latter concerns helped spawn calls to move away from predominately "academic" research about quality of care toward applied methods to assess performance and hold each organization more accountable for its performance – at least via public reporting. Similarly, work that today is called comparative effectiveness was initiated to better understand the real impact of new treatment technologies on care outcomes and costs.

The Stanford School of Organizational Sociology launched a number of theoretical developments relevant to the environments of HCOs. These included: (1) attempts to refine theories of resource dependence and the development of organizational dependency relationships between organizations (Pfeffer & Salancik, 1978; Zucker, 1986; Cook, 1976; Hannan & Freeman, 1977) and the building of networks of linkages across HCOs (Fennell & Warnecke, 1988; Powell, 1990; Scott, 1982); (2) the development of theories about how hierarchies across organizations help deal with uncertain markets (Ouchi, 1980; Williamson, 1975); and (3) major advances in institutional theory, to understand the forces and consequences of organizational responses to technical and/or institutional environments (Meyer & Rowan, 1977; Scott, 1983; DiMaggio & Powell, 1983; Fennell & Alexander, 1987; Zucker, 1977, 1987).

Resource dependency theory begins with a focal organization and its efforts to ensure survival in a changing, complex environment; thus, this theory is conceptualized at the organizational level of analysis. The basic premise of resource dependence is that no single organization can generate all the resources it needs for survival; instead, it is necessary to take action to ensure access to needed resources (Aldrich & Pfeffer, 1976). To control the environment by linking, the organization attempts to acquire a broader resource base by building linkages to other organizations. Within the healthcare arena of the 1980s and 1990s, a multitude of linking strategies emerged, including dyadic relationships like strategic alliances and voluntary affiliations, to more complex interorganizational links within confederations and consortia (Kaluzny, Morrissey, & McKinney, 1990; Zuckerman & D'Aunno, 1990).

The next contribution of the Stanford School to HCO theory was to expand the theory to accommodate complex interactions of HCOs through networks. This conceptual contribution opened new areas of inquiry about organizations and their environments and it also helped transform how administrators and policy-makers thought about HCOs. Since then, healthcare organizational theorists have used insights from resource dependency to examine networks of HCOs to study how treatment innovations diffuse within federally sponsored networks (Fennell & Warnecke, 1988; Kaluzny et al., 1990). More recently Shortell and Rundall (2003) proposed a set of hypotheses on the diffusion of clinical process innovations across networks of physician–organization partnerships. Network structures have also been linked to the examination of resource exchanges (Cook, 1976), of the development of trust in exchange relationships (Zucker, 1986; Cook & Whitmeyer, 1992), and between subunits of organizations (Flood et al., 1998). The contemporary turmoil in HCOs, such as the rapid realignments and dissolution of networks and the closure and turnover of HCOs, provides ripe opportunities to revisit and update these healthcare organizational theories.

The Stanford School had a particularly important impact on the development of institutional theory, building on Meyer and Scott's (1983) identification of two categories of environmental constraints: technical and institutional. Technical environments relate primarily to market structures and production concerns, but include demographic characteristics of local communities and technological concerns. These provide more direct, measurable feedback to the organization about how well it is performing. Institutional environments involve the social and political structures to which organizations must conform, including professional and public opinion, legal structures (Edelman & Suchman, 1997), ideologies and regulatory structures (Alexander & Scott, 1984; Fennell & Alexander, 1987; Cook, Shortell, Conrad, & Morrissey, 1983; Fennell & Campbell, 2007). Feedback from these environments may be explicit (such as being accredited) or normative (adopting practices of benchmark hospitals), but they are at best indirectly related to how well the organization is performing. Although both sets of constraints are important for HCOs, each category involves a variety of environmental influences and spawns differing responses to them. See Scott (1987) for a particularly helpful summary of institutional theory through the mid-1980s and Flood and Fennell (1995) for a review of organizational sociology's contributions to understanding how HCOs work.

Although market structures are a predominant factor in the technical environments of organizations, they are also linked to resource dependence notions of exchange relationships and market transactions. As such, the development of transaction cost economics (or transaction cost analysis [TCA]) in the mid-1970s and 1980s was singularly important for pulling together notions about contracts (voluntary transactions) and how organizational structures (hierarchies) act to govern various contracts. When the marketplace fails to provide the most efficient mode of exchange for goods or services, governance structures (organizations) arise to permit buyers to minimize the transaction costs associated with exchanges with suppliers (Williamson, 1975, 1986).

Transaction cost economics provide a useful framework for several aspects of healthcare delivery, such as the study of Medicaid case management of primary care (Hurley, 1986; Hurley, Freund, & Taylor, 1989), case management in the delivery of mental health services (Bassuk, 1986; Mechanic, 1986), and long-term care (Capitman, Haskins, & Bernstein, 1986). For example, Hurley and Fennell (1990) discussed case management as one such type of governance structure in healthcare that has arisen to combat the notoriously uncertain and failure-prone healthcare markets for third-party payers. Using Williamson's terminology, case management is a "buyer approach" that arises to help minimize transaction costs because the market per se does not work to contain the costs of certain suppliers.

Rarely are both technical and institutional constraints considered jointly in research on HCOs. Most of the earlier research in this tradition attempted to identify and measure a single environmental factor (or at most two) and traced the impact of change in that factor on change in HCOs. Complicating the situation, of course, is the fact that environmental factors in healthcare are themselves subject to change, particularly regulatory programs (Fennell & Campbell, 2007) and market conditions. Thus, the impact of one factor can change over time, and different factors can gain or lose influence over a relatively short period of time. For example, research by Wilke and Choi (1988) demonstrated that models to explain hospital acquisition by multihospital systems differed over a five-year period, underscoring the need for multiple models to capture the changing dynamics of the healthcare environment.

Alexander and D'Aunno (1990) provide an excellent discussion of such changing environmental dynamics, with particular attention to comparing and contrasting both technical and institutional environments. They convincingly argue that institutional theory has tended to focus on the easier cases: industries where one or the other set of pressures is predominant. It has not, however, adequately addressed the issue of change in organizational sectors where institutional and technical environments are either both strong (such as the healthcare sector) or both weak (such as in mental healthcare delivery). As a result, we do not understand well how they interact with each other. The authors illustrate this by tracing the corporatization of US healthcare and argue that the resultant transformation of institutional systems could have occurred as the result of two different scenarios: the entropy of institutional factors followed by the ascendance of technical demands, or the changing content of the belief systems embedded within institutional forces. Both scenarios are worth considering again with an eye toward advancing institutional theory in healthcare, given the magnitude of changes occurring in health policy and the reopening of the political window for healthcare reform in the US with the election of President Obama.

BREAKING DOWN OLD BOUNDARIES: ORGANIZATIONAL SYSTEMS OF CARE AND MULTIPLE LEVELS OF INFLUENCE

Following the explosion of theoretical developments in the 1990s related to organizational environments, we now find ourselves in a period of "reconstruction," that is, rebuilding both our understanding of micro-level care processes, of macro systems of HCOs, and multilevel models of organizations nested within multiple layers of environmental contexts. Alexander and D'Aunno's (1990) ideas concerning the entropy of previously held institutional beliefs within healthcare and their replacement by corporate-inspired norms of competition has provided a framework for understanding the remarkable shift in values from community service to the "bottom line." Non-profit HCOs now look remarkably like HCOs in the for-profit sector (Fennell & Alexander, 1993), and the vocabulary of HCOs has changed from a focus on systems to a focus on "industry" (Mick, 1990).

A number of other long-held distinctions have also eroded, for example, the separation of acute care delivery and chronic or long-term care into distinct organizational sectors; the distinction between primary care and specialty care; and the blurring of the separation between public health and traditional primary care (particularly in the age of pandemics and the possibility of bioterrorism). These eroded distinctions have not been fully replaced by alternate values or belief systems; instead they are areas in need of continued monitoring and analysis.

Although the conceptual direction of much of the HCO literature covered in this review has developed historically from a focus on the organization, to interorganizational linkages, to the macro level (environments and networks), it would be a mistake to assume that little of theoretical or empirical excitement is happening at all of these levels in healthcare today. Indeed, we began this review with a consideration of healthcare organizational performance, tracking early developments in conceptualizing and measuring patient-level outcomes and the impact of HCO structures and processes on those outcomes. Recent work on cancer care systems has developed a more finely focused analysis of the continuum of cancer care services, examining in detail the interfaces and transitions between each stage of the continuum (Zapka, Taplin, Solberg, & Manos, 2003; Zapka, 2008).

This kind of modeling and analysis provides a grounded approach to the design of cancer care delivery interventions, which increases the likelihood that such interventions will improve patient outcomes as well as patient satisfaction with care. In many ways, this type of work represents an important complement to current emphases on "patient centered care" (Sepucha, Fowler, & Mulley, 2004; Bergeson & Dean, 2006).

Interventions in care delivery, however, are not designed solely at the organizational level (e.g., improvements in care delivery also need to focus on transitions between providers). Nor is it possible to adequately understand why organizational-level changes succeed or fail without fully appreciating the multiple layers of organizational and environmental influences surrounding patient care. Instead, we need to turn our theoretical attention to evaluating complex intermediary impacts and designing interventions at multiple levels.

Multilevel interventions can be conceptualized as attempts to impose change within systems of patient care that involve multiple levels of influence and interactions between relevant variables. For example, changes may need to simultaneously consider effects and influences at the patient level, which is embedded in a patient-provider dyad (or series of dyads), that are in turn embedded in one or more HCOs, which are all influenced by macro levels of system context like the local market, community, multihospital system, networks of HCOs linked by cooperative joint ventures or temporary alignments, state or regional initiatives, and state or federal levels of reimbursement and regulation. No matter which aspect of the care continuum is targeted, the implementation and evaluation of treatment interventions need to be framed by a broader focus on the multiple levels of influences that can impede or facilitate the intended effect of interventions on patient outcomes, including pressures from the technical and institutional environments of all of the organizations involved.

There is a growing literature on multilevel modeling in the healthcare sector, particularly in assessments of quality improvement programs in chronic illness care (Cretin, Shortell, Keeler, 2004), community demonstration programs for AIDS care (Needle, Coyle, Normand, Lambert, & Cesari, 1998), smoking cessation (Duncan, Jones, & Moon, 1996), and innovations in the delivery of mental health services (Kimberly & Cook, 2008; Alexander et al., 2005). A few authors have even linked multilevel modeling statistical techniques (such as hierarchical linear modeling [HLM]) to discussions of performance accountability in healthcare (O'Connell & McCoach, 2004; Gordon & Heinrich, 2004). There are also several comprehensive "case studies" of specific instances of system-level transformations that examine federally sponsored programs to diffuse treatment innovations (Kaluzny & Warnecke, 2000; Fennell & Warnecke, 1988), and change over time in the healthcare delivery system (such as Scott, Ruef, Mendel, & Caronna's, 2000 study of the San Francisco Bay Area and Flood & colleagues', 1998, 2000 study of a large multibranch clinic in the Midwest).

Within the cancer literature, there are few models available that explicitly examine system-level interventions on patient outcomes using an HLM approach (with the notable exception of recent work on breast cancer screening by Zapka referenced above). Comparative data on compliance with guidelines for breast cancer care (such as data using linked Seer-Medicare Claims and data on provider linkages in National Cancer Institute research networks) has been used to estimate the effects of network linkage and type of treatment facility (e.g., ownership, teaching program, location) on the likelihood of receipt of guideline-compliant care (Laliberte, Fennell, & Papandonatos, 2005).

All of these studies placed particular emphasis on simultaneously considering multilevel impacts on patient-level care patterns and outcomes, such as the influence of contextual layers of change within HCO structures, in network connections between HCOs, and in clinical decision-making. In many ways, these researchers are following paths laid out earlier by Stanford scholars of HCOs who pioneered including multilayered perspectives, linking performance based on patient outcomes with organizational structures, and actively considering environmental pressures and influences on performance and structure.

IMPLICATIONS FOR CURRENT AND FUTURE DEBATES IN HEALTHCARE AND HEALTH SERVICES RESEARCH

This review of the Stanford legacy within the field of HCO research has primarily focused on contributions made to HCO theory and research. That body of work has also had some impact on the development of contemporary health policy and has been (and will be) part of the debate on future health policy issues as well. We close this chapter with a very brief review of some of these issues.

Translational research has frequently been presented as the combination of two distinct foci: (1) "the transfer of new understandings of mechanisms gained in the laboratory into the development of new methods for diagnosis, therapy, and prevention, and their first test in humans" (known as T1 research) and (2) "the translation of results from clinical studies into everyday clinical practice and health decision making" (known as T2 research) (Sung et al., 2003). The resources needed to successfully implement T1 research are typically found in many academic medical settings, where molecular biology, genetics, highly trained clinical scientists, well-equipped labs, and a supportive research infrastructure exist. T2 research, however, requires the evaluation of T1 findings for their application to *the real world* of healthcare delivery.

"Implementation sciences" are being identified to carry out T2 research and involve a wide range of disciplines and research methodologies, including clinical epidemiology and evidence synthesis, communication theory, behavioral science, public policy, finance, organizational theory, system redesign, informatics, and evaluation methods. However, we argue that an appreciation of the important translational work of T2 research is impossible without including the contributions of healthcare organizational theory. As reviewed above, the adoption and diffusion of treatment innovations occurs within the setting of HCOs, and those diffusion processes are best understood when framed by multilevel theories contextualized by organizational networks, technical and institutional environments. This area offers a rich and important opportunity for healthcare organizational theorists to make important contributions to theory, practice, and policy.

A second emerging policy issue that HCO theories can inform is the notion of "pay for performance" (P4P) applied to health services delivery. The core idea behind P4P is to link healthcare payments – not just to evidence that a service was delivered as is current practice, but to require evidence that certain levels of performance were achieved. For example, payment could be contingent on showing that the patient's health improved or more likely that the HCO on average achieved acceptable rates (or improved rates) of best practices in the delivery of care. As described by Kimberly and Minvielle (2003): "Payment weighted by quality represents the next logical phase in the evolution of how quality is taken into account in health." Further, the Institute of Medicine clearly signaled that payment policies need to be linked to quality improvement (Hurtado, Swift, & Corrigan, 2001). We argue that this essential linkage of payment and performance could not be imagined without the gains made in conceptualizing and measuring healthcare performance that began with the IDS in the mid-1970s, and its success will continue to benefit from further HCO research.

Finally, although major health policy reform is an elusive goal, no lasting reform of the healthcare system can occur without influencing HCOs and the delivery of care. Even reforms such as those being considered by the US Senate in 2009 to reform healthcare by altering tax law will impact HCOs and related institutions such as health insurance and employers as purchasers of healthcare insurance. Reformers may prefer to ignore the multilevel impact of their intended changes and may prefer to target politically more vulnerable targets than providers and HCOs. However, despite those who argue that the United States has no "healthcare system," its networks and linkages across organizations are strong, and HCOs are critical to any solution. For that reason, the future of healthcare organizational theory is vital to this policy discussion.

In summary, the Stanford legacy has made important contributions to healthcare organizational research and theory. This highly successful and rich effort needs to continue to evolve and grow by producing new ideas and new scholars who will in turn energize the field of HCOs.

REFERENCES

Aldrich, H. E., & Pfeffer, J. (1976). Environment of organizations. *Annual Review of Sociology*, 2, 79–105.

Alexander, J. A., & D'Aunno, T. A. (1990). Transformations of institutional environments: perspectives on the corporatization of U.S. Health Care. In: S. M. Stephen & Associates (Eds), *Innovations in health care delivery: Insights for organization theory* (pp. 53–85). San Francisco, CA: Jossey-Bass Publishers.

Alexander, J. A., & D'Aunno, T. A. (2003). Alternative perspectives on institutional and market relationships in the US health care sector. In: S. M. Stephen & E. W. Mindy (Eds), *Advances in health care organization theory* (pp. 45–78). San Francisco, CA: Jossey Bass.

Alexander, J. A., & Scott, W. R. (1984). The impact of regulation on hospital administrative structure: Toward an analytic framework. *Hospital and Health Services Administration*, 29(3), 71–85.

Alexander, J. A., Lichtenstein, R., Jinnett, K., Wells, R. R., Zazzali, J., & Liu, D. (2005). Cross-functional team processes and patient functional improvement. *Health Services Research*, 40(5), 1335–1355.

Bassuk, E. L. (1986). Concluding comment, in Special Issue of *New Directions in Mental Health Services*, 30, 95–98.

Bergeson, S. C., & Dean, J. D. (2006). A systems approach to patient-centered care. *The Journal of the American Medical Association*, 296(23).

Brook, R. H. (1973). *Quality of care assessment: A comparison of five methods of peer review*. HRA-74-3100. Washington, DC: Bureau of Health Services Research and Evaluation.

Brook, R. H., Davies-Avery, A., Greenfield, S., Harris, L. J., Lelah, T., Solomon, N. E., & Ware, J. E., Jr. (1977). Assessing the quality of care using outcome measures: An overview of the method. *Medical Care*, 15(Suppl. 9), 1.

Brook, R. H., & Lohr, K. N. (1985). Efficacy, effectiveness, variations, and quality: Boundary-crossing research. *Medical Care*, 23(5), 710–722.

Capitman, J. A., Haskins, B., & Bernstein, J. (1986). Case management approaches in coordinated community-oriented long-term care demonstrations. *The Gerontologist*, 26(4), 398–404.

Comstock, D. E., & Scott, W. R. (1977). Technology and the structure of subunits: Distinguishing individual and workgroup effects. *Administrative Science Quarterly*, 22(2), 177–202.

Cook, K. S. (1976). Exchange and power in networks of interorganizational networks. *Sociological Quarterly*, 18(Winter), 62–82.

Cook, K. S., Shortell, S. M., Conrad, D., & Morrissey, M. (1983). A theory of organizational response to regulation: The case of hospitals. *Academy of Management Review*, *8*(2), 193–205.

Cook, K. S., & Whitmeyer, J. M. (1992). Two approaches to social structure: exchange theory and network analysis. In: W. R. Scott (Ed.), *Annual Review of Sociology*, *18*, 109–127.

Cretin, S., Shortell, S. M., & Keeler, E. B. (2004). An evaluation of collaborative interventions to improve chronic illness care: Framework and study design. *Evaluation Review*, *28*(1).

DiMaggio, P. J., & Powell, W. W. (1983). The iron cage revisited: institutional isomorphism and collective rationality in organizational fields. *American Sociological Review*, *48*(2), 147–160.

Donabedian, A. (1980). Methods of deriving criteria for assessing the quality of medical care. *Medical Care Review*, *37*(7), 653–698.

Dornbusch, S. M., & Scott, W. R. (1975). *Evaluation and the exercise of authority*. San Francisco, CA: Jossey-Bass Publishers.

Duncan, C., Jones, K., & Moon, G. (1996). Health-related behaviour in context: A multilevel modeling approach. *Social Science in Medicine*, *42*, 817–830.

Edelman, L. B., & Suchman, M. C. (1997). The legal environments of organizations. *Annual Review of Sociology*, *23*, 479–515.

Fennell, M. L., & Alexander, J. A. (1987). Organizational boundary spanning in institutionalized environments. *Academy of Management Journal*, *30*(3), 456–476.

Fennell, M. L., & Alexander, J. A. (1993). Perspectives on organizational change in the US medical care sector. *Annual Review of Sociology*, *19*, 89–112.

Fennell, M. L., & Campbell, S. E. (2007). The regulatory environment and rural hospital long-term care strategies from 1997 to 2003. *The Journal of Rural Health*, *23*(1), 1–9.

Fennell, M. L., & Leicht, K. T. (1997). The changing organizational context of professional work. *Annual Review of Sociology*, *23*, 215–231.

Fennell, M. L., & Warnecke, R. B. (1988). *The diffusion of medical innovation: An applied network analysis*. Plenum Press.

Flood, A. B., Bott, D. M., & Goodrick, E. (2000). The promise and pitfalls of explicitly rewarding physicians based on patient insurance. *The Journal of Ambulatory Care Management*, *23*(1), 55–70.

Flood, A. B., & Fennell, M. L. (1995). Through the lenses of organizational sociology: The role of organizational theory and research in conceptualizing and examining our health care system. *Journal of Health and Social Behavior*, *36*, 154–169.

Flood, A. B., Fremont, A. M., Jin, K., Bott, D. M., Ding, J., & Parker, R. C., Jr. (1998). How do HMOs achieve their savings? The effectiveness of one organization's strategies. *Health Services Research*, *33*(1), 79–99.

Flood, A. B., & Scott, W. R. (1987). *Hospital structure and performance*. Baltimore, MD and London, England: The Johns Hopkins University Press.

Flood, A. B., Scott, W. R., & Ewy, W. (1984a). Does practice make perfect? I: The relation between hospital volume and outcomes for selected diagnostic categories. *Medical Care*, *22*(2), 98–114.

Flood, A. B., Scott, W. R., & Ewy, W. (1984b). Does practice make perfect? II: The relation between volume and outcomes and other hospital characteristics. *Medical Care*, *22*(2), 115–124.

Freidson, E. (1970a). *Professional dominance: The social structure of medical care*. New York: Atherton Press.

Freidson, E. (1970b). *Profession of medicine: A study of the sociology of applied knowledge.* New York: Dodd, Mead & Co.

Freidson, E. (1975). *Doctoring together: A study of professional social control.* New York: Elsevier Scientific Publishing.

Galbraith, J. K. (1973). *Designing complex organizations.* Addison Wesley.

Georgopoulos, B. S., & Mann, F. C. (1962). *The community general hospital.* New York: MacMillan.

Goodrick, E., Flood, A. B., & Fremont, A. M. (1998). Models of culture in physician group practices. In: H. Lopata (Ed.), *Current research on occupations and professions* (Vol. 10, pp. 135–156). Greenwich, CT: JAI Press Inc.

Gordon, R. A., & Heinrich, C. J. (2004). Modeling trajectories in social program outcomes for performance accountability. *American Journal of Evaluation, 25*(2), 161–189.

Hannan, M., & Freeman, J. (1977). The population ecology of organizations. *American Journal of Sociology, 82*(March), 95–115.

Hurley, R. E. (1986). Toward a behavioral model of the physician as case manager. *Social Science and Medicine, 23*(1).

Hurley, R. E., & Fennell, M. L. (1990). Managed care systems as governance structures: A transaction cost interpretation. In: S. S. Mick & Associates (Eds), *Innovations in health care delivery: Insights for organization theory* (pp. 241–268). San Francisco, CA: Jossey-Bass Publishers.

Hurley, R. E., Freund, D., & Taylor, D. (1989). Gatekeeping the emergency room: Impact of a medicaid primary care case management program. *Health Care Management Review, 14*(2), 63–71.

Hurtado, M. P., Swift, E. K., & Corrigan, J. M. (Eds). (2001). *Committee on the national quality report on health care delivery, board on health care services. Institute of Medicine.* Envisioning the National Health Care Quality Report. Washington, DC: National Academy Press.

Kaluzny, A. D., & Warnecke, R. B. (2000). *Managing a health care alliance: Improving community cancer care.* Beard Books.

Kaluzny, A. K., Morrissey, J. P., & McKinney, M. M. (1990). 'Emerging organizational networks: The case of the community clinical oncology program. In: S. S. Mick & Associates (Eds), *Innovations in health care delivery: Insights for organization theory.* San Francisco, CA: Jossey-Bass Publishers.

Kimberly, J., & Cook, J. M. (2008). Organizational measurement and the implementation of innovations in mental health services. *Administration Policy in Mental Health, 35,* 11–20.

Kimberly, J. R., & Minvielle, E. (2003). Quality as an organizational problem. In: S. S. Mick & M. E. Wyttenbach (Eds), *Advances in health care organization theory.* San Francisco, CA: Jossey Bass.

Laliberte, L., Fennell, M. L., & Papandonatos, G. (2005). The relationship of membership in research networks to compliance with treatment guidelines for early-stage breast cancer. *Medical Care, 43,* 471–479.

Leicht, K. T., & Fennell, M. L. (2001). *Professional work, a sociological approach.* Blackwell Publishers.

Luft, H. S., Bunker, J. P., & Enthoven, A. C. (1979). Should operations be regionalized: The empirical relation between surgical volume and mortality. *New England Journal of Medicine, 301*(25), 1364–1369.

Luft, H. S., Garnick, D. W., Mark, D. H., & McPhee, S. J. (1990). *Hospital volume, physician volume and patient outcomes: Assessing the evidence.* Ann Arbor, MI: Health Administration Press.

Mechanic, D. (1986). The concept of illness behaviour: Culture, situation and personal predisposition. *Psychological Medicine, 16*(1), 1–7.

Meyer, J. W., & Rowan, B. (1977). Institutionalized organizations: Formal structures as myth and ceremony. *American Journal of Sociology, 83*(2), 340–363.

Meyer, J. W., & Scott, W. R. (1983). *Organizational environments: Ritual and rationality.* Beverly Hills: Sage Publications.

Mick, S. S. (1990). Themes, issues, and research avenues. In: S. S. Mick & Associates (Eds), *Innovations in health care delivery: Insights for organization theory* (pp. 1–19). San Francisco, CA: Jossey-Bass Publishers.

Mick, S. S., & Associates (Eds). (1990). *Innovations in health care delivery: Insights for organization theory.* San Francisco, CA: Jossey-Bass Publishers.

Mick, S. S., & Wyttenbach, M. E. (Eds). (2003a). *Advances in health care organization theory.* San Francisco, CA: Jossey Bass.

Mick, S. S., & Wyttenbach, M. E. (2003b). Research and policy implications. In: S. S. Mick & M. E. Wyttenbach (Eds), *Advances in health care organization theory* (pp. 1–22). San Francisco, CA: Jossey Bass.

Moses, L. E., & Mosteller, F. (1968). Institutional differences in postoperative death rates. Commentary on some of the findings of the national halothane study. *The Journal of the American Medical Association, 203*(7), 492–494.

Needle, R. H., Coyle, S., Normand, J., Lambert, E., & Cesari, H. (1998). HIV prevention with drug-using populations – Current status and future prospects: Introduction and overview. In: R. H. Needle, S. Coyle & H. Cesari (Eds), *HIV prevention with drugusing populations – current status and future prospects. Public Health Reports, 113*(Suppl. 1), 4–19.

O'Connell, A. A., & McCoach, D. B. (2004). Applications of hierarchical linear models for evaluations of health interventions: Demystifying the methods and interpretations of multilevel models. *Evaluation and the Health Professions, 27,* 119–151.

Ouchi, W. G. (1980). Markets, bureaucracies, and clans. *Administrative Science Quarterly, 25*(1), 129–141.

Pfeffer, J., & Salancik, G. R. (1978). *The external control of organizations.* New York: Harper and Row.

Powell, W. W. (1990). Neither market nor hierarchy: Network forms of organizations. In: B. M. Shaw & L. R. Cummings (Eds), *Research in organizational behavior* (pp. 295–336). Greenwich, CT: JAI Press.

Roemer, M. I., & Friedman, J. W. (1971). *Doctors in hospitals: Medical staff organization and hospital performance.* Baltimore and London: Johns Hopkins Press.

Schoonhoven, C. B. (1981). Problems with contingency theory: Testing assumptions hidden within the language of contingency theory. *Administrative Science Quarterly, 26*(3), 349–377.

Schoonhoven, C. B., Scott, W. R., Flood, A. B., & Forrest, W. H., Jr. (1980). Measuring the complexity and uncertainty of surgery and postsurgical care. *Medical Care, 18*(9), 893–915.

Scott, W. R. (1982). Managing professional work: Three models of control for health organizations. *Health Services Research, 17,* 213–240.

Scott, W. R. (1983). Health care organizations in the 1980s: The convergence of public and professional control systems. In: J. M. Meyer & W. R. Scott (Eds), *Organizational environment: Ritual and rationality* (pp. 99–114). Beverly Hills: Sage.

Scott, W. R. (1987). The adolescence of institutional theory. *Administrative Science Quarterly*, *32*(4), 493–511.

Scott, W. R. (2003). The old order changeth: The evolving world of health care organizations. In: S. S. Mick & M. E. Wyttenbach (Eds), *Advances in health care organization theory* (pp. 23–43). San Francisco, CA: Jossey Bass.

Scott, W. R. (2004). Reflections on a half-century of organizational sociology. *Annual Review of Sociology*, *30*, 1–21.

Scott, W. R., & Backman, E. (1990). Institutional theory and the medical care sector. In: S. S. Mick & Associates (Eds), *Innovations in health care delivery: Insights for organization theory* (pp. 20–52). San Francisco, CA: Jossey-Bass Publishers.

Scott, W. R., Ruef, M., Mendel, P. J., & Caronna, C. (2000). *Institutional change and healthcare organizations, from professional dominance in managed care*. Chicago and London: The University of Chicago Press.

Sepucha, K. R., Fowler, F. J., Jr., & Mulley, A. G., Jr. (2004). Policy support for patient centered care: The need for measurable improvements in decision quality. *Health Affairs*, 54–62.

Shortell, S. M., & Rundall, T. G. (2003). Physician-organization relationships: Social networks and strategic intent. In: S. S. Mick & M. E. Wyttenbach (Eds), *Advances in health care organization theory*. San Francisco, CA: Jossey Bass.

Sung, K. S., Crowley, W. F., Genel, M., Salber, P., Sandy, L., Sherwood, L. M., Johnson, S. B., Catanese, V., Tilson, H., Getz, K., Larson, E. L., Scheinberg, D., Reece, E. A., Slavkin, H., Dobs, A., Grebb, J., Martinez, R. A., Korn, A., & Rimoin, D. (2003). Central challenges facing the national clinical research enterprise. *Journal of American Medical Association*, *289*(10), 1278–1287.

Wilke, C. L., & Choi, T. (1988). Changing criteria for hospital acquisitions. *Health Care Management Review*, *13*(3), 23–34.

Williamson, O. E. (1975). *Markets and hierarchies, analysis and antitrust implications: A study in the economics of internal organization*. New York: Free Press.

Williamson, O. E. (1986). *Economic organizations: Firms, markets and policy control*. New York: University Press.

Zapka, J. G. (2008). Innovative provider – and health system-directed approaches to improving colorectal cancer screening delivery. *Medical Care*, *46*(9), S62–S67.

Zapka, J. G., Taplin, S. H., Solberg, L., & Manos, M. M. (2003). A framework for improving the quality of cancer care: The case of breast and cervical cancer screening. *Cancer Epidemiology Biomarkers Prevention*, *12*(1), 4–13.

Zucker, L. G. (1977). The role of institutionalization in cultural persistence. *American Sociological Review*, *42*, 726–743.

Zucker, L. G. (1986). Production of trust: Institutional sources of economic structure. *Research in Organizational Behavior*, *8*, 53–111.

Zucker, L. G. (1987). Institutional theories of organization. *Annual Review of Sociology*, *13*, 443–464.

Zuckerman, H. S., & D'Aunno, T. A. (1990). Hospital alliances: Cooperative strategy in a competitive environment. *Health Care Management Review*, *15*(2), 21–30.

PART II
FACULTY

CHAPTER 9

ADMINISTRATION IS NECESSARY – BUT RESEARCH RULES

W. Richard Scott

I served as the director/coordinator of the National Institutes of Mental Health (NIMH) research training program from 1972 to 1989 and from 1988 through 1995 as director of the Stanford Center for Organization Research (SCOR). I also served as vice-chair of the Department of Sociology from 1968 to 1972 and as chair from 1972 to 1975. In these and other ways, I served my time as an administrator of academic programs. In the NIMH program, I was heavily involved in the selection of trainees and post-doctoral fellows; ran the weekly trainee seminar; helped to plan the colloquia, workshops, and conferences; and oversaw administrative matters ranging from annual reports and budgets to preparing for regular site visits from NIMH officers. As director of SCOR, I managed the program budgets, helped to select and appoint post-doctoral scholars, and participated in a range of program and conference planning activities (see Chapter 31).

All of these activities, however, were secondary to the research in which I was involved throughout this period. During the decades 1970–2000, I pursued projects with various colleagues and students in four related but distinct arenas: (1) the organization of educational systems; (2) the organization and effectiveness of health care systems; (3) the organization of mental health systems; and (4) the diffusion of personnel reforms – due

Stanford's Organization Theory Renaissance, 1970–2000
Research in the Sociology of Organizations, Volume 28, 173–189
Copyright © 2010 by Emerald Group Publishing Limited
All rights of reproduction in any form reserved
ISSN: 0733-558X/doi:10.1108/S0733-558X(2010)0000028013

process, equal opportunity, internal labor market – across a range of public agencies and private firms.Because I organize my review topically – emphasizing the substantive nature of the organizational system being examined – it might appear more diverse than I believe it was. In my own mind, the portfolio of projects exhibits a number of connected and overlapping interests and common themes:

- First, the studies were related in that, in one way or another, all dealt with the determinants and/or consequences of the structuring of professional work, a life-long interest of mine. Professionals organize their work in distinctive ways and, even when they are employed by more conventional bureaucratically administered organizations, their work arrangements remain somewhat distinctive (Scott, 1965, 1982, 2008b). Moreover, because of the nature of the work that professionals undertake, considerable care must be taken in developing valid measures to assess the quality or effectiveness of their efforts.
- Second, virtually all of the research is informed by an institutional perspective. Even my early concern with professional structures, I would argue with the benefit of hindsight, can be interpreted as focusing on two different institutional logics, two different approaches – the professional and the bureaucratic – to rationalizing complex work. My interest in better understanding how institutional forces – regulative, normative, cultural-cognitive – operate to shape organizational structures and systems – has grown stronger over time, enormously aided by my long-term collaboration with John Meyer and my years-long conversations with Jim March.
- Finally, although my research began at what was then treated as the very macro level of studying organizational structures, the trajectory of my work over time has moved relentlessly higher, to examine organizational populations, fields, and societal sectors. (Indeed, I am now studying transnational systems of organization [Orr & Scott, 2008].) I believe that too many contemporary organization scholars still fail to take into account the effects of the wider cultural and social environment on the structure and functioning of organizations.

I turn now to review research carried out in the four areas.

EDUCATIONAL SYSTEMS

Most of my work focusing on educational systems – including universities, public elementary schools, private schools, and training programs in organizations – was supported by Stanford University centers and grants separate from the Training Program, for example, the Stanford Center for Research and Development in Teaching (1968–1977) and the Institute for Research on Educational Finance and Governance (1979–1986). Faculty collaborators in these studies included Elizabeth Cohen and Terrence Deal in the School of Education, and John W. Meyer, my colleague in Sociology. A number of NIMH trainees participated in these studies, including Andrew Creighton, Margaret Davis, and Brian Rowan. Other doctoral students involved in this research included Sally Cole, Joanne Intili, Suzanne E. Monahan, E. Anne Stackhouse, and Marc Ventresca.

My earliest research on schools commenced late in the 1960s when I was collaborating with another colleague in Sociology, Sanford M. Dornbusch. In research supported by the National Science Foundation, we studied a range of organizations including professionals in a university faculty, pastors in a Diocesan clergy, nurses, and principals and teachers in both public and alternative schools. The studies focused on modes of work control, differentiating between attempts to manage inputs and processes, such as certification, vs. those evaluating outcomes, such as math scores. An important early finding of this research was that, compared to nurses in hospitals, teachers in schools believed that neither peers nor authority figures were able to effectively evaluate the quality of their performance. Nurses reported that their work was much more visible to their colleagues and superiors than did classroom teachers (except for the relatively few teachers engaged in team teaching) (Dornbusch & Scott, 1975, Chap. 6). This research provided an early glimpse into the phenomenon of "loose-coupling" in some types of organizations.

During the mid-1970s, Cohen, Deal, Meyer, and I collaborated on research examining the effects of open-space classrooms on the structuring of work in elementary schools. The design of these studies reflected the then-dominant paradigm of contingency theory, suggesting that the adoption of more complex technologies (e.g., curricular materials) would be associated with the development of more complex collaborative structures among teachers and administrative structures within schools. Longitudinal surveys were conducted in a sample of elementary schools in the San Francisco Bay area. We did find, as expected, that the use of more complex classroom curricula, materials, and methods was associated with more complex patterns of classroom organization (e.g., group work and teaming), but, to our surprise, school and district properties seemed to bear little or no relation to the characteristics of classrooms (Cohen, Deal, Meyer, & Scott, 1979). We had uncovered even stronger evidence of loose coupling.

If macro-organizational structures were not shaped by the nature and complexity of work being performed at more micro levels, what were their determinants? The now canonical explanation, first advanced in Meyer and Rowan (1977), was that institutional forces were shaping these more peripheral structural components (see also Meyer, Scott, Cole, & Intili, 1978; Meyer, Scott, & Deal, 1981).

Positing the importance of the previously neglected role of regulative, normative, and cultural forces in shaping organization structures, the institutional perspective emphasized the extent to which the environment of organizations, far from being chaotic or a set of disembodied, amorphous "dimensions" was itself highly organized – into distinctive "organization fields" (DiMaggio & Powell, 1983) or "societal sectors" (Scott & Meyer, 1983, 1991a). Much of my agenda for the next three decades was devoted to elaborating this level of analysis (see, e.g., Meyer & Scott, 1983; Scott, 1983, 1987, 1994a, 1995, 2001, 2008a; Scott & Christensen, 1995; Scott & Meyer, 1994) and applying it to a variety of arenas, including education, health care, and mental health services, as discussed below. In addition to empirical studies of public school and district organizations (Meyer et al., 1978; Meyer, Scott, & Strang, 1987, Meyer, Scott, Strang, & Creighton, 1988), we also compared the structures supporting private and public schools (Scott & Meyer, 1988) and examined the technical and institutional forces shaping the curriculum of training programs in firms and agencies (Monahan, Meyer, & Scott, 1994) and the diffusion of these programs across varying types of organizations (Scott & Meyer, 1991b).

HEALTH CARE SYSTEMS

During the mid-1970s, I was enticed to join a group of medical school collaborators, including Dr. John Bunker and Dr. William Forrest, Jr., Anesthesiology, and Dr. Byron William Brown and Dr. Wayne Ewy, Biostatistics, to examine organizational differences among hospitals in the effectiveness of their surgical care. (It was a time when many organization scholars were focusing attention on organizational effectiveness (Goodman & Pennings, 1977; Scott, 1977). Our medical and biostatistical colleagues were indispensable in enabling us to develop valid measures of quality of care. Since surgical outcomes are greatly dependent on nature and stage of disease and the condition of the patient at the time of surgery, we needed to take into account a wide array of differences among individual patients and diagnostic condition, adjusting observed outcomes accordingly

(Ewy, Flood, Brown, & Scott, 1987; Scott, 1979). I was able to enlist a highly talented collection of doctoral and post-doctoral trainees to help carry out a multi-faceted research program that extended over the next decade and a half. Participating trainees included Joan R. Bloom, Donald Comstock, Mary L. Fennell, Ann Barry Flood, and Claudia Kaye Schoonhoven; other doctoral students working with us included Jeffrey Alexander and Thomas Rundall. This work was carried out under the auspices of the Stanford Center for Health Care Research, supported by grants and contracts from the National Research Council and the National Center for Health Services Research.

The major components of our research were based on (1) an "intensive" study of selected surgical cases within 17 hospitals, chosen to be roughly representative of non-profit, acute care hospitals in the United States, and (2) an "extensive" study of 1,224 hospitals participating in the Professional Activity Study that collected data based on patient records including outcome at the time of discharge. In both studies, we focused on the outcomes associated with 15 selected diagnostic categories, most of which were treated surgically. For the intensive study, we employed a technician in each hospital to gather additional patient-level data as well as to administer questionnaires to surgical ward and intensive care staff, operating room staff, pathologists, radiologists, and surgeons. We depended on data from the American Hospital Association's annual survey of hospitals to obtain measures of hospital characteristics for the extensive study.

In addition to these patient-level data and measures of professional qualifications and hospital structure, another study, spearheaded by Trainee Kaye Schoonhoven, gathered data from a stratified random sample of surgeons, all members of the American College of Physicians and Surgeons, who were asked to rate the complexity of 71 surgical procedures, as well as from a sample of ward nurses drawn from a national sample of hospitals, who were asked to rate complexity of post-surgical care (Schoonhoven, Scott, Forrest, & Flood, 1980). These measures, which showed very high reliability among raters, were utilized to create assessments of the level of complexity of patient mix confronting specific hospitals and surgical units. (It has long been observed that hospitals vary greatly in the average level of complexity associated with the patients served.)

A study conducted in collaboration with Trainee Don Comstock employed the data gathered from the intensive hospital study and these complexity scores to examine the varying relations between complexity and organizational structure as we move from the individual worker level (e.g., qualifications, specialization) to hospital subunit structure (e.g., standardization, centralization) (Comstock & Scott, 1977). As expected, task complexity was positively correlated with staff qualifications and specialization. At the level of subunit structure, greater workflow complexity was associated with lower levels of standardization of procedures and higher level of centralization. Data from the intensive hospital study were also employed by Kaye Schoonhoven (1981) to examine contingency predictions linking technology, structure, and effectiveness. In an influential critique of contingency theory, Schoonhoven found that standard arguments under-represented the complexity present in these relations, many of which proved to be nonlinear, nonmonotonic, and asymmetric.

Together with Ann Flood, one of the few students that was both a pre- and post-doctoral trainee in the program, as well other sociology, education, and medical school colleagues, I carried out a wide range of studies examining the effects of both professional qualifications and structural characteristics of hospitals on medical outcomes for surgical patients – mortality and numerous measures of morbidity. It is not possible here to summarize these studies and their findings, but let me mention a few major results. Like other researchers (e.g., Brook et al., 1977), we found only weak and inconsistent associations between differing types of measures of effectiveness – structural, process, and outcome indicators. Characteristics of hospitals had a greater impact on surgical outcomes than did the characteristics of individual physicians. Hospital served by a medical staff exercising more stringent controls over surgeons provided better quality care. Hospitals and surgical units with higher levels of differentiation and more resources devoted to coordination of work activities exhibited better outcomes. And, our results were greatly affected by the time unit selected to measure post-surgical outcomes: immediately following surgery, after intensive care, 7 days or 30 days post-operatively (Flood, Ewy, Scott, Forrest, & Brown, 1979; Flood, Scott, Ewy, & Forrest, 1982; Flood & Scott, 1978, 1987; Flood, Scott, & Ewy, 1984a, 1984b; Scott & Flood, 1984; Scott, Flood, & Ewy, 1979; Scott, Flood, Ewy, & Forrest, 1978).

Working at a higher level – that of the organization set – Trainee Mary L. Fennell, who also participated in our research on surgical care, conducted under my supervision a study of hospitals "clusters" – hospitals located in the same metropolitan area. She examined the range of services offered and the degree of differentiation among these hospitals. One of her most interesting findings was that range of cluster services was more strongly related to characteristics of community physicians (the supply side) than to characteristics of patients (the "demand" side). Apparently the most salient set of "customers" for hospitals were physicians (Fennell, 1980).

Moving to the field level of analysis (Scott, 1994a), I served as a consultant to the Health Care Finance Administration and conducted research on the Professional Standard Review Organizations (PSRO) program, created in the late 1970s as a national system for monitoring health care outcomes in hospitals. Together with Trainee Robert Bies and doctoral student Mitchell LaPlante, we developed an analytic model for assessing the effectiveness of this innovative governance structure (Scott, Bies, & LaPlante, 1980). And subsequently, together with Trainee Elaine Backman, I crafted an early version of a theoretical model for examining the structure of the field of health care organizations (Scott & Backman, 1990), a model which I later elaborated and pursued in carrying out a longitudinal study of the structuration of this field in the United States during the period 1945–1995 (Scott, 1993).

The study of changes in the structure of the health care field was undertaken in 1995, sometime after the NIMH Training Program had ended. However, with the help of an Investigator Initiated Award from the Robert Wood Johnson Foundation received in 1995, I recruited a talented cadre of doctoral students as collaborators on this project. Doctoral students engaged in one or another phase of this work included Randy Cohen, Kathy Kuipers, Elaina Kyrouz, Seth Pollack, Sammie Speigner, and Junko Takagi. A large collection of master's level and undergraduate students also participated in one or another aspect of the study. However, my primary research compatriots, who began as my doctoral students and ended as co-authors, were Carol A. Caronna, Peter J. Mendel, and Martin Ruef (Scott, Ruef, Mendel, & Caronna, 2000).

The study was designed to explore a then-neglected aspect of field dynamics. Although a number of studies had explored the emergence and construction of an organization field (e.g., Dezalay & Garth, 1996; DiMaggio, 1991; Rao, 1998), few if any studies had examined the disintegration (de-structuration) of a previously coherent field. We believed that developments in health care in the United States during the last decades of the 20th century presented such a pattern. To explore these field-level changes in a manageable way, we concentrated attention on the case of one metropolitan community, collecting systematic data on changes in the numbers and types of acute health care delivery organizations in the San Francisco Bay Area, as affected by changes occurring in local demographics, modes and levels of funding, state-wide systems, national policies, and societal beliefs affecting health care. We relied primarily on archival data to assess not only changes in organizational and occupational systems, but in state and national policies, professional and public discourse, and amounts and sources of health care expenditures.

Employing empirical indicators, we identified three periods or "eras" – a period of professional dominance, of federal involvement, and of market-managerial orientation – each characterized by differing belief systems and values (institutional logics), differing governance systems (combinations of public and private oversight bodies), and differing collections of organizational and professional actors. We observed that the destructuration of the field was associated with increasing differentiation and fragmentation of interests within the American Medical Association. Their hegemony, at its height during the era of professional dominance, was challenged by the rise of competing powers and alternative logics – federal bodies demanding greater access to health care for marginalized groups during era two, and market advocates and managerial interests calling for greater efficiency and responsive of health care systems to consumer demands during era three. Because none of the actors and associated logics were able to prevail, the once coherent field became more conflicted and differentiated (Scott et al., 2000, Chap. 10). As the 20th century was coming to an end, in the health care field in the United States:

> Governance structures have become less unified. Structural isomorphism has been reduced so that a greater diversity of organizational forms now operate in the field. The coherence of organizational boundaries has been greatly reduced, and many blended and hybrid forms have been created. Consensus on institutional logics has been reduced: patients are confused by the multitude of plans; providers are less secure in their practice arrangements; and there is disagreement as to how health care should be funded. Field boundaries have become more permeable. The health care sector is no longer seen as a distinctive and protected arena and is more subject to external influences and alien logics and actors. Destructuration of the field has proceeded in all of these ways during the past fifty years. (Scott, 2004, p. 283)

MENTAL HEALTH SYSTEMS

Not only because it was a programmatic requirement but also because it was a topic of genuine intellectual interest, some of us devoted scholarly attention to the dramatic changes taking place in the organization of services for the mentally ill. During the late 1950s–early 1960s in the United States, dramatic changes took place in the organization of mental health services. The primary locus of care shifted from vast centralized state institutions to smaller, more varied community-based facilities (Foley & Sharfstein, 1983; Lerman, 1982; Levine, 1981; Scull, 1977). This process was greatly facilitated by initiatives taken by the Kennedy administration, culminating in the passage of the Community Mental Health Services Act of 1963. Dr. Lorrin Koran, a psychiatrist in the medical school at Stanford, as a member of our Training faculty, provided invaluable expertise to trainees and other faculty on these developments. A trainee, Patricia Thornton, also had previous work experience in the mental health services area, and I worked with her on an analysis she conducted of changes over time in psychiatric diagnosis categories in relation to changes in both technical advances and institutional forces (Thornton, 1992).

Given the deinstitutionalization movement, my research interests were in examining changes in the mental health services system at the field level. This work was advanced when Dr. Kenneth Lutterman, Associate Director for Mental Health Services Planning, Research and Research Training at NIMH, invited me to organize a conference to bring together organizational theorists and researchers studying mental health agencies and systems. The conference took place in Washington DC in September of 1984 and provided the basis for a special journal issue and a book devoted to the organization of mental health services at the community and societal level. Trainee Bruce Black contributed to this research effort and served as co-editor for the special issue and the book (Scott & Black, 1985, 1986).

My own work attempted to place changes in the mental health services system in a broader historical context as field-level processes involving a shift in the locus of control from state to federal authorities as well as the emergence within the profession of psychiatry of factions favoring community and rehabilitation approaches in contrast to more traditional clinical modes of care. Also, whereas public providers had long dominated in-patient care for the mentally ill and private providers specialized in out-patient services, with the Community Mental Health Centers Program, public providers more than tripled their volume of out-patient services during the decade 1970–1980.

These were significant changes, but, as I argued, perhaps the most important insight into the problems confronting this field was a realization of the extent to which specialized professional providers of mental health services constituted a distinct minority of those providing treatments. Of the roughly 30 million persons in the United States with mental disorders in 1975, only about 20 percent received treatment in the mental health sector. The great majority received no care or were seen in general hospitals or "treated" by other non-specialist providers, such as members of the clergy or social welfare agents (Koran, 1981; Regier, Goldberg, & Taub, 1978; Scott, 1986).

Comparing the mental health with the (acute) medical care field, the former appears to lack both a strong and well-accepted technical foundation to support its practice as well as a coherent and unified institutional base. The absence of both types of environmental support systems renders it difficult to construct and maintain strong and viable organizations (Scott & Meyer, 1983, p. 141). Trainee John C. Lammers and I compiled systematic data regarding changes in the major occupational and organizational forms and connections between them within the two sectors over a 30-year period (Scott & Lammers, 1985). Both sectors grew rapidly between 1950 and 1980, considerably exceeding the growth of the population, and the connections between organizations and occupations became more highly coupled. For example, by 1980, over 50 percent of physicians were salaried employees of organizations. The federal role in both sectors also expanded during this period, including support for research, aid in the expansion of hospitals, and the launching of community mental health centers. However, responsibility for mental health services remained primarily a state rather than a federal responsibility, resulting in greater fragmentation and inconsistency in policies. The large influx of federal dollars also stimulated the growth of private providers in both sectors: for-profit hospitals and specialized providers such as dialysis centers in health, and for-profit clinics, nursing homes, and board-and-care facilities in mental health. As previously noted, our comparison underlines the point that the mental health sector is far less specialized or sequestered from more general purpose forms, such as nursing homes, and the sector is much less under the control of the major claimant for dominance: psychiatrists.

Our major research project on mental health systems focused on variations among states within the United States in their responses to a federal initiative in 1977 providing incentives to create "Community Support Programs" (CSP). This project enlisted collaboration from four trainees: Bruce Black, Valerie Montoya, Sharon G. Takeda, and David A. Weckler, and was supported by funds from the CSP under a contract administered by the Department of Mental Health, State of California. The CSP program was a federal effort to induce states to take the initiative in improving services for the mentally ill at the community level, in particular, by improving the coordination of services across varying sectors (e.g., welfare, health, housing, criminal justice). In this respect, the initiative was similar in many respects to a range of "great society" programs initiated by democrats during the late 1960s, including Community Action Agencies associated with the poverty program and Health Systems Agencies in the health care sector (Sundquist, 1969). Demonstration projects were federally funded, but the implementation of the full program rested on the assumption that states would shift funds from large state facilities, as they were phased out, to community programs (Scott, Weckler, Takeda, & Montoya, 1983).

We viewed this program as an opportunity to consider its implementation in a complex sector-wide system, charting the number and locus of levels at which organizational units develop and the degree of centralization or fragmentation in decision making at each level (Scott & Meyer, 1983). We examined factors affecting state responses to the program, in particular, (1) whether states applied for a CSP demonstration grant; (2) the overall level of state expenditure for mental health programs; and (3) the proportion of state expenditure allocated to community-based mental health programs. We found that the best predictors of these variables were the extent of centralization of funding for mental health at the state level, the ratio of psychiatrists to the state's population, the rate of deinstitutionalization within the state, and number of interest groups lobbying for mental health services (Scott, Takeda, & Black, 1988).

This program along with more ambitious initiatives underway to strengthen mental health delivery systems at the community level ended with the coming of the conservative revolution of the 1980s under Ronald Reagan. These are, by the way, the same forces that brought to an end our Training Program funding from NIMH (see Chapter 31).

DIFFUSION OF PERSONNEL REFORMS

During the early 1980s, I worked together with a number of collaborators, including John W. Meyer and Ann Swidler, colleagues in sociology and members of the Training Faculty, and several trainees, including Frank R. Dobbin, Lauren Edelman, Anne S. Miner, and John R. Sutton, to examine the spread of various personnel reforms within organizations, including both private firms and public agencies. We were particularly interested in types of reforms that organizations instituted in response to changes in legal requirements. Given this substantive focus, we sought and received research support from the Russell Sage Foundation, which focused at that time on the impact of law on society.

Our research design examined two kinds of reforms, the adoption of grievance procedures, a procedural reform which gained impetus from the National Labor Relations Act of 1935, and affirmative action policies, a substantive reform mandated by the Civil Rights Act of 1964

(Dobbin, Edelman, Meyer, Scott, & Swidler, 1988). A convenience sample
of 52 organizations was selected from eight sectors, including manufacturing, financial, retail, and government. Data were gathered by a survey
instrument administered to personnel officers or general managers.
Consistent with previous research, larger organizations exhibited higher
levels of formalization, including due process protections. However, we also
found that unionization stimulated the adoption of these protections as
did public visibility and connections to the federal government. And the
adoption of these reforms was strongly linked to the existence of a
specialized personnel office.

Encouraged by this exploratory study, we crafted a more ambitious
design to expand the sample of organizations and to examine the effect of
variation in legal environments among states. Our focus was on the
adoption of internal labor market systems (often associated with union
pressures) and equal opportunity programs. We sampled organizations
located in California, New Jersey, and Virginia – states varying from liberal
to more conservative legal climates – and gathered information by telephone
interview from a stratified random sample of public, for-profit, and
nonprofit organizations ($n = 270$). The study was supported by a grant
from the National Science Foundation.

In addition to replicating many of the findings from our exploratory
study, this effort expanded the theoretical framework to examine the ways in
which environmental pressures that begin as legal (regulatory) requirements
do not function as predicted by formal legal or other instrumental theorists,
but set in motion a set of cognitive processes among responsible
organizational authorities (in this case, personnel officers), who attempt to
"make sense" of the situation. Once this sense-making process formulates
an "appropriate" response and a legitimating rationale, the reform quickly
diffuses through the field of organizations, now fueled by normative
pressures (Dobbin, Sutton, Meyer, & Scott, 1993; Edelman, 1992; Sutton,
Dobbin, Meyer, & Scott, 1994). Dobbin and Sutton (1998) later elaborated
this account to explain the unexpectedly strong effects of legal mandates
from a "weak" state. And in their innovative study of a representative
national sample of organizations in the United States, Kalleberg, Knoke,
Marsden, and Spaeth (1996) adopted and adapted many of our indicators
and replicated most of our findings.

This research program examining the interdependence of legal and
organizational processes has been further pursued and elaborated by
Trainee Lauren Edelman and by Mark Suchman, another doctoral student
with whom I worked, as well as by Trainees Robert Bies and Sim Sitkin

(Edelman & Suchman, 1997; Edelman, Uggen, & Erlanger, 1999; Suchman, 1995; Suchman & Edelman, 1997; Sitkin & Bies, 1994a). Edelman and Suchman emphasize the multiple ways in which legal environments impact organizations (e.g., in facilitative, regulative, and constitutive ways) (Edelman & Suchman, 1997); while Bies and Sitkin focus attention on the domination of organization decision-making by a "concern for what is legally defensible" (Sitkin & Bies, 1994b, p. 20). I believe that these research directions are among the most promising of the many strands of work linking organizations and institutional environments (Scott, 1994b).

CONCLUDING COMMENT

I hope that this brief survey of the principal research projects in which I was involved during this period provides evidence that, for me, administration was secondary to research. In my view, it is not possible to train people in research unless one is conducting research. Research is as much (if not more) art as science, and an apprenticeship system – learning to do by doing – is a vital ingredient in any training effort.

Preparing this review of (some of) the research in which I was involved during the past three decades, I was surprised to find what a large role NIMH trainees played in my research portfolio (although, as discussed, I also worked with a number of other students). Like many Stanford faculty – probably more than most – I was the beneficiary of a Training Program that provided financial support for a range of highly qualified doctoral students and enticed to Stanford many young professionals from other universities for post-doctoral training. Faculty and students alike profited from the program.

All of my work and my intellectual development over the years was greatly enabled by and is hugely indebted to the collegial culture established and maintained at Stanford for more than three decades. I cannot conceive of a more supportive and stimulating environment in which to conduct research, teach, and learn than was afforded by the multiple social structures and networks we – participating faculty and students alike – constructed at Stanford University between 1970 and 2000.

REFERENCES

Brook, R. H., Davies-Avery, A., Greenfield, S., Harris, L. J., Lelah, T., Solomon, N. E., & Ware, J. E., Jr. (1977). Assessing the quality of medical care using outcome measures: An overview of the method. *Medical Care, 15*(Suppl. 9), 1–165.

Cohen, E. G., Deal, T. E., Meyer, J. W., & Scott, W. R. (1979). Technology and teaming in the elementary school. *Sociology of Education, 52*, 20–33.

Comstock, D. E., & Scott, W. R. (1977). Technology and the structure of subunits. *Administrative Science Quarterly, 22*, 177–202.

Dezalay, Y., & Garth, B. G. (1996). *Dealing in virtue: International commercial arbitration and the construction of a transnational legal order.* Chicago: University of Chicago Press.

DiMaggio, P. J. (1991). Constructing an organizational field as a professional project: U.S. art museums, 1920–1940. In: W. W. Powell & P. J. DiMaggio (Eds), *The new institutionalism in organizational analysis* (pp. 267–292). Chicago: University of Chicago Press.

DiMaggio, P. J., & Powell, W. W. (1983). The iron cage revisited: Institutional isomorphism and collective rationality in organizational fields. *American Sociological Review, 48*, 147–160.

Dobbin, F. R., Edelman, L. B., Meyer, J. W., Scott, W. R., & Swidler, A. (1988). The expansion of due process in organizations. In: L. G. Zucker (Ed.), *Institutional patterns and organizations: Culture and environment.* Cambridge, MA: Ballinger.

Dobbin, F. R., & Sutton, J. R. (1998). The strength of a weak state: The rights revolution and the rise of human resources management divisions. *American Journal of Sociology, 104*, 441–476.

Dobbin, F., Sutton, J. R., Meyer, J. W., & Scott, W. R. (1993). Equal opportunity law and the construction of internal labor markets. *American Journal of Sociology, 99*, 396–427.

Dornbusch, S. M., & Scott, W. R. (1975). *Evaluation and the exercise of authority.* San Francisco, CA: Jossey-Bass. (With the assistance of B. C. Busching & J. D. Laing.)

Edelman, L. B. (1992). Legal ambiguity and symbolic structures: Organizational mediation of civil rights law. *American Journal of Sociology, 97*, 1531–1576.

Edelman, L. B., Uggen, C., & Erlanger, H. S. (1999). The endogeneity of legal regulation: Grievance procedures as rational myth. *American Journal of Sociology, 105*, 406–454.

Edelman, L. B., & Suchman, M. C. (1997). The legal environment of organizations. *Annual Review of Sociology, 23*, 479–515.

Ewy, W., Flood, A. B., Brown, B. W., & Scott, W. R. (1987). A methodology for assessing hospital performance. In: A. B. Flood & W. R. Scott (Eds), *Hospital structure and performance* (pp. 127–173). Baltimore, MD: Johns Hopkins University Press.

Fennell, M. L. (1980). The effects of environmental characteristics on the structure of hospital clusters. *Administrative Science Quarterly, 25*, 485–510.

Flood, A. B., Ewy, W., Scott, W. R., Forrest, W. H., Jr., & Brown, B. W. (1979). The relationship between intensity and duration of medical services and outcomes for hospitalized patients. *Medical Care, 17*, 1088–1102.

Flood, A. B., & Scott, W. R. (1978). Professional power and professional effectiveness: The power of the surgical staff and the quality of surgical care in hospitals. *Journal of Health and Social Behavior, 19*, 240–254.

Flood, A. B., & Scott, W. R. (1987). *Hospital structure and performance.* Baltimore, MD: Johns Hopkins Press.

Flood, A. B., Scott, W. R., & Ewy, W. (1984a). Does practice make perfect? I. The relation between hospital volume and outcome fo selected diagnostic categories. *Medical Care, 22*, 98–114.

Flood, A. B., Scott, W. R., & Ewy, W. (1984b). Does practice make perfect? II. The relation between volume and outcomes and other hospital characteristics. *Medical Care, 22*, 115–124.

Flood, A. B., Scott, W. R., Ewy, W., & Forrest, W. H., Jr. (1982). Effectiveness in professional organizations: The impact of surgeons and surgical staff organization on the quality of care in hospitals. *Health Services Research, 17,* 341–366 (with commentaries, 376–385).

Foley, H. A., & Sharfstein, S. S. (1983). *Madness and government: Who cares for the mentally Ill?* Washington, DC: American Psychiatric Press.

Goodman, P. S., & Pennings, J. M. (Eds). (1977). *New perspectives on organizational effectiveness.* San Francisco, CA: Jossey-Bass.

Kalleberg, A. L., Knoke, D., Marsden, P. V., & Spaeth, J. L. (1996). *Organizations in America: Analyzing their structures and human resource practices.* Thousand Oaks, CA: Sage.

Koran, L. M. (1981). Mental health services. In: S. Jonas (Ed.), *Health care delivery in the United States* (pp. 235–271). New York: Springer.

Lerman, P. (1982). *Deinstitutionalization and the welfare state.* New Brunswick, NJ: Rutgers University Press.

Levine, M. (1981). *The history and politics of community mental health.* New York: Oxford University Press.

Meyer, J. W., & Rowan, B. (1977). Institutionalized organizations: Formal structure as myth and ceremony. *American Journal of Sociology, 83,* 440–463.

Meyer, J. W., Scott, W. R., Cole, S., & Intili, J. (1978). Instructional dissensus and institutional consensus in schools. In: M. W. Meyer (Ed.), *Environments and organizations* (pp. 233–263). San Francisco, CA: Jossey-Bass.

Meyer, J. W., Scott, W. R., & Deal, T. E. (1981). Institutional and technical sources of organizational structure: Explaining the structure of educational organizations. In: H. D. Stein (Ed.), *Organization and the human services* (pp. 151–178). Philadelphia, PA: Temple University Press.

Meyer, J. W., & Scott, W. R. (1983). *Organizational environments: Ritual and rationality.* Beverly Hills, CA: Sage.

Meyer, J. W., Scott, W. R., & Strang, D. (1987). Centralization, fragmentation, and school district complexity. *Administrative Science Quarterly, 32,* 186–201.

Meyer, J. W., Scott, W. R., Strang, D., & Creighton, A. (1988). Bureaucratization without centralization: Changes in the organizational system of American public education. In: L. G. Zucker (Ed.), *Institutional patterns and organizations: Culture and environment.* Cambridge, MA: Ballinger.

Monahan, S. E., Meyer, J. W., & Scott, W. R. (1994). Employee training: The expansion of organizational citizenship. In: W. R. Scott & J. W. Meyer (Eds), *Institutional environments and organizations: Structural complexity and individualism* (pp. 255–271). Thousand Oaks, CA: Sage.

Orr, R. J., & Scott, W. R. (2008). Institutional exceptions on global projects: A process model. *Journal of International Business Studies, 38,* 562–588.

Rao, H. (1998). Caveat emptor: The construction of nonprofit consumer watchdog organizations. *American Journal of Sociology, 103,* 912–961.

Regier, D. A., Goldberg, I. D., & Taub, C. A. (1978). The de facto U.S. mental health services system. *Archives of General Psychiatry, 35,* 685–693.

Schoonhoven, C. B. (1981). Problems with contingency theory: Testing assumptions hidden within the language of contingency 'theory'. *Administrative Science Quarterly, 26,* 349–377.

Schoonhoven, C. B., Scott, W. R., Forrest, W. H., Jr., & Flood, A. B. (1980). Measuring the complexity and uncertainty of surgical and post-surgical care. *Medical Care, 18,* 893–915.

Scott, W. R. (1965). Reactions to supervision in a heteronomous professional organization. *Administrative Science Quarterly, 10,* 65–81.

Scott, W. R. (1977). Effectiveness of organizational effectiveness studies. In: P. S. Goodman & J. M. Pennings (Eds), *New perspectives on organizational effectiveness* (pp. 63–95). San Francisco, CA: Jossey-Bass.

Scott, W. R. (1979). Measuring outputs in hospitals. In: Panel to Review Productivity Statistics (Ed.), *Measurement and interpretation of productivity* (pp. 255–275). Washington, DC: National Academy of Sciences.

Scott, W. R. (1982). Managing professional work: Three models of control for health organizations. *Health Services Research, 17,* 213–240.

Scott, W. R. (1983). The organization of environments: Network, cultural and historical elements. In: J. W. Meyer & W. R. Scott (Eds), *Organizational environments: Ritual and rationality* (pp. 155–175). Beverly Hills, CA: Sage.

Scott, W. R. (1986). Systems within systems: The mental health sector. In: W. R. Scott & B. L. Black (Eds), *The organizational of mental health services: Societal and community systems* (pp. 31–52). Beverly Hills, CA: Sage.

Scott, W. R. (1987). The adolescence of institutional theory. *Administrative Science Quarterly, 32,* 493–511.

Scott, W. R. (1993). The organization of medical care services: Toward an integrated theoretical model. *Medical Care Review, 50,* 271–302.

Scott, W. R. (1994a). Conceptualizing organizational fields: Linking organizations and societal systems. In: H.-U. Derlien, U. Gerhardt & F. W. Scharpf (Eds), *Systemrationalität und partialinteresse [System rationality and partial interests]* (pp. 203–219). Baden-Baden, Germany: Nomos Verlagsgesellschaft.

Scott, W. R. (1994b). Law and organizations. In: S. B. Sitkin & R. J. Bies (Eds), *The legalistic organization.* Thousand Oaks, CA: Sage.

Scott, W. R. (1995/2001/2008a). *Institutions and organizations* (1st ed. 1995; 2nd ed. 2001; 3rd ed. 2008.). Thousand Oaks, CA: Sage.

Scott, W. R. (2004). Competing logics in healthcare: Professional, state, and managerial. In: F. Dobbin (Ed.), *The sociology of the economy* (pp. 295–315). New York: Russell Sage Foundation.

Scott, W. R. (2008b). Lords of the dance: Professionals as institutional agents. *Organization Studies, 29,* 219–238.

Scott, W. R., & Meyer, J. W. (1988). Environmental linkages and organizational complexity: Public and private schools. In: T. James & H. M. Levin (Eds), *Comparing public and private schools, Vol. 1: Institutions and organizations* (pp. 128–160). Philadelphia, PA: Falmer Press.

Scott, W. R., & Meyer, J. W. (1991a). The organization of societal sectors: Propositions and early evidence. In: W. W. Powell & P. J. DiMaggio (Eds), *The new institutionalism in organizational analysis* (pp. 164–182). Chicago: University of Chicago Press.

Scott, W. R., & Meyer, J. W. (1991b). The rise of training programs in firms and agencies: An institutional perspective. In: B. M. Staw & L. L. Cummings (Eds), *Research in organization behavior* (Vol. 13, pp. 297–326). Greenwich, CT: JAI Press.

Scott, W. R., & Backman, E. V. (1990). Institutional theory and the medical care sector. In: S. S. Mick (Ed.), *Innovations in health care delivery: Insights for organization theory* (pp. 20–52). San Francisco, CA: Jossey-Bass.

Scott, W. R., Bies, R., & LaPlante, M. (1980). Organizational effectiveness: models and measures for assessing PSRO effectiveness. *Professional Standards Review Organizations 1979 Program Evaluation,* Research Report. Washington, DC: Health Care Financing Administration, Office of Research, Demonstrations and Statistics, pp. 139–151.

Scott, W. R., & Black, B. L. (Eds). (1985). Organizational of mental health systems: Macro and micro perspectives. *American Behavioral Scientist, 28,* 579–720.

Scott, W. R., & Black, B. L. (Eds). (1986). *The organization of mental health services: Societal and community systems.* Beverley Hills, CA: Sage.

Scott, W. R., & Christensen, S. (Eds). (1995). *The institutional construction of organizations: International and longitudinal studies.* Thousand Oaks, CA: Sage.

Scott, W. R., & Flood, A. B. (1984). Cost and quality of hospital care: A review of the literature. *Medical Care Review, 41,* 213–261.

Scott, W. R., Flood, A. B., & Ewy, W. (1979). Organizational determinants of services, quality and cost of care in hospitals. *Milbank Memorial Fund Quarterly/Health and Society, 57,* 234–264.

Scott, W. R., Flood, A. B., Ewy, W., & Forrest, W. H., Jr. (1978). Organizational effectiveness and the quality of surgical care in hospitals. In: M. Meyer (Ed.), *Environments and organizations* (pp. 290–305). San Francisco, CA: Jossey-Bass.

Scott, W. R., & Lammers, J. C. (1985). Trends in occupations and organizations in the medical care and mental health sectors. *Medical Care Review, 42,* 37–75.

Scott, W. R., & Meyer, J. W. (1983). The organization of societal sectors. In: J. W. Meyer & W. R. Scott (Eds), *Organizational environments: Ritual and rationality* (pp. 129–153). Beverly Hills, CA: Sage.

Scott, W. R., & Meyer, J. W. (Eds). (1994). *Institutional environments and organizations: Structural complexity and individualism.* Thousand Oaks, CA: Sage.

Scott, W. R., Ruef, M., Mendel, P. J., & Caronna, C. A. (2000). *Institutional change and healthcare organizations: From professional dominance to managed care.* Chicago: University of Chicago Press.

Scott, W. R., Takeda, S. G., & Black, B. L. (1988). *State systems and community mental health.* Unpublished Paper, Department of Sociology, Stanford University.

Scott, W.R., Weckler, D.A., Takeda, S.G., & Montoya, V. (1983). *State responses to the community support program.* Unpublished Paper, Department of Sociology, Stanford University.

Scull, A. T. (1977). *Decarceration.* Englewood Cliffs, NJ: Prentice-Hall.

Sitkin, S. B., & Bies, R. J. (1994a). *The legalistic organization.* Thousand Oaks, CA: Sage.

Sitkin, S. B., & Bies, R. J. (1994b). The legalization of organizations. In: S. G. Sitkin & R. J. Bies (Eds), *The legalistic organization* (pp. 19–49). Thousand Oaks, CA: Sage.

Suchman, M. A. (1995). Localism and globalism in institutional analysis: The emergence of contractural norms in venture finance. In: W. R. Scott & C. Christensen (Eds), *The institutional construction of organizations: International and longitudinal studies* (pp. 39–63). Thousand Oaks, CA: Sage.

Suchman, M. A., & Edelman, L. B. (1997). Legal rational myths: The new institutionalism and the law and society tradition. *Law and Social Inquiry, 21,* 903–941.

Sundquist, J. L. (1969). *Making federalism work.* Washington, DC: Brookings Institution.

Sutton, J. R., Dobbin, F. R., Meyer, J. W., & Scott, W. R. (1994). The legalization of the workplace. *American Journal of Sociology, 99,* 944–971.

Thornton, P. (1992). Psychiatric diagnosis as sign and symbol: Nomenclature as n organizing and legitimating strategy. In: G. Miller & G. Holstein (Eds), *Research on social problems* (Vol. 4). Greenwich, CT: JAI Press.

CHAPTER 10

SILICON VALLEY, THEORIES OF ORGANIZATION, AND THE STANFORD LEGACY

Kathleen M. Eisenhardt

THE "OTHER" REVOLUTION

In the late 1970s, the much beloved tradition of Asilomar began. But then, of course, it was not even located at Asilomar. Rather it was a much smaller event that was held at Pajaro Dunes. Nonetheless, it featured what ultimately became the traditional blend of informal sessions that mixed students and faculty from around the University. The most memorable conference of that time featured working papers by Jeff Pfeffer and Jerry Salancik, John Meyer and Brian Rowan, and Mike Hannan and John Freeman. Each of these pairs of authors presented fledgling work that would go on to become keystone statements for three highly influential theories: resource dependence (Pfeffer & Salancik, 1978), "new" institutional theory (Meyer & Rowan, 1977), and population ecology (Hannan & Freeman, 1977).

Yet at the same time, there was a second revolution occurring in a very proximate geographic space, but in a very distant intellectual one. Members of the Home Brew computing club were founding Apple Computer, thereby launching the personal computer industry. Scientists at Genentech were working on the first biotechnology applications. Intel engineers had

Stanford's Organization Theory Renaissance, 1970–2000
Research in the Sociology of Organizations, Volume 28, 191–205
Copyright © 2010 by Emerald Group Publishing Limited
All rights of reproduction in any form reserved
ISSN: 0733-558X/doi:10.1108/S0733-558X(2010)0000028014

designed a Silicon Valley icon, the first microprocessor. Yet despite their early lead, these engineers were locked in a war with other local upstarts like Zilog and National Semiconductor for processor supremacy. Atari innovators would soon launch with the first video gaming consoles with "hit" products like Pong. And an even bigger torrent of entrepreneurial firms was about to flood the Valley. Some of these ventures such as Adobe, Cisco, Autodesk, Sun, LSI Logic, Cypress, and Symantec would ultimately "make it" in diverse technology-based industries ranging from software, computing hardware, networking, and semiconductors to biotechnology, medical devices, and disk drives. Many more of these ventures would die along the way. Meanwhile back in Washington D.C., crucial activities were occurring that further ignited this other revolution. The Prudent Man legislation of the late 1970s loosened the investment rules for pension funds, and thereby created a landslide of venture capital firm formations and capital inflows. The Bayh-Dole Act of 1980 changed the patenting rules for the commercialization of federally funded innovations by universities. So side-by-side, but worlds apart, two separate revolutions began.

Many students and faculty at Stanford followed the lure of the first revolution. So, they examined questions from institutional theory such as why hospitals, governments, and schools had seemingly useless "non-rational" processes, or focused on the "vital rates" of foundings and deaths from ecology theory in restaurants, newspapers, and similar types of simple organizations. Although fewer studied resource dependence theory, researchers would bring back its core focus on dependence between firms with the rise of social network theory in the late 1980s. There was also burgeoning interest in learning theory and agency theory, a nascent approach being developed at this time by Stanford economists and others. All of these efforts were an ideal fit with the cultural emphasis within the Stanford organizations community on theory-driven research.

But, there was also a much smaller group of students and faculty who followed the second revolution of technological and entrepreneurial ferment within Silicon Valley and beyond. As a result, these researchers developed a distinctive research style of field-oriented, process-focused, and often case-based research that frequently broke away from the dominant theories and methods. They blurred the sharp distinction between rigor and relevance, and added managerial agency and the perspective of the firm. And some of them formed a sub-community of organizational scholars at Stanford with an unusual home base, the School of Engineering.

HIGH-TECH INDUSTRIES AND
ENTREPRENEURIAL FIRMS

The signals of scholarly interest in this second revolution first showed up in the choice of research setting. The *technology-based companies* of Silicon Valley became not only the research setting of convenience, but also the research setting of choice. Sometimes these companies were large incumbents (e.g., Burgelman, 1991; Eisenhardt & Tabrizi, 1995; Galunic & Eisenhardt, 1996; Hansen, 1999). For example, Jelinek and Schoonhoven (1990) studied how Hewlett-Packard, Intel, and several other technology giants continuously created innovative products and brought them to commercial success. Their prescient book, *The Innovation Marathon: Lessons from High-Technology Firms*, chronicled insights about flexible organizational structures. Similarly, Bill Ouchi was one of the first to study Silicon Valley firms in his research that contrasted the autocratic organizational culture of Fairchild Semiconductor with the egalitarian culture at Hewlett-Packard. This comparison formed the basis of Bill's important article on the distinctions among markets, clans, and bureaucracies (Ouchi, 1980), and his blockbuster book, *Theory Z: How American Business Can Meet the Japanese Challenge* (Ouchi, 1981).

But just as often, the research setting of choice was entrepreneurial firms (e.g., Roure & Maidique, 1986; Eisenhardt & Bourgeois, 1988; Schoonhoven, Eisenhardt, & Lyman, 1990; Baron, Hannan, & Burton, 1999; Stuart, Hoang, & Hybels, 1999). The early 1980s saw an explosion of entrepreneurial firms within Silicon Valley and beyond that was primarily based upon the opportunities created by the microprocessor and biotechnology innovations. So, for example, Kaye Schoonhoven and I took advantage of the wealth of just-begun, semiconductor ventures. We gathered longitudinal data on the entire population of U.S. semiconductor ventures that were founded between 1978 and 1985, most of which were born in Silicon Valley. We then went on to write a series of publications on processes such as organizational growth (Eisenhardt & Schoonhoven, 1990), regional development (Schoonhoven & Eisenhardt, 1992, 1993), product innovation (Schoonhoven et al., 1990), and alliance formation (Eisenhardt & Schoonhoven, 1994, 1996; Schoonhoven & Eisenhardt, 1995) that tracked the development of the industry and the entrepreneurial firms within it. More broadly, as is well-known, Silicon Valley became the global hub of the venture capital industry, and the birthplace of numerous technology-based ventures in a broad swath of industries including semiconductors, biotechnology, medical devices, networking, software, and more recently, Internet and clean-technologies.

FRESH IDEAS AND REVERSE ASSUMPTIONS

But the research setting was just a superficial difference. Early on, signals came that pointed to the need for fresh perspectives on theories of organizations, their assumptions, and key constructs. In Silicon Valley's technology-based firms, change was vital. Executives at most of these firms were well-attuned to the demands of shifting technologies, customers, business models, strategies, organizational structures, products, and so forth. So out went the theoretical assumption of organizational inertia that characterized some theories of the time, and in came assumptions of flexibility and the possibility of effective change. Indeed, without change, technology-based firms typically went nowhere. The term *high-velocity environment* (Eisenhardt, 1989a) was coined to capture the turbulence occurring in these technology-based industries where the pace of change was so fast, and the uncertainty and ambiguity were so high that it was enormously challenging for top management teams to understand and track relevant technologies, competitors, complementers, products, and customers.

Also vanishing was the theoretical emphasis on selection within ecology theory. It was not credible to focus solely on selection when change within the technology-based firms of Silicon Valley was so apparent. After all, Hewlett-Packard executives really did re-invent the firm – going from an instruments firm to a computer firm and then later on to become the world leader in both ink-jet and laser-jet printing. Symantec entrepreneurs really did launch an artificial intelligence venture, morphed it several times, and ended up with a dominant computer security firm. Intel executives really did drop their very successful DRAM products in order to focus on their fledgling line of microprocessors, and then went on to champion more attempts to change. Robert Burgelman was an early observer of these activities at Intel, and wrote a series of publications on the emergence of strategies in technology-based firms based on his Intel research (Burgelman, 1991, 1994, 2002). Robert also developed a deep teaching and research partnership with Intel's long-time chairman and CEO, Andy Grove. Overall, the focus on technology-based companies brought change and related phenomena such as product and process innovation to the foreground of research interest (e.g., Schoonhoven et al., 1990; Eisenhardt & Tabrizi, 1995; Sutton & Hargadon, 1996; Brown & Eisenhardt, 1997; Stuart, 1998;

Hansen, 1999; Sorenson, 2000; Miner, Bassoff, & Moorman, 2001; Katila & Ahuja, 2002).

Another theoretical casualty was the emphasis on isomorphism and conformity within institutional theory. Success in technology-based firms came from *being unique*, not from being the same. And speaking of success, it too changed. Survival was a much too crude measure of success, and vital rates kind of missed the point. Indeed, few executives aspired to survival if survival meant joining the limbo of the "living dead," a popular term for barely alive ventures. Rather, success was defined much more in terms *scaling and growth*. So, research interest often centered on which firms grew and why (Eisenhardt & Schoonhoven, 1990; Powell, Koput, & Smith-Doerr, 1996), not simply on survival. *Speed* was also recognized as essential for creating success within technology-based firms because of the high-velocity nature of the environments in which they competed. So the speed at which technology-based firms engaged in a variety of activities such as strategic decision-making (Eisenhardt, 1989a), product innovation (Schoonhoven et al., 1990; Eisenhardt & Tabrizi, 1995; Hansen, 1999), and reaching particular milestones such as initial public offering (IPO) (Stuart et al., 1999) became central.

Given this interest in change, uniqueness, growth, and speed, there was, not surprisingly, also an emphasis on *managerial agency* – that is, on what executives, managers, engineers, and scientists were actually doing and how they did it. While it may be true that leaders make little difference in many settings, they appeared to matter within technology-based firms of the Silicon Valley (e.g., Ouchi, 1981; Eisenhardt, 1989a; Burgelman, 1991). The nature of technology-based industries created a significant role for managerial action, especially within entrepreneurial firms where small-scale and nascent markets often meant high influence for senior executives.

An important insight was to replace the focus on a single executive such as the CEO with an emphasis on the top management team (e.g., Roure & Maidique, 1986; Eisenhardt & Schoonhoven, 1990, 1996; Burton, Sorensen, & Beckman, 2002; Beckman, Burton, & O'Reilly, 2007). For example, Jay Bourgeois and I exploited the opportunity of roughly 100 hardware computing ventures that began in the early 1980s in the Bay Area to study the top management teams in twelve of those firms. By focusing on these teams, we were able to develop insights into the politics, speed, and conflict that occurred within them, and that were critical to their ventures' outcomes (e.g., Eisenhardt & Bourgeois, 1988; Eisenhardt, 1989a; Eisenhardt, Kahwajy, & Bourgeois, 1997). Similarly, Diane Burton, Christine Beckman, and their colleagues analyzed the Stanford Project on Entrepreneurial Companies (SPEC) database of Silicon Valley ventures to understand whether top management teams shaped important human resource practices, the composition of future teams, and various indicators of success (e.g., Baron et al., 1999; Burton et al., 2002; Beckman et al., 2007; Beckman & Burton, 2008).

CHALLENGES TO THE AGENDA

But while the focus on technology-based firms as a setting dramatically shifted research questions, assumptions about organizations and environments, and key constructs, there were clearly some serious challenges. First, there was a major data problem. There were few (if any) archival data sets that could be used for large-scale, empirical tests within the context of technology-based firms. Later on, large, archival data sets became available, especially related to the biotechnology sector and venture capital-backed entrepreneurial firms. But initially, there were virtually none. In fact, databases that relied on traditional standard industrial classification (SIC) codes did not fit well because Silicon Valley's technology-based industries were often too new to be adequately covered by a coding system that was based on categorizing mature, manufacturing-based sectors.

This lack of existing, archival data sets had significant ramifications for research. For one, researchers had to "get out" into real companies to gather data. So this drove research to become field-based. And given the intense effort involved in data collection, field-based typically meant a relatively small number of observations. So deductive studies necessarily often had relatively small sample sizes based on painstakingly captured original, field data (e.g., Eisenhardt & Tabrizi, 1995; Hansen, 1999; Burton et al., 2002). So, for example, Kaye Schoonhoven and I used a sample size only slightly over 100 in our semiconductor industry study. Hansen's research (1999) on internal firm networks for product innovation and my and Tabrizi's (Eisenhardt & Tabrizi, 1995) study of product development in the computer industry were based on similarly small sample sizes as was the SPEC research on human resource practices in technology-based ventures (e.g., Burton et al., 2002). So researchers were forced to place a premium on careful measures and deep understanding of the research setting to compensate for their relatively small number of observations. After all, significance had to be real, not just statistical, when the sample size hovered around 100. So, knowing the setting very well was essential. The need for field data also encouraged researchers to consider the practical implications of their work. The reality was that company executives rarely agreed to let their firms be studied if they were not also intrigued by the relevance of the research. So, research questions had to resonate with these executives. This need for industry cooperation did, however, offer the unexpected benefits of closer engagement with practice, and softened tension between rigor and relevance.

The even bigger problem with studying research questions that were relevant to technology-based firms was the lack of theory. It was not so much that researchers who were caught up in the technology revolution consciously chose to avoid theory. Rather, there was more of a frustration that extant theories simply did not have much insight into the phenomena of interest within technology-based firms. Even the new organizational theories that were showcased at the early Asilomar conferences were developed primarily in the contexts of universities, school systems, restaurants, and foreign newspapers. As a result, they were not particularly relevant for technology-based firms, the environments in which they operated, or the intriguing challenges that their executives faced. Given the cultural emphasis on theory-driven research within Stanford's organizations community, it was a bit embarrassing to be phenomenon-driven. But the reality was that the existing theories were not particularly germane to many of the most intriguing aspects of technology-based firms.

MULTIPLE-CASE, THEORY-BUILDING

Given the lack of theory and the need for field data, the new method became *multiple-case, theory-building* studies among many of those studying organizational and strategic phenomena within technology-based firms. Bob Sutton was among the first members of the organizations community at Stanford to conduct rigorous research using this method. Bob brought this method to Stanford when he joined the Department of Industrial Engineering (now Management Science and Engineering) in the early 1980s. His theory-building, case-based dissertation examined the death processes of about eight organizations (Sutton & Callahan, 1987). Bob and his Ph.D. students went on to study a variety of phenomena using this method, including his important work with Andy Hargadon on brainstorming and brokering in the creative processes at the iconic Silicon Valley product design house, Ideo (Sutton & Hargadon, 1996; Hargadon & Sutton, 1997; Hargadon, 2003). Robert Burgelman (1991, 1994, 2002), who studied the strategy making process at Intel, was another early member of the organizations community who employed multiple-case, theory-building methods as were Bill Ouchi (1981), Kaye Schoonhoven

(Jelinek & Schoonhoven, 1990), and I (Eisenhardt & Bourgeois, 1988; Eisenhardt, 1989a). Later, Steve Barley added to the bench strength related to this method when he moved from Cornell to Stanford. Steve, Diane Bailey, and their Ph.D. students (Bechky, 2003; O'Mahony, 2003) contributed a more ethnographic approach to the method in their study of work within engineering firms in Silicon Valley and beyond. In fact, multiple-case, theory-building studies became a signature method for Stanford, and the University became a world-leading institution in the development of this method for conducting organizational research.

The usual approach to multiple-case, theory-building was to carve a theoretical gap for which there was either no prior theory or conflicting theories, theoretically sample between about 4 and 12 cases, gather extensive field data, and develop theory using comparative case and grounded theory-building analytic techniques (Eisenhardt, 1989b; Eisenhardt & Graebner, 2007). Somewhat ironically, the method had surprising similarities to that used in the empirical studies on "old" institutional theory with their emphasis on a careful comparison of small number of cases. Throughout the 1990s, a string of Ph.D. students including Beth Bechky, Shona Brown, Kim Elsbach, Charlie Galunic, Andy Hargadon, and Mark Zbracki completed Ph.D. dissertations that relied on this method.

Surprisingly, the multiple-case, theory-building method found its Stanford home in the Department of Industrial Engineering. So, this most qualitative of methods wound up being developed in the most quantitative of schools at the University. But while the qualitative features of this method did not fit with engineering, the method's emphasis on staying closely in touch with real-world phenomena in actual companies did fit very well with the problem-solving ethos of engineering. So via a very emergent process that was rather like the processes in the technology-based firms being studied, a vibrant, field-oriented, case-based research community with two research centers (i.e., Stanford Technology Ventures Program and the Center for Work, Technology, and Organization) cropped up in the School of Engineering.

ORGANIZATIONAL PROCESSES, SEMI-STRUCTURES, AND NETWORKS AT THE "EDGE OF CHAOS"

As it turned out, the multiple-case, inductive method was particularly well-suited to studying *organizational processes*. Such processes could typically only be studied well with field data. So, researchers converged on using field-based data, a relatively small sample size, and often theory-building cases to study organizational process phenomena such as product development (Schoonhoven et al., 1990; Brown & Eisenhardt, 1997; Hansen, 1999; Miner et al., 2001), technology brokering (Hargadon & Sutton, 1997; Hargadon, 2003), strategic decision making (Burgelman, 1991, 2004; Eisenhardt & Bourgeois, 1988; Eisenhardt, 1989a), being acquired (Graebner, 2004), technical work (Bechky, 2003; O'Mahony, 2003), and creating networks (Hallen, 2008).

A good example is the research of Anne Miner, who studied the process of job creation for her Ph.D. at Stanford, and later improvisation in product development processes (Miner et al., 2001). Her work on improvisation is particularly intriguing. She and her colleagues used rich case studies of innovation in several firms to develop new insights about improvisation, to distinguish it from other forms of learning, and to clarify its short- and long-term implications for successful (and not so successful) product development processes (Miner et al., 2001). Similarly, Charlie Galunic relied on the multiple-case, theory-building method to study how the senior executives at a major Silicon Valley firm engaged in a "charter change" process to shift very frequently the architecture of product-market responsibilities among the firm's business units (Galunic & Eisenhardt, 1996, 2001). This process was especially striking because it was the keystone for this firm's stunning track record as the most consistently high-performing, technology-based firm over a three-decade period. Overall, the point is that the multiple-case, inductive method was essential for tackling research questions when appropriate theory was limited or even non-existent, and organizational processes were particularly relevant.

Over time, research in technology-based companies led to fresh insights and new theories. Among the most important theoretical developments was fleshing out the theoretical implications for organizations as *complex adaptive systems,* and more generally, complexity theory. Complex adaptive systems are sets of loosely coupled, unique actors such as jazz bands, basketball teams, multi-business corporations, and networks of people, groups, and organizations. The core insights focus on moderately connected systems of agents that act using simple rules (i.e., complex adaptive systems). These systems have emergent properties that originate from agent actions and generate complex behaviors such that they out-perform both more and less structured systems in dynamic environments (Brown & Eisenhardt, 1998).

Important themes about emergence and complexity came from studies of *loosely coupled, modular networks* including the work on technology brokering at Ideo (Sutton & Hargadon, 1996; Hargadon & Sutton, 1997) and on charter change across business units at a major Silicon Valley-based technology firm (Galunic & Eisenhardt, 1996, 2001). Morten Hansen (1999, 2002) developed particularly key insights in his study of the network connections among business units within a large, technology-based corporation in Silicon Valley. He found that loosely coupled networks not only accelerated product innovation, but also created the core tradeoff between searching for opportunities and executing them. Working at a higher level of analysis, Woody Powell and his colleagues focused their attention on networks as the source of innovation within the biotechnology industry (Powell et al., 1996; Owen-Smith & Powell, 2004). By studying how networks of innovation collaboration among partially connected organizations emerged, these researchers clarified the evolution of networks, the growth paths of particularly successful firms, and the role of loose coupling in generating network-wide innovations.

Important themes about emergence and complexity also came from studies of *semi-structures* and *simple rules* within highly innovative, adaptive organizations. Jelinek and Schoonhoven (1990) were among the first to recognize that effective organizations in dynamic environments were not completely unstructured as had been asserted in earlier contingency theory. Rather, they were semi-structured. Without structures, organizations in dynamic environments fell apart. Their work foreshadowed later research that more explicitly focused on the semi-structures and simple rules that are the central to the emergent, improvised behavior that characterizes complex adaptive systems (Eisenhardt & Tabrizi, 1995; Miner et al., 2001). Related research highlighted the role of simple rules and dynamic capabilities in the strategies of technology-based firms (Eisenhardt & Martin, 2000). For example, Shona Brown and I examined organization and strategy at the "edge of chaos" by studying 12 global computing firms. We explored the roles of semi-structures, modularity, and simple rules in the emergence of cross-business synergies, business strategies, experimentation, and timing. Illustrative of the value placed on rigor and relevance, we published in both Administrative Science Quarterly (ASQ) (Brown & Eisenhardt, 1997) and Harvard Business Review (Eisenhardt & Brown, 1999). Shona went on to apply the "edge of chaos" insights as Senior Vice-president cum organizational architect for Google.

Collectively, the legacy and critical acclaim of the Stanford research on emergence and complexity themes is striking. In addition to numerous Ph.D. dissertation awards and book awards, three of the above papers won ASQ's scholarly contribution award (i.e., Eisenhardt & Tabrizi, 1995;

Powell et al., 1996; Hansen, 1999). More broadly, Stanford scholars working in technology-based firms were among the leaders in the new thinking about organizations and networks of organizations using the complexity sciences.

CLASSIC THEORIES FROM THE ENTREPRENEUR'S LENS

The convergence of technological innovations during the Internet boom once again prompted a surge of foundings of technology-based ventures. Much of the related research at Stanford used the lens of the entrepreneurial firm to refresh a variety of existing theories. By taking the entrepreneur's perspective in relationships with larger and more established firms, this research flipped the usual dominant-firm perspective of theories such as social network, agency, resource dependence, and institutional approaches. So, for example, Ph.D. dissertations by Fabrizio Ferraro, Melissa Graebner, Ben Hallen, Andrew Nelson, Pinar Ozcan, Jeff Rosenberger, and Filipe Santos adopted the entrepreneurial lens on phenomena such as being acquired, pioneering nascent markets, gaining venture capital ties, attracting corporate venture capital, and building portfolios of alliances with large partner firms. In so doing, these more recent researchers often refreshed existing theories, particularly by illuminating the role of ostensibly low-power actors (i.e., entrepreneurial firms) in nascent markets and in their relationships with major corporations (Graebner, 2004; Hallen, 2008). Other researchers from the Stanford organizations community also began to take advantage of technology-based firms in Silicon Valley and beyond by extending extant theories to examine topics that were relevant within this context such as the social network factors that influenced the speed of IPO's (Stuart et al., 1999), an evolutionary perspective on product evolution (Sorenson, 2000; Katila & Ahuja, 2002), and the institutional implications of Silicon Valley law firms (Suchman, 1995).

STANFORD'S ORGANIZATIONAL COMMUNITY

The organizational community at Stanford with its interdisciplinary emphasis and organizational training was essential to the emergence of this more slowly developing research that found its inspiration in the other revolution of technology-based firms of Silicon Valley and beyond. It is a tribute to the openness of Dick Scott and the rest of the organizations community that this research was able to flourish despite its orthogonal research style of field data, relatively small sample sizes, and multiple-case, theory-building studies. Its alternative research questions and constructs, and its newer, more emergent theories were distinctly different from those of others in the community. Yet, the much-beloved Asilomar conferences provided particularly significant opportunities to learn from others and to test ideas. The training grants and associated get-togethers also provided very welcome financial aid, camaraderie, and guidance.

If there is a recipe to be learned from the rich theoretical and methodological legacy of Stanford's organizational research from 1970 to 2000, then it is probably a simple one. Mix researchers together from diverse areas and interests, place them in a relaxing venue with some yummy nibbles and tasty drinks, and let the magic happen. In fact, come to think of it, that sounds a lot like how effective adaptation and rich innovation quickly emerge in the technology-based firms of Silicon Valley.

REFERENCES

Baron, J. N., Hannan, M. T., & Burton, M. D. (1999). Building the iron cage: Determinants of managerial intensity in the early years of organization. *American Sociological Review*, *64*(4), 527–547.

Bechky, B. A. (2003). Sharing meaning across occupational communities: The transformation of understanding on a production floor. *Organization Science, 14*, 312–330.

Beckman, C. M., & Burton, M. D. (2008). Founding the future: The evolution of top management teams from founding to IPO. *Organization Science, 19*(1), 3–24.

Beckman, C. M., Burton, M. D., & O'Reilly, C. (2007). Early teams: The impact of team demography on VC financing and going public. *Journal of Business Venturing, 22*(2), 147–173.

Brown, S. L., & Eisenhardt, K. M. (1997). The art of continuous change: Linking complexity theory and time-paced evolution in relentlessly shifting organizations. *Administrative Science Quarterly, 42*(1), 1–34.

Brown, S. L., & Eisenhardt, K. M. (1998). *Competing on the edge: Strategy as structured chaos.* Boston: Harvard Business School Press.

Burgelman, R. A. (1991). Intraorganizational ecology of strategy making and organizational adaptation. *Organization Science, 2*(3), 239–262.

Burgelman, R. A. (1994). Fading memories: A process theory of strategic business exit in dynamic environments. *Administrative Science Quarterly, 39*(1), 24–56.

Burgelman, R. A. (2002). Strategy as vector and the inertia of coevolutionary lock-in. *Administrative Science Quarterly, 47*(2), 325–357.

Burton, M. D., Sorensen, J. B., & Beckman, C. M. (2002). Coming from good stock: Career histories and new venture formation. In: M. Lounsbury & M. Ventresca (Eds), *Research in the sociology of organizations* (Vol. 19). Greenwich, CT: JAI Press.

Eisenhardt, K. M. (1989a). Making fast strategic decisions in high-velocity environments. *Academy of Management Journal, 32*(3), 543–576.

Eisenhardt, K. M. (1989b). Building theories from case study research. *Academy of Management Review, 14*(4), 532–550.

Eisenhardt, K. M., & Bourgeois, L. J. (1988). Politics of strategic decision making: Toward a mid-range theory. *Academy of Management Journal, 14*(4), 737–770.

Eisenhardt, K. M., & Brown, S. L. (1999). Patching: Restitching business portfolios in dynamic markets. *Harvard Business Review* (May–June), 72–82.

Eisenhardt, K. M., & Graebner, M. E. (2007). Theory building from cases: Opportunities and challenges. *Academy of Management Journal, 50*(1), 25–32.

Eisenhardt, K. M., Kahwajy, J. L., & Bourgeois, L. J. (1997). How top management can teams have a good fight. *Harvard Business Review* (July–August), 77–84.

Eisenhardt, K. M., & Martin, J. A. (2000). Dynamic capabilities: What are they? *Strategic Management Journal, 21*(Special Issue), 1105–1121.

Eisenhardt, K. M., & Schoonhoven, C. B. (1990). Organizational growth: Linking founding team, strategy, environment and growth among U.S. semiconductor. *Administrative Science Quarterly, 35*(3), 504–529.

Eisenhardt, K. M., & Schoonhoven, C. B. (1994). Triggering strategic alliances in entrepreneurial firms: The case of technology-sharing alliances. In: W. Bygrave. S. Birley, N. Churchill, E. Gatewood, F. Hoy, R. Keeley & W. Wetzel (Eds), *Frontiers of entrepreneurship research*. Babson Park, MA: Babson College Publishers.

Eisenhardt, K. M., & Schoonhoven, C. B. (1996). Resource-based view of strategic alliance formation: Strategic and social effects in entrepreneurial ventures, 1978–1988. *Organization Science, 7*(2), 136–150.

Eisenhardt, K. M., & Tabrizi, B. N. (1995). Accelerating adaptive processes: Product innovation in the global computer industry. *Administrative Science Quarterly, 40*(1), 84–110.

Galunic, D. C., & Eisenhardt, K. M. (1996). The evolution of intracorporate domains: Divisional charter losses in high-technology. *Organization Science, 7*(3), 255–282.

Galunic, D. C., & Eisenhardt, K. M. (2001). Architectural innovation and modular corporate forms. *Academy of Management Journal, 44*(6), 1229–1249.

Graebner, M. E. (2004). Momentum and serendipity: How acquired leaders create value in the integration of technology firms. *Strategic Management Journal, 25*(8–9), 751–777.

Hallen, B. L. (2008). The causes and consequences of the initial network positions of new Organizations: From whom do entrepreneurs receive investments? *Administrative Science Quarterly, 53*(4), 685–715.

Hannan, M. T., & Freeman, J. H. (1977). The population ecology of organizations. *American Journal of Sociology, 82*, 929–964.

Hansen, M. T. (1999). The search-transfer problem: The role of weak ties in sharing knowledge across organization subunits. *Administrative Science Quarterly, 44*(1), 82–112.

Hansen, M. T. (2002). Knowledge networks: Explaining effective knowledge sharing in multiunit companies. *Organization Science, 13*(3), 232–248.

Hargadon, A. B. (2003). *How breakthroughs happen: The surprising truth about how companies innovate*. Boston: Harvard Business School Press.

Hargadon, A. B., & Sutton, R. I. (1997). Technology brokering and innovation in a product development firm. *Administrative Science Quarterly, 42*(4), 716–749.

Jelinek, M., & Schoonhoven, C. B. (1990). *The innovation marathon: Lessons from high technology firms.* Oxford, UK: Blackwell.

Katila, R., & Ahuja, A. (2002). Something old and something new: A longitudinal study of search behavior and new product introduction. *Academy of Management Journal, 45*(3), 1183–1194.

Meyer, J. W., & Rowan, B. (1977). Institutional organizations: Structure as myth and ceremony. *American Journal of Sociology, 83*, 340–363.

Miner, A. S., Bassoff, P., & Moorman, C. (2001). Organizational improvisation and learning: A field study. *Administrative Science Quarterly, 46*(2), 304–337.

O'Mahony, S. (2003). Guarding the commons: How community managed software projects protect their work. *Research Policy, 32*(7), 1179–1198.

Ouchi, W. G. (1980). Markets, clans, and bureaucracies. *Administrative Science Quarterly, 25*(1), 129–141.

Ouchi, W. G. (1981). *Theory Z: How American business can meet the Japanese Challenge.* Reading, MA: Addison-Wesley.

Owen-Smith, J., & Powell, W. W. (2004). Knowledge networks as channels and conduits: The effects of spillovers in the Boston biotechnology community. *Organization Science, 15*(1), 5–21.

Pfeffer, J., & Salancik, G. (1978). *The external control of organizations.* New York: Harper & Row.

Powell, W. W., Koput, K. W., & Smith-Doerr, L. (1996). Interorganizational collaboration and the locus of innovation: Networks of learning in biotechnology. *Administrative Science Quarterly, 41*(1), 116–145.

Roure, J., & Maidique, M. (1986). Predictors of success in new technology-based ventures. *Journal of Business Venturing, 1*(3), 295–306.

Schoonhoven, C. B., & Eisenhardt, K. M. (1992). Regions as industrial incubators of new technology-based firms: Implications for economic growth. In: E. S. Mills & J. F. McDonald (Eds), *Sources of metropolitan growth.* New Brunswick, NJ: Center for Urban Policy Research.

Schoonhoven, C. B., & Eisenhardt, K. M. (1993). Entrepreneurial environments: Incubator region effects on the birth of new technology-based firms. In: L. Gomez-Mejia & M. Lawless (Eds), *Advances in global high-technology management: High technology venturing.* Greenwich, CT: JAI Press Inc.

Schoonhoven, C. B., & Eisenhardt, K. M. (1995). Effects of founding conditions on the creation of manufacturing alliances in U.S. semiconductor firms. In: H. Thomas, D. O'Neal & E. Zajac (Eds), *Integrating strategy: The power of synthesis.* New York: John Wiley & Sons.

Schoonhoven, C. B., Eisenhardt, K. M., & Lyman, K. (1990). Speeding products to market: Waiting time to first product introduction in new firms. *Administrative Science Quarterly, 35*(1), 177–207.

Sorenson, O. (2000). Letting the market work for you: An evolutionary perspective on product strategy. *Strategic Management Journal, 21*(5), 577–592.

Stuart, T. E. (1998). Network positions and propensities to collaborate: An investigation of strategic alliance formation in a high-technology industry. *Administrative Science Quarterly, 43*(3), 668–698.

Stuart, T. E., Hoang, H., & Hybels, R. C. (1999). Interorganizational endorsements and the performance of entrepreneurial ventures. *Administrative Science Quarterly, 44*(2), 315–349.

Suchman, M. C. (1995). Localism and globalism in institutional analysis: The emergence of contractual norms in venture finance. In: W. R. Scott & S. Christensen (Eds), *The institutional construction of organizations.* Thousand Oaks, CA: Sage Publications.

Sutton, R. I., & Callahan, A. L. (1987). The stigma of bankruptcy: Spoiled organizational image and its management. *Academy of Management Journal, 30*(3), 405–436.

Sutton, R. I., & Hargadon, A. B. (1996). Brainstorming groups in context: Effectiveness in a product design firm. *Administrative Science Quarterly, 41*(4), 685–718.

CHAPTER 11

WHEN THEORY MET PRACTICE: COOPERATION AT STANFORD

Roderick M. Kramer

In this brief, reflective chapter, I provide an overview of what is now a 30 year program of research on the antecedents and consequences of cooperative behavior. I trace the development of this research program from its inception in 1980, where I was then a graduate student in experimental social psychology at the University of California at Santa Barbara, to the quarter century I have spent subsequently at the Stanford Graduate School of Business.

Although one aim of this chapter is to communicate some (hopefully) interesting and useful academic insights and understandings from that program of research, a more salient and personal aim is to acknowledge the substantive contributions of the many talented graduate students and professional colleagues whose presence and support contributed greatly to this research. For a scholar studying cooperative behavior, one could not imagine a more perfect place to work. The vibrant and inclusive research atmosphere I encountered as a newly minted assistant professor arriving at Stanford in 1985 was an enormous catalyst to my work as a scholar and my development as a teacher. When it came to cooperation, I found that the Stanford organizations community was a place where theory and practice converged. Appropriately, therefore, I begin by talking about the people.

Stanford's Organization Theory Renaissance, 1970–2000
Research in the Sociology of Organizations, Volume 28, 207–219
Copyright © 2010 by Emerald Group Publishing Limited
All rights of reproduction in any form reserved
ISSN: 0733-558X/doi:10.1108/S0733-558X(2010)0000028015

THE PEOPLE WHO MADE THE PLACE

In their original invitation, editors Kaye Schoonhoven and Frank Dobbin urged the contributors to this volume to be substantive and scholarly in their approach to their essays. I have tried to honor their request by summarizing the results of a programmatic line of scholarly inquiry on a thorny academic problem. It is also a problem of enormous and enduring real-world importance: As the world continues to confront divisive and escalating conflicts over how to share increasingly scarce global resources, we need to have a better understanding of when and why people are willing to cooperate to solve such problems.

I have to confess, however, that I instantly agreed to participate in this volume not because it would provide a chance to wax on about my research. Rather, my ready acquiescence to their request reflected two motives that were more personal than scholarly. The first motive was simply an acute sense of indebtedness to the place. Stanford has been an exceptionally good place for me to develop as an organizational theorist and I am grateful for the many experiences it has provided. Thus, I viewed the writing of this chapter as an opportunity for me to acknowledge the formative role that Stanford University played in my development as an young (and, in fact, completely naïve) organizational scholar. I was trained as a "pure," and at that time intendedly die-hard, experimental social psychologist. I never ever anticipated during my four years of doctoral training ending up in a business school. In fact, when I joined the Graduate School of Business, there were only a very small handful of active social psychologists situated in business schools. These included Joel Brockner at Columbia, Blair Sheppard at Duke, and Joanne Martin at Stanford.

A second motive for participating in this volume is that I thought I might be able to offer a somewhat different – and perhaps unique – perspective on organizational theory development at Stanford during this period. Because I studied cooperative decision making in experimental settings, I was a bit of an "odd duck" when I first came to the campus in 1985. At that time, the norm for our small organizations group in the business school seemed to be "hire one of everything." So, I felt myself (happily) to be one of these "one's." As an experimental social psychologist, and a latent behavioral decision theorist, I was hardly paddling center stream in the flourishing macro-organizational currents flowing through the Farm at the time. Indeed, the disciplinary waters seemed flush with sociologists. But the excitement these organizational sociologists generated was infectious; it was the intellectual equivalent of whitewater all the time. Moreover, they were an amazingly welcoming and generous group – thanks in large measure to the unlimited enthusiasm and inclusive spirit of our organizations community leader, Dick Scott. I also benefited from the ever-generous "Buzz" Zelditch in Sociology, who made his lab available to me for running experiments (the business school had no laboratory facility at the time and when I inquired of our Associate Dean Gene Webb as to the prospects for even a one-room lab space, his response was a warm but instant, "It ain't gonna happen. Find some lab space elsewhere." I emphasize warm here because Gene was one of the most supportive Associate Deans I have experienced in all my years at Stanford).

On the more micro-side of our small OB group, Hal Leavitt, Gene Webb, and Joanne Martin warmly drew me into their fold and helped me learn the ropes. Social psychologist Peter Wright, in our marketing group, became a steadfast friend and we spent many hours sharing ideas and talking about exciting experiments. Joanne Martin helped me learn the ropes. She was extraordinarily generous with her time and gracious with her patience. We took many walks to the Stanford bookstore and I learned a great deal about how the wheels turned from those walks. Jeffrey Pfeffer and Robert Sutton each deserve special nods themselves – Bob for seducing me into the joys of qualitative work, and Jeff for inviting me to teach power and influence with him. Bob was one of the first scholars to invite me to do collaborative work at Stanford. We had a great deal of fun writing a paper together about impression management within the Reagan administration. Jeffrey Pfeffer was a source of endless narratives – about where the field had gone, where it was today, and where it might go. I think I have learned more about creative work from Jeff than anyone else at Stanford. He inspires, intimidates, and challenges by his industry, depth, and breadth of scholarship. Sociologists Jim Baron and Don Palmer were endlessly generous with their time in terms of helping me learn to teach the core course in organizational behavior at the business school. I also developed two new MBA electives that first year – the first scholarly elective at the business school on negotiations and the second an elective on small group dynamics and decision making. Both benefited enormously from Jim, Don, Joanne, Hal, Jeff, and Bob. On a personal level, I think of those early years as halcyon years in the Stanford organizations community – and for me personally those years were made all the more golden by the presence of such incredible colleagues.

I was also fortunate to work in those critical pre-tenure years with some truly wonderful graduate students – Debra Meyerson, Gerald Davis, Pamela Pommereneke, Elizabeth Newton, and Kimberly Elsbach.

Each contributed immeasurably to the development of my research. And they offered warm and enduring friendships that continue to this day.

The research I dutifully summarize in the next section could not have been done without their earnest and enthusiastic cooperation.

COOPERATION THEORY CIRCA 1985

Situations where social actors exert fate control over each other are known formally as *interdependence dilemmas*. When I first joined Stanford's organizational theory community in 1985, an atmosphere of intense intellectual excitement existed for social scientists studying such dilemmas. At least three important scholarly developments fueled this excitement. The first was the publication of Hardin's (1968) influential article on the "tragedy of the commons." Hardin's short but evocative essay created an enormous stir among researchers across a variety of disciplines. It was immediately evident that the simple parable of the commons constituted a powerful analog for a variety of vexing real-world collective action problems. The second development was Axelrod's (1980a, 1980b, 1984; Axelrod & Dion, 1988) innovative and insightful work on the evolution of cooperation. Almost single-handedly, his innovative computer tournament methodology – and the intriguing results it spawned – revitalized interest in the prisoner's dilemma game. The third development was Kelley and Thibaut's (1978) powerful and rich social psychological framework for understanding how social actors construe and respond to interdependence dilemmas.

At the heart of, and common to, all three of these major streams of research were a preoccupation with the foundations of cooperation among interdependent social decision makers. My research in this arena has focused on identifying psychological, social and structural determinants of cooperative choice across a variety of such dilemmas. These include the commons dilemma (Kramer & Brewer, 1984; Kramer & Goldman, 1995; Kramer, McClintock, & Messick, 1986; Messick et al., 1983; Parker et al., 1983), public goods dilemma (Brewer & Kramer, 1986), security dilemma (Kramer, 1987, 1989; Kramer, Meyerson, & Davis, 1990a, 1990b), two-person and *n*-person forms of negotiation dilemmas (Kramer, 1991b; Kramer & Messick, 1998; Kramer, Newton, & Pommerenke, 1993; Kramer, Pommerenke, & Newton, 1993; Kramer, Pradhan-Shah, & Woerner, 1995), organizational resource dilemmas (Kramer, 1991a; Kramer & Messick, 1996a, 1996b), noisy repeated prisoner's dilemmas (Bendor, Kramer, & Stout, 1991), and both dyadic and *n*-person trust dilemmas (Kramer, 1994, 1996, 1998; Messick & Kramer, 2001).

In their comprehensive catalog of interdependence dilemmas, Kelley et al. (2003) provided a systematic and exhaustive taxonomy of the myriad forms such dilemmas take. To set the stage for my discussion of the individual studies described in more detail below, a brief overview of the general anatomy of an interdependence dilemma may be useful. Trust dilemmas represent a prototypic example of interdependence problem, and I will use them to illustrate some major psychological and structural features of such situations.

Formally, trust dilemmas possess a deceptively simple decision structure. A social actor *S*, hoping to realize some perceived benefit, is tempted to engage in some form of trusting behavior with one or more other social actors. Engaging in such behavior, however, exposes *S* to the prospect that his or her trust might be exploited or betrayed by the other party or parties with whom *S* is interdependent. Hence, most starkly stated, the choice dilemma for *S* is whether to trust or not to trust.

Although the logical structure of choice in trust dilemmas can be expressed in such simple terms, the decisions themselves are psychologically more complex. First of all, such decisions resemble other forms of approach-avoidance conflict, in that a decision maker is simultaneously attracted to the prospect of reaping some desired benefit, while also hoping to avoid disappointment or loss. The psychological complexity of choice in trust dilemmas is further animated, of course, by the inherent and inescapable uncertainties we face whenever we find ourselves trying to assess the trustworthiness of other people on whom we must rely or depend. We can never know with complete certainty, for example, another person's true character or underlying motivation. Nor can we ever fully comprehend their intentions towards us. And we can never completely monitor all of their relevant actions, and especially those behaviors they might engage in behind our backs. As trust theorist Diego Gambetta (1988) once noted in this regard, "The condition of ignorance or uncertainty about other people's behavior is central to the notion of trust. It is related to the limits of our capacity ever to achieve a full knowledge of others, their motives, and their responses" (p. 218). However much we might desire transparency and clarity in our relations with others, there will always be a curtain of doubt interposed between self and other.

From the standpoint of contemporary theory and research on social decision making, Gambetta's observation raises a variety of cogent but analytically vexing questions. First and foremost, on what basis do they assess another person's trustworthiness or lack of trustworthiness? What counts as sufficient evidence to push one towards trust? Under what circumstances are we likely to decide to give someone the benefit of the doubt when entering into a potentially profitable trust relationship? In short, on what psychological grounds do we trust others and decide, in turn, to cooperate with them? These are some of the central questions addressed by the research my graduate students and I have done over the years, and which this chapter reviews. In the next section, I discuss some of these collaborative ventures and what we learned from them.

UNTYING THE KNOT: UNDERSTANDING WHEN AND WHY PEOPLE COOPERATE

I had the extra-ordinary good fortune to begin my graduate training as an experimentalist under the guidance of two outstanding experimental social psychologists – Marilynn Brewer and David Messick. Both were faculty members at the University of California at Santa Barbara and both were interested in studying social dilemma behavior. To do so, they put together an amazing team of young researchers, including Scott Allison and Charles Samuelson. As new doctoral students, we were eager to unravel the mysteries of cooperation. Those were exciting days – and equally exciting but long nights. We developed one of the very first computer-interactive behavioral labs for studying social dilemma behavior. Setting up such a lab today would be child's play. But back then the programming needed just to get six computer terminals linked together and capable of interacting in real-time was no mean task. The laboratory paradigm we developed (Parker et al., 1983) was so successful that it became a prototype for many other labs and remains in use today.

In one of our first studies using this new lab (Messick et al., 1983), we investigated how decision makers' *expectations of reciprocity* influence their willingness to exercise personal self-restraint in a commons dilemma. Such expectations represent one important cognitive component of trust. Similarly, people's willingness to exercise personal self-restraint when consuming shared resource pools can be viewed as a behavioral indicator of trust in others. Consistent with our theoretical expectations, we found that individuals who expected reciprocal restraint from other group members were more likely to exercise personal self-restraint themselves. This restraint was especially evident, moreover, under conditions of increasing resource scarcity. Thus, we showed (at least in the context of a laboratory simulation) that people were willing to do their part in cooperating to preserve an endangered collective resource so long as they believed others were willing to do so as well.

In a subsequent set of experiments, Marilynn Brewer and I (Brewer & Kramer, 1986; Kramer & Brewer, 1984) extended this investigation by examining the effects of *group-based trust* on personal restraint in social dilemmas. Drawing on Brewer's previous work on ingroup stereotyping and favoritism, we reasoned that individuals within small, cohesive social groups might possess a generalized or "depersonalized" form of trust that extends to other ingroup members. Even within the context of our minimal laboratory groups, our data provided some support for this notion, although the data revealed a more complex picture than we had theorized. In particular, we found that a variety of psychological and structural factors influenced both people's trust-related expectations and their actual choice behavior in these circumstances. These factors included such variables as (1) the decision structure or framing of the choice dilemma, (2) the size of the group confronting the dilemma, and (3) the level of salient social categorization. In terms of their relevance to the present essay, the results served to indicate just how psychologically complex individuals' responses to uncertainty about others' intentions and motives can be. In particular, when doubt exists regarding others' trustworthiness, decision makers tend to try to "fill in the holes" in their understanding, using whatever social information and situational cues are available.

The next set of experiments we conducted explored in more detail the effects of these psychological variables on another form of dilemma known as a security dilemma. In a security dilemma, decision makers must choose between cooperative restraint and potentially escalatory security moves. As in our earlier studies, we found that decision framing, level of salient social categorization, and mental simulation on judgment and choice produced strong effects on cooperative choice, in full accord with our theoretical expectations (Kramer, 1989; Kramer et al., 1990a). Specifically, we explored how the framing of a risky decision (i.e., whether resource allocation decisions were framed in terms of prospective gains versus losses) influenced decision makers' preferences for different outcome distributions. We also investigated how engaging in "best-case" versus "worst-case" mental simulations about an opponent's actions affected judgment and choice. Interestingly, we found that simply having people think about worst-case possibilities regarding their opponents' intentions and behaviors increased their willingness to allocate resources to protect against those imagined threats.

Using a different and new laboratory paradigm – this one designed to
simulate an *n*-person trust dilemma – an additional study explored the
effects of social uncertainty on a variety of social cognitive processes that
contribute to distrust and suspicion of other social actors (Kramer, 1994).
A basic premise of this study was that, under appropriate circumstances,
uncertainty about others' cooperative or competitive intentions might
contribute to paranoid-like suspicion and distrust of others. In accord with
this premise, the results of this experiment demonstrated that situationally
induced self-consciousness – which can be construed as a psychological
proxy for perception of social threat – led decision makers to over-estimate
others' lack of trustworthiness. Similarly, the results showed that providing
study participants an opportunity to ruminate about others' potentially
devious motives and intentions also increased suspicion and distrust of other
study participants. Construed broadly, these results suggested how
normatively "irrational" psychological factors can nonetheless influence
judgment and choice in such situations.

To summarize, the results of these laboratory studies identified a wide
range of social psychological variables that influence cooperative judgment
and choice across a variety of different kinds of interdependence dilemma.

CONCLUSIONS AND CAVEATS

Viewed in aggregate, the results from these studies reveal the significant
extent to which decision makers' psychological construal of their
interdependence with other people is affected by both psychological and
situational factors. In particular, whether decision makers perceive social
opportunity or risk in their encounters with others is largely influenced by a
variety of basic cognitive processes – such as the initial perception of the
nature of their interdependence, the framing of their choices, and the
salience of various social identities or categories. The experiments also
implicate a variety of situational factors, including the salience feedback
about others' decisions, the structure of opportunity and vulnerability (e.g.,
institutional norms and constraints on choice), and level of uncertainty
inherent in the situation.

The results of these studies also reveal some of the creative responses
decision makers make when attempting to cope with such interdependence.
One way of thinking about these responses is that they represent decision
makers' intendedly *adaptive* or *compensatory* actions. In other words, they
reflect decision makers' explicit "on-line" assessments as to how best to

manage the inherent trade-offs between perceived risks and perceived opportunities in situations involving uncertainty about others' motives and intentions. In this respect, these results accord nicely with prior arguments by Messick and his students regarding the utility of what he termed *social decision rules* for solving various kinds of interdependence dilemmas (e.g., Allison & Messick, 1990; Samuelson & Messick, 1995).

In the case of interdependence dilemma situations, the present research suggests that at least two different kinds of adaptive rules are important in helping decision makers respond to interdependence and uncertainty. One subset of rules can be thought of as predominantly cognitive in nature, and pertains to the social auditing heuristics individuals use when trying to assess opportunity and vulnerability in a given situation. This includes the search for evidence that individuals rely on when trying to assess others' trustworthiness and cooperativeness. These cognitive rules constitute, in a fashion, "social auditing" rules that decision makers employ to facilitate sense-making in dilemma situations. Such social auditing rules presumably reflect individuals' beliefs regarding what different behaviors by other people mean (e.g., how verbal and non-verbal behaviors should be interpreted or decoded). The social auditing rules people use reflect, in this sense, their *a priori* beliefs regarding the expressive attributes presumably correlated with, and predictive of, others' trustworthiness and cooperativeness.

A second subset of rules might be characterized as more behavioral in nature, and operates as prescriptive guidelines that support intendedly adaptive decision making. In other words, these prescriptive rules guide decision makers who are trying to determine how they ought to respond to a given situation, *given* their construal of it. These behavioral rules can be viewed as intendedly adaptive in the sense that their use presumably helps decision makers reap the benefits of trust and cooperation when they happen to be dealing with trustworthy and cooperative others. At the same time, they help minimize the costs of misplaced trust and cooperation when they happen to be interacting with untrustworthy or uncooperative others. As noted throughout this chapter, research by many scholars have documented the versatility and power of even very simple decision rules for navigating social dilemmas (Axelrod, 1984; Gigerenzer, 2000).

One of the major goals of these studies has been to explicate some of the cognitive processes associated with social judgment in the face of interdependence and uncertainty. We can conceptualize decision makers' judgments in these dilemma situations as forms of embedded or "situated" cognition. Situated cognitions locate our choices about whom to trust and cooperate with within a much larger class of judgments that have been extensively studied by behavioral decision theorists. Their prior research takes as a starting point the recognition that human beings are imperfect information processors who must often render judgments before all of the relevant and desired facts are known. This fundamental idea was first articulated by Simon (1957) in the notion of *satisficing*. In contrast to conceptions of decision making that presumed thorough and exhaustive search, Simon argued that people often are satisfied with alternatives that are perceived as acceptable or good enough under the prevailing circumstances.

Stimulated by the pioneering work of Kahneman and Tversky (1984), the study of heuristic reasoning was enjoying a period of considerable vogue at the time we conducted our studies on cooperation. It then, however, went through a period of spirited scrutiny. In particular, a number of decision theorists – most notably Hogarth (1981) and von Winterfeldt and Edwards (1986) – began to suggest that the contemporary focus on the ways in which heuristic processes led to judgmental biases misrepresents reality and constituted "a message of despair" (von Winterfeldt & Edwards, 1986, p. 531). To be sure, the predominant emphasis of experimental research for several decades did seem to be the documentation of judgmental short-comings. However, some responded; perhaps the baby had been thrown out with the bath water. In this spirit, a variety of studies have undertaken the task of rehabilitating the notion of heuristic information processing (e.g., Allison & Messick, 1990). Of particular note, there has been a movement away from thinking that heuristics are necessarily sources of biased or flawed cognition, and instead toward thinking of heuristics as adaptive cognitions (Gigerenzer, 2000; Gigerenzer & Todd, 1999). These studies, and many others, converge on the proposition that in some contexts even very simple decision heuristics can produce highly efficient and satisfactory results for a variety of important information processing tasks.

From the perspective of such work, it would be easy to construe such heuristic-based modes of judgment as somewhat shallow or "quick and dirty." They might seem to occur in the "blink" of an eye or, more literarily perhaps, a blink of the mind (Gladwell, 2005; Gigerenzer, 2007). But there are many circumstances where judgments about who to trust or cooperate with must be rendered swiftly, even if not all of the relevant or desired information is available to decision makers (Gambetta & Hamill, 2005).

These are only first steps, of course, on the road to a more complete understanding of how decision makers think about and respond to interdependence dilemmas. In the final analysis, I remain optimistic about people's prospects for solving such dilemmas. If people can think their way into dilemmas, they can also think their way out of them.

A PARTING REFLECTION

This chapter has provided an opportunity for me to cast an affectionate glance back at what seems like a long scholarly odyssey. Although I have highlighted the importance of the Stanford organizations community in this narrative, I should acknowledge that this odyssey has been physical as well as intellectual. Over the past 30 years, I have had the good fortune to spend time at the Russell Sage Foundation, the Center for Advanced Studies, Bellagio, Oxford, Cambridge, the London Business School, the Hoover Institution, and Harvard's Kennedy School of Government. Each of these places, and the people who inhabit them, are obvious extra-ordinary centers of intellectual life and commitment. But I am always mindful (and grateful) for the long shadow that Stanford has cast over my academic life. When I think now about my formative days at Stanford, I recall what Ernest Hemingway once said about his early years as a struggling writer in Paris. "If you are lucky enough to have lived in Paris as a young man, then wherever you go and for the rest of your life, Paris goes with you, for Paris is a moveable feast." For me, Stanford has been just such a moveable feast.

REFERENCES

Allison, S., & Messick, D. (1990). Social decision heuristics in the use of share resources. *Journal of Behavioral Decision Making, 3*, 195–204.

Axelrod, R. (1980a). Effective choice in the prisoner's dilemma. *Journal of Conflict Resolution, 24*, 3–25.

Axelrod, R. (1980b). More effective choice in the prisoner's dilemma. *Journal of Conflict Resolution, 24*, 379–403.

Axelrod, R. (1984). *The evolution of cooperation*. New York: Basic Books.

Axelrod, R., & Dion, D. (1988). The further evolution of cooperation. *Science, 242*, 1385–1390.

Bendor, J., Kramer, R. M., & Stout, S. (1991). When in doubt: Cooperation in the noisy prisoner's dilemma. *Journal of Conflict Resolution, 35*, 691–719.

Brewer, M. B., & Kramer, R. M. (1986). Choice behavior in social dilemmas: Effects of social identity, group size, and decision framing. *Journal of Personality and Social Psychology, 50*, 543–549.

Gambetta, D. (1988). Can we trust trust? In: D. Gambetta (Ed.), *Trust* (pp. 213–238). New York: Blackwell.

Gambetta, D., & Hamill, H. (2005). *Streetwise: How taxi drivers establish their customers' trustworthiness*. New York: Russell Sage Foundation.

Gigerenzer, G. (2000). *Adaptive thinking: Rationality in the real world*. New York: Oxford University Press.

Gigerenzer, G. (2007). *Gut feelings: The intelligence of the unconscious*. New York: Viking.

Gigerenzer, G., & Todd, P. M. (1999). *Simple heuristics that make us smart*. New York: Oxford University Press

Gladwell, M. (2005). *Blink*. New York: Penguin.

Hardin, G. (1968). The tragedy of the commons. *Science, 162*, 1243–1248.

Hogarth, R. M. (1981). Beyond discrete biases: Functional and dysfunctional aspects of judgmental heuristics. *Psychological Bulletin, 90*, 197–217.

Kahneman, D., & Tversky, A. (1984). Choices, values, and frames. *American Psychologist, 39*, 250–341.

Kelley, H. H., Holmes, J. G., Kerr, N. L., Reis, H. T., Rusbult, C. E., & van Lange, P. (2003). *An atlas of interpersonal situations*. New York: Cambridge University Press.

Kelley, H. H., & Thibaut, J. W. (1978). *Interpersonal relations. A theory of interdependence*. Reading, MA: Addison-Wesley.

Kramer, R., Meyerson, D., & Davis, G. (1990a). How much is enough? Psychological components of "guns versus butter" decisions in a security dilemma. *Journal of Personality and Social Psychology, 58*, 984–993.

Kramer, R., Pommerenke, P., & Newton, E. (1993). The social context of negotiation: Effects of social identity and accountability on negotiator judgment and decision making. *Journal of Conflict Resolution, 37*, 633–654.

Kramer, R. M. (1987). Cooperation in security dilemmas. *Social Science, 72*, 144–148.

Kramer, R. M. (1989). Windows of vulnerability or cognitive illusions? Cognitive processes and the nuclear arms race. *Journal of Experimental Social Psychology, 25*, 79–100.

Kramer, R. M. (1991a). Intergroup relations and organizational dilemmas: The role of categorization processes. In: L. L. Cummings & B. M. Staw (Eds), *Research in Organizational Behavior* (Vol. 13, pp. 191–228). Greenwich, CT: JAI Press.

Kramer, R. M. (1991b). The more the merrier? Social psychological aspects of multi- party negotiations. In: R. Lewicki, B. Sheppard & M. Bazerman (Eds), *Research on Negotiation in Organizations* (Vol. 13, pp. 307–332). Greenwich, CT: JAI Press.

Kramer, R. M. (1994). The sinister attribution error. *Motivation and Emotion, 18*, 199–231.

Kramer, R. M. (1996). Divergent realities and convergent disappointments in the hierarchic relation: The intuitive auditor at work. In: R. M. Kramer & T. R. Tyler (Eds), *Trust in organizations: Frontiers of theory and research* (pp. 216–245). Thousand Oaks, CA: Sage Publications.

Kramer, R. M. (1998). Paranoid cognition in social systems. *Personality and Social Psychology Review, 2*, 251–275.

Kramer, R. M., & Brewer, M. B. (1984). Effects of group identity on resource use in a simulated commons dilemma. *Journal of Personality and Social Psychology, 46*, 1044–1057.

Kramer, R. M., & Goldman, L. (1995). Helping the group or helping yourself? Determinants of cooperation in resource conservation dilemmas. In: D. A. Schroeder (Ed.), *Social dilemmas*. New York: Praeger.

Kramer, R. M., McClintock, C. G., & Messick, D. M. (1986). Social values and cooperative response to a simulated resource conservation crisis. *Journal of Personality, 54*, 576–592.

Kramer, R. M., & Messick, D. M. (1996a). *Negotiation as a social process.* Thousand Oaks, CA: Sage Publications.

Kramer, R. M., & Messick, D. M. (1996b). Ethical cognition and the intuitive lawyer: Organizational dilemmas and the framing of choice. In: D. M. Messick & A. Tenbrunsel (Eds), *Codes of conduct: Behavioral research and business ethics.* New York: Russell Sage Foundation.

Kramer, R. M., & Messick, D. M. (1998). Getting by with a little help from our enemies: Collective paranoia and its role in intergroup relations. In: C. Sedikides, J. Schopler & C. Insko (Eds), *Intergroup cognition and intergroup behavior* (pp. 233–255). Hillsdale, NJ: Lawrence Erlbaum.

Kramer, R. M., Meyerson, D. M., & Davis, G. (1990b). Deterrence and the management of international conflicts: Cognitive aspects of deterrent decisions. In: A. Rahim (Ed.), *Conflict Management* (pp. 188–208). New York: Praeger.

Kramer, R. M., Newton, E., & Pommerenke, P. (1993). Self-enhancement biases and negotiator judgment: Effects of self-esteem and mood. *Organizational Behavior and Human Decision Processes, 56,* 110–133.

Kramer, R. M., Pradhan-Shah, P., & Woerner, S. (1995). Why ultimatums fail: Social identity and moralistic aggression in coercive bargaining. In: R. M. Kramer & D. M. Messick (Eds), *Negotiation as a social process* (pp. 123–146). Thousand Oaks, CA: Sage Publications.

Messick, D. M., & Kramer, R. M. (2001). Trust as a form of shallow morality. In: K. S. Cook (Ed.), *Trust in society* (pp. 89–118). New York: Russell Sage Foundation.

Messick, D. M., Wilke, H., Brewer, M. B., Kramer, R. M., Zemke-English, P., & Lui, L. (1983). Individual adaptations and structural change as solutions to social dilemmas. *Journal of Personality and Social Psychology, 44,* 294–309.

Parker, R., Lui, L., Messick, C., Messick, D. M., Brewer, M. B., Kramer, R. M., Samuelson, C. P., & Wilke, H. (1983). A computer laboratory for studying resource dilemmas. *Behavioral Science, 28,* 298–304.

Samuelson, C. D., & Messick, D. M. (1995). Let's make some new rules: Social factors that make freedom unattractive. In: R. M. Kramer & D. M. Messick (Eds), *Negotiation as a social process* (pp. 48–68). Thousand Oaks, CA: Sage.

Simon, H. A. (1957). *Models of man.* New York: Wiley.

von Winterfeldt, D., & Edwards, W. (1986). *Decision analysis and behavioral research.* Cambridge: Cambridge University Press.

CHAPTER 12

NIMH-SCOR: A PIONEERING CENTER AT STANFORD

Raymond E. Levitt

This chapter is a very personal set of reflections about how a traditionally trained civil engineer seeking new insights about the organization and management of complex, fast-paced projects found inspiration, guidance, and lifelong friendships through the Stanford Consortium on Organizational Research (SCOR). I will try to describe how, at several mileposts along my intellectual journey, the people, ideas, and intellectual and social community created by the SCOR challenged, nurtured, and refined the work of my research team. Moreover, I will show that SCOR was a forerunner of multiple cross-disciplinary, problem-focused Centers in the School of Engineering for which Stanford has been become famous and has been widely emulated.

BEFORE STANFORD

I received a traditional undergraduate degree in Civil Engineering from the University of Witwatersrand in South Africa. Under the very inflexible British system of higher education then in place in South Africa, my civil engineering degree allowed me just one elective in four years – either German-English or French-English technical translation. I was not allowed to enroll in courses in such "irrelevant" fields as economics or law, much less sociology.

Stanford's Organization Theory Renaissance, 1970–2000
Research in the Sociology of Organizations, Volume 28, 221–231
Copyright © 2010 by Emerald Group Publishing Limited
All rights of reproduction in any form reserved
ISSN: 0733-558X/doi:10.1108/S0733-558X(2010)0000028016

After graduation I worked for a marine construction company in Cape Town. This company was led by multiple brilliant engineers, several with PhD degrees, who had invented a string of innovative marine construction technologies. I was, therefore, very surprised to find that the organization and management of this company was haphazard to say the least, and led to numerous missed opportunities for the firm. I resolved to pursue graduate study in areas that could give me insights about how to organize and manage projects and project-based firms like this to be more effective. I considered two alternatives: the Politics, Philosophy and Economics degree at Oxford, or the MS degree in Construction Engineering and Management at Stanford. After talking to people who had attended both programs I opted for Stanford.

1972–1973: MS DEGREE

The organizations community at Stanford was forming when I arrived at Stanford in the Autumn of 1972 to start work on my MS degree. *The National Institute of Mental Health (NIMH) Organizations Research Training Program* at Stanford had just been launched with the awarding of the first cohort of NIMH traineeships and funding for a part-time administrator.

Because of my technically rigorous undergraduate engineering degree, I was exempted from many of the required MS courses in Civil Engineering, and thus had the chance to take multiple free electives as part of the MS degree. I began to roam around the intellectual terrain of Stanford University and was extremely fortunate to land up in an organizational theory course taught by Victor Baldridge in the School of Education, a first-year MBA course on organizational behavior taught at the Graduate School of Business (GSB) by William Ouchi, and subsequently a course on organizational decision-making by Jim March, again in the School of Education.

These courses on organizations exposed me to a superb group of faculty and doctoral students from multiple departments and schools who were part of the NIMH organizations community. Some of them were the initial NIMH trainees, and several of them have authored other chapters in this volume. They introduced me to multiple elements of well-formed organization theory that convinced me the social world could be modeled and analyzed in ways that had some parallels to – and some notable differences from – engineering models of the physical world with which I was familiar. The March and Simon ideas about bounded rationality seemed especially applicable to explaining breakdowns in the engineering project organizations in which I had worked.

1973–1975: PhD DISSERTATION

I was excited enough about the opportunity for applying these kinds of ideas to the problems of creating more effective project teams that I decided to continue on for a PhD Moreover, my faculty adviser in Civil Engineering, Clark Oglesby, was so impressed with the insights that I had gained through my interaction with the NIMH Program community that he decided to hire an industrial psychologist, Dr. Nancy Morse Samelson, co-author of the famous Morse and Reimer (1956) experiment at Michigan on the link between worker satisfaction and productivity, as a Research Associate on our team.

Jim March's exquisite class, *Introduction to Models in the Social Sciences*, using the eponymous textbook that he had authored with Richard Lave, fired me up to do applied social science research based on models of human behavior in the construction industry, and pointed me down the intellectual path that I would follow for the next three decades. This class dazzled me with insight after insight about how relatively simple logical and mathematical models of social phenomena like decision-making, diffusion through social networks, trial and error learning, and economic exchange could be assembled and exercised to make powerful predictions of micro- and meso-level organizational outcomes that could, in turn, be tested, and the models progressively refined. I was thus inspired and emboldened to use this kind of approach in my own PhD research on the ways in which senior managers of construction firms could create policies and practices to promote the safety of construction workers.

The scholars who formed the *NIMH Organizations Research* community enriched my studies as a doctoral student in many ways: sparkling seminars on cutting edge work by Stanford and outside organizations scholars; a dense web of strong and weak ties between organization faculty and students from across the campus that could be tapped to direct a confused student to experts, ideas, critiques, and answers to vexing research questions; social events like Jim March's wine tasting soirées on Tolman Drive; informal student seminars at which my fellow SCOR students and I could forge and hone our own research ideas; and the Asilomar conferences at which we could break bread, drink wine, and attend fireside chats with top organizations scholars from Stanford and elsewhere.

Building on ideas from this class, and with Jim March having agreed to serve on my PhD dissertation committee, I first created a simple decision analysis model in which a worker traded off the extra cost of using more costly, but safer, work methods against the cost of infrequent accidents resulting from using less costly, but also less safe, work methods. Other models we developed looked at the effects of incentives for accident-free work, and a computer simulation of the effect of infrequent but potentially severe accidents and Occupational Safety and Health Administration (OSHA) citations for safety violations on workers' decisions about whether to use safe vs. hazardous work methods.

These mathematical and computational models made it clear that "recordable" accidents were statistically infrequent enough that the most commonly used incentives in the industry – that is, worker rewards for working one week with no accidents – were of limited value. Workers would be rewarded most weeks even for using unsafe work practices that were 10 times as likely to cause accidents as the safest practices. They also made it clear that citations and accidents by themselves would be unlikely to drive consistently safe worker behavior. A financial model of the way in which the costs of preventing accidents and the costs of having accidents were, or were not, captured in traditional project and company accounting metrics provided additional insights about policies and practices that managers might use to encourage investments in safety that could return many times their value in reduced accident costs, disruptions, and human costs (Levitt & Parker, 1976).

The predictions from these models were used to develop a set of hypotheses that were then tested through a mail survey and subsequent set of in-depth interviews with managers. Again the SCOR community facilitated access to an enormous breadth and depth of expertise in designing, administering, and analyzing questionnaires and surveys. The findings from these surveys and interviews turned out to be very exciting, confirming many of the hypotheses developed from the models. They provided insights that we used to develop a set of senior management policies and practices that have had a significant impact on reducing accidents among construction workers in the following three decades (Levitt & Samelson, 1993).

1975: ORGANIZATIONS RESEARCH
AT MIT–HARVARD: A STUDY IN CONTRASTS

Following my PhD degree, I joined the faculty of the newly formed *Construction Engineering and Project Management Program* in the Department of Civil Engineering at MIT, hoping to find a similar organizational community that might link organizations scholars at the Sloan School of Management, Harvard Business School, and other schools and departments at MIT and Harvard. I did find some individual labor economists to collaborate with at the Sloan School of Management, Harvard Business School, and Harvard-MIT Joint Center for Urban Studies, but I never found anything like the community of organizational scholars from multiple schools that had existed at Stanford to inspire, stress-test, select, and refine each others' organizational research ideas.

1980: JOINING THE STANFORD FACULTY

When an opportunity arose to move back to Stanford in 1980, I jumped at the chance. To my delight, I found the NIMH community of organizational scholars at Stanford was still just as vibrant and active as it had been in the early 1970s. Moreover, I found a new set of colleagues in the emerging Artificial Intelligence area of computer science, including Edward Feigenbaum, Barbara Hayes-Roth, Nils Nilsson, Michael Genesereth, and Terry Winograd, whose interests in human cognition, learning, problem-solving, and decision-making overlapped significantly with the interests of Stanford social scientists in Sociology, Psychology, Linguistics, Political Science, Education, Business, and other nooks and crannies around the campus, including the newly formed Engineering Management Department (later reconstituted as the Management Science and Engineering Department) and the marvelous undergraduate program in Symbolic Systems encompassing Computer Science, Psychology, Linguistics, and Philosophy, from which we drew several superb undergraduate researchers, including William Hewlett III and Yul Kwon.

Drawing on the deep and rich pool of both Artificial Intelligence and Organization scholars across the campus, my research group began to develop an agent-based simulation model of information flow in project organizations. Our computational, boundedly rational agents in the "Virtual Design Team" (VDT) processed tasks, generated and resolved exceptions (Galbraith, 1974) and resolved coordination issues (Thompson, 1967) in project teams that were attempting to execute complex, interdependent tasks under tight time constraints. Developing and validating the VDT methods and tools subsequently involved over a dozen PhD students over more than 15 years, and faculty from Computer Science, Communications, Education, MS&E, Sociology, Psychology, and Business (Levitt et al., 1999).

By 1995, we had developed and validated VDT to the point that it was accurately predicting bottlenecks in project teams that caused delays, cost overruns, and quality breakdowns on complex projects. Starting in 1996, we worked with Stanford's Office of Technology Licensing to commercialize VDT as SimVision®, which is now used by organization design consultants to analyze and design organizations for major projects around the world, and which was awarded a US patent in 2009.

In 1989, at about the same time this research effort was launched, the SCOR had been formed to take over the community building role of the NIMH program when it expired. Again, this community of organization's scholars played critical roles in our success. Its seminars provided forums for my students to test out their ideas and find new ideas, classes taught by SCOR community members provided key theoretical elements of our framework, and one or more SCOR faculty served on all of my students' dissertation committees.

CREATING AN INTERDISCIPLINARY CENTER TO STUDY GOVERNANCE OF GLOBAL PROJECTS (2002)

Once VDT had been commercialized, I decided to direct my research group towards a new challenge – understanding how the clash of institutions on global projects to develop infrastructure creates new kinds of "cross-institutional transaction costs" resulting in delays, cost overruns, and reputational damage, both for foreign entrant firms working on these projects and for host country governments and populations. This required augmenting the "organizational information flow physics" model of VDT with several flavors of "organizational chemistry" related to clashing institutions, development of trust in global teams, and related issues.

In 2002, Dick Scott and I began looking around the University to identify a group of scholars who wanted to participate in a new "Collaboratory for Research on Global Projects" (CRGP) http://crgp.stanford.edu. We sought to understand and ultimately help to address the long-term organization and governance challenges that arise for global infrastructure projects involving public and private financiers, regulators, developers, and users from multiple countries. These projects typically have physical and investment life cycles ranging from 35 to 50 years, so they must span multiple changes in host country governments; and they must hold up against cycles of local and global economic and geopolitical upheavals in order to pay off their loans and thus render them financially viable.

Neoclassical contracting, using contingent claims contracts and trilateral governance with arbitrators in third countries *a la* Williamson (1979), has proven far too brittle to address these kinds of unforeseeable risks for transactions that are enacted over multiple decades. Long, risky projects like this need much richer governance frameworks that allow the multiple stakeholders involved to renegotiate costs and benefits continuously among each other over the long term. The issues in designing more effective forms of governance for such projects span a broad range of management, engineering, and social science disciplines.

Once again Stanford's unique organizational community and its global network turned out to be a deep well of resources:

- Dick Scott, the godfather of SCOR, agreed to come out of retirement to be CRGP's *Institutions* guru and help build the community.
- Stephen Barley from the Management Science and Engineering Department agreed to teach our students how to do ethnography rigorously.
- Douglass North, a Nobel laureate institutional economist from Washington University in St. Louis who spends winter quarters at the Hoover Institute, joined the Collaboratory and the PhD committee of Ryan Orr, the first doctoral graduate of CRGP.
- We lassoed Doug McAdam just as he was stepping down from his stint as Director of the Center for Advanced Study in the Behavior Sciences to contribute his knowledge of the activation of social movements such as the ones that frequently arise to oppose large infrastructure projects like dams.
- Avner Greif, Roger Noll, other economists, sociologists, political scientists and even a historian, Gordon Chang, have contribute their expertise by engaging in our seminars and agreeing to serve on students' dissertation committees.

Moreover, we tapped into the network of the Scandinavian Consortium for Organizational Research to identify a group of scholars on project-based organizations at the Helsinki University of Technology and a sociologist at the Helsinki School of Economics who are studying the challenges of global projects in Finland's export-oriented heavy industrial equipment industry.

Funding for this new multinational, multidisciplinary research venture came from a seed grant out of Stanford's Freeman-Spogli Institute for International Research, a startup grant from the deans of Engineering and Humanities & Social Sciences and annual contributions from industrial affiliates from around the world. The first cohort of PhD students from CRGP graduated about 2006 and the fruits of the cross-disciplinary organizations research in this center, inspired by SCOR, (Scott, Levitt, & Orr, 2010).

SCOR is no longer, but the ethos and spirit of SCOR live on at Stanford in this new millennium, even as it takes on new forms, with new organizing vehicles and new funding sources.

NIMH-SCOR: A PIONEERING "CENTER" EMBEDDED IN – AND SHAPING – STANFORD'S UNIQUE INSTITUTIONS

Stanford University's distinctive *Ideation* – the university's purpose, identity and long range vision (Malek, Levitt, & Morgan, 2008) was embedded in the University's founding charter by Leland and Jane Stanford. Stanford's *Ideation* includes the following purposes: *"to qualify its students for personal success, and direct usefulness in life"* and *"to promote the public welfare by exercising an influence in behalf of humanity and civilization...."*

Stanford's uniquely pragmatic *Ideation* expressed in its charter distinguishes it from that of universities like Harvard, whose charter defines its *Ideation* as: *"the advancement of all good literature, arts, and sciences; the advancement and education of youth in all manner of good literature, arts, and sciences; and all other necessary provisions that may conduce to the education of the ... youth of this country...."*

As I have worked at Stanford for more than three decades, it has become increasingly clear to me that this pragmatic charter, the Stanford's choice of the University's first president, and Jane Stanford's strong guiding hand in the initial decades of the University's life laid the groundwork for a unique set of institutions that promote cross disciplinary collaboration at Stanford, compared to any of its peer research universities. At Stanford, the search for knowledge that is not just academically novel and scientifically rigorous, but also serves to *"promote the public welfare"* has generated a culture in which disciplinary silos have always been rendered semi-permeable to its faculty, and non-existent for its students, in the service of public welfare.

Cross-disciplinary centers focused on a set of real world problems are often believed to have evolved initially in the Engineering School at Stanford. Centers at Stanford are simply "problem-focused research communities of practice" that cut across departmental lines to engage faculty, students, and research staff from multiple disciplines to collaborate. Centers do not generally admit students or hire faculty; rather they create a weak matrix structural overlay and support a cross-departmental and cross-school collaborative culture at Stanford (Malek et al., 2008).

Departments still admit students, grant degrees, hire and promote faculty. However, overlaid on what would otherwise be rigid departmental silos, Centers exert an integrative influence for promoting the public welfare in various problem-focused institutional fields: advancing semiconductor design and manufacturing (Center for Integrated Systems); spurring new kinds of design and manufacturing automation for manufactured goods (Product Realization Network); spurring standardized data modeling to promote integration via automation and product-process-organization simulation and visualization in the fragmented construction industry (Center for Integrated Facility Engineering); exploring the integration between digital media and society (Media-X), and most recently, applied biological sciences (Bio-X).

In all of these Centers, *Industrial Affiliates* (from both government and the private sector) provide problem definition, funding through membership subscriptions, direct research support, access for researchers to real world data and settings, and employment opportunities for the graduates. Alongside these Industrial Affiliates, governmental or private entities such as the National Science Foundation, US Department of Defense, National Institute of Health, major private foundations and others provide basic research funding, along with peer group review and legitimacy. Reinforcing the Centers, Stanford's widely admired – and often slavishly emulated – *Office of Technology Licensing* helps faculty, students, departments, and schools to commercialize and monetize the results of successful applied research. Commercialization of research results has worked so well at Stanford in fields like computers, data networking, manufacturing, and construction that education and science ministers and academic adminis-trators make ongoing pilgrimages to Stanford to study the nuances of how Stanford executes technology transfer so effectively, to help their institutions emulate it.

Interestingly, the *NIMH Organizations Research Training Program's* "problem-focused community of practice" predated all or most of the Engineering School's Centers at Stanford. Founded in 1972, this Center obtained "problem-focused" funding from the National Institutes of Mental Health; it provided a community of practice to link and nurture students from both theoretical and applied fields: it supported students in traditionally descriptive social science fields like Sociology to work on applied organizational problems related to mental health administration and educational administration, as well as general management. At the same time, the NIMH program – and subsequently SCOR – provided a rich organization theory community of practice for students from applied fields like construction management (the author) or management of mineral exploration (Dr. Alan Campbell) to learn about social science-based models of behavior that could support their research. And SCOR encouraged faculty to secure multiple courtesy appointments in schools and departments such as Sociology, Economics, Education, and Business to further strengthen the weak ties across departments.

Embedded within Stanford's uniquely supportive culture for this kind of venture, SCOR empowered my students, me, and many others to cross departmental and school boundaries effortlessly in assembling coursework and committee support for interdisciplinary organizational research; and this was a key enabler of its success.

The SCOR ended its formal existence after 1996. But, as writers like Anthony Giddens (1986) understand so well, SCOR had both thrived under and helped to shape and mould Stanford's unique structure and culture – nurtured by its entrepreneurial, problem-focused institutions dating back to the University's founding charter – for assembling cross-disciplinary teams of scholars on-demand to tackle scientifically and practically important problems.

As the CRGP story above illustrates, even though SCOR had ceased to exist after 1996, it was relatively easy for a group of faculty, starting in 2002, to form and grow the *Collaboratory for Research on Global Projects,* a new collaboration among organizations scholars from multiple Engineering and Social Science disciplines to tackle yet another set of organizational problems to advance human welfare – finding new governance approaches for delivering sustainable civil infrastructure for the billion additional travelers on our planet in the next decade. Clearly, many of the institutions supporting collegial organizational scholarship forged by NIMH and SCOR have survived their formal demise and live on into this millennium.

Vive la SCOR!

REFERENCES

Galbraith, J. R. (1974). Organization design: An information processing view. *Interfaces, 4*(3), 28–36.
Giddens, A. (1986). *The constitution of society: Outline of the theory of structuration.* University of California Press.
Levitt, R. E., & Parker, H. W. (1976). Reducing construction accidents – Top management's role. *ASCE Journal of the Construction Division, 102*(CO3), 465–478.

Levitt, R. E., & Samelson, N. M. (1993). *Construction safety management.* John Wiley and Sons.

Levitt, R. E., Thomsen, J., Christiansen, T. R., Kunz, J. C., Jin, Y., & Nass, C. (1999). Simulating project work processes and organizations: Toward a micro-contingency theory of organizational design. *Management Science, 45*(11), 1479–1495.

Malek, W., Levitt, R. E., & Morgan, M. (2008). *Executing your strategy: How to break it down and get it done.* Harvard Business School Press.

Morse, N. C., & Reimer, E. (1956). The experimental change of a major organizational variable. *Journal of Abnormal Psychology, 52*(1), 120–129.

Scott, W. R., Levitt, R. E., & Orr (Eds). (2010). *Global projects: Institutional and political challenges,* Forthcoming.

Thompson, J. D. (1967). *Organizations in action.* McGraw-Hill.

Williamson, O. E. (1979). Transaction cost economics: The governance of contractual relations. *Journal of Law and Economics, 22*(2), 223.

CHAPTER 13

A FELLOW FROM KANSAS

James G. March

Intellectual and academic institutional histories are combinations of events and speculations, the latter often cloaked in recollections that are garbled mixes of wishful self-adulation, vivid memories of dubious veracity, and legends honed by previous occasions for articulation. This does not distinguish such histories from other histories except that the recollections are those of professional idea mongers who have considerable experience weaving their speculations into tempting generalities that substitute the simplicities of imagination for the complexities and contradictions of reality.

This chapter displays those attributes abundantly. It is one person's prejudicial recollection of ancient history without even the minimal checks on memory provided by a decent diary. It revels in a history that was seriously entwined with my own, thus undoubtedly significantly colored by self-indulgence. It makes a simple argument on the basis of a murky memory of more complex events.

The simple argument is that the main instruments for creating an intellectual community in a research university are not direct devices for integrating or stimulating faculty. They are devices for bringing students from several departments together in their search for ideas and self-discovery. Such devices require a combination of favorable times and the altruistic dedication of faculty members, requirements that are unlikely to be met and, if met, unlikely to be sustained; but it is the brief moments of unlikely scholarly communities that shape our intellectual histories.

Stanford's Organization Theory Renaissance, 1970–2000
Research in the Sociology of Organizations, Volume 28, 233–239
Copyright © 2010 by Emerald Group Publishing Limited
All rights of reproduction in any form reserved
ISSN: 0733-558X/doi:10.1108/S0733-558X(2010)0000028017

AN UNLIKELY COMMUNITY

For many years, Stanford University has had a major organizations research faculty distributed across at least four schools and numerous departments. By its existence, that faculty has recruited others of similar quality. It has attracted a strong group of students who in due course have gained their doctorates at Stanford and have populated North American, European, and Asian universities.

However, for about 25 years (1970–1995 roughly), Stanford University's organizations research community was not just a superior collection of faculty. It was an exceptional intellectual enclave. Faculty and students in engineering management, civil engineering, business, sociology, and education – with small outposts in psychology, political science, and economics – maintained a research community of unusual variety, depth, and spirit.

No department, school, center, or institute planned that good fortune, or could claim either to have led the development or to have anticipated it. It was unlikely, but it happened. Those of us who were fortunate enough to have been involved were (and are) grateful for it.

THE STANFORD CONTEXT

The flowering of the organizations research community at Stanford in the two decades after 1970 was not implicit in either the history, or the structure, or the incentives of the university. Conspicuous features of the Stanford situation and experience militate against such a community. During this period, Stanford was a campground for faculty whose commitments to the profession were, in most cases, greater than their commitments to the university. They camped at Stanford for an assortment of reasons and most probably hoped to spend the remainder of their professional lives at the university; but the incentives for collaboration among faculty were small.

Most active Stanford faculty members were better connected to colleagues outside the university than to Stanford colleagues outside their own departments. There were multiple parallel doctoral programs, not conspicuously influenced by each other. Thus, a single faculty member was ordinarily connected more productively and persistently to his or her own doctoral students than to other faculty members or to other students. The structure of relations was not perverse. Productive faculty members were members of an international collection of contributors to the field and saw their primary comparative advantages and responsibilities as involving maximizing their research productivity through a time-demanding focus on their own work.

Students tied themselves to faculty who could provide immediate support and who could facilitate subsequent employment in a department of choice (normally the one in which the student was currently enrolled). The support levels for graduate students varied substantially among departments, with support being more problematic and more conditional in sociology and education than in business or psychology, thus requiring more imaginative relationships in the former than in the latter.

Faculty without resources to support research assistants were disadvantaged in the search for student colleagues, but those with money were generally not compulsively possessive of students; so it was possible for students who wished to do so to maintain various kinds of discreet polygamous faculty relationships, and for underfunded faculty to poach on the largess of others.

BUILDING A COMMUNITY

The structure of incentives at Stanford and the realities of commitments to research, disciplines, and careers dictated a culture dominated by multiple bilateral relations between individual faculty members and individual students. It was a proven structure for producing good research and did not invite extensive tampering. Building a lively multi-disciplinary research community depended on creating a structure that tied the bilateral relations between individual faculty members and individual students into a larger network without weakening them. In principle, this might have been done by tying the faculty members together. There undoubtedly have been situations in which such a strategy has worked, but it was made almost impossible in this instance by the strong centrifugal properties of a good faculty at a good university.

On the other hand, tying students together was a more promising direction. Individual faculty members had few incentives to join together; students had more. Faculty members were generally in a process of narrowing and refining their foci; students were more likely to be in a process of broadening theirs. Faculty members were defending their reputations in competition with each other; students were building their reputations in a somewhat less zero-sum way. For a research scholar, life as a senior faculty member at Stanford was too good to make most investments in broadening personal or intellectual horizons seem attractive; but a community might be built if students were connected with each other as they tried to make sense of their aspirations and their faculty mentors.

Stanford doctoral study was strongly departmentalized. Research was located within particular departments with little effort to expand beyond the department. However, in general, doctoral students were given substantial freedom to develop individual interests once departmental demands were met. In most cases, of course, individual interests were as localized as the programs were, but those students who wished to expand outside the department could do so. As a result, enrollment in courses outside the focal department was possible, as was the participation of faculty members from outside the department in dissertation committees.

The development of organization studies as a field encouraged such contact. In the years after the Second World War, organizational economics, organizational psychology, and organizational sociology continued to evolve as self-contained disciplinary specialties; but they evolved in a scholarly world in which a multi-disciplinary field of organization studies (some kind of amalgam) was increasingly recognized as a quasi-discipline increasingly located in business schools. Research reports were increasingly published in "organization" journals rather than standard disciplinary journals; and students of organizations (particularly those from psychology and sociology) increasingly found jobs on the faculties of business schools.

THE STUDENT FOCUS

In spite of these trends in organization studies toward finding a home in business schools, the Stanford faculty group of organizations scholars was led by, and consisted predominantly in, faculty scholars not at the Stanford Graduate School of Business but at the Department of Sociology. A small handful of faculty members in other departments and schools were active; but any memory of the glory years as exhibiting active, sustained participation by a large group of faculty from multiple disciplines is fictitious.

A student community was built around the Organizational Research Training Program (ORTP) funded by the National Institute for Mental Health (NIMH). In concrete terms, the NIMH program consisted simply of a set of doctoral and post-doctoral fellowships and a seminar. The fellowships supplemented graduate student support resources, particularly in the Department of Sociology and the School of Education; however, their primary purpose was to define a community of scholars organized around the ORTP seminar. Other students (e.g., students from the Graduate School of Business who were already well-supported by that school's resources) were co-opted into the group.

The ORTP provided exposure to multi-disciplinary conversations and ideas, as well as informal contacts that were independent of a student's department, thus reduced departmental control in a gentle way. The program thrived intellectually and socially; but from the start, it struggled to invent links with mental health that were sufficiently obvious to overcome skepticism on the part of key people and panels at the NIMH; and it ultimately abandoned the effort. While it endured, the program owed a great deal to the support of program officers at NIMH who supported it despite the manifest difficulty in detecting relevance of the research training for mental health.

The iconic artifact of the Stanford organizations research community of the 1970s and 1980s was the annual Asilomar Conference run at the conference center in Pacific Grove on the Pacific coast. It is easy to romanticize Asilomar in memory. You tend to forget the food. The romance, however, is real in important respects. Asilomar conferences displayed the community at its best. They were the constructions of students. Students invented the themes, devised the sessions, prepared most of the papers, and managed the discussions. Insofar as faculty members were present, they were (somewhat) honored guests. They could enjoy the brilliance of their students, colleagues, bask in the pleasures of contemplating whatever responsibility they might claim, and walk along the beach.

Asilomar was a demonstration of professional competence and scholarly breadth by students. Students seemed to feel comfortable in a way that few faculty members did in wandering from sessions on meaning and narrative to sessions on multi-variate models and heteroscedasticity. They moved from hyperbolic functions to hyperbolic statements without visible distress. Although the main fulcrum was sociology, the programs extended considerably beyond a narrow sociological emphasis.

Asilomar was also a symbol. It symbolized the notion that organization studies was a serious field of study. It symbolized the idea that the field was (or at least might be) multi-disciplinary, multi-institutional, multi-methodological, multi-national, and probably multi-global. It symbolized that the profession of organization researchers included graduate students as significant colleagues. And it symbolized that it was possible both to be a serious professional and to enjoy walks in the moonlight, the comforts of wine, and soft moments of collegial intimacy.

All of this was made possible by a fortuitous combination of events that cannot be produced arbitrarily. It was an unusual time in the development of a field: Organization studies was booming. An unusual collection of faculty members was present at Stanford, hired for idiosyncratic reasons by autonomous departments and schools. It was a time of optimism about scholarship and the importance of academe.

A FELLOW FROM KANSAS

Neither the conditions nor the Stanford locale would have produced the environment they did if it were not for one man: W. Richard Scott. Dick Scott was the father, the nurse, the patron, the scold, and the symbol of a broad conception of Stanford organization studies. The rest of us enjoyed the largess of his contributions and the generosity of his spirit. Without him and the community he created and nurtured, our lives would have been poorer.

Organization studies at Stanford was the loosest possible association of faculty and students, most of whom were quite parochial in their departmental allegiances. Quite a few faculty members were nominally involved in the ORTP effort in the sense of allowing their names to be associated with it; some were important assets for individual students; and for some years a few successfully solicited funds from the deans at the business school in support of Asilomar conferences and other activities; but most nominal participants were inactive in collective community building efforts and were rarely present at events such as the research training seminar or Asilomar. This was not because they were disaffected, antagonistic, or immoral; for the most part, they simply did not see such a multi-departmental community as providing sufficient professional benefit to justify the costs of involvement.

The only two organized attempts to provide a formal organizational home for the community were the ORTP that secured its support primarily from the NIMH and the Stanford Center for Organizations Research (SCOR). SCOR played a role briefly but shut down after only a few years. Both SCOR and ORTP depended critically on the totally altruistic willingness of one faculty member, Dick Scott, to do all of the practical negotiations and write all of the applications required to make it work.

When he grew tired of sustaining the unfavorable balance of altruistic contributions that his relationship with SCOR and his colleagues exhibited, Dick Scott sought to find a replacement as director of SCOR and leader of the community from among those who had so long benefited from his generosity. There were no volunteers and, despite some sturdy efforts to twist arms, no willingness to succumb to observations about duty, collegial responsibilities, and fairness.

In the end, the ORTP died for lack of funds and SCOR collapsed. The community dissipated, though the organizations research faculty at Stanford continued to be strong as the old guard retired, and new heads filled their places. The program and the community did not survive; but they contributed to the graduate education of scholars of distinction; they stimulated emulation in seminars and centers throughout North America and Europe; and they nurtured ideas that subsequently left visible marks on organizations scholarship.

THE MORAL OF THE STORY

There is a quintuple moral in all of this: First, if the times and conditions are not right, neither wishes, nor creativity, nor collective efforts will create an exciting scholarly community. Second, in a modern university, the main hope for constructing a serious, intellectual community that combines disciplines and departments lies in bringing students together. Third, developing an exceptional research community requires that not only that the conditions be right but also the altruistic self-sacrifice of someone from Kansas. Fourth, if you find yourself in one of these rare communities, enjoy it, exploit it, and be grateful for the fellow from Kansas; but do not expect it to last. Fifth, if you are from Kansas, do not expect the world to replicate you, but take glory in the many ways your colleagues and their students are better than they would have been without you.

CHAPTER 14

A CULTURAL VIEW OF THE ORGANIZATIONAL COMMUNITY AT STANFORD UNIVERSITY

Joanne Martin

In this multiauthored volume, the story of the organizational community at Stanford University has been told in numerous ways. Some chapters offer a substantive review of a research topic, while others give an historical version of a part of the community's development. In this chapter, I am going to offer a cultural description of our community, hopefully drawing attention to aspects of the community's functioning that were seen differently or not included in other chapters. Readers of this chapter will have a whirlwind tour of the cultures of the community, with snapshots of our working lives. In the cultures I will describe, research excellence was the name of the game; collaborative relationships were a norm, but they were embedded in a sometimes fierce, but usually tacit and intermittent competitiveness.

THE CREATION OF AN ORGANIZATIONAL COMMUNITY

Cultural portraits usually begin with a description of the context, but as this material is covered elsewhere in this volume, this introduction will be mercifully brief. At any time during the last four decades, there have been

Stanford's Organization Theory Renaissance, 1970–2000
Research in the Sociology of Organizations, Volume 28, 241–262
Copyright © 2010 by Emerald Group Publishing Limited
All rights of reproduction in any form reserved
ISSN: 0733-558X/doi:10.1108/S0733-558X(2010)0000028018

dozens, perhaps even hundreds, of Stanford University faculty and doctoral students interested in studying organizations. They have been scattered across the campus, often in small groups within larger schools and departments. They have been based in the Sociology Department and the Organizational Behavior and Strategy areas at the Graduate School of Business. There were always a handful at the Education and Engineering schools, as well as a scattering of individuals doing related work in Psychology, Political Science, and Anthropology. In spite of their numbers, before the Stanford Center for Organizational Research (SCOR) was founded in 1972, many of these faculty, postdoctoral fellows, and doctoral students felt rather isolated. They had little contact with colleagues across campus who shared their interest in organizations and little collective clout when resources were being distributed.

With the goal of bringing these scholars together, Professor of Sociology, Dick Scott, designed the interdisciplinary structure of SCOR and got funding for an annual conference, frequent colloquia, some short topic-specific conferences, some research and graduate student fellowships, and visiting faculty member and postdoctoral fellows. The hope was that these organizational scholars would help each other, enjoy each other's company, and collaborate on research, teaching, and doctoral dissertations. Ultimately, the goal was that the existence of SCOR would improve the quality and quantity of our research and increase our collective power and access to resources in our schools and departments and across the campus. By the middle 1980s, the existence of SCOR had catalyzed an interdisciplinary organizational studies community at Stanford that persists to this day. This chapter will focus on that community, as Dick Scott's leadership and the participants' contributions created something larger and perhaps longer lasting than SCOR itself.

CAVEATS AND LIMITATIONS

Space in a volume like this is limited, so I will only be able to give a glimpse of the rich detail and systematic analysis that a cultural portrait usually provides. Because of the limits of my spotty knowledge of the many visitors, postdoctoral fellows, and doctoral students who passed through Stanford, many working outside my areas of expertise, this chapter focuses predominantly on a subset of tenured and tenure-line faculty. This account includes material from 1972 to 2007. There will be no attempt to document a chronology within that time frame, as keeping track of the exact dates of the arrivals and departures of temporary visitors and "permanent" community members is beyond my resources at this time. Because the cast of characters was always changing, I will attempt to focus on aspects of the cultures in our community that were relatively constant. Because I am a member of the collectivity being described, no objectivity can be claimed – only the advantages and disadvantages of an insider's view.

INTRODUCING CULTURAL THEORY:
THREE PERSPECTIVES

I am a cultural researcher, so I have decided to use some parts of my own cultural theory to structure this description. When I first reviewed many of the hundreds of studies of organizational culture, I was dismayed to find their results were starkly contradictory. A systematic review (Martin, 1992, 2002) of these studies revealed that most cultural researchers were using one (or sometimes two) of three diametrically opposed theoretical perspectives. Researchers' choice of theoretical perspective(s) influenced what data they collected and thus, what results they found. In contrast, I have argued that a cultural study is richer and more complete when a culture is described using all three perspectives, one after another. With various co-authors, of them doctoral students, many cultural researchers have used the three perspectives to study several large corporations, some small start-up companies, a company-funded community in Turkey, a doctoral seminar, non-profit organizations, and even the Peace Corps (e.g., Baburoglu & Gocer, 1994; Damon, 1997; Enomoto, 1993; Koot, Sabelis, & Ybema, 1996; Martin, 2002; Meyerson & Martin, 1987; Stevenson & Bartunek, 1996; Takahashi, 1997). In this chapter, I will give a taste of the three perspective approaches, applied to the organizational community at Stanford.

A three perspective view results in a complex cultural portrait: some ideas and practices seem clear and consistent and are shared by most members of the organization (this is the Integration perspective). Some ideas and practices are shared primarily within subcultures that coexist in overlapping and nested forms, in supportive, conflicting, or orthogonal relationships with each other (the Differentiation perspective). And, in the interstices between these cultural and subcultural islands of apparent clarity and unity, ambiguities flourish, bringing irony, paradox, and constant flux (the Fragmentation perspective). Each of the three perspectives highlights quite different aspects of the experience of being a member of the organizational community at Stanford – the joys of working together to foster innovative interdisciplinary scholarship, clashing theoretical and methodological assumptions that triggered subcultural alliances and rivalries, and the ambiguities that permitted us to coexist, cooperate, take risks, innovate, and even thrive.

INTEGRATION: INTERDISCIPLINARY HARMONY AND COOPERATION

Defining the Integration Perspective

An Integration view of a culture is built around a set of themes (often values espoused by leaders). In a cultural study conducted from the Integration perspective, each theme is clearly stated and apparently unambiguous; those themes are described as being enacted consistently – in formal structures and written rules; in informal practices and norms of behavior; in rituals, stories, culture-specific jargon, jokes only cultural insiders would find amusing; and in the physical arrangements of people's work spaces. In an Integration study, the culture is characterized by consistency, clarity, and consensus; it is seen as being homogeneous and monolithic (e.g., Kotter & Heskett, 1992; Martin, Feldman, Hatch, & Sitkin, 1983; O'Reilly, Chatman, & Caldwell, 1991; Ouchi, 1981; Pascale & Athos, 1981; Peters & Waterman, 1982; Porras & Collins, 1994; Schein, 1985; Siehl & Martin, 1984).

An Integration View of the Organizational Community at Stanford

A few content themes serve as the unifying backbone of an Integration portrait of a culture. Such themes, in an Integration study, are usually highly abstract and phrased in bland terms that are the rough equivalent of singing the praises of motherhood and apple pie. You can see this platitudinous quality in the most common themes that emerge in large corporations: the need for the company to be fiscally responsible, to have a concern for employee well being, to foster customer satisfaction, to work to maximize the quality of goods and/or services produced, and, less frequently, to protect the natural environment and behave in a socially responsible manner (Siehl & Martin, 1990). In an Integration account of a culture, themes phrased at this high level of abstraction can be interpreted in a variety of consistent ways, thus fostering a seeming organization-wide consensus.

An Integration study of the organizational community might include themes such as:

1. Research excellence: It is important to do original rather than derivative research that is nationally (and later, internationally) recognized as first rate. Publishing, often, in top tier journals is essential.
2. Originality: Excellent research must be innovative rather than derivative; as one doctoral student handbook put it, "A doctoral dissertation must make an original contribution to theory."
3. Interdisciplinarity: Cross-disciplinary research collaborations have the capacity to foster innovative research.

Integration studies explore how a given theme is consistently enacted across a variety of cultural manifestations. Given this volume's focus on the interdisciplinary aspects of organizational research at Stanford, it might be appropriate to focus here on the cultural manifestations consistent with the third, interdisciplinary theme mentioned above. The formal Stanford rules that permitted interdisciplinary work were all regularly enacted by members of the organizational community. Organizational faculty often held courtesy or joint appointments in other fields, actively participating in faculty meetings and committee work outside their own departments and schools. Professor Jim March set records in this regard, having had, at one time or another, basic or joint appointments in Sociology, Political Science, the Graduate School of Business, the Education School, and the Hoover Institute. Organizational doctoral students were often required by their home departments to take courses in other departments and schools. Doctoral, some MBA, and some undergraduate courses taught by organizational faculty were often cross listed in several departments. An organizational student's dissertation committee members were often drawn from two or three different departments. Interdisciplinary contacts were a big part of most faculty and doctoral students' daily activities at Stanford, as we walked and bicycled across campus from one department to another.

Interdisciplinary relationships were fostered at the annual SCOR conference, held most years at Asilomar, a state park located on the sea in Monterey, California. Organizational faculty, doctoral students, post-doctoral fellows, and visitors attended, and later, alumni/ae joined as well. We slept in houses on park grounds. Some of these houses were sprawling relics from the early 1900s, others were new, but all had living rooms where we gathered for informal panel discussions, formal lectures (usually by visitors from a variety of disciplines and universities), and more private chats. We ate our meals together, at large tables, in the park's central dining room. The food was generally absymal, but conversations ranged far and were often fascinating. At night, those living rooms were party sites, with music and laughter sometimes lasting until the wee hours.

Each year small gatherings of faculty and students would walk the beach at Asilomar, talking about organizational issues with colleagues who came from all kinds of departments and professional schools. For some faculty and students, Asilomar and the SCOR colloquia held regularly at Stanford provided our first introduction to some of the major organizational research paradigms. At Asilomar, we all attended formal presentations on the latest empirical developments in these areas. We also got to hear Professors Deb Meyerson and Woody Powell from Education argue with Dale Miller, Jim Phills, and Jerry Porras from the business school about whether non-profit organizations were more or less socially responsible than corporations. We watched as Professors Nancy Tuma (Sociology at Stanford), John Freeman (a sociologist from Berkeley), Bill Barnett (Graduate School of Business), and Michael Hannan (Sociology and later, Graduate School of Business), and their students disputed the fine points of event history analysis. We witnessed Professor Jeff Pfeffer debate vociferously with faculty like Professors Jim Baron and Joel Podolny (all from the Graduate School of Business with ties to the Sociology Department) about whether it was worthwhile to find an accommodation between sociology and economics. Jeff Pfeffer was the naysayer.

Our talk was not all about work. I fondly remember one night, after dinner, when John Freeman entertained a living room of colleagues with tales of fishing under the Golden Gate Bridge – tales of dubious veracity and considerable wit. After dinner, we would adjourn to one of the parties (sort of) organized by the students, where we might find out that Pfeffer could dance, some doctoral students (especially Jerry Davis) could be very funny, and almost everyone liked wine. The social side effects of such interdisciplinary gatherings, large or small, should not be underestimated. They fostered interdisciplinary collaboration across departmental and school boundaries, and helped to loosen, somewhat, the strong status differences between tenured and untenured faculty, and between faculty and doctoral students. In addition, they were a fine way to help introduce and integrate the constant influx of visitors, postdoctoral fellows, and others new to Stanford into the organizational community.

An Integration View of Cultural Consequences

Many Integration researchers have argued that a strongly integrated culture sets off a cascade of positive consequences in corporate settings, such as enthusiasm, loyalty, commitment, increased productivity, and greater profitability (e.g., Kotter & Heskett, 1992; Ouchi, 1981; Pascale & Athos, 1981; Peters & Waterman, 1982; Schein, 1985). You can imagine, if you have not seen, how welcome these ideas are to audiences of MBA students or executives. They are, in essence, being promised a kind of organizational immortality. If leaders clearly articulate a set of value themes, backing them up with formal and informal practices, as well as rituals, stories, jargon, etc., their personal values would be adapted and reproduced by their employees, and the holy grail of greater productivity and profitability would be found – quite a promise.

In the organizational community similar positive consequences could be seen. This was a culture of competition as well as interdisciplinary collaboration. When others were shocked that we had not read a classic or the latest important journal article, we would find it, fast. Eventually we became literate and conversant in a shared library of ideas. Because we were exposed to the latest developments in many aspects of organizational research, broadly defined, many of these ideas came to inform and broaden our own research agendas. We built friendships with faculty and students from across campus, and found those whose research interests coalesced with our own, fostering an interdisciplinary research environment. When we collaborated with some of these colleagues, their disparate expertise made our work more innovative and theoretically original (the second of the themes above). The organizational community became a large and powerful collectivity, full of intense arguments and affectionate friendships.

Consistent with the first theme listed above, the community published dozens, even hundreds of new (and often collaborative) books and papers every year. Just being exposed to so many fine scholars, all blasting full speed ahead into their work, made all of us stimulated and most of us, more productive than we ever thought possible. The competition, as we tried to outdo each other or beat our own goals of excellence, just served to raise the bar. From an Integration point of view, the organizational community was unified and, even sometimes when we were competing for a tenured job or the best new publication, generally harmonious. We all were aiming to be highly productive, first rate organizational researchers.

There is some evidence that this intensely collaborative and competitive culture had positive consequences in terms of productivity, defined as research excellence based on innovation/originality and, often, interdisciplinary collaboration. At the risk of immodesty (the Integration view of a culture does not tend to foster modesty), Stanford faculty were central to the creation or advancement of many of the central research areas of organizational theory. An incomplete list of (sometimes vaguely defined) topics and faculty would include work by the following individuals (this is an interdisciplinary list of professors associated with SCOR):

- Altruism and justice (John Jost, Joanne Martin, Dale Miller, and others).
- Ambiguity in decision making and other challenges to the rational model (Jon Bendor, Jim March, and Serge Taylor; and others).
- Organizational culture (Tony Athos, Steve Barley, Joanne Martin, Charles O'Reilly, Bill Ouchi, Tom Peters, Jerry Porras, Bob Sutton, and others).
- Race, gender, and organizational demographics (Roberto Fernandez, Deb Gruenfeld, Brian Lowery, Joanne Martin, Maggie Neale, Jeff Pfeffer, Jim Phills, Charles O'Reilly, and others).
- Institutional theory (John Meyer, Woody Powell, Dick Scott, and others);.
- Labor markets (Jim Baron, Roberto Fernandez, Jeff Pfeffer, and others).
- Networks (Mark Granovetter, Don Palmer, Joel Podolny, Ezra Zuckerman, and others).
- Planned organizational change (Charles O'Reilly, Jerry Porras, and others).
- Population ecology (Bill Barnett, Glenn Carroll, Mike Hannan, Susan Olzack, and allied others, such as Nancy Tuma, Jesper Sorenson, Huggy Rao, and Martin Ruef).
- Power, trust, and status (Deb Gruenfeld, Rod Kramer, Don Palmer, Jeff Pfeffer, Joel Podolny, Cecilia Ridgeway, Lara Tiedens, and others).
- Resource dependence (Jeff Pfeffer and others).

DIFFERENTIATION: SUBCULTURAL ALLIANCES AND CONFLICTS

Defining the Differentiation Perspective

Anyone familiar with a university can suggest ways this Integration view presents an idealized, overly homogenized, functionalist, and therefore incomplete view of an academic environment (e.g., Barley, Meyer, & Gash, 1988).

A Differentiation view of the organizational community alleviates some of these shortcomings. When an organizational culture is viewed from a Differentiation perspective, clarity and consensus are observed, but only within the boundaries of a subculture. Subcultures often have distinctive themes, as well as unique manifestations consistent with those themes. Sometimes, however, subcultures are overlapping or nested within each other, which results in some similarities of subcultural content. From the Differentiation perspective, any apparently homogeneous culture is riddled with subcultural differences. It is important to explore how an organization's subcultures relate to each other because this opens the door to understanding alliances, intergroup conflicts of interest, and pressures toward organizational change (e.g., Bartunek & Moch, 1991; Martin & Siehl, 1983; Martin, Sitkin, & Boehm, 1985; Rosen, 1991; Van Maanen, 1991; Van Maanen & Kunda, 1989; Young, 1991).

A Differentiation View of Stanford's Organizational Community

Drawing boundaries around subcultures is a tricky business. In a systematic cultural study, all (or a systematic sample of) organizational members would be observed, interviewed, and/or surveyed to determine how they interpreted the meanings of organizational stories, rituals, informal and formal practices, etc. The content themes that emerged from this analysis would be used to determine where subcultural boundaries were, and whether those subcultures were overlapping or nested within each other (Martin, 1992). Some subcultures would take congruent or opposing positions on these themes, placing the subcultures in supportive or conflicting relationships; other independent subcultures would be orthogonal in their relationships with other subcultures (Louis, 1985). Sometimes subcultural boundaries follow formal structural lines, reflecting departmental distinctions or status differences, and sometimes informal groupings cross these formal lines, as when a subculture evolves around an individual or a project (Martin, 2002). A Differentiation view of a culture, then, is complex; it surfaces conflicts and alliances, shows how and sometimes why an organizational environment is politicized – quite a contrast to the harmonious and cooperative image projected in an Integration view.

Space and time limitations preclude a full subcultural analysis of the organizational community. To simplify and shorten this section of the chapter, I will describe only a few subcultures that I am most familiar with, and I will name only some of the tenure-line faculty members who belonged to each of these subcultures. Even with these major limitations, the complexity of a subcultural analysis will quickly become evident.

The Sociology Department had two major subcultures (roughly 1990–2005). The first subculture included the social psychologists in the department, lead by Professors Joe Berger, Bernie Cohen, Sandy Dornbusch, Cecilia Ridgeway, and Buzz Zelditch, among others. They were known for their precisely expressed, rigorous experimental work. The second subculture was more organizational in focus, and was lead by Professors Mark Granovetter, Michael Hannan, John Meyer, Susan Olzack, Dick Scott, and others. There were silent struggles and later fierce fights for resources and reputational status between these subcultures in the Sociology department, resulting eventually in the departure of Michael Hannan to a primary appointment in the Graduate School of Business.

At the same time, the Organizational Behavior group within the Graduate School of Business was informally split between the "micros" and the "macros." The micros were generally psychologists, trained either in Social Psychology departments (John Jost, Rod Kramer, Brian Lowery, Joanne Martin, Dale Miller, Lara Tiedens, and others) or in Organizational Psychology/Organizational Behavior (Deb Gruenfeld, Hal Leavitt, Maggie Neale, Charles O'Reilly, Jerry Porras, Eugene Webb, and others). This division, roughly correlated with educational background and a less or more applied focus, sometimes created nascent nested subcultures within the micro subculture of the Organizational Behavior group. The macros, in contrast, studied organizations at higher levels of analysis, from a sociological point of view (Bill Barnett, James Baron, Glenn Carroll, Roberto Fernandez, Michael Hannan, Pam Haunschild, Bill Ouchi, Don Palmer, Jeff Pfeffer, Joel Podolny, Huggy Rao, Martin Ruef, Jesper Sorenson, Ezra Zuckerman, and others).

As you might expect, there were tacit and overt struggles for resources (Who will we hire? Who will we admit to the doctoral program?) between and sometimes within the micros and the macros in the Graduate School of Business. Over time, these subcultures learned to dampen their conflicts by co-teaching core courses, working together on committees and sometimes even research, and developing formal rules for sharing resources (e.g., specifying in advance of admissions or hiring decisions, the approximate number of new individuals each subculture could choose). Links between the social psychologists in the Sociology Department and in the Graduate School of Business were friendly, but relatively weak on a subcultural level. In contrast, the macros in the business school and the organizational scholars in the Sociology Department were closely linked, creating overlapping subcultures with most members having formalized courtesy

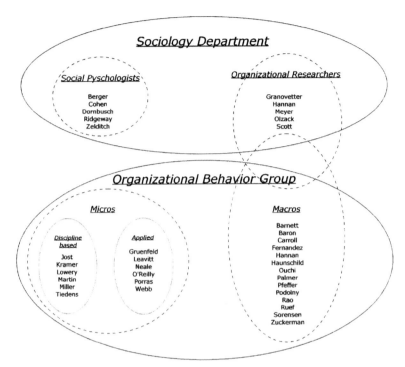

Fig. 1. A Map of Subcultures in the Sociology Department and the Organizational Behavior Group in the Graduate School of Business, Stanford Univesity. *Note:* This map is incomplete. Only a few representative tenure track faculty are named in each subculture. Subculture identities of some individuals are more multifaceted this diagram indicates.

appointments in both groups. This nexus of nested and overlapping subcultures is diagrammed in Fig. 1.

The content of the conflicts and alliances between these subcultures sometimes echoed discipline-based loyalties. These were particularly evident during contested reviews at tenure time or in arguments about the quality of the research of job applicants. For example, publication in a top psychology journal usually required a series of tightly designed, theoretical focused experiments (generally only two or three independent variables). While psychologists might have no hesitation in claiming this kind of work to be excellent and original, others might dismiss it as theoretically too narrow to be important. Some faculty (and their students, whose opinions were often more polarized echoes of the views of their mentors) believed that higher levels of analysis produced work of greater importance, or that micro level analysis of thought or beliefs could open the "black box" that sometimes could be found at the heart of a sociological theory, explaining why individuals behaved, en masse, in a certain way. These kinds of discipline-associated difference of opinion were promulgated within subcultures, fostering alliances and conflicts described above.

These subcultural conflicts and alliances add a layer of understanding to the three themes discussed in the Integration view of the organizational community. What is being argued about is how to define excellence and (sometimes) originality in research, the first and second of the three themes. Because these differences of opinion were reflected in subcultural alliances and conflicts, and because they stemmed from disciplinary differences in training and preferred level of analysis, the existence of these subcultures undermines claims of interdisciplinarity, the third theme in the Integration view. In this way, the Differentiation perspective directly challenges the simplistic claims of unity and harmony of the Integration view of this community's culture. The Differentiation view, however, does more than just challenge Integration; it also contributes additional kinds of complexity that come from acknowledging and seeking to understand difference.

Sometimes subcultures emerged, at least for a time, that cross-cut the subcultures described immediately above. For example, some status-associated subcultures cross-cut disciplinary allegiances. The biggest status difference, of course, was between faculty and students. Faculty statuses differed as well; there were times when a subculture of senior faculty saw things differently than a subculture of junior faculty, and often faculty who did not have tenure track jobs (lecturers and adjunct professors) seemed to live in a different world. Additionally, within and sometimes across these status subcultures, sometimes cohorts would create a healthy competitive environment. For example, sometimes a particular cohort of graduate students would create a subculture in which members would strive to outdo each other in the quality of their dissertations, the length of their vitae, and the number of job interview invitations they received from top schools.

The organizational community also had several orthogonal subcultures that evolved as separate, independent groups with distinctive values and cultural practices. Perhaps the best example of this is the Work and Technology Group founded by Professor Steve Barley in the Engineering School. Their renowned colloquium series draws faculty and students from across campus, as well as executives from the industrial park that surrounds Stanford University. At this series, research presentations generally focus on work group cultures and the technology industry.

Usually, research associated with the Work and Technology Group utilizes ethnographic methods, making this subculture a Mecca for organizational scholars interested in qualitative research methods. This subculture also prides itself on a rare combination of strong applied focus and strong scholarly values.

In addition, faculty members attracted postdoctoral fellows and doctoral students, creating transient or constantly evolving subcultures focused on particular theories. For example, each of the topic areas listed at the conclusion of the Integration description above was associated with one or more subcultures, each headed by one or more faculty members and evolving cohorts of doctoral students.[1] In addition, sometimes a research project would evolve into a subculture. For example, Mike Hannan and Jim Baron spearheaded a study of the technology industry, creating a large data set that was analyzed in various ways by different subgroups of a temporary subculture. Jim March attracted a larger and more diverse group to his subculture; their research generally involved some reference to March's large body of work, but the topics covered were as diverse as the subculture's interdisciplinary membership. This subculture gathered late Friday afternoons in March's large office at the Hoover Institute, drinking wine of varying quality out of glasses that were always small, accompanied by conversation that was often stimulating or at least funny. These social gatherings were supplemented by other more work-focused discussions and research presentations. The combination of frequent socializing and hard work produced some fine papers, making this one of the most productive of the informal, faculty-centered subcultures that evolved within the organizational community.

A Differentiation View of Cultural Consequences

A seemingly endless process of subcultural proliferation dictated the texture of our everyday working lives. There were times when subcultural rivalries and competition for resources created unpleasantness and dysfunction. Nevertheless, this plethora of subcultures within the community had its advantages. Because the community had so many subcultures, most of us could find one or more subcultural homes, where we could find like-minded colleagues. Most of us were members of several, often overlapping or nested subcultures. Because the Differentiation perspective preserves, honors, and reifies the intellectual, political, and social commitments that drove this constantly evolving process of subcultural development, it is a particularly useful way to view the organizational community.

This subcultural analysis, however, does not offer adequate explanation for the roles of all individuals. Some organizational scholars bridged the subcultural groupings described above or belonged to none of these subcultures. For example, I am trained as a social psychologist, I worked in the micro group at the business school, but my research is generally at the organizational level of analysis, and I have a courtesy appointment in Sociology. Other faculty, such as Jeff Pfeffer and Jerry Porras, generally work at the organizational or interorganizational levels of analysis, and yet have close ties with both micro and macro colleagues. In the Sociology Department, John Meyer collaborated with Dick Scott on institutional research (e.g., Meyer, Scott, & Deal, 1983), but allied himself politically with population ecologists in some departmental struggles, while Dick Scott made repeated attempts to bridge subcultural gaps within and beyond the boundaries of the Sociology Department. Jim March is undefinable in subcultural terms, as he is considered as an honorary member, with a solid research track record, in any and all subcultures imaginable in the organizational community. A subcultural analysis is complicated by individuals who fall between the cracks or bridge subcultural boundaries with ease. These individuals, and the fact that any analytic categorization scheme omits some complexities, suggest the need for a third way to view cultures in organizations.

FRAGMENTATION: AMBIGUITIES, IRONY, PARADOX, AND CONSTANT FLUX

Defining the Fragmentation Perspective

Looking beyond the apparent harmony and uniformity of Integration, the Differentiation perspective opens the door for the study of supportive alliances, clashing intergroup rivalries, and the struggle for subcultural autonomy. Differentiation refuses to squeeze differences of belief into the single, apparently dominant world view of the Integration perspective. However, the Differentiation view echoes the unities of Integration, albeit on a smaller scale, offering a view of culture that is clear and consistent – within the bounds of a subculture.

A third, Fragmentation, perspective challenges these simplifications and acknowledges the pervasiveness of ambiguity and uncertainty within cultures and subcultures (e.g., March & Olsen, 1976; Starbuck, 1983; Weick, 1991). Because cultural themes are highly abstract, they can be and are interpreted in a myriad of ways. Manifestations associated with a theme are often only tangentially related. Interpretations of a manifestation's connection with a theme therefore are ambiguous, multiple, often paradoxical or ironic – no clarity or consistency here (e.g., Brunsson, 1989; Feldman, 1989; Hatch, 1999; Meyerson, 1994; Martin & Meyerson, 1988; Perrow, 1984; Sabelis, 1996; Weick, 1991). This is a Fragmentation view of culture. There is a lack of consensus everywhere, never coalescing into organization-wide or subcultural agreement. In addition, beliefs and behaviors are in constant flux; nothing is stable.

A Fragmentation View of the Organization Studies Community

Of the three perspectives, the Fragmentation view is most complex and hardest to write coherently (for more on Fragmentation, see Martin, 2002). Here, given space constraints, I will simply offer an illustration of four of the concepts central to Fragmentation: ambiguity of meaning, paradox, irony, and constant flux. A more complete Fragmentation description would focus on a series of transiently activated themes that attract attention from a changing cast of individuals, some opposed, some in favor, some confused, and some looking for a context where their own concerns can be aired, in much the same way Cohen, March, and Olsen (1972) describe a decision opportunity as a garbage can that attracts many unrelated issues.

Ambiguity of Meaning
Two of the themes of central importance to the organizational community were the importance of original and excellent research. However, as discussed above, within the community there was a wide variety of opinions about what originality and excellence entailed. Methods choices were particularly problematic. There was no general consensus on this issue and opinions did not cluster in subcultural groupings associated with status or departmental, school, or disciplinary affiliation.

You can imagine the kinds of arguments that ensued whenever a dissertation had to be designed, a new faculty member hired, or a tenure case evaluated. Some scholars preferred quantitative approaches – the more statistical sophistication the better, whether one was analyzing archival data or doing an experiment. Some even liked computer simulations and math models. Some preferred experimental methods because of their ability to pin down causality; others claimed experimental studies of organizational phenomena lacked external validity (reflecting an inability to represent accurately the complexities of organizational life within a laboratory setting). Some experimentalists criticized multivariate regression studies, labeling them atheoretical number crunching ("correlation is not causality"). Others dismissed any attempts at quantitative precision as theoretically and empirically naïve ("Garbage in, garbage out"). Some advocates of qualitative methods claimed that most quantitative studies are severely limited because they focus on questions asked by researchers, rather than letting study participants reveal what they think is important through unstructured interviews and long-term participant observation. Ethnographic methods, these qualitative researchers argued, have the capacity to reveal deeper kinds of knowledge, less affected by researchers' preconceptions. Others disagreed, dismissing qualitative studies as no better than journalism ("for example is not proof").

Given these differences of opinion, it is not surprising that discussions about methods often dissolved into cacophony. Some community members believed that theory had to be built on multiple observations of multiple instances in multiple settings, while others preferred in-depth studies of single contexts. Some insisted that theory building required the testing of specific, disprovable hypotheses, while others questioned the neo-positivist epistemology associated with such preferences. Original and excellent researches were highly ambiguous terms, meaning many irreconcilable things to different people.

Paradox
These ambiguities in interpretation, which reflected disagreements on very important methodological issues, did not prevent members of the organizational community from agreeing that excellent and original research was crucially important. Even though we could not agree about which research methods were appropriate, arguing this issue helped all of us improve the rigor of our data collection and interpretation. At colloquia and dissertation defenses, any method choice could and often would be strongly challenged. The resulting debates strengthened the diverging convictions of most parties to an argument, as well as their ability to defend their views. Doctoral students often echoed the opinions of their teachers and advisors, sometimes coming to hold even more extreme views about which kinds of methods were preferable. Ultimately, anticipating objections to one's methods choices strengthened one's work. The more fiercely we fought intellectual opponents about methods choices, paradoxically, the more we

helped them to clarify their thinking. We could not win, or to put it differently, we all won.

Irony

Interdisciplinary work requires a lot of organization. It is hard to schedule. Interdepartmental and interschool differences in administrative require-ments need to be accommodated. Scheduling a dissertation committee meeting or an oral exam is complex when participants are likely to come from four or five different departments. Organizational scholars, both students and faculty, are generally frantically busy, in part because of the multiplicity of demands from the interdisciplinary work we do. No wonder that, when we needed to meet, we were reliant on skilled and patient administrative assistants who made sure we all were going to the same room, for the same purpose, at roughly the same time, and that once there, the audio visual equipment would work. We may have studied organization, but many of us were personally, hopelessly disorganized, and, as our assistants would claim, "unorganizable." Herding cats was their favorite metaphor.

Constant Flux

Most organizational faculty and doctoral students joined several different collaborative research projects at once. We tried to manage our research "pipelines," so that as one project waned, another began. Ideally, the pipeline was never blocked and never empty. In addition, junior faculty tended to get promoted or leave. Students graduated or dropped out, senior faculty moved or retired, and the research interests of everyone changed all the time. The casts of characters on our various projects was constantly evolving, demands of members' other projects waxed and waned, and therefore any research group's skill mix fluctuated, making planning and execution difficult. Constant flux was our constant companion.

As these examples illustrate, any cultural theme, including the three themes that have been the focus of this chapter, has to be constantly reintroduced and reinterpreted for newcomers. Subcultures emerge, change, and disappear, while their borders fluctuate in unanticipated ways. The stolid clarity of the Integration perspective and the clearly defined lines of conflict and alliance that emerge from a Differentiation analysis of subcultures are dissolved when cultures are viewed from a Fragmentation perspective. Ambiguities proliferate, uncertainties are pervasive, and change takes the shape of constant flux.

A Fragmentation View of Cultural Consequences

Individuals differ in their tolerance for ambiguity. And it is undoubtedly the case that there can be too much of a potentially good thing. However, when we laugh at a good joke, chuckle at an irony, suddenly see a paradox, or wallow in the ambiguities caused by endlessly different interpretations of what just happened, or what would be best, or what causes what, we taste a moment of uncertainty, when the horizons of our thought are expanded. In addition, awareness of constant flux undermines the certainties that come with the illusion that truth has been discovered, once and for all, and that change will come slowly if at all. Once those false certainties are removed, innovation is required, risk taking seems more worthwhile, and creativity is encouraged. A Fragmentation view of the organizational community acknowledges the ambiguities and uncertainties that pervaded our daily working lives, enabling the intellectual innovation that is a prerequisite for original, excellent research to flourish.

A CONCLUSION: BRINGING THE THREE PERSPECTIVES TOGETHER

Integration views of culture are comforting to many, offering a vision of unity and harmony. In contrast, the Differentiation perspective draws attention to issues that cause differences of opinion, opening the door to serious clashes between groups, conflicts of interest, and possibilities of outright war, secession, and rebellion of various academic sorts. Were the subcultures of community so divisive that we could not hold together? A Fragmentation view is equally uncomfortable for some; it suggests the organizational community might become lost in a haze of endlessly multiple interpretations, everything so confused and vague that coordinated action is increasingly impossible. Was the community caught in a perfect storm, overwhelmed by intergroup conflicts and the ambiguities of endlessly multiple points of view?

The answer, I believe, is no. And not because of the positive cultural consequences outlined in the Integration view of the community's culture. Certainly, we do have common beliefs, shared commitments, and tacit premises that we can fall back on whenever conflict or confusion becomes too much; these comforts of consensus were and continue to be very important.

But to think that the positive consequences revealed in the Integration view would suffice for community's survival is too simple a conclusion. When members of a culture place primary emphasis on Integration – seeking strong consensus around clear values, consistently enacted – they may try to repress some subcultures, deny the validity of differing interpretations, and create a façade of conformity and clarity. When dissent and ambiguity are hidden, they can thrive in the shadows and cracks, growing dramatically.

There is more to a three perspective view than a lesson about the advantages or disadvantages of Integration. The Differentiation and Fragmentation views of the organizational community point to strengths that permit it to transform itself and find new ways to flourish. The Differentiation perspective legitimates and reifies subcultural differences, rather than challenging their right to exist and trying to force dissenting individuals into an oppressed silence. Almost everyone in the community could find relatively enduring as well as transient subcultures where they could feel comfortable and supported, at least for a critical time period.

A Fragmentation view sidesteps the oversimplified certainties and clarities of the Integration and Differentiation views. In the interstices between (sub)cultural islands of clarity and shared values, Fragmentation draws attention to the ways ambiguities proliferate. Ambiguities create room for uncertainty, paradox, irony, ambivalence, humor, and even the unknowable – all precursors to that invaluable creative leap, enabling the risk taking that permits intellectual innovation to occur. In short, without the strengths that are the focus of the Differentiation and Fragmentation perspectives, the organizational community would never have produced the research track record that made the organizational community so productive. Perhaps these same strengths will enable it to continue to thrive, in a constantly transforming state, in years to come.

If this cultural portrait had left out any one of the three perspectives, our view of the organizational community would be falsely and unnecessarily oversimplified, in misleading ways. Without the community's unifying commitments, without the fact that the community's strong subcultural differences were allowed to survive and even flourish, and without the creativity-fostering haze of ambiguity and constant flux that floated through our everyday working lives – the organizational community would never have created so much high quality, original scholarship or sustained and trained such a diverse group of fine scholars. We are all indebted to each other, and above all, to Dick Scott who initiated the structures that enabled the contacts and networks that created the work. Thank you all.

NOTE

1. Doctoral students were at the heart of the organizations community and it is difficult to omit them from this manuscript. I would like to mention those I worked most closely with: Kathy Anterasian, Christine Beckman, Bob Bies, Michael Boehm, Martha Feldman, Joe Harder, Mary Jo Hatch, Kathy Knopoff, Barbara Levitt, Deb Meyerson, Alan Murray, Greg Northcraft, Mandy O'Neill, Kerry Patterson, Melanie Powers, Ray Price, Majken Schultz, Maureen Scully, Caren Siehl, Sim Sitkin, and Alan Wilkins. We created quite a series of subcultures. My sincere apologies to all who have not been mentioned. The length of my list of students makes it clear why including doctoral students where they belong, throughout this manuscript, would have made it very long and, given the limits of records in the various relevant departments and the limits of my knowledge, it would still have been incomplete.

ACKNOWLEDGMENTS

I am grateful for helpful comments from Frank Dobbin, Mary Jo Hatch, Deb Meyerson, and Beau Sheil.

REFERENCES

Baburoglu, O., & Gocer, A. (1994). Whither organizational culture? Privatization of the oldest state-owned enterprise in Turkey. *Industrial and Environmental Crisis Quarterly*, *8*, 41–54.
Barley, S., Meyer, G., & Gash, D. (1988). Cultures of culture: Academics, practitioners, and the pragmatics of normative control. *Administrative Science Quarterly*, *33*, 24–61.
Bartunek, J., & Moch, M. (1991). Multiple constituencies and the quality of working life intervention at FoodCom. In: P. Frost, L. Moore, M. Louis, C. Lundberg & J. Martin (Eds), *Reframing organizational culture* (pp. 104–114). Newbury Park, CA: Sage.
Brunsson, N. (1989). In: N. Alder (Trans.), *The organization of hypocrisy: Talk, decisions, and actions in organizations*. New York: John Wiley.
Cohen, M., March, J., & Olsen, J. (1972). A garbage can model of organizational choice. *Administrative Science Quarterly*, *17*, 1–25.
Damon, C. (1997). *Making sense of meridian: A cultural analysis of organizational life in a new television station*. Unpublished manuscript. University of Kent, Canterbury, UK.
Enomoto, E. (1993). In-school truancy in a multi-ethnic urban high school examined through organizational culture lenses. Doctoral dissertation, University of Michigan. *UMI Dissertation Services, 9331999*.
Feldman, M. (1989). *Order without design: Information processing and policy making*. Stanford, CA: Stanford University Press.
Hatch, M. J. (1999). Exploring the empty spaces of organizing: How improvisational jazz helps redescribe organization structure. *Organizational Studies*, *20*, 75–100.

Koot, W., Sabelis, I., & Ybema, S. (Eds). (1996). *Contradictions in context*. Amsterdam, The Netherlands: Vrej University Press.

Kotter, J., & Heskett, J. (1992). *Corporate culture and performance*. New York: Free Press.

Louis, M. (1985). An investigator's guide to workplace culture. In: P. Frost, L. Moore, M. Louis, C. Lundberg & J. Martin (Eds), *Organizational culture* (pp. 73–94). Newbury Park, CA: Sage.

March, J., & Olsen, J. (Eds). (1976). *Ambiguity and choice in organizations*. Bergen, Norway: Universitetsforlagert.

Martin, J. (1992). *Cultures in Organizations: Three Perspectives*. London: Oxford University Press.

Martin, J. (2002). *Organizational culture: Mapping the terrain*. Newbury Park, CA: Sage.

Martin, J., Feldman, M., Hatch, M. J., & Sitkin, S. (1983). The uniqueness paradox in organizational stories. *Administrative Science Quarterly, 28*, 438–453.

Martin, J., & Meyerson, D. (1988). Organizational cultures and the denial, channeling, and acknowledgment of ambiguity. In: L. Pondy, R. Boland & H. Thomas (Eds), *Managing ambiguity and change* (pp. 93–125). New York: Wiley.

Martin, J., & Siehl, C. (1983). Organizational culture and counter culture: An uneasy symbiosis. *Organizational Dynamics, Fall*, 52–64.

Martin, J., Sitkin, S., & Boehm, M. (1985). Founders and the elusiveness of a cultural legacy. In: P. Frost, L. Moore, M. Louis, C. Lundberg & J. Martin (Eds), *Organizational culture* (pp. 99–124). Newbury Park, CA: Sage.

Meyer, J., Scott, W. R., & Deal, T. (1983). Institutional and technical sources of organizational structure: Explaining the structure of educational organizations. In: J. Meyer & W. R. Scott (Eds), *Organizational environments: Ritual and rationality* (pp. 45–70). Beverly Hills, CA: Sage.

Meyerson, D. (1994). Interpretations of stress in organizations: The cultural production of ambiguity and burnout. *Administrative Science Quarterly, 39*, 628–653.

Meyerson, D., & Martin, J. (1987). Culture change: An integration of three different views. *Journal of Management Studies, 24*, 623–648.

O'Reilly, C., Chatman, J., & Caldwell, D. (1991). People and organizational culture: A profile comparison approach to assessing person-organization fit. *Academy of Management Journal, 34*, 487–516.

Ouchi, W. (1981). *Theory Z: How American business can meet the Japanese challenge*. Reading, MA: Addison-Wesley.

Pascale, R., & Athos, A. (1981). *The art of Japanese management; applications for American executives*. New York: Simon and Schuster.

Perrow, C. (1984). *Normal accidents*. New York: Basic Books.

Peters, T., & Waterman, R. (1982). *In search of excellence: Lessons from America's best-run companies*. New York: Harper and Row.

Porras, J., & Collins, J. (1994). *Built to last*. Harper Business: New York.

Rosen, M. (1991). Breakfast at Spiro's: Dramaturgy and dominance. In: P. Frost, L. Moore, M. Louis, C. Lundberg & J. Martin (Eds), *Reframing organizational culture* (pp. 77–89). Newbury Park, CA: Sage.

Sabelis, I. (1996). Temporal paradoxes: Working with cultural diversity in organizations. In: W. Koot, I. Sabelis & S. Ybema (Eds), *Contradictions in context* (pp. 171–192). Amsterdam, The Netherlands: Vrej University Press.

Schein, E. (1985). *Organizational culture and leadership*. San Francisco, CA: Jossey-Bass.

Siehl, C., & Martin, J. (1984). The role of symbolic management: How can managers effectively transmit organizational culture? In: J. Hunt, D. Hosking, C. Schriesheim & R. Stewart (Eds), *Leaders and managers: International perspectives on managerial behavior and leadership* (pp. 227–239). Elmsford, NY: Pergamon.

Siehl, C., & Martin, J. (1990). Organizational culture: A key to financial performance? In: B. Schneider (Ed.), *Organizational culture and climate* (pp. 241–281). San Francisco: Jossey-Bass.

Starbuck, W. (1983). Organizations as action generators. *American Sociological Review, 48*, 91–102.

Stevenson, W., & Bartunek, J. (1996). Power, interaction, position, and the generation of cultural agreement in organizations. *Human Relations, 49*, 75–104.

Takahashi, S. (1997). Organizational culture and innovation: Theoretical modeling and statistical testing. *Journal of Economics, 62*, 27–67.

Van Maanen, J. (1991). The smile factory: Work at Disneyland. In: P. Frost, L. Moore, M. Louis, C. Lundberg & J. Martin (Eds), *Reframing organizational culture* (pp. 58–76). Newbury Park, CA: Sage.

Van Maanen, J., & Kunda, G. (1989). Real feelings: Emotional expression and organizational culture. In: L. Cummings & B. Staw (Eds), *Research in organizational behavior* (pp. 43–103). Greenwich, CT: JAI Press.

Weick, K. (1991). The vulnerable system: An analysis of the Tenerife air disaster. In: P. Frost, L. Moore, M. Louis, C. Lundberg & J. Martin (Eds), *Reframing organizational culture* (pp. 117–130). Newbury Park, CA: Sage.

Young, E. (1991). On the naming of the rose: Interests and multiple meanings as elements of organizational culture. In: P. Frost, L. Moore, M. Louis, C. Lundberg & J. Martin (Eds), *Reframing organizational culture* (pp. 90–103). Newbury Park, CA: Sage.

CHAPTER 15

EXPLAINING THE IMPACT OF THE STANFORD ORGANIZATION STUDIES COMMUNITY

Donald Palmer

INTRODUCTION

This chapter attempts to explain why the community of scholars at Stanford University generated an unparalleled amount of highly influential theory and research on organizations in the last three decades of the 20th century.[1]

The Stanford organizations studies community (SOC) developed three broad theoretical perspectives that continue to shape the field today; the resource dependence perspective (Pfeffer & Salancik, 1978), the population ecology approach (Hannan & Freeman, 1977), and the new institutional view (Meyer & Rowan, 1977; Meyer, Scott, Rowan, & Deal, 1983; Scott, 1995).[2] It also developed a number of lines of inquiry that remain vibrant today; including work on organizational learning and decision-making (March & Olsen, 1976), culture (Martin, 1992), organizational demography and stratification (Baron & Bielby, 1980), corporate networks (Haunschild, 1993), status (Podolny, 1993), technology management (Barley, 1990), emotions (Sutton, 1991), innovation (Sutton & Hargadon, 1996; Eisenhardt & Tabrizi, 1995), and strategy (Eisenhardt & Schoonhoven, 1996).[3]

This is not to say that other centers of organization studies (OS) scholarship did not exist outside the SOC. There were important practitioners

Stanford's Organization Theory Renaissance, 1970–2000
Research in the Sociology of Organizations, Volume 28, 263–288
Copyright © 2010 by Emerald Group Publishing Limited
All rights of reproduction in any form reserved
ISSN: 0733-558X/doi:10.1108/S0733-558X(2010)0000028019

of SOC-identified theory and research located elsewhere. For example, Howard Aldrich (first in the Cornell University, School of Industrial and Labor Relations and later in the University of North Carolina, Sociology Department) was an important contributor to the ecological tradition (Aldrich, 1999). And other important OS theory and research was developed at other academic institutions. For example, the embeddedness perspective was pioneered at the upstart SUNY Stony Brook by Mark Granovetter (1985) and network research with which this perspective was associated was actively practiced at Stony Brook (Mintz & Schwartz, 1983) as well as at Harvard University, Columbia University, and the University of Chicago (Burt, 1983; Mizruchi, 1982; Laumann, Galaskiewicz, & Marsden, 1978; White, Boorman, & Breiger, 1976).

But the SOC's contributions to OS theory and research overshadow those of other centers with respect to breadth and impact. Further, the SOC was able over time to incorporate OS scholars doing important work elsewhere. For example, Mark Granovetter, who moved from SUNY Stony Brook to Northwestern University in 1994, joined the Stanford Sociology Department in 1995. Woody Powell, a graduate of SUNY Stony Brook before becoming a faculty member at Yale University, MIT, and the University of Arizona, who along with Paul DiMaggio, a faculty member at Princeton, penned a foundational piece in new institutional analysis (DiMaggio & Powell, 1983), joined the Stanford School of Education in 1999. And Doug McAdam, another SUNY Stony Brook graduate, who provided important impetus for the recent integration of social movement and organization theory (Davis, McAdam, Scott, & Zald, 2005), joined the Stanford Sociology Department in 1998.

My explanation of the SOC's extraordinary contribution to OS in the last three decades of the late 20th century draws on classic urban economic theory. I argue that the SOC benefited from an agglomeration process that allowed it to accumulate a large number of smart and productive scholars. A few exceptionally talented, productive, and prominent OS scholars who were located on the Stanford campus in the late 1970s attracted a greater number of exceptional graduate students and other faculty, who in turn attracted still more outstanding graduate students and faculty, all the while developing an academic infrastructure that served to attract still more high quality OS scholars.

My explanation also draws on classic organizational and urban sociological theory as well as recent organizational extensions of this theory. I argue that the SOC's internal structure and network embeddedness provided its members with a wide variety of benefits. The SOC was structurally differentiated and both formally and informally integrated. Further, it was centrally located in the national organization studies community (NOC). And this allowed SOC members to interact in ways that enhanced their ability to develop new and innovative ideas, get those ideas into print, advertise those ideas and publications widely, and sustain and advance themselves in their respective disciplines so that they could continue to create, publish, and thrive professionally.

Before embarking on my analysis, though, one caveat is in order. I have not let the systematic collection of evidence get in the way of my analysis. I develop arguments based on my recollections, without taking into account the twin certainties that these recollections are biased by my primary appointment in Stanford's Graduate School of Business (GSB) and my secondary appointment in its Sociology Department during the 1980s and the certainty that these recollections have weathered and warped with the passage of time.[4]

THE SOC AS AN AGGLOMERATION ACADEMY

Urban economists contend that agglomeration processes underpin the ascendance of economic centers (Marshall, 1890). Firms locate near other firms that can provide them with inputs and absorb their outputs, especially when proximity facilitates inter-firm exchange. As firms emerge in or move to a center, opportunities for beneficial exchange among potential entrants and migrants increase at a geometric rate. Further, as firms concentrate in a center, an infrastructure develops to support the center's business inhabitants and becomes an additional source of attraction for even more entrants and migrants. Agglomeration processes that underpin the ascendance of corporate headquarters centers are fueled by the exchange of corporate headquarters' principal input and output – strategic information (Pred, 1977). Strategic information is proprietary and generated stochastically. As a result, senders are only willing to offer up strategic information when they trust the recipient and recipients can only access this information if they are in continuous contact with senders. And proximity facilitates the development of trust and continuous contact between senders and recipients.

I think an agglomeration process similar to the one that underpins the growth of corporate headquarters centers fueled the growth of the SOC. The presence of talented, productive, and prominent scholars on the Stanford University campus attracted other talented, productive, and prominent senior faculty, promising junior faculty, and gifted graduate students to the campus. The new faculty and graduate students joined the talented, productive, and prominent scholars already on campus to benefit from interacting with them. They also joined to take advantage of the academic infrastructure that arose to support them. And with the addition of each new talented, productive, and prominent senior faculty member, promising junior faculty member, and gifted graduate student, the likelihood that other exceptional faculty and graduate students would come to Stanford increased.

Dick Scott, John Meyer, and Jim March provided the initial spark for this agglomeration process and Mike Hannan and Jeffrey Pfeffer added fuel to the fire. This core group of five scholars generated a gravitational force that attracted a second wave of younger (but now senior) scholars, such as Joanne Martin, Jim Baron, Rod Kramer (Elsbach & Kramer, 1996), Joel Podolny, Bob Sutton, Steve Barley, and a host of other talented scholars too numerous to list. And this growing group of senior and junior scholars attracted a remarkable array of graduate students who went on to make major contributions to the field of organization studies. In addition to the students mentioned elsewhere in this chapter there were: Kathy Eisenhardt, Kaye Schoonhoven (1981), Mary Jo Hatch (1987), Allison Davis-Blake (Davis-Blake & Uzzi, 1993), Jerry Davis, Jitendra Singh (Singh, House, & Tucker, 1986), Dev Jennings (Jennings & Zandbergen, 1995), Marc Ventresca (Washington & Ventresca, 2004), Christine Beckman (Beckman & Haunschild, 2002), Toby Stuart (1998), Olav Sorenson (Sorenson & Audia, 2000), Damon Philips (2002), Willie Ocasio (1999), and Henrich Greve (Greve, 1998), to name just a very few.

OS scholars at nearby universities also contributed to and benefited from this academic agglomeration process. UC Berkeley (an hour drive away) had John Freeman (Freeman & Hannan, 1983). UC Davis (a two-hour drive away) had Gary Hamilton and Nicole Wholsey Biggart (Hamilton & Biggart, 1988). San Jose State University (a 30 minute drive away) had Kaye Schoonhoven. And the more distant UCLA (an hour plane ride away) had Lynn Zucker (Zucker, 1977). Further, interactions among these "peripheral" (relative to the SOC core) OS scholars and between these peripheral scholars and members of the SOC contributed to the SOC's growth. Some OS scholars undoubtedly joined the peripheral institutions to have access to the SOC core. A few scholars might have joined the SOC core to be close or have access to scholars in the peripheral institutions.

The scholarly agglomeration process that I describe above, though, was not (as neo-classical economic theory would have it) a disembodied one.

Rather it unfolded through organizational structures and network connections that accelerated the SOC's growth and facilitated its productivity, creativity, and impact.[5] I elaborate these structures and connections below.

THE SOC AS A COMMUNITY
AND AN ORGANIZATION

Urban sociologists believe that city centers become industrially diverse and administratively intense as they increase in size (Hawley, 1986). Similarly, organizational sociologists believe that organizations become structurally differentiated and formally integrated as they grow (Blau, 1970). Both theories are based on functionalist assumptions. Urban sociologists assume that increased size generates competitive pressures that are reduced by differentiation. Organizational sociologists assume that increased size generates opportunities to increase efficiency that are exploited by differentiation. And both assume that increased differentiation generates control problems that are solved by the creation of coordination devices. City centers that do not become industrially diverse and administratively intense and organizations that do not become structurally differentiated and integrated tend to languish and fail. I think the SOC became structurally differentiated and integrated as it grew and this structural differentiation and integration accelerated the agglomeration process I described above and increased its members' productivity, creativity, and impact.

Differentiation

The SOC exhibited considerable horizontal differentiation. Its members hailed from a variety of disciplinary backgrounds; including psychology, sociology, economics, political science, anthropology, and management. Further, they were spread out across a large number of different academic units. The Department of Sociology (which in the beginning included Scott, Meyer, and Hannan) and the GSB (which in the early years included Pfeffer, Martin, and Baron) were home to the bulk of Stanford's organization scholars. But other schools also provided homes for organizational scholars. Most notably, the School of Engineering included a large number of scholars who studied organizational phenomena, including faculty such as Steve Barley, Bob Sutton, and Kathy Eisenhardt and a host of graduate students that included Kim Elsbach (1994), Beth Bechky (2003),

Andy Hargadon (Hargadon & Sutton, 1997), and Siobhan O'Mahony (O'Mahony & Ferraro, 2007). Also noteworthy, the School of Education included a number of faculty who pursued lines of inquiry and theoretical approaches that were relevant to organization studies; including David Tyack (1974), Martin Carnoy (1975), and Francisco Ramierez (Ramirez & Meyer, 1980) as well as one graduate student who later moved into OS proper, Marc Ventressca. Several independent entities also provided homes for OS scholars, including the Hoover Institute (where Jim March was ensconced) and later Scandinavian Consortium for Organizational Research (SCANCOR) (of which Jim March was the founding director and Woody Powell was a recent director). Finally, the Center for Advanced Study in the Behavioral Sciences (CASBS) provided a temporary home for SOC members on leave (including Jim Baron, John Meyer, and Dick Scott).[6]

The dispersion of OS scholars across many different disciplinary backgrounds reduced competition for status. Scholars were evaluated relative to their disciplinary peers. Thus, if an SOC member wanted to be held in high esteem by his or her Stanford colleagues, s/he did not have to be considered among the best OS scholars on campus, s/he only (and here I am being a bit flippant) had to be considered among the best organizational economists or political scientists or sociologists on campus (or even the best organizational economist, political scientist, or sociologist in a particular academic unit). The dispersion of OS scholars across multiple academic units also increased the community's access to campus resources. Thus, if an SOC member wanted to bring a new OS scholar to campus, s/he could tap open faculty positions in multiple academic units. Over the years, the School of Education has become the home to an increasing number of OS scholars, including Woody Powell and Debra Meyerson (Meyerson, 1994).

The SOC also exhibited significant vertical differentiation. Universities differ substantially in the degree to which they segregate administrative and intellectual labor. The University of California, which likely anchors one end of the spectrum, self-consciously embraces the concept of "shared governance," in which faculty members are expected to participate extensively in the administrative affairs of the institution. For example, junior and senior faculty members at each of the nine full-service UC campuses are expected to review and vote on the personnel actions of all of their departmental colleagues. Stanford University, at least during the 1980s when I was on campus, anchored the other end of the continuum. There Assistant and even Associate Professors had few administrative responsibilities, playing, for example, essentially no role in the personnel process. The segregation of intellectual from administrative labor allowed most SOC members to devote the vast majority of their time to intellectual matters, including interacting with their colleagues, developing their work, getting into print, and advancing their ideas and findings.

Integration

While SOC members hailed from a wide variety of disciplinary backgrounds and were dispersed among a wide range of schools and departments, there were numerous mechanisms for integrating scholars with different back- grounds and situated in different academic units. Perhaps most elemental, each of the different units were integrative mechanisms themselves, providing homes for scholars from different disciplinary backgrounds. The GSB was particularly noteworthy in this respect, providing a home for organizational economists, such as David Teece (Armour & Teece, 1978), sociologists (Jim Baron and Joel Podolny), social psychologists such as Harold Leavitt (Leavitt, 1996) and Joanne Martin, and political scientists (Bendor, 1985) as well as scholars trained in business schools such as Jeffrey Pfeffer and Jerry Poras (Collins & Poras, 1994).

There were also multiple formal mechanisms that linked OS scholars situated in different units. Many faculty members held multiple appoint- ments in different academic units. Thus, faculty members whose principal appointment was in one unit would associate on a regular basis with faculty members in other units in which they held secondary appointments. While my main appointment was in the GSB, I also held a "by courtesy" appointment in the Sociology Department. Further, most OS courses were cross-listed. Thus graduate students from the GSB, the Sociology Department, and the School of Education sat side-by-side in elective courses such as the Organizations and Environment course I taught in the GSB. Finally, graduate students sometimes obtained degrees from multiple departments, the most common combination being a masters in Sociology and a PhD in one of the professional schools. Partly as a result, faculty members often found themselves sitting on dissertation committees along- side colleagues with other disciplinary backgrounds and/or from other schools and departments.

Perhaps most important, Dick Scott's National Institutes of Mental Health (NIMH) training grant sponsored weekly seminars that training grant recipients were expected to attend and in which other graduate students and faculty were encouraged to participate. As a result, sociologists in the GSB such as myself congregated regularly with sociologists from the

Sociology Department, as well as with graduate students, post-doctoral fellows, and faculty members from other disciplines in other units on campus (e.g., with industrial engineers from the Engineering School's Industrial Engineering and Engineering Management Department).

Also important, the NIMH training grant and several academic units (from a financial standpoint, most notably the GSB) sponsored an annual retreat at the Asilomar Conference Grounds on the Monterey peninsula each spring. This three-day retreat included panels in which faculty and students from across the Stanford campus presented and discussed their work. And because the conference was intentionally "under scheduled," it provided participants with a considerable amount of free time during which they could engage in more spontaneous intellectual discussions.

In addition to these formal integrative mechanisms, there were a number of informal gatherings that were convened on a regular basis at Stanford. Foremost among these were Jim March's Friday afternoon wine and cheese parties, where (to the best of my recollection) guests were explicitly but unsuccessfully discouraged from "talking shop." There were also physical locations that served as places where graduate and post-doctoral students convened on an occasional basis. Foremost among these was an old house-like structure known as the "Hannan Hilton," which provided temporary office space for graduate students, most of whom were associated with research projects sponsored by Mike Hannan, while the building that served as the Sociology Department's permanent home underwent seismic retrofitting.

THE SOC AS A NODE IN A NETWORK

It is now widely recognized that economic action, like other forms of human activity, is embedded in social networks (Granovetter, 1985). Sociologists have drawn on this fundamental insight and the foundational ideas of economic and urban sociology to analyze a city's growth and decline as a function of its position in the network of inter-city relationships, many of which are organizational or inter-organizational in nature (Romo & Schwartz, 1995; Palmer & Friedland, 1987; Freeman & Audia, 2006). I think that the SOC was linked by a variety of network connections to other actors in its environment. And these network connections were partly responsible for the community's dramatic growth and its members' productivity, creativity, and impact.

Among the most important ties between the SOC and other actors were those that linked the community to sources of financial support. And arguably the most important of these connections was Dick Scott's NIMH training grant. Also important were the National Science Foundation (NSF) grants won by Mike Hannan, John Meyer, and others. Last but certainly not least were the GSB's ties to donors, which allowed it to provide ample research support to its faculty. These ties provided funds that attracted and supported top graduate students and post-doctoral students. Further, the way these funds were allocated reinforced the internal integrative mechanisms discussed above.

Most important, graduate students in one academic unit sometimes found themselves employed by a faculty member in another. For example, Frank Dobbin (Dobbin & Dowd, 1997) and Dev Jennings, graduate students in Sociology, worked with Jim Baron, a GSB faculty member, on a now very well known study of the diffusion of human resource management policies in the mid-20th century (Baron, Dobbin, & Jennings, 1986). And sometimes graduate students from different academic units found themselves working together on the same project, sponsored by a faculty member situated in their or a different academic unit. For example, Dev Jennings and Melanie Powers (a GSB graduate student) worked together with me, a faculty member in both the GSB and (by courtesy) Sociology, on a project on the multi-divisional form (Palmer, Friedland, Jennings, & Powers, 1987). In addition, NIMH training grant fellowships were awarded to graduate students in a variety of departments and to post-doctoral students with a variety of disciplinary backgrounds and who thus found homes in a variety of academic units. For example, Yinon Cohen (an NIMH post-doc who was a sociology PhD from SUNY Stony Brook) worked with Jeffrey Pfeffer (a GSB faculty member) on several papers on stratification and inequality in organizations (Pfeffer & Cohen, 1984).

In addition, most of the integrative mechanisms discussed in the previous section also provided opportunities for SOC members to develop social relationships with OS scholars situated across the nation. Perhaps most important, as indicated above, the fact that SOC members were situated in multiple academic units increased the opportunities to bring in NOC scholars for invited lectures and increased the opportunities to support visiting NOC scholars (on sabbatical from other institutions). For example, the GSB awarded a visiting professorship to Mark Granovetter, then a member of the Northwestern Sociology Department, in 1986; his only responsibility being to conduct a high level seminar (attended by graduate students, post-doctoral fellows, and faculty members from across campus) devoted to exploring his embeddedness perspective.

The NIMH training grant seminar and the Asilomar Conference provided further opportunities to establish connections with OS scholars at other institutions. These integrative activities served to link SOC members to faculty and graduate students at nearby institutions, including UC Berkeley, UC Davis, UCLA, and the Naval Post Graduate School in Monterey, California. For example, John Freeman was among the faculty and Bill Barnett (Barnett & Carroll, 1987), Heather Haveman (Haveman & Rao, 1997), and Jenny Chatman (1991) were among the graduate students from UC Berkeley who regularly attended the Asilomar Conference. These integrative mechanisms also served to link SOC members to colleagues in more far flung locations. Among the outsiders invited to deliver keynote speeches at Asilomar were Edward Lauman from the University of Chicago, John Kimberly from Wharton (Kimberly, 1979), and, again, Mark Granovetter.

The CASBS provided additional opportunities to forge links with OS scholars in distant places. Among those who spent time at the CASBS were Stewart Clegg (1981), then located at Griffith University in Australia; Ronald Burt, then situated at Columbia University; and Charles Perrow (Perrow, 1984), then positioned at Yale University but who now holds a regular visiting position at Stanford.

Finally, the SOC was central in the network of inter-university personnel flows. Some personnel flows involved movement of faculty from the SOC to nearby communities of OS scholars. For example, David Teece moved from Stanford to UC Berkeley and I moved from Stanford to UC Davis. Other personnel flows involved movement of faculty from the SOC to more distant communities of OS scholars. For example, Joel Podolny left the Stanford GSB for Harvard University. Earlier, Mike Hannan left Stanford for Cornell University, but returned to Stanford within a period of a few years.

Often the inter-university career paths of individual scholars created complex connections between the SOC on the one hand and neighboring and more distant OS communities on the other. This was particularly the case for graduate students trained at Stanford and UC Berkeley. Some OS scholars graduated from Stanford, began their careers in distant locations, and returned to Stanford. For example, Jeffrey Pfeffer graduated from the Stanford GSB, began his career at the University of Illinois, moved to UC Berkeley, and then returned to the Stanford GSB. Similarly, Glenn Carroll graduated from the Stanford Sociology Department, joined the Brown University Sociology Department, moved to UC Berkeley's Haas School, and then returned to the Stanford GSB (after two years at Columbia University's Business School).

Some OS scholars graduated from Stanford, began their careers in distant locations, and returned to a nearby OS community. For example, a host of students who graduated from the Stanford Engineering School's program in Engineering and Engineering Management and left for distant locales, including Kim Elsbach, whose first job was at Emory University, Beth Bechky, whose first position was at Wharton, Andy Hargadon, whose first employment was at the University of Florida, and Siobhan O'Mahony, whose began her career at Harvard, all eventually settled at the UC Davis Graduate School of Management.

Some OS scholars graduated from UC Berkeley, began their careers elsewhere, and ended up at Stanford. For example, Charles O'Reilly (O'Reilly, Chatman, & Caldwell, 1991; O'Reilly, Caldwell, & Barnett, 1989) received his PhD from UC Berkeley, took a position at UCLA, returned to Berkeley, and eventually moved to Stanford where he currently serves in the GSB. Bill Barnett (Barnett & Carroll, 1987) graduated from the Haas School, took a position at the University of Wisconsin, School of Business, and returned as a faculty member to the Stanford GSB.

Finally, there were personnel flows among nearby OS communities that created second-order (two-step) network connections from the vantage point of the SOC. Some OS scholars graduated from Berkeley and moved to another nearby OS community. For example, Nicole Biggart graduated from UC Berkeley and moved to UC Davis. Other OS scholars graduated from UC Berkeley, started their careers in more distant locations, and returned to UC Berkeley. For example, Jennifer Chatman graduated from the UC Berkeley Haas School and assumed a position at the Northwestern Kellogg School of Management, only to return as a faculty member to the Haas School. And Heather Haveman graduated from the Haas School of Business, moved to Cornell University, then to Duke, and then to Columbia University, only to return to the UC Berkeley Sociology Department. Finally, at least one OS scholar graduated from UC Berkeley, started his career elsewhere, and returned to a nearby OS community. Anand Swaminathan (Swaminathan, 1996), now at Emory, graduated from UC Berkeley, began his career at the University of Michigan, and moved to UC Davis.

IMPLICATIONS FOR THE STIMULATION OF RESEARCH PRODUCTIVITY AND THE DEVELOPMENT AND ADVANCEMENT OF THEORETICAL PERSPECTIVES

The SOC members were physically proximate to a large number of highly diverse OS scholars. They were also linked to these many diverse proximate scholars through many integrative mechanisms. In addition, the SOC members were connected to OS scholars in distant locales. I think that this proximity, these local linkages, and these extra-local connections facilitated social interaction among SOC members and between SOC members and distant OS scholars that in turn stimulated the productivity, creativity, and impact of SOC members. Below I elaborate this argument in greater detail.

Developing New and Innovative Ideas

Since the inception of organization studies, the leading figures in the field have advocated the pursuit of methodological rigor and theoretical progress, viewing the two as centerpieces of scientific inquiry (Palmer, 2006). While this orientation has been the subject of much criticism, it remains very influential in our field.

One cannot employ up-to-date methods and go beyond prior theory without developing a comprehensive understanding of current methods and theory. The relationships among SOC members and between SOC and NOC members provided SOC members with information about intellectual developments taking place in the field. And the disciplinary diversity of the SOC's membership, both with respect to background and current location, and the range of its network connections guaranteed that this information was comprehensive.

One cannot employ up-to-date methods and go beyond prior theory without also developing a subtle understanding of current methods and theory and this often requires the acquisition of tacit knowledge about these methods and theory. The relationships among SOC members and between SOC and NOC members provided SOC members with the opportunity to have face-to-face discussions with the authors of prior work, or those intimately acquainted with them; an effective means to obtain the tacit knowledge upon which subtle understandings are built.

Thus, members of the SOC were aware of and intimately familiar with the full range of state-of-the-art research methods, in vogue theoretical ideas, and recent empirical findings in organization science. This allowed them to more convincingly formulate and pitch their work as new; that is, as an advance over prior work. But, the relationships among SOC members and between SOC and NOC members also provided SOC members with another key benefit: the opportunity for the combination of diverse methodological and theoretical ideas. Hargadon and Sutton (1997) contend that technical and product innovation results from the combination of existing ideas in new ways. I think the same can be said for scholarly innovation. As indicated above, SOC scholars frequently interacted with other SOC and NOC scholars who possessed different intellectual resources; scholars who differed in their overall focus (methodological versus theoretical), who had expertise on different methodological techniques, who adhered to different theoretical perspectives, and/or who possessed different disciplinary backgrounds. And these exchanges allowed SOC members to combine existing ideas in new ways.

There were many exchanges that lead to the introduction of new methods into existing lines of inquiry. In most cases, these exchanges only left traces in acknowledgments. But in some cases they culminated in co-authorships. Most notable among these was the collaboration of Nancy Tuma, who studied social stratification systems, and Mike Hannan, who studied organizational populations. Both were interested in modeling discrete state transitions. For example, Tuma was interested in modeling the movement of individuals from one job to another and Hannan was interested in modeling the movement of organizations from birth to death. Their *Social Dynamics* (Tuma & Hannan, 1984) articulated a method for analyzing longitudinal categorical data that dominated the field in the 1980s and 1990s and remains highly influential today.

In addition, like-minded theorists spurred each other on and combined to produce joint work. Most notable among these is the stream of work that flowed from John Meyer and Dick Scott that evolved into the new institutional analysis of organizations. If one considers interaction between core SOC members and more peripheral members, other collaborations quickly come to mind, most notably the seminal pieces in the ecological tradition produced by Mike Hannan and John Freeman and the early strategic management work of Kathy Eisenhardt and Kaye Schoonhoven.

Also important, though, were the exchanges that took place between theorists adhering to different theoretical perspectives. Some of the exchanges between scholars with different theoretical orientations left no visible traces, but can be inferred. The co-habitation in the Stanford Sociology Department of Hannan on the one hand and Meyer and Scott on the other likely facilitated the incorporation of institutional ideas into the ecological model; most evident in the density-dependent selection model (Ranger-Moore, Banaszak-Holl, & Hannan, 1991; Hannan, Carroll, Dundon, & Torres, 1995), which predicts that organizational birth and survival rates will increase at low population density (when increases in population size legitimate a population form) and decline at high density levels (when increases in population size intensify competition). Similarly,

the invited lectures at Asilomar of Edward Laumann and Mark
Granovetter, major figures in network theory, likely facilitated Scott's
incorporation of network ideas into the institutional perspective; most
evident in the raft of diffusion of innovation studies that were produced by
Stanford graduate students and flooded the journals toward the end of the
last century (Mezias, 1990; Davis, 1991).

Some of the exchanges between scholars adhering to different theoretical
orientations, though, left traces in collaborations. Some collaborations
arose between faculty with the same disciplinary background in the same
academic unit. When Hannan (a population ecologist) and Meyer (a new
institutionalist) were both located in the Sociology Department, they
collaborated on *National Development and the World System* (1979). Later,
when Hannan moved to the GSB, he collaborated with Jim Baron (who
comfortably embraced a wide range of theoretical perspectives) on a series
of studies on high technology start-up companies in California's Silicon
Valley (Baron, Burton, & Hannan, 1999; Baron, Hannan, & Burton, 1999).
Some collaborations arose between faculty with different disciplinary
backgrounds situated in the same academic unit, such as the partnership
between Jim Baron (a sociologist) and Peter Reiss (an economist), that led
to an article on imitative homicide (Baron & Reiss, 1985). Finally, as already
noted above, there were many collaborations between faculty members
and graduate students from different disciplinary backgrounds and thus
implicitly different theoretical orientations, such as the collaboration
between Pfeffer and Cohen.

Getting into Print and Getting Noticed

Of course, ideas that advance the state-of-the-art, even innovative ideas that
advance the state-of-the-art, have little impact unless they are published.
The relationships among SOC members and between SOC and NOC
members helped community members get their work into print. They
provided SOC members, especially junior faculty, post-doctoral fellows, and
graduate students, with information and advice about which publication
outlets to pursue, how to write papers that resonated with reviewers at those
outlets, and how to respond to reviewer criticisms. This information and
advice supplemented the information and advice passed from SOC
members' immediate mentors.[7]

Further, publications, even publications in top journals, have little impact
if they are not read and taken into account. The average article in our field,

even the average top-tier journal publication in our field, is cited by less than a handful of other authors. The relationships among SOC members and between SOC and NOC members helped here as well. These connections provided SOC members with opportunities to advertise themselves and their ideas to local and distant OS scholars. SOC members talked among themselves about their current work. They also presented their ideas to NOC members who visited Stanford. And NOC members who visited Stanford reciprocated by inviting SOC members to speak at their institutions, where SOC members could further promote their ideas.

Getting Professional Opportunities

The relationships among SOC members and between SOC and NOC members also provided OS scholars, especially junior faculty, post-doctoral fellows, and graduate students, with information about and access to professional opportunities. Perhaps most important, these relationships provided SOC members with knowledge of and the inside track for visiting and permanent academic positions, both locally and elsewhere (e.g., the CASBS and the Russell Sage Foundation in New York City). Indeed, a number of Stanford graduates found their way back to Stanford at key moments in their careers (as post-doctoral fellows or visiting professors) after their initial appointments failed to pan out for one reason or another. This, of course, by definition enhanced the SOC's centrality in the interuniversity personnel flows discussed earlier.

Also important, being a member of the SOC afforded OS scholars with superior information about and access to funding opportunities locally and elsewhere (e.g., government and foundation grants). It also provided scholars with superior knowledge about and the inside track for publication opportunities, again both locally and elsewhere (e.g., with respect to planned edited volumes, proposed special issues of academic journals, and journals with momentarily short publication queues).

As a result of these relatively material benefits, SOC members were better equipped to suffer the slings and arrows of outrageous fortune that sometimes bruise and skewer young academics, allowing them to survive and publish for another day.[8] And, to make a point that should resonate with organizational ecologists, the ideas championed by surviving and publishing OS scholars (those that were able to obtain tenure at research universities with low teaching loads and service responsibilities) proliferated while the ideas of failing OS scholars (those who left the field or ended up at non-research institutions with heavy teaching loads and service responsibilities) fell by the wayside. Put simply, the methods and theories developed in the SOC came to dominate the field partly because they had more vigorous soldiers to carry their flags.

Emotions, Expectations, Standards, Identity, and Friendships

Finally, the relationships among SOC members provided community members with a variety of relatively intangible but important benefits. First, these relationships provided SOC members with intellectual stimulation. This stimulation took three forms, which can be characterized as lessons that were imparted to SOC members via social comparison processes and the expectations of others. SOC members learned that it was exciting to be an OS scholar (e.g., my colleagues seemed invariably up-beat about the enterprise in which they were engaged). They also learned that they were capable of being successful (e.g., several of my senior colleagues told me matter-of-factly that Stanford did not make hiring mistakes). And they learned that the bar against which success was measured was very high (e.g., my colleagues seldom offered effusive praise for top tier journal publications and, instead, left the impression that they expected them). In short, SOC members were socialized to embrace an emotional state, efficacious self-concept, and evaluative framework that, for the most part, facilitated the production of a high quantity and quality of scholarly output.

Relationships among SOC members also provided community members with the opportunity to develop a heightened sense of their own theoretical identity. Adherents to the organizational ecology perspective refined their sense of self by sparring with the proponents of the resource dependence perspective, perceiving themselves as having escaped the limitations of a theoretical approach that naively personified organizations. And proponents of the emerging new institutional analysis of organizations refined their self-concept by sparring with the adherents to the organizational ecology and the resource dependence perspectives, perceiving themselves as having escaped the limitations of views that, respectively, underestimated and overestimated organizations' capacity for strategic action. And as organizational scholars who study identity understand, the possession of a strong self concept can be empowering.

Lastly, membership in the SOC also provided community members with the opportunity to develop personal relationships of varying strength, from casual contact to deep friendship. These relationships sustained members of the community in the face of the challenges that confront any scholar – prospective, junior, or senior. They also served as glue that held the community together. I will consider the significance of this glue, and the lack thereof, in the next section.

TWO REMAINING QUESTIONS

Why Stanford University and Not another University?

I have explained why the SOC grew and generated an extraordinary quantity of highly influential macro-organizational behavior theory and research. But one might ask why another campus did not grow and generate a similar extraordinary quantity of highly influential theory and research? It is, of course, possible that the co-location of scholars of the caliber of Dick Scott, John Meyer, Jim March, Mike Hannon, and Jeffrey Pfeffer was both unique and sufficient to produce the developments I describe above. But I think that two other factors might have also come into play.

First, the Stanford GSB was close to the center of the business school reform movement of the 1950s, which pushed business schools to develop a more research-oriented focus; in particular, a research-oriented focus rooted in the social science disciplines, which valued the sort of methodological and theoretical rigor for which the SOC became known (Khurana, 2007). This reform movement began at the Harvard Business School (HBS) and the Carnegie Mellon Graduate School of Industrial Administration (GSIA). But it quickly spread to the business schools at Columbia University, the University of Chicago, and Stanford University. And the Stanford GSB was a central actor in the SOC.

Further, several of the SOC satellites were also central to the business school reform movement. After spreading to the business schools at Columbia, Chicago, and Stanford, the movement diffused to the business schools at UC Berkeley, UCLA, and the Massachusetts Institute of Technology (MIT), before finding its way to the business schools of the University of Michigan, the University of Pennsylvania (Wharton), and Northwestern University – and ultimately to the vast majority of tier-one US universities.

Stanford is an hour's drive from UC Berkeley. And UC Berkeley, because it is a member of the University of California system, is linked through administrative relationships to UCLA.

But there were other centers among the central players in the business school reform movement that were similarly advantaged. Most obviously,

HBS was proximate to MIT, which was also a major player in the business school reform movement. And Carnegie's GSIA was relatively close to the University of Pennsylvania's Wharton School, which also was an important player in the business school reform movement. And both HBS and GSIA were relatively close to the business school at Columbia University.

I suspect that two things set the Stanford-UC Berkeley-UCLA triad apart from the Harvard-MIT and Carnegie-University of Pennsylvania dyads. First, developments unique to HBS and the GSIA caused their enthusiasm for the business school reform movement to wane and thus likely inhibited their ability to become centers of macro-organizational behavior theory and research comparable to the SOC. Perhaps most importantly, despite the fact that Harvard was a leader of the business school reform movement, it was slow to relinquish its case-based orientation to business education and research.

Second, the strength of the sociology departments at Stanford, UC Berkeley, and UCLA likely provided a push to the SOC that the Sociology departments at other potential centers of OS scholarship could not provide. Sociology, rather than other social sciences such as political science, anthropology, and economics, has provided the disciplinary foundation for contemporary macro-organizational behavior theory and research. While the authors who published in *Administrative Science Quarterly* early in the journal's history exhibited a diversity of disciplinary backgrounds, the authors who published in *ASQ* in the last three decades have exhibited a much narrower range of disciplinary backgrounds. *ASQ* authors in this later period tend to possess PhDs in Sociology, Business/Management, or Organizational Studies/Science (Palmer, Dick, & Freiburger, 2009).

Stanford University and two of its satellites, UC Berkeley and UCLA, had highly respected sociology departments in the last three decades of the 20th century. Harvard University's Department of Sociology was renowned in this period, but I suspect that the sociology departments at nearby academic institutions did not enjoy reputations that equaled those of UC Berkeley and UCLA. And I suspect that the sociology departments at Carnegie Mellon and the University of Pennsylvania were not as strong as those at Stanford, UC Berkeley, and UCLA.

Has the Gap between the SOC and Competing Centers
of OS Scholarship Narrowed and, if so, Why?

I have explained why the SOC developed into a center of unparalleled macro-organizational behavior theory and research in the last three decades of the 20th century. The SOC remains an exceptionally vibrant community of OS scholars today. And I suspect that many of the factors that I identify above as a source of the community's development are responsible for its resiliency. With this said, I also think that there are today a good number of other concentrations of highly productive OS scholars that rival the SOC for preeminence, among them communities located at the University of Michigan, Northwestern University, Harvard University, the University of Chicago, and outside the United States at the University of Toronto, the University of Alberta, and INSEAD. This raises the question, why has the gap between the SOC and competing centers of OS scholarship narrowed in recent years? I offer two speculations on this score.

First, I suspect that the SOCs unparalleled success at the end of the 20th century is one reason for its partial eclipse today. The SOC has served as a veritable fountain of graduate students, post-doctoral fellows, and faculty members who have gone on to populate the global intellectual landscape. And each of these scholars has sought to develop communities of productive OS scholars, in some cases mimicking the structural arrangements and activities (such as annual conferences that were modeled on the Asilomar conference) that underpinned the SOC's growth, productivity, and impact.

Second, I suspect that the pattern of friendships among members of the SOC left it ill-equipped to respond to the decline in federal funding for the social sciences that accompanied the fiscal conservatism that was ushered in by the Reagan administration between 1981 and 1989 and carried on by the first Bush administration between 1989 and 1993. Mathew Stafford (2009) has analyzed the different paths taken by Allentown and Youngstown in the wake of the deindustrialization of America's heartland in the late 20th century. He contends that Allentown was able to survive the crisis of deindustrialization by transforming its local business community to meet the challenges of a high tech and global economy, because members of its economic elite were connected by civic ties that persisted even as the economic ties that previously sustained the community disintegrated. I think that a variety of work-related ties among the different academic units at Stanford withered as the NIMH training grant funding dried up. And I suspect that the network of friendship ties in the SOC, which was organized into academic unit clusters, did not provide a basis for concerted action between academic units. As a result, conflict arouse between formerly friendly units, such as between the GSB and the Department of Sociology.

CONCLUSION

I have attempted to explain why the SOC grew and produced an
extraordinary amount of influential theory and research on organizations
in the last three decades of the 20th century, why other communities of
scholars did not grow and develop to the same extent, and why the gap
between the SOC and competing centers of OS scholarship has narrowed
in recent years. As noted at the end of the introduction, my analysis is
speculative, being based on recollections that almost certainly are biased by
my location in the SOC and have degraded with the passage of time. My
analysis also suffers from two other potential shortcomings, which I need to
acknowledge because they will be readily apparent to scholars who were
members of the SOC in the last decades of the 20th century.

First, my analysis is theoretically eclectic. The SOC exemplified the norm
of theoretical purity. SOC scholars for the most part plied a single theory
(e.g., population ecology theory or resource dependence theory, but not
both), taking into account other theories only for the purpose of exposing
their limitations. I have, though, employed a large number of theoretical
arguments, without taking care to make sure that they belonged to the same
family of theories or even to make sure that they were consistent with one
another. While this approach will likely grate on some of my former
colleagues, it is consistent with the recent move towards using ideas about
social mechanisms drawn from multiple theoretical perspectives to construct
explanations of organizational phenomena (Davis & Marquis, 2005).

Second, my analysis does not place much weight on human agency. Many
of the theories developed by the SOC have been criticized for their failure to
take into account agency (c.f. DiMaggio and Powell's (1991) assessment of
the new institutional perspective). A more complete analysis of the SOC
might draw on recent theory on entrepreneurship to investigate the role that
intellectual entrepreneurship played in the development of the SOC. While
I do not have the space to pursue this line of argument here, I should at least
note that some core SOC members engaged in activities designed to advance
their own theoretical and research agendas, which in turn redounded to the
benefit of the SOC as a whole. And I must acknowledge that some members
of the SOC engaged in entrepreneurial activities that were primarily
intended to advance the SOC as a whole, rather than their own agendas. The
activities of Jim March and especially Dick Scott stand out among all others
in this respect. Jim and Dick clearly had their own theoretical axes to grind.
But, they also provided a number of grinding stones upon which others
could sharpen their analytical skills and fashion their theoretical edifices.

And the many members of the SOC, including those who like me only passed through the community in a relatively short period of time, owe them a large debt of gratitude for doing so.

NOTES

1. By "theory and research on organizations" I mean theory and research that is conventionally identified with "macro-organizational behavior." Such theory and research focuses on the organization as the unit of analysis or on organizational processes as the level of analysis.

2. Here and throughout this chapter I use citations to point to publications that I consider illustrative of the type of work to which I am referring in the text. These citations are not comprehensive (there is much more work in the traditions to which I point than I present here) and they do not identify the most exemplary pieces in each type of work (one could easily claim that work not cited here is more important than the work cited).

3. This list is intended to be illustrative of the many important theories that were developed and lines of inquiry that were explored at Stanford and is not intended to be comprehensive.

4. I was a faculty member in the Stanford GSB and Sociology Department from 1980 to 1989, where I conducted research on corporate networks.

5. I use the word creativity to connote the ability to develop ideas that others in the field considered at the least an advance over previous work and at most an innovative break from prior thinking. I consider this ability to be distinct from the ability to get one's ideas into print. And I consider that ability to be distinct from the ability to convince others of the worth of one's ideas and publications.

6. There were also a handful of students of organizations in other academic departments, foremost among them Terry Moe (1982) in the Political Science Department. The interaction between these scholars and the rest of the SOC, though, was relatively minimal.

7. My experience with my first publication in a management journal provides a good illustration of how a junior scholar's membership in the SOC helped him/her to get into print. I submitted a manuscript, cannibalized from my dissertation, to a sociology journal, *Social Problems*, which had solicited it. However, after a rather long review process in which the manuscript was lost, that journal rejected it. On hearing of this outcome, Jeffrey Pfeffer advised me to submit the piece to *Administrative Science Quarterly*, instructing me that this is where I should have submitted the paper in the first place. Among the reviews on the *ASQ* submission was one that I immediately recognized was written by Ron Burt (who was in the Department of Sociology at UC Berkeley at the time). This review endorsed my paper's main thrust but criticized its use of an antiquated simple tabular analysis and went so far as to reanalyze my data using a log-linear model, which was a state-of-the art statistical technique at the time. I revised the paper, taking into account Pfeffer's reading of the reviews and employing Burt's method. The revision, "Broken Ties" (1983) was accepted for publication and remains among my most cited papers.

284   DONALD PALMER

Had I not been in the SOC at the time, I would not have enjoyed the benefit of
Pfeffer helpful advice and, I strongly suspect, that I would not have been the
recipient of Burt's generous guidance.

   8. I strongly suspect that I was appointed to the editorial board of the
Administrative Science Quarterly (a journal of which I later became editor) in my
second year at the Stanford GSB because one of my senior colleagues recommended
me for the position. And I was interviewed for the position I now hold at UC Davis,
after failing to assemble a record worthy of receiving tenure at Stanford, because of
the acquaintance I made of Gary Hamilton and Nicole Woolsey Biggart at an early
Asilomar Conference.

REFERENCES

Aldrich, H. (1999). *Organizations evolving*. London: Sage Publications Ltd.
Armour, H. O., & Teece, D. J. (1978). Organizational structure and economic performance:
    A test of the multidivisional hypothesis. *The Bell Journal of Economics, 9*(1), 106–122.
Barley, S. (1990). The alignment of technology and structure through roles and networks.
    Administrative Science Quarterly, 35, 61–103.
Barnett, W. P., & Carroll, G. R. (1987). Competition and mutualism among early telephone
    companies. *Administrative Science Quarterly, 32*(3), 400–421.
Baron, J. N., & Bielby, W. T. (1980). Bringing the firms back in: Stratification, segmentation,
    and the organization of work. *American Sociological Review, 45*, 737–765.
Baron, J. N., Burton, D. M., & Hannan, M. T. (1999). Engineering bureaucracy: The genesis of
    formal policies, positions, and structures in high-technology firms. *Journal of Law,
    Economics, & Organization, 15*, 1–41.
Baron, J. N., Dobbin, F. R., & Jennings, P. D. (1986). War and peace: The evolution of modern
    personnel administration in U.S. industry. *American Journal of Sociology, 92*, 350–383.
Baron, J. N., Hannan, M. T., & Burton, D. M. (1999). Building the iron cage: Determinants of
    managerial intensity in the early years of organizations. *American Sociological Review,
    64*(4), 527–547.
Baron, J. N., & Reiss, P. C. (1985). Same time, next year: Aggregate analyses of the mass media
    and violent behavior. *American Sociological Review, 50*(3), 347–363.
Bechky, B. A. (2003). Object lessons: Workplace artifacts as representations of occupational
    jurisdiction. *American Journal of Sociology, 109*, 720–752.
Beckman, C. M., & Haunschild, P. R. (2002). Network learning: The effects of partners'
    heterogeneity of experience on corporate acquisitions. *Administrative Science Quarterly,
    47*(1), 92–124.
Bendor, J. (1985). *Parallel systems: Redundancy in government*. Berkeley, CA: University of
    California Press.
Blau, P. (1970). A formal theory of differentiation in organizations. *American Sociological
    Review, 35*, 201–218.
Burt, R. S. (1983). *Corporate profits and cooptation*. New York: Academic Press.
Carnoy, M. (1975). *Schooling in a corporate society*. New York: McKay.
Chatman, J. A. (1991). Matching people and organizations: Selection and socialization in public
    accounting firms. *Administrative Science Quarterly, 36*, 459–484.

Clegg, S. (1981). Organization and control. *Administrative Science Quarterly, 26*(4), 545–562.

Collins, J., & Poras, J. (1994). *Built to last: Successful habits of visionary companies.* New York: Harper Collins Publishers.

Davis, G. E. (1991). Agents without principles? The spread of the poison pill through the intercorporate network. *Administrative Science Quarterly, 36,* 583–613.

Davis, G. E., & Marquis, C. (2005). Prospects for organizational theory in the early twenty-first century: Institutional fields and mechanisms. *Organization Science, 16,* 232–343.

Davis, G. E., McAdam, D., Scott, W. R., & Zald, M. N. (2005). *Social movement organizations.* New York: Cambridge University Press.

Davis-Blake, A., & Uzzi, B. (1993). Determinants of employment externalization: A study of temporary workers and independent contractors. *Administrative Science Quarterly, 38*(2), 195–223.

DiMaggio, P. J., & Powell, W. W. (1983). The iron cage revisited: Institutional isomorphism and collective rationality in organized fields. *American Sociological Review, 48,* 147–160.

DiMaggio, P. J., & Powell, W. W. (1991). Introduction. In: W. W. Powell & P. J. DiMaggio (Eds), *The new institutionalism in organizational analysis.* Chicago: University of Chicago Press.

Dobbin, F., & Dowd, T. J. (1997). How policy shapes competition: Early railroad foundings in Massachusetts. *Administrative Science Quarterly, 42,* 501–529.

Eisenhardt, K. M., & Schoonhoven, C. B. (1996). Resource-based view of strategic alliance formation: Strategic and social explanations in entrepreneurial firms. *Organization Science, 7*(2), 136–150.

Eisenhardt, K. M., & Tabrizi, B. N. (1995). Accelerating adaptive processes: Product innovation in the global computer industry. *Administrative Science Quarterly, 40*(1), 84–110.

Elsbach, K. (1994). Managing organizational legitimacy in the California cattle industry: The construction and effectiveness of verbal accounts. *Administrative Science Quarterly, 39*(1), 57–88.

Elsbach, K., & Kramer, R. (1996). Members' responses to organizational identity threats: Encountering and countering the Business Week Rankings. *Administrative Science Quarterly, 41*(3), 442–476.

Freeman, J., & Audia, P. (2006). Organizational foundings in community context: Instrument manufacturers and their interrelationship with other organizations. *Administrative Science Quarterly, 51,* 381–419.

Freeman, J. H., & Hannan, M. T. (1983). Niche width and the dynamics of organizational populations. *American Journal of Sociology, 88,* 1116–1145.

Granovetter, M. (1985). Economic action and social structure: The problem of embeddedness. *American Journal of Sociology, 91,* 481–510.

Greve, H. R. (1998). Performance, aspirations, and risky organizational change. *Administrative Science Quarterly, 43,* 58–86.

Hamilton, G., & Biggart, N. W. (1988). Market, culture, and authority: A comparative analysis of management and organization in the far east. *American Journal of Sociology, 94*(Suppl.), S52–S94.

Hannan, M. T., Carroll, G. R., Dundon, E. A., & Torres, J. C. (1995). Organizational evolution in a multinational context: Entries of automobile manufacturers in Belgium, Britain, France, Germany, and Italy. *American Sociological Review, 60*(4), 509–528.

Hannan, M. T., & Freeman, J. (1977). The population ecology of organizations. *American Journal of Sociology, 82,* 929–964.

Hargadon, A., & Sutton, R. (1997). Technology brokering and innovation in a product development firm. *Administrative Science Quarterly, 42,* 716–749.

Hatch, M. J. (1987). Physical barriers, task characteristics, and interaction activity in research and development firms. *Administrative Science Quarterly, 32,* 387–399.

Haunschild, P. R. (1993). Interorganizational imitation: The impact of interlocks on corporate acquisition activity. *Administrative Science Quarterly, 38,* 564–592.

Haveman, H., & Rao, H. (1997). Structuring a theory of moral sentiments: Institutional and organizational coevolution in the early thrift industry. *American Journal of Sociology, 102,* 1606–1651.

Hawley, A. (1986). *Human ecology: A theoretical essay.* Chicago: University of Chicago Press.

Jennings, P. D., & Zandbergen, P. A. (1995). Ecologically sustainable organizations: An institutional approach. *Academy of Management Review, 20*(4), 1015–1052.

Khurana, R. (2007). *From higher aims to hired hands.* Princeton, NJ: Princeton University Press.

Kimberly, J. R. (1979). Issues in the creation of organizations: Initiation, innovation, and institutionalization. *Academy of Management Journal, 22*(3), 437–457.

Laumann, E. O., Galaskiewicz, J., & Marsden, P. V. (1978). Community structure as interorganizational linkages. *Annual Review of Sociology, 4,* 455–484.

Leavitt, H. J. (1996). The old days, hot groups, and managers' Lib. *Administrative Science Quarterly, 41*(2), 288–300 (40th Anniversary Issue).

March, J. G., & Olsen, J. P. (1976). *Ambiguity and choice in organizations.* Bergen, Norway: Universitetsforlaget.

Marshall, A. (1890). *Principles of economics.* London: Macmillan.

Martin, J. (1992). *Organizational cultures: Three perspectives.* New York: Oxford University Press.

Meyer, J. W., & Rowan, B. (1977). Institutionalized organizations: Formal structure as myth and ceremony. *American Journal of Sociology, 83,* 340–363.

Meyer, J. W., Scott, W. R., Rowan, B., & Deal, T. E. (1983). *Organizational environments: Ritual and rationality.* Beverly Hills, CA: Sage.

Meyerson, D. (1994). Interpretations of stress in institutions: The cultural production of ambiguity and burnout. *Administrative Science Quarterly, 39*(4), 628–653.

Mezias, S. (1990). An institutional model of organizational practice: Financial reporting at the fortune 200. *Administrative Science Quarterly, 35,* 431–457.

Mintz, B., & Schwartz, M. (1983). *Bank hegemony, corporate networks and intercorporate power: A study of interlocking directorates in American business.* Chicago: University of Chicago Press.

Mizruchi, M. (1982). *The American corporate network, 1904–1974.* Beverly Hills, CA: Sage Publications, Inc.

Moe, T. M. (1982). Regulatory performance and presidential administration. *American Journal of Political Science, 26,* 197–224.

Ocasio, W. (1999). Institutionalized action and corporate governance: The reliance on rules of CEO succession. *Administrative Science Quarterly, 44,* 431–457.

O'Mahony, S., & Ferraro, F. (2007). The emergence of governance in an open source community. *Academy of Management Journal, 50,* 1079–1106.

O'Reilly, C., III., Caldwell, D., & Barnett, W. (1989). Work group demography, social integration, and turnover work group demography, social integration, and turnover. *Administrative Science Quarterly, 34*(1), 21–37.

O'Reilly, C., III., Chatman, J., & Caldwell, D. (1991). People and organizational culture: A profile comparison approach to assessing person-organization fit. *Academy of Management Journal, 34*(3), 487–516.

Palmer, D. (2006). Taking stock of the criteria we use to evaluate one another's work: ASQ 50 years out. *Administrative Science Quarterly, 51*, 535–559.

Palmer, D., Dick, B., & Freiburger, N. (2009). Rigor and relevance in organization studies. *Management Inquiry, 18*, 265–272.

Palmer, D., & Friedland, R. (1987). Corporation, class and city system. In: M. Mizruchi & M. Schwartz (Eds), *Structural analysis of business* (pp. 145–184). Cambridge, UK: Cambridge University Press.

Palmer, D., Friedland, R., Jennings, P. D., & Powers, M. E. (1987). The economics and politics of structure: The multidivisional form and the large U.S. corporation. *Administrative Science Quarterly, 32*(1), 25–48.

Perrow, C. (1984). *Normal accidents*. New York: Basic Books.

Pfeffer, J., & Cohen, Y. (1984). Determinants of internal labor markets in organizations. *Administrative Science Quarterly, 29*, 550–572.

Pfeffer, J., & Salancik, G. (1978). *External control of organizations*. New York: Harper & Row.

Phillips, D. J. (2002). A genealogical approach to organizational life chances: The parent-progeny transfer among Silicon Valley law firms, 1946–1996. *Administrative Science Quarterly, 47*(3), 474–506.

Podolny, J. (1993). A status-based model of market competition. *American Journal of Sociology, 98*(4), 829–872.

Pred, A. (1977). *City systems in advanced economies*. London: Hutchinson.

Ramirez, F., & Meyer, J. (1980). Comparative education: The social construction of the modern world system. *Annual Review of Sociology, 6*, 369–399.

Ranger-Moore, J., Banaszak-Holl, J., & Hannan, M. T. (1991). Density-dependent dynamics in regulated industries: Founding rates of banks and life insurance companies. *Administrative Science Quarterly, 36*(1), 36–65.

Romo, F. P., & Schwartz, M. (1995). The structural embeddedness of business decisions: The migration of manufacturing plants in New York state, 1960 to 1985. *American Sociological Review, 60*(6), 874–907.

Schoonhoven, C. B. (1981). Problems with contingency theory: Testing assumptions hidden within the language of contingency 'theory'. *Administrative Science Quarterly, 2*(3), 349–377.

Scott, W. R. (1995). *Institutions and organizations*. London: Sage Publications.

Singh, J. V., House, R. J., & Tucker, D. J. (1986). Organizational change and organizational mortality. *Administrative Science Quarterly, 31*(4), 587–611.

Sorenson, O., & Audia, P. (2000). The social structure of entrepreneurial activity: Geographic concentration of footwear production in the United States, 1940–1989. *American Journal of Sociology, 106*(2), 424–461.

Stafford, M. (2009). *Why the garden club couldn't save Youngstown*. Cambridge, MA: Harvard University Press.

Stuart, T. (1998). Network positions and propensities to collaborate: An investigation of strategic alliance formation in a high-technology industry. *Administrative Science Quarterly, 43*(3), 668–698.

Sutton, R. I. (1991). Maintaining norms about expressed emotions: The case of bill collectors. *Administrative Science Quarterly, 36*, 245–268.

Sutton, R. I., & Hargadon, A. (1996). Brainstorming groups in context: Effectiveness in a product design firm. *Administrative Science Quarterly, 41*, 685–718.

Swaminathan, A. (1996). Environmental conditions at founding and organizational mortality: A trial-by-fire model. *Academy of Management Journal, 39*(5), 1350–1377.

Tuma, N., & Hannan, M. (1984). *Social dynamics*. New York: Academic Press.

Tyack, D. (1974). *The one best system: A history of American urban education*. Cambridge, MA: Harvard University Press.

Washington, M., & Ventresca, M. J. (2004). How organizations change: The role of institutional support mechanisms in the incorporation of higher education visibility strategies, 1874–1995. *Organization Science, 15*(1), 82–96.

White, H. C., Boorman, S. A., & Breiger, R. L. (1976). Social structure from multiple networks: 1. Blockmodels of roles and positions. *American Journal of Sociology, 81*, 730–780.

Zucker, L. G. (1977). The role of institutionalization in cultural persistence. *American Sociological Review, 42*, 726–743.

CHAPTER 16

SPEAKING WITH ONE VOICE: A "STANFORD SCHOOL" APPROACH TO ORGANIZATIONAL HIERARCHY

Ezra W. Zuckerman

INTRODUCTION

I am honored to contribute to this volume on the Stanford Organization Theory Renaissance, though I must admit that I am a bit sheepish about being listed as a faculty member. I was indeed on the Stanford faculty, from 1997 to 2001. However, the experience for me was more of a developmental one in which I learned from my colleagues, who consisted of the leading lights in the sociology of organizations and organization theory generally. This period was as formative for me as was the prior period, when I was a student in the formal sense. I find it easy to point to specific ideas that I encountered during my stay at Stanford and to trace how they shaped my perspective on key questions of social and economic organization. In the following, I will discuss one example of this Stanford influence. In particular, I build on ideas developed at Stanford during the 1970s and 1980s (and which I came to appreciate during the 1990s) to make progress on a puzzle that did not occupy center stage there and then. Nothing testifies

Stanford's Organization Theory Renaissance, 1970–2000
Research in the Sociology of Organizations, Volume 28, 289–307
Copyright © 2010 by Emerald Group Publishing Limited
All rights of reproduction in any form reserved
ISSN: 0733-558X/doi:10.1108/S0733-558X(2010)0000028020

to the value of a theory or approach than its ability to generate insight well beyond the original questions for which it was originally developed.

The puzzle that forms the focus of this essay is the question of why formal organizations tend to be hierarchical, such that certain key rights are concentrated in the hands of a small fraction of organization members, with sub-rights (the general rights as they pertain to specific functions or divisions) delegated in highly restricted ways. The puzzle as to why these key rights – which Williamson (1975) summarizes as "fiat" and which encompass (a) membership-rights (the right to control the organization's boundary through hiring and firing) and (b) decision-rights (the right to issue orders to those lower in the hierarchy, with the expectation by all concerned that such orders are legitimate) – are concentrated, has never occupied center stage among organizational sociologists. Perhaps this neglect is justified. Especially if one begins with Weber's definition of bureaucracy (see Scott, 2002, pp. 43–50), formal organizations seem to be hierarchical by definition. But even if it is tautological to assert that formal organizations are hierarchical, this begs the question of *why and in what respects* this tautology holds. Many business firms are now described as eschewing formal hierarchy, with such deviations from hierarchy often cited as being responsible for such firms' success.[1] And even organizations that look quite hierarchical "on paper" tend to feature much behavior that deviates from the formal hierarchy. As Granovetter (1985, p. 502) quipped, "it hardly needs repeating that observers who assume firms to be structured in fact by the official organization chart are sociological babes in the woods."

And yet, even if formal organizations are less hierarchical (or more effective when less hierarchical) than a naïf might suppose, it still appears that all formal organizations share certain hierarchical features. Note, in particular, that while managers may choose not to exercise their member-ship- or decision-rights, *those rights still belong to them.* As Baker, Gibbons, and Murphy (1999, p. 56) stress, "subordinate decision-rights are loaned, not owned." That is, even the most avowedly egalitarian organization only *suppresses* its rights to control membership and give orders; it cannot constitutionally give up these rights. As Perrow (1986, p. 129) puts it, "direct controls... always exist." But why is this? Why are formal organizations fundamentally hierarchical?

In this brief essay, I develop an answer to this question by focusing on a third right, which is analytically distinct from membership- and decision-rights, and which (I contend) is invariably concentrated in the hands of a very small fraction of organization members – that is, the *right to speak on behalf of the organization.* I argue that the concentration of this right (as well as the right to delegate it) follows as an unrecognized implication of Hannan and Freeman's (1984) sociological theory of formal organizations, which they present (but do not really present as such) in their classic article "Structural Inertia and Organizational Change" (henceforth, HF84). In short, HF84 argue that structural inertia is a byproduct of what makes formal organizations evolutionarily adaptive – that is, their "accountability and reliability." I argue that two key factors are necessary to make organizations accountable and reliable – (a) the ability to credibly commit to outside stakeholders and (b) the ability to converge on common routines for coordination – and each requires that the organization have a *clear identity*, either to outsiders (to achieve external commitment) and/or to insiders (to provide the basis for internal accountability and thereby achieve internal coordination). And insofar as a collective actor will not have a clear identity unless it is clear who can speak on its behalf, it follows that such rights will be highly concentrated, and the delegation of sub-rights (e.g., who can speak on behalf of a division) will be sharply delimited as well. Finally, just as HF84 understand inertia to be a byproduct of accountability and reliability, I argue that the more obvious hierarchical features of formal organizations (e.g., the concentration of membership-rights and decision-rights) can be derived from the more subtle but more basic need to concentrate voice-rights.

In what follows, I will fill in this outline a bit more. In the first section, I summarize the contribution of HF84 and distill the elements that can be applied to the current problem. In so doing, I will make the case that HF84 should be read as part of a broader Stanford-based sociological theory of the formal organization, in that it developed from engagement with other lines of thinking that were based at Stanford. I then propose a modified form of their argument, which suggests why organizations tend to concentrate their "voice-rights" in a small number of hands, and then draw out the implications for the puzzle at hand. I conclude by briefly treating objections.

HF84: STRUCTURAL INERTIA AS BYPRODUCT OF FORMAL ORGANIZATION

To recall, the central objective of HF84 was not to propose a theory of the formal organization and it certainly was not to clarify why such organizations tend to be hierarchical. Rather, their goal was to defend the main premise of organization ecology, as articulated in their classic 1977 article – that is, that organizations could be assumed to be "structurally inert" such that "most of the variability in organizational structures comes about through the creation of new organizations and new organizational forms and the replacement of old ones" (HF84, p. 150). Why might such a premise need defense? For starters, HF were clearly under the impression that this premise was not popular on The Farm. They cite both Pfeffer and Salancik's (1978) resource dependence theory and Meyer and Rowan's (1977; cf., DiMaggio & Powell, 1983) new institutionalism as "variants ... (of) rational adaptation theory... (which propose) that organizational variability reflects designed changes in strategy and structure of individual organizations in response to environmental changes, threats, and opportunities" (*ibid.*). Moreover, they see themselves as answering a challenge by March (1981), who appears to reject the assumption of structural inertia out of hand: "... it is not that organizations are rigid and inflexible, but that they are impressively imaginative" (p. 150).

While Stanford-based organization theorists may not have been on the same page when it came to organizational change/inertia, it is clear that they were engaging with one another. And especially in hindsight, such engagement seems to have been highly productive. In particular, it is noteworthy that HF84 credit Scott (1981, p. 204) for the suggestion (which they then develop further) that structural inertia pertains to "core" features of organizations rather than peripheral ones. And HF84 argue that March's observations on organizational change are in fact compatible with their view that while organizations undergo significant change, such change is effectively "random with respect to adaptive value" (HF84, p. 150). Moreover, two related and central elements of HF's approach clearly echo Meyer and Rowan (1977): (a) the idea that technical efficiency is not the right address to seek the basis for commonly shared features of formal organization; and (b) the emphasis on how organizations legitimize or account for their actions quite apart from what they actually do.

Yet, while HF84 clearly owes much to Stanford-based influences, it is important to appreciate its signal contribution. In particular, whereas HF's landmark 1977 article (Hannan & Freeman, 1977) was premised on the observation that organizations tend to be inert (i.e., they change slowly relative to the pace of environmental change), HF84 make the theory more compelling by *transforming structural inertia from an axiom into a theorem.* That is, they derive structural inertia from more basic principles. They accomplish this by hoisting themselves on their own petard and addressing a challenge to their work which no one had actually raised but which, they argue convincingly, needed to be addressed: Since features of organizations should not survive for long if they are not adaptive, it follows that if organizations tend to be structurally inert, then inertia is adaptive. But why would this be? And *how* could this be, when it seems plain that organizations *should change* when they face significant environmental threats.

HF's inspired move is to suggest that while inertia itself is not adaptive, it is a *byproduct* of organizational characteristics, which are adaptive. In particular, they stress that modern society and economy favor actors that are reliable and/or accountable. By *reliability*, they mean the "capacity to generate collective actions with small variance in quality" (HF84, p. 153). And they argue that while "from the perspective of the performance of a single, complex collective action, it is not obvious that a permanent organization has any technical advantage" (*ibid.*), it is the "distinctive competence of (permanent, formal) organization" that it is highly reliable in the above sense. By *accountability*, they mean the ability "to document how resources have been used and ... reconstruct the sequences of... decisions" to show that "appropriate rules and procedures" were followed (*ibid.*). And as did Meyer and Rowan (1977), HF84 observe the spread of "general norms of rationality in the modern world," which increase the demand for accountable actors in the above sense. Finally, since the organizational features necessary to produce reliability and accountability also produce structural inertia as a byproduct, it follows that organizations will tend to be structurally inert. HF84 summarize these features as "reproducibility," which they define as satisfaction of the imperative that "structures of roles, authority, and communication must be... very nearly the same today [as] yesterday" (p. 154). Fig. 1 is a sketch of their argument.

It is worth underlining two key features of HF's approach. First, while their goal was the perhaps modest one of justifying the assumption of structural inertia (by turning it into a theorem derived from the more primitive axiom of selectivity), they developed a sociological theory of the formal organization, one that is clearly compatible with other Stanford-based approaches, particularly the institutionalism of Meyer and Rowan

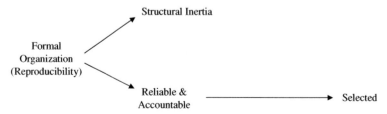

Fig. 1. Based on Hannan and Freeman (1984): Formal Organization due to Reliability and Accountability.

(1977).[2] Second, the form of their argument, whereby common features of formal organizations (and entities generally) are explained not as adaptive in themselves but as *byproducts* of adaptive features, represents a useful model that can be applied to other problems.

In what follows, I build on each of these features to make some progress on the question of why formal organizations are hierarchical. In particular, I follow the basic form of HF84's argument, albeit while suggesting that we recast the organizational characteristics that make organizations reliable and accountable. I then sketch how this modified version of HF84's framework suggests that: (a) in order to be reliable and accountable (and thereby enhance selectivity), formal organizations must concentrate the right to speak on behalf of the organization; and (b) the need to concentrate "voice-rights" creates, as a byproduct, a need to concentrate control of membership- and decision-rights.

CLEAR IDENTITY AS PRECONDITION
FOR REPRODUCIBILITY

As depicted at the right of Fig. 2, my first modification of HF84's model is to distinguish reliability from (external) accountability as distinctive criteria for selection. The main reason for doing so is to highlight the fact that they solve different problems. Reliability is demanded of an actor when those who turn to that actor for goods or services seek to minimize their risk of a bad draw. Such "audiences" will place a premium on actors who can consistently meet a quality threshold. The preference for accountable actors is related to the demand for reliability but is distinct from it.

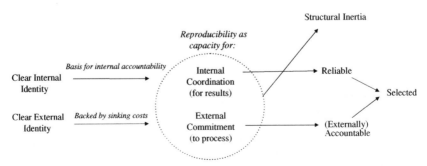

Fig. 2. Modified based on Hannan and Freeman (1984): Clear Identity as Basis for Reliability and Accountability.

To paraphrase March (1994), the issue is one of "appropriateness" rather than "consequences." If performance always reached the desired threshold, there would be no reason for the audience to question the procedures that were followed. But even a highly reliable actor may sometimes fail to reach such a threshold. Moreover, in many cases, performance criteria are ambiguous or are subject to change ex post by those who review the audience's decisions. Under such conditions, it is useful to be able to "take cover" in the appropriateness of the procedures followed. To be sure, appropriate procedures are not random with respect to consequences. Rather, these procedures seem appropriate because they are the reasonable, most accepted ways of generating the desired performance – even if they often do not work for the specific task.

The second reason for distinguishing reliability from accountability in this way is that we can more clearly see that "reproducibility" addresses two related but distinct organizational challenges, which are distinguished in Fig. 2: (a) to coordinate action among employees in such a way as to generate reliable (high) performance and (b) to commit the organization to following reasonable procedures. While this first challenge is evident to anyone who has ever tried to "herd cats," the second challenge is perhaps more subtle. It can be stated as follows: insofar as actors will be preferred when they can "document how resources have been used and ... show that appropriate rules and procedures" have been followed (HF84, p. 153), this raises the question as to how an audience will know ex ante that the organization will be accountable in this fashion ex post. To address this issue, the actor must take steps to *commit* itself, in the (Schelling, 1956; cf., Becker, 1960; Selznick, 1957) sense of making it more costly to act "inappropriately." That is, outsiders can count on an actor to follow appropriate procedures when we see that it would be more costly for it to act inappropriately (see King, Felin, & Whetten, 2010, pp. 292–294).

What is then about formal organizations, as distinct from (sets of) actor(s) that are not formal organizations, which allows them to coordinate internally sufficiently well to perform reliably? And what allows them to commit themselves to acting appropriately? HF84 do not address these questions directly, but they provide a critical lead when they distinguish between the organizational core and periphery and suggest why core elements are so difficult to change:

> Universities, for example, are constantly changing the textbooks used for instruction. They do so in an adaptive way, keeping up with the constantly evolving knowledge bases of their various fields. Persuading a university faculty to abandon liberal arts for the sake of vocational training is something else again. Why would the university's curriculum be

so difficult to change? A number of answers come quickly to mind. The *curriculum embodies the university's identity* with reference both to the broader society and to its participants (i.e., faculty, students, staff, administration, alumni). The kinds of courses offered and the frequency with which they are offered serve as a statement of purpose....
(p. 155; italics added)

Thus, HF84 suggest that an organization's identity is at the heart of its capacity for reproduction (via internal coordination and external commitment), and this thereby increases its survival prospects (via greater reliability and accountability) and correlatively, its structural inertia. But what is an organizational identity and how does it help the organization achieve such feats?

Following Zuckerman (2010), we may define identity as *consistent placement*, where such placements (Stone, 1962) pertain both to extension (i.e., how much space does the entity take up?) and location (where is it relative to other entities?), and where such consistency pertains both to its stability over time and agreement among observers (including but not limited to the subject of that identity). HF84 suggest two sets of observers: internal members (e.g., employees) and external stakeholders (e.g., customers, investors). That is, it is useful to distinguish between an organization's internal identity and its external identity (e.g., Bouchikhi & Kimberly, 2003; Tripsas, 2009; cf., Dutton, Dukerich, & Harquail, 1994), which may be sharply decoupled from one another (Meyer & Rowan, 1977). Of course, it is possible for either insiders or outsiders to be utterly confused (individually and/or collectively) as to how to place the organization relative to others (e.g., Gioia & Thomas, 1996; Tripsas, 2009). And clearly, such confusion is highly problematic.

Indeed, if observers disagree as to the boundaries of an organization and how it should be placed relative to others (Is it a church, a synagogue, or a mosque? Does it sell high-end or low-end products?), they will not be able to decide which actions to attribute to the organization and how to judge whether such actions are appropriate. In this basic sense then, a clear identity is a precondition for external commitment. And both the strength of such commitment and the clarity of the organization's identity are increasing in the extent to which the actor has sunk investments in that identity – for example, in a distinctive logo and marketing materials; in equipment that can be used to produce one product but not others. As Selznick (1957, p. 40) writes concerning the foundations of organizational "character" (which he characterizes as involving "a distinct identity" and is the basis for its "distinctive competence"):

A great deal of management practice, as in the hiring of personnel, may be viewed as an effort to hold down the number of irreversible decisions that must be made. On the other hand, a wise management will readily limit its own freedom, accepting irreversible commitments, when the basic values of the organization and its direction are at stake. The acceptance of irreversible commitments is the process by which the character of the organization is set.[3]

A clear identity in the eyes of external observers, which is constructed via such irreversible commitments, is thus the basis for external accountability.

But if a clear identity seems necessary for achieving external accountability, its importance for achieving reliability is less obvious. It is instructive in this regard to note what HF84 *do not say* when discussing how organizations are able to (coordinate internally and thus) achieve reliability: they do not reference the most obvious instrument for such coordination: fiat. Rather, they draw on the lessons of the Carnegie School (March & Simon, 1958; Cyert & March, 1963; Nelson & Winter, 1982) to suggest that internal coordination is achieved via convergence on a set of *roles* that organization members occupy and a set of *routines* for managing communication and exchanges among roles. HF84's lack of emphasis on fiat reflects a broad theme in organizational sociology, which has long noticed the absence of direct control in organizations (Child, 1972) and expressed skepticism regarding its effectiveness (on the latter, see especially Freeland, 1996, 2001). As Perrow (1986, p. 128) stresses (in his review of the work of March and Simon), "the vast proportion of the activity in organizations goes on without personal directives and supervision – and even without written rules – and sometimes in permitted violation of the rules." Moreover, he argues that "unobtrusive controls," which are rooted in a shared "premises" or a common "definition of the situation" (March & Simon, 1958; cf., Thomas & Thomas, 1928; Merton, 1995), can be highly effective in coordinating action and are superior to "direct controls" in that the latter are more "expensive and reactive." Selznick (1957) echoes these observations. He agrees with Kaufman that internal coordination ("unity" or "conformity of action") can be achieved in one of two ways: (a) by requiring that "the members… take all matters to a central point for a decision" or (b) by "carefully instill(ing) in the minds of its members an *identity of outlook*, a sameness of objectives, a sense of mutual obligation and of common identification and common values" (Kaufman, 1950, p. 226, quoted in Selznick, 1957, p. 114; italics added). However, he stresses that the former, fiat-based approach, "may well yield (less) flexible and efficient types of decision-making" with a lower capacity for "discretion in the application of policies to special circumstances" (Selznick, 1957, p. 114). In sum, while formal organizations *can* achieve coordination via fiat, most coordination is achieved without the use of direct controls, and this is as it should be since direct controls are blunt instruments.

Moreover, Kaufman's notion of an "identity of outlook" suggests how a clear internal identity facilitates coordination even in the absence of direct controls. Insofar as all members have the same view of the boundaries of the organization and how it is (or should eventually be) placed relative to other organizations, much coordination can be achieved without need for fiat or even explicit discussion of the organization's purpose. Note finally that the achievement of such an identity of outlook is considerably easier than is suggested by received organization theory. The emphasis in such theory has largely been on recruitment and socialization processes, which are designed to develop a cadre of personnel that have similar views of the world (e.g., March, 1991; Harrison & Carroll, 2006; Perrow, 1986, pp. 127–128). But there are obvious limits to such processes (e.g., Wrong, 1961) and clear downsides to having all organization members believe the same things (such conformity would limit the variation that facilitates innovation).

The good news then is that everyone need not actually have the same outlook in order for them to act as if they do. Coordination does not occur on the basis of private (or "first order"; Ridgeway & Cornell, 2006) beliefs – after all, how can we ever know what others really believe? Rather, the foundation of coordination is *common knowledge* ("third-order beliefs") – that is, what "everyone" knows about what "everyone knows" (see especially Chwe, 2001). For example, while faculty members may vary considerably in how they think about the university (e.g., Do we really need this or that department?), they will suppress such beliefs (and thereby convey the false impression they endorse common knowledge) as long as they believe that they are in the minority and they depend on the majority for resources. This last stipulation, that organization members will deviate from common knowledge if they feel sufficiently independent, suggests why we do see gadflies among the tenured faculty of universities. But it also suggests why university faculty, and employees of organizations, generally, often *act as if* they share the same views even when they do not. In particular, the heart of "unobtrusive control" (Perrow, 1986) is *internal* accountability – the expectation by organizational members that their actions will be reviewed according to their appropriateness. As with external accountability, the reason appropriateness matters is because performance is highly ambiguous and difficult to anticipate ex ante. And so, organizational members "take cover" by following convention. We keep department x because everyone knows that we are a university of type X and all such universities have such a department – even when many, if not most, faculty privately believe that the department could be removed with little loss.[4]

WHY A VOICE HIERARCHY?

To this point, we have developed HF84 to suggest how a clear identity is the basis for the formal organization's achievement of reliability and accountability, and how these may be achieved without resort to direct controls. But how do insiders or outsiders ever come to any level of agreement as to what any organization "is"? Indeed, given the fact that a large organization encompasses many human beings, with heterogeneous appearance, skills, personalities, etc., and perhaps especially given the fact that outside observers are free to place an organization in any way they like, it is astounding that any organization can attain a relatively clear identity. Perhaps even more remarkable, it seems that the most consistent identities are those attributed to formal organizations rather than individuals.[5] For example, while it is often unclear whether an individual who stands accused of a war crime is the "same person" as the individual who perpetrated the crimes (e.g., was Ivan Demjanjuk "Ivan the Terrible" of Treblinka, another "terrible Ivan" who committed atrocities at Sobibor, or just John Demjanjuk, a mild-mannered retired auto worker from Cleveland?; see Kulish, 2009), there are fewer such doubts when it comes to organizations (e.g., I.G. Farben; Volkswagen; the German government), who can sometimes be induced into accepting blame for past sins even when there has been complete turnover in the biological persons who comprise them.

What is responsible then for the relative consensus that typically pertains to the identity of formal organizations? As depicted in Fig. 3, I suggest that the key ingredient is that while formal organizations may have many members and many stakeholders, the *right to speak on behalf of the*

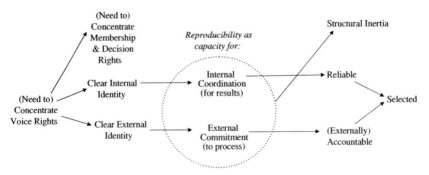

Fig. 3. Why Hierarchy?

organization is always strictly controlled. This follows from the foregoing discussion regarding the importance of common knowledge for coordination. To repeat, coordination can occur despite wide variation in private beliefs. What matters is what is expressed publicly (see Adut, 2005). Accordingly, two related "voice-rights" are crucial: the right to speak on behalf of the organization and the right to speak *publicly* within the organization. Consider in any organization who is allowed to send emails to all other members and who can claim that they are speaking on the organization's behalf in such communications. Observe further how the right to speak to outsiders (e.g., the press, Wall Street analysts) in an official capacity is strictly controlled. And consider what would occur were these rights to be broadly shared. Suddenly, the organization reverts to being a collection of individuals rather than a coherent "actor." Since anyone can speak, and can say that they represent the organization, it becomes highly unlikely that there will be a consistent message about the organization's identity. As a result, the common knowledge that is the basis for coordination (in the absence of fiat) internally, and external commitment, evaporates.

Note further that insofar as organizations engage in decoupling in order to deal with external demands without having to change their procedures (Meyer & Rowan, 1977), the concentration of voice-rights plays a key role in making this possible. Such decoupling would be threatened if internal actions and conversations were freely broadcast to the outside and/or if representations to the outside had equal weight regardless of which organization member makes them. That is, not only does the consistency of internal identity (upon which internal coordination is predicated) and the consistency of external identity (upon which external commitments are predicated) depend on a voice hierarchy, but so too does the capacity for maintaining a public face that differs from one's private face.

FIAT AS BYPRODUCT

We can now return to the question of why organizations are hierarchical. Building on HF84, I have argued that the key rights that must be concentrated in order for formal organizations to achieve the reliability and accountability that gives them their selective advantage are voice-rights. And once we recognize that voice-rights must be concentrated in order for organizations to achieve a clear (internal or external) identity, it follows why membership- and decision-rights ("fiat") must be concentrated as well, even if they are often "loaned" out (Baker, Gibbons, & Murphy, 1999). As discussed above, it is problematic to view fiat as the basis for effective internal coordination. And it does nothing (directly) to shape outsiders' orientation to the organization since such outsiders are outside the purview of such fiat. But as depicted in Fig. 3, the concentration of such rights is a *byproduct* of the need to concentrate voice-rights. That is, just as HF84 asserted that structural inertia confers no particular advantage on organizations, it seems reasonable to conjecture that fiat confers no *general* advantage on organizations. However, the right to direct employee behavior, and perhaps the ultimate right of firing noncompliant employees, must be concentrated if voice-rights are to be concentrated.[6] What ultimately prevents an employee from speaking to the media, or broadcasting her/his views on the organization on a company-wide email if not that she/he can be fired for speaking out of turn?

The logic of this argument can also be developed from an external perspective. Ultimately, the manager's right to fire employees is backed by the (monopoly over force enjoyed by) the state. If the manager fires an employee and the (now former) employee does not leave the premises, the police may be enlisted to remove her/him. To be sure, the state will enforce this right only if the employer abides by its rules for employer conduct. But every employer enjoys a certain latitude or "sovereignty" (Coleman, 1982; see also King et al., 2010) whereby it is recognized that employees are expected to obey orders (see Masten, 1988; Freeland, 2009). But why does the state give such autonomy to organizations? Consider the counterfactual. If employees were free to act as they saw fit – and to claim that such actions represent the organization – then the organization could no longer be held *accountable* for its actions. And it may be said that the ultimate reason why accountability confers selective advantage upon formal organizations is that the state is thereby willing to treat them as fictive persons (Coleman, 1982; see also King et al., 2010). But this fiction would not hold if the persons involved were a hydra-headed organism, with each mouth telling a different story about its past or future actions. Thus insofar as the state wishes to imbue organizations with accountability, the very charter of the organization must spell out who controls the right to act on behalf of the organization, and it must correspondingly be willing to enforce such rights. Finally, insofar as actions can be understood as being undertaken on behalf of an organization only when they are *announced* as such, the ultimate right (which must be strictly controlled) is that of voice.

EXCEPTIONS?

The foregoing discussion is obviously too brief a treatment to do full justice to the question of why formal organizations tend to be hierarchical. At the very least, a full treatment must deal with variation in the degree of such hierarchy. Some aspect of this variation is captured in this observation by yet another famous resident of The Farm:

> Stanford students often asked me about the differences between managing in business, in government, and in the university. I had a somewhat flip answer. "In business," I said, "you have to be very careful when you tell someone working for you to do something, because chances are high that he or she will actually do it. In government, you don't have to worry about that. And in the university, you aren't supposed to tell anyone to do anything in the first place. (Shultz, 1993, p. 34 quoted in Galaskiewicz, 2008)

Clearly, the difference in the low level of compliance in government and universities (at least by tenured faculty) is driven by the employees' perception that managers cannot penalize them for disobedience. But then does the weakness of hierarchy in these cases imply that they are not formal organizations? Clearly not. How then do we reconcile such weakness with the current framework?

Two final points may be made in response to this question. First, while fiat may be weak in such organizations, control of voice-rights is just as concentrated as in any organization. Government bureaucrats face sharp restrictions on their ability to speak to the press on behalf of the government. Moreover, even tenured faculty cannot (credibly) speak on behalf of a university; they speak for themselves. Second, such weakness in control reflects the penetration of alternative bases for external accountability and internal coordination (cf., Galaskiewicz, 2008). In the case of government bureaucrats, civil service rules and regulations govern conduct. In the case of university faculty, conduct is governed by professional norms. Were these alternative sources of coordination and accountability not to govern, the weakness of fiat would indeed undermine the reliability and accountability of these formal organizations. And since they do govern, they simultaneously undermine the organizational hierarchy and make it relatively unimportant for achieving the reliability and accountability needed for the organization to survive.

Thus we ultimately return to the lynchpin of HF84's analysis, with its accompanying echoes of Meyer and Rowan (1977) – that is, the selective advantage conveyed by reliability and accountability. Insofar as reliability and accountability can be attained without a formal organization, it should be relatively unimportant to take on the guise of a formal organization. And this in turn should weaken the hierarchical features that make the formal organization possible – in particular, the concentration of voice-rights. In this sense then, the Stanford School of Organizations teaches us, if implicitly, that *who says organization says one voice* (cf., Michels, 1962).

In reaching this conclusion, I hope I have not done an injustice to Hannan and Freeman's theory and have made at least a token gesture of repayment for all that I learned during my time on The Farm.

NOTES

1. For examples, see Baron, Hannan, and Burton (1999) on "community," "engineering," and "star" models of employment; Foss (2003) and Zenger (2002) on "intenal hybrids"; Nickerson and Zenger (2004) on "consensus-based hierarchy"; Ouchi (1980) on "clan" organizations; and Williamson (1996) on "relational team" organization. And see Freeland (1996, 2001) on how the use of fiat undermines organizational effectiveness.

2. It seems an important task, though outside the scope of this essay, to compare the empirical implications of this theory with existing theories of the "firm" (i.e., market-oriented organization). One possible implication (based on the modified version of the theory, presented in the next section) is that insofar as firms are more likely to incorporate transactions when they involve specific investments or assets (cf., Williamson, 1996; Hart, 1995), the reason is due less to how it changes bargaining between the parties than outsourcing such assets makes it less clear, both to insiders and outsiders, who is responsible for what. And this in turn hinders the capacity to project accountability to external audiences. More generally, this perspective shifts our attention away from the parties to a transaction and directs it to the third-parties (other organizational members; outside stakeholders such as customers and investors) who seek to interpret the transaction in order to decide how they will interact with those parties. See Freeland (2009) for a line of argument consistent with this implication.

3. It is noteworthy that while Selznick's concept of distinctive competence had much influence on the resource-based view (RBV) of the firm that emerged in the mid-1980s (see, e.g., Snow & Hrebiniak, 1980; Henderson & Cockburn, 1994), HF84 use this term in a different way than did Selznick – that is, as the *distinctive level of reliability that formal organizations as a class are able achieve* rather than a set of *distinctive set of actions that a particular organization is able to achieve*. It is also worth noting that while Hannan and Freeman's argument that organizations are structurally inert was highly controversial at the time, it is now basic to the RBV that any organizational competence/capability implies a corresponding inability to (change so as to) succeed at other tasks (e.g., Leonard-Barton, 1992). This too hearkens back to Selznick, who wrote that "Perhaps the most obvious indicator of organizational character as a palpable reality is the abandonment of old organizations and the creation of new ones when changes in general orientation are required"

(1957, p. 41). Note finally that this implies that one does not need HF84 to explain why organizations are structurally inert. Yet, it is still an insightful framework for explaining the selective advantage of formal organizations and it can therefore be used for the current investigation of why formal organizations are hierarchical.

4. Bob Freeland points out (private communication) that such dissembling may support a minimal level of effort at coordination ("perfunctory performance"), but that high levels of effort ("consummate performance") require that members internalize organizational myths and strongly identify with them.

5. Organizations are also the bases for the least *consistent* identities (e.g., the American Can Corporation "became" Citigroup through a series of mergers).

6. One could reasonably argue that decision-rights are thus relatively unimportant, with fiat essentially consisting of membership-rights only. This may be true to a certain extent, but the control of both membership-rights and decision-rights ultimately flow from the same legal foundation (and are therefore difficult to separate), which is the master–servant relationship (see Masten, 1988; Freeland, 2009).

ACKNOWLEDGMENTS

Thanks to Frank Dobbin, Brayden King, and Jesper Sorensen, and participants in the MIT Organization Economics Lunch for their feedback. Special thanks are owed to Bob Freeland, who provided incisive feedback and who began teaching me about the nature of organizations during our time together on The Farm. The usual disclaimer applies.

REFERENCES

Adut, A. (2005). A theory of scandal: Victorians, homosexuality, and the fall of Oscar wilde. *American Journal of Sociology, 111*(1), 213–248.

Baker, G., Gibbons, R., & Murphy, K. (1999). Informal authority in organizations. *Journal of Law, Economics and Organization, 15*(1), 56–73.

Baron, J. N., Hannan, M. T., & Burton, M. D. (1999). Building the iron cage: Determinants of managerial intensity in the early years of organizations. *American Sociological Review, 64*(4), 527–547.

Becker, H. S. (1960). Notes on the concept of commitment. *American Journal of Sociology, 66*(1), 32.

Bouchikhi, H., & Kimberly, J. R. (2003). Escaping the identity trap. *MIT Sloan Management Review, 44*(3), 20–26.

Child, J. (1972). Organization structure and strategies of control: A replication of the Aston study. *Administrative Science Quarterly, 17*, 163–177.

Chwe, M. S. (2001). *Rational ritual: Culture, coordination, and common knowledge.* Princeton, NJ: Princeton University Press.

Coleman, J. S. (1982). *The asymmetric society* (1st ed.). Syracuse, NY: Syracuse University Press.

Cyert, R., & March, J. (1963). *Behavioral theory of the firm* (1st ed.). Englewood Cliffs, NJ: Prentice Hall.

DiMaggio, P. J., & Powell, W. W. (1983). The iron cage revisited: Institutional isomorphism and collective rationality in organizational fields. *American Sociological Review, 48*(2), 147–160.

Dutton, J. E., Dukerich, J. M., & Harquail, C. V. (1994). Organizational images and member identification. *Administrative Science Quarterly, 39*(2), 239–263.

Foss, N. J. (2003). Selective intervention and internal hybrids: Interpreting and learning from the rise and decline of the oticon spaghetti organization. *Organization Science, 14*(3), 331–349.

Freeland, R. F. (1996). The myth of the M-form? Governance, consent, and organizational change. *The American Journal of Sociology, 102*(2), 483–526.

Freeland, R. F. (2001). *The struggle for control of the modern corporation: Organizational change at general motors, 1924–1970.* New York: Cambridge University Press.

Freeland, R. F. (2009). The social and legal bases of managerial authority. *Entreprises et Histoire, 57.*

Galaskiewicz, J. (2008). Is leadership ever not important? Yes, but unfortunately not often. *Presentation at the Wharton Conference on Governance, Leadership, and Networks.* September 19. Philadelphia, PA.

Gioia, D. A., & Thomas, J. B. (1996). Identity, image, and issue interpretation: Sensemaking during strategic change in academia. *Administrative Science Quarterly, 41*(3), 370–403.

Granovetter, M. (1985). Economic action and social structure: The problem of embeddedness. *The American Journal of Sociology, 91*(3), 481–510.

Hannan, M. T., & Freeman, J. (1977). The population ecology of organizations. *The American Journal of Sociology, 82*(5), 929–964.

Hannan, M. T., & Freeman, J. (1984). Structural inertia and organizational change. *American Sociological Review, 49*(2), 149–164.

Harrison, J. R., & Carroll, G. R. (2006). *Culture and demography in organizations.* Princeton, NJ: Princeton University, Press.

Hart, O. D. (1995). *Firms, contracts, and financial structure.* New York: Oxford University Press.

Henderson, R., & Cockburn, I. (1994). Measuring competence? Exploring firm effects in pharmaceutical research. *Strategic Management Journal, 15,* 63–84.

Kaufman, H. (1950). *Field man in administration.* Unpublished doctoral dissertation, Columbia University.

King, B. G., Felin, T., & Whetten, D. A. (2010). Finding the organization in organizational theory: A meta-theory of the organization as a social actor. *Organization Science, 21,* 290–305.

Kulish, N. (2009). Accused Nazi arrives in Munich. *New York Times,* May 13, 2009.

Leonard-Barton, D. (1992). Core capabilities and core rigidities: A paradox in managing new product development. *Strategic Management Journal, 13,* 111–125.

March, J. G. (1981). Footnotes to organizational change. *Administrative Science Quarterly, 26*(4), 563–577.

March, J. G. (1991). Exploration and exploitation in organizational learning. *Organization Science, 2*(1), 71–87.

March, J. G. (1994). *A primer on decision making: How decisions happen.* New York: Free Press.

March, J. G., & Simon, H. (1958). *Organizations.* New York: John Wiley & Sons, Inc.

Masten, S. E. (1988). A legal basis for the firm. *Journal of Law, Economics, and Organization,* 4(1), 181–198.

Merton, R. K. (1995). The Thomas theorem and the Matthew effect. *Social Forces,* 74(2), 379–422.

Meyer, J. W., & Rowan, B. (1977). Institutionalized organizations: Formal structure as myth and ceremony. *The American Journal of Sociology,* 83(2), 340–363.

Michels, R. ([1911]1962). In: E. Paul & C. Paul (Trans.), Zur Soziologie des Parteiwesens in der modernen Demokratie. Untersuchungen über die oligarchischen Tendenzen des Gruppenlebens. [*Political parties: A sociological study of the oligarchical tendencies of modern democracy.*] New York: Free Press.

Nelson, R. R., & Winter, S. G. (1982). *An evolutionary theory of economic change.* Cambridge, MA: Belknap Press of Harvard University Press.

Nickerson, J. A., & Zenger, T. R. (2004). A knowledge-based theory of the firm: The problem-solving perspective. *Organization Science,* 15(6), 617–632.

Ouchi, W. G. (1980). Markets, bureaucracies, and clans. *Administrative Science Quarterly,* 25(1), 129–141.

Perrow, C. (1986). *Complex organizations: A critical essay* (3rd ed.). New York: Random House.

Pfeffer, J., & Salancik, G. R. (1978). *The external control of organizations: A resource dependence perspective.* New York: Harper & Row.

Ridgeway, C. L., & Cornell, S. J. (2006). Consensus and the creation of status beliefs. *Social Forces,* 85(1), 431–453.

Schelling, T. C. (1956). An essay on bargaining. *The American Economic Review,* 46(3), 281–306.

Scott, R. W. (1981). *Organizations rational, natural, and open systems* (2nd ed.). Englewood Cliffs, NJ: Prentice Hall.

Scott, R. W. (2002). *Organizations: Rational, natural, and open systems* (5th ed.). Upper Saddle River, NJ: Prentice Hall.

Selznick, P. (1957). *Leadership in administration: A sociological interpretation.* New York: Harper & Row.

Shultz, G. P. (1993). *Turmoil and triumph: My years as secretary of state.* New York: Charles Scribner's Sons.

Snow, C. C., & Hrebiniak, L. G. (1980). Strategy, distinctive competence, and organizational performance. *Administrative Science Quarterly,* 25(2), 317–336.

Stone, G. P. (1962). Appearance and the self: A slightly revised version. In: A. Rose (Ed.), *Human nature and social process* (pp. 86–118). Boston: Houghton Mifflin Company.

Thomas, W. I., & Thomas, D. S. (1928). *The child in America: Behavior problems and programs.* New York: Alfred A. Knopf.

Tripsas, M. (2009). Technology, identity, and inertia through the lens of 'The Digital Photography Company'. *Organization Science,* 20, 441–460.

Williamson, O. E. (1975). *Markets and hierarchies, analysis and antitrust implications: A study in the economics of internal organization.* New York: Free Press.

Williamson, O. E. (1996). *The mechanisms of governance.* New York: Oxford University Press.

Wrong, D. H. (1961). The oversocialized conception of man in modern sociology. *American Sociological Review, 26*(2), 183–193.

Zenger, T. R. (2002). Crafting internal hybrids: Complementarities, common change initiatives, and the team-based organization. *International Journal of the Economics of Business, 9*(1), 79–95.

Zuckerman, E. A. (2010). *Why identity? A prolegomenon to any account of social organization or human action.* Unpublished manuscript, MIT Sloan School of Management.

PART III
FORMER DOCTORAL STUDENTS, POST-DOCS, AND A VISITOR

CHAPTER 17

HOW I SPENT THE SUMMER OF 1973: IT WAS NOT A VACATION

Howard E. Aldrich

A summer spent at Stanford University in 1973 contributed significantly to my emerging perspective on organizations and generated the spark I needed to begin working on what became *Organizations and Environments* (Aldrich, 1979). Dick Scott invited me to be the second visiting scholar to participate in the Research Training Program on Organizations and Mental Health, following my Cornell colleague, Karl Weick, who had done it the year before. Curiously enough, Paul Hirsch, a former colleague of mine in graduate school, was the third visiting scholar in the program. I taught an organizational theory course to a class that included Chuck Snow, Kaye Schoonhoven, and a number of Mike Hannan and John Meyers' students. I suspect that I learned as much over those three months as did the students in my course.

For my contribution to the program, I rather foolishly designed an organization theory course that compressed a semester's worth of material into less than a dozen class meetings. On top of that, I asked the students to conduct an empirical analysis of a huge data set I brought with me from Cornell. The data were from a multi-city study that focused on inter-organizational relations in the manpower training field in New York State, featuring surveys, information on resource flows between commercial organizations and public agencies, and network relations data between all the organizations within about 10 cities. We did not get the data in shape to run on the Stanford computing system until the term was half over!

Stanford's Organization Theory Renaissance, 1970–2000
Research in the Sociology of Organizations, Volume 28, 311–317
Copyright © 2010 by Emerald Group Publishing Limited
All rights of reproduction in any form reserved
ISSN: 0733-558X/doi:10.1108/S0733-558X(2010)0000028021

Nonetheless, the students persevered and finished their papers on time. As I recall, Kaye Schoonhoven was a particularly diligent student and kept after me to produce a clean data set. Surprisingly, none of those papers turned into co-authored papers with me, which I take as a sign that the problems motivating my inter-organizational relations project were far removed from the health-care system problems most of the students found interesting.

Despite the mismatch between my empirical interests and those of Dick Scott's students, the Stanford experience rekindled my interest in a more comparative and political view of organizations, an interest that had lain dormant since I had left the University of Michigan after earning my PhD in sociology in 1969. I had entered Michigan in 1965 intending to study social psychology, but after beginning an apprenticeship with Albert J. Reiss, my interest gravitated to organizational studies. He had put me to work coding tape recordings of calls from citizens of the Chicago Police Department, matching up those calls to other recordings of what the police dispatchers did in response to the calls. I was intrigued by the harsh reality of the administrative rules and regulations that intervened between citizens' appeals for help and the provision of justice. Another project that I worked on involved interviews of small business owners in the high crime rate areas of three American cities, and through coding the owner's responses I began to learn about organizational survival in hostile environments. My first formal course in organizational sociology was a seminar taught by Edward Laumann, who had arrived at Michigan as an assistant professor the year before I enrolled. I had some familiarity with the subject because I had been a teaching assistant for Laumann's undergraduate organizational sociology class.

Laumann gave us free reign to explore the classics in organizational studies, and beyond providing us with three- or four-page single-spaced list of suggested readings, he provided minimal direction. When I told one of my friends about my growing interest in organizational analysis, he suggested we enroll together in a new course being taught by Dan Katz. As luck would have it, Katz was just finishing up his book with Robert Kahn on *The Social Psychology of Organizations*, and we read it in manuscript form. Katz introduced me to the work of Karl Weick and I began to see the potential of a multilevel approach to studying organizations. Through Katz, I met Stan Seashore and eventually convinced him to be on my dissertation committee. At the same time I was finishing up the requirements of my minor in social psychology, I was also being taught to think "big thoughts" in courses, on comparative economic development, cross-cultural analysis of societies, and political sociology. Bill Gamson's course was particularly instructive in that regard, as the five two-page papers he required forced me to find ways to frame big ideas in quickly comprehensible packages. Those were heady days to be at the University of Michigan, and I also took courses in economic behavior with George Katona, political behavior with Philip Converse and Donald Stokes, and college-level math for social science with Jack Goldberg.

I hoped to find something similar when I took a job at the School of Industrial Labor Relations at Cornell in 1969, and was pleasantly surprised by the supportive colleagues I found. William Foote Whyte was chair of the Organizational Behavior Department and was very encouraging of my interests in ethnographic research, although after publishing several papers from my fieldwork-based M.A. paper at Michigan, I drifted away from that research method. Bill Starbuck only remained at Cornell for two more years after I arrived, but reviewing manuscripts for the *Administrative Science Quarterly* (ASQ) (which Bill edited) and having my own papers rejected were bracing lessons for a junior scholar! Karl Weick arrived in 1972 and immediately made a huge difference in the organization studies community on campus. Although I had minored in psychology as an undergraduate and in social psychology as a graduate student, I made little use of it in my work. Nonetheless, Karl and I enjoyed a very productive exchange via sitting on joint graduate student committees. Marshall Meyer, a student of Peter Blau, was the other assistant professor in my cohort and very much into what we would call today a "structural approach" to sociological analysis. Until he left in 1973, he was a forceful presence at our after-lunch coffee sessions in the Statler Inn, insisting that we needed to publish papers in "A-level" journals every year!

In the summer of 1973, Dick Scott was away in Europe, I believe, and so I spent a lot of time with his students, as well as those of Mike Hannan and John Freeman. In addition to studying the health care system, their students were working on a variety of "world systems" topics and I found their projects fascinating. Through these students, I met Jane Weiss and we began a collaboration that was cut short by her premature death in 1981. Jane challenged me to rise above the fairly empirical approach I was schooled in at Michigan and broadened my horizons, as reflected in the papers we published on class analysis (Aldrich & Weiss, 1981) and world systems theory (Weiss & Aldrich, 1977).

My lunchtime companion during much of the summer of 1973 was Nancy Tuma, whom I had met back in the 1960s when I was studying at Michigan and she was still a graduate student at Michigan State. As I recall, she was teaching part-time in the Sociology Department and was not yet on a tenure-track line, which seems incredible today, given all that she subsequently accomplished. Through Nancy I learned some of the inside stories about the department and also got to meet Francesca Cancian, Murray Webster (who I think was a visitor in the department), and a few other faculty. Some of the graduate students, including Chris Chase-Dunn and Richard Rubinson, were working on their dissertations and I had occasional opportunities to chat with them in their offices.

To put my Stanford experience into the context of the early 1970s, I would say that the type of organization theory popular in the 1960s emphasized structure at the expense of genesis and process. The paradigm shift of the 1970s challenged these earlier approaches, as theorists on both coasts developed distinctive ideas about organizational analysis. At Stanford and UC-Berkeley, three new views of organizational analysis emerged: resource dependence, population ecology, and "new" institutional theory. Pfeffer had begun working on resource dependence ideas when he was at the University of Illinois with Salancik, and he brought those ideas to Berkeley and then Stanford. Hannan and Freeman knew each other from their days at the University of North Carolina, and when Freeman moved from Riverside to Berkeley, they were just down the road from each other. More opportunities to debate resource dependence issues came my way when Salancik became a second associate editor at ASQ and made occasional visits to Ithaca.

I had hoped to spend time with Pfeffer that summer, as he had just moved to UC-Berkeley, but I think the only contact we had was over the phone a few times. Those discussions helped me think about how my views of organization theory differed from his and led to our collaboration, a few years later, on a paper in the *Annual Review of Sociology* (Aldrich & Pfeffer, 1976). That paper, in turn, fostered ideas that appeared in his book with Salancik, *The External Control of Organizations* (Pfeffer & Salancik, 1978), and in my book, *Organizations and Environments* (Aldrich, 1979). Indeed, my papers in the early 1970s drew heavily upon the concept of resource dependence. For example, in our 1975 paper in *ASQ*, Sergio Mindlin and I wrote that "the major axiom of the resource dependence perspective on the study of organizational behavior is that organizations must be studied in the context of the population of organizations with which they are competing and sharing resources" (Mindlin & Aldrich, 1975, p. 382). Following up my earlier papers, we laid out the premises of a resource dependence model, building on Stanford graduate Karen Cook's (Cook, 1977) work and on work by Dick Scott's mentor, Peter Blau (1964). (Karen Cook was an assistant professor at the University of Washington in Seattle in 1973 and graciously loaned us the use of her house for a family summer holiday.) Note that Mindlin and I combined the ideas of "populations" and "resource dependence" and thus our model was unlike that subsequently proposed by Pfeffer and Salancik.

During the mid-1970s, additional approaches to organizational analysis were flowering in other parts of the world. Curiously enough, I found that my Stanford experience was better preparation for understanding these new approaches than what I was exposed to on the East Coast, in Ivy League sociology. As I discovered during stints at various European universities, Marxist scholars of organizational change saw organizations as a critical battleground between capital and labor. Scholars analyzed organizational structures in terms of struggle, conflict and domination, and exploitation, rather than in the neutral terms found in American organizational texts. Scandinavian approaches to organizational analysis were much more problem-focused and pragmatic, and scholars were willing to use whatever conceptual principles they could to shed light on specific issues. Differences in methodological presuppositions generated a great deal of tension between the United States and European scholars, and I often found myself defending one group to the other, leaving me uncertain of where I stood myself. I remember a UK scholar telling me during a Paris conference in 1975 that, as associate editor of ASQ, "You have a lot to answer for!"

Less than a year after returning to Cornell from Stanford, I wrote the prospectus for *Organizations and Environments*. Before my Stanford experience, I had proposed to call the book *The Organization and Its Environment*, but I realized that using the definite article (the) implied a homogeneity and singularity in which I no longer believed. Instead, I turned to plural words – "organizations" and "environments" – as a way of expressly recognizing heterogeneity and diversity. Perhaps subtly influenced by the Stanford group's terminology, I rather carelessly used the label "population ecology" interchangeably with "natural selection" throughout my 1979 book, but my views would have been better described as a sociological approach, strongly informed by evolutionary principles.

The extent to which what I was doing differed from the perspective on organizations being developed at Stanford is apparent in the preface I wrote to *Organizations and Environments*. I said:

> In trying to write a book on organizational sociology for both students and colleagues, I decided there was no point in either reviewing all of the 'perspectives' advanced by theorists in the past two decades, or in re-creating the seemingly endless debates over measurement and method that have plagued the field. Rather, I have attempted to present a perspective that integrates concepts and research findings from all social

science disciplines studying organizations, while retaining the gains made by historically
and politically sensitive investigators in the United States and abroad. With a slight shift
of emphasis from an original investigator's intentions, I found that a great deal of the
literature in economic history, industrial economics, the social psychology of
organizations, organizational sociology, and political sociology could be integrated
into an encompassing framework.

The fundamental axiom of the approach in my 1979 book was that
explanations for organizational change must explicitly incorporate organizational properties and environmental characteristics. I argued that neither
organizational nor environmental attributes, by themselves, were sufficient
grounds for building explanations. In this respect, my argument differed
significantly from that of organizational ecologists, whose early statements
heavily emphasized the role of external constraint over organizational
variation and strategy. Although Hannan and Freeman (1977) cited my
papers with Pfeffer and Reiss in their iconic *American Journal of Sociology*
presentation of population ecology, their examples were nearly all from the
United States and they focused mainly on explaining the uses of selection
logic in formal modeling of organization population growth.

By contrast, many of the explanations in my book were historical and
comparative and explicitly invoked resource dependence principles, beginning with my proposal that environments could be defined as resource
controllers. I made the point that "selection" is not just the working out
of an impersonal invisible hand, but rather that power and domination
were the keys to understanding organizational change. I wrote that we
needed to understand the distribution of resources in environments and the
terms on which they were available to organizations. I drew on Peter Blau's
reworking of Richard Emerson's ideas concerning the association between
dependence, autonomy, and power, and I used resource dependence ideas to
argue that organizations use interorganizational relations to manage their
interdependencies. Thus, the book was thoroughly infused with resource
dependence concepts and principles. However, unlike Pfeffer's work, my
perspective was much more comparative and historical.

Although I knew about Dick Scott's research program and John Meyer's
programs on institutional analysis, their specific projects did not figure
prominently in my preparation for this book. At that time, I saw the
emerging neo-institutional perspective primarily as a vehicle allowing
mainstream sociologists to insinuate fundamental sociological concepts
into the curricula of management departments in business schools. Little did
I know that years later, Dick and I would commiserate over the apparently
unstoppable drain of our best organizational sociologists to business

schools! No matter how many other issues we disagree on, Dick and I have made common cause on this one.

REFERENCES

Aldrich, H. E. (1979). *Organizations and environments.* Englewood Cliffs, NJ: Prentice-Hall.

Aldrich, H. E., & Pfeffer, J. (1976). Environments of organizations. In: A. Inkeles, J. Coleman & N. Smelser (Eds), *Annual review of sociology* (Vol. 2, pp. 79–105). Palo Alto, CA: Annual Reviews.

Aldrich, HE., & Weiss, J. A. (1981). Differentiation within the United States capitalist class: Workforce size and income differences. *American Sociological Review, 46*(3), 279–290.

Blau, P. M. (1964). *Exchange and power in social life.* New York: John Wiley.

Cook, K. S. (1977). Exchange and power in networks of interorganizational relations. *Sociological Quarterly, 18*(1), 62–82.

Hannan, M. T., & Freeman, J. H. (1977). The population ecology of organizations. *American Journal of Sociology, 82*(5), 929–964.

Mindlin, S., & Aldrich, H. E. (1975). Interorganizational dependence: A review of the concept and a re-examination of the findings of the Aston group. *Administrative Science Quarterly, 20*(3), 382–392.

Pfeffer, J., & Salancik, G. (1978). *The external control of organizations.* New York: Harper & Row.

Weiss, J. A., & Aldrich, H. E. (1977). The supranational organization of production. *Current Anthropology, 18*(December), 630–631.

CHAPTER 18

THE CONTRIBUTIONS OF ORGANIZATIONAL THEORY TO HEALTH CARE

Joan R. Bloom

During my tenure at Stanford University, as a graduate student and post-doctoral fellow, I followed the development of at least four of the theoretical formulations that form the core of this volume. It was a very exciting time to be on campus, as we not only had opportunities to read about these theoretical ideas, but also had the opportunity to discuss these theories with faculty, visiting faculty, and students, and for some, the opportunity to contribute to their development. Having a cluster of faculty focused on organizational theory at Stanford meant that others around the country chose to spend time at Stanford University, thereby, enriching the intellectual environment. In addition, having another major research university nearby (University of California, Berkeley) facilitated collaboration in theory development and provided additional stimulation.

For most of us, involvement in the development of one of these theories formed the direction for our academic career and we became an ecologist or an institutionalist. Some became fascinated with a particular area of application such as the educational system or the health care system and predominately used only one theory and/or methodology to study the system of interest; other's argued that a solo focus is limiting and were eclectic and used several theories to conceptualize parts of the system of interest.

Stanford's Organization Theory Renaissance, 1970–2000
Research in the Sociology of Organizations, Volume 28, 319–327
Copyright © 2010 by Emerald Group Publishing Limited
All rights of reproduction in any form reserved
ISSN: 0733-558X/doi:10.1108/S0733-558X(2010)0000028022

I followed the latter path and have studied organizational questions as they apply to health care organizations. While the field of health care organizations initially had weak and indeterminate boundaries, over the years it has become institutionalized and is recognized as a separate field of inquiry. Not only does it have its own section within the Academy of Management, but also has developed a smaller, independent, and loosely affiliated organization known as the Health Organizations Research Association (HORA). Both meet annually; the former focuses on the socialization of advanced doctoral students and new graduates; the latter focuses on the development of researchers following an academic career path in health care organizations and management (there are multiple opportunities to follow a research path).

My journey to the field of studies of health care organizations commenced with Dick Scott receiving funding of the organizations research training program in 1972–1973 by National Institute of Mental Health. The first cohort of pre- and post-doctoral students in the program began in July, 1973. There were three members of the first cohort of post-doctoral scholars; they were Ed Deci, Charles Snow, and myself. As most of my doctoral training had focused on micro-organizational theory I applied for the fellowship to learn about structural approaches to organizational theory applied to hospitals. A major portion of my time during the post-doctoral fellowship was spent working on Dick Scott's Institutional Differences Study (IDS). The year spent as a post-doc at Stanford was pivotal in my career as it led to my current position at the School of Public Health, University of California, Berkeley.

Following are my reflections on teaching organizational theory to the next generation of scholars, the contributions that organizational theory has made to understanding health care organizations, and the contributions of organizational theory to my own research.

ORGANIZATIONAL THEORY APPLIED
TO HEALTH CARE

Two courses that focus on organizational theory are taught for doctoral students and two others are taught for Masters of Public Health students; only the former are relevant. The development and theses of macro-organizational theory are reviewed along with empirical applications to health care organizations like hospitals, nursing homes, and community mental health centers.

The doctoral seminars in the School of Public Health differ from courses taught elsewhere on the Berkeley campus (e.g., the Hass School of Business, Department of Political Science, and Department of Sociology) because the students not only read the seminal contributions of each theory and analyze the theories, but also study the empirical applications to health care. All students in our PhD program in Health Services and Policy Analysis are required to take a minimum of two courses in organizational theory (micro and macro). Additional coursework and demonstrations of competence is required for those whose focus is on the field of health organizations. For the sake of parsimony, I will restrict my reflections on the contributions of three theories, resource dependence, institutional theory, and population ecology, as these were being developed at Stanford during my pre- and post-doc years that form the core of our course.

Resource Dependence Theory

Resource Dependence Theory (RDT) (Pfeffer & Salancik, 1978) is the most easily understood by the students, especially those with a strong economics background. Inevitably, the question arises as to whether RDT is a subset of Transaction Cost Economics (TCE, Williamson, 1981) or vice versa. The answer given to this question is "it depends" – on who is answering the question. Most readers of this volume will concur that TCE is an extension of resource dependence.

The contributions of RDT to health care include: explaining the composition of hospital governing boards (Pfeffer, 1973); the effects of regulation on hospital organizations (Cook, Shortell, Conrad, & Morrisey, 1983); responses of hospitals to resource constraints in the environment resulting in contract management (Alexander & Morrisey, 1989); vertical integration within hospitals (Lerman & Shore, 1998); staffing strategies and hospital efficiency (Bloom, Alexander, & Nuchols, 1997); nursing home participation in Total Quality Management (TQM) (Zinn, Weech, & Brannon, 1998); and explaining referral patterns of clients between organizations (Provan, Sebastian, & Milward, 1996). The application of RDT to health care studies in the past decade have been fewer, perhaps due to Casciaro's and Piskorski's (2005) argument that RDT needs selective theoretical development or because of ongoing changes to the US health care delivery systems. Given the state of the US economy in 2009, the issues of resource constraints and resource dependence are likely to become more important in studying the health sector.

New Institutional Theory

The *New Institutional Theory* asks why are so many organizations so similar and how do organizations relate to their environments (Meyer & Rowan, 1991; DiMaggio & Powell, 1991; Scott, 1995). Students with a sociological background have little difficulty understanding this theory, but those from different backgrounds have more difficulty and eventually embrace it. Once understood, the theory is extended to consider more complex phenomena such as organizational change and diffusion, conflicting institutional environments, the instability of mimetic isomorphism compared to other sources of isomorphism.

One of its major contributions to health care is providing a framework for understanding why organizational innovations are adopted and how the adoption diffuses, a topic of interest to many health researchers (Tolbert & Zucker, 1983). Until Tolbert and Zucker's seminal article, most research on innovation had focused on the characteristics of individuals, especially those who were early adopters of innovations. Adoption by an organization is a far more complex process. It also is often combined by health services researchers with other theories such as Social Networks. Some of the specific studies that use the network framework and develop it still further include the adoption of TQM (Westphal, Gulati, & Shortell, 1997), and HIV prevention efforts by drug abuse treatment units (D'Aunno, Vaughn, & McElroy, 1999).

Another contribution of institutional theory has been in understanding complexity of the environment of some health organizations such as hospitals that exist in both a technical and an institutional environment (Scott & Meyer, 1983; Alexander & Scott, 1984). For example, the paper written with Jeff Alexander and two former graduate students (Bloom, Alexander, Lerman, & Norrish, 1994) provided empirical validation for the argument that hospitals exist in both a technical and an institutional environment which are of equal importance in determining staffing strategies in hospitals. Two other papers explaining the complexities of institutional environments in health organizations are, first, D'Aunno and colleagues' (1991) work which explored how community mental health centers respond to conflicting institutional environments when they provide drug abuse treatment as well as mental health services. The second paper, by Burns and Wholey (1993), studied the effect of mimetic forces on organizations in the form of how fads like matrix management diffused throughout US hospitals (Burns & Wholey, 1993).

Popululation Ecology

Population ecology (Hannan & Freeman, 1977, 1984; Carrol, 1984) has contributed to health care organizational research by providing a way to understand changes in the type of organizations that deliver health care and to understand the conditions under which organizations grow and survive (Alexander, Kaluzny, & Middleton, 1986) and how these might relate to the stability of new forms of health care delivery. Focusing on the health and survival of populations of organizations rather than single ones is a challenge for the students.

In the 1970s, the Health Maintenance Organization (HMO) Act was passed by Congress providing the impetus for the growth of HMOs. Population ecology provided a lens to view the rapid growth of this form of organization and a way to understand which populations of HMOs were likely to survive (Wholey, Christianson, & Sanchez, 1992). The population ecology of state mental hospitals has also been a focus of study (Dowdall, 1996).

Another concern in health services research of consequence to managers is that not all hospitals or health systems are alike. For example, Alexander, Anderson, and Lewis (1985) used cluster analysis to classify hospital systems on multiple dimensions, and they found that simplistic dichotomies of for-profit or not-for-profit are not adequate to understanding the taxonomy of organizational populations in the health sector. They added the dimension of presence of a religious affiliation as well as the type of religious affiliation. They found 15 different organizational forms and three families. Within the 50 Catholic systems, 41 were characterized by the same form. However, populations (clusters) differed organizationally and operationally from other homogeneous populations including system ownership, centralization of governance, hospital-related decision-making, medical staff organization, proportion of contract-managed systems, and the extent of corporate involvement in medical affairs.

In addition to population ecology's focus on mortality of organizational forms, in health care many have been interested in organizational births. Considering organizational births rather than mortality is important as many of the new forms of health organizations have evolved and grown due to legislation (Tucker, Singh, & Meinhard, 1990). For example, legislation in the 1970s enabled the growth of HMO's. Other populations have also been enabled by legislation. For example, the Johnson Administration's Great Society Program in the 1960s created both community health centers and community mental health centers. Legislation also created the rapid growth of federally qualified community health centers from about 500 to 1,200 during the Bush Administration (2001–2009), an organizational population that had been relatively stable since the 1960s. Additionally, how organizations are born can also be learned from health care. Thus, while many of these community mental health centers started de novo as a result of the Great Society program, a large number of what came to be community mental health organizations were already in existence but in a different form. Work in this area is not only a contribution to health organizational research, but also to the field of population ecology. The study of the evolution of organizational populations is likely to have a resurgence given the continued federal interest in the financing and delivery of health during the current era of health care reform.

PERSONNEL REFLECTIONS ON THE USING ORGANIZATION THEORY IN THE STUDY OF HEALTH CARE

Doctoral training with Elizabeth Cohen at Stanford focused on applied research, but a special type of applied research. For her applied research meant the conceptualization of "real world problems" in health care organizations, for example, as instances of one or more organizational theories. As a consequence, designing research projects entails intimate knowledge of a "bag of organizational theories." For example, in studying hospitals and nurse staffing patterns, Scott and Dornbusch's analysis and interpretation of technology as task conceptions seemed to be particularly useful in understanding the unionization of nurses and labor disputes of nurses in hospitals in their efforts to improve staffing ratios and quality of care (Alexander & Bloom, 1987; Bloom, Alexander, & Nuchols, 1992). Conceptualizing hospital staffing in terms of Pfeffer and Salancik's RDT and Williamson's TCE was helpful in explaining the efficiency of using part-time staffing for nurses in hospitals (Bloom et al., 1997). Interestingly, the use of part-time nurses is more efficient than the use of nurses hired from a nursing registry albeit part-time nurses are rarely used by hospitals. Finally, Scott and colleagues' notions of the effects of both technical and institutional environments on organizations such as hospitals was so intriguing that we set out to empirically test this argument and found that hospitals exist in both environments and that each explains approximately half of the variance (Bloom et al., 1994). In studying community mental health centers undergoing change in their reimbursement policy from fee-for service to capitation, a profound organizational as well as economic change, the organization's culture has been as important for this transition for the staff of the organization as well as for the quality of the care provided to the population being served (Morris & Bloom, 2002, 2007).

STANFORD UNIVERSITY DURING AN ERA OF INTENSE CREATIVITY

One of the goals of this volume on Research in the Sociology of Organizations is to better understand why Stanford was such a fertile source of organizational theories. Clearly, Stanford's exant faculty were a very important factor. During my six years at Stanford as both a doctoral student and post-doctoral fellow, opportunities to learn organizational theory were available from courses, lectures, and conversations with Michael Hannan, Dick Scott, Sandy Dornbush, Ann McMahon, Jim March, Buzz Zelditch, and my mentor, the late Elizabeth Cohen. Howard Aldrich spent a summer at Stanford during this period and Jeff Pfeffer was a frequent visitor from Berkeley. This mix of faculty provided an exceptionally rich intellectual environment. There was also an exceptional bright and creative group of doctoral students in Sociology with whom I had the opportunity to interact, and these included Ann Barry Flood, Kaye Schoonhoven, Don Comstock, Ruth Cronkite, Lynn Zucker, Mary Fennell, Jeff Alexander, and Tom Rundall. The development of a network of scholars has also kept this intellectual stimulation alive over time.

In addition, Dick Scott provided the leadership to make the intellectual environment at Stanford grow and develop. I am deeply grateful that he had the foresight to secure funding for pre-doctoral and post-doctoral fellows through the National Institutes of Health (NIH) training grant and he and others on the faculty developed an infrastructure across the campus for increasing the interaction between students and faculty from the Schools of Education, Business, Engineering, the Medical School, and the Department of Sociology.

I left for Berkeley before the annual meetings at Asilomar were instituted and was able to join the group only once. However, these annual meetings were also important as they allowed graduate students as well as former students to continue to collaborate and learn from each other, that is, to keep the excitement of theory development alive.

It is not a surprise to conclude that while having the right people is important, but so is the development of a design and structure of the environment.

REFERENCES

Alexander, J. A., Anderson, J. G., & Lewis, B. (1985). Toward an empirical classification of hospitals in multihospital systems. *Medical Care, 23*(7), 913–932.

Alexander, J. A., & Bloom, J. R. (1987). Collective bargaining in hospitals: An organizational and environmental analysis. *Journal of Health and Social Behavior, 28*(1), 60–73.

Alexander, J. A., Kaluzny, A., & Middleton, S. (1986). Organizational growth, survival and death in the US hospital industry: a population ecology perspective. *Social Science and Medicine, 22,* 303–308.

Alexander, J. A., & Morrisey, J. (1989). A resource dependence model of hospital contract management. *Heath Services Research, 24*(2), 259–284.

Alexander, J. A., & Scott, W. R. (1984). Impact of regulation on the administrative structure of hospitals: Toward an analytic framework. *Hospitals and Health Services Administration, 29,* 72–85.

Bloom, J. R., Alexander, J. A., Lerman, S., & Norrish, B. (1994). *Institutional and environmental influences on staffing strategies.* Dallas, TX: Academy of Management.

Bloom, J. R., Alexander, J. A., & Nuchols, B. A. (1992). The effect of the social organization of work on the voluntary turnover rate of hospital nurses in the United States. *Social Sciences and Medicine, 34*(12), 1413–1424.

Bloom, J. R., Alexander, J. A., & Nuchols, B. A. (1997). Nurse staffing patterns and hospital efficiency in the U.S. *Social Science and Medicine, 44*(2), 147–155.

Burns, L. R., & Wholey, D. R. (1993). Adoption and abandonment of matrix management programs: Effects of organizational characteristics and interorganizational networks. *Academy of Management Journal, 36*(1), 106–138.

Carrol, G. (1984). The specialist strategy. *California Management Review, 26,* 126–137.

Casciaro, T., & Piskorski, M. J. (2005). Power imbalance, mutual dependence, and constraint absorption: A closer look at Resource Dependence Theory. *Administrative Science Quarterly, 50,* 167–199.

Cook, K., Shortell, S. M., Conrad, D., & Morrisey, M. (1983). A theory of organizational response to regulation. *Academy of Management Review, 8*(2), 193–205.

D'Aunno, T., Sutton, R. I., & Price, R. H. (1991). Isomorphism and external support in conflicting institutional environments: A study of drug abuse treatment units. *Academy of Management Journal, 34*(3), 636–661.

D'Aunno, T., Vaughn, T. E., & McElroy, P. (1999). An institutional analysis of HIV prevention efforts by the nation's outpatient drug abuse treatment units. *Journal of Health and Social Behavior, 40*(2), 175–192.

DiMaggio, P. J., & Powell, W. W. (1991). The iron cage revisited: Institutional isomorphism and collective rationality in organizational fields. In: W. W. Powell & P. J. DiMaggio (Eds), *The new institutionalism in organizational analysis* (pp. 61–82). Chicago: The University of Chicago Press.

Dowdall, G. (1996). The natural history of an organizational form: The state mental hospital. *The eclipse of the state mental hospital* (Chapter 2, pp. 226–249). New York:The State University of New York Press.

Hannan, M., & Freeman, J. (1977). The population ecology of organizations. *American Journal of Sociology, 82*(5), 929–964.

Hannan, M., & Freeman, J. (1984). Structural inertia and organizational change. *American Sociological Review, 49,* 149–164.

Lerman, S., & Shore, K. (1998). Hospitals' vertical integration into skilled nursing: A rational approach to controlling transaction costs. *Inquiry, 35,* 303–314.

Meyer, J. W., & Rowan, B. (1991). Institutionalized organizations: Formal structure as myth and ceremony. In: W. W. Powell & P. J. DiMaggio (Eds), *The new institutionalism in organizational analysis.* Chicago: The University of Chicago Press.

Morris, A., & Bloom, J. R. (2002). Contextual factors affecting job satisfaction and organizational commitment in Community Mental Health Centers undergoing system changes in the financing of care. *Mental Health Services Research, 4,* 71–83.

Morris, A., & Bloom, J. R. (2007). Organizational and individual factors affecting consumer outcomes of care in mental health services. *Mental Health Services Research, 34,* 243–253.

Pfeffer, J. (1973). Size, composition and function of hospital boards of directors: A study of organization environment linkage. *Administrative Science Quarterly, 19,* 349–364.

Pfeffer, J., & Salancik, G. (1978). *The external control of organizations.* New York: Harper and Row.

Provan, K. G., Sebastian, J. G., & Milward, H. B. (1996). Cooperation in community mental health: A resource based explanation of referrals and case coordination. *Medical Care Research and Review, 53,* 95–119.

Scott, W. R. (1995). *Institutions and organizations.* Thousand Oaks, CA: Sage Publications.

Scott, W. R., & Meyer, J. W. (1983). The organization of societal sectors: Propositions and early evidence. In: J. W. Meyers & W. R. Scott (Eds), *Organizational environments: Ritual and rationality* (pp. 129–153). Chicago: University of Chicago Press.

Tucker, D. J., Singh, J. V., & Meinhard, A. G. (1990). Organizational form, population dynamics, and institutional change: The founding patterns of voluntary organizations. *Academy of Management Journal, 30,* 151–178.

Tolbert, P. S., & Zucker, L. G. (1983). Institutional sources of change in the formal structure of organizations: the diffusion of civil service reform, 1880–1935. *Administrative Science Quarterly, 30,* 22–39.

Westphal, J. D., Gulati, R., & Shortell, S. M. (1997). Customization or conformity? An institutional and network perspective on the content and consequences of TQM adoption. *Administrative Science Quarterly, 42,* 66–394.

Wholey, D. R., Christianson, J. B., & Sanchez, S. M. (1992). Organization size and failure among health maintenance organizations. *American Sociological Review, 57,* 829–842.

Williamson, O. E. (1981). The economics of organization: The transaction cost approach. *Journal of Sociology, 87,* 548–587.

Zinn, J. S., Weech, R. J., & Brannon, D. (1998). Resource dependence and institutional elements in nursing home TQM adoption. *Health Services Research, 33,* 261–273.

CHAPTER 19

THE DEVIL'S WORKSHOP

Jacques Delacroix

In the late 1960s and early 1970s, the world was bursting at the seams. There were several political struggles going on at the same time, and many more existential ones. I now think it mostly boiled down to a formidable explosion of youthful energy, starting in the United States and spreading to much of the world, like rock-and-roll and fast-food. I suspect it was largely demographically impelled. I am not expressing contempt toward my youth here. Much of what we were doing or trying to do was right-minded. Some of it even needed to be done. It turns out now that of the many revolutions taking place at the time, the ones with lasting effects were the Civil Rights Movement, the radical spread of the use of cannabis, and Steve Jobs'. Yet, the collective mood was such that if there had been no dragons to slay, we would have invented some, out of exuberance. It was the generation of the Rolling Stones and of Bob Dylan. It was also the generation after the pill and before HIV. (I shall say no more!) It was the same generation that now insists on a Medicare program it never paid for, of course. I am on the older edge of that generation and that may influence my retrospective under-standing of what was happening at the time. At any rate, inventive destructiveness was in the air we breathed.

I have thought hard about writing a real discursive sociological paper on the Stanford Sociology Department's outburst of creativity in the 1970s. I could not. The topic is too close to home. All I can come up with is an autobiographical essay. I hope it contains enough pop-sociology to be entertaining if not enlightening. By the way, my memory of the period seems

Stanford's Organization Theory Renaissance, 1970–2000
Research in the Sociology of Organizations, Volume 28, 329–337
Copyright © 2010 by Emerald Group Publishing Limited
All rights of reproduction in any form reserved
ISSN: 0733-558X/doi:10.1108/S0733-558X(2010)0000028023

clear to me but that's no guarantee of accuracy. Much water has run under my bridge and there have been several discontinuities in my life. It is possible I am unconsciously filling in the blanks. There are also some blanks I could not fill if I tried, especially as concerns persons. There are zones of unexplained obscurity. However, I am writing honestly. Anything I affirm below that is not true to fact proceeds from genuine ignorance or forgetfulness. To make my testimony worse, I was at Stanford both as an undergraduate, 1966–1967, and again, with only a one-year interval, as a doctoral student, both times in Sociology. I may be confusing the two experiences. I apologize in advance if I do. I received my PhD in the summer of 1974.

TRAINERS

Those who were students in the Stanford Sociology Department at the time received first, a top-quality grounding in basic methods (using the term broadly), and second, in clear thinking. It took me long to understand how exceptional that was. For years, in academia, I did not realize how many of my colleagues and competitors lacked exactly such a grounding. I was puzzled by the combination of their hard work and low productivity. (I am retired; I can afford to tell the mean, pitiless truth.) How did this happen? First, in this case, people and personalities mattered. I do not think they always do.

Dick Scott gave me the desire to become a Sociologist. (I forgave him for that long ago.) His lectures first drew my attention to the fact that organizations are important and interesting. His example of hard work, boundless inquisitiveness, and intellectual honesty inspired me as an undergraduate, as a doctoral student, and through my academic life. It still inspires me now. I am not even trying to emulate him. He is just an implicit standard in my brain.

Joseph Berger taught me how to think straight in 10 brisk weeks. His explanation of what constitutes a theory has served me like a lighthouse a mariner in the storm. (Sorry for the cliché; sometimes, clichés are exactly right.) Understanding the meaning of the word is like doubling your neural connections. You would be surprised how many social scientists have no idea.

Bernie Cohen, Sandy Dornbusch, and Morris Zelditch, each in his own highly personal way, helped me understand what methods make for rigor. I did not digest everything they taught on the spot. Much of it, I ruminated in later years. I realized early in the game though that there was zero chance I would have begun to understand the link between appropriateness of design and methods and rigor without them, or without others just like them.

Jim March, with whom I had few working contacts, nevertheless played an important role as a distant example of breadth of vision and intellectual bravura.

I owe an unusual personal debt of gratitude to the late St Clair Drake. I took deeply into my heart his frequent demonstrations of the didactic power of story-telling. It brightened all my teaching and it is moving me now, in my third or fourth career, when I am doing little more than telling stories.

Looking back, the most astonishing thing about this group of people is that they knew exactly what they were doing. Unlike many of us, they were not effective teachers by sheer luck. These good teachers, and others I did not know personally, packed the barrel of powder that fed the Stanford Sociology explosion. There were others, to whom I refer below, who lit the fuse.

SIZE AND CREATIVITY AND THE GERMAN DEMOCRATIC REPUBLIC

Any or most social systems generative of much talent of any kind are either large or they operate as variants of the old East German Olympic model. The relationship between size and achievement is self-evident: If the distribution of talent were perfectly random and of equal frequency in all social systems, the larger systems would turn out more talent. These conditions are weakly satisfied in the Olympics where a large country, the United States, accounts for a high percentage of medals, and China, another large country comes close. There are noteworthy exceptions to this rough model, in both directions. First, India, the second most populated country, managed only one gold medal in more than 20 years (in air rifle target shooting!) and just three total in Beijing. Second, some relatively small countries, such as Australia, perform much better than their population size would predict. In fact, on a medals-per-capita basis, the over-all winner of the Beijing Olympics was Jamaica. Now, on to the East German model that goes a long way, but not all the way, toward explaining deviations from the large-size benchmark.

For those too young, or too old, to remember: the Communist-ruled, German, so-called Democratic, so-called Republic, the part of Germany under Soviet control, turned out a prodigious number of Olympic winners between about 1965 and its dissolution in 1990. Here is the East German model: Test everyone who has four limbs at an early age. Select the ones that seem endowed for a particular sport; train them intensively. Test again, select again, train again. And so forth, until you have 50 subjects you have good reasons to believe are world-class. Give those a pseudo-job so they can train full-time. Keep a steely eye on all their doings. If some of the girls appear a little weak, give them hormones until they become girl-boys or boy-girls. (But, that is another story that does not need to be told here perhaps. It is pretty clear East Germany would have garnered impressive numbers of medals even without the help of hormone injections.)

The Stanford Sociology Department in the 1970s was not large and it stood at the antipodes of the East German Olympic model, except in one way: it gave many graduate students pseudo-jobs thus freeing them from the undermining effects of extreme poverty. Yet, in the next 30 years, its graduates and its graduates' intellectual children, and grandchildren, and great-grandchildren, and on till now, would garner a preponderance of the medals in Sociology and perhaps in the social sciences broadly defined.

THE SHOP

Back in those days, there was a great deal of research money around. What happened was that two youngish scholars, John Meyer and Michael Hannan (the latter new at Stanford), grabbed some of that money. They used it to create an enchanted environment for doctoral students.

I suspect my experience was typical: One day Hannan, whom I knew only from one methods class where I had performed no better than OK, approached me and offered to support the rest of my graduate studies. I had passed my qualifying exams; I was then about three years from finishing, I think. What would I have to do in return, I asked? (My mother did not raise a fool!) His answer was something like this:

> You can do what you wish but John Meyer and I, and some other graduate students, are building some data sets you can use. Also, if you need help with research or writing, you can ask me.

At the time, I had some vague ideas about doing something in Human Ecology, as defined by the precursor Amos Hawley. I had yet vaguer ideas about what a doctoral thesis was. I can add without bragging because it was so long ago that I am almost describing a different person, that I was then a well-educated, well-read man, with a good basic training (see above) but no sense of purpose and no compass. I was a pure dilettante.

I accepted what was clearly a generous offer and joined the Meyer/ Hannan research shop-in-the-making. Within a few weeks, my life took a decisive turn.

First, I discovered the existence of large data banks. I had no reason to pay attention to them before because they were useless without a computer. There was a good mainframe computer at Stanford but I did not know what it was for. I was only peripherally aware of the fact that the engineering students with whom I partied were using it. I did not have the curiosity to inquire further because I did not know of large data banks. And so forth.

Second, I was suddenly again in the presence of people who were allowing themselves to envisage really big questions. Big questions were not alien to me because of my familiarity with broadly discursive social philosophers such as the Three Musketeers, Max Weber, Karl Marx, Emile Durkheim, and Joseph Schumpeter. But, I had been tempered in the forge of Stanford's culture of evidence. That put the big questions pretty well out of reach. You could either deal with big questions or you could be serious about facts. The loquaciousness of my French background had vaccinated me against endless speculative wordiness; I was mistrustful of those who did not squarely choose facts. I was going to avoid the big questions, and even the mid-sized ones, all in the interest of empirical sturdiness.

In that budding group of budding scholars, I realized quickly that one did not have to choose. I could ask big questions and satisfy my desire for empirical verification, both. Like a glutton, I embarked quickly on a dual intellectual course: I would deal with big issues of economic development that interested me because I had a heart; I would do it within an ecological framework. I knew little about the first and the framework was just being developed at that moment.

Overnight, I felt that everything was possible. I had emigrated to the United States indirectly but ultimately in large part because of my utter inability to satisfy French high-school math requirements. That had made me a high-school dropout in the French system of the day. (I spent three years as a high-school senior actually, but that is yet another story.) In spite of this built-in history of failure in quantitative anything, I have a clear memory of embarking on the computing and analysis phase of my dissertation in a merry mood. I remember working with the mainframe manual on my left knee, the Statistical Package for the Social Sciences (SPSS) manual on the right knee, and the statistics books on the table next to the computer terminal. I was doing that with enthusiasm and joyously, only eight or nine years after being thrown by the educational system of my country of origin.

CREATION

And God, said, let there be light: and there was light...And God divided the light from
the darkness. (King James' Bible, pp. 1–3, 4)

The Meyer/Hannan shop invented Institutional Theory and Organizational Ecology in a few years. (My description may be unfair because I was unaware, and still may be ignorant, of inputs from outside the shop that may have been determining.)

Each of these new schools of thought rested on a minuscule number of concepts. These few concepts began early to shatter received ideas. But this is a long-term retrospective. This handful of ideas is so profoundly original that older scholars, including many of my age peers today, still seem constitutionally unable to contemplate them. Several have told me that they were evil inventions, even devilish, or words to that effect. Accordingly, I would venture that most Management textbooks published in the past 10 years give both approaches a cursory, usually under-informed attention or that they ignore them completely. In spite of the fact that a hundred articles in good journals have demonstrated the common-place nature of organizational failure, many Business textbooks still adopt the triumphalist tone that was the rule from 1950 to 1970: The well-informed, knowledgeable manager leads his organization from summit to ever higher summit, blah, blah. (I wonder if the Fall 2008 corporate disaster is going to be enough to change this *Weltanschaung*.) The Stanford-based advent of Institutional Theory and Organizational Ecology may thus have inadvertently widened the chronic separation between scholarly research and ordinary teaching. Sorry for the digression. After teaching business undergraduates and MBAs for years in a decidedly non-elite university, I think textbooks matter, not least for the harm they do.

Young scholars are often not shy about trying to make their elders irrelevant, fortunately. Many of them at the time readily adopted these two ways of thinking. Some were Stanford graduate students inside the Sociology Department and in other departments. Some were outsiders who just caught the bug. The late John Freeman infected UC Berkeley early on because of his founding role. Stanford PhDs soon propagated the thinking and the training to several good schools.

Quickly, the new ideas dominated the best journals. I do not mean this in a strict numerical sense. Rather, it seems to me that it has long been almost impossible for scholarly students of organizations to approach most issues as if these few concepts did not exist. They adopt them, or they fight them, or they risk irrelevancy. Even young scholars who did not take an interest in either school got a lift because the methods they popularized are readily adaptable to other endeavors. Organizational Theory broadly defined experienced sudden growth.

Later, as it spread pretty well to the limit of the known world, I thought Organizational Ecology took on some tribal features. It reminded me of the Zulu Kingdom – arising out of undifferentiated groups through the vision and strength of a handful – it did not know its own power and decimated its neighbors. In time, I think it also developed a kind of theoretical dogmatism that I regretted.

I now think that the inherent power of these basic concepts would have been insufficient to account for their dominance. I believe rather that the adoption of new methods simultaneous with the invention of these concepts gave them instant force. Without the quick schooling of many graduate students in the methods of regression analysis applied to large archival data sets, the fate of these ideas would have been different. They would have remained at the center of brilliant but soon forgotten theoretical articles, perhaps to be re-discovered by a few in each new cohort of social scientists.

The sudden emergent practice of centering papers on powerful empirical findings produced through methods difficult but accessible to those who cared enough also generated a rare on-going multi-generational conversation. About 35 years later, I have been drawn to other pursuits. Some of the statistical sophistication in empirical articles eludes me but the prevailing form remains familiar. After studying the tables of findings, I am still generally able to engage in discussions with my scholarly great, great, great-grandchildren.

APPRENTICESHIP

I got only two explicit lessons personally from Mike Hannan, my thesis adviser. One was face-to-face, the other was diffuse and possibly unintentional.

One day when I was whining because of the huge pile of computer printouts awaiting my scrutiny (Do you know what a mainframe computer printout is?), Mike asked me point-blank: "Can you write one page in three hours? Are you crazy, I replied, of course I can. Here is what you do, then: Every morning, you get to work at 6. You write until 9. After three months, you will have 90 pages. That's probably more than you have to say."

"What do I do with the rest of the day, I asked? Oh, you just go and play."

I followed this advice to the letter. It worked exactly as described. I had so much play time that I finished a trade book the same day I finished my dissertation. (It was a book on free-diving, co-authored with Eric Multhaup – MA, Sociology, *circa* 1969. It is still sold on the Internet. Thanks for asking!) I practiced early morning laboriousness faithfully for years and until an evening teaching schedule made it impractical.

The second counsel Hannan gave to all around him through his pernicious example. He was the one who debauched graduate students early on each Friday afternoon, urging them to go drink beer with him at the Dutch Goose. That was at the same time as he was laying the foundations of Organizational Ecology as well as publishing right and left. I absorbed that particular lesson easily because it suited my temperament: Creativity requires leisureliness.

And always, there was the regretted omnipresent John Freeman, like the ideal cousin, quietly in the background, discretely lending a hand, whispering an idea, or the right suggestion to thaw a frozen imagination.

John Meyer's declarations frequently puzzled me; they forced me to think deeply, usually in vain. Being puzzled was one of the best things that could have happened to a bunch of upstart, know-it-all graduate students.

INTO THE WORLD

My completed doctoral thesis, the product itself, was quite bad because it reached so much. If my mother had been a publisher, she would have turned it down. Producing the same doctoral thesis was priceless. I tried nearly everything I was interested in trying. I failed at many. I staggered on to interesting facts. I learned to deal with the peculiar disappointments serious empirical research always dishes out. I stumbled on strengths and small talents I would have never suspected I possessed. It was a superior apprenticeship. It was also the last time I did scholarly work supervised by someone who was both friendly and more knowledgeable than I. Later in my career, people who were both hostile and ignorant tried to direct my work. It was not good for me, obviously. They did not have a great time of it either.

The general benevolence prevailing during that formative era created a short-term problem for me for which there was probably no solution: When I emerged in 1974, I was unprepared for the sometimes vicious realities of the real world, in academia and elsewhere.

Now, 35 years later, I am still a dilettante but I like to think I am a rigorous kind of dilettante because of what I learned at Stanford. My *caca de taureau* detector works excellently, even when I am the *taureau* myself. In an unexpected, paradoxical way, I believe the same formal training feeds my imagination in unrelated endeavors. Above all, my passage through the Stanford Sociology Department in the 1970s gave me the gift of productive effortlessness. Thanks a million.

CHAPTER 20

LEGACIES FROM GROWING UP ON THE FARM

P. Devereaux Jennings

Law school or sociology? Law school or sociology? I was working nights in a hospital in Hanover, N.H., trying to figure out what to do as a next step. After all, pushing around injured bodies on a gurney is not really much of future. A few months before I had finished my undergraduate thesis on Max Weber's philosophy of the cultural science, at the heart of it was my own symbolic logic "proof" of how *verstehen* captures the other's inner world. Seriously. Everyone I knew in my history honors group at Dartmouth was headed to law school, and all of my engineering and math buddies seemed headed for some kind of computer-related job. Better do something else – sociology. Now, who would be broad-minded enough to admit me, given my eclectic background, my age (barely 22), and my penchant for being out-of-doors much more than in?

STANFORD

Nine months later, after four days and nights on a bus, I was dropped off on El Camino Real, walked into campus with my backpack, and navigated my way to the Sociology Department, temporarily housed in three residential buildings, a volleyball net outside. Wow, now this is laid back, which was totally fine with me as a then legal resident of ski area. So I thought, until

Stanford's Organization Theory Renaissance, 1970–2000
Research in the Sociology of Organizations, Volume 28, 339–349
Copyright © 2010 by Emerald Group Publishing Limited
ISSN: 0733-558X/doi:10.1108/S0733-558X(2010)0000028024

I started talking in more depth to Larry Wu, with whom I was rooming for the first few days. Larry had come from Harrison White's group at Harvard. Like others from that group (e.g., David Strang), he already had essentially completed a math major, along with several math-social science courses. My heart sank. Lucky, I thought, that Stanford is willing to give a Master's degrees to those who want to leave Ph.D. program!

THE FIRST YEAR

My first week of class included an overview theory course with Buzz Zelditch, a basic methods course with Mike Hannan and Nancy Tuma, a research design class with Bernie Cohen, and Dick Scott's famous organization theory course. Someone in this list of illustrious names told me four trimester courses would be no problem.

Most of our cohort of 15 plus were in a similar predicament. The overview course was required of everyone in the fall; theory construction, in the winter. After basic methods, we were required to take static and then dynamic analysis. Finally, everyone had to choose an elective, based on his or her potential areas of specialization. In those days, there were dozens of options in organization theory alone: decision making with Jim March, population ecology with Mike Hannan, power and organizations with Jeff Pfeffer, demographics with Nancy Tuma, stratification with Cy (WJ) Goode, culture with Ann Swidler, politics and social issues with Marty Lipset, institutions and the world economy with John Meyer, and on and on. Little balkanization along intellectual lines existed in the organization group. In part, this was because the professors were collaborating a great deal with each other. For example, John Meyer and Mike Hannan had been working for a few years on world systems dynamics (Meyer & Hannan, 1979). Mike was also working with Nancy on their dynamic methods book (Tuma & Hannan, 1984), and John was working with Dick Scott on the first institutional compilation (Meyer & Scott, 1983). Consequently, a student could take a stratification course and population ecology and culture without anyone thinking much of it. In the first year, I ended up taking a course on culture and joining the world systems seminar.

In the spring was the dreaded first-year review of new students. Each of us was assessed on our performance in the required and elective courses, then encouraged to go forward, put on probation for a year, or subtly discouraged from continuing. I guess every program has such make-or-break periods, if at different times. Four or five of my cohort were put on probation and soon decided to leave Stanford. In some case, this was "for the better," and in some cases, for the worse. One particularly brilliant friend of mine was put probation because he could not finish writing his papers (he had writer's block). He had aced his methods and elective statistics courses, but in spite of receiving help from his advisor and from on-campus writing courses, he could not resolve the issue in a timely matter. He left at the end of his second year. Fortunately for me, I was allowed to go forward.

WORKING AS AN RA

I went forward, but I was broke. After applying for admissions in the winter of 1980, I had missed the spring deadline for receiving the four-year entry funding. I was off skiing in Utah due to lack of snow at the Dartmouth Skiway where I had planned to coach again and did not receive notification of my acceptance to Stanford until I returned in late April to New England. By then I had to beg Ann Swidler, who was in charge of sociology admissions that year, to be allowed to join the group. She had graciously agreed, but said no money could be provided after my first year. Having come form a VERY large blended family and having put myself through college, I was used to finding work. I asked around. Dick Scott and others suggested that I go over to the business school and try there.

That is where I met Donald Palmer. Don was there in his office, as I recall, pouring over printout. He looked up with his whimsical smile and asked "can I help you?" (In those days his hair was long, to match his beard, and he probably had his string tie on too.) I explained my predicament, and said that I had some math background and had done fine in the sociology methods courses, plus I was willing to stay the summer to work on his data (i.e., not go back and work on contract for the Forest Service). In other words, I totally over-stated my qualifications and commitment, but Don did not blow my cover. Instead, he hired me. Don had a lot of network data from Stonybrook, where he had done his dissertation, and wanted to get these up and running on the Stanford mainframe. Along with doing this, my job was to create new network variables for Fortune 500 to measure direct and indirect interlocks.

Later my jobs included more theoretical, and not just methodological, tasks, as longer term research assistant (RA) jobs typically do. Don and I would frequently meet to discuss research design issues, variable construction, results, and next papers. At the time (the mid-1980s), neo-Marxism and critical theory were still quite hot theoretical areas in sociology, partly because it was still the Post-Vietnam Era and prior to the fall of the Berlin Wall. Stonybrook was one of the homes of this tradition, as well as home to Perrow's brand of institutional theory (e.g., Perrow, 1972). From this power perspective on organizations, important managerial and economic outcomes, like the use of the multidivisional form, mergers and acquisition, and headquarter location, were viewed primarily as outcomes of elite network dynamics, embedded in different eras of economic development. We were busy surfacing the theoretical nuances of this view and trying to demonstrate the claims empirically, especially while doing a good job of controlling for the normally hypothesized economic effects on such outcomes (Palmer, Friedland, Jennings, & Powers, 1987).

But in summer of 1984 I needed even more funds. My significant other was in the social work program at UCLA, and we had to travel back and forth to see each other. Don was kind enough to recommend me as a part-time, summer RA to Jim Baron, the stratification expert recently arrived from Wisconsin who was in the office beside Don. Jim and Frank Dobbin had just begun an historical study of personnel practice evolution, one devoted to detailing the impact of the State on the development of modern industrial relations system. This system had been taken for granted since the 1950s as being "modern" and "advanced," but its origins were less functionalist and deterministic than believed. Unlike the research with Don, on the personnel project, I was given more specific pieces to pursue, one which would then be incorporated into the paper being developed. My first part was on the professionalization of practices, which I sought to document via a variety of industry sources, particularly the Personnel Journal. This worked out relatively well, leading to a larger, second part built on extensive factor analyses of various employment relations systems in the 1928–1940 period: the simple, technical, and bureaucratic systems (Baron, Dobbin, & Jennings, 1986).

DISSERTATION TIME

My work with Don and Jim continued through my time at Stanford, with a hiatus in late 1985 when I took a Master's Degree and temporarily tried to relocate to Los Angeles. Upon returning from LA, the question for me was the same one for most of my cohort, "what should I write my dissertation on?"

The beguiling thing about Stanford in the 1980s was that there appeared to be so much work to be done within each theoretical area of research (paradigm or theory) that doing *any* research seemed to be a contribution.

In addition, most of us had worked on two research projects, simultaneously or sequentially. As part of those projects, we normally collected a lot of data. Consequently, those ideas and data seem like the natural first place to start the thesis.

That was a mistake that the best graduate students did not make. Whether by circumstance, personal persuasion, or via encouragement from their advisors, the best tried to distance themselves from their advisors, looking elsewhere for ideas and data. One student, Glenn Carroll, was legendary in this regard. I remember hearing about this really talented student of Mike Hannan. We would occasionally see him laughing with Mika, the departmental administrator, or kidding around with Terry Amburgey, his buddy. Then it seemed like he had disappeared; the word was, "Glenn's gone underground to write." Upon his return, drafts of his great papers on inertia, specialization and niche width, and density dependence (e.g., Carroll, 1985) appeared, the guts of the 1992 population ecology book with Mike Hannan. Now, some might say Glenn was only doing work with Mike, but to many of us younger graduate students it seemed that he was demonstrating his independence and his ability to make a unique contribution.

Frank Dobbin and Jerry Davis were similar in this regard. Frank received an National Science Foundation (NSF) scholarship and brokered that money into additional funding to study railroads in France, Britain, and the United States (Dobbin, 1994). The funding was to do on-site, original research, which Frank did, for the better part of a year, first in France (*en francasis*), then in England. Jerry built a data set by hand on interlocks and F500 covariates to test his poison pill idea, spending endless hours in Jackson Library, where the data were housed, mostly in hardcopy, which he pecked into e-files, key-by-key (Davis, 1991).

My own dissertation was much more of an extension of work being done with Don. I was quite intrigued by how de-industrialization was furthered by investment decisions of the Fortune 500 in the US city system. The thesis was simple: family and bank-owned firms would make or keep their manufacturing investments near prior investment locations and their headquarter (HQ) cities as elite enclaves, rather than following the "managerialist" moves to the less elite Southwest or lower wage, Right to Work (union-busting) states in the South. It appeared that there were good over time investment (plant) data collected by Roger Schmenner (1982), then at Duke, which I could purchase. I bought the data, with Don's help. But most of the time codes were either missing or inaccurate. (Schmenner, in all fairness, had never really used the codes much in his own study, hence had not set them up well.) By then it was early 1986. I had three options: (1) re-start data collection, which would take a year or so; (2) create and defend a new thesis proposal, which would take an additional two years; or (3) do what I could with the non-temporal data, which would take six to nine months. My committee was quite split on the matter. Given that I was involved in so much other research work with Don and Jim already, they allowed me to choose the third option. One of the hallmarks of Stanford in those days was that even though it relied heavily on "shops," apprentices had the freedom to make their own choices and suffer the consequences. In my case it was short-term graduating gain, with longer-term publishing pain.

JOBS

The stock market "crashed" in 1987, making all dissertations look less valuable and putting a temporary brake on the expansion of sociology into business schools. Those of us considering the market in 1987–1989 – for example, Frank, Larry Wu, Kathy Grey, Chikako Usui, and a few others from the original sociology cohort – had to scale back our expectations and think about doing two years of search to get a job that would be a good fit. In the end, most of us found good jobs in just one year. Frank went to Indiana, Larry to Wisconsin, Kathy to Deleware, Chickako to Tulane. I went to the University of British Columbia (in business). The Stanford Business School cohort also fared well, with Jerry Davis going to Northwestern, Steve Mezias to Yale, Theresa Lant to New York University, Deb Meyerson to Michigan, Peter Robertson to University of Southern California (USC), and Joe Harder to Wharton.

But many of the 1987–1989 graduating class have since said to me that their first job was a jolting experience. Few universities had as much going on in the area of organization studies as Stanford did at the time. Suddenly, we were faced with being the lone macro person in a micro group or one of a few behaviorists in a department dominated by neo-classical economists. In addition, we were not formally trained to teach. Stanford had teaching assistantships (TAs), but TAs rarely taught more than a class or two and did not design courses. We primarily ran labs, mini-tutorials, and graded. (As was explained to me by one professor, "the Stanford students are paying so much money in tuition and are being told that they are 'the best of the best', so they do not want graduate students as instructors.")

In spite of these challenges, things have worked out well for most of us. All of the individuals mentioned still have good (or great) jobs, some even at the same places where they started. Most of us have been able to publish in our areas of expertise, and many have joined editorial boards, started journals, and written recognized books. We can proudly say that we have joined the broader Stanford collective – the so-called "Stanford Mafia."

REFLECTING BACK ON STANFORD'S LEGACIES

Reflecting back on my experiences as a sort of mini case study, there are a few more general points about the legacies from Stanford with which I would like to end this chapter. I will limit myself to those involving unique features in graduate student selection, training, and placement process for elite networks in the academic field. My assessment will be based primarily on those theories that we were being taught at the time, thus capturing some of what we saw through those lens.

Selection as Experimentation

In hindsight, the Sociology Department's selection process seemed to be based on creating a large size, diverse cohort, one that would then be winnowed down by half within three years. The cohort was *not* based on prior elite ties, particular forms of education and high test scores, contrary to what is often claimed to be the primary path to professionalization (e.g., see Larson, 1977). Some of us were from elite universities, some not; some of us had taken sociology, others (like myself), very little; some had Graduate Record Exams (GREs) in the high 700s, some in the low 600s. Instead, each of us seemed to have a set of qualities that the selection committee was willing to bet on. More than once, we quipped that the population ecology models being taught (e.g., see Hannanm & Freeman, 1977) were actually being applied to us as a form of Social Darwinism for selecting cohort members. We were generalists and specialists of all varieties in a brand new field (organization studies), one whose nature would only be known post hoc based on who among us survived!

In the case of my business school friends, whose selection committees I later observed and whose admissions advisor I knew fairly well, there were stronger elite university connections, a smaller numbers experiments, and more involvement of faculty in the selection procedure. Both the Sociology Department and business school method seemed to have produced successes, but there were fewer failures with the latter than the former.

Indeed, this second model seems to have gained more legitimacy at Stanford and among other universities as time has gone on, as is common once a professional specialty becomes accepted within the system of professions (Abbott, 1988).

Training Apprentices

The training of students was partly through course work, and partly through the advisor–advisee (apprentice) system (Merton & Storer, 1979). The coursework, as mentioned above, was relatively standardized in the first two years, with a heavy emphasis on formal theory and formal methods, run by the departments involved. This training has been labeled "positivist" and "objectivist" by some critics in the program and of Stanford's legacy in general. In some ways, the training was a holdover from the scientific and structuralist approaches to sociology and business begun in places like Carnegie Mellon, Chicago, Princeton, and Harvard. But from a student's point of view, it was one of the important attributes for applying to the program. I reckoned that even if I did not stay for a Ph.D., I would be employable afterwards. Human capital improvements, in other words, were well aligned with our professional investments (Becker, 1993).

The apprenticeship system had at least three unique qualities, often common of "craft" systems (Edwards, 1979). First, the apprenticeship was relatively informal and open-ended. Upon entry, a student was temporarily assigned an advisor, but a student was free to approach anyone to see if the person had some work for to do, or if the faculty member was willing to offer advice on a student's work. I suppose there were turn-downs, but none that I heard about. Then, if the match was going well, it might continue for an indefinite period of time. Second, the apprenticeship was interdisciplinary. Most of us had at least four-year funding, so we felt free to move across research shops and schools, sometimes to the annoyance of our advisors. Third, the apprenticeship had some checks and balances. Dissertation committee members, department heads, and former members seemed to have some idea of what was going on with advisors and advisees and would intervene if necessary. For example, one friend of mine who was working as an RA for a particularly tough and testy advisor was approached in the middle of the department Christmas party by the advisor to go do some more computer runs, now. My friend did so immediately. But this story circulated, and my understanding is the advisor was discretely discouraged by a few well-placed heads in the department from making such demands in the future and my friend remained in the advisor's employ.

Placement among the Elites

The main job strategy of graduating students was to shoot for the best job available, hope to get tenure – but expect otherwise – then go to the next "tier" down for a job, hopefully with tenure. The alternative, if less common strategy, was to shoot for the best fit in a very good, if perhaps not great, school, but one with a reasonable chance of tenure; then hope to move upward if things went well. Both placement strategies served the individual and Stanford well. Being placed in elite universities, or working your way upwards into them, meant that individuals were more likely to have similar experiences and face the same criteria for success as they did at Stanford. At the same time, by placing students in other elite universities, Stanford's own elite status was retained, plus it ensured a quality source of new students and faculty in the future (Podolny, 2001).

Apart from where a person was placed, joining the Stanford Mafia had implications. Of course, several other universities have well-known alumni groups among their professionals – Northwestern, Michigan, Harvard, Carnegie-Mellon, Chicago, to name a few. In every case, in order to remain cohesive, such groups require some form of common understanding (Meyer & Scott, 1983; Swidler, 1986). The Stanford group had a common understanding of theory and method that it considers to be "state-of-the-art," and the group was driven by the belief in creativity as the means of pushing the boundaries of knowledge outward.

Such collectives also require norms of exchange and reciprocity (Goode, 1973). One that seems to be well-known about Stanford is that, all other things being equal, coming from the Farm will be counted in a decision being made by another Stanford person. A related norm is that commitment to one's research group, colleagues, and friend does not end when you leave the Farm, it is much longer term. Don, who is known for his fairness and ethical standards, has, nevertheless, been enormously helpful in pushing some opportunities my way. Jim Baron was also quite willing to work with Frank and me after we left Stanford. And Dick Scott has remained supportive through the years, even though I did not work directly for him.

What then can be summed up as the "Stanford Legacy"? A critic viewing these selection, training, placement, and career advancement processes might say "nothing more than elites perpetuating elites," a grand form of network homophily in which cliques compete over narrow gradations in status (Perrow, 1972; Mizruchi, 1993). My own view is somewhat more positive. Having a diverse incoming group, egalitarian funding, interdisciplinary training, an appreciative culture, and enduring norms has helped create a relatively rich, open, robust, and benevolent network of scholars in the academic field (Bellah, Madsen, Sullivan, Swidler, & Tipton, 1985; Scott, 1980). If other readers agree with my observation, then the Stanford Legacy is one that I hope will continue.

REFERENCES

Abbott, A. (1988). *The system of professions: An essay on the division of expert labor.* Chicago: The University of Chicago Press.

Baron, J. N., Dobbin, F. R., & Jennings, P. D. (1986). The evolution of modern personnel administration in US industry. *American Journal of Sociology, 92*(2), 350–383.

Becker, G. S. (1993). *Human capital: A theoretical and empirical analysis, with special reference to education* (3rd ed.). Chicago: University of Chicago Press.

Bellah, R. N., Madsen, R., Sullivan, W. M., Swidler, A., & Tipton, S. M. (1985). *Habits of the heart: Individualism and commitment in American life.* Berkeley, CA: University of California Press.

Carroll, G. (1985). Concentration and specialization: Dynamics of niche width in populations of organizations. *American Journal of Sociology, 90*(6), 1262–1283.

Davis, G. (1991). Agents without principles? The spread of the poison pill through the intercorporate network. *Administrative Science Quarterly, 36*(3), 583–613.

Dobbin, F. (1994). *Forging industrial policy: The United States, Britain and France in the railway age.* Cambridge, MA: Cambridge University Press.

Edwards, R. (1979). *Contested terrain: The transformation of the workplace in the twentieth century.* New York: Basic Books.

Goode, W. J. (1973). *Explorations in social theory.* London: Oxford University Press.

Hannanm, M. T., & Freeman, J. (1977). The population ecology of organizations. *American Journal of Sociology, 82*(5), 929–964.

Larson, M. S. (1977). *The rise of professionalism: A sociological analysis.* Berkeley, CA: University of California Press.

Merton, R. K., & Storer, N. W. (1979). *The sociology of science: Theoretical and empirical investigations.* Chicago: University of Chicago Press.

Meyer, J., & Hannan, M. (1979). *National development and the world system.* Chicago: University of Chicago Press.

Meyer, J., & Scott, W. R. (1983). *Organizational environments.* Thousand Oaks, CA: Sage.

Mizruchi, M. S. (1993). Cohesion, equivalence, and similarity of behavior: A theoretical and empirical assessment. *Social Networks, 15*(3), 275–307.

Palmer, D. P., Friedland, R., Jennings, P. D., & Powers, M. E. (1987). The economics and politics of structure: The multidivisional form and the large U.S. corporation. *Administrative Science Quarterly, 32*(1), 25–48.

Perrow, C. (1972). *Complex organizations: A critical essay.* Glenview, IL: Scott, Foresman.

Podolny, J. M. (2001). Networks as pipes and prisms of the market. *American Journal of Sociology, 107*(1), 33–60.

Schmenner, R. W. (1982). *Making business location decisions.* New York: Prentice-Hall.

Scott, W. R. (1980). *Organizations: Rational, natural and open systems.* New York: Wiley.

Swidler, A. (1986). Culture in action: Symbols and strategies. *American Sociological Review, 51*(2), 273–286.

Tuma, N. B., & Hannan, M. T. (1984). *Social dynamics: Models and methods.* Orlando, FL: Academic Press.

CHAPTER 21

SITUATED LEARNING AND BROKERAGE AS KEYS TO SUCCESSFUL KNOWLEDGE PRODUCTION: AN EXPERIENTIAL REVIEW

Stephen Mezias and Theresa Lant

We both arrived at Stanford in September 1982 to begin the Ph.D. program at the Graduate School of Business (GSB). The beginning was not auspicious; it rained heavily during orientation, an unusual event in itself, but a fitting precursor to one of the worst El Niño's on record. By February of our first winter in California, there was one period in which it rained 60 of the prior 63 days. The cold and the wet did not dampen our curiosity or that of our cohort, however, as we began the required Organizational Behavior class with GSB Professor James March in January 1983. We emerged from the shock of the first semester of graduate school into a course that powerfully underscored the interdisciplinary nature of the doctoral program at the GSB. Because the syllabus actively engaged the literature of rational choice in making the case for behavioral perspectives, students from all disciplines were drawn into the discussion. We learned more about rational choice in the many discussions that ensued in this cross-disciplinary climate than in our graduate economics classes. More importantly, we learned

Stanford's Organization Theory Renaissance, 1970–2000
Research in the Sociology of Organizations, Volume 28, 351–357
Copyright © 2010 by Emerald Group Publishing Limited
All rights of reproduction in any form reserved
ISSN: 0733-558X/doi:10.1108/S0733-558X(2010)0000028025

through experience that the individual mind is not an adequate level of analysis to understand the dynamics of the organizations community at Stanford in the early 1980s. Only in retrospect, though, can we appreciate fully the uniqueness of that time and place, and the resulting impact of scholarship that emerged from this context. For this reason, our discussion will emphasize a situated learning perspective to comprehend the Stanford phenomenon. The resulting de-emphasis of the individual mind as the focal repository of knowledge and emphasis on interactions among actors and sources of embedded knowledge is not intended to slight the role of incredibly intelligent individuals and the stellar intellects that surrounded us. Rather, we adopt a situated perspective because it provides a mechanism for traversing the large Stanford community and its multiple levels of analysis without resorting to aggregation, dominant coalitions, or anthropomorphized learning units. Although we will confine our examples of activities and dynamics to the community at the GSB that we knew best, we also believe that other communities of practice were similar to varying degrees. The importance of these other communities will be implicit in our discussion of the role of bridges linking these dense networks of situated learning.

Our experience in being part of the community of practice at the GSB was a cogent demonstration of Greeno and Moore's (1993, p. 49) argument that cognitive activities "... should be understood primarily as interactions between agents and physical systems and with other people." The housing of the Ph.D. students together, in portable trailers outside the GSB proper, without regard to discipline and the use of seminar spaces for the primary disciplinary courses, which were required for *all* students, made this point. The way we came to understand new perspectives, such as resource dependence, population ecology, and institutional theory, reinforced the view that interpretation and meaning are created through webs of social interaction. We not only read the articles, but actively discussed them and saw them applied in a variety of settings. The redesign of the Ph.D. curriculum to be both cross-disciplinary within the GSB and require a broad array of courses for those majoring in organizational behavior, including graduate courses in sociology and psychology, was also important. In leading this redesign, the prior head of the doctoral program, GSB Professor Jeffrey Pfeffer, had enacted Pea's (1993) view that human cognition and knowledge are created across time and space, and must take into account people, practices, artifacts, and symbols. Throughout the slightly more than four years we took to complete the doctoral program, we were reminded on a regular basis that knowledge resides not just in people's heads but also in the structure of the environment.

Wenger (1998) argued that knowledge and its meaning are negotiated and constructed by actors who interact within a community with which they identify and with which they enact shared practices. This observation helps us to understand an important aspect of what happened at Stanford during this era. Various processes that were in place allowed information and knowledge to be shared across multiple communities of situated learners, amplifying and extending the value of interactions and shared practices within the communities. Individual faculty members acted as strong bridges across communities: Professor Jim March linked the GSB to education, political science, and sociology. Professor Pfeffer linked the GSB to sociology and Stanford University to UC Berkeley, which was particularly important in motivating the interuniversity organizations community that was assembled each year at the Asilomar Conference Center on the Pacific coast at Monterey Bay. Professor W. Richard Scott, in sociology, being an active integrator in his own right, was also important, particularly given his strong ties with Professors Pfeffer and March. The hiring of junior faculty from discipline based Ph.D. programs, including Professor Joanne Martin in social psychology and Professors Don Palmer and Jim Baron in sociology, also created bridges to the departments of their disciplines. The interaction of these strong bridges with the strong norms of interdisciplinary collegiality within the GSB community was particularly powerful. The newly revised Ph.D. curriculum, the handiwork of Professor Pfeffer and steadfastly maintained by Marketing Professor Seenu Srinivasan, his successor as school-wide head of the doctoral program, also played an important role. A steady stream of OB students taking Professor Scott's sociology of organizations course, the graduate level introduction to social psychology with Professors Marc Lepper and Lee Ross in Psychology, as well as elective courses taught by thought leaders such as the late Professor Amos Tversky, famous for helping launch the field of behavioral decision making, and Professor Mike Hannan who introduced ecological views on organizations, created additional bridges for ideas. This was reinforced on the sociology side by the fact that Professors Don Palmer and Jim Baron both hired sociology graduate students to work as their research assistants. In addition to impactful work produced by these collaborations, the physical presence of students such as Dev Jennings, Frank Dobbin, and many others at the GSB fostered relationships of all kinds. Funding by the National Institutes of Health to the sociology department allowed Dick Scott to run a seminar series that brought renowned sociologists Paul DiMaggio, Neil Fligstein, Mark Granovetter, and Woody Powell, among others, to campus. Here the entire community saw papers presented at their early stages that were to become classics of organizational theory over the ensuing 20 years.

As Lave (1988, 1993) has noted, learning to become a community member is not simply the individual adoption of socially shared cognition, but a process of situated learning whereby the individual develops an identity as a member of a community. The genius of the Stanford system in this era was that it established boundaries firmly enough to ensure that we were socialized effectively as members of the GSB community while simulta- neously having sufficient interactions outside of the GSB to ensure the possibility of broader overlapping identities. Both identities and knowledge developed reciprocally through these interaction processes (Lant, 1999). To use the terminology of Brown and Duguid (1991, p. 47), these interactions created a "community of interpretation" in which the "shared means of interpreting complex activity" were "formed, transformed, and trans- mitted." The presence of cohesive communities of practice connected by strong bridges facilitated the legitimate peripheral participation (Lave & Wenger, 1991) of novices in multiple communities.

The irony of applying a situated learning perspective to understand what happened at Stanford during this era is that the focus of much of this literature has been on boundaries, particularly erecting and maintaining them. Much of the research has emphasized how shared histories of learning create boundaries between those who participate in a community and those who do not. Researchers highlight the processes by which participation is channeled and limited and by which reification can produce boundaries. There have been studies of both the formal markers of membership, such as reified titles, dress, and language as well as the informal boundaries such as cliques and friendship networks. Perhaps just due to the accident of focusing on the emergence of learning communities, at least as a way of differentiating this perspective from other perspectives on learning and group phenomenon, there has been less attention to the means of enabling connections across boundaries. We interpret the Stanford we experienced as suggesting that, at least in a university setting with well-established disciplinary identities, the problem of crossing boundaries turns out to be more difficult than the process of erecting boundaries. It may also be that business schools, in the wake of the Ford Foundation report of two decades earlier and the phenomenal success of the Carnegie School at professionalizing business academics, were at the cusp of new possibilities. By luck and happenstance, these new possibilities for cross-disciplinary, cross-academic community learning reached an incredible fruition at the Stanford we knew.

The real magic of Stanford in this era was the strength with which members of a variety of communities of learning and practice recognized the extent to which they belonged to multiple communities. Most importantly, there was a shared willingness to do the hard work of sustaining enough mutual engagement to assure that the communities enriched one another even as they nurtured their own perspectives and identities. We will conclude by arguing that much of this can be understood in terms of success in creating mechanisms for linking communities across boundaries. Rather than descending into professionalized jargon that separated communities, participants in these situated learning enclaves worked hard to create boundary objects that crossed communities. Rooming patterns at the annual Asilomar Conference mixed people up; documents and working papers were widely circulated. Much of this shared activity was focused on developing terms, concepts, and other forms of language that facilitated cross-community interactions. Brokering activities were widely pursued by senior faculty and doctoral students alike, and there seemed to be a shared ethic of valuing the connections provided by people who could introduce elements of one practice into another. Much of this happened because of the constant production, reproduction, and renewal of boundary encounters. Hardly a week would go by in the academic year without meetings, conversations, and other opportunities to negotiate meaning across community boundaries. Those community members who actively created boundary practices, and established ongoing boundary encounters and ongoing forms of mutual engagement, were valued throughout the Stanford and Bay Area organizations community. Because reputations were enhanced by doing the hard work of and establishing routine boundary encounters there were multiple opportunities for mutual engagement. This turned into a self-reinforcing process by which sets of practices emerged to create permeable boundaries and sustain connections among the people and practices within the individual communities.

In closing, we would emphasize that the most important lesson of the Stanford decades is that one needs to constantly renew cross-community ties and reward the hard work that goes into maintaining them. As noted by Elsbach, Barr, and Hargadon (2005), situated cognitions, which depend upon both context and shared schemas of interpretation, are transitory. The "magic" that emerged during a situated time and place of organization studies at Stanford University could evaporate as mysteriously as it appeared. With a long history of well-defined disciplinary boundaries, universities can be very hard places to encourage collaboration across these boundaries. There are constant pressures to focus one's research as narrowly as possible to make a contribution to a well-defined area. From this point of view, there is little value to knowing what those from other perspectives think and believe. As rankings and other criteria for performance have developed outside their control, the leaders of faculties, schools within universities, and universities themselves, have felt incredible pressure to centralize and have (at least the illusion of) control. It is often easiest to do this by dividing and conquering; emphasizing pre-existing disciplinary boundaries and enacting zero sum games is too often the route chosen to accomplish this (questionable) goal. Once the larger university system has gone this route, it is hardly surprising that cross-community and even cross-disciplinary collaboration quickly fades. We are all too familiar with cross-boundary appointments that run into trouble because the constituent groups cannot agree on appropriate candidates. One colleague told us about an entrepreneurship chair that was given to another department because members of the first department could not agree on the type of research that was required. We know of another case where a chair was supposed to be shared across two schools, but the search was scrapped in the first year because the representatives could not agree on even the criteria for choosing. While understanding the internal dynamics of communities is crucial to any successful situated learning activity, understanding how to create brokerage across communities seems to be the more difficult task. We believe other institutions can learn from what happened at Stanford during the era in question. While we would hardly contend that slavish imitation of the cross-community mechanisms observed there guarantees success, we would suggest that spectacular success in knowledge production at the modern university likely cannot occur without a simultaneous emphasis on creating communities and crossing boundaries between them.

REFERENCES

Brown, J. S., & Duguid, P. (1991). Organizational learning and communities of practice: Toward a unified view of working, learning, and innovation. *Organization Science*, 2, 40–57.

Elsbach, K., Barr, P., & Hargadon, A. (2005). Identifying situated cognition in organizations. *Organization Science*, 16, 422.

Greeno, J. G., & Moore, J. L. (1993). Situativity and symbols: Response to Vera and Simon. *Cognitive Science*, 17, 49–60.

Lant, T. (1999). A situated learning perspective on the emergence of knowledge and identity in cognitive communities. In: R. Garud & J. Porac (Eds), *Advances in management cognition and organizational information processing* (Vol. 6 pp. 171–194). Greenwich, CT: JAI Press.

Lave, J. (1988). *Cognition in practice*. Cambridge, UK: Cambridge University Press.

Lave, J. (1993). Situated learning in communities of practice. In: L. Resnick, J. Levine & S. Teasley (Eds), *Perspectives of socially shared cognition* (pp. 63–82). Washington, DC: American Psychological Association.

Lave, J., & Wenger, E. (1991). *Situated learning: Legitimate peripheral participation.* Cambridge, UK: Cambridge University Press.

Pea, R. D. (1993). Practices of distributed intelligence and designs for education. In: G. Solomon (Ed.), *Distributed cognitions: Psychological and educational considerations* (pp. 47–87). Cambridge, UK: Cambridge University Press.

Wenger, E. (1998). *Communities of practice: Learning, meaning, and identity.* Cambridge, UK: Cambridge University Press.

CHAPTER 22

A RELATIONAL APPROACH TO ORGANIZATIONAL LEARNING

Martha S. Feldman

Recently, Lee Sproull contacted me as she prepared to write her contribution to this volume on learning. Much of my work is on the relationship between organizational routines and the learning process. As we talked, I was aware that I was not saying much about the relationship between my work and the work of people I studied with at Stanford. How could this be? In writing this essay, I hope to show that part of what made Stanford a powerhouse of organization theory is also part of what allows Stanford Ph.D.s to develop in their own directions.

I was a graduate student at Stanford between 1976 and 1983, an incredibly vibrant time to be there. I had many interactions with amazing people during these years. My dissertation advisor was James G. March, well known for his insight and theorizing about organizational learning, among many other things. I co-authored an article with Jim. Joanne Martin was another important influence. I was invited to be part of a team of researchers working with her. Sim Sitkin, MaryJo Hatch, and I learned from Joanne as we wrote about the uniqueness paradox in organizational stories. Other students I knew well who continue to work on topics that I work on include Anne Miner and Dan Levinthal. While I wrote my dissertation, visitors who came to Stanford for long or short periods were a big help. Michael Cohen, Lee Sproull, and Elisabeth Hansot each spent hours reading what I wrote, then walking and talking about it and numerous other ideas. I was a political

Stanford's Organization Theory Renaissance, 1970–2000
Research in the Sociology of Organizations, Volume 28, 359–363
Copyright © 2010 by Emerald Group Publishing Limited
All rights of reproduction in any form reserved
ISSN: 0733-558X/doi:10.1108/S0733-558X(2010)0000028026

science student so people like Seymour Martin Lipset, Jonathon Bendor, Terry Moe, Daniel Okimoto were important influences. Ultimately, I graduated and went to work at the University of Michigan in Political Science and Public Policy. No doubt, the publications with Stanford co-authors and letters of recommendation from James G. March and Seymour Martin Lipset helped (a lot).

I am, of course, grateful for these many blessings and, though my scholarship may have moved theoretically from what I learned at Stanford, much of what I learned at Stanford has been incorporated into my practices as a scholar and professor. Theoretically, I have moved to practice theories from the behavioral theory of the firm and the institutional theories that I learned at Stanford. That is, in part, because of my methodological grounding in ethnography, not the typical methodological base for Stanford students at that time. The book I published based on my dissertation, *Order without Design,* was very much based in the ambiguity and choice literature that built on the behavior of the firm. My ethnographic data, however, allowed me to produce an argument that leaned in the direction of practice theory even before I knew of it. Later, I found that without additional theoretical input, I had nothing new to say using the kind of data I had. Practice theory provided the input I needed, and I now find myself making contributions to conceptualizing organizational routines in ways that sometimes extend, sometimes challenge, and sometimes just raise different questions than the theories I learned at Stanford and particularly those of my mentor.

So, what made Stanford such a powerful force in the field of organization theory and in my intellectual development? Though I may be an outlier in theoretical and methodological inclinations, I think that many of the features of Stanford at the time that I was there and that have helped me and stayed with me are also features that made Stanford such a generative intellectual environment. I can immediately point to three features: supportive faculty, a community of scholars, and a combination of openness and high standards.

SUPPORTIVE FACULTY

In retrospect, one of the most extraordinary features of the support from faculty was that they encouraged me to follow my interests rather than being concerned about making sure that I would contribute to enlarging their research agenda. I say, in retrospect, because it has only been in seeing how often graduate students are given limited options by faculty that I have understood the model that I was taught at Stanford. Each faculty member I interacted with knew that I was developing a different agenda either because of my interest in ethnography or because of my interest in different disciplines than theirs. Seymour Martin Lipset, similarly, could clearly see that I was not following in his footsteps, yet hired me as a research assistant and provided important input for my dissertation work. When I returned from doing fieldwork in Washington, DC, Joanne Martin's expertise in studying culture and narratives helped me to make sense of my data and helped provide a different perspective to the ambiguity and choice scholarship. My work was more closely related to that of my dissertation advisor, Jim March, though he was also in a position to see how my ethnographic leanings would uncover issues that required me to move in directions other than his work. Yet, he defended and supported my choice even to the point of walking me through the conundrums that arose while I was working as a policy analyst and doing fieldwork.

Jim March was an extraordinary advisor. I said something to that effect at one of the many events that have been held over the past decade to celebrate Jim's career and there were snickers from many of the men in the room. They were, of course, snickering because it was well known that Jim enjoyed the company of young women. But what their snickers belied was what they did not understand – namely that at that time it was not easy to find powerful academics who would take seriously the intellectual development and careers of women scholars and push them to be their best just as others did for the students who were men. Jim did. That was a gift. And I am not looking that gift horse in the mouth.

I worked with Jim as a research assistant and as a teaching assistant, we developed and co-taught a course toward the end of my doctoral student days and we co-authored our article, *Information in Organizations as Signal and Symbol*. I learned from each of these opportunities.

Being his teaching assistant provided a couple of events that I still have not forgotten. One happened when my dog upstaged Jim in the middle of a lecture. The other happened when I could not bring myself to finish *War and Peace* even though I had to grade papers based on the novel. (I ended up relying on Jim's summary and the Cliff notes.) I hope that, on the whole, I was pretty reliable and helpful, but Jim's forebearance through these mishaps (he never appeared even to be angry) gave me a model for how to treat students and people who work for me. His observation in relation to the *War and Peace* reading (and probably others) was that I like to have read more than to read. This insight is still largely true and is still an important challenge for me to be aware of. I learned that being honest about people's weaknesses is important and does not diminish your support for them. Later, I learned how to be honest about people's strengths, too.

The lessons I remember most came from working with Jim on the course and on the article. I learned, for instance, that "everything is always up for grabs," a phrase I have annoyed co-authors with for years. Though I am not sure Jim ever used these words, he enacted them. I remember, for instance, that we rearranged the syllabus the day before the course started. While that is a level of chaos I have tried to resist in later years, I do believe that for learning it is (almost) never too late to incorporate a good idea and that continuing to think about the topic you are working on is always important was a useful lesson.

I learned to recoil at the phrase "careful analysis" and to insist that, of course, analysis must always be careful and that what is not careful should not be called analysis. I learned to shudder at split infinitives and phrases such as "the data is" or "the data has been." Were these nit-picky complaints? Certainly they did not come from a lack of incisive critical comments about the content of the work. Instead, these were part and parcel of learning to pay attention to what I was saying and how I was saying it. Learning these lessons have been critical to the kinds of contributions my scholarly work has made. Indeed, being aware of the assumptions embedded in my own words and in the words of others has been essential to being able to open up concepts like routines and resources (see, e.g., Feldman, 2000, 2004; Feldman & Pentland, 2003).

COMMUNITY OF SCHOLARS

As a graduate student, I experienced Stanford as a community of scholars. I do not know whether it felt that way to the faculty, but they did provide many opportunities for graduate students to meet scholars across the many disciplines that constitute organization theory. Two important institutional manifestations of the community were the Natioal Institute of Mental Health (NIMH) supported seminar series (and the graduate student fellowships that supported many of us) and Scandinavian Consortium of Organization Studies (SCANCOR). The seminar series brought in scholars from around the world and gave graduate students a broad education in organization theory. SCANCOR brought a flow of Scandinavian social scientists who enriched the conversation by introducing both new theoretical questions and closer proximity to organizational practice.

These institutional efforts made a huge contribution to the intellectual environment that I gained from and have motivated me to be part of creating such efforts at the two institutions I have belonged to since leaving Stanford. At the University of Michigan, I helped to start and was on the executive committee for the Interdisciplinary Committee on Organizational Studies, more commonly known as ICOS. At the University of California, Irvine, I helped to start and have been director or co-director for the Center for Organizational Research. I continue to have a deep appreciation for the importance of such institutions and now understand just how much effort they take to keep going.

OPENNESS AND HIGH STANDARDS

Perhaps the most important thing I learned at Stanford from both the support of the faculty and the community of scholars approach to learning is that having high standards is not the same as being exclusive. Over the time I have been a professor, I have heard "standards" used as a proxy for endorsing a particular theoretical or methodological stance, but I did not experience the expectations of me while I was at Stanford in this way. Indeed, I learned that having high expectations was about taking seriously the research enterprise and thinking deeply about the work that you are doing and its implications. I learned that the work we do is worth doing well, and I had the opportunity to learn several different ways of doing it well.

My Stanford experience has provided a model for graduate student learning that has many features I have tried to recreate for graduate students I encounter. It was expansive, interdisciplinary, engaging, and fun, and at the same time provided a great base for my career. That is a high standard worth emulating.

REFERENCES

Feldman, M. S. (2000). Organizational routines as a source of continuous change. *Organization Science, 11*(6), 611–629.

Feldman, M. S. (2004). Resources in emerging structures and processes of change. *Organization Science, 15*(3), 295–309.

Feldman, M. S., & Pentland, B. T. (2003). Reconceptualizing organizational routines as a source of flexibility and change. *Administrative Science Quarterly, 48*, 94–118.

CHAPTER 23

THE STANFORD ORGANIZATIONAL STUDIES COMMUNITY: REFLECTIONS OF A TEMPERED RADICAL

Debra E. Meyerson

I was a doctoral student in the Organizational Behavior (OB) Ph.D. program in the Graduate School of Business (GSB) from 1984 to 1989 and a faithful participant in the annual Stanford Organizations Conference at Asilomar, on the shores of the Pacific. I worked under the guidance of Professors Joanne Martin, Rod Kramer, Robert Sutton, and James March. I also benefited from the support and guidance of sociology professor Richard Scott in his capacity as director of the National Institute of Mental Health (NIMH) and National Institute of Aging (NIA) Fellows Training Program in which I was a pre-doctoral fellow from 1985 to 1988. The reflections that follow are based primarily on my experience as a student during this vibrant period, although, as a current a faculty member within the School of Education at Stanford, I cannot resist drawing occasional comparisons between the organizations community then and now.

Most striking in this comparison is the extraordinary sense of community among organizational scholars during the earlier era. Boundaries of membership in the community were defined not by discipline or school, theoretical tradition, or epistemology, but by a shared sense of being part of a vibrant

Stanford's Organization Theory Renaissance, 1970–2000
Research in the Sociology of Organizations, Volume 28, 365–372
Copyright © 2010 by Emerald Group Publishing Limited
All rights of reproduction in any form reserved
ISSN: 0733-558X/doi:10.1108/S0733-558X(2010)0000028027

intellectual community that was "onto something," however broadly defined. As students with few points of comparison, we probably did not fully appreciated the unique qualities of our community, but I believe we knew that we were privileged to be part of it all – we knew that our young faculty (e.g., Rod Kramer, Joanne Martin, Robert Sutton) were on the way up, our established faculty had authored the core textbooks (e.g., Pfeffer, 1982; Scott, 1987) and theories of our field, and our peers were landing jobs in the top OB and organizational sociology programs in the country. Most students belonged to different research projects and subgroups. Despite our separate cohort and project affiliations, we identified with something larger than the sum of our groups.

It is worth noting that, as a student, I felt a strong sense of affinity and shared identity with other organizational scholars around campus even as I felt at odds with many of its dominant values and norms. Motivated by this tension, Maureen Scully and I introduced the notion of "tempered radicalism" (Meyerson & Scully, 1995) to conceptualize our experience of simultaneously identifying and feeling misaligned with our professional community, and we discovered that several of our peers and mentors shared this sense of ambivalence. We were very much "insiders" in that we felt part of the organizations community at Stanford and wanted to fit in and succeed within our institution and the academy at large, but in important self-defining ways we also perceived ourselves to be "outsiders" who deviated from the dominant values and approaches and we aspired to change some of the criteria that marked success (Meyerson, 2001). As a student in the business school (focused on businesses), I wanted to become a valued member of the scholarly community by becoming fluent in quantitative methods and steeped in the macro-theories of organizations, such as neo-institutional theory, population ecology, and resource dependence that were the mainstay of the field, even as my choice of subjects (social workers, feminist executives), theories (culture and interpretative approaches), methods (ethnography), and ideology (feminism and radical humanism) were marginalized within the field.

Feeling at once an insider and an outsider characterized my experience as a student at Stanford and has continued to define my career as an organizational scholar within various institutional settings. This stance also provides a vantage point from which to reflect on the qualities of the Stanford organizational studies community in the late 1980's that drew so many of us in – the stuff of community and shared identity – which enabled deviation and innovation.

What was it about the organizations community at Stanford during this period that fostered a collective identity among scholars from different disciplines, schools, and research groups, across different status levels, theoretical orientations, and values? While others will undoubtedly offer other accounts, I boil it down to four conditions that fostered a sense of belonging while encouraging experimentation and deviation: an abundance of different types of resources, close mentoring ties between students and faculty, forums for intellectual engagement and cross-fertilization, and opportunities to socialize in ways that built informal ties.

First, there was a perceived sense of abundance among students and, I suspect, faculty: abundant opportunities for students to collaborate with faculty on new and important research topics; an abundant pool of material resources to fund research; and, importantly, abundant job opportunities. This is not to suggest that the organizational studies community, even during its heyday, was flooded with resources and void of competition and political jockeying. From a student's perspective, however, I recall only a sense of plenty. This made for minimal competition and significant collaboration among peers within and between schools at Stanford. The perceived abundance of resources may have also contributed to the significant experimentation and innovation during the period, although the relationship between slack resources and risk taking and innovation has been the subject of a good deal of scholarly debate (see Christensen & Bower, 1996; Nohria & Gulati, 1996; Ajuja, Gautam, & Tandon, 2008 for discussions of resources and innovation).

A number of factors combined to create a real and perceived sense of resource availability. As Scott (this volume) describes in more detail, beginning in the 1960s, the federal government played an important role in supporting the expansion of social science research in general, and this fueled the growth of organizational studies. The expansion of Stanford's organizational studies community was a beneficiary of this wider trend within the academy, but it may have benefited disproportionately as well. Under the leadership of Dick Scott, multi-year training grants from the NIMH became available to support the study of all types of organizations. From 1972 through 1989, these grants combined with a comparable grant from the NIA from 1986 to 1989 supported, on average, five pre-doctoral and five post-doctoral fellows in organizational studies annually. As a condition of funding, each fellow was required to work directly with a faculty member in organizational studies, which meant that the NIMH and NIA grants supported the research and cultivated the loyalty of most of the organization studies faculty around campus (Scott, this volume).

These funds were supplemented by other pools of resources that seemed to be readily available to Stanford organizational scholars. For instance, with a five-page proposal, Maureen Scully and I secured a $50,000 grant from the Haas Foundation to study ethics officers in the defense industry, a role we believed mirrored the structural ambivalence of tempered radicals' position (Scully & Meyerson, 1993). The funding was part of a larger program to support research on corporate ethics on the tail of ethics scandals in the defense and other industries in the mid-1980s. Because it was our first independent field project, we took for granted the seamless access we were granted to the officers and top executives in all of the major defense contractors as well as the relative ease with which we secured funding to support our study. I believe that we were not alone in our sense of abundant opportunities and resources, and, in reflection, I would conjecture that these resources encouraged intellectual risk taking; we did not have to "play it safe" to secure resources and legitimacy.

It is difficult not to compare this sense of abundance with the current resource conditions facing organizations scholars and social scientists more generally. Although business school faculty and students at elite schools may be insulated from the implications of a shrinking pool of research funding, organizational scholars in sociology, education, and engineering have had to rely on a variety of funding sources, some with significant strings attached. Many of us worry about how we will support our doctoral students who tend to stay in graduate school longer because there are fewer jobs. And, because of the shrinking pool of resources to fund organizational research, students must now compete with peers to land sponsored research assistantships. How the diminishing pool of resources will affect scholars' choice of topics and the risks they are willing to take is an empirical question.

Second, as a stipulation of the NIMH and NIA training grants and a norm within the OB program (and I believe other organizations programs at Stanford), graduate students worked closely with faculty in an apprenticeship or mentoring relationship (Kram, 1983; Kramer & Martin, 1996). Cohorts within the OB program were very small (between one and three students were admitted per year), which meant that each faculty member mentored only a few students at a time and collaborated closely with them on research and publications. Virtually all of my peers left graduate school with several co-authored publications and multiple methods in their quiver. I learned to do laboratory research by working with Rod Kramer on several experiments and picked up qualitative methods in my collaborations with Joanne Martin and Bob Sutton. Although the apprenticeship model was not unique to Stanford during this period, these relationships were pivotal in cultivating students' and advisors' identification with a broader community as well as providing the psychological safety that allowed for experimentation and innovation (Edmondson, 1999). This was certainly true in my case. My advisors, starting with Joanne Martin, transmitted the norms and expectations of the local and national scholarly communities and, at the same time, provided the permission and safety to deviate from them.

Third, a number of intellectual forums brought together organizational scholars across schools, research areas, disciplines, and status levels that enabled the cross-fertilization of ideas that enriched the intellectual experience (e.g., Saxenian, 1996). The GSB presented regular colloquia, which were well attended by scholars from across campus. For example, the NIMH and NIA training programs held regular seminars and convened post-doctoral and pre-doctoral fellows from different disciplines to discuss research on a routine basis under Richard Scott's leadership. In addition, the Scandinavian Consortium of Organization Studies (SCANCOR), founded 20 years ago and first led by James March, and now Woody Powell, attracted visiting organizational scholars from Scandinavia and other parts of Europe to Stanford for lengths of stay that varied from a few days to a year. In the early days, the Scandinavian visitors were integral members of the organization community. A favorite among the organization students from around campus was Jim March's Friday afternoon wine and cheese party, ostensibly a party thrown for the visitors, but, like other occasions, served also to bring together local scholars. Most renowned for its cross-fertilization, was the conference at Asilomar – the annual intellectual gathering of organizational scholars. After initially being restricted to members of the Stanford community, the conference later opened to include organizational scholars from neighboring universities and alumnae-turned-faculty. These participants organized their calendars to show up at Asilomar and affirm their identities as Stanford organizational insiders, whether they were interested in the themes of that year's conference or not. In retrospect, there seemed to be a sufficient variety of intellectual gatherings to create what Scott (this volume) calls "collegial capital," but not so many forums that faculty and students would segregate into sub-communities by theoretical taste, school, or discipline.

Today, like two decades ago, there are organizational studies students and faculty in the schools of engineering, business, and education as well as in sociology. The numbers have grown significantly. The GSB alone now has 19 tenure-line organizations faculty. Today, most schools, as well as SCANCOR, host their own organizational studies colloquia with regular participants and a few people who occasionally attend multiple forums. There is no gathering equivalent to Asilomar. Thus, while Stanford can still boast a first-rate collection of organizational scholars and students, we are now, at best, multiple communities linked together by idiosyncratic relational ties between individuals from different schools and disciplines.

Fourth, there were a number of opportunities for informal socializing across status-level and disciplinary boundaries, particularly at the Asilomar Conference, which built different types of relationships and trust, the raw materials of social capital (e.g., Coleman, 1988; Podolny & Baron, 1997). Parties late into the night leveled status distinctions and smoothed over theoretical and epistemological contests, at least for the weekend. My memories of Asilomar are punctuated by the two years Don Palmer (then a faculty member in the GSB) and I made our way down the coast by bicycle. The pretense for showing up at Asilomar was the intellectual exchange, but the parties, the walks on the beach, and the rides down the coast, were the reasons for coming back year after year. Undoubtedly, these status-leveling social experiences helped build the trust and multiplex connections that characterized the community.

These last two conditions – forums for intellectual exchange across boundaries and opportunities to socialize – helped build the "collegial capital" that contributed to the extraordinary degree of innovation that came out of Stanford's organizational scholars during this period. According to Scott (this volume), the process involved "not so much co-production, as mutual stimulation – one person's ideas stimulating or building upon another's." This is only possible if people have regular opportunities to interact with one another and "play" with ideas (March, 1976). In contrast, when organizational scholars from different disciplines or schools come together to play with ideas or socialize in the current context, it is strictly the result of personal ties rather than ritualized forums that enable these rich exchanges and cultivate collegial relationships.

In sum, I have proposed that four factors – perceived resource abundance, strong mentoring ties between students and faculty, forums for cross-fertilization and intellectual exchange, and opportunities to socialize and build multi-plex ties across traditional divisions – cultivated a sense of community and shared identity among organizational scholars from disparate disciplines and schools. I posited that these same conditions created a fertile ground for members' capacity to take risks, deviate, and innovate. I will leave it to others to speculate about what it would take to replicate this sense of community in the context of a much larger and fragmented group of organizational faculty and students with fewer resources to go around. But a strong funded cross-department fellowship program coupled with an annual bash at Asilomar would probably be a good start.

It seems fitting to conclude with a reflection of my experience at the SCANCOR 20th Anniversary celebration held in November of 2008. As might be expected, the main celebration was attended by dozens of Stanford organizational studies alumnae representing different generations and disciplines. Although some of us from different cohorts had not seen each other in several years, we found each other and made sure to sit together at the gala dinner. We had developed different interests and taken divergent professional paths. Some had left academia; some, like Martha Feldman, Gerry Davis, and Michael Cohen, had built or contributed to impressive interdisciplinary organizations communities in their own universities; others, like myself, had led non-linear academic careers. I have little doubt that all who have remained in the academy continue to draw upon and benefit immeasurably from the collegial capital we acquired during our years at Stanford.

REFERENCES

Ajuja, G., Gautam, A., & Tandon, V. (2008). Moving beyond Schumpeter: Management research on the determinants of technological innovation. *The Academy of Management Annals*, 2(1), 1–98.

Christensen, C. M., & Bower, J. L. (1996). Customer power, strategic investment and the failure of leading firms. *Strategic Management Journal*, 17, 197–218.

Coleman, J. S. (1988). Social capital in the creation of human capital. *American Journal of Sociology*, 94, 95–120.

Edmondson, A. (1999). Psychological safety and learning behavior in work teams. *Administrative Science Quarterly*, 44(2), 350–383.

Kram, K. (1983). Phases of the mentor relationship. *Academy of Management Journal*, 26, 608–625.

Kramer, R., & Martin, J. (1996). Transitions and turning points in faculty and doctoral student relationships. In: P. Frost & M. Taylor (Eds), *Rhythms of academic life: Personal accounts of careers in academia* (pp. 165–180). Thousand Oaks, CA: Sage Press.

March, J. G. (1976). The technology of foolishness. In: J. G. March & J. Olsen (Eds), *Ambiguity and choice in organizations*. Bergen, Norway: Universitetsforlaget.

Meyerson, D. (2001). *Tempered radicals: How people use difference to inspire change*. Boston: Harvard Business School Press.

Meyerson, D., & Scully, M. (1995). Tempered radicalism and the politics of ambivalence and change. *Organization Science*, 6, 585–600.

Nohria, N., & Gulati, R. (1996). Is slack good or bad for innovation? *Academy of Management Journal*, 39(5), 1245–1264.

Pfeffer, J. (1982). *Organizations and organization theory*. Cambridge, MA: Pitman.

Podolny, J. M., & Baron, J. J. (1997). Resources and relationships: Social networks and mobility in the workplace. *American Sociological Review*, 62, 673–693.

Saxenian, A. (1996). Beyond boundaries: Open labor markets and learning in Silicon Valley. In: M. B. Arthur & D. M. Rousseau (Eds), *The boundaryless career: A new employment principle for a new organizational era* (pp. 23–39). New York: Oxford University Press.

Scott, W. R. (1987). *Organizations: Rational, natural, and open systems*. Englewood Cliffs, NJ: Prentice Hall.

Scott, W. R. (this volume). Collegial capital: The organizations research community at Stanford, 1970–2000. In: F. Dobbin, & C. B. Schoonhoven (Eds), *Research in the sociology of organizations: Stanford's organization theory renaissance, 1970–2000*. Bingley, UK: Emerald.

Scully, M., & Meyerson, D. (1993). The separation of law and justice: Managing impressions of corporate ethics programs. *The Employees Rights and Responsibilities Journal, 17*, 32–59.

CHAPTER 24

UNPACKING THE STANFORD CASE: AN ELEMENTARY ANALYSIS

Mark C. Suchman

The unifying goal of this assembly of recollections is simple: To offer an organizational account for the remarkable success of the Stanford organizations community – both in generating new ideas and in training new researchers – during its heyday in the last quarter of the 20th century. But simple goals are not always simply achieved, and there are risks to seeking general lessons in the inevitably idiosyncratic recollections of a few relatively successful alumni of a single relatively successful intellectual community. The sample is small, nonrandom, and selected on the dependent variable; the data are partial, skewed by the vantage points of the informants, and distorted by retrospective reconstruction; and the conclusions are colored by self-esteem biases and social-desirability effects. "Anecdote," as they say, is not the singular of "data."

Given that the Stanford organizations community was known for the rigor of its methodological training, it seems fitting, at the very least, for me to begin by acknowledging the limitations that my particular trajectory places on me as an "auto-ethnographer." My account of the Stanford experience is necessarily situated in time, in social-network space, and in cultural-logic space. I arrived at Stanford as a graduate student in Sociology in Fall 1984, at a time when many of the hallmark Stanford paradigms – resource

Stanford's Organization Theory Renaissance, 1970–2000
Research in the Sociology of Organizations, Volume 28, 373–386
Copyright © 2010 by Emerald Group Publishing Limited
All rights of reproduction in any form reserved
ISSN: 0733-558X/doi:10.1108/S0733-558X(2010)0000028028

dependence, institutional theory, organizational ecology, behavioral decision theory – were already established features (dare I say "institutions"?) of the intellectual landscape. Other traditions – organizational culture, organizational learning, workplace stratification, and organizational impression management – were still nascent, but by the time I received my Ph.D. in 1994, they too had progressed well down the road toward taken-for-grantedness in their own right. The Stanford that I saw was thus an ongoing, routinized enterprise, not anymore an entrepreneurial "prospector," although also by no means an ossified "reactor." It was, to continue the Miles and Snow (1978) analogy, an "analyzer," leveraging its strength in established domains to enter and systematize new domains as they emerged.

Unlike some of my cohorts, I did not arrive at Stanford as an "organizations person"; I was interested in legislative and judicial decision-making, which at the time I saw as being closer to political sociology than to organizational studies. But like many Stanford graduate students of the era, I was attracted and ultimately captivated by the rich array of opportunities (intellectual, professional, and social) that the organizations community had to offer. My time at Stanford was cushioned by external funding and interrupted by stints at law school on the East Coast – and as a result, I never became quite as attuned to the administrative and political intricacies of the place as my less itinerant compatriots. But I, nonetheless, came away with a strong identity as an organizations researcher, and with an ingrained sense of the desirability and appropriateness of the Stanford way of doing things. I had, some might say, internalized the legitimacy-claims of the Stanford "rational myth" (Meyer & Rowan, 1977).

ELEMENTS OF ORGANIZATION

Charged with a daunting task of organizational analysis, the good Stanford graduate of my era dutifully turns for inspiration to Dick Scott's *Organizations: Rational, Natural and Open Systems*. It is not quite the Bible, but it has a far more useful index and bibliography. And, as a beginning, I often encourage my own students to consider the basic "elements of organizations" that Scott presents in the form of a simple "diamond" typology, originally attributed to Harold Leavitt (1965) and in the most recent edition (Scott & Davis, 2007) updated to reflect the work of Nadler, Tushman, and Nadler (1997). This typology directs attention to five key components of any organizational phenomenon: (1) the participants; (2) the formal structure; (3) the informal structure; (4) the technology; and

(5) the environment. Considering each of these elements may shed some light on the Stanford experience.

Participants

Any well-trained sociologist is honor-bound to disdain "great individual" explanations of social life. Unfortunately, such disdain would be a significant handicap in the present endeavor. During the period of its ascendancy, Stanford was fortunate to house an unusually productive mix of intellects, personalities, and talents. John Meyer, Jeff Pfeffer, Mike Hannan, and Joanne Martin all brought richly conceptualized and thoroughly differentiated personal visions. Jim March brought this and also immense conviviality and an irrepressible intellectual playfulness, like a kitten with a ball of yarn. Dick Scott brought a vision of his own; but even more importantly, to this medley of distinctive visions he brought an enormous capacity for integration, juxtaposition, and synthesis. Through his teaching, his writing, and his institution-building, he gathered together the partially unraveled balls of yarn, tied them end to end, and started weaving a fabric.

More prosaically, an organizational demographer might note that Stanford was fortunate not just in the talents but also in the age-structure of this core participant group. Most were old enough to be tenured, but young enough to have long careers ahead of themselves. And because Stanford was a desirable "terminal position," most could plausibly expect to remain embedded for the rest of their careers in the community that they were building together. In game-theoretic models of cooperation and trust, the "shadow of the past" and the "shadow of the future" (Voss, 2001; Batenburg, Raub, & Snijders, 2003) are often presented as being consequences of distinctive interaction patterns (to which I will turn shortly); but time-horizons also reflect individual life-course trajectories, and Stanford's hey-day corresponded to a period when both temporal shadows loomed large for much of the core faculty.

To this group of central, long-term participants, one could add a long list of students, visitors, colleagues, and collaborators – including most of the authors in this volume. By the mid-1980s, Stanford had become a convening ground for organizational scholars of virtually every stripe. Some found the environment more congenial than others (critical scholars on the left and traditional management theorists on the right were notably scarce; minorities were under-represented at least relative to the general population, if not relative to peer campuses; quantitative researchers outnumbered qualitative researchers by a substantial margin); however, across a significant swathe of the field, Stanford's talent pool was remarkably deep – and remarkably focused on *organizational studies* as an autonomously valuable pursuit, not simply as the handmaid to some other, more topical, investigation.

The sociologist in me must note, of course, that many campuses house brilliant intellects, committed paradigm-pushers, and assiduous institution-builders. These individual traits are only raw materials. To adequately explain the Stanford phenomenon, one must go on to posit that they needed to be present in a critical mass, that they needed to be arrayed in a particular orientation toward one another, that they needed to be animated by particular customs and amplified by particular routines, and that they needed to be energized by and engaged with particular environmental streams. But even if Stanford might have thrived equally well with some other set of participants, it surely would have thrived quite differently. Emergent properties notwithstanding, compositional effects do matter.

Formal Structure

Stanford was and is an elite private research university, with the usual complement of academic departments, professional schools, and administrative offices. Its hiring, promotion, compensation, and disciplinary procedures are largely isomorphic with its peers. It certainly was never an organizational-studies Los Alamos; not a skunkworks (Rich & Janos, 1994); not even a UC-Irvine. Taken as a gestalt, Stanford's formal structure during the period in question was rather conventional, with few idiosyncrasies large enough to account for the distinctiveness of its outcomes. Nonetheless, several features deserve mention, at least as facilitating factors, if not as fundamental causes:

First, Stanford was and is a relatively wealthy university, and during the period in question, a series of ambitious (and occasionally iconoclastic) fundraising and investment strategies helped to fuel a significant expansion of Stanford's faculty, campus, and mission. I assume that the organization studies community experienced its share of battles over budgets, boundaries, and priorities, but the general atmosphere was one of growth not retrenchment, symbiosis not competition. Second, compared to most US schools of equivalent status, Stanford was relatively young – particularly in its incarnation as a major research university with international pretensions. Tradition weighed more lightly at Stanford than at many of its peers, and inherited roles were less sacrosanct. Together, these elements of rapid expansion and low inertia combined to erode outmoded hierarchies and foster the entrepreneurial recombination of old organizational forms into new intellectual spaces (cf. Stark, 1996).

One place where this structural flexibility showed up was in Stanford's relatively high number of interdisciplinary appointments and initiatives. Perhaps one should not overstate this point; these days, it seems that virtually every university professes to be uniquely interdisciplinary. But the Stanford organizations community did seem to have an unusual number of faculty who held – and exercised – voting appointments in multiple units. And jointly sponsored institutes, programs, and events were the norm rather than the exception. Indeed, graduate students of the era often had trouble identifying official departmental boundaries, tracing lines of authority, distinguishing appointment-holders from fellow-travelers, and differentiating hosts from guests. To us, at least, Stanford seemed closer to an interwoven "matrix" (or at times a maze) than to a collection of "silos," each on its own bottom (Galbraith, 1971; Davis, Lawrence, Kolodny, & Beer, 1977).

A related feature of Stanford's formal structure was the linkage of the professional schools to the academic disciplines, and vice versa. The Graduate School of Business (GSB) was particularly notable in this regard. The rise of the Stanford organizations community corresponded to a period of both expansion and identity-formation for American business schools, and the Stanford GSB was situated quite far toward the "academic" end of the continuum. This does not mean that the GSB abjured practitioner adjunct faculty, or cookbook MBA skills courses, or network-building mixers; however, alongside these concessions to the realities of running a professional school, the GSB also operated an unusually large, sophisticated, and rigorous Ph.D. program, and hired an unusually high number of faculty members with disciplinary, rather than management, backgrounds and interests. A similar pattern of engagement with – and respect for – disciplinary social science also prevailed (albeit somewhat less pervasively) at the School of Education and the School of Engineering. As a result, the Stanford organizations community was spared much of the status-driven border skirmishing that divided and distracted researchers on many other campuses.

During the period when I passed through Stanford, the paragon of all these structural attributes – the flexibility, the interdisciplinarity, and the spanning of professional schools and social science departments – was the Stanford Center for Organizational Research (SCOR). SCOR was housed in the GSB and directed by Dick Scott from Sociology. To this day, I have no idea who "owned" it or what its governance structure was, despite the fact that I was briefly employed by it and served on its student advisory committee. But SCOR acted as a clearinghouse and coordinating body; it administered an outstanding interdisciplinary colloquium series; and it convened a wide array of mini-conferences and training workshops. It was the classic "liaison" unit, an internal bridge that facilitated horizontal integration and countered the centrifugal forces of disciplinary differentiation (cf. Lawrence & Lorsch, 1967). In an increasingly complex academic environment, SCOR provided the Stanford organizations community with an integrated identity and a capacity for resource sharing, information exchange, and conflict resolution that many other campuses lacked.

Perhaps most importantly, SCOR organized the annual "Asilomar Conference" – a weekend-long retreat at a rustic but spectacularly sited ocean-front conference facility near Monterey. Over a period of two decades, the Asilomar Conference grew from being a small workshop-like gathering into being a major organizational undertaking, drawing well over 100 participants not only from Stanford but from Berkeley, UCLA, and beyond. Although the atmosphere was unswervingly casual (shorts and sandals, shared accommodations, cafeteria-style meals, and evening parties that often ended with semi-legal campfires on the beach), the Asilomar Conference was formalized and carefully planned. But like a ritual feast-day, the "function" that this formal structure served was less technical than cultural: The Asilomar Conference symbolized and enacted a particular set of normative commitments and cognitive schemas, reinforcing the structural interdisciplinarity described above, and encouraging collegiality, informality, creativity, and eclecticism. Virtually everyone in the community participated, and with the exception of a few keynote addresses, most activities – from paper sessions to rooming assignments – were configured to minimize distinctions of field and rank.

Informal Structure

As the Asilomar Conference illustrates, if Stanford's formal structures were primarily facilitating factors, the most important thing that they facilitated was Stanford's *informal* structure. Three elements of Stanford's culture stand out in my recollection:

The first, to which I have already alluded, was a near-universal assumption that organizational analysis was a coherent and worthy intellectual enterprise in its own right, transcending any particular empirical domain. No one questioned whether a study of restaurants (Freeman & Hannan, 1983) could be as "serious" as a study of semiconductor manufacturers (Eisenhardt & Schoonhoven, 1990), or whether a study of bill collectors (Sutton, 1991) could be as "important" as a study of nuclear war planners (Eden, 2004). Nor did anyone question whether these disparate studies could be relevant to one another, or whether they could cumulate into a single interconnected body of knowledge. To some degree, this neo-positivist ahistoricism (like many articles of faith) may have been a mythical conceit; but as a cognitive institution, it served to bind together a remarkably diverse array of projects, and to undergird a collective identity that encompassed students of both the private sector and the public, of large organizations and small, of social services and high-technology, of science and art. And because no one doubted that these disparate studies constituted a common enterprise, people were eager to attend to work from multiple empirical domains, and to couch their arguments at a level of theoretical generality that would "travel" well. This, I suspect, is one of the most important reasons why Stanford tended to produce paradigms, while many other campuses tended to produce case studies.

A second crucial element of Stanford's informal organization was the prevalence of collaborative work, both among faculty and between faculty and students. Buffered by material munificence, supported by structural interdisciplinarity, and encouraged by cultural inclusiveness, Stanford researchers co-authored at a prodigious rate. The most famous of these collaborations included Dornbusch and Scott (1975), Meyer and Hannan (1979), Meyer and Scott (1983), Meyer, Boli, Thomas, and Ramirez (1997; Thomas, Meyer, Ramirez, & Boli, 1987), Tuma and Hannan (1984), Hannan and Carroll (1992), Meyerson and Martin (1987), Levitt and March (1988), Eisenhardt and Schoonhoven (1990), Elsbach and Sutton (1992), and Dobbin and Sutton (1998). Moreover, these collaborations were not only frequent but interactionally dense: Several of the most active collaborators – Dick Scott, John Meyer, and Mike Hannan, in particular – formed cross-cutting ties, creating "bridging social capital" (Gittell & Vidal, 1998; Putnam, 2000) by working with colleagues from several parts of the community, rather than from only one congenial research shop.

A third noteworthy aspect of Stanford's informal organization was less a matter of lofty normative commitments, pervasive cognitive frameworks, or intricate relational networks than a matter of learned emotional responses and emergent self-images: Through some rare alchemy of personality, place, experience, and interpretation, organizational studies simply became fun. People took themselves less seriously than they took their ideas. Jim March held Friday afternoon wine-and-cheese "office hours," published quirky poetry, and (thanks to a mail-order ordination) presided at student weddings. Mike Hannan held office hours and research meetings at a downscale local bar. Don Palmer made frequent appearances on the

Sociology graduate-student intramural softball team. Dick Scott routinely treated his undergraduates (who were required to buy his text) to a lavish end-of-semester "royalties party," and occasionally gathered his research team over games of backyard croquet. The unifying theme of all these otherwise idiosyncratic escapades was a sense that good scholarship required playfulness, conviviality, and iconoclasm as much as it required angst, introspection, and caution. This outlook may not always have produced the most rigorous investigations of specific propositions, but it produced more than its share of intriguing new propositions to be investigated – and it attracted more than its share of eager young graduate students to investigate them.

Technology

For a "people-processing" organization such as a university, technology – broadly conceived as the instrumental techniques for accomplishing work – inevitably blurs into formal and informal structure. The Asilomar Conference, one could argue, was a technology for building interdisciplinary fluency; wine-and-cheese office hours, a technology for encouraging identity-formation; and so on through most of the features mentioned above. But for brevity I will set aside these ambiguities and focus only on one core aspect of technology: graduate pedagogy. And, in a concession to the limits of my first-hand knowledge, I will confine myself primarily to the Ph.D. program in Sociology.

In pedagogy as in formal structure, Stanford's approach was less a radical departure from the norm than a felicitous variation on familiar themes. Stanford's program covered most of the usual graduate subjects – theory, statistics, a professionalization seminar – and imposed most of the usual hurdles – preliminary exams, teaching and research experience, a thesis proposal, etc. Admittedly, compared to its peers, Stanford's formal requirements were arguably somewhat light – there was, for example, no qualitative methods requirement, no master's thesis, and no final dissertation defense. But I see no clear line from these idiosyncracies to Stanford's success in producing organizations scholars.

More significantly, unlike some larger programs elsewhere, the Stanford Sociology Department treated graduate training as craftwork rather than as mass processing. This arguably had important consequences both for students and for faculty. Students were allowed (and tacitly encouraged) to chart their own paths; and faculty, confronted with the need to support advisees with a wide range of substantive interests, tended to focus their own intellectual personas around a metatheoretical toolkit, rather than around a particular empirical phenomenon. John Meyer and Dick Scott, for example, routinely served on a myriad of far-flung prelim and dissertation committees – not out of interest in a particular empirical context, but out of willingness to offer an organizational and institutional perspective on *any* empirical context. In theoretical terms, Stanford's reluctance to screen out, pre-process, or ignore variations in its (human) throughput stream placed a premium on cultivating flexibility, cognitive complexity, and professional discretion in its frontline workforce; and because throughputs and workforce were both composed of social actors linked in a shared community, those traits ultimately came to define a distinctive Stanford work style.

Three more concrete pedagogical features may also merit notice: The first, consistent with the arguments of the preceding sections, was a high rate of interdisciplinary course-taking: Even the most parochial Sociology student could not have passed through the Stanford Ph.D. program, without having numerous classes – including quite a few advanced seminars – with students from Business, Education, Engineering, and Political Science. The result was a truly interdisciplinary graduate community, in which learning to communicate across departmental boundaries became a crucial survival skill.

A second potentially significant quirk of the Stanford training program was the way it handled theory training. The norm within the discipline was (and largely still is) for theory courses to focus on Theory with a capital "T," emphasizing heavy exegetical analyses of Marx, Weber, and Durkheim, perhaps along with a few more recent big-T thinkers such as Parsons, Giddens, Foucault, and Bourdieu. Stanford, in contrast, emphasized what Merton ([1949] 1968) termed "theories of the middle range": Drawing on Kuhn (1962) and Lakatos (1968), students were encouraged to read big-T Theory not for exegesis but for a window into a particular metatheoretical perspective. Metatheoretical perspectives, in turn, were presented not simply as abstract intellectual constructs, but as the underpinnings of "theoretical research programs," recursive dialogs between theory and evidence in specific empirical contexts. The resulting imagery reduced the gap between theoretical and empirical work and encouraged students to see the two not as competing career trajectories, but as mutually justifying aspects of a well-balanced scholarly identity. This indoctrination had its drawbacks: Some Stanford students pushed themselves to generate both theory and evidence, even though their skills might have been better used by focusing on one or the other alone. But for students with a suitable combination of aptitudes and interests, Stanford's "theoretical research program" model provided an effective recipe for making a lasting mark on the field.

Finally, no account of Stanford's pedagogy would be complete without at least a brief nod to the program's close identification with the statistical technique of Event History Analysis (EHA). Although EHA did not originate at Stanford, Tuma and Hannan (1984) were largely responsible for introducing the technique both to sociology and to organizational studies. As a method for analyzing the timing of discrete-state transitions, EHA was particularly well-suited to the hallmark Stanford paradigms of the 1980s, organizational ecology and neo-institutional theory. In addition, EHA resonated with larger trends in the field, favoring dynamic models and longitudinal data. All Stanford students were required to learn EHA, and it gave them a highly prized calling-card on the job market. Although EHA was not formally treated as proprietary "intellectual property," it was informally protected by a mixture of mystification and tacit knowledge (cf. Suchman, 1989) – and it became a source of sustained competitive advantage (Barney, 1991) for Stanford graduates from the mid-1970s until at least the mid-1990s.

Environment

It is difficult to imagine discussing Stanford's accomplishments without considering the role of the organizational environment – because no campus was as thoroughly infused with an "organization-and-environment" sensibility as was Stanford. There is, however, an irony here: To caricature somewhat, Stanford stood out from its environment precisely by questioning the ability of organizations to stand out from their environments. From this, one might glibly conclude that Stanford's success disconfirms one of the unifying assumptions behind many of Stanford's most influential paradigms. But, in fact, the Stanford case merely illustrates some often-overlooked subtleties in the organization-environment relationship.

First, one must note that the Stanford organizations program was, in fact, every bit a product of its environment. Stanford's core participants (with the exception of Jeff Pfeffer) received their training elsewhere, and their early non-Stanford experiences – whether Dick Scott's exposure to the structuralism of Peter Blau, or Mike Hannan's exposure to the human ecology of Amos Hawley – clearly influenced their later scholarship. Stanford's formal structure and Stanford's pedagogical technology, as noted above, borrowed heavily from the familiar institutionalized scripts of

American academia, and a few fillips notwithstanding, Stanford's training programs were well within the mainstream of its peer universities, in virtually every regard. Stanford's informal culture was perhaps somewhat more distinctive, but it was hardly unprecedented. Moreover, many elements that distinguished Stanford from peer organizations in the *institutional* field of higher education resulted, at least in part, from Stanford's immersion in the *geographic* field of Silicon Valley: Certainly, no account of Stanford's history would be complete without an acknowledgment of how the local environment provided both (a) material resources that facilitated growth and buffered conflict, and (b) cultural orientations that encouraged informality and broke down hierarchy (cf. Saxenian, 1994). Thus, there is little about the Stanford experience that, upon sober consideration, fundamentally undermines the thesis that organizations are open systems, profoundly conditioned by their environments.

At the same time, however, Stanford's distinctive accomplishments do highlight an intriguing alchemy of sustained competitive advantage: Although environmental forces generally produce isomorphism among similarly situated organizations, different aspects of the environment are not always neatly aligned: Industries, professions, factor markets, regions, and social networks are rarely fully coterminous, and when such environmental divisions cross-cut, the numbers of organizations in any given intersection can become quite small. Under these conditions, it is hardly impossible for an organization's attributes to be simultaneously environmentally determined and yet largely inimitable. Stanford was the only elite private university in Silicon Valley; if that particular environmental intersection offered competitive advantages (or disadvantages, of course), they were uniquely Stanford's, for better or worse.

In addition, Stanford perhaps serves as a reminder that, in a world of path-dependent increasing returns (Arthur, 1989; Krugman, 1991; cf. Merton, 1968), large differences in outcomes can often arise from small differences in inputs – especially when those inputs generate non-linear synergies. From 20,000 feet, Stanford looked indistinguishable from other elite private research universities, and virtually every visible feature was environmentally determined; on the ground, at T_0, Stanford was recognizable as an instance of a familiar archetype, but it also showed idiosyncrasies, as one might expect in a small-numbers sample from a complex intersection of environmental pools. As Stanford's history played out, environmental sampling continued, and some of those early idiosyncrasies equilibrated and gradually disappeared. However, going enterprises do not always sample their environments neutrally. They selectively attract some inputs more than others; they selectively screen both what inputs they perceive and what inputs they accept; and they selectively project both their preferences and their expectations onto the sites from which their inputs are drawn (cf. Weick, 1979). Through such feedback loops, a subset of Stanford's early idiosyncrasies became self-reinforcing, sharpened over time, and eventually gave the campus its distinctive character. These two dynamics – regression to the mean and deviation amplification – are countervailing, but not contradictory. They constitute the basic rhythm of identity and embeddedness in any open system.

CONCLUSION

Empirically, there can be little doubt that the Stanford organizations community did, in fact, become a (positive) outlier from most of its peers during the period between 1975 and 2000. This unique outcome, however, had no single, unique cause. Stanford recruited and attracted a productive, relatively young faculty that meshed well and that shared a commitment to organizational scholarship as a coherent field of study. However, these participants could not have thrived without formal structures that facilitated flexibility and interdisciplinarity, and informal practices that encouraged dialog, collaboration, and an element of intellectual playfulness. All of this was amplified by a small-batch pedagogy that preserved individuality and intellectual ambition while imparting solid "middle-range" research values and flashy cutting-edge research tools. And the entire combination of participants, structures, practices and technologies was sustained – and its distinctive properties preserved – by a munificent niche at a sheltered intersection of sectoral and regional environments.

How many building blocks could one remove from this foundation before the edifice would crumble? And how many alternative materials could one substitute, and to what effect? We can never know the answers to such questions for sure. However, as grateful as I am to have had the good fortune of witnessing such an intricate and glorious architecture, I hope for the sake of organizational studies that it was but one of many equally felicitous configurations. At a hundred campuses around the globe, organizational scholars are busily building new research communities every day. They should take the Stanford experience neither as a rigid blueprint nor as an unattainable ideal, but simply as a demonstration of how much is possible when all the elements of organization stand in balance.

REFERENCES

Arthur, W. B. (1989). Competing technologies, increasing returns, and lock-in by historical events. *The Economic Journal, 99*(394), 116–131.

Barney, J. B. (1991). Firm resources and sustained competitive advantage. *Journal of Management, 17*, 99–120.

Batenburg, R. S., Raub, W., & Snijders, C. (2003). Contacts and contracts: Dyadic embeddedness and the contractual behavior of firms. *Research in the Sociology of Organizations, 20*, 135–188.

Davis, S. M., Lawrence, P. R., Kolodny, H., & Beer, M. (1977). *Matrix*. Addison-Wesley series on organization development, 1115. Reading, MA: Addison-Wesley.

Dobbin, F., & Sutton, J. R. (1998). The strength of a weak state: The rights revolution and the rise of human resources management divisions. *American Journal of Sociology, 104*(2), 441–476.

Dornbusch, S. M., & Scott, W. R. (1975). *Evaluation and the exercise of authority*. San Francisco: Jossey-Bass Publishers.

Eden, L. (2004). *Whole world on fire*. Ithaca, NY: Cornell University Press.

Eisenhardt, K. M., & Schoonhoven, C. B. (1990). Organizational growth: Linking founding team, strategy, environment, and growth among U.S. semiconductor ventures, 1978–1988. *Administrative Science Quarterly, 35*(3), 504–529.

Elsbach, K. D., & Sutton, R. I. (1992). Acquiring organizational legitimacy through illegitimate actions: A marriage of institutional and impression management theories. *The Academy of Management Journal, 35*(4), 699–738.

Freeman, J., & Hannan, M. T. (1983). Niche width and the dynamics of organizational populations. *American Journal of Sociology, 88*(6), 1116–1145.

Galbraith, J. R. (1971). Matrix organization designs: How to combine functional and project forms. *Business Horizons, 14*(1), 29–40.

Gittell, R. J., & Vidal, A. (1998). *Community organizing: Building social capital as a development strategy*. Thousand Oaks, CA: Sage Publications.

Hannan, M. T., & Carroll, G. R. (1992). *Dynamics of organizational populations*. New York: Oxford University Press.

Krugman, P. (1991). Increasing returns and economic geography. *Journal of Political Economy, 99*(3), 483.

Kuhn, T. S. (1962). *The structure of scientific revolutions*. Chicago: University of Chicago Press.

Lakatos, I. (1968). Criticism and the methodology of scientific research programmes. *Proceedings of the Aristotelian Society, 69*, 149–186.

Lawrence, P. R., & Lorsch, J. W. (1967). *Organization and environment*. Boston: Harvard University, Graduate School of Business Administration.

Leavitt, H. (1965). Applied organizational change in industry: Structural, technological, and humanistic approaches. In: J. G. March (Ed.), *Handbook of organizations* (pp. 1144–1170). Chicago: Rand McNally.

Levitt, B., & March, J. G. (1988). Organizational learning. *Annual Review of Sociology, 14*, 319–340.

Merton, R. K. ([1949] 1968). On sociological theories of the middle range. In: R. K. Merton (Ed.), *Social theory and social structure* (pp. 39–72). New York: Free Press.

Merton, R. K. (1968). The Matthew effect in science: The reward and communication systems of science are considered. *Science, 159*(3810), 56–63.

Meyer, J. W., & Hannan, M. T. (1979). *National development and the world system: Educational, economic, and political change, 1950–1970.* Chicago: University of Chicago Press.

Meyer, J. W., & Rowan, B. (1977). Institutionalized organizations: Formal structure as myth and ceremony. *The American Journal of Sociology, 83*, 340–363.

Meyer, J. W., & Scott, W. R. (1983). *Organizational environments: Ritual and rationality.* Beverly Hills, CA: Sage.

Meyer, O. W., Boli, J., Thomas, G. M., & Ramirez, F. O. (1997). World society and the nation-state. *American Journal of Sociology, 103*(1), 144–181.

Meyerson, D., & Martin, J. (1987). Cultural change: An integration of three different views. *Journal of Management Studies, 24*(6), 623–647.

Miles, R. E., & Snow, C. C. (1978). *Organizational strategy, structure and process.* New York: McGraw-Hill.

Nadler, D., Tushman, M., & Nadler, M. B. (1997). *Competing by design.* New York: Oxford University Press.

Putnam, R. (2000). *Bowling alone: The collapse and revival of American community.* New York: Simon & Schuster.

Rich, B. R., & Janos, L. (1994). *Skunk works: A personal memoir of my years at lockheed.* Boston: Little, Brown.

Saxenian, A. (1994). *Regional advantage: Culture and competition in Silicon Valley and route 128.* Cambridge, MA: Harvard University Press.

Scott, W., & Davis, G. (2007). *Organizations and organizing: Rational, natural and open system perspectives* (International Edition). Upper Saddle River, NJ: Pearson Education.

Stark, D. (1996). Recombinant property in East European capitalism. *American Journal of Sociology, 101*(4), 993–1027.

Suchman, M. C. (1989). Invention and ritual: Notes on the interrelation of magic and intellectual property in preliterate societies. *Columbia Law Review, 89*(6), 1264–1294.

Sutton, R. I. (1991). Maintaining norms about expressed emotions: The case of bill collectors. *Administrative Science Quarterly, 36*(2), 245–268.

Thomas, G. M., Meyer, J. W., Ramirez, F. O., & Boli, J. (1987). *Institutional structure: Constituting state, society and the individual.* Newbury Park, CA: Sage.

Tuma, N. B. (1984). *Social dynamics: Models and methods.* Orlando, FL: Academic Press.

Tuma, N. B., & Hannan, M. T. (1984). *Social dynamics: Models and methods.* New York: Academic Press.

Voss, T. (2001). Game-theoretical perspectives on the emergence of social norms. In: M. Hechter & K. Opp (Eds), *Social norms* (pp. 105–136). New York: Russell Sage Foundation.

Weick, K. E. (1979). *The social psychology of organizing* (2nd ed.). Reading, MA: Addison-Wesley Pub. Co.

CHAPTER 25

"LET A HUNDRED FLOWERS BLOSSOM": THE CROSS-FERTILIZATION OF ORGANIZATION STUDIES AT STANFORD

Martin Ruef

When I arrived at Stanford in the fall of 1993, the university was a thriving site of organizational research. The department of sociology served as a sort of epicenter, with workshops on organizational ecology (led by Mike Hannan), organizations in the world polity (John Meyer and Francisco "Chiqui" Ramirez), and healthcare organizations (Dick Scott). In the school of education, Jim March was intriguing a new generation of students with his puzzles and wisdom. In addition to Mike Hannan's joint appointment, the Graduate School of Business featured such luminaries as Jeff Pfeffer, Joanne Martin, Jim Baron, Joel Podolny, and Bill Barnett. Slightly further afield, Ray Leavitt and Michael Fehling had begun to train engineers to think about organizational issues, as they developed computer simulations with nuanced attention to cognitive and decision-making processes. Steve Barley would join (what was then) the department of industrial engineering in 1994 and Mark Granovetter would join the department of sociology in 1995, adding fresh insights from the sociology of work and economic sociology,

Stanford's Organization Theory Renaissance, 1970–2000
Research in the Sociology of Organizations, Volume 28, 387–393
Copyright © 2010 by Emerald Group Publishing Limited
All rights of reproduction in any form reserved
ISSN: 0733-558X/doi:10.1108/S0733-558X(2010)0000028029

respectively, to what was already a firm foundation for organization studies. The umbrella organization that linked many of these efforts was the Stanford Consortium on Organizational Research (SCOR), which had been guided by Dick Scott's able leadership since 1988 and hosted an annual organizations conference at the beautiful Asilomar retreat in Monterey, California.

I remain deeply appreciative that my own apprenticeship in organizational research also began with Dick. Shortly before my second year in graduate school, I had been assigned to serve as a teaching assistant for an undergraduate course in "Formal Organizations" and naively assumed that a steady stream of such pedagogical assignments would serve to fund me throughout much of the year. Thankfully, I was quickly disabused of this notion by the faculty member in charge of TA assignments, a rudder adjustment that helped steer me toward the numerous research opportunities that were then available at Stanford. Partially as a matter of serendipity, I heard that Dick was initiating a historical study of the healthcare field in the San Francisco Bay area, funded by the Robert Wood Johnson Foundation. Over the next six years, I would join Dick and an intrepid group of Ph.D. students – including Peter Mendel, Carol Caronna, Sammie Speigner, Junko Takagi, Seth Pollack, and Randi Cohen – in weekly meetings.[1] This exceedingly enjoyable and fruitful collaboration culminated in the publication of *Institutional Change and Healthcare Organizations* (University of Chicago Press) in 2000.

I think it is worth dwelling a bit on the process of writing this book, since it provides some insights into the state of organizational sociology at Stanford and, perhaps, in the United States more generally during the 1990s. (The book's influence can also be measured by the awards it received, particularly the Max Weber and Eliot Freidson awards from the American Sociological Association in 2001 and 2002, respectively.) With some risk of simplification, the late 1970s and early 1980s can be characterized as the watershed years of "West Coast" organizational theory, in which the paradigms of organizational ecology, institutional theory, resource dependence, and organizational learning were developed at Stanford.[2] The subsequent decade was devoted to more incremental and integrative efforts, culminating in such landmark summaries as Hannan and Freeman (1989), DiMaggio and Powell (1991), and Cohen and Sproull (1995), each of which provided a clear statement of the state-of-the-art for a given framework of organizational analysis. Thus, by the time of my arrival at Stanford, many of the "West Coast" paradigms had entered the phase of mature research programs. But given this stage of development, where would these research programs go next? How could they avoid the fate of what Imre Lakatos (1978) has dubbed "degenerative" research programs, in which a scientific approach to a substantive phenomenon becomes incapable of generating novel insights. Going forward, would organizational ecologists dutifully apply the tenets of density dependence arguments to yet another industry, institutional scholars analyze the effects of yet another historical epoch, and analysts of organizational networks address the diffusion of yet another management fad or fashion through corporate interlocks?

The open-minded approach that Dick Scott laid out in our research project on medical organizations offers one possible response. Although the project was animated from the start by the intuition that changing institutional logics affect the behavior and life chances of organizations in profound ways, we were not bound to neo-institutional theory as our exclusive theoretical lens. The project drew explicitly on a variety of frameworks – ranging from ecological and resource dependence perspectives to transaction cost economics – in seeking to understand how an organizational field evolves over a period of half a century. Analytically, we sought an explicit cross-fertilization of these perspectives: not just a juxtaposition in terms of competing hypotheses, but the idea that the processes from one perspective would *interact* with the processes that were posited by another. For instance, one chapter tested the proposition that the salience of performance metrics for hospital survival varied depending on the nature of the institutional environment that these organizations operated within. Consistent with a tenet of strategic management perspectives, we found that relevant measures of performance (e.g. capacity utilization) had a large effect on hospital survival during recent decades, when healthcare organizations adopted a logic of managerial and market orientation. However, this effect was negligible between the late 1940s and 1970s, when the field was dominated by medical practitioners and supportive federal initiatives (Scott, Ruef, Mendel, & Caronna, 2000, pp. 258–263). More generally, a number of quantitative findings reported in the book suggested that concerns about particular metrics of organizational viability (e.g. competition, performance, and even legitimacy) were historically contingent on institutional conditions.

The hybridization of frameworks in our study of healthcare organizations was not limited to theories but extended to matters of method as well. Much of the previous research on the topic had employed either detailed case study materials on specific healthcare facilities – painstakingly collected through interviews, site observations, and examinations of historical archives – *or* systematic statistics on a wide range of organizations available through oversight bodies (such as the American Hospital Association). Although our project began with a largely quantitative slant, this one-sided approach to data collection was soon abandoned in favor of a mixed method perspective, in which qualitative inquiry occurred alongside quantitative analysis. Thanks to Carol Caronna and Seth Pollack, we discovered that the case studies not only helped to ground and breathe life into our regression models, but also that they identified many of the nuances of organizational processes – exceptions to empirical generalizations, extensions of existing theories, and complex organizational dynamics – that would have been missed otherwise (see also Caronna, Pollack, & Scott, 2009).

We applied a similar eclecticism in our levels of analysis. During the 1960s, the rise of "open systems" theory had been marked by a strong emphasis on the organizational environment and the proliferation of distinctive material and symbolic dimensions that called for the attention of organizational scholars. The next wave of open system theories in the 1970s and 1980s largely displaced these taxonomies of environmental dimensions. Instead, environmental properties were increasingly derived as aggregate properties of organizational populations – with density being the most familiar example in organizational ecology and the (isomorphic) adoption of a structure or practice serving a similar conceptual function in institutional approaches. Rather than privilege either organizations or environments as our primary units for purposes of data collection, we informally split our research team into two groups, one of which was responsible for developing a detailed understanding of the material resource and institutional environments across counties in the San Francisco Bay area (drawing on both quantitative and qualitative sources) and the other group taking responsibility for developing a detailed profile of the medical organizations that populated these counties (again, using mixed methods).

In retrospect, the multitheory, multilevel, mixed method approach we adopted in the project was characteristic of the evolution of organization studies during the 1990s. A number of scholars found themselves too constrained by the conventional frameworks of "West Coast" organizational sociology and now experimented with hybrids that would feature elements from several of them. For instance, Joel Baum and his colleagues coined the term "institutional ecology" to refer to the promise of a new approach that would combine insights from ecological and institutional perspectives (e.g. Baum & Oliver, 1996), an effort at hybridization that led to a lively debate on the pages of the *American Sociological Review* (see Baum & Powell, 1995 and response by Hannan and his colleagues). Similarly, network analysts began to abandon the simple exchange-theoretic framework of the resource dependence paradigm in order to incorporate more institutional processes, just as institutional analysts began to accord more attention to interorganizational networks and diffusion processes

(Strang & Meyer, 1993). Even interpretive approaches to organizational phenomena, long side-lined by the Stanford tradition, enjoyed a renaissance as organizational sociologists experienced a new-found interest in culture and the micro-foundations of the "West Coast" frameworks.

More tellingly, the 1990s witnessed substantial changes in the core concepts of the classic Stanford paradigms of organizational analysis. Consider the traditional approaches to defining *organizational forms* within the ecological perspective, which emphasized either internal "blueprints" – routines for transforming inputs into organizational products or responses (Hannan & Freeman, 1977, p. 935) – or external "resource niches" – combinations of social, political, or economic conditions that would sustain a particular type of organization (Hannan & Carroll, 1995). By the end of the decade, both conceptions had largely been replaced by constructivist definitions of organizational forms that hewed more closely to institutional ideas. For instance, I defined forms as (potentially empty) cells in a discourse space among field participants who were advocating ways of organizing their activities in a specific arena (Ruef, 2000). Pólos and his colleagues introduced the idea of "cultural codes" to denote ways that audiences classify organizations and sanction deviance from categorical schemata (Pólos, Hannan, & Carroll, 2002). Both definitions reflected a bricolage of pre-existing ideas in organizational ecology and institutional theory, as well as in fields outside of sociology (especially, cognitive psychology).

In Stanford's lineage of organization studies, if the 1990s were an era of mixing organizational paradigms in order to launch new concepts and hypotheses or rework old ones, what would the future bring? While some might argue that an assessment of the latest decade of "West Coast" organizational sociology is premature, I would submit that many of the most exciting recent developments have occurred not *within* organization studies, per se, but at the *intersection* of this field with other major domains in sociology and economics. This cross-fertilization was already in abundant display when I returned to Stanford in 2002, as a faculty member in the Graduate School of Business. The rapprochement between the sociology of organizations and social movement analysis, spearheaded at Stanford by Dick Scott and Doug McAdam, was one prominent example (see Davis, McAdam, Scott, & Zald, 2005). Another was the intersection of the sociology of science and organization theory, in particular, the research by Woody Powell and his colleagues around the topic of university–industry interfaces (e.g. Colyvas & Powell, 2007). The subfields of social stratification and education also come to mind, though these have a longer heritage of cross-fertilization with organization studies at Stanford (as evidenced by Jim

Baron's early interest in the "new structuralism" and John Meyer's abiding interest in the sociology of education, for instance).

To summarize, we might describe the development of Stanford's frameworks of organizational analysis in four rough stages: (a) initial development of three or four central paradigms (starting in the 1970s); (b) incremental refinement and integration of ideas *within* each paradigm (1980s); (c) cross-fertilization *across* paradigms (1990s); and (d) cross-fertilization with other subfields of sociology (various starting points, but with an increasing number of subfields over time). Other chronologies are possible, of course, but the question I would pose is whether this particular sequence offers a successful recipe for scientific research programs, considered at a more abstract level. Based on my experiences as a graduate student at Stanford between 1993 and 1998, I would suggest that it does. Having a critical mass of competing schools of thought – more than one but no more than half-a-dozen in Randall Collins' (1998) "law of small numbers" – seems crucial to most intellectual movements. By the time of my entry into Stanford's Ph.D. program, this critical mass provided plenty of energy and lively debates among grad students, but not an excess of material to master on qualifying exams. Having the intellectual founders of these schools of thought in the same geographic location also mattered, since it encouraged cross-fertilization among paradigms at a point when many research programs enter a degenerative phase. Finally, I think it propitious that the carriers of the Stanford tradition have embraced a growing interest in the impact of formal organizations on society as a whole. This will serve to identify points of intersection with other subfields of the discipline and highlight the relevance of organizational sociology for future generations of students.

NOTES

1. The PhD students in Dick's "medical organizations group" have since gone on to become professors of sociology or senior researchers themselves. Carol Caronna teaches sociology at Towson University in Maryland and Junko Takagi teaches at the ESSEC Business School in Paris. Peter Mendel works as a social scientist at the RAND corporation. Seth Pollack is a faculty member and director of the Service Learning Institute at California State University, Monterey Bay. Randi Cohen leads Beetrix, a research and consulting firm she started in 2000. Sammie Speigner taught at Birmingham Southern College, but died tragically in 2005.

2. The scare quotes around "West Coast" are not merely incidental but reflect the complicated geography of the Stanford tradition of organization studies. Some key contributors, such as Michael Hannan, who was at Cornell from 1984 until 1991, spent a considerable amount of time at other institutions during the formative years of their frameworks for organizational analysis. Other scholars associated with

a "West Coast" paradigm, such Oliver Williamson, actually developed their ideas at East Coast institutions (the University of Pennsylvania and Yale in the case of Williamson and transaction cost economics). Still others who have occasionally been identified with the Stanford tradition (e.g. John Freeman or Paul DiMaggio) were never at the university. A unifying geographic feature of the tradition, however, involves the elder statesmen – W. Richard Scott, Jim March, and John Meyer – who spent most (or all) of their careers at Stanford University.

REFERENCES

Baum, J., & Oliver, C. (1996). Toward an institutional ecology of organizational founding. *Academy of Management Journal, 39*, 1378–1427.

Baum, J., & Powell, W. W. (1995). Cultivating an institutional ecology of organizations: Comment on Hannan, Carroll, Dundon, and Torres. *American Sociological Review, 60*, 529–538.

Caronna, C., Pollack, S., & Scott, W. R. (2009). Organizations, populations, and fields: Investigating organizational heterogeneity through a multilevel case study design. *Research in the Sociology of Organizations, 26*, 249–270.

Cohen, M., & Sproull, L. (1995). *Organizational learning*. Thousand Oaks, CA: Sage.

Collins, R. (1998). *The sociology of the philosophies: A global theory of intellectual change*. Cambridge, MA: Harvard University Press.

Colyvas, J., & Powell, W. W. (2007). From vulnerable to venerated: The institutionalization of academic entrepreneurship in the life sciences. *Research in the Sociology of Organizations, 25*, 219–259.

Davis, G., McAdam, D., Scott, W. R., & Zald, M. (2005). *Social movements and organization theory*. Cambridge: Cambridge University Press.

DiMaggio, P., & Powell, W. W. (Eds). (1991). *The new institutionalism in organizational analysis*. Chicago: University of Chicago Press.

Hannan, M. T., & Carroll, G. R. (1995). An introduction to organizational ecology. In: G. Carroll & M. Hannan (Eds), *Organizations in industry: Strategy, structure, and selection* (pp. 17–31). New York: Oxford University Press.

Hannan, M. T., & Freeman, J. (1977). The population ecology of organizations. *American Journal of Sociology, 82*, 929–964.

Hannan, M. T., & Freeman, J. (1989). *Organizational ecology*. Cambridge, MA: Harvard University Press.

Lakatos, I. (1978). *The methodology of scientific research programmes: Philosophical papers* (Vol. 1). Cambridge: Cambridge University Press.

Pólos, L., Hannan, M. T., & Carroll, G. R. (2002). Foundations of a theory of social forms. *Industrial and Corporate Change, 11*, 85–115.

Ruef, M. (2000). The emergence of organizational forms: A community ecology approach. *American Journal of Sociology, 106*, 658–714.

Scott, W. R., Ruef, M., Mendel, P., & Caronna, C. (2000). *Institutional change and healthcare organizations: From professional dominance to managed care*. Chicago: University of Chicago Press.

Strang, D., & Meyer, J. (1993). Institutional conditions for diffusion. *Theory and Society, 22*, 487–511.

CHAPTER 26

CHANCE ENCOUNTERS, ECOLOGIES OF IDEAS, AND CAREER PATHS: A PERSONAL NARRATIVE OF MY STANFORD YEARS ☆

Jitendra V. Singh

CHANCE EVENTS AND CAREER PATHS

As I have reflected upon the last thirty years, since it was precisely thirty years ago that I started as a student at Stanford, I have wondered if there is an overall theme to how my professional career has unfolded and the role Stanford played in it. I believe Albert Bandura's (1982) paper, *The Psychology of Chance Encounters and Life Paths*, provides a good descriptive framework to work with. I am persuaded that at various points of time as I stood at the proverbial fork in the road, due to one chance factor or another, my decision was tipped one way. This is not to suggest that my

☆This first draft of this chapter was written while I was Dean of Nanyang Business School at Nanyang Technological University in Singapore. Prof. W. Brian Arthur, who was visiting that institution as Nanyang Professor at the time, made many useful suggestions on an earlier draft, and Frank Dobbin offered several judicious editorial suggestions, which have improved the chapter. I am grateful to both for their help.

Stanford's Organization Theory Renaissance, 1970–2000
Research in the Sociology of Organizations, Volume 28, 395–408
Copyright © 2010 by Emerald Group Publishing Limited
All rights of reproduction in any form reserved
ISSN: 0733-558X/doi:10.1108/S0733-558X(2010)0000028030

career has been a sequence of random events; quite the contrary. While the specific fortuitous events occurred largely outside my control, my responses to them were quite systematic; some fortuitous events had lasting influence, and some even changed my life trajectory. But, what I am struck by, ex post, is that in 1973, as I was just finishing my undergraduate education in India, the ex ante probability of my ending up some years later as a professor at an Ivy League university was essentially zero. Yet, this did eventually happen.

What is intriguing is how with each one of these sequentially occurring chance encounters or events, my career trajectory got changed just a little, my intellectual capital accreted just a little differently over the next few years, and the opportunity landscape got altered in turn, quite significantly on occasion. And I, of course, by putting one foot in front of the other, eventually arrived at the present. Of course, it goes without saying that being part of the dense intellectual ecology at Stanford significantly raised my base rate of encountering ideas and opportunities to innovate.

I believe the descriptive narrative of my career, such as it has been, bears testimony to the power of evolutionary processes, and the complex roles played by chance factors, the occasional decision points, and my ongoing attempts to learn from experience, sometimes successfully, given the noisy world we live in, and the always present and important shaping influence of environmental contexts. Given this world view, perhaps it was not entirely surprising that I ended up as a student of Jim March.

I arrived at Stanford in fall 1979 as a doctoral student in *Organizational Theory and Behavior* in the Graduate School of Business and stayed there until the end of 1982. Truth be told, I did not have much of a history of thinking seriously about theoretical ideas, much less doing research. I had until recently before Stanford been a practicing executive in India after my MBA. Indeed, even my introduction to the world of business schools was of recent vintage and rather accidental. I had been a student of Physics, Mathematics, and Statistics as an undergraduate at Lucknow University in my hometown in India, the capital city of the largest state in India, and I was rather inclined to pursue the beauty and elegance of particle Physics as a career choice. But chance intervened.

Even as I was wondering as a teenager about what to do with the rest of my life, I heard from a fellow student about a new institution, the Indian Institute of Management, Ahmedabad (IIMA), located out in western India. As I gathered more information about IIMA, I was quite struck by how, once there, I would have the opportunity to learn about all kinds of interesting new subjects like Psychology and Economics, quite in addition to the usual disciplines of business. This seemed to be a splendid opportunity to learn in new areas; not entirely coincidentally, it was also a convenient excuse to leave home for the first time and journey out on my own into the world beyond.

My two years at IIMA were a life altering experience. It was then, as now, the most selective business school in the world (the current admit percentage is a small fraction of one percent; it was just above one percent back in 1973 when I entered their MBA program) and the quality of the top students was quite exceptional. But the most enduring influence for me was of one of my OB professors, Pulin Garg, who went on to become my mentor and lifelong friend. I stayed in touch with him until his death a few years ago. He was a veritable genius when it came to his understanding of human behavior. I believe it was his influence as a role model that brought me to the US a few years later as a Ph.D. student at Stanford GSB, since he was himself a UC, Berkeley Ph.D.

Just as I was quite privileged to spend two years at IIMA, I believe I was equally fortunate to study at Stanford. Given the early links of IIMA with Harvard Business School, HBS was spoken of almost reverentially back in India, and was often the natural first choice for IIMA graduates. Indeed, in fall 1979, I had to choose between Stanford GSB, HBS, and Carnegie Mellon's GSIA, among other schools, for my Ph.D. I chose to come to Stanford, and, in retrospect, I believe it was the right decision. This gave me the chance to become a member of one of the most productive organizational research communities anywhere in the world at a time when this community was, as some have later observed, near or at its most fertile. This was for me a great opportunity to learn and be a minor participant in a superlative ecology of ideas.

In this short essay, I want to trace back to its roots in the Stanford community the evolution of my own development as a scholar. I will address four themes in the rest of this essay: one, in the rich intellectual context of the Stanford community, which paradigms and people were most influential in shaping both the content and process of my thinking; two, what were the main theoretical ideas that had the most enduring influence on my later research; three, what did I learn about the process of doing research that has stayed with me over the years, or, put differently what was the Stanford imprint on me; and, finally, what were the reasons, from my perspective as a graduate student, for the unusual success of the Stanford organizations research community, and what lessons might this experience hold for others.

PARADIGMS AND PERSONALITIES

One of the most remarkable aspects of the Stanford context was the sheer richness of the intellectual resources that were available not only within the organizations research community, but in several conjugate areas. I thrived in the diversity of it all. As will become clearer below, these became the building blocks of my own later intellectual development.

One of my earliest introductions to the organizations area was Dick Scott's introductory course (Formal Organizations, SOC 160, if I remember right), a masterful survey of organizational sociology. I had as an MBA some years earlier been introduced to organization theory in the form of Charles Perrow's introductory textbook, but this was an opportunity to dive deeper. The content of this course eventually became Dick Scott's Organizations: Rational, Natural and Open Systems, now a must read textbook for all graduate students of organization theory. As I recall, Dick did not permit classroom discussion, since the course was in lecture format. But I do remember that I used to ask many questions, perhaps breaking his rule, although I hope I was not an inordinate nuisance.

One other set of early influences came from the Psychology department. Kahneman and Tversky had recently published their paper on prospect theory in *Econometrica* (Kahneman & Tversky, 1979). There was a buzz in the Stanford air that they would one day win the Nobel Prize in Economics, since Herbert Simon had won it just the previous year, signaling an openness by the Nobel Prize committee to Economics related work in conjugate areas such as behavioral research in decision making (as had been predicted by many, this did eventually happen in 2002 although, unfortunately, Amos Tversky had died prematurely a few years earlier in 1996; Kahneman publicly acknowledged that surely both would have been awarded the Nobel Prize for their joint work, if only Amos were still alive, and this cast a shadow on his own award). So I enrolled in Tversky's Psychology of Decision Making course (PSYCH 256, as I recall) and was quite struck by the simplicity and elegance of the experimental work he had done with Daniel Kahneman, among others, showing how decision-making behavior frequently departed from some fundamental assumptions about human rationality commonly used in economic approaches. In time, as I learned more about Jim March's work and the Carnegie tradition of research in behavioral decision making, some of it done together with stalwarts like Herbert Simon and Dick Cyert, among others, I was quite influenced by it. I was later to integrate parts of these two bodies of work into one important pillar of my own thinking in my dissertation research.

I took yet another foray into experimental social psychology in a graduate course with Lee Ross and Mark Lepper, both professors at the Stanford Psychology department. This was a fascinating introduction for me to the experimental approach in psychology. Some of this body of work was synthesized in Nisbett and Ross' quite well-known book, *Human Inference: Strategies and Shortcomings in Social Judgment* (Nisbett & Ross, 1980.) While I chose eventually to go in a more "macro" direction for my Ph.D. thesis, in my first two years I had been equally steeped in both Psychology and Sociology, and could just as easily have gone in a more "micro" direction, likely ending up with a rather different career path.

After Dick Scott's introductory course in organization theory, my next in-depth experience of organizations research was a graduate course with Jeff Pfeffer at GSB where I was first introduced to his work on resource dependence theory (Pfeffer & Salancik, 1978), Meyer and Rowan's work on institutionalization theory (Meyer & Rowan, 1977), Williamson's theories of transaction cost economics (Williamson, 1975), and Hannan and Freeman's paper on population ecology (Hannan & Freeman, 1977), among others. While every perspective had interesting insights to offer, I was particularly taken with institutionalization theory on the one hand and population ecology on the other. In time, these ideas were also to become building blocks of my own thinking, although I did not quite know it at the time.

Rather early during my stay at Stanford, I had encountered some of Jim March's writings. As I recall, one of his first papers I read was "The Technology of Foolishness." I was quite entranced. It was not just the substance of the paper, which was clearly deep, perhaps even profound. I was also quite taken with his elegant writing style. There seemed to be wisdom in his words.

Never having been much of a shrinking violet, I figured I would go and meet the man. With some trepidation in my heart, one fine morning I went and knocked at the door of his GSB office. At the time, I did not even know what he looked like. He opened the door and stood there, looking rather quizzically, though not unkindly, at me. As I remember, in a not particularly sophisticated manner, I blurted out how much I admired his writings and how much I would like to work with him on some research. He smiled and said that he did not have any research assistant openings at the time, but he would be glad to keep me in mind. In the meantime, he invited me to attend his doctoral seminar which was in progress at the time. This was the rather humble beginning to what was to become for me the most important intellectual relationship at Stanford. Both intellectually and socially, Jim was a constant positive factor during my stay there. I have always been grateful for him having taken me under his wing. It was with him, on our many regular walks together through Stanford campus under the fragrant eucalyptus trees that I really learned to think on my own and how to pursue a research idea to its conclusion, a remarkable echo of the millennia old *guru-shishya parampara* (literally, teacher–student tradition) Indian tradition.

Although I did not work directly with Mike Hannan, who was a professor in the Stanford Sociology department, I did take a research methods course with him. That was my introduction to structural models and issues of research design in nonexperimental studies. Later, just as I was finishing my dissertation at Stanford, one of the last courses I did was with Nancy Tuma, also from the Stanford Sociology department, on dynamic modeling. Terry Amburgey was her teaching assistant and a general factotum on their new program for estimating transition rate models, RATE. He went on in later years to become a good friend and coauthor. This material for this course eventually became Tuma and Hannan's influential textbook on dynamic models (Tuma & Hannan, 1984). Although I did not know it at the time, this knowledge of dynamic modeling would later become quite critical in my future research.

There were as well other influences at GSB that were not all directly linked with the organizations research community but which gave me a solid background in behavioral research, in research inquiry, and in econometrics and multivariate statistics. Some of this coursework in behavioral issues was with Peter Wright and Michael Ray in Marketing and Joanne Martin in OB, and there were outstanding foundations provided in econometrics by Dave Montgomery and in multivariate statistics by Seenu Srinivasan, both professors of Marketing at Stanford GSB. The last two have remained friends and colleagues to this day, with our paths crossing several times in different parts of the world.

I also have very fond memories of the late Gene Webb, who taught a Ph.D. seminar in individual behavior. What I remember most distinctly is one incident that influenced my subsequent thinking on how to ask research questions. One day in class, he asked us rhetorically, "Colleagues, how do you think a geologist decides what rock he should study? Does he just walk out of his front door and pick up any which rock, and then proceed to study it?" Pausing for effect, he then said, "No. What makes a rock worthy of study is *what questions intersect in the existence of that rock?*" This was quite a revelation to me, because it meant that even before starting to research a topic, it was important to consider whether the research question was worth asking. Clearly, some questions were more worthwhile than others, with only some questions worthy of serious, careful attention. By implication, effort, energy and time were more fruitfully deployed in some directions than in others. This was another important building block for me.

SOME INFLUENTIAL IDEAS

I noted earlier that I reveled in the intellectual diversity of the Stanford community. While some of the directions I pursued were voluntary, as with my forays into the Psychology and Sociology departments, I was required as a graduate student in the business school and as part of the Ph.D. program at GSB to take certain courses. This included Microeconomics, which I did with Larry Lau from the Economics department (I met him recently out in Asia, where he is now President of Chinese University of Hong Kong), and Single Person Decision Theory, which I did with Dave Kreps, an Economics professor at GSB. While these domains were not directly related to my subsequent research, they did provide me with some appreciation for the more formal, analytical approach often taken by economists. Clearly, my first two years at Stanford gave me a quite broad theoretical background ranging from Sociology to Psychology, with foundations in research methods, both experimental and nonexperimental, and tools from econometrics, multivariate statistics, and dynamic analysis to help answer research questions in rigorous ways. In retrospect, this was one thing that the Stanford GSB doctoral training did extremely well: provide strong methodological foundations, and a broad exposure to diverse theoretical ideas which would create fertile ground for the creation of new ideas. The organizations research community provided a rich ecology of ideas in which to put this training to good use. In part, this occurred in the form of very productive research assistantships with Jerry Porras and Don Palmer, both OB faculty members at GSB.

The next question was what I should do for my dissertation. Several factors were instrumental in my ultimate choice of thesis topic. By now, I had a strong, supportive mentoring relationship with Jim March, so it was natural that I sought him out as my thesis adviser. As for the other committee members, I would, almost certainly, have wanted Jeff Pfeffer as a member of my thesis committee, since I had also been his research assistant. (He had very kindly created space for me to work on my own research.) Unfortunately, he was on sabbatical at Harvard Business School the year (1981–1982) I was ramping up work on my thesis (I also had this somewhat fixed, though, in retrospect, perhaps unwise, idea, that I should graduate from Stanford as quickly as possible, hopefully in three years, which meant that I would have been nearing completion by the time he returned from Harvard.) Dick Scott, who had also been my mentor at Stanford, was another member of my thesis committee. Jay Bourgeois, a member of the Strategy group at GSB, had done some work on operationalizing the measurement of organizational slack, and I had also been doing some research with him. Since my thesis involved organizational slack as a variable in the model, I invited Jay to be the third member of my thesis committee.

In my thesis, I asked at the organizational level the question Kahneman and Tversky (1979) had raised at the individual level in their prospect theory: do firms that perform below aspiration levels take riskier strategic decisions? Clearly, Cyert and March (1963) had also raised this question several years ago. And, more recently, March and Shapira (1982) had reiterated this. My contribution was to create a structural model in which this direct effect of risk seeking by firms performing below aspiration levels was supplemented by an indirect effect by which better performing firms had more organizational slack, which, in turn, influenced risk taking positively. A test of this model in a secondary analysis of cross-sectional field data showed broad support for the main predictions. I successfully defended my dissertation in March 1983. I am proud to this day that Amos Tversky was the Chairman of my university oral defense. He asked some quite tough questions but I did manage to pass muster. A paper based in this work appeared in print some years later (Singh, 1986), and became, in time, part of a small body of work in Strategy on related questions.

The real strength of my Stanford training was to provide me with significant "genetic variety," as it were, and an approach to research inquiry that was not unduly fettered by disciplinary boundaries. What mattered most was asking interesting questions, and I was happy to go wherever they led me. My thesis research was just the first of several instances in which I recombined some building blocks from the proximate ecology of ideas at Stanford in ways to create new insights. Other such ideas would follow in time.

While my exposure to the world of ideas at Stanford was quite broad, some of them influenced my thinking much more than others. One influential theme was the behavioral critique of neoclassical economic thinking, starting with March and Simon (1958) and continuing in the work of March and other colleagues, and joined more recently in the work of Kahneman and Tversky. But I also found very appealing Meyer and Rowan's (1977) paper on institutionalization theory, particularly the importance of legitimacy for organizational survival. I found Hannan and Freeman's (1977) essay on the population ecology of organizations remarkably original and provocative, with a vision of organizational evolution that I was quite sympathetic to myself. These ideas would keep featuring in my work over the next few years.

In early 1983, even as I was just about finished with my thesis research, I took an Assistant Professor position at the University of Toronto in what is now the Rotman School of Management. Almost immediately upon my arrival, I was invited by Bob House, a senior colleague at University of Toronto and a well-known leadership researcher, and David Tucker, who was housed upstairs in the same building in the Social Work department, to join their research team on a project studying a cohort of voluntary social service organizations (VSSOs) in Toronto. Although I did not at the time know much about their research, I said "yes" anyway. It later transpired that all the coursework I had been doing on dynamic models with Nancy Tuma and Mike Hannan was exactly what was needed next in this project. Dave Tucker had very diligently gathered data of the creation and demise of these VSSOs, and I brought to the table a complementary set of theoretical and modeling skills that culminated successfully in a stream of several papers (see, for example, Singh, House, & Tucker, 1986; Singh, Tucker, & House, 1986; Singh, Tucker, & Meinhard, 1991; Tucker, Singh, & Meinhard, 1990). Howard Aldrich from UNC, Chapel Hill, and Paul DiMaggio, then at Yale, were valuable external resources in our research efforts. Since this was still an early stage in the history of organizational ecology, ours were among a few of the earliest empirical studies in the literature, and this attracted some favorable critical attention from the research community. As I think back, the interplay of institutional factors and ecological dynamics played a significant role in several of these papers, emphasizing once again the crucial importance of the theoretical and methodological building blocks I had acquired as a graduate student at Stanford.

LESSONS LEARNED AT STANFORD

At the risk of sounding overly formulaic, even mechanistic, I want to turn my attention next to some lasting lessons that have stayed with me over the years from my Stanford experience. But first, a brief detour: I want to address whether there was a signature Stanford approach to organizations research. In my view, while there was not one singular Stanford paradigm as far as the content of the theories went, there was perhaps a greater unity of beliefs around the process of doing research, which I address below. There were multiple theoretical approaches – resource dependence theory, population ecology theory, institutionalization theory, behavioral decision making, to pick a few – and they all had their adherents, including doctoral students doing the next generation of research. What was notable, however, was the tolerance, even encouragement, in the research community for quite different ideas. The overarching commitment, as I experienced it, was to rigor and high quality.

As for values about the research process, it is unclear to me if anyone had actually consciously planned for students to graduate with a particular set of beliefs in this domain, although the GSB doctoral program did insist on the general program requirements (to some, the dreaded GPRs), a sequence of required courses that laid a common foundation for all doctoral students, regardless of their chosen field. Given the emergent quality of these research values, it was likely that that no two students took away exactly identical lessons. What I learned was as much my way of integrating the multiple influences that surrounded me as it was a product of the environment; it was an active rather than a passive process.

Although I cannot definitively trace the origins of each one of the values below to specific events or people at Stanford, below are some of the process lessons that I took away from my experience. Inevitably, they are just as likely the result of role modeling by people I particularly admired, as the result of papers that were particularly influential in my thinking:

- *The importance of quality over quantity.* It is all right to have some ideas that do not see the light of day if they are not good enough; a quality distribution in the output of the creative process is inevitable, with a right and a left tail; the trick is to sample from the right tail; Jim March was the best exemplar for me here.
- *the importance of not taking disciplinary boundaries too seriously.* What is important is to focus on the phenomenon, and to follow the questions where they lead; the ultimate goal is understanding and insight, and that is what matters; once again, Jim March was a role model here.
- *The importance of testing competing theoretical models.* Such a "strong inference" (Platt, 1964) approach may not always be feasible, but, when feasible, it is a powerful way to go; Jeff Pfeffer emphasized this repeatedly in his seminar.
- *The importance of hardnosed empirical evidence over ideology or favorite theories.* If rigorous study suggests that a theory is wrong, and most alternative explanations can be ruled out, it probably is wrong, as discomfiting as that may be; this was an important theme in Jeff Pfeffer's seminar.
- *Creative ideas do not happen in a vacuum.* One mother lode process underlying innovative thinking consists of Schumpeterian recombinations

of existing blocks or "chunks," and then selecting from among them the more interesting or insightful ones; but there is no shortcut to acquiring those blocks in the first place, which takes persistent effort.

• *There are no superior or inferior research methods, which method is most appropriate depends on the question being asked.* Each method, even when executed to perfection, has its limitations; if one wants to be really complete and rigorous, it is useful to use multiple methods to tackle the same question in different ways. This was crystallized in Joanne Martin's introduction to Joseph McGrath's work on the "dilemmatics of research" in her Ph.D. seminar.

It is now over 26 years since I left Stanford. As I reflect back on the body of work that I have done, I believe these values above are often reflected in it. I have enjoyed working on questions in organizational decision making, organizational ecology, organizational learning, technology, strategy, entrepreneurship, multinational organizations, and health care using quantitative and qualitative methods, simulation techniques and direct interviews, theory building, and case studies. My interests have led me in recent years into China and India, and, with a group of Wharton colleagues I have just finished a book on Indian business leadership called "The India Way" (Cappelli, Singh, Singh, & Useem, 2010) It has been an enjoyable journey of discovery. And I believe the journey is not quite over yet.

So, What Was the Secret Sauce at Stanford?

I think there would be little argument from most people in the organizations area that the Stanford example stands out as one of the great flowerings of organizational research in recent decades. Perhaps the only other comparable setting may have been Carnegie Mellon in its heyday, although that body of work was arguably built around a tighter paradigm, without quite the theoretical diversity of the Stanford community. I suspect that is arguable, but, importantly, it does not take away from the success of either institution.

I want to offer here my speculations for what had made the Stanford organizations research community as successful and influential as it has been. While I recognize that others may have different views that may also be valid, to me some of the highlights were:

• Perhaps by design, during the years I was at Stanford, and I think some years before and after, I think there was *a healthy, thriving ecosystem* supporting the pursuit of organizational ideas; there were multiple actors involved, every one of them playing specialized, complementary roles, but a small number of actors played critical roles and were the quiet anchors of the community.

- In my experience (while I have no desire to make less of anyone's contributions, some people stood out), *two of the key anchors of the community were Dick Scott and Jim March*; their roles sometimes required altruistic actions on their part, usually at significant personal cost, but they could always be counted on to deliver.
- There was also a very *important cultural component*, I think, of respect for diverse, even differing points of view; it was not necessary for someone to be wrong in order for someone else to be right; and this was communicated and reinforced by quite public role modeling behavior by key players on numerous occasions.
- As is often the case in robust, thriving ecosystems, there was *a great deal of "genetic variety" of ideas*; the clear implication here, of course, is that if that genetic variety were diminished, with any one particular perspective dominating the discourse, the health of the ecosystem would falter, making it more vulnerable, overall.
- But this *tolerance of differences was never a defense against poor quality*; there was always a quality of hardheadedness about the usual discourse, with clear norms of calling a spade a spade, though sometimes with a deft, even diplomatic touch, and a dash of humor, as I saw Jim March, for instance, demonstrate on multiple occasions.

By way of lessons for other institutions, I would underscore the metaphor of a thriving ecosystem, a healthy ecology of ideas. The spirit of designing the community is much less akin to building a cathedral, and much more to growing a bazaar, which, while sometimes appearing disorganized, even chaotic, continually adapts dynamically at the edges to an uncertainly changing context, often through decentralized experimentation. While many interconnected building blocks and resources are necessary, the cultural component is critical, with community leaders playing crucial roles as models. Clearly, this is not easy to accomplish, which is perhaps why we do not see such intellectual flowerings with greater frequency. Yet it can and does happen, though the perspective involves a modesty of ambition, an acknowledgement of the limits of human prescience, and a belief in the power of evolutionary processes.

In summary, I believe I was very fortunate to have been a member of the Stanford organizations community, and it proved a turning point in my career. The simplest way to put it is this: my stay at Stanford was like being in an orchard which was planned and planted by others, with the full realization that they would not be the prime beneficiaries of the fruit; while the costs were largely theirs, the benefits would go mainly to others. And I and many others who benefited from this thank them for their generosity, even altruism. What I am left with is the keen recognition that this debt cannot be repaid; it can only be passed on to the next generation. Perhaps that is why I have been involved in recent years in the creation of the Indian School of Business in Hyderabad, India, and in the founding of Singapore Management University in Singapore, both with help from Wharton, and why I was for the last two years (2007–2009) Dean of Nanyang Business School in Singapore. Perhaps these are my modest efforts to pay it forward.

REFERENCES

Bandura, A. (1982). The psychology of chance encounters and life paths. *American Psychologist, 37*(7), 747–755.

Cappelli, P., Singh, H., Singh, J. V., & Useem, M. (2010). *The India Way: How India's business leaders are revolutionizing management.* Boston, MA: Harvard Business Press.

Cyert, R. M., & March, J. G. (1963). *A behavioral theory of the firm.* Englewood Cliffs, NJ: Prentice Hall.

Hannan, M. T., & Freeman, J. (1977). The population ecology of organizations. *American Journal of Sociology, 82*(5), 929–964.

Kahneman, D., & Tversky, A. (1979). Prospect theory: An analysis of decision making under risk. *Econometrica, 47*(2), 263–292.

Nisbett, R. E., & Ross, L. (1980). *Human inference: Strategies and shortcomings of social judgment.* Englewood Cliffs, NJ: Prentice Hall.

Pfeffer, J., & Salancik, G. R. (1978). *The external control of organizations: A resource dependence perspective.* New York: Harper & Row.

Platt, J. R. (1964). Strong inference. *Science, 146*(3642), 347–353.

March, J. G., & Shapira, Z. (1982). Behavioral decision theory and organizational decision theory. In: G. Ungson & D. Braunstein (Eds), *New directions in decision making.* Boston, MA: Kent Publishing Co.

March, J. G., & Simon, H. A. (1958). *Organizations.* New York: Wiley.

Meyer, J. W., & Rowan, B. (1977). Institutionalized organizations: Formal structure as myth and ceremony. *American Journal of Sociology, 83*(2), 340–363.

Singh, J. V. (1986). Performance, slack and risk taking in organizational decision making. *Academy of Management Journal, 29*, 562–585.

Singh, J. V., House, R. J., & Tucker, D. J. (1986). Organizational change and organizational mortality. *Administrative Science Quarterly, 31*, 587–611.

Singh, J. V., Tucker, D. J., & House, R. J. (1986). Organizational legitimacy and the liability of newness. *Administrative Science Quarterly, 31*, 171–193.

Singh, J. V., Tucker, D. J., & Meinhard, A. G. (1991). Institutional change and ecological dynamics. In: W. W. Powell & P. DiMaggio (Eds), *The new institutionalism in organizational analysis* (pp. 390–422). Chicago, IL: University of Chicago Press.

408   JITENDRA V. SINGH

Tucker, D. J., Singh, J. V., & Meinhard, A. G. (1990). Organizational form, population dynamics, and institutional change: A study of founding patterns of voluntary organizations. *Academy of Management Journal, 33,* 151–178.

Tuma, N. B., & Hannan, M. T. (1984). *Social dynamics: Models and methods.* Orlando, FL: Academic Press.

Williamson, O. E. (1975). *Markets and hierarchies: Analysis and antitrust implications.* New York: Free Press.

CHAPTER 27

SENSE-MAKING IN ORGANIZATIONAL RESEARCH

Sim B. Sitkin

Two strikingly distinct perspectives on organizations are captured well by the distinction between logics of "rationality" and logics of "appropriateness" (March, 1994; March & Olsen, 2006). In this essay, I will focus on the latter perspective as reflecting an important theme running through the work at Stanford starting with the late 1970s, and a theme that has provided a guiding lens through which virtually all of my work has viewed organizations and their members. The logic of appropriateness is essentially a sense-making approach (Weick, 1995) that builds on the recognition that individuals are most typically boundedly rational and guided by habit and norm, and that organizations are more typically guided by rules and practices grounded in institutional logics than economic rationality (March & Simon, 1958; Meyer & Rowan, 1977; Scott, 1987, 2008).

Such an approach does not deny the value of the rational – not for the organizational member, the organizational manager, nor the observing organizational scholar – but it does suggest that even when there is a desire to be rational, the complex and changing world of organizations can make it all but impossible to do better than rely upon history, habits, and heuristics to cope ... thus implying that the main task at hand is that of sense-making rather than truth-finding.

Stanford's Organization Theory Renaissance, 1970–2000
Research in the Sociology of Organizations, Volume 28, 409–418
Copyright © 2010 by Emerald Group Publishing Limited
All rights of reproduction in any form reserved
ISSN: 0733-558X/doi:10.1108/S0733-558X(2010)0000028031

SEEING MY OWN WORK THROUGH
A SENSE-MAKING LENS

My own work reflects an attempt to understand organizational processes as, at their core, the process of pursuing or facilitating sense-making. Organizational members make sense of complex, changing conditions. Organizational systems and organizational leaders can be seen as serving the role of facilitating or impeding sense-making (Sitkin, Lind, & Siang, 2006).

Control in Organizations

My more macro research has examined formal and informal control systems and how those emerge from and guide individual and collective cognition, behavior, and effect. In my work on "legalistic organizations" (e.g., Sitkin, 1995; Sitkin & Bies, 1993, 1994), I drew on Stanford's institutional theory and resource dependence traditions to examine how organizations facing uncertainty adopt the trappings of the formal legal system in order to obtain legitimacy. In my work on the adoption of formal control systems (e.g., TQM), I examined how the mere development of a shared terminology, set of expectations, and commonly framed objectives could have significant clarifying and legitimating effects on organizational innovations (e.g., Sitkin, Sutcliffe, & Schroeder, 1994; Sutcliffe, Sitkin, & Browning, 2000). By taking ambiguous – or sometimes even clearly negative – circumstances (e.g., keeping shame-laden secrets and hiding illegal acts) and draping them in the cloak of formal appropriateness, organizations can obtain and sustain trust and support from internal and external constituencies (Sitkin & Sutcliffe, 1991; Sitkin, Sutcliffe, & Reed, 1993).

In my more recent work on how formal and informal control systems and their component parts emerge, reconfigure, and are eliminated, I build on roots in Stanford's organizational ecology (Hannan & Freeman, 1977) and organization design (Pfeffer, 1978) work. The evolutionary process of variation–selection–retention was not distinctive to Stanford, but its application to understanding organization change processes was significantly influenced by Stanford's work. So too was my emphasis on combining the formal and informal drawn directly from roots in Stanford's intellectual climate of the 1980s in which organizational sociology's focus on the establishment of formal structures and procedures that foster perceived legitimacy (e.g., Meyer & Rowan, 1977; Scott, 1987, 1995) was coupled with a strong stream of work focusing on how cultural norms were manifest in a variety of informal social mechanisms that conveyed and sustained a sense of organizational legitimacy (e.g., Martin, Feldman, Hatch, & Sitkin, 1983; Martin, Sitkin, & Boehm, 1985).

Organizational research on control has gone underground for nearly three decades, in part because Ouchi's (1977, 1978, 1979) strong research contribution unintentionally created an impression in the field that research on control had been largely explored, and also because the generative implications of his markets, hierarchies, and clans framework were under-appreciated. Over the past two decades, I have initiated efforts to revitalize this area of the field as being one of the fundamental aspects of organizations. As demonstrated in a recent volume on new directions in organizational control (Sitkin, Cardinal, & Bijlsma-Frankema, 2010), this is a potentially vibrant and burgeoning area of research – and one that derived a good deal of its intellectual energy from a Stanford legacy.

Stanford faculty and former students have contributed in numerous ways to specific theories and findings concerning organizational structure, procedures, and culture. Yet, at its core, the reemergence of control research in organizations is, in my view, about the role that control plays in helping organizational members and external constituencies to make sense of the organization. Structures and practices reflect mission and strategy, manifest underlying assumptions and norms, and help direct attention and guide interpretation. In short, what control systems do in organizations is make sense of the confusing, and channel belief and behaviors in ways that are more readily interpretable. This framing of control owes a debt to the Stanford legacy.

Leadership in Organizations

Most recently, I have begun working on issues concerning how organizational leader's actions influence follower responses. This work has obvious roots in Stanford-based research on legitimate authority (Dornbusch & Scott, 1975), symbolic management (Martin et al., 1985; Peters, 1978; Pfeffer, 1977, 1981a), and power (Cohen & March, 1974; March, 1966; Pfeffer, 1981b).

While the Stanford approach to leadership typically involved a great skepticism about the power of leaders and instead emphasized the power of organizational conditions (Davis-Blake & Pfeffer, 1989; March, 1966; Martin et al., 1983, 1985), I have come to see that work in a new light as I began to do more research myself in this domain. Specifically, one critical aspect of leader effects concerns the ability of the leader to help others see more clearly and coherently, to understand more deeply. In a sense, this view of leadership is that of a teacher and guide, helping others in and around the organization to fill in missing information, correct misunderstandings, and see otherwise hidden or obtuse connections – in other words, the leader as a sense-maker.

Strong situations (Davis-Blake & Pfeffer, 1989) may channel organizational member and even leader actions, but even strong situations are not necessarily transparent or readily interpreted. If they were, we would see more articles on managers as intuitive sociologists, but I have come across very few such articles. Thus, leaders function as much to shape the interpretation of organizational conditions as to strategically guide them. This view of leadership is less of the strategic master of the universe and much more of an active thought leader or a tacit puppeteer, shaping the ways in which attention is directed (Ocasio, 1997; March & Simon, 1958) and stories and symbols shape ideas, practices, and effect (Feldman & March, 1981; Martin, 1982; Martin & Powers, 1983; Martin et al., 1983; Peters, 1978; Pfeffer, 1981a). Even when the leader's strategic legacy is elusive (Martin et al., 1985), their framing of language and process can continue to guide the organization and its members for many years (Bies & Sitkin, 1992; Cardinal, Sitkin, & Long, 2004; Sitkin & Bies, 1993, 1994; Sitkin & Stickel, 1995).

Risk Taking, Failure, and Learning in Organizations

Learning is at its core a sense-making process. It does not necessarily require conscious human agency, although it also does not preclude it. My work on learning flowed very naturally from the Stanford traditions in this regard. While some approaches (e.g., Hannan & Freeman, 1977) were pretty explicit about sidestepping individual agency, exploratory variation, the selection of courses of action, and the retention of some paths over others can simply unfold or can be explicitly pursued. But the sense-making aspect of these processes and the factors that can make these processes more or less illuminating was what guided much of my research in this domain. For example, I became interested in better understanding the familiar notion that we learn more from failure than from success (Sitkin, 1992). If failure provided us with more data and experience to make sense of complex issues, then how did that take place? This led me to ask how formal systems of trial and error, learning, and improvement might function in the face of success and failure under more or less clear and understandable conditions (Sitkin et al., 1994).

I also began to question whether dominant notions of risk taking (e.g., Kahneman & Tversky, 1979; Tversky & Kahneman, 1981) were as non-contingent as they were being represented at that time. This led me to explore whether, over time and experience, individuals and organizations might build up a propensity to take or avoid risk (Sitkin & Pablo, 1992; Sitkin & Weingart, 1995) that could also affect the organization's capacity to learn from those risks and successes/failures (Pablo, Jemison, & Sitkin, 1996; Sitkin, Miller, See, Lawless, & Carton, 2009b). It is noteworthy that at the same time I was exploring these issues, Jim March was pursuing very similar themes in the now familiar exploration/exploitation dichotomy (March, 1991; Levinthal & March, 1993).

Critically influential, in terms of my own thinking, was a core notion driving March's early work on learning in organizations (Cyert & March, 1963) as well as his later work (e.g., Levitt & March, 1988; March & Olsen, 1976): the idea that learning is a sense-making process. Learning is not an outcome, but a step along the way. This influenced how I thought about the formulation of corporate acquisition deals (Jemison & Sitkin, 1986; Pablo et al., 1996), and how I thought about error reduction efforts (Sitkin, 1992; Sitkin et al., 1994) and goal setting (Sitkin, 1992; Sitkin et al., 2009a, 2009b). Learning is a set of hypotheses that are tested through action and the acting organism can then either learn or not, and retain the learning or not – but it is an ongoing process of sense-making.

Trust in Organizations

Trust involves the acceptance of "vulnerability based on positive expectations of the intentions or the behavior of another" (Rousseau, Sitkin, Burt, & Camerer, 1998, p. 395), whereas distrust involves the avoidance of vulnerability resulting from "negative expectations of intentions or the behavior of another due to perception of incongruent core values" (Bijlsma-Frankema, Sitkin, & Weibel, 2009). Just how is that acceptance or avoidance of vulnerability and underlying expectations formulated? What determines when trust or distrust is evoked?

My work on trust also builds on the notion of sense-making, especially in terms of perceived values as framed in the organizational culture (Martin, 1992) and institutional theory (Scott, 1995) streams of work. In particular, I draw on March's (1994) logic of rationality/logic of appropriateness typology to distinguish the foundations and functions of trust from those of distrust.

While most of the field views distrust as simply the low end of a single continuum, where the high end is anchored by trust, my view is that they are distinct constructs. I view trust as being grounded in the logic of rationality. Sometimes that rationality is framed as a willingness to rely upon a trustee who is demonstrably competent, reliable, and/or benevolent (Mayer, Davis, & Schoorman, 1995). I suggest that willingness to be vulnerable is qualitatively different when the other party is viewed as "not like me" than when they are seen as similar. If another party does not share my core values or my world view, then a high level of competence or reliability is small comfort since those attributes could simply make for a more effective adversary. Thus, the question I pose with respect to trust and distrust is whether the amelioration of distrust is a necessary prerequisite for trust assessment to commence, or whether trust and distrust can be assessed independently of each other and their joint product determines how high trust can go.

This conception of trust and distrust has clear roots not only in March's distinction, noted above, but also in the conception of an organization having multiple cultures with core and peripheral values that align to varying degrees (Martin, 1992). It also has roots in the notion that institutional indicators of normative legitimacy can have unexpected effects when they also send a signal of non-prototypicality and mismatched core values. These are the issues I continued to explore in terms of institutional stigma (Sitkin & George, 2005; Sitkin & Roth, 1993; Sitkin & Stickel, 1995), the adoption of the normative trappings of legitimacy at the individual (Bies & Sitkin, 1991; Sitkin & Bies, 1993; Sitkin & Sutcliffe, 1991; Sitkin et al., 1993) and organizational levels (Sitkin & Bies, 1994).

THE STANFORD LEGACY: MAKING
SENSE OF AND IN ORGANIZATIONS

I have discussed how four streams of my own work were influenced by one relatively under-emphasized aspect of the Stanford legacy: the pervasive emphasis on sense-making in organizations. I could have just as easily stressed what I see as the distinctive norms and expectations concerning multi-level analysis, the use of multiple research methodologies, and drawing upon a range of disciplinary literatures. But all four streams of my research were influenced significantly by the fundamental role of sense-making in organizations – a conceptual thread that I was not aware of until I began to prepare to write this short essay and make sense of Stanford's influence on my own work.

I would suggest that this notion – that even the seemingly clear and definitive is laced with ambiguity – is a motif that reappears through the work produced by Stanford faculty, students, and visitors during this period and in the years that followed. And it certainly was a motivating force in my own interests and research since that time.

Although I did not realize it until much later in my career, I viewed individual action and organizational processes as working through a filtered glass. That filter made even the sharpest image appear fuzzy and in need of active processing and interpretation. Sometimes the filter distorted in a biased way; sometimes it merely made the signals more faint or fuzzy. But my view was that organizations and their members were always trying to interpret their circumstances in an attempt to ascertain what was happening and how to act.

A single theoretical lens is inadequate for understanding how individuals and organizations make sense of an uncertain, complex, and changing world. Stanford during this period was a fertile research context precisely because it was period of very diverse disciplinary, theoretical, and empirical perspectives. Fiercely argued, but with an open eye to important other work that challenged assumptions. As a PhD student at Stanford during this period, it was almost literally impossible to avoid putting on different lenses in that it was impossible to try to formulate what was an interesting question, a well-grounded theory, or a strong test without anticipating how a fellow student or faculty member would challenge the ideas or results from a stance very different from one's own. This is the way a rigorous intellectual environment is supposed to work but rarely does in practice.

REFERENCES

Bies, R. J., & Sitkin, S. B. (1991). Explanation as legitimation: Excuse-making in organizations. In: M. McLaughlin, M. Cody & S. Read (Eds), *Explaining one's self to others: Reason-giving in a social context* (pp. 183–198). Hillsdale, NJ: Lawrence Erlbaum Associates.

Bijlsma-Frankema, K. M., Sitkin, S. B., & Weibel, A. (2009). *Distrust in balance: Evolution and resolution of inter-group distrust between judges and administrators in a Court of Law.* Working paper. Duke University, Durham, NC.

Cardinal, L. B., Sitkin, S. B., & Long, C. P. (2004). Balancing and rebalancing in the creation and evolution of organizational control. *Organization Science, 15*(4), 411–431.

Cohen, M. D., & March, J. G. (1974). *Leadership and ambiguity: The American college president.* Boston: Harvard Business School Press.

Cyert, R. M., & March, J. G. (1963). *A behavioral theory of the firm.* Englewood Cliffs, NJ: Prentice Hall.

Davis-Blake, A., & Pfeffer, J. (1989). Just a mirage: The search for dispositional effects in organizational research. *Academy of Management Review, 14*, 385–400.

Dornbusch, S. M., & Scott, W. R. (1975). *Evaluation and the exercise of authority*. San Francisco: Jossey-Bass.

Feldman, M. S., & March, J. G. (1981). Information in organizations as signal and symbol. *Administrative Science Quarterly, 26*(2), 171–186.

Hannan, M. T., & Freeman, J. H. (1977). The population ecology of organizations. *American Journal of Sociology, 82*, 929–964.

Jemison, D. B., & Sitkin, S. B. (1986). Corporate acquisitions: A process perspective. *Academy of Management Review, 11*(1), 145–163.

Kahneman, D., & Tversky, A. (1979). Prospect theory: An analysis of decision under risk. *Econometrica, 4XLVII*(1979), 263–291.

Levinthal, D., & March, J. G. (1993). The myopia of learning. *Strategic Management Journal, 14*, 95–112.

Levitt, B., & March, J. G. (1988). Organizational learning. In: W. R. Scott & J. Blake (Eds), *Annual review of sociology* (Vol. 14, pp. 319–340). Palo, CA: Annual Reviews Inc.

March, J. G. (1966). The power of power. In: D. Easton (Ed.), *Varieties of political theory* (pp. 39–70). New York: Prentice-Hall.

March, J. G. (1991). Exploration and exploitation in organizational learning. *Organization Science, 2*(1), 71–87.

March, J. G. (1994). *A primer on decision making*. New York: Free Press.

March, J. G., & Olsen, J. P. (1976). *Ambiguity and choice in organizations*. Universitetforlaget, Bergen, Norway.

March, J. G., & Olsen, J. P. (2006). The logic of appropriateness. In: M. Moran, M. Rein & R. E. Goodin (Eds), *Oxford handbook of public policy*. Oxford: Oxford University Press.

March, J. G., & Simon, H. A. (1958). *Organization*. New York: Wiley.

Martin, J. (1982). Stories and scripts in organizational settings. In: A. H. Hastorf & A. Isen (Eds), *Cognitive social psychology*. New York: Elsevier.

Martin, J. (1992). *Cultures in organizations: Three perspectives*. Oxford: Oxford University Press.

Martin, J., Feldman, M., Hatch, M. J., & Sitkin, S. B. (1983). The uniqueness paradox in organizational stories. *Administrative Science Quarterly, 28*(3), 438–453.

Martin, J., & Powers, M. (1983). Truth or corporate propaganda: The value of a good war story. In: L. Pondy, P. Frost, Morgan & T. Dandridge (Eds), *Organizational symbolism*. Greenwich, CT: JAI.

Martin, J., Sitkin, S. B., & Boehm, M. (1985). Founders and the elusiveness of a cultural legacy. In: P. Frost, L. Moore, M. Louis, C. Lundberg & J. Martin (Eds), *Organizational culture* (pp. 99–124). Beverly Hills, CA: Sage.

Mayer, R. C., Davis, J. H., & Schoorman, D. (1995). An integrative model of organizational trust. *Academy of Management Review, 20*, 709–734.

Meyer, J. W., & Rowan, B. (1977). Institutional organizations: Formal structure as myth and ceremony. *American Journal of Sociology, 83*, 340–363.

Ocasio, W. (1997). Towards an attention-based view of the firm. *Strategic Management Journal, 18*(Summer Special Issue), 187–206.

Ouchi, W. G. (1977). The relationship between organizational structure and organizational control. *Administrative Science Quarterly, 22*(1), 95–113.

Ouchi, W. G. (1978). The transmission of control through organizational hierarchy. *Academy of Management Journal, 21*(2), 173–192.

Ouchi, W. G. (1979). A conceptual framework for the design of organizational control mechanisms. *Management Science, 25*(9), 833–848.

Pablo, A. L., Sitkin, S. B., & Jemison, D. B. (1996). Acquisition decision-making processes: The central role of risk. *Journal of Management, 22*(5), 723–746.

Peters, T. J. (1978). Symbols, patterns and settings: An optimistic case for getting things done. *Organizational Dynamics, 7*(2), 3–23.

Pfeffer, J. (1977). The ambiguity of leadership. *Academy of Management Review, 1*, 104–112.

Pfeffer, J. (1978). *Organizational design*. Arlington Heights, IL: AHM Publishing.

Pfeffer, J. (1981a). Management as symbolic action: The creation and maintenance of organizational paradigms. In: L. L. Cummings & B. M. Staw (Eds), *Research in organizational behavior* (Vol. 3, pp. 1–52). Greenwich, CT: JAI Press.

Pfeffer, J. (1981b). *Power in organizations*. Marshfield, MA: Pitman.

Rousseau, D. M., Sitkin, S. B., Burt, R. S., & Camerer, C. (1998). Not so different after all: A cross-discipline view of trust. *Academy of Management Review, 23*(3), 393–404.

Scott, W. R. (1987). The adolescence of institutional theory. *Administrative Science Quarterly, 32*, 493–511.

Scott, W. R. (1995). *Institutions and organizations*. Thousand Oaks, CA: Sage.

Scott, W. R. (2008). Approaching adulthood: The maturing of institutional theory. *Theoretical Sociology, 37*, 427–442.

Sitkin, S. B. (1992). Learning through failure: The strategy of small losses. *Research in Organizational Behavior, 14*, 231–266.

Sitkin, S. B. (1995). On the positive effect of legalization on trust. *Research on Negotiation in Organizations, 5*, 185–217.

Sitkin, S. B., Lind, E. A., & Siang, S. (2006). The six domains of leadership. *Leader to Leader* (Special Supplement), 27–33.

Sitkin, S. B., & Bies, R. J. (1993). Social accounts in conflict situations: Using explanations to manage conflict. *Human Relations, 46*(3), 349–370.

Sitkin, S. B., & Bies, R. J. (1994). The legalization of organizations: A multi-theoretical perspective. In: S. Sitkin & R. Bies (Eds), *The legalistic organization* (pp. 19–49). Newbury Park, CA: Sage.

Sitkin, S. B., Cardinal, L. B., & Bijlsma-Frankema, K. M. (Eds). (2010). *Control in organizations: New directions in theory and research*. Cambridge: Cambridge University Press.

Sitkin, S. B., Carton, A. M., Emery, J. D. (2009a). *"How" and "why" are leaders inspirational?: Moving beyond the "what" of inspirational motivation*. Duke University Working paper, Durham, NC.

Sitkin, S. B., & George, E. (2005). Managerial trust-building through the use of legitimating formal and informal control mechanisms. *International Sociology, 20*(3), 307–338.

Sitkin, S. B., Miller, C. C., See, K., Lawless, M., & Carton, A. M. (2009b). *The paradox of stretch goals: Pursuit of the seemingly impossible in organizations*. Duke University Working paper, Durham, NC.

Sitkin, S. B., & Pablo, A. L. (1992). Reconceptualizing the determinants of risk behavior. *Academy of Management Review, 17*(1), 9–38.

Sitkin, S. B., & Roth, N. L. (1993). Explaining the limited effectiveness of legalistic remedies for trust/distrust. *Organization Science, 4*(3), 365–390.

Sitkin, S. B., & Stickel, D. (1995). The road to hell … : The dynamics of distrust in an era of "quality" management. In: R. Kramer & T. Tyler (Eds), *Trust in organizations* (pp. 196–215). Thousand Oaks, CA: Sage.

Sitkin, S. B., & Sutcliffe, K. M. (1991). Dispensing legitimacy: Professional, organizational, and legal influences on pharmacist behavior. *Research in the Sociology of Organizations, 8*, 269–295.

Sitkin, S. B., Sutcliffe, K., & Reed, G. L. (1993). Prescriptions for justice: Using social accounts to legitimate the exercise of professional control. *Social Justice Research, 6*(1), 87–103.

Sitkin, S. B., Sutcliffe, K. M., & Schroeder, R. G. (1994). Distinguishing control from learning in total quality management: A contingency perspective. *Academy of Management Review, 18*(3), 537–564.

Sitkin, S. B., & Weingart, L. R. (1995). Determinants of risky decision making behavior: A test of the mediating role of risk perceptions and risk propensity. *Academy of Management Journal, 38*(6), 1573–1592.

Sutcliffe, K. M., Sitkin, S. B., & Browning, L. D. (2000). Tailoring process management to situational requirements: Beyond the control and exploration dichotomy. In: R. Cole & W. R. Scott (Eds), *The quality movement in America: Lessons for theory and research* (pp. 315–330). Thousand Oaks, CA: Sage.

Tversky, A., & Kahneman, D. (1981). The framing of decisions and the psychology of choice. *Science, 211*(4481), 453–458.

Weick, K. E. (1995). *Sensemaking in organizations.* Thousand Oaks, CA: Sage.

CHAPTER 28

SCHOOL AND SUPER-SCHOOL

David Strang

Since the late 1970s, Stanford-based research and researchers have been absolutely central to the field of organizational studies. Cohen, March, and Olsen's "A garbage can model of organizational choice," Meyer and Rowan's "Institutionalized organizations: formal structure as myth and ceremony" (1977), Hannan and Freeman's "The population ecology of organizations" (1978), Pfeffer and Salancik's "The external control of organizations" (1978), and Scott's "Organizations: rational, natural, and open systems" (first edition, 1981) defined distinctive perspectives that shaped and continue to shape the scholarly conversation. It is hard to underestimate the influence of these authors and of the many other students of organizations who have taught and/or been trained at Stanford.

It is thus of interest that references to "the Stanford school" are relatively few and far between. One main reason is that Stanford is home, not to a school, but to a collection of schools – a super-school! Adaptive learning, institutionalism, population ecology, resource dependence, and more: each can well be described as a school in its own right.[1] All have their own charismatic leaders, central and peripheral participants linked by graduate training and personal collaboration, gangs of student apprentices, and long and distinguished traditions of scholarly production. While scholars often patrol the "school" concept to keep out the small-fry, organizational studies at Stanford could be excluded because it is too big.

The distinction is relevant when we consider the dynamics of spatial concentration. Most schools form around one or two individuals who

Stanford's Organization Theory Renaissance, 1970–2000
Research in the Sociology of Organizations, Volume 28, 419–424
ISSN: 0733-558X/doi:10.1108/S0733-558X(2010)0000028032

combine the attributes of intellectual leadership and personal appeal. Much like communal groups founded by charismatic religious leaders, these schools are in many ways the natural reflection of the stature, capacity, and magnetism of a central figure or duo. Adding the reinforcing effects of interlocking joint recruitment and the staying power of a critical mass, we have dynamic stability as well as its basin of attraction. Schools in this sense are commonplace, though they cannot grow too large. Their gravitational pull is countered by the expanding distance of the average member from the school's charismatic center as well as by field-wide resistance to concentrated power and privilege.

A super-school involves not only these dynamics within its component schools but also exchange and rivalry between them. The various intellectual subgroups share ideas, techniques, and fringe members, and provide knowledge of cutting-edge developments that more isolated scholars must labor to keep abreast of. Mutual success spurs a healthy competition and a sense that more can and should be accomplished. If component schools unite around their common interests rather than struggle destructively over control of local resources, each will gain from the presence of others.

From an individual perspective, the pull of the super-school is particularly strong, as personal experience makes clear to me. I came to Stanford with a mild interest in organizations. But my fate was sealed when Dick Scott asked me if I wanted to serve as a research assistant on a project that he and John Meyer were conducting on schools; sealed again when I took Jim March's early morning seminar; yet again when Jim Baron presented his work on gender segregation in California state government; and yet again at a kumbaya-moment at a bonfire at Asilomar.[2] (Actually, that last one left me cold.) It is really not apropos of organizational studies, but the related memory I will always treasure is of the conversation when I first found myself following John Meyer's train of thought. The ocean of organizational studies was so large that little fish didn't even know they were all wet, or that there was anything outside that deserved real attention. Talk about conditions for successful recruitment and retention!

For a super-school to emerge and be stable, however, positive interdependence and centripetal forces cannot be too strong. Participants must gain from a shared institutional identity while resisting movement towards a convergent intellectual identity. Unlike the simple school grounded in the gravitational field formed by a single individual, a super-school involves a complex equilibrium whose component groups remain both proximate and distinct. Charismatic leaders must define themselves as allied free agents and followers must breed true.

A problem with the notion of a super-school is that its substance as an intellectual enterprise is hard to define. A centralized simple school, organized around a few leaders, will always have a conceptual and intellectual core, often one that can be meaningfully linked to its time and place. A super-school, by contrast, is a messy business. Since it is formed out of the institutional proximity of multiple intellectual leaders whose interests connect but do not coincide, a super-school lacks a unified scholarly profile. It is marked instead by broad commonalities and consistencies, sufficient to keep members of the several tribes at peace though insufficient to impel them to merge.

What are these substantive commonalities, in the case of Stanford? It is easier to begin with scholarly themes that are generally absent, before describing the super-school in more positive terms. First, organizational studies at Stanford seldom takes "work" as a central concern. Stanford researchers are not much interested in the job experience of those on the assembly line or even on the phone lines. Stanford-based research diverges sharply from industrial sociology's attention to structural sources of alienation, the union movement, industrial relations, and new forms of emotional labor. Exceptions occur, for example, in Jeff Pfeffer's work on labor unions and more recently in the impact of Steve Barley, but nevertheless work in Stanford's organizational tradition is notably not about work.

The Stanford super-school has also generally displayed little theoretical attention to the other side of the equation – to the elites who own and manage American corporations. There is little work on the social class bases of corporate leadership and the prospects for classwide rationality, though Don Palmer's work on social networks (a concern more compatible with the super-school's general theoretical proclivities) provides another exception that proves – demonstrates – the rule. Likewise, what managers do all day is seldom a topic of interest, and there is limited attention to the substantive content of managerial practice. The Stanford school differs greatly here from the focal concerns of institutions as disparate as Michigan and Harvard, which have characteristically sought to identify and broadcast conceptions of enlightened corporate leadership. Still less have Stanford organizational researchers aimed to take up the banner of the besieged middle manager, the politically thwarted engineer, or the belittled human resources expert.

If the Stanford super-school turns away from work and class, what does it turn towards? Organizations are treated as sites of generic social processes. Jim March and other students of organizational learning his students stress routine adaptation to experience and the virtues and pitfalls of simple forms of bounded rationality. Resource dependence views organizations from the perspective of a field of power and strategic networks. Ecology studies vital events that reshape organizational populations through selection. Institutionalism focuses on formal structure, seen as symbolic displays emblematic of broader cultural forces at work. The operative principles in these lines of inquiry are highly variable – from cognition to power to culture – but their deepest intellectual commitments are not so different.

This preference for the abstract and structural can also be seen when we consider how Stanford organizational research has approached the core sociological issue of inequality. Very general forms of discrimination linked to individual identity replace the particulars of class and occupation. This is visible in Jim Baron's close analyses of racial and gender segregation in the workplace; it appears as well in institutionalism's concern with the way organizations interpret and respond to equal employment laws. Ecological research on the way organizational founding and failure generate employment opportunities provides yet another highly structural analysis of individual-level outcomes.

A second source of intellectual coherence across the Stanford super-school is methodological, where a taste for formal and quantitative dominates. There is little in the way of case-specific research or focused small N comparisons – the goal is instead to characterize general tendencies and sources of variation across many cases. (Students can be especially doctrinaire here; I recall a workshop where Mike Hannan noted the benefits of an exploratory case study but aspiring ecologists would have none of it.) Stanford's bent for clean generalization also leads methodologically to simulation analysis, especially in research on learning, and to formal logical methods.

The most prominent common thread at Stanford, of course, is its causal focus on the "environment." This is almost emblematic of the main lines of theoretical analysis that make up the super-school – resource dependence, ecology, institutionalism, and adaptive decision-making. Their complex object of study is not the individual organization made up of multiple interdependent sub-systems, routines, or actors, but a larger network, field, or population within which the organization forms a relatively undifferentiated node. (This shift is especially clear in Dick Scott's textbook introduction to the field; Scott's brilliant conceptualization of rational, natural, and open systems perspectives integrates and celebrates the multiple forms of environment-centered analysis, that is, Stanford's hallmark.) I recall a comment made by a fellow doctoral student in sociology in the mid-80s to the effect that the contemporary turn towards environmental effects would presumably soon be balanced by a return to interest in what went on inside the firm. If so, the corrective will not come from Stanford.

In many ways, the collective approach of the Stanford super-school represents the application of modern social consciousness and modern social scientific consciousness to the organizational setting. We live less of a work-a-day life than we once did, a world where most of us contribute more as consumers than producers.[3] Organizations do indeed to crowd in on each other, and in John Meyer and Brian Rowan's wonderful language their building blocks come to be littered around the environment. Management is increasingly routinized and standardized, and grows distant from industry- or organization-specific traditions. In tracking these phenomena, the Stanford super-school updates Weber while slighting Durkheim and Marx.

What conditions led a modernist perspective on organizations to flourish so vigorously at Stanford, of all places? Stanford is a fairly young university, founded with a strong engineering emphasis, and at considerable geographic distance from most centers of social scientific scholarship. Youth and pragmatism separated Stanford from many traditional sociological and managerial concerns and towards a highly contemporary mindset. Spatial distance also made it easier for Stanford researchers to diverge from well-established lines of scholarship elsewhere. As in other settings, a little isolation promotes a lot of speciation.

Even more telling, however, is Stanford's location in San Francisco's South Bay, as theorists of open systems would have already surmised. When faculty and doctoral students ventured down Palm Drive, they ran into the agglomeration of electronics and software companies that turned had farming towns into Silicon Valley. The organizational/occupational community that these high-tech firms generated shows many affinities with themes dominant at Stanford. Hero managers and deep-seated internal conflict were out, exchange and adaptive learning among densely connected organizations were in. Idiosyncratic organizational traditions were out, a cookie-cutter façade protecting substantive innovators was in. Agonized organizational surgery was out, fruitfully high birth and death rates in.

A final consideration, perhaps the most important, is with the personal qualities of the leaders who brought the Stanford super-school into being, not only through their scholarship but through their work as institution builders. The flip side of environmental conditions and generic social processes are the constructive activities of particular individuals who locate opportunities for mutual gain, find harmony where others hear only cacophony, and form connections rather than extinguish them. But as a good Stanford student of organizations, of these putative "actors" and "actions" I can have little to say.

NOTES

1. On the concept of school as a central unit of scholarship, see Tiryakian (1979). Collins (1998, and elsewhere) finds that intellectual inquiry is often structured by four to six schools that compete with and define each other. Perhaps not coincidentally, Stanford's super school is also made up of four to six schools that compete with and define each other.
2. From the 1970s through the 1990s Stanford organizational scholars – led by Dick Scott via an NIMH training grant that involved some 20 faculty – held an annual conference at Asilomar in Pacific Grove. The conference grew from a Stanford affair to include faculty and students at Berkeley and other universities across the country, and seamlessly combined intellectual stimulation, community building, and recreation.
3. A good indicator of this is the way studies of boutique consumer goods providers like wineries and movie studios have replaced studies of auto manufacturers and industrial plants. Academic research always follows leading sectors and sites of supernormal profits.

REFERENCES

Collins, R. (1998). *The Sociology of Philosophies*. Cambridge, MA: Harvard University Press.
Tiryakian, E. A. (1979). The significance of schools in the development of sociology. In: W. E. Snizek, E. R. Fuhrman & M. K. Miller (Eds), *Contemporary Issues in Theory and Research* (pp. 211–233). Westport, CN: Greenwood.

CHAPTER 29

REFLECTIONS ON THE STANFORD ORGANIZATIONS EXPERIENCE

Amy S. Wharton

I was at Stanford from 1984 to 1986 as a post-doctoral fellow in the NIMH Organizations and Mental Health Training Program. I never thought of myself as a sociologist of organizations or of mental health. As a student of feminist sociologist Joan Acker, my interests were firmly in the area of gender inequality and work, and I went to Stanford primarily for the opportunity to collaborate with Jim Baron. I had been very much influenced by Baron and Bielby's (1980) call to "bring firms back in" to the study of work and inequality. Baron and Bielby's research on job- and firm-level gender segregation and their efforts to probe its underlying organizational dynamics seemed to offer exciting new vantage points from which to understand gender inequality in the workplace.

During the past 25 years, much has been written about the tensions and discontinuities between the sociology of work and organizational studies (Barley & Kunda, 2001; Parker, 2000; Whyte, 1987). One manifestation of this division was the movement of organizational researchers out of sociology departments and into business schools, a trend that was well underway in the mid-1980s. Like the boundaries between "male" and "female" jobs that were my research focus, the boundaries between work and organizations seemed, from the outside at least, fairly impenetrable. I thus arrived at Stanford apprehensive about how a feminist sociologist of work would fare in an organizational studies world.

Stanford's Organization Theory Renaissance, 1970–2000
Research in the Sociology of Organizations, Volume 28, 425–427
Copyright © 2010 by Emerald Group Publishing Limited
All rights of reproduction in any form reserved
ISSN: 0733-558X/doi:10.1108/S0733-558X(2010)0000028033

The tension between the sociology of work and organizational studies continues to exist and may have even become more entrenched over the years. However, my time at Stanford provided me opportunities for intellectual boundary spanning that were enriching and unlike anything I experienced in my career before or since. I trace these opportunities to several factors, not the least of which was an environment in which boundary spanning was more norm than exception and where its potentially negative consequences were largely mitigated.

Post-doctoral fellowships such as mine played an important role in this process. Among those in my Stanford post-doctoral cohort was a sociologist of education doing ethnographic research, a conversational analyst, and a medical sociologist. Early on I discovered that, like me, each came to the field of organizations through a research interest in another substantive area; none of us came to Stanford as organizational sociologists per se. During our time there, however, each of us found a bridge that connected our work to this field.

These bridges were facilitated by the existence of a large cross-disciplinary network of organizational scholars on the Stanford campus. I will leave it to others to explain how this network was built and sustained. Perhaps its vitality was a reflection of some of its central players. This includes Dick Scott, whose own studies of organizations were wide-ranging in their foci and approach, or Jim Baron who, despite his business school location, viewed the workplace through an organizational and sociological lens. Whatever the reasons, the Stanford network functioned effectively as a way to link together organizationally minded people with disparate interests and backgrounds.

Because of their pervasiveness, organizations are inherently well-suited to cross-disciplinary study. But crossing boundaries is difficult even under the best circumstances, and collaborations cannot be sustained without participants sharing some common purpose or commitment. This sense of common purpose was what made the Stanford organizational experience unique and valuable. All forms of cross-disciplinary collaboration are intellectually fashionable right now, but I have yet to see one that works quite as successfully as at Stanford during my short time there.

Boundary spanning plays an important role in organizations, though it is often associated with negative consequences, such as role conflict for individuals or communication disruptions in relationships. My efforts at Stanford to personally straddle the divide between the sociology of work and organizational studies were not without some discontent. I was disappointed that there was not more space at Stanford (or in sociology of work and organizations more generally) for systematically connecting the concerns of both streams of research. For example, Arlie Hochschild's (1983) book *The Managed Heart* had only recently been published when I arrived at Stanford in 1984, and her critique of the commodification of emotion was resonating in sociology of work circles. A short time later I had the opportunity to hear Bob Sutton discuss his research on the relations between store clerks' display of positive emotions and sales receipts (see Sutton & Rafaeli, 1988). While both represented important contributions to understanding the role of emotion in organizational life, the organizations-based and work-based explorations of this topic were even then moving along different tracks.

This disconnect was not unique to Stanford, of course, and was likely less deeply rooted there than in other places. Twenty-five years later, however, the gap between the sociology of work and the study of organizations remains. In a pattern similar to the shifting of gender boundaries in the workplace, just as organizational research became formally incorporated into the American Sociological Association's section on work and occupations, some organizational researchers formed a new section on Economic Sociology. As a result of my time at Stanford, I can say that I have friends and colleagues on both sides of the work and organizations divide. And while boundary spanning has its challenges, the opportunity to immerse myself in organizational sociology at Stanford is one that this sociologist of work continues to appreciate.

REFERENCES

Barley, S. R., & Kunda, G. (2001). Bringing work back in. *Organization Science, 12*, 76–95.
Baron, J. N., & Bielby, W. T. (1980). Bringing the firms back in: Stratification, segmentation and the organization of work. *American Sociological Review, 45*, 337–365.
Hochschild, A. R. (1983). *The managed heart: Commercialization of human feeling*. Berkeley: University of California.
Parker, M. (2000). The sociology of organizations and the organization of sociology: Some reflections on the making of a division of labor. *The Sociological Review, 48*, 124–146.
Sutton, R., & Rafaeli, A. (1988). Untangling the relationship between displayed emotions and organizational sales: The case of convenience stores. *Academy of Management Journal, 31*, 461–487.
Whyte, W. F. (1987). From human relations to organizational behavior: Reflections on the changing scene. *Industrial & Labor Relations Review, 40*, 487–500.

CHAPTER 30

TOUCHSTONES: THE STANFORD SCHOOL OF ORGANIZATION THEORIES, 1970–2000

Patricia H. Thornton

I reflect on the origins and development of the Stanford school of organization theories (1970–2000) as one who received her Ph.D. in Sociology in 1993 from Stanford University. I stress four of the many explanations why so many important ideas in organization theory can be traced to a single school: (1) institutional leadership and legitimacy; (2) resource-dependent faculty networks across departments, schools, and universities; (3) touchstones provided by the ritual and ethos of routine science supported by the core teaching of cumulative research programs; and 4) cultural and infrastructural conformity between the university and the larger institutional environment of Silicon Valley.

The Stanford organizations community during the years 1970–2000 was a unique force in the development of the field of organization theory and I have from time to time pondered why this is so. In offering my views on this question, I will draw on several different analytical lenses. First, I will highlight some of the contributions of Dick Scott's "institutional leadership" (Selznick, 1957) in creating an intra- and inter-university network that played a part in the development of an interdisciplinary community of organizations training, research, and theory building. In subsequent analysis, I refer to this as the Stanford phenomenon. Second, I will draw

Stanford's Organization Theory Renaissance, 1970–2000
Research in the Sociology of Organizations, Volume 28, 429–437
Copyright © 2010 by Emerald Group Publishing Limited
All rights of reproduction in any form reserved
ISSN: 0733-558X/doi:10.1108/S0733-558X(2010)0000028034

on resource dependence (Pfeffer & Salancik, 1978) and institutional theories (Scott, 2001) in explaining how institutional leadership, new sources of legitimacy, and conformity with the larger institutional environment may account for the Stanford phenomenon. Third, I will discuss the Stanford phenomenon in relation to the concept of cumulative research programs promulgated by two Stanford sociologists, Berger and Zelditch (1993). Zelditch's core course on theory construction and growth created a pedagogy that reached beyond the classroom and in my view was a salient factor in originating and shaping student and faculty communities of theorists. Last, as the title of my essay foreshadows, I liken the Stanford organization theories to touchstones. I use the metaphor of touchstones to represent what good research should look like to make a contribution to the discipline. This "good research" had other characteristics – both a ritual and routine science functions that may explain why for so many years the Stanford organizations community produced a high level of creative ideas that were systematically codified and spread across different disciplines, universities, and geographies.

INSTITUTIONAL LEADERSHIP AND RESOURCE-DEPENDENT NETWORKS

Dick Scott's "statesmanship" stands out as an obvious factor in explaining the Stanford phenomenon. By statesmanship, I refer to what Selznick (1957) meant by the institutional leader who plays a fundamental role in making an organization an institution that has the capacity to develop, adapt, and endure over time. Perhaps this goes without saying; Dick's statesmanship has been recognized elsewhere with the aim that he will know how much he is appreciated for his vital role.

The study of organizations is interdisciplinary and this gave legitimate license for cross-discipline organizing both at Stanford University and at other schools as well. In this endeavor, Dick Scott was masterful in applying institutional and resource-dependence theories. He employed institutional theory as he himself was the institutional leader and he had a key role in legitimating what was and was not a part of organization studies. He also applied resource-dependence theory in his efforts to weave together a labyrinth of internal and external funding to provide training and collegial opportunities for graduate and post-doctoral students and faculty in Sociology and other departments and schools outside of Sociology and

Stanford University.[1] Andy Van de Ven (2005) succinctly summarizes these attributes in his personal notes introducing Dick to the Academy of Management Fellows by commenting on how Dick organized and directed a Ph.D. research training program, Asilomar Conferences, the Stanford Center for Organization Research (SCORE), several consortiums involving other schools throughout the United States and Scandinavian countries, and many other initiatives that provided an inclusive and supportive community for intellectual development in the study of organizations. With his NIMH grant, Dick generously funded the Ph.D. students of other faculty! I believe that much of Dick's tireless efforts at building intra- and inter-university networks of organizations scholars were in hopes that they would "take on a life of their own."

This resource network had a tremendous impact on jump starting the careers of many and enhanced their ability to build their respective scholarly communities. Dick knew how to wisely bootstrap and leverage Stanford's resources and reputation. He and his colleagues at Stanford went about recruiting and collecting joint appointments in various departments and schools around the campus, for example, in sociology, business, education, and medicine, among others. They then filled those faculty offices with a network of visiting scholars from around the world. These post docs and senior fellows came to attend and give seminars and participate in research. Eventually, they left Stanford and like Johnny Appleseeds spread in wider circles what they had learned about the Stanford ways of thinking. This resulted in the scholarly world knowing much more about the Stanford brands of organization theory than would typically be the case.

SOURCES OF LEGITIMACY

There is another aspect of Dick Scott's institutional leadership that may be unintended and under recognized. While Dick self-deprecatingly paints the authors of textbooks as the Rodney Dangerfields of the academic world (Scott, 2006, p. 899), I would argue that it depends on the state of development of the field and of course the quality of the book. In my view, Dick's textbooks have been a powerful force in organizing and legitimating organizations studies as a field and in earmarking and legitimating sets of colleagues through his citations of their work. It is not that there was little competition for his position as author of well-selling organizations books on the market – as there was and still is. However, the creativity and universality of Dick's typology of rational, natural, and open systems has stood up under such market forces and the test of time as measured by many successive editions.

What other attributes might explain the success of the Stanford-branded organizations theories and why they spread – why they became touchstones? The definition of a touchstone is that it is a criterion for testing and measuring quality. The word stems from a hard black stone, such as jasper, which is used to test the quality of gold or silver by comparing the streak left on the stone to one left by a standard alloy (Morris, 1969). Several attributes made the Stanford experience for students the touchstone that authenticated their future research and teaching endeavors.

CUMULATIVE RESEARCH PROGRAMS

Stanford sociology taught us students how to learn – not what to learn. It stressed understanding the role of metatheory, typologies, and ideal types as interpretive schemes and organizing categories. It taught us how to glean from the literature the abstractions and generalizations that were applicable across different contexts, how to develop theory and evaluate propositions, and how to apply them across time and space. While the basic mechanics were the focus of a two-course theory sequence led by Buzz Zelditch and Bernie Cohen, this style of pedagogy was embedded in a series of required and voluntary courses and workshops. Remarkably, it seemed to be a value held by the near entirety of the faculty. Not until after leaving for my first job as an assistant professor, did I realize how rare it was to have such agreement on the underlying fundamentals of acquiring ideas and building knowledge. Moreover, I realized how this value was held across a broad range of faculty across departments and schools at Stanford. Agreement on such a philosophy can trickle down to all sorts of critical departmental and institution-building decisions from graduate student admissions, to junior faculty hires, to joint faculty grant writing.

In the Zelditch theory sequence at Stanford, we did not spend class time interpreting the works of Marx, Weber, and Durkheim and other long-gone founding fathers of the disciplines. If students were not accomplished in reading this metatheory, it was expected that they should do so. Instead, the theory course required that we students select a thriving or nearly dead theoretical research program (TRP) and trace its growth back to its roots and suggest how it might develop in the future. This meant figuring out who planted the seeds, who stimulated the growth of the trunk, why the tree branched in the directions that it did, why some branches withered and the twigs died out, and who was doing the pruning to force new growth – and why. As students, we presented these trees of knowledge in class so our fellow students could experience the life course of all the theories. Moreover, Zelditch encouraged us to go interview the faculty working in the TRP we had selected and to ask for their working papers. This practice had secondary gains for building student and faculty introductions and networks.

Not only did we learn to understand the birth, growth, and decay of theory, we also learned how to construct a new theory from an empirical observation without explanation in the literature. Combined, this style of teaching showed how others had come up with an explanation to a puzzle and made a difference in the literature. This style of learning was indeed powerful – it made students feel like there was important work happening in real time and that they themselves could participate in building sociological and organization theory.

For example, as a student in Zelditch's theory course, I selected to trace the origins and growth of population ecology theory. This exercise enabled me to recognize the ecologists' contribution to formalizing theoretical concepts and their development of rigorous methods of analysis (Pfeffer, 1993). It enabled me to borrow and import some of the ecologist's ideas into my research on institutional changes in higher education publishing. For example, I learned to focus on a population of organizations, which I applied not to an industry as had been the case in ecology theory, but to a product market. This also was distinct from prior institutional theorizing focusing on organizational fields of nonprofit organizations such as schools, hospitals, and museums that were driven at the time more by the state and the professions than by market forces. Moreover, this free-spirited training on theoretical research programs led me to extract ideas from the contingency theory literature on strategy and structure of the firm. This literature seemed rich in empirical observations, yet impoverished in theory, but the empirical problems helped me to think about sociological theory of business strategy in markets (Thornton, 2004) – a subfield empirically driven by narrower economic views.

RITUAL AND ROUTINE SCIENCE

Overall, the main point I want to emphasize is that this style of pedagogy provides a set of touchstones that have ritual and routine science functions (Stinchcombe, 1982) in motivating continuous scientific work. By ritual it is meant that they bind together groups of researchers telling them that they have a common scholarly identity. By routine science it is meant that they create important ongoing puzzles with applications in a number of different arenas. The Ph.D. training on cumulative research programs and its inherent view on the progress of social science was the code behind the user interface, so to speak. I argue this way of thinking about organization studies had a hand in shaping how and why communities of scholars at Stanford focused on theory construction, not description – and on independent variables and causal models. This training is what enabled my colleague William Ocasio and me, both having benefited from Zelditch's theory course, to fertilize the seed corn that Friedland and Alford (1991) planted, contributing to the development of the cumulative research program on institutional logics (Thornton & Ocasio, 1999, 2008; Thornton, 2004).

If my argument is valid, it implies that the recent turn toward descriptive case studies and problem-focused research identified by Davis and Marquis (2005), which does not as easily lend itself to the cumulative research program pedagogy, may be missing the strong legs needed for continuously developing organization theories.[2]

This culture of teaching, learning, and researching means that Stanford was unusually fertile soil for the development of new theories. I would argue that this culture of theory construction propelled the marquee of theories discussed in this volume. This view of the growth of social science, embedded in the teaching and researching functions of the time, is an important part of the explanation for why Stanford is known for the proliferation of organization theories. The overarching focus of the theory training of Ph.D. students was on universality of theoretical mechanisms and explanations across contexts – not on particular descriptions of contexts.[3]

In addition, there was a ritual function meaning that the routine science ethos bound together groups of students and faculty, telling them they had a common scholarly identity (Stinchcombe, 1982). At the time in other universities, it would be unusual for an engineering or graduate business student to take a theory course in the Department of Sociology. At Stanford, this was not the case; students in psychology and the business, education, and engineering schools, among other areas around the campus were either encouraged or required to take the theory and the methods sequences of courses in sociology. The extension of this pattern of course work was to create for students an unusually rich set of peers to talk and network with during our education at Stanford with the potential to continue after we had left to the far away corners of different schools and disciplines. It also meant that these Ph.D. students took these ideas back to their respective home bases across the departments and schools at Stanford creating a trickle up effect to their faculty advisers. This flat network, compared to the hierarchical silos existing at many universities, was essential to the proliferation and widespread acceptance of many of the ideas and theories at Stanford.

CONFORMITY WITH THE LARGER INSTITUTIONAL ENVIRONMENT

Last, any institutional analysis coming from a Stanford person of my era is not complete without locating the focal context in some larger arena. The institutional environment at Stanford was a microcosm of the larger Silicon Valley flat and open network culture. Perhaps the shortest way to make this point is to mention that the Stanford phenomenon is validated by its analogy to Saxenian's (1994) explanation for the faster growth of Silicon Valley as an engine of entrepreneurship than that of Boston's Route 128.

CONCLUSION

I have discussed how the success and legacy of the Stanford organizations research community is dependent on the institutional sources of leadership and legitimacy during the years of 1970–2000; the resource dependence among faculty across departments, schools, and other universities; touchstones provided by the ritual and ethos of routine science supported by the teaching of cumulative research programs; and the larger institutional environment of Silicon Valley that encouraged a culture of creativity through open networks.

  In addition to the substantive contributions of the theories and other reasons for the success of the Stanford organizations paradigms, this essay is also shaped by the biases of my own personal experience. I did not realize until I had left Stanford University in 1993 that my Stanford experience was a touchstone to help guide my subsequent work in organizations research and teaching. In reflecting back, I cherish and appreciate the opportunity to participate in and learn from the sociology and organizations community of scholars at Stanford. I am thankful to many at Stanford for the opportunity, knowledge, and guidance they gave.

NOTES

1. One could argue a structural explanation among others for the waning of the Stanford phenomenon is that at the disequilibrium point resource dependence and external network expansion resulted in the Department of Sociology being externally controlled (Pfeffer & Salancik, 1978).

2. Or it may be the case that my observation period is not long enough to see more generally that discourse has an underlying cyclical or dialectic functional form that undulates between a focus on the micro or macro, and a focus on particular empirical problems or universal general theories (Barley & Kunda, 1992). This undulation may be partially evidenced over longer stretches of time in the development of sociological theory in terms of the corrective shifts in levels of analysis for example in bringing back individuals (Homans, 1964), organizations (Baron & Bielby, 1980), and society (Friedland & Alford, 1991) into sociological analysis.

3. The style of teaching is perhaps more understandable by knowing that Zelditch was a Ph.D. student of Talcott Parsons at Harvard.

REFERENCES

Barley, S. R., & Kunda, G. (1992). Design and devotion: surges of rational and normative ideologies of control in managerial discourse. *Administrative Science Quarterly*, 363–399.

Baron, J. M., & Bielby, W. T. (1980). Bringing the firms back in: stratification, segmentation, and the organization of work. *American Sociological Review*, 45, 737–765.

Berger, J., & Zelditch, M., Jr. (1993). *Theoretical research programs: Studies in the growth of theory*. Stanford, CA: Stanford University Press.

Davis, G. F., & Marquis, C. (2005). Prospects for organization theory in the early twenty-first century: institutional fields and mechanisms. *Organization Science*, 16(4), 332–343.

Friedland, R., & Alford, R. (1991). Bringing society back in: symbols, practices, and institutional contradictions. In: W. W. Powell & P. J. DiMaggio (Eds), *The new institutionalism in organizational analysis* (pp. 232–263). Chicago, IL: University of Chicago Press.

Homans, G. C. (1964). Bringing men back in. *American Sociological Review*, 29, 809–818.

Morris, W. (Ed.) (1969). *The American Heritage Dictionary of the English Language*. Boston, MA: American Heritage and Houghton Mifflin.

Pfeffer, J. (1993). Barriers to the advance of organization science: Paradigm development as a dependent variable. *Academy of Management Review*, 19, 599–620.

Pfeffer, J., & Salancik, G. (1978). *The external control of organizations*. New York, NY: Harper & Row.

Saxenian, A. (1994). *Regional advantage: Culture and competition in Silicon Valley and route 128*. Cambridge, MA: Harvard University Press.

Scott, W. R. (2001). *Institutions and organizations* (2nd ed.). Thousand Oaks, CA: Sage.

Scott, W. R. (2006). Ad astra per aspera: A journey from the periphery. *Organization Studies,* 27(6), 877–897.

Selznick, P. (1957). *Leadership in administration.* New York, NY: Harper & Row.

Stinchcombe, A. L. (1982). Should sociologists forget their mothers and fathers. *American Sociologist, 17,* 2–11.

Thornton, P. H. (2004). *Markets from culture: Institutional logics and organizational decisions in higher education publishing.* Stanford, CA: Stanford University Press.

Thornton, P. H., & Ocasio, W. (1999). Institutional logics and the historical contingency of power in organizations: Executive succession in the higher education publishing industry, 1958–1990. *American Journal of Sociology, 105,* 801–843.

Thornton, P. H., & Ocasio, W. (2008). Institutional logics. In: R. Greenwood, C. Oliver, S. K. Andersen & R. Suddaby (Eds), *Handbook of organizational institutionalism* (pp. 99–129). Thousand Oaks, CA: Sage.

Van de Ven, A. (2005). Personal notes, *Introduction of W. Richard Scott to the Academy of Management Fellows,* Honolulu, Hawaii, August 9.

PART IV
CONCLUSION

CHAPTER 31

COLLEGIAL CAPITAL: THE ORGANIZATIONS RESEARCH COMMUNITY AT STANFORD, 1970–2000 [*]

W. Richard Scott

Organization studies emerged as an academic discipline during the late 1950s, when a few scholars began to pull together various scattered and fugitive ideas from engineers (Taylor, 1911), scholars of administrative systems (Weber, 1924/1968; Gulick & Urwick, 1937; Barnard, 1937; Drucker, 1946), social psychologists (Mayo, 1933, 1945), students of public administration (Simon, Smithberg, & Thompson, 1950), and industrial sociologists (Dubin, 1951; Whyte, 1946). A number of well-crafted case studies – including those of Selznick (1949), Gouldner (1954), Blau (1955), Lipset, Trow, and Coleman (1956), and Dalton (1959) heightened attention to organizational structures and processes. The field began to coalesce when a handful of texts and treatises – e.g., March and Simon (1958), Etzioni (1961), Thompson (1961), and Blau and Scott (1962) – endeavored to define its scope and limits. These efforts were both consolidated and advanced with

[*] An early version of this paper was presented to the Stanford Historical Society on November 16, 2005. This paper benefited from the constructive suggestions of Ray Bacchetti, Hal Leavitt, Jim March, Jeff Pfeffer, and Patricia Thornton.

Stanford's Organization Theory Renaissance, 1970–2000
Research in the Sociology of Organizations, Volume 28, 441–457
Copyright © 2010 by Emerald Group Publishing Limited
All rights of reproduction in any form reserved
ISSN: 0733-558X/doi:10.1108/S0733-558X(2010)0000028035

the publication of March's (1965) *Handbook of Organizations*. Centered during the early period primarily in the academic departments of sociology and psychology and, subsequently, migrating to management schools (Augier, March, & Sullivan, 2005), organization studies has from its earliest beginnings to the present remained an interdisciplinary enterprise.

This is, of course, largely a function of timing. By not congealing as a subject area until the mid-twentieth century, organization studies arrived long after the academic boundaries of schools and departments within universities had been institutionalized. As a consequence, the study of organizations was (and remains) fragmented with its practitioners scattered throughout the university. Scholars in different schools and departments focus on different kinds of organizations: management school faculty concentrate on firms, education school scholars on schools and colleges, political scientists on public organizations, sociologists on non-profits and voluntary associations, and so on. In addition, organizational scholars work on varying problems. For example, political scientists are likely to focus on power and decision-making processes; economists on the acquisition and allocation of scarce resources and on financial indicators of performance; psychologists, on variations of perception, cognition, and motivation among participants; and sociologists, on status and legitimation processes. Moreover, scholars focus on varying levels of analysis: some on decision-making processes by individuals within firms; some on the sources of diversity in organizational forms; others on power processes among organizations; and still others on industry structure and the dynamics of wider organization fields.

While no one scholar or study can comprehend all facets and perspectives, to be reminded of the variety and complexity of matters surrounding and, potentially, affecting one's subject is always useful and sometimes of critical importance. Because organization studies is intrinsically interdisciplinary, its strength and development depends greatly on the quality of the scholars in supporting schools and departments and on the number and intensity of connections among them. As the study of organizations advanced during the last decades of the twentieth century, Stanford University and its wider context provided a highly supportive environment.

THE STANFORD CONTEXT

Operating as a promising regional university well into the 1960s, Stanford witnessed a "great leap forward" in the 1970s and 1980s. Guided by the visionary leadership of its president, Wallace Sterling, and provost,

Frederick Terman, Stanford began its meteoric climb into the ranks of the nation's top tier universities. This more general history has been told and retold in numerous publications (e.g., Lowen, 1997; Gillmor, 2004) and need not be recounted here.

Like all organizational histories, Stanford's story reflects developments both within and outside the boundaries of the University. Externally, the federal government had emerged, during the decade of the 1960s, as a major player in strengthening the foundations of basic research – in both the natural and the social sciences – by investing in direct support for research and research-training programs in public and private universities (Graham & Diamond, 1997). For the social sciences, key supporting agencies included the Office of Naval Research (ONR) – a forerunner of the National Science Foundation – and the National Institute of Mental Health (NIMH). Both agencies supported research, but NIMH also made large investments in research infrastructure, funding research training programs across the social sciences.

Beginning in the 1960s, Stanford's social science departments and professional schools commenced their march to prominence. It was also at about this time that professional schools such as business and education, following the successful model of medical schools, began to shift their orientation from vocationalism and reliance on experienced practitioners to focus more on discipline-based theories and research-based scholarship (Augier, March, & Sullivan, 2005; Gordon & Howell, 1959; Schlossman, Gleeson, Sedlak, & Allen, 1994). A wide range of organization scholars were drawn to the Stanford campus, beginning with social psychologists and economists but soon including political scientists and sociologists. During the 1980s, the engineering school elected to extend its curriculum to management training, and thus another professional school attracted prominent organization scholars to the campus. The range of faculty talent assembled at Stanford from the early 1960s to the beginning of 1990 is suggested by the list of scholars (see Appendix A) affiliated with Stanford's organization training program, which I describe later. This collection of scholars constituted what my colleague Jim March described as an expanding "density of competence."

However, an aggregate of individual scholars, no matter how talented, does not comprise a scientific community.

COLLEGIAL CAPITAL

Exactly what is it about being surrounded by a dense collection of scholars that seems to produce new insights and approaches? Many would argue that it has nothing to do with interaction and everything to do with assembling smart individuals capable of conjuring up new insights or combining existing ideas into new combinations through bricolage. It is "obvious" to many that individuals are the sole source of creativity.

However, as a card-carrying sociologist, I have always believed in the generative power of social interaction. In general terms, I imagined that the process involved not so much co-production, as mutual stimulation – one person's ideas stimulating or building upon another's. Recently, however, I came across a paper coauthored by Lee Fleming, a former doctoral student in engineering at Stanford, now at Harvard Business School, who had participated in SCOR's programs and returned to the campus for SCANCOR's 20th anniversary celebration.[1] Lee embraces an evolutionary view of creativity, wisely noting that to develop, ideas must not only be generated – the "variation" phase – but also be "selected" – evaluated by others – and then, if of promise, "retained" (Fleming & Singh, 2008). The latter two stages are inevitably social, the former at least sometimes. As Csikszentmihalyi (1999) argues, "To be creative, a variation must somehow be endorsed by the field … Creativity involves social judgment."

Positing that we treat creative ideas as a distribution ranging from being more to less fruitful, Fleming and Singh argue that collaboration with others can create value both by reducing the probability of less promising or fruitful outcomes and also by increasing the probability of highly successful outcomes. They provide empirical validation for their arguments by examining U.S. patent data for a recent 10-year period, distinguishing between those involving collaboration and those produced by lone inventors. They assessed "promise" or "fruitfulness" in terms of the number of citations received by a patent. They found support for the hypothesis that "collaboration improves the sorting and identification of promising new ideas" both by trimming the lower tail and "shifting the mass of creative outcomes toward extremely successful outliers" – patents receiving higher numbers of citations (Fleming & Singh, 2008, p. 3).

This view of the creative process – as involving not simply the generating but also the sifting and sorting of more from less creative ideas – seems to me to capture the essence of what I mean by "collegial capital." Colleagues stimulate us to generate ideas but, perhaps more importantly, guide our efforts by recognizing, rewarding, and encouraging us to retain and develop our good ideas, and abandon those less viable. In this sense, I have long regarded the scientific process as being constructed with an "open architecture." Science advances as one scholar stimulates another by sharing his ideas, but also as scientists collectively sort for and select out the more promising ideas among the large pile of hopeful contenders.

ORGANIZATIONAL RESEARCHERS GET ORGANIZED

Early in the 1970s, a small number of Stanford faculty came together to seek funding to support a research training program. A proposal was submitted in 1971 to the National Institute of Mental Health (NIMH) to fund training in "Organizations and Mental Health." The first proposal listed 21 Stanford faculty members as participants of the Training Faculty. The program proposed to develop training procedures to further the investigation of mental health systems – which at that time were undergoing a major transition from reliance on the services of isolated "total institutions" (asylums and mental hospitals) to the creation of community-based programs (Goffman, 1961; Scull, 1977; Lerman, 1982). But in addition, the proposal advocated inquiry into the effects that *all* types of organizations – firms, agencies, and voluntary associations – have on the mental health of their participants, both positive and negative. In short, we defined the goals of the Training Program quite broadly to encompass a wide range of topics and methodologies.

Our Research Training proposal was approved by NIMH, and so commenced in 1972 a program that provided vital resources allowing us to build a more stable network of organization researchers on the campus. I served as the director – more accurately, coordinator – of this program, which operated at Stanford for 18 years, from 1972 until 1989. The program was augmented between 1986 and 1989 by a second training grant from the newly established National Institute on Aging (NIA). In combination, throughout the period, the programs supported each year, on average, five pre-doctoral and five post-doctoral fellows, each working under the supervision of a member of the Training Faculty. In addition, during the early years, largely because of the efforts of William Ouchi, a faculty member in the School of Business, we received additional funds through 1975–1978 from Booz-Allen & Hamilton, Inc. to support a seminar series and associated publications.

In designing the training program we were careful to define it as an augmentation of, not a replacement for, existing school and departmental programs and requirements. The typical pre-doctoral trainee entered the two-year program in the third year of graduate school, after completing the course and exam requirements of his or her home department. Training seminars, colloquia, workshops, and conferences were put in place to enrich disciplinary preparation and to inform dissertation research. Social events were hosted to facilitate interaction and build community.

The NIMH and NIA trainees constituted the core of a much larger cohort of doctoral students drawn from all the participating schools and departments. In this manner, the Training Program was not an enclave, but a leavening agent enhancing opportunities for a sizable collection of doctoral students and faculty.

During the 1970–1980s, training program events annually attracted the involvement of shifting cohorts of roughly 40 Stanford faculty and 80 doctoral student participants.

ASILOMAR

Without question, our most successful and visible collective enterprise was an annual conference, which we hosted beginning in 1975. Guided by a faculty committee, the conference was largely planned and organized by graduate students – led by but not limited to NIMH Trainees. After trying out alternative locations, Atherton House and Pajaro Dunes, in 1979 we moved our venue to the Conference Center at Asilomar in Pacific Grove, a rustic collection of lodges and assembly rooms located on the shores of the Pacific ocean – a welcoming facility we utilized for almost 20 years. The format each year was roughly the same. We invited three leading scholars to keynote the event, which began on Friday late afternoon during the spring quarter and ended Sunday after lunch. Faculty, both visiting and local, hosted evening fire-side chats – devoted to topics ranging from research design and professional development to research ethics. Trainees and other graduate students presented and discussed research papers. And, of course, there were parties in the evening, beginning at 9 and continuing (for some) well into the next morning.

In the early years of the Asilomar tradition, attendees were primarily Stanford faculty and graduate students, 60 or 70 of us. Student attendance was subsidized by the Training Program. As the reputation of the conference grew, students from other California schools sought to be included. We began to be joined by students and faculty from University of California (UC) Berkeley, UC San Francisco, UC Davis, and Santa Clara University, followed soon after by students from UCLA and University of Southern

California. Then, as the tradition extended over time, students who had graduated – alumni of the program – found ways to come back, year after year, so that the community expanded both geographically and temporally, including successive cohorts of doctoral and post-doctoral students and junior faculty. In order to preserve some of the intimacy and informal character of the event, we capped attendance at 125. During the latter years, we found we could not accommodate all interested students and faculty, and were obliged to create a waiting list.

The Asilomar conference continued from the late 1970s until well into the mid-1990s. To this day, I rarely attend a professional meeting without being intercepted by some grateful conference alum who wants to nostalgically recall some memorable if not transcendent organizational moment experienced among the cypress groves on the shores of the Pacific. Between 1975 and 1995, Asilomar played a critical role in creating a community of scholars, one that continues to help shape and define the direction of the field's development. Connecting junior and senior scholars across the country and internationally, this conference exerted substantial influence on the fledging field of organization studies.

While the formal title was "the NIMH Research Training Program,"[2] I believe that what was going on in the seminars, workshops and conferences was by no means "training" in the narrow sense. Rather, interaction between students and faculty was engendering and reinforcing the norms of a scholarly community, the values of basic research, the importance of interdisciplinary discourse, and collegial community. The community was driven more by shared identities than by narrow incentives.

The great bulk of the funding was deployed to pay tuition and stipends of trainees – although these trainees were only a small proportion of the students involved. However, since trainees, both pre- and post-doc, were expected to work with faculty members, NIMH funding served as a significant resource for faculty research. The remaining funds provided support for a half-time administrator. Throughout most years of the program's existence, Mai Lam, a bright and talented recent immigrant from Vietnam, served as administrator and effectively managed the many appointment processes and papers, reports, and accounts. All faculty, including the directors of the program, served without salary.

The structure of the program was not sustained by a conventional unified hierarchy but by a loosely connected network – a form that subsequently has become quite trendy. We were 20 years ahead of the times in the design of our own organization! A shifting coalition of faculty provided oversight and leadership, all participating because they identified with the goals of the program. Faculty participants were linked more by a shared vision and culture rather than a formal administrative apparatus or the lure of financial incentives.

PROOF OF THE PUDDING

The fruits of this community were not only to be seen in the increasing quality of university-wide faculty – the existence of the program allowed Stanford to recruit superior scholars to participating schools – or in the impressive group of doctoral and post-doctoral students who found their way to Stanford during this period. One important output was the many trainees who went on to become highly productive scholars in their own right. (A list of pre- and post-doctoral trainees appears in Appendices B and C).

An even more important indicator, I believe, was the creative outpouring of seminal theoretical perspectives and research approaches produced during this period by program faculty (described in more detail in Section 2 of this volume). Of the five major theoretical perspectives that dominated organization studies during the 1970s–1990s, four of them were pioneered by the work of Stanford faculty.[3] Earlier theoretical approaches to organizations emphasized their rational and technical character. Organizations were viewed as rationally designed instruments for the achievement of specified objectives. By contrast, most Stanford researchers examined organizations as political, social, and cultural systems. Also, most early work in organization studies took an organization-centric view, viewing the world from the vantage point of a single "focal" organization. By contrast, the bulk of Stanford researchers sought to raise the level of analysis from a single organization up to a "population" of similar organizations or a "field" of varying but interdependent organizations operating in the same institutional arena.

Graduate School of Business (GSB) Professor Jeff Pfeffer was the chief architect of the *resource dependence* approach that recognized that a given organization was dependent on other organizations for necessary resources and technical information but stressed the extent to which the economic dependencies created by unequal resource exchanges give rise to power processes that are often managed by political strategies (Pfeffer, 1972; Pfeffer & Salancik, 1978).

Raising the level of analysis, Sociology Professor Mike Hannan pioneered the *organizational ecology* approach, which considers the ways in which collections of similar organizations – organizational populations – arise, become more numerous, compete, and eventually subside or fail (Hannan & Freeman, 1977, 1989). Adapting the concepts and methods of biological ecologists, these scholars examined the history of populations of organizations, such as newspapers, universities, and biotech firms. In this work, organizations are not presumed to maximize effectiveness or productivity, but to be primarily driven by an interest in survival.

Sociology Professor John Meyer and I, and, independently, Professor Jim March (with appointments in several departments) and his colleague, Johan Olsen, helped to develop an *institutional* approach to organizations that emphasized the role of cultural and normative factors in shaping the formal structures and strategies of organizations (March & Olsen, 1984, 1989; Meyer & Rowan, 1977; Meyer & Scott, 1983; Scott, 1995, 2008). This approach stresses the importance of ideas – for example, templates for organizing and social logics that guide work patterns – and normative pressures – such as professional standards – that govern the structure and operation of organizations.

Jim March pioneered the study of *organizational learning* (March & Olsen, 1975; Levitt & March, 1988). Not only do their individual members engage in learning, but organizations themselves exhibit learning as they code the results of their own and others' experiences into the design of their structures and routines. March is careful not to treat learning as necessarily leading to improvement: learning can be "superstitious" and based on a faulty selection or interpretation of one's experience, or it may serve as a form of intelligence and improvement.

Observe that all of these general perspectives treat political, social, and cultural factors not as occasional sources of disruption or disturbance affecting these rational systems, but as omnipresent, continuing forces shaping the structure and functioning of organizations. This attention to "non-rational" factors has been the hallmark of the "Stanford school."

In addition to these comprehensive perspectives, which continue to be utilized and elaborated up to the present time, other important theoretical frameworks developed by Stanford faculty during this period include GSB Professor Bill Ouchi's "Theory Z," accounting for the differences between Asian and Western organizing forms (Ouchi, 1981), his GSB colleague Jim Baron's work on organizational stratification – examining the ways in which organizational structures and processes mediate mobility processes (Baron & Bielby, 1980) – Jim March's analysis of organizational decision making, including decisions made under uncertainty and with poorly defined objectives (March, 1981, 1988; Cohen, March, & Olsen, 1972); GSB Professor Joanne Martin's work on organizational culture – the ways in which particular organizations develop shared understandings and common sets of symbols – (Martin & Siehl, 1983; Martin, 1992); GSB Professor Rod Kramer's examination of trust relations in organizations (Kramer & Tyler, 1996); Jeff Pfeffer's analysis of organizational demography, dealing with the consequences of varying age and gender distributions of the work force on organizational structure (Pfeffer, 1983); GSB Professor Podolny's (1994) explorations of the effects of status processes among organizations on market exchanges; engineering school Professor Robert Sutton's work on organizational decline processes (Sutton & Callahan, 1987); engineering school Professor Kathleen Eisenhardt's analysis of project team structures associated with firms specializing in rapid product development (Eisenhardt & Tabrizi, 1995); GSB Professor Pam Haunschild's work on the various forms and effects of corporate interlocks (Haunschild, 1993); and my examination with several colleagues and trainees of the occupational and organizational structure of mental health systems (Scott & Lammers, 1985; Scott & Black, 1986) and other studies examining the effects of hospital and medical staff professional structures on surgical care outcomes (Flood & Scott, 1987). These and other contributions are described in Section 2 of this volume.

END OF THE TRAINING PROGRAM

In the midst of this considerable success, the national policy climate for federal support of the social sciences had begun to change. With the election of Ronald Reagan in 1980, political support within the federal bureaucracy for social science training and research began to erode (Institute for Scientific Analysis, 1999). Within the mental health profession, those advocating the clinical medical model distanced themselves from those stressing a social, community approach (Thornton, 1992). Political appointees within the funding agencies generally challenged the use of federal funding for basic social science research, and NIMH officers, in particular, insisted that mental health problems had specific individual etiologies that bore no relation to social conditions. It was decreed that social organization and/or disorganization had no relevance to mental illness. Under these conditions, NIMH, which had been a central focus for the support of a broad range of social science training, began to shut down most of its training programs, and, we decided not to apply for renewal. Our training programs supported by NIMH and NIA ended in 1989.

Summing over the roughly 20 years of this program, more than 75 pre-doctoral and 50 post-doctoral trainees received an average of two years support from the program. And, allowing for comings and goings over the years, more than 80 members of the Stanford faculty were affiliated with the training faculty (see Appendices A–C).

ORIGINS OF SCOR

Anticipating the end of federal support, the core members of the Training Faculty began during the late 1980s to craft an alternative framework to support our joint venture. We began early in 1987 to initiate discussions with University administrators, the various deans and the Provost, Jim Rosse, to attempt to secure greater recognition and modest but stable internal funding for our research community. We proposed the creation of the Stanford Center for Organizations Research (SCOR), an inter-disciplinary center intended to "provide education and training opportunities for students at all levels: undergraduate, graduate, post-graduate, and visiting scholars" (SCOR Charter, 1988). In addition to my involvement, faculty leadership for this initiative was provided by Jim March and Jeff Pfeffer.

I believe it is accurate to say that the University's endorsement at this juncture was, at best, half-hearted. We received moral support from all the participating schools but financial support only from the Provost's office and, because of Dean Bob Jaedicke's endorsement, from the School of Business. Critical to our success in getting the Center off the ground was the enthusiastic support of Ray Bacchetti, Vice Provost, ably assisted by Lowell Price. Ray served as the cognizant administrative officer.

SCOR formally opened its doors in February 1988, with offices for a half-time administrator and several post-doctoral students in the Graduate School of Business. I was appointed Director and Robert Sutton, engineering, Associate Director. The first faculty Steering Committee included, in addition to Bob and me, Milbrey McLaughlin, education, James March, education and business, and Jeff Pfeffer, GSB.

SCOR's resources were also greatly enhanced by an influx of new talented scholars coming to Stanford during the 1990s, including Stephen Barley, engineering management, Glenn Carroll and Charles O'Reilly, GSB, Mark Granovetter, sociology, and Walter Powell, education and sociology.

Although we had lost financial support for pre- and post-doctoral students, the visibility of Stanford as a leader in organization studies continued to attract a large number of highly qualified post-doctoral scholars from around the world and all parts of the United States. Between 1988 and 1995 SCOR hosted more than 60 postdoctoral visitors (who arrived with their own financial support). We continued with our colloquia series, training workshops, and the Asilomar Conference and were ably supported in these ventures by the effective efforts of Lisa Hellrich, administrative assistant for SCOR and beloved "den-mother" for active doctoral and visiting post-doctoral students. However, the absence of financial support for doctoral and post-doctoral students reduced our influence and attractiveness for some faculty participants.

THE STANFORD COMMUNITY AS MODEL

As word of the success of the Stanford organizations community spread and as our graduates moved to occupy faculty positions at other institutions, several universities began to develop similar or related programs. Early "imitators" include the University of Michigan and the University of Texas. Stanford faculty were interested in fostering such developments so that, in 1990, another network organization – the Consortium of Centers for Organizations Research (CCOR) – was formally launched. In addition to my efforts, important leadership for this initiative was provided by Andrew Van de Ven, University of Minnesota; Marshall Meyer, University of Pennsylvania; and Janice Beyer and George Huber, University of Texas.

CCOR grew from a few, fledgling members in 1990 to eight U.S. members and a number of international affiliates in 1996 (for a list of CCOR participants, see Appendix D). Programs were developed in this country at Carnegie Mellon, Northwestern, Michigan, Illinois, Pennsylvania, Minnesota, and Texas. Our efforts were governed by two major objectives. First, we met to share with one another the fruits of our experience: What activities work? What connections are productive? How can research training be fostered? How should local university networks be structured? Second, since no one university can do everything, we sought ways to take advantage of the natural strengths of each university program and facilitate the movement among campuses of faculty and students to participate in courses, seminars, and joint training ventures of shorter or longer duration. A number of such programs were created and well attended.

DECLINE, DEATH, AND AUTOPSY

In 1993, SCOR moved out from the purview of the Vice-Provost's office to report to the Dean of Research, and later in that year, we became an Independent Research Center – one of nine such units on the Stanford campus. But as is characteristic of all too many organizations throughout history, this pinnacle of official recognition coincided closely with the onset of decline.

Vigorous attempts at fund raising targeted for public agencies and private foundations proved unsuccessful, and a leadership succession crisis hastened the end.

How can we understand the causes of SCOR's demise? To be sure, it is difficult to sustain informal networks over long periods of time. Inter-disciplinary efforts always confront the head-winds of disciplinary purity and associated departmental incentives. Faculty commitments are vital but fragile. Some schools and departments, such as business and engineering that had initially been small and hosted only a handful of organizational scholars, grew significantly and elected to operate more independently. The decision by the federal government to eliminate funding for basic research training in the social sciences affected not only ours, but many university programs. This loss of external funding for doctoral and post-doctoral students reduced the attraction of involvement for some faculty. There were the inevitable interpersonal frictions, and age also took its toll: several of the early champions of the program were approaching retirement.

More generally, the organizations program appears to have suffered from a problem opposite to that which besets many university-based activities. Often, university programs are initiated by the interests of donors, developers, and administrators, who then endeavor to craft incentives to entice faculty and students into new pursuits. But, we all know, faculty are not easily seduced from their own agendas, and externally generated efforts can end up creating centers operating mostly as façade, the formal structures loosely-coupled from the actual work of teaching and research. By contrast, the organizations group, in retrospect, perhaps depended too much on faculty energy and had too little connection with the administrative structures of the University. We were successful in involving faculty and students, but less so in obtaining administrative backing.

Although SCOR has disappeared, two more limited, but related centers of organization research now flourish on campus. Under the initial leadership of founding director Jim March and current director Walter Powell, the Scandinavian Consortium on Organization Research (SCANCOR) hosts international scholars from Scandinavia and other countries for study leave in this country as well as stimulating Stanford scholars to connect to overseas research. In 2008, SCANCOR celebrated its 20th year of operation. And the Center for Work, Technology, and Organization, housed in the school of engineering and led by Stephen Barley, who arrived at Stanford in 1992, focuses scholarly attention on the development and impact of the new information and communication technologies on organizations. Both are important centers of cross-disciplinary conversation on organizations.

LEGACY

How should we interpret the legacy of this research community? There is no question that Stanford can claim a special place in the history of organization studies. During the late 1950s when organizational studies was just emerging as a specialized field of study, the two leading centers were Columbia University, where Robert Merton and colleagues, including Philip Selznick, Alvin Gouldner, James Coleman, and Peter Blau, were launching the empirical study of bureaucratic systems, and Carnegie Institute of Technology (now Carnegie-Mellon University), where Herbert Simon, together with Richard Cyert, Jim March, and Oliver Williamson, were examining the ways in which organizational structures support "boundedly rational" decision making. During the 1960s, there was no dominant center although several universities – including Harvard, Chicago, and Michigan – hosted productive collections of scholars. However, by the late 1970s and continuing well into the 1990s, I believe that Stanford University emerged as the unchallenged powerhouse at which organizational studies were being advanced.

The Stanford history appears to me to testify to the value of genuinely interdisciplinary research and education when carried out in a supportive and interactive collegial community of scholars. While it may seem ironic that the interdisciplinary organization studies program floundered for lack of organizational support, it is important not to overlook its successes. Our history suggests that faculty-initiated programs have strengths as well as vulnerabilities, and that low profile activities can have broad and significant effects. On balance, remarkable things took place at Stanford University in the recent past involving a wide range of organizational scholars that need to be recognized, remembered, and celebrated. That is why I am so pleased by the appearance of this volume.

NOTES

1. These organizations, SCOR and SCANCOR, are described later in this chapter.
2. Informally, the program was frequently referred to as ORTP – the Organization Research Training Program.
3. The fifth, transaction cost economics, was pioneered by Oliver Williamson, at the University of California, Berkeley.

REFERENCES

Augier, M., March, J. G., & Sullivan, B. N. (2005). Notes on the evolution of a research community: Organization studies in Anglophone North American, 1945–2000. *Organization Science, 16,* 85–95.

Barnard, C. I. (1937). *The functions of the executive.* Cambridge, MA: Harvard University Press.

Baron, J. N., & Bielby, W. T. (1980). Bringing the firms back in: Stratification, segmentation, and the organization of work. *American Sociological Review, 45,* 737–765.

Blau, P. M. (1955). *The dynamics of bureaucracy.* Chicago: University of Chicago Press.

Blau, P. M., & Scott, W. R. (1962). *Formal organizations: A comparative perspective* (Reissued by Stanford University Press, 2003). San Francisco: Chandler.

Cohen, M. D., March, J. G., & Olsen, J. P. (1972). A garbage can model of organizational choice. *Administrative Science Quarterly, 17,* 1–25.

Csikszentmihalyi, M. (1999). *Creativity.* New York: Harper Collins.

Dalton, M. (1959). *Men who manage.* New York: Wiley.

Drucker, P. F. (1946). *Concept of the corporation.* New York: John Day.

Dubin, R. (1951). *Human relation in administration.* New York: Prentice-Hall.

Eisenhardt, K. M., & Tabrizi, B. N. (1995). Accelerating adaptive processes: Product innovation in the global computer industry. *Administrative Science Quarterly, 40,* 84–110.

Etzioni, A. (1961). *A comparative analysis of complex organizations.* New York: Free Press of Glencoe.

Fleming, L., & Singh, J. (2008). *Lone inventors as sources of breakthroughs: Myth or reality?* Unpublished paper presented to the SCANCOR 20th Anniversary Conference, Stanford University, November 21–23.

Flood, A. B., & Scott, W. R. (1987). *Hospital structure and performance.* Baltimore, MD: Johns Hopkins University Press.

Gillmor, C. S. (2004). *Fred Terman at Stanford: Building a discipline, a university, and Silicon Valley.* Stanford, CA: Stanford University Press.

Goffman, E. (1961). *Asylums.* Garden City, NY: Doubleday.

Gordon, R. A., & Howell, J. E. (1959). *Higher education for business.* New York: Columbia University Press.

Gouldner, A. W. (1954). *Patterns of industrial bureaucracy.* Glencoe, IL: Free Press.

Graham, H. D., & Diamond, N. (1997). *The rise of American Research Universities: Elites and challenges in the postwar era.* Baltimore, MD: Johns Hopkins University Press.

Gulick, L., & Urwick, L. (Eds). (1937). *Papers in the Science of Administration*. New York: Institute of Public Administration, Columbia University.

Hannan, M. T., & Freeman, J. (1977). The population ecology of organizations. *American Journal of Sociology, 82*, 929–964.

Hannan, M. T., & Freeman, J. (1989). *Organizational ecology*. Cambridge, MA: Harvard University Press.

Haunschild, P. (1993). Interorganization imitation: The impact of interlocks on corporate acquisition activity. *Administrative Science Quarterly, 38*, 564–592.

Institute for Scientific Analysis. (1999). Thirty Year Report, 1968–1998.

Kramer, R., & Tyler, T. R. (Eds). (1996). *Trust in organizations: Frontiers of theory and research*. Thousand Oaks, CA: Sage.

Lerman, P. (1982). *Deinstitutionalization and the welfare state*. New Brunswick, NJ: Rutgers University Press.

Levitt, B., & March, J. G. (1988). Organizational learning. *Annual Review of Sociology, 14*, 319–340.

Lipset, S. M., Trow, M. R., & Coleman, J. S. (1956). *Union democracy*. Gleocoe, IL: Free Press.

Lowen, R. S. (1997). *Creating the Cold War University: The transformation of Stanford*. Berkeley: University of California Press.

March, J. G. (Ed.) (1965). *The handbook of organizations*. Chicago: Rand-McNally.

March, J. G. (1981). Decision in organizations and theories of choice. In: A. H. Van de Ven & W. F. Joyce (Eds), *Perspectives on organization design and behavior* (pp. 205–244). New York: Wiley-Interscience.

March, J. G. (1988). *Decisions and organizations*. Oxford: Basil Blackwell.

March, J. G., & Olsen, J. P. (1975). The uncertainty of the past: Organizational learning under ambiguity. *European Journal of Political Research, 3*, 147–171.

March, J. G., & Olsen, J. P. (1984). The new institutionalism: Organizational factors in political life. *American Political Science Review, 78*, 734–749.

March, J. G., & Olsen, J. P. (1989). *Rediscovering institutions: The organizational basis of politics*. New York: Free Press.

March, J. G., & Simon, H. A. (1958). *Organizations*. New York: Wiley.

Martin, J. (1992). *Cultures in organizations: Three perspectives*. New York: Oxford University Press.

Martin, J., & Siehl, C. (1983). Organizational culture and counterculture: An uneasy symbiosis. *Organizational Dynamics, 12*, 52–64.

Mayo, E. (1933). *The human problems of an industrial civilization*. New York: Macmillan.

Mayo, E. (1945). *The social problems of an industrial civilization*. Boston: Graduate School of Business Administration, Harvard University.

Meyer, J. W., & Rowan, B. (1977). Institutionalized organization: Formal structure as myth and ceremony. *American Journal of Sociology, 83*, 340–363.

Meyer, J. W., & Scott, W. R. (1983). *Organizational environments: Ritual and rationality*. Beverly Hills, CA: Sage.

Ouchi, W. (1981). *Theory Z: How American business can meet the Japanese challenge*. New York: Addison-Westley.

Pfeffer, J. (1972). Size and composition of corporate boards of directors: The organization and its environment. *Administrative Science Quarterly, 17*, 218–228.

Pfeffer, J. (1983). Organizational demography. In: L. L. Cummings & B. M. Staw (Eds), *Research in organizational behavior* (Vol. 5, pp. 299–357). Greenwich, CT: JAI Press.

Pfeffer, J., & Salancik, G. R. (1978). *The external control of organizations* (Reissued by the Stanford University Press, 2003.). New York: Harper & Row.

Podolny, J. M. (1994). Market uncertainty and the social character of economic exchange. *Administrative Science Quarterly, 39*, 458–483.

Schlossman, S., Gleeson, R., Sedlak, M., & Allen, D. (1994). *The beginnings of graduate management education in the United States.* Santa Monica, CA: Graduate Management Admission Council.

Scott, W. R. (1995). *Institutions and organizations.* Thousand Oaks, CA: Sage.

Scott, W. R. (2008). *Institutions and organizations: Ideas and interests* (3rd ed). Thousand Oaks, CA: Sage.

Scott, W. R., & Black, B. L. (Eds). (1986). *The organization of mental health services: Societal and community systems.* Beverly Hills, CA: Sage.

Scott, W. R., & Lammers, J. C. (1985). Trends in occupations and organizations in the medical care and mental health sectors. *Medical Care Review, 42*(Spring), 37–76.

Scull, A. T. (1977). *Decarceration.* Englewood Cliffs, NJ: Prentice-Hall.

Selznick, P. (1949). *TVA and the Grass Roots.* Berkeley: University of California Press.

Simon, H. A., Smithberg, D. W., & Thompson, V. A. (1950). *Public Administration.* New York: Knopf.

Stanford Center for Organization Research (SCOR). (1988). Charter. Unpublished document, Stanford University.

Sutton, R. I., & Callahan, A. L. (1987). The stigma of bankruptcy: Spoiled organizational image an its management. *Academy of Management Journal, 30.*

Taylor, F. W. (1911). *The principles of scientific management.* New York: Harper.

Thompson, V. A. (1961). *Modern organization.* New York: Knopf.

Thornton, P. (1992). Psychiatric diagnosis as sign and symbol: Nomenclature as an organizing and legitimating strategy. In: G. Miller & G. Holstein (Eds), *Research on social problems* (Vol. 4). Greenwich, CT: JAI Press.

Weber, M. (1924/1968). Economy and society: An interpretive sociology (2 Vols). In: G. Roth & C. Wittich (Eds). New York: Bedminister Press.

Whyte, W. F. (1946). *Industry and society.* New York: McGraw-Hill.

PART V
APPENDIXES

APPENDIX A: STANFORD FACULTY
IN ORGANIZATIONS

Table A1. List of Participants in the Organizations Research Training
Program, Stanford University National Institute of Mental Health
(1972–89) and National Institute of Aging (1986–89).

List of Participants

Training faculty

Paul S. Adler, IE
Victor Baldridge, Ed
James N. Baron, GSB
Jonathan Bendor, GSB
Robert A. Burgelman, GSB
Ruth Cronkite, Soc & VA
Carol Conell, Soc
Sanford M. Dornbusch, Soc
Lynn R. Eden, Pol Sci
Kathleen M. Eisenhardt, IE
Roberto Fernandez, GSB
Brian Fry, Pol Sci
Francine Gordon, GSB
Michael T. Hannan, Soc
Thomas W. Harrell, GSB
Albert H. Hastorf, Psy
Pamela R. Haunschild, GSB
Thomas R. Hofstedt, GSB
Alex Inkeles, Soc
James V. Jucker, IE
Roderick Kramer, GSB
Lorrin Koran, Psychiatry
Harold J. Leavitt, GSB
Raymon E. Levitt, CE
Milbrey McLaughlin, Ed
Ann M. McMahon, Soc
James G. March, Ed, GSB, Soc, Pol Sci

Joanne Martin, GSB
John W. Meyer, Soc
James R. Miller, III, GSB
William G. Ouchi, GSB
Donald A. Palmer, GSB
Jeffrey Pfeffer, GSB
Joel Podolny, GSB
Jerry I. Porras, GSB
Francisco O. Ramirez, Ed
Condoleeza Rice, Pol Sci
James A. Robins, GSB
Scott Sagan, Pol Sci
W. Richard Scott, Soc
William H. Simon, Law
Myra Strober, Ed
Robert I. Sutton, IE
Ann Swidler, Soc
Joan Talbert, Ed
J. Serge Taylor, GSB
Nancy B. Tuma, Soc
David B. Tyack, Ed
Henry A. Walker, Soc
Robert A. Walker, Pol Sci
Eugene J. Webb, GSB
Steven Weiner, Ed
Morris Zelditch, Jr., Soc

Table A1. (*Continued*)

List of Participants

Administration
W. Richard Scott, Director
Mai Lam, Administrator
Kenneth Lutterman, Program Officer, NIMH
Richard Suzman, Program Officer, NIA

Notes: GSB, Graduate School of Business; IE, Industrial Engineering; VA, Veterans'
Administration Hospital.

APPENDIX B: STANFORD GRADUATE STUDENTS IN ORGANIZATIONS

Table B1. List of Participants in the Organizations Research Training Program, Stanford University (1972–89), National Institute of Mental Health (1972–89), and National Institute of Aging (1986–89).

List of Participants	

Pre-doctoral trainees

Terry Amburgey, 1978–80, Soc	Robert LeDuc, 1973–74, GSB
Victoria Alexander, 1986–87, Soc	Virginia V. Lee, 1979–81, Ed
Elaine Backman, 1982–83, Soc	Mary Ann MaGuire, 1972–73, Soc
Jerry Beasley, 1972–74, Ed	Paul McCright, 1985–87, IE
Robert Bies, 1978–80, GSB	Patricia McDonnah, 1987–89, Ed
Kennett Benedict, 1975–77, PS	Curtis L. Manns, 1973–76, Soc
Michael Boehm, 1985–86, GSB	Debra Meyerson, 1985–87, GSB
Glenn R. Carroll, 1979–80, Soc	Anne S. Miner, 1979–81, GSB
Lisa Catanzarite, 1988–89, Ed	Theodore Mitchell, 1980–81, Ed
Donald E. Comstock, 1972–75, Soc	Valerie Montoya, 1985–86, Soc
Andrew Creighton, 1985–87, Soc	James Newton-Shane, 1975–76, Psy
John R. Curry, 1974–75, Ed	Sorca O'Conner, 1981–83, Ed
Gerald F. Davis, 1987–89, GSB	Elizabeth Ozer, 1988–89, Psy/Ed
Margaret Davis, 1976–77, Soc	Rodney B. Plimpton, 1972–73, GSB
Alison Davis-Blake, 1985–86, GSB	Melanie E. Powers, 1979–81, GSB
Sarah M. Corse, 1985–86, Soc	Raymond Price, 1977–79, GSB
Charles Denk, 1981–82, Soc	Holly Prigerson, 1986–87, Soc
Frank Dobbin, 1983–84, Soc	Robert Rosenbloom, 1973–74, PS
Carla Edlefson, 1976–77, Ed	Stephen Rosenholtz, 1977–79, Ed
Kathleen Eisenhardt, 1976–77, GSB	Amy Roussel, 1988–89, Soc
Martha Feldman, 1978–79, PS	Brian Rowan, 1975–76, Soc
Mary L. Fennell, 1975–77, Soc	Claudia Kaye Schoonhoven, 1972–75, Soc
Phillip C. Fisher, 1972–75, GSB	Caren Siehl, 1981–83, GSB
Mary K. Garrett, 1982–84, Soc	Sim Sitkin, 1983–84, GSB
David Gibson, 1976–77, Soc	Lee L. Sproull, 1974–76, Ed
Jane Hannaway, 1973–76, Ed	William L. Stallworth, 1974–76, Soc

Table B1. (*Continued*)

List of Participants

Joeseph Harder, 1987–89, GSB	Suzanne Stout, 1988–89, GSB
Reuben T. Harris, 1972–73, GSB	Sharon Takeda, 1983–84, Soc
Scott Herriot, 1982–83, IE	Michal Tamuz, 1980–82, Soc
Polly E. Hildebrand, 1977–79, Ed	Patricia Thornton, 1988–89, Soc
Alfred M. Jaeger, 1974–76, GSB	William Tobin, 1987–79, Ed
Stephen Lee Jerrell, 1973–74, GSB	Caroline Turner, 1985–87, Ed
Jerry B. Johnson, 1975–77, GSB	Alan Wilkins, 1976–77, GSB
Alice L. Kaplan, 1974–76, GSB	Ronald R. Williams, 1972–73, GSB
Michael Knapp, 1978–80, Ed	Alan Wilkins, 1976–78, GSB
	Sylvia M Yee, 1985–87, Ed

Notes: GSB, Graduate School of Business; IE, Industrial Engineering; VA, Veterans' Administration Hospital.

APPENDIX C: STANFORD POST-DOCS IN ORGANIZATIONS

Table C1. List of Participants in the Organizations Research Training Program, Stanford University (1972–89), National Institute of Mental Health (1972–89), and National Institute of Aging (1986–89).

List of Participants

Postdoctoral trainees

Joan R. Bloom, 1973–74, Ed
Bruce L. Black, 1984–86, Soc
Deirdre Boden, 1984–86, Soc
Karen Christensen, 1980–81, PS
Adele Clark, 1987–89, Soc
Yinon Cohen, 1982–84, Soc
Martin Davidson, 1988–89, Bus
Nanette Davis, 1978–79, Soc
Edward L. Deci, 1973–74, Psy
Jacques Delacroix, 1978–80, Soc
Elaine Draper, 1985–87, Soc
Nancy Durbin, 1988–89, Soc
George Ecker, 1973–74, Ed
Tammy Feldman, 1987–88, PS
Mary Fennell, 1982–83, Soc
Ann Barry Flood, 1977–79, Soc
Joan Fujimura, 1987–88, Ant
Sandra Goff, 1975–76, Psy
Marilyn Goldberg, 1977–78, Econ
Andrew J. Grimes, 1974–75, Bus
Alice Handley-Isaksen, 1979–80, Psy
Clifton D. Hollister, 1978–79, Soc Wk
Elizabeth Hansot, 1976–77, PS
Helga Hernes, 1974–75, PS
David G. Hopelain, 1976–77, Bus
Nancy Howell, 1986–88, Ant
Xandra Kayden, 1978–79, PS

Alison Konrad, 1986–88, Soc
Susan Krieger, 1980–82, Com
John C. Lammers, 1983–84, Soc
Nancy Langton, 1986–88, Soc
Annette Lareau, 1984–86, Soc
Anne Lawrence, 1985–87, IR
James P. McNaul, 1975–76, Bus
Rodney Ogawa, 1979–80, Ed
Geanne T. Pankey, 1978–79, Soc
Brian Powers, 1987–89, Soc
Francisco Ramirez, 1979–81, Soc
Susan Rosenholtz, 1978–79, Ed
James Rounds, 1979–80, Ant
Jerry Ross, 1980–82, Psy
John Scholz, 1981–82, PS
Charles Snow, 1973–74, Bus
Lee Sproull, 1982–83, Ed
Jerome Steinman, 1973–75, Bus
David Stevenson, 1986–87, Soc
John Sutton, 1981–83, Soc
Richard Suzman, 1978–80, Soc Psy
David Weckler, 1981–83, Psy
Janet Weiss, 1986–87, PS
Amy Wharton, 1985–86, Soc
Mark Wolfson, 1988–89, Soc
Julie Zatz, 1982–83, PS

Notes: GSB, Graduate School of Business; IE, Industrial Engineering; VA, Veterans' Administration Hospital.

APPENDIX D: AFFILIATED CENTERS FOR ORGANIZATION RESEARCH

Table D1. List of University Participants in the Consortium of Centers for Organization Research (CCOR), 1995.

Member centers

Center for Management of Technology, Carnegie Mellon University

General Motors Center for Research in Strategy, Kellogg School of Management, Northwestern University

Interdisciplinary Committee on Organizational Studies (ICOS), University of Michigan

Office of Organizational Research (OOR), College of Commerce and Business Administration, University of Illinois

Reginald Jones Center, Wharton School of Management, University of Pennsylvania

Stanford Center for Organizations Research, Stanford University

Strategic Management Research Center, University of Minnesota

Texas Center for Organizations Research, University of Texas, Austin

International affiliates

Center for Public Organization and Management, COS Center, Copenhagen Denmark

Centre de Recherche en Gestion (CRG), De L'Ecole Polytechnique, Paris, France

Helsinki Center for Management and Organizational Studies, Helsinki, Finland

Norwegian Research Center in Organization and Management, LOS, Bergen, Norway

Stockholm Center for Organizations Research (SCORE), Stockholm, Norway